Sixth Edition

# GROWING ARTISTS

## Teaching the Arts to Young Children

## Dr. Joan Bouza Koster
### Broome Community College

CENGAGE
Learning

Australia • Brazil • Japan • Korea • Mexico • Singapore • Spain • United Kingdom • United States

**CENGAGE**
Learning·

**Growing Artists: Teaching the Arts to Young Children, Sixth Edition**
**Dr. Joan Bouza Koster**

Product Manager: Mark Kerr

Content Developer: Nicolas Albert

Outsource Development Manager:
Jeremy Judson

Outsource Development Coordinator:
Joshua Taylor

Product Assistant: Nicole Bator

Media Developer: Renee C. Schaaf

Marketing Manager: Kara Kindstrom

Production Management, and Composition:
Preeti Longia Sinha, MPS Limited

Manufacturing Planner: Doug Bertke

Rights Acquisition Specialist (Text, Image):
Don Schlotman

Art and Cover Direction: Carolyn Deacy,
MPS Limited

Cover images: Photos ©Cengage Learning;
Butterfly and Xylophone ©Dreamstime/
Dr. Joan Bozua Koster

Xylophone photo on section opener:
Stock Connection / SuperStock

For product information and technology assistance, contact us at
**Cengage Learning Customer & Sales Support, 1-800-354-9706**
For permission to use material from this text or product,
submit all requests online at **www.cengage.com/permissions**
Further permissions questions can be emailed to
**permissionrequest@cengage.com**

Library of Congress Control Number: 2013947725

ISBN-13: 978-1-285-74314-1

ISBN-10: 1-285-74314-8

**Cengage Learning**
200 First Stamford Place, 4th Floor
Stamford, CT 06902
USA

Cengage Learning is a leading provider of customized learning solutions with office locations around the globe, including Singapore, the United Kingdom, Australia, Mexico, Brazil and Japan. Locate your local office at **www.cengage.com/global**

Cengage Learning products are represented in Canada by Nelson Education, Ltd.

For your course and learning solutions, visit **www.cengage.com**

Purchase any of our products at your local college store or at our preferred online store **www.cengagebrain.com**

Printed at CLDPC, USA, 11-20

# Contents

Reflection Page Guide    viii

Preface    ix

Acknowledgments    xix

## Section 1  Introduction to the Arts    1

### Chapter 1  The Arts and Young Children    2

Who are the young artists?    3

What are the creative arts?    4

Why should the arts be taught to young children?    5

How do the creative arts help children learn?    10

  Teachsource Video Case:
  0-2 Years: Piaget's Sensorimotor Stage    11

  Teachsource Video Case:
  5-11 Years: Lev Vygotsky, the Zone of Proximal Development, and Scaffolding    12

  Digital Download: MI Planning Web    13

What does a well-designed arts curriculum look like?    13

  Digital Download: Learning Standards Resources    18

What is the teacher's role in creative arts education?    18

Conclusion: The well-designed arts program    18

  Digital Download: Online Resources    19

Reflection Pages 1–4    22

### Chapter 2  Nurturing Creativity    26

What is creativity?    27

  Teachsource Video Case:
  Kindergarten Curriculum    29

What does creativity look like in children?    29

What is the creative process?    30

  Digital Download: Books that Celebrate Creativity    33

How do teachers foster the creative process?    38

  Digital Download: Thinking About Thinking    44

  Digital Download: Creative Thinking Routines    47

  Digital Download: Sample Letter to Family    49

Conclusion: Creativity in teaching    50

  Digital Download: Online Resources    51

Reflection Pages 5–8    52

### Chapter 3  Artistic Development    56

How do children develop in the arts?    57

What is known about child development in the arts?    58

What is known about each child's individual development?    62

What is known about the social, emotional, and cultural context in which children live?    64

How do we make sense of children's artistic development?    66

How do we select the best DAP arts activities?    68

How do we assess children's growth in the arts?    69

  Teachsource Video Case:
  Progress Monitoring: Using Transitional Time in an Early Childhood Classroom    70

  Digital Download: Examples of Checklists and Anecdotal Records    71

  Digital Download: Digital Portfolios    71

Digital Download: Sample Model Release   72

Digital Download: Suggested Content for an Arts Portfolio   72

Digital Download: Making a Folder Portfolio   72

How can we share the arts with families?   75

Digital Download: Digital Portfolio   77

How can we practice reflective teaching?   77

Digital Download: Example of Reflective Assessments   78

Conclusion: The child artist   80

Digital Download: Online Resources   80

Reflection Pages 9–12   81

**Chapter 4   Awakening the Senses   85**

What is sensory perception?   86

Why is sensory perception important?   88

How should sensory perception activities be selected?   91

Digital Download: Sensory Activity Plans   92

Digital Download: Examples of Sensory Stimuli   94

Digital Download: Sample Letter to Family   94

How should sensory perception activities be presented?   96

Digital Download: Sensory Perception Arts Activities   98

How do we create sensory interactions?   98

What are the elements of the arts?   100

Digital Download: Guide to Mixing Colors   102

Digital Download: Arts Elements Activities   105

How can we use children's literature?   106

Digital Download: The Annotated Book List of Children's Books   106

Conclusion: The sensitive teacher   107

Digital Download: Online Resources   107

Digital Download: Sample Plans for a Celebratory Presentation   107

Reflection Pages 13–16   109

**Section 2   Teaching the Arts   113**

**Chapter 5   Coming Together Through the Arts   114**

How can young artists work together?   115

Teachsource Video Case: 2-5 Years: Play in Early Childhood   118

How do we create a positive social-emotional climate through the arts?   118

Digital Download: Community Building Arts Activities   119

How should group arts activities be organized?   120

Digital Download: Shared Experiences and Group Arts Activities   124

How are children with special needs included in the arts program?   125

Digital Download: Examples of Ways to Adapt Arts Activities   128

How can the arts be used in anti-bias activities?   130

How do we address cultural differences through arts activitiy?   133

Digital Download: Books that Make a Difference   134

Digital Download: Substitutions for Food in Art Activities   136

Conclusion: Caring for each other   137

Digital Download: Online Resources   139

Reflection Pages 17–20   141

**Chapter 6   Creating a Place for the Arts   146**

What kind of environment is needed for the arts?   147

How do we create an arts-infused learning environment?   148

Teachsource Video Case: Reggio Emilia Approach and Preschool Appropriate Learning Environment and Room Arrangement   152

How is an aesthetic environment created?   153

Digital Download: Planning an Outdoor Environment   156

How should materials be presented?   157

Digital Download: Materials for Young Children   159

Digital Download: Assessing the Arts Environment   161

Digital Download: Sample Letter to Family    161

How can we share children's arts learning?    162

    Digital Download: Mounting 2-D and 3-D Artworks    164

Conclusion: Creating a sense of place    167

    Digital Download: Online Resources    167

Reflection Pages 21–24    169

## Chapter 7   Introducing the World's Arts    173

How do children learn respond to the arts?    174

How do we engage children with artistic works?    177

    Digital Download: Major Styles of Music, Dance and Visual Arts    181

    Digital Download: Multicultural Artifacts    185

    Digital Download: Exemplary Illustrated Chilren's Books    185

    Digital Download: Books About Other Cultures    185

    Digital Download: Making a Big Book    185

    Digital Download: Books About the Arts    186

    Digital Download: Online Resources    186

How can we talk about artistic works?    187

How do we incorporate writing responses to artistic works?    190

    Digital Download: Arts Games    191

    Digital Download: Suggestions for Art Bags    192

How can children be introduced to community arts resources?    193

Conclusion: Becoming a lover of the arts    199

    Digital Download: Online Resources    199

Reflection Pages 25–28    201

## Chapter 8   Integrating the Arts into the Curriculum    205

Where do the arts belong?    206

What is emergent curriculum?    208

What is the project approach?    209

What is an integrated learning unit?    213

    Digital Download: Questions for Integrated Units    213

    Digital Download: What is Water? Example of a Unit Web Organized by DAP Skills    214

Teachsource Video Case: Exploring Math Concepts through Creative Activities    216

    Digital Download: Our Bodies: A Sample MI Web    217

    Digital Download: What is Water Integrated Unit Weekly Plan    218

    Digital Download: Integrated Unit Weekly Planning Sheet    218

    Digital Download: Sample Family Newsletter    221

How can we share learning through the arts?    222

    Digital Download: Online Resources    223

Conclusion: Making the connection    226

    Digital Download: Online Resources    226

Reflection Pages 29–32    228

## Section 3   Exploring the Arts    233

## Chapter 9   Creating Visual Art    234

What are the visual arts?    235

How do the visual arts help children grow?    235

How do children develop in two-dimensional expression?    236

How are two-dimensional activities designed?    238

The drawing experience    239

    Digital Download: Open-Ended Drawing Activities for Young Children    240

    Digital Download: Books Celebrating Drawing    241

The painting experience    242

    Digital Download: Open-Ended Painting Activities for Young Children    245

    Digital Download: Books Celebrating Painting    245

    Digital Download: Sample Letter to Family    246

The collage experience    246

    Digital Download: Open-Ended Collage Activities    250

    Digital Download: Collage Materials    250

Digital Download: Books celebrating Collage   250

Digital Download: Sample Visual Arts Plans   251

## The printmaking experience   251

Digital Download: Making a Print-Drying Box   252

Digital Download: Open-Ended Printmaking Activities   254

## The fiber art experience   254

Digital Download: Books Celebrating Fiber Art   257

## The digital art experience   257

Digital Download: Digital Media Resources   259

## How are three-dimensional activities designed?   260

## The modeling experience   260

Digital Download: Firing Pottery Clay   263

Digital Download: Pottery Clay Activities   265

Digital Download: Books About Modeling and Clay   265

## The constructed sculpture experience   266

Digital Download: Books About Building   269

## How do we share children's artwork with families?   269

## Conclusion: The power of the visual arts   270

Digital Download: Online Resources   270

## Reflection Pages 33–36   271

## Chapter 10 Making Music   275

## What is music?   276

## How do children develop musically?   277

Digital Download: Music Development in Young Children   279

## How does music help children grow?   280

## How are music activities designed?   283

## The listening experience   284

Digital Download: Music for Listening and Study   285

Digital Download: Lullabies from Around the World   285

Digital Download: Musical Forms   287

Digital Download: Books about Music and Musicians   287

Digital Download: Listening Activities for Young Children   288

## The rhythmic experience   288

Digital Download: Books with a Rollicking Rhythm   292

Digital Download: Rhythmic Activities for Young Children   293

## The musical instrument experience   293

Digital Download: Music Software   295

Digital Download: Activities with Tonal Instruments   298

Digital Download: Books about Musical Instruments   298

Digital Download: Steps to Music Literacy   299

Digital Download: Open-Ended Music   300

## The singing experience   300

Digital Download: Fingerplays and Jump Rope Rhymes   302

Digital Download: Songs for Children   305

Digital Download: Books Based on Popular Songs   306

## How do we share children's music with families?   306

Digital Download: Making Instruments for Children   306

## Conclusion: Becoming musical   307

Digital Download: Online Resources   307

## Reflection Pages 37–40   308

## Chapter 11 Moving Creatively   312

## What is creative movement and dance?   313

## How does creative movement and dance help children grow?   316

Digital Download: Physical Milestones   316

## How are creative movement activities designed?   319

## The creative movement experience   322

Digital Download: Props for Moving   322

Digital Download: Music for Moving   322

Digital Download: Inclusive Practices for Creative Dance   323

Digital Download: Open-Ended Creative Movement for Infants and Toddlers   325

Digital Download: Guided Creative Movement Explorations   325

Digital Download: Creative Dance Activities for Preschool and Up   327

Digital Download: Creative Dance Plans   328

**The creative dance experience   328**

Digital Download: Music for Dancing   329

Digital Download: Dances for Children   331

Digital Download: Books that Celebrate Dance   333

Digital Download: Online Resources   333

Digital Download: Online Resources   334

**Conclusion: Let's dance!   334**

Digital Download: Online Resources   335

**Reflection Pages 41–44   336**

## 12 Nurturing the Imagination   341

**What are the dramatic arts?   342**

**What are the elements of the dramatic arts?   343**

Digital Download: Dramatic Elements in Children's Play   343

**What is the relationship between the dramatic arts and children's play?   344**

**How do children grow through the dramatic play?   346**

Digital Download: Sequence of Development in the Dramatic Arts   348

**How do we address special needs?   350**

**What is the teacher's role in children's play?   351**

Teachsource Video Case: School Age Cognitive Development   352

**How are dramatic arts activities designed?   353**

Digital Download: Open-Ended Dramatic Play Centers   354

Digital Download: Outdoor Prop Boxes   354

Digital Download: Guided Imagery: A Peaceful Cave   356

**The pantomime experience   357**

Digital Download: Ideas for Simple Descriptive Pantomimes   357

Digital Download: Open-Ended Dramatic Arts Activity Plans   358

**The improvisation experience   361**

Digital Download: Ideas for Open-Ended Improvisations   361

Digital Download: Ideas for Role Plays   361

**The story play experience   364**

Teachsource Video Case: Infant & Toddlers: Emotional Development   365

Digital Download: Finger plays   365

Digital Download: Puppetry Resources   367

Digital Download: Making Costumes, Hats, and Jewelry   369

**How do we introduce children's theatre?   369**

**How do we use the dramatic arts to assess growth?   371**

**Conclusion: Imagine it!   372**

Digital Download: Online Resources   372

**Reflection Pages 45–48   373**

## Appendix A   378

Safety guidelines   378

Safe substitutions   379

Ways to help children distinguish food from art supplies   381

## Appendix B   383

Planning arts activities   383

Who? Group composition   383

When? Time frame   383

Why? Goals and objectives   383

Where? Set up   386

What? Materials   386

How? Procedure   386

What to do   387

What to say   387

Transition out   387

Assess the learning   388

Writing an arts activity plan   388

## Appendix C   391

Teacher resources   391

Artifact sources   391

Sources of prints and posters   391

Music supplies   392

## Appendix D   394

Recipes   394

References   397

Glossary   406

Index   415

# Reflection Page Guide

Reflection 1   Why the arts?   22

Reflection 2   How to have a successful observation   23

Reflection 3   Observation: The arts and the child   24

Reflection 4   Analysis: The arts and the child   25

Reflection 5   Experiencing the creative process: What is in a name?   52

Reflection 6   Self-exploration: My first arts experience   53

Reflection 7   Self-exploration: My personal arts time line   54

Reflection 8   Self-exploration: Defining creative behavior   55

Reflection 9   Factors affecting your artistic work   81

Reflection 10   Looking at children's artistic development   82

Reflection 11   Documenting artistic behavior   83

Reflection 12   Observation: Observing children and the arts   84

Reflection 13   Reviewing sensory perception   109

Reflection 14   Selecting sensory objects, materials, and experiences   110

Reflection 15   Designing a big book that entices the senses   111

Reflection 16   Observation: A sensory experience   112

Reflection 17   Exploring ourselves   141

Reflection 18   Shared experiences   142

Reflection 19   Dealing with difficult situations   143

Reflection 20   Observation: Bias in the environment   144

Reflection 21   Becoming sensitive to our environment   169

Reflection 22   Observation: Aesthetics of an environment   170

Reflection 23   Designing the environment   171

Reflection 24   Scaled furniture pieces   172

Reflection 25   Artwork study   201

Reflection 26   Comparing creative works   202

Reflection 27   Self-exploration: My artistic heritage   203

Reflection 28   Self-exploration: My view of the arts now   204

Reflection 29   MI integrated unit framework   228

Reflection 30   Arts activity plan   229

Reflection 31   Preparing a documentation panel   230

Reflection 32   Planning a celebration of the arts   231

Reflection 33   The elements of art   271

Reflection 34   Planning an art center   272

Reflection 35   Observation: Children drawing   273

Reflection 36   Observation: Children and modeling   274

Reflection 37   Discovering one's musical heritage   308

Reflection 38   Selecting appropriate music activities   309

Reflection 39   Meeting special needs   310

Reflection 40   Supporting music education for young children   311

Reflection 41   The elements of dance   336

Reflection 42   Meeting special needs   337

Reflection 43   Selecting appropriate creative movement and dance activities   338

Reflection 44   Observation: Children moving creatively   339

Reflection 45   The importance of play   373

Reflection 46   Using guided imagery   375

Reflection 47   Designing a play center or prop box   376

Reflection 48   Telling a story   377

# Preface

## Introduction to the Sixth Edition

The arts have always served as the distinctive vehicle for discovering who we are. Providing ways of thinking as disciplined as science or math and as disparate as philosophy or literature, the arts are used by and have shaped every culture and individual on earth. They continue to infuse our lives on nearly all levels—generating a significant part of the creative and intellectual capital that drives our economy. The arts inform our lives with meaning every time we experience the joy of a well-remembered song, experience the flash of inspiration that comes with immersing ourselves in an artist's sculpture, enjoying a sublime dance, learning from an exciting animation, or being moved by a captivating play . . . Nurturing our children, then, necessarily means that we must provide all of them—not just those identified as "talented"—with a well-rounded education that includes the arts. By doing so, we are fulfilling the college and career readiness needs of our nation's students, laying the foundations for the success of our nation's schools and, ultimately, the success of our nation.

(National Core Arts Standards: A Conceptual Framework for Arts Learning, 2013. p. 3)

In recent years the arts have often been neglected in the curriculum, with the increasing focus placed on academic learning in English language arts and mathematics. However, with the development of the National Common Core Arts Standards attention has again turned to the immense importance of the arts in our lives. The NCCAS has set out the following lifelong goals for the education of artistically literate citizens:

1. **The Arts as Communication**—Be able to use a variety of arts media, symbols, and metaphors to create ways to communicate with others and in turn to be able to respond to the communication of others.

2. **The Arts as Personal Creative Realization**—Be competent in at least one art form and continue to be involved with that art form as an adult.

3. **The Arts as Culture, History, and Connection**—Know and understand the arts from diverse times and cultures and be able to identify patterns and connection between the arts and all areas of learning.

4. **The Arts as a Means to Well-Being**—Find joy, inspiration, peace, health, and life-enhancement through the arts.

5. **The Arts as Community Engagement**—Participate in and support the arts in their community, state, country, and the world.

Reaching these goals starts in infancy. Babies are born ready to respond to music, movement, story, and visual images. Therefore, caregivers and teachers play a tremendous role in nurturing children's artistic and creative potential. They do so by deciding actively to provide the best arts experiences they can for the children with whom they work, and by carefully planning those activities. *Growing Artists: Teaching the Arts to Young Children* provides the framework that early childhood educators need in order to design effective arts programs for children from infancy to age eight, which respect the individual pace of young artists. Throughout there is an emphasis on understanding how to foster children's development in the arts by offering open-ended arts activities and by creating a safe, sensory-appealing environment in which creativity will be nurtured. It presents an approach to arts education in which the inclusion of the visual arts, music, dance, and dramatic works created by diverse peoples and cultures is valued, and where arts activities are integrated into the total curriculum in a wide variety of engaging ways.

## What Is the Approach of this Book?

In order that this relationship between child artists and guiding adults can be deep and meaningful, this book provides a theoretical perspective, grounded in the work of Piaget, Vygotsky, Gardner, and Kindler, and suggests effective practices drawn from the National Coalition for Core Arts Standards and the National Association for the Education of Young Children's recommendations for developmentally appropriate curriculum.

## What Is the Plan of this Book?

This book is designed to be an easy-to-use resource for both those preparing to be early childhood teachers and those currently working in the field. The ideas, methods, and suggested practices found in each chapter provide a springboard for readers to design their own curriculum. As such, this book goes beyond the presentation of isolated "projects." It provides child-tested, traditional, and innovative open-ended arts experiences that serve as both a resource and model for those creating their own repertoire of activities.

To accomplish this, the book is divided into three sections of four chapters each, which address the interrelated areas of knowledge needed in order to successfully introduce young children from birth to age 8 to the arts. The first section, "Introduction to the Arts," presents the theory and practice upon which exemplary arts education is based. It looks at learning theory, creativity, developmentally appropriate practice (DAP), reflective teaching, and sensory development in young children. The second section, "Teaching the Arts," examines the components that make up a vibrant, inclusive arts program. It explains how to create an integrated arts program in a welcoming physical and social environment in which all children, including those from diverse backgrounds and those with special needs, can be successful. The third section, "Exploring the Arts," looks at the basic elements and concepts of music, creative movement, drama, and visual art, and presents ways to teach these to young children. The four chapters in this section are rich in activity ideas that show how to incorporate the theory, creative processing, developmentally appropriate practice, assessment methods, and inclusive teaching methods explained in the previous two sections.

Each of the 12 chapters is structured around learning objectives based on effective developmental appropriate practice. These provide a guide for meaningful reading and discussion. Here is an overview of each chapter and the new content for this 6th edition.

Chapter 1 sets the stage for developing a rich, integrated arts program for young children by introducing current research on how the arts influence young children's brain development and linguistic and social-emotional growth. It presents educational theory as it relates to the development of young children and the teaching of art. It includes descriptions of exemplary programs and gives an example of how such a program would look in an early childhood program.

The ensuing chapters delve into topics related to the effective teaching of art to infants, toddlers, preschoolers, kindergarteners, and primary school students.

Chapter 2 introduces the creative process as a way of understanding why children create the art they do and as a framework for structuring arts activities to allow creative growth. It addresses the role of the teacher and positive ways teachers can respond to young artists in the context of creative development.

Chapter 3 reviews what is known about the artistic development of young children and identifies the physical and environmental factors that influence how children approach arts activities. Authentic assessment using a variety of methods, including portfolios, is provided.

Chapter 4 examines the sensory experience of the arts from infancy on and presents activities to develop children's sensory perception and their awareness of the arts elements in the environment around them. Creating a community of caring artists is addressed in Chapter 5, which focuses on how arts activities can enhance social growth. It presents practices that increase cooperative behaviors, accommodate children with special needs, use art to deal with bias, and provide holiday art activities that are inclusive and open-ended. How to create a setting conducive to the growth of children in the arts and how to present children's arts learning is detailed in Chapter 6. This chapter emphasizes the need to see the arts as an integral part of how both the indoor and outdoor teaching space is designed and arranged.

Chapter 7 provides exciting hands-on activities that open children's eyes to the varied artworks and performances created by musicians, dancers, actors, and artists from many cultures, times, and places. It provides information on organizing field trips and arranging guest artists' visits. Integrating the arts into the curriculum is the focus of Chapter 8, which offers ways to teach an arts-rich curriculum through emergent curriculum design, integrated teaching, multiple intelligences, and the project approach. Ways to celebrate learning with families are shared, including creating documentation panels and holding arts

celebrations. Chapter 9 introduces the teaching of the visual arts and provides practical ways to help children express themselves through drawing, painting, modeling, constructed sculpture, collage, printmaking, computer art, and the fiber arts.

Chapter 10 focuses on the elements of music and how to introduce young children to music making and appreciation through listening to music, playing instruments, and singing. In Chapter 11 creative movement and open-ended dance activities are explored. Finally, Chapter 12 examines the role of children's pretend play and the dramatic arts, including pantomime, guided imagery, narrative drama, and storytelling in the literacy development of young children and presents creative ways to foster dramatic play through puppetry, mask making, and performance.

## In-Text Features

Within each chapter, specific information has been highlighted in order to attract attention to important ideas, present supplementary material, and provide an easy reference for the reader. Look for the following featured material.

**Across Cultures.** Multicultural and bilingual issues are addressed in this section.

**Integrating the Arts.** Here will be found ways to incorporate the arts into other subject areas. Activities that integrate the arts into math, science, social studies, and language activities are suggested.

**Special Needs.** Suggestions are given for adapting arts activities to make them accessible to all children.

**Reflection Pages.** Each chapter ends with reflective activities designed to help readers think further about the information presented in each chapter. These include answering questions about personal beliefs and experiences, applying information from the chapter to real-life situations, and carrying out and reflecting on systematic observations in actual classroom settings.

 **Teacher Tip.** This is a brief, practical idea that may prove helpful to teachers who are just starting out.

**Teaching in Action.** These descriptions of teaching illustrate how the ideas in this book work in the reality of the classroom. They are taken directly from practicing teachers' lesson plans, teaching journals, and taped interviews.

**Classroom Technology** Find suggested ways to incorporate digital media into the arts program here.

**Making Plans.** Throughout the book are sample activity plans designed to help beginning teachers better picture how arts activities are organized from beginning to end. Each plan details what to do and say as well as suggests authentic ways to assess the children's progress and is linked to similar model plans available through *Digital Downloads*.

**Teacher to Family.** Sample letters to families are included in many chapters to provide examples of the ways teachers should reach out to the families of the children they teach.

**Young Artists Creating** Short vignettes, based on the author's observations of real children in real situations, provide a vivid picture of the kind of child-art interactions most teachers can expect to find in their rooms. These vignettes lead into discussions of the philosophical basis and organizational needs of a creative and an open-ended arts program.

# New Features in the Sixth Edition

The following new features will be found in this edition :

**Arts for the Whole Child Chapter Web.** Each chapter opens with a graphic presentation of developmentally appropriate learning objectives related to the topics covered in the chapter. These objectives are based on the five key interrelated areas of DAP practice. (1) creating a caring community of learners, (2) teaching to enhance development and learning, (3) planning curriculum to achieve important goals, (4) assessing children's development and learning, (5) establishing reciprocal relationships with families (Copple & Bredekamp, 2009). After completing the chapter,

students should be able to demonstrate how they can use and apply their new knowledge and skills.

**Standards Alignment.** A correlation chart to the latest NAEYC Standards for Early Childhood Professional Preparation helps students make connections between what they are learning in the textbook and the standards. New and improved coverage of NAEYC and DAP standards includes callouts to help students identify where key standards are addressed in the text. These callouts, the Arts for the Whole Child Chapter Web, and the standards correlation chart helps students make connections between what they are learning in the textbook and the standards.

**Digital Downloads.** Digital Downloads include annotated lists of great children's literature, open-ended activity ideas for infants through primary age, charts, graphics, activity plans, web resources, and complete versions of the forms in the textbook for students to download, often customize, and use to review key concepts and in the classroom! Look for the Digital Downloads label that identifies these items.

**TeachSource Video Cases.** The TeachSource Video Cases feature footage from the classroom to help students relate key chapter content to real-life scenarios. Critical-thinking questions, artifacts, and bonus video help the student reflect on the content in the video.

In addition new material and resources have been added to each chapter as indicated here.

## Chapter 1: The Arts and the Young Child

Importance of the 2013 National Core Arts Standards and the relationship with to National Common Core Standards

Introduction to intentional teaching

The arts and English-language learners

Up-dated discussion of NAEYC Developmentally Appropriate Practice for the Arts

New *Teach Source Video* Cases featuring the work of Piaget and Vygotsky

- New *Digital Downloads* including the 2013 National Core Arts Standards and the Highscope developmental key.
- New *Photo Story*: An integrated arts unit: Ocean life

## Chapter 2: Nurturing Creativity

- New introduction to creativity and an expanded section on the definition of creativity
- New section on the importance of creativity
- New section on creativity and play
- Expanded definition of open-ended activities
- Increased coverage of flow, its importance, and ways to nurture it
- Using soliloquy for language development
- New research on the importance of teacher-child verbal interactions
- Coverage of ways to set the stage for creativity using brainstorming, uncertainty, and other practices
- New materials on creativity and children with special needs
- In-depth discussion of intentional teaching
- New section on thinking about thinking and using thinking routines in responding to the arts.
- New *Teach Source Video* Case examining state requirements and the effect on children's creativity
- New *Digital Downloads* including a Creative Process Wheel and an annotated list of children's literature celebrating creativity
- New *Photo Story* An emergent child-initiated project: A playground for our mouse

## Chapter 3: Artistic Development

- Updated coverage of Developmentally Appropriate Practice
- Expanded coverage of cultural and environmental influences on artistic development and the importance of valuing home cultures

- Updated coverage of assessing children's growth in the arts
- Updated and expanded coverage of using observation tools, digital and online media, and digital portfolios in assessment
- Expanded coverage of how to practice reflective teaching
- New *Teach Source Video* Case illustrating progress monitoring
- New *Digital Downloads* including an example of a digital portfolio and reflective assessments
- New *Photo Story*: Viewing individual development: At the playground

## Chapter 4: Awakening the Senses

- New research on sensory perceptual development and the effectives of sensory deprivation
- New focus infancy and the importance of experiences with the arts from birth
- New research on brain development and ways to build focus and deep meaning through the arts
- New arts activities to promote sensory perceptual development and selective attention in infants and children with special needs
- New *Digital Downloads* including examples of sensory stimuli and annotated children's literature featuring the elements of the arts

## Chapter 5: Coming Together Through the Arts

- New research on socio-emotional development and the role of the arts in creating a positive social-emotional environment
- Expanded section on socio-emotional skills and children's play
- Updated discussion of positive guidance
- Expanded coverage of organizing and facilitating group arts activities including examples
- Updated modifications for children with special needs in the arts

- New coverage of using digital technology to capture the creative process

- New section on cultural differences and respecting family cultures using a multicultural lens

- Expanded discussion of the use of food products in arts activities

- New *Teach Source Video* Case illustrating the different stages of play

- New *Digital Downloads* including community building arts activities and annotated children's literature that celebrate working together

- New *Photo Story* :We all have feelings

## Chapter 6: Creating a Place for the Arts

- Updated coverage of Developmentally Appropriate Practice in designing positive learning environments

- Updated and expanded coverage of the aesthetic design of the instructional space

- New section on designing outdoor spaces to include the nature and arts

- More coverage of how open-ended "intelligent" arts materials should be organized and presented, particularly to infants and toddlers

- New discussion of the use of computers and other digital media in early childhood classrooms

- Expanded discussion of ways to share children's arts activities with families

- New *Teach Source Video* Case illustrating the Reggio Emilia Approach to environment

- New *Digital Downloads* including planning outdoor learning centers and rubrics for assessing the arts environment

- New *Photo Story:* An emergent project: An addition to our school

## Chapter 7: Introducing the Worlds Arts

- New coverage of the foundational guidelines of National Core Arts Standards and ways to respond aesthetically to the arts

- New coverage of the Common Core ELA Curriculum and artistic works as texts

- New discussion of what engagement with the arts looks like and expanded ways to increase that engagement

- Updated coverage of making selections for musical and dance experiences

- New focus on the teacher as mediator of the arts

- Expanded section on how to talk to children about artistic performances and how to incorporate literacy development through aesthetic responsive activities

- New Section on audience etiquette

- New *Digital Downloads* including making a big book about the arts and children's books about the arts of other cultures

- New *Photo Story*: At the Museum

## Chapter 8: Integrating the Arts into the Classroom

- Coverage of the value of cultivating the interests of children

- New examples of how to connect the arts and literacy activities

- New focus on creating documentation panels

- New *Teach Source Video* Case on connecting the arts and mathematical knowledge

- New *Digital Downloads* including a continuum of teaching interactions and examples of integrated units and activity plans

- New *Photo Story*: Documenting an emergent project

## Chapter 9: Creating Visual Art

- Expanded sections on children's development in two- and three-dimension visual art

- More focus on visual art activities for infants and toddlers

- New sections of reading and responding activities for each art medium with questions to ask about each.

- Revised section on fiber arts

- New coverage of the NAEYC position on technology and young children with an expanded look at the benefits and disadvantages of using digital

- Updated section on digital art media

- Expanded coverage of modeling activities for infants

- More suggestions for construction activities

- Ways to connect visual art activities and the Common Core Standards in ELA and mathematics

- New *Digital Downloads* including suggested activities, model activity plans, children's literature about the visual arts, and listings of digital media resources

## Chapter 10:  Making Music

- Expanded coverage of the elements of music

- Expanded discussion of the ways children develop musically based on current research in the field

- Increased coverage of music activities for infants and toddlers

- Expanded sections on listening activities and rhythm activities

- Ways to connect music activities and the Common Core Standards in ELA and mathematics

- New section on ways to share music activities with families

- New coverage of music software

- Expanded coverage of adapting music activities to children with special needs, including the use of assistive technology

- New sections on reading, writing, and talking about music, rhythm, musical instruments, and singing

- New *Digital Downloads* including suggested activities, model activity plans, children's literature about music, and directions for making musical instruments

## Chapter 11:  Moving Creatively

- New coverage of the Common Core Standards in the Arts for dance and the core processes

- Expanded coverage of the elements of dance

- Expanded coverage of children's development in dance

- New section on developmentally appropriate practice and the role of the reflective teacher

- New coverage of assessing proficiency in creative movement activities

- Expanded coverage of open-ended creative movement activities

- New coverage of technology and digital media and dance

- New coverage of reading about, responding to, and connecting with dance

- Expanded coverage of ways to teach children how to respond to arts performances and make connections between the arts and their own lives

- New *Digital Downloads* including a Circle of Dance graphic, movement starters, suggested activities, model activity plans, suggested music for dancing, and children's literature on dance.

## Chapter 12: Nurturing the Imagination

- New coverage of the Common Core Standards in the Arts for the theater arts

- New section on the elements of drama

- New section on the relationship between children's play and the dramatic arts

- New coverage and research on children's play, flexible thinking, and the brain

- Expanded section on adapting dramatic play activities for children with special needs and to address bias

- New section on teachers' role in children's play

- Increased focus on open-ended, playful activities for infants and toddlers

- Expanded coverage of improvisational experiences
- New section on responding to dramatic performances
- Expanded coverage of ways to teach children how to respond to arts performances and make connections between the arts and their own lives.
- New section on using dramatic activities to assess children's growth
- New *TeachSource Video* Case on the teacher's role in children's imaginative play
- New *Digital Downloads* featuring a continuum of teacher roles in children's play, suggested dramatic activities, model activity plans, puppetry resources, prop boxes, finger plays, and dramatic play center designs

### Appendices

- Expanded coverage of recipes for safe, effective arts materials

## Appendices

The following information has been presented in the form of appendices for ease of use.

**Appendix A: Safety guidelines.** These guidelines detail ways to make arts activities safe for young children. It includes a table of substitutions for hazardous arts supplies.

**Appendix B: Planning arts activities.** This section explains the purpose of activity planning and provides guidance in writing an arts-based activity plan. Placing this information in an appendix allows readers to find it quickly and easily when writing plans, and permits instructors to introduce activity plan designs at the point they feel best fits their instruction.

**Appendix C: Teacher resources.** A list of updated sources for the special art supplies, computer software, art prints, and artifacts mentioned in the text.

**Appendix D:** An expanded resource of teacher-tested recipes for arts activities.

**Glossary.** A listing of terms used in the text. These terms are highlighted in bold the first time they appear in the text.

## Ancillary Materials

### Instructor Resources

Cengage Learning's Education CourseMate brings course concepts to life with interactive learning, study, and exam preparation tools that support the printed textbook. CourseMate includes the eBook, quizzes, Digital Downloads, TeachSource Video Cases, flashcards, and more—as well as EngagementTracker, a first-of-its-kind tool that monitors student engagement in the course. The accompanying instructor website, available through login.cengage.com, offers access to password-protected resources such as PowerPoint® lecture slides and the online Instructor's Manual with Test Bank. CourseMate can be bundled with the student text. Contact your Cengage sales representative for information on getting access to CourseMate.

### PowerPoint® Lecture Slides

These vibrant Microsoft® PowerPoint lecture slides for each chapter assist you with your lecture, by providing concept coverage using images, figures, and tables directly from the textbook!

### Online Instructor's Manual with Test Bank

An online Instructor's Manual accompanies this book. It contains information to assist the instructor in designing the course, including sample syllabi, discussion questions, teaching and learning activities, field experiences, learning objectives, and additional online resources. For assessment support, the updated test bank includes true/false, multiple-choice, matching, short-answer, and essay questions for each chapter.

### CourseMate

Cengage Learning's Education CourseMate brings course concepts to life with interactive learning, study, and exam preparation tools that support the printed textbook. Access the eBook, Did You Get It? quizzes, Digital Downloads, TeachSource Video Cases, flashcards, and more in your Education CourseMate. Go to CengageBrain.com to register or purchase access.

## Digital Downloads

Digital Downloads include information and complete versions of the forms in the textbook for students to download, often customize, and use to review key concepts and in the classroom! Look for the Digital Downloads label that identifies these items.

## Did You Get It? Quizzes

Did You Get It? quizzes allow students to measure their performance against the learning objectives in each chapter. Questions encourage students to go to CengageBrain.com, take the full quiz, and check their understanding.

## TeachSource Video Cases

The TeachSource Video Cases feature footage from the classroom to help students relate key chapter content to real-life scenarios. Critical-thinking questions, artifacts, and bonus video help the student reflect on the content in the video.

# What Do the Terms Mean?

## Young Artist

In this book, young artist (or child) is used to refer to children from birth to eight years old. This age range is based on the mode of delivery for art education in our society. Most children ages eight and under are in settings such as child care, preschool, nursery school, play groups, kindergarten, primary programs, or at home, where art activities take a wide range of directions depending on the training and knowledge of the adult in charge.

In addition, these years also form an artistically and conceptually unified whole, because during this span children develop their first graphic symbol system through art. Children in the midst of this process need a nourishing environment in which to explore the arts.

## Educational Settings

Programs for young children meet in many different locations, from private homes and church basements to public and private school buildings. For simplicity, classroom refers to the inside area used by the children, and outdoor area refers to any contiguous outside play area. Adaptations are included for activities in the home, as are suggestions about when to use the outdoor area.

## Guiding Adults

Throughout the text, guiding adult is used interchangeably with teacher, parent, aide, and caregiver. The role of the adult in the arts is to be a guide—someone who selects and prepares the supplies, maps out the possible routes, provides encouragement along the way, takes time for side trips, and celebrates each milepost the child reaches.

# About the Author

Joan Koster is an instructor in early childhood education at Broome Community College, Binghamton, New York, and holds degrees in art education and elementary education from Adelphi University and Temple University, and a doctorate in education from Binghamton University. Over the past 43 years, she has taught art at all levels, from preschool through college. She is the author of *Bringing Art into the Elementary School Classroom* and *Handloom Construction: A Practical Guide for the Non-Expert*. Her work in early childhood education has been published in various journals, including *Young Children*, and she has presented numerous workshops to teachers' organizations. In addition, with her family she operates a small sheep farm in upstate New York and is a professional hand-weaver, whose uniquely dyed work has been exhibited and marketed widely.

# Acknowledgments

In addressing all the arts in this new full-color edition I have found myself drawing not only on my own expertise in the areas of music, drama, and dance, but also the knowledge and resources of others. First of all, I wish to thank my husband, not only for his patience over the many months I have worked on this book, but also for his deep knowledge and love of music of all styles. I could always count on him to answer my questions about music. Second, I want to thank my sister, with her flair for the dramatic arts, for contributing her expertise on integrating all the arts into wonderful mind-expanding experiences for children. I also appreciate the continuing kindness of my fellow teachers who have allowed me to photograph in their classrooms, helped obtain permissions, and offered wonderful suggestions.

Finally, I wish to acknowledge the critical feedback I have received over the years from my undergraduate students who have pointedly told me what they love about the book, as well as what I should improve. I also want to thank my editor, Mark Kerr; Joshua Taylor; Renee Schaaf; and the staff at Cengage for their support in producing this sixth edition. In addition, my appreciation goes to all of the members of my publishing team who have seen this work through to completion.

Last, the thoughtful and detailed advice of the following reviewers was invaluable in helping me revise this book to make it more clear and more usable.

Ann Renee Guy,
*Lawson State Community College*

Sheri Leafgren,
*Miami University at Ohio*

Yash Bhagwanji,
*Florida Atlantic University*

Michelle Keast,
*University of Texas of the Permian Basin*

Jamie Harmount,
*Ohio University*

Johnny Castro,
*Brookhaven College*

Alan Weber,
*Suffolk County Community College*

Leigh Ann Atkins,
*Zane State College*

Angela Raines,
*Oconee Fall Line Technical College*

Susan Griebling,
*Northern Kentucky University*

Eileen Yantz,
*Gaston College*

Patricia Ashford,
*Cleveland State University*

Gail Multop,
*Northern Virginia Community College*

Sharon Carter,
*Davidson County Community College*

Dawn Levasseur,
*MassBay Community College*

Cindy Calenti,
*Pima Community College*

Laura Wilhelm,
*University of Central Oklahoma*

Jennifer Andrade,
*Wenatchee Valley College*

Kathy Kemp,
*Mohawk College*

Pam Geer,
*Woodland Community College*

Josephine Wilson,
*Bowie State University*

Sandy Putnam-Franklin,
*University of Massachusetts, Boston*

Evelyn Nelson-Weaver,
*Nova Southeastern University*

Betsy Squibb,
*University of Maine at Farmington*

Mayra Almodovar,
*Oklahoma State University*

Mary Jane Eisenhauer,
*Purdue University North Central*

Wendy Fletcher,
*Wiregrass Georgia Technical College*

Linda Hockenberry,
*Daytona State College*

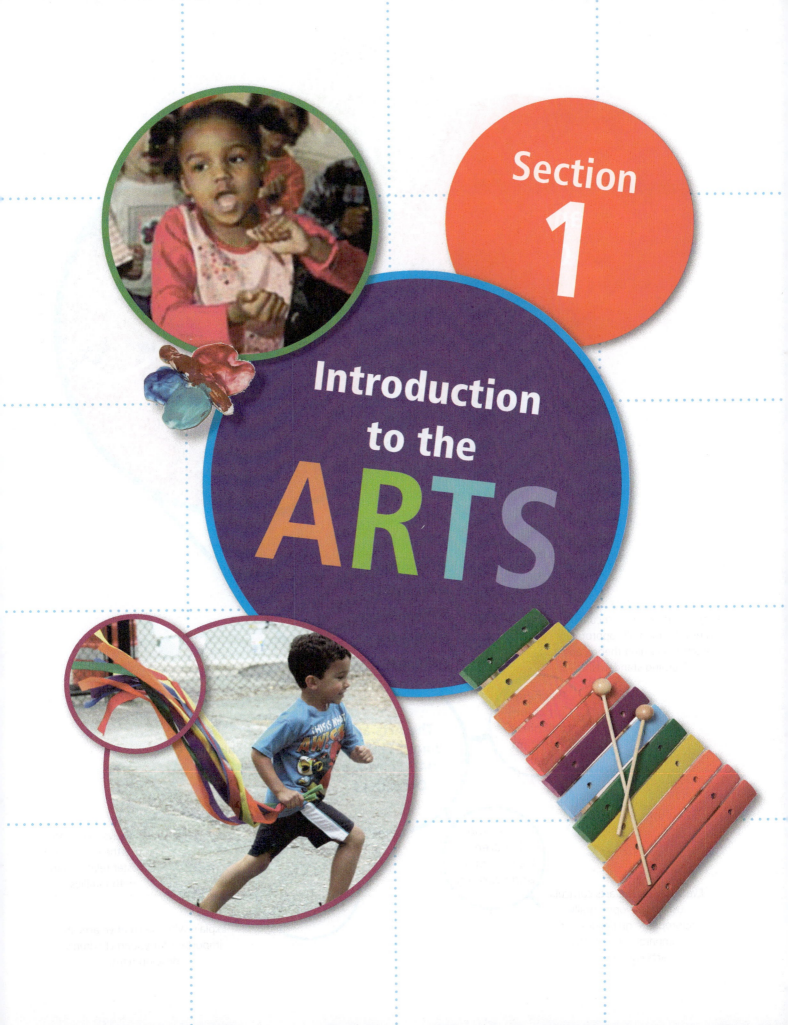

# Section 1

# Introduction to the ARTS

# The Arts and Young Children

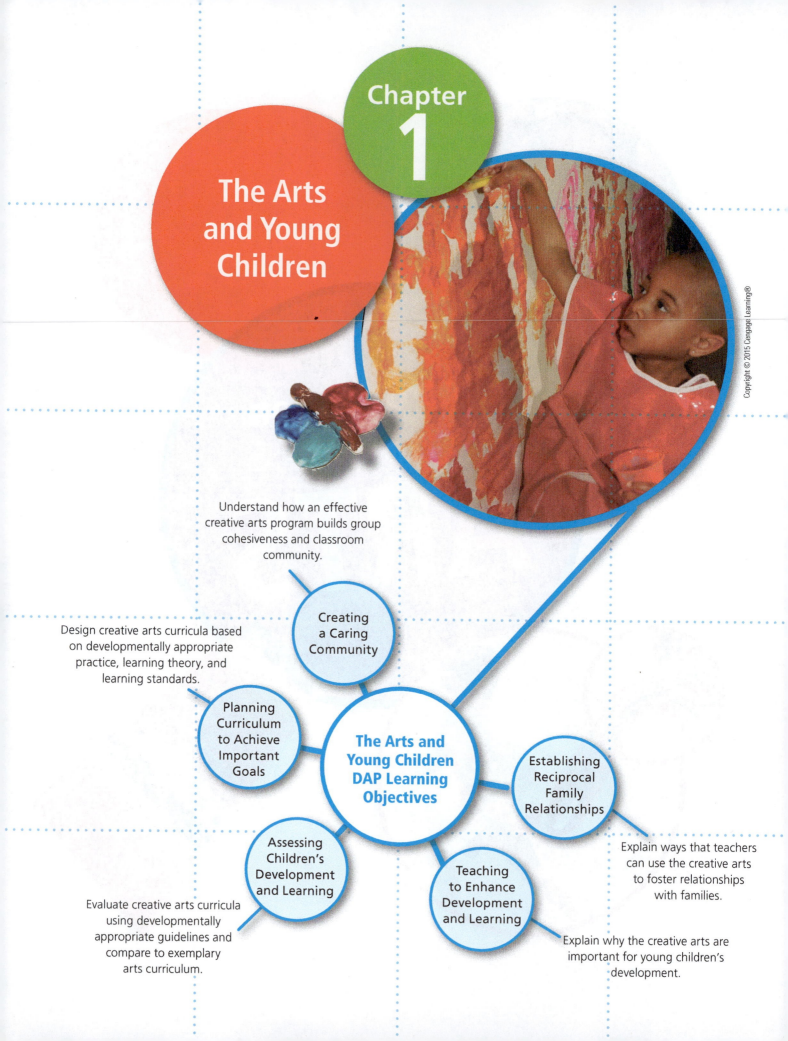

Understand how an effective creative arts program builds group cohesiveness and classroom community.

Design creative arts curricula based on developmentally appropriate practice, learning theory, and learning standards.

Creating a Caring Community

Planning Curriculum to Achieve Important Goals

**The Arts and Young Children DAP Learning Objectives**

Establishing Reciprocal Family Relationships

Assessing Children's Development and Learning

Teaching to Enhance Development and Learning

Evaluate creative arts curricula using developmentally appropriate guidelines and compare to exemplary arts curriculum.

Explain ways that teachers can use the creative arts to foster relationships with families.

Explain why the creative arts are important for young children's development.

## Young Artists Creating

Maria, age one, pulls her finger through a drop of spilled cereal and then licks her finger.

Steve, age two, hums a tune as he amuses himself during his bath by decorating the tub with handfuls of bubbly white soap foam.

Lorna, age four, splashes through a puddle and then with careful deliberation makes a pattern of wet footprints on the pavement. With every step she looks back to see her "trail."

Paul, age six, spends a busy day at the beach building sand mountains and decorating them with broken shells and beach pebbles. Other children join in his fun and watch excitedly as the surf slowly creeps up and then finally washes each mountain away.

## Who Are the Young Artists?

Each of these children is a young artist, investigating elements of the arts—line, shape, color, texture, form, movement, melody, rhythm, and pattern. They are making the same artistic discoveries and decisions that all of us have made in our own lives. In doing so, they are repeating a process that has gone on as long as people have inhabited the earth. Like the circles, swirls, and lines on the walls of the caves and cliffs that were the canvasses of the earliest humans, the stone-smoothed satin black pot of a Pueblo potter, the intense sound of a jazz musician, and the flowing movement of a Chinese lotus dancer, the art of young children expresses their personal and cultural history. Their art reflects who they are at this moment in time.

Children from birth to age eight are busy discovering the nature of their world. They are not consciously artists in the way an adult is. They do not stop and say, "Now I am creating a piece of art." They are not creating a product—they are involved in a process!

They are at play. They enjoy manipulating the many materials that they find around them and expressing their creative power to change a piece of their world. In doing so they communicate their feelings and what they are learning. As they learn, they grow and develop.

In this process they gain control over their large and small muscles. Their skill in handling their bodies and artistic tools improves. Their repertoire of lines,

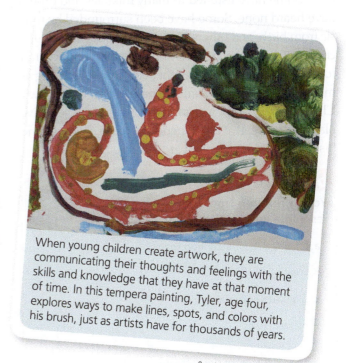

When young children create artwork, they are communicating their thoughts and feelings with the skills and knowledge that they have at that moment of time. In this tempera painting, Tyler, age four, explores ways to make lines, spots, and colors with his brush, just as artists have for thousands of years.

Copyright © 2015 Cengage Learning®

shapes, sounds, movements, and patterns expands. They repeat their successes over and over and learn to use artistic symbols that have meaning not just to themselves but also to others around them. By the time these young artists reach age eight, they already know a great deal about the world of creative expression.

But these growing artists are also still very young. They do not yet have skillful control over their bodies and the materials they use. They make messes. They sing out of tune and bump into things. They cry if they spill paint on their shoes.

Young children have short attention spans and are infinitely curious. They get distracted by a noise and run off, leaving their paintbrush in the middle of their picture. They do not always do things in an orderly sequence. Sometimes they glue their paper to the table. Sometimes they drop clay on the floor and unintentionally step on it when trying to pick it up. Anyone working with these children soon learns that great patience is needed.

But most importantly, each child is unique. As young as they are, they each bring to the creative arts experience their own personalities as well as their family and cultural heritage. Some are timid. Others are bold. Some have listened to many folktales and others have heard none. Some have been surrounded by music from birth, and others have rarely heard a tune. One child may have been taught not to get dirty and will not touch fingerpaint, while another child revels in being as messy as possible and smears paint up to the elbows. Children grow at their own pace, but through sensitive planning of creative arts experiences, each child can find his or her personal joy and growth through the arts.

---

**Did You Get It?**

**Young children from birth to age eight most resemble adult artists when they:**

   a. display a short attention span

   b. create a product

   c. play with materials

   d. make messes

**Take the full quiz on CourseMate**

---

## What Are the Creative Arts?

The arts exist in all societies and have been part of human existence since prehistoric times. Ellen Dissanayake (1995) points out that art creation is taking ordinary things and making them special. She argues that making art is part of being human—a normal behavior in which all people participate. Jessica Davis (2008) notes that as long as people have made tools

they have also made art. Through the creative manipulation of visual, auditory, dramatic, and spatial elements, the arts express the history, culture, and soul of the peoples of the world, both past and present.

## A World Without the Arts

The arts are so much a part of our lives that we can recognize their existence only by imagining their absence. Envision our homes and clothing without patterns, textures, and colors; our books without stories; advertisements without pictures; a drive in the car without music; and our feet never dancing to the rhythm of a pop tune. Their purpose can be practical—as in the interior design of a home; communicative—as in an illustration or a television advertisement; or aesthetically and spiritually expressive—as in the swirling colors of a Van Gogh painting or the power of a Beethoven symphony.

In the same way, the creative arts are a part of every activity we offer children, through the clapped rhythms we use to catch their attention, in the box of blocks we give them to build with, and in the picture books we choose to read to them. The colors, textures, and forms of the toys we purchase, the pictures we hang on the walls, the patterns on our floors, and the sounds and rhythms they hear all form the artistic environment of the child. The arts surround us constantly. We can choose to ignore them, or we can select activities for children with an awareness of the role the arts play in our lives.

## The Unique Arts

All of the arts incorporate creative problem solving, playfulness, and the expression of feelings and ideas. The term **the arts** encompasses all the different ways of doing this. In this text, the term **art form** is used to refer to the unique disciplines of creative movement or dance, drama, music, and visual art. However, these art forms should not be viewed as static, rigid categories. What makes them powerful is that they are expansive, and complementary, readily intermingled to create something new.

## Creative Dance

**Creative dance** explores the movement and position of the body in space. Children involved in creative movement activities discover ways to physically control and coordinate the rhythmic movement of their bodies in a specific environment, alone and in cooperation with others. Specific information on creative dance and how to introduce young children to creative movement activities is provided in Chapter 11.

## Drama

**Drama** is based on the presentation of ideas and actions through pantomime, improvisation, play acting, literature, and storytelling to create a visual and auditory performance. Dramatic activities and dramatic play engage children in verbal and physical communication through imitative role behavior, make believe, and social interaction with real and imaginary others. Chapter 12 presents many ways to interact with children through the dramatic arts and play.

## Music

**Music** is organized sound. Music activities provide opportunities for children to learn how to control and respond to voices and instruments as they create rhythmic and melodic patterns through song and sound. Chapter 10 looks at ways to increase children's skill in listening to music, making music, and creating music.

## Visual Arts

The **visual arts** draw on visual and tactile elements in order to communicate ideas and feelings. Children involved in visual arts activities use hand-eye coordination as they become skilled at manipulating materials and tools in symbolic ways. Two-dimensional and three-dimensional art activities for young children are provided in Chapter 9.

### Did You Get It?

Creative dance, dramatic play, music, and visual art all share which feature?

a. colorfulness

b. playfulness

c. story structure

d. sound play

Take the full quiz on CourseMate

## Why Should the Arts Be Taught to Young Children?

We need to teach the arts to young children, first of all, because the arts are an integral part of our lives as human beings. Second, and just as important, the arts help children grow and develop into learners who are stronger in the key developmental areas—intellectually, linguistically, physically, emotionally, perceptually, socially, and creatively.

### The Arts Stimulate Intellectual Growth

Because the arts are multisensory and interactive, they are an ideal way to help young children develop **cognitively**. Infants are born ready to make sense of the world. From birth, their brains absorb and process sensory and spatial information. Billions of neural connections grow rapidly as the child interacts with the environment. The arts can play an important role in enhancing this process.

**The arts enrich learning.**  Eric Jensen (2005, 2008) suggests the following ways to strengthen learning based on recent brain research.

1. **Provide multisensory, interactive activities.** Because the brain is capable of simultaneously processing information from many senses, we learn best when sensory, visual, and spatial information are combined. Providing hands-on arts activities stimulates the senses and makes learning more memorable.

2. **Create an enriched environment.** Young children, and infants in particular, constantly seek stimulation and are attracted to novelty—loud noises, sudden movements, bright colors, and unique textures. Unusual events call forth excitement and curiosity. Enriched learning environments have been found to have a positive effect on brain development, physically changing the brain. Animals provided with many toys, for example, develop more brain connections than animals in bare environments (Carey, 2002, p. 11). Hanging intriguing artworks on the wall for children to look at, singing a wide variety of songs, offering intriguing props for dramatic play, and providing

colorful, tactile art materials for them to explore are ways to enrich the learning environment and foster young children's brain development.

3. **Establish connections.** Searching for meaning is an innate process. The brain constantly examines incoming information, finding and creating patterns as it creates links to previous experiences. We help children learn when we draw on what they already know and present new information in integrated ways, such as when after a trip to the supermarket we set up a play store so that children can learn more about money through their dramatic play.

4. **Build on individual interests.** Every child is unique. A child's memories are constantly changing as new connections are made between past experience and incoming information. Making and talking about their creative work is a positive way for children to share what they know and like. Based on what they tell us, we can create a more personalized curriculum.

**The arts help children develop logical thinking.** To grow intellectually means to become skilled at finding patterns, organizing them logically, and using reasoning to solve problems.

For example, arts activities invite counting, sorting, and classifying. Through questioning, children involved in arts activities can become aware of numerical concepts. They can count the number of flowers they have drawn. They can graph the shapes in their collages and sort the leftover paper scraps by color. They can represent the rhythm of a song with symbols, or map the pattern in the steps in a dance.

Well-designed arts activities require children to make their own decisions and to order their behavior to accomplish a goal. Children who are busy creating develop skill in planning and sequencing. They learn that they must put glue on the paper before attaching the piece of yarn. They must dip the brush in the water to clean the paint off of it. They must beat the drum in a regular pattern if they want to follow the rhythm of the song. They must move their arms in a special way to imitate flapping wings. When they are done, they must put their artistic tools in the proper place so they will be ready to use again.

Arts activities provide children with experiences in identifying how properties change and in discovering

By participating in creative movement activities, these young children are not only increasing physical control over their bodies in space, but are also improving their health and well-being.

examples of cause and effect. Visual arts activities allow children to examine the properties of different substances—sticky glue, damp clay, shifting sand. Music activities let children play with changes in pitch, rhythm, and dynamics. Cause and effect are discovered when children explore how their fingers can change the shape of their play dough, or discover that spinning around makes them feel dizzy. Through discussion and questioning, we can help children formulate math and science concepts about these results.

## The Arts Are a Child's First Language

Long before they can put their ideas into spoken and written words, children can demonstrate their concept of the world through the arts. It is through the creative exploration of their bodies, the materials and tools of the art form, and the environment that child artists begin to develop visual, auditory, kinesthetic, and graphic symbols with which to represent their thoughts.

Children's language abilities are enhanced through the arts in many ways.

1. **Listening.** All of the arts require children to attend carefully to directions in order to be successful.

2. **Communicating.** Children share their art creations in a variety of ways—some nonverbally, some through sound effects or movements, and others with intricate oral explanations and stories. This is an important part of language development—the prewriting stage.

3. **Vocabulary.** Children learn new words and develop fluency when describing arts materials, processes, their own work, and the works of others.

4. **Symbolically.** Between the ages of two and eight, children acquire the ability to make symbols and learn that these symbols can communicate to others. Children develop writing skills by creating a graphic symbol system to record their inner and outer observations. When children are asked to respond creatively in response to an experience, they are being challenged to communicate their ideas and thoughts in a symbolic mode. Responsive arts activities, such as imitating the movement of animals after a visit to the zoo and then talking or writing about it or keeping an illustrated journal, help them use this developing symbol system and refine the nature of their communication.

## Special Needs

### • ENGLISH LANGUAGE LEARNERS [ELLS] AND THE ARTS •

Because the arts are a nonverbal way to communicate feelings and ideas, arts activities are an ideal way to integrate non–English speaking children or those beginning to learn English into the community of the classroom. Directions for many arts activities can be given through modeling, physical clues, and hands-on demonstrations. Activities that are open-ended with no preconceived correct responses and that incorporate an element of play can allow ELLs to develop self-confidence and to gain acknowledgment from peers. For example, creative movement allows all children to express themselves nonverbally, so it provides an ideal communication tool for children who are nonnative speakers or who have trouble expressing themselves orally (Koff, 2000).

## The Arts Improve Physical Well-Being

Physical activity promotes fitness and health. This is particularly important at a time when our children are becoming increasingly sedentary. A 2006–2007 study found that 20 percent of two-year-olds watch two or more hours of television a day, which can lead to childhood obesity and slowed development (Kent, Murphy & Stanton, 2010, p. 837; Louv, 2008, p. 7).

The arts are a motivating way to get children moving. Arts activities help children improve their ability to control large and small muscles and refine hand-eye coordination. An infant shaking a bell, a preschooler jumping up and down to music, and a first grader acting out a nursery rhyme are all learning to manage the way their bodies move.

Soft, pliable play dough and clay improve finger strength. Using brushes at an easel develops control of the arm and wrist. Large and small muscles are exercised and challenged through the manipulation of materials and tools when children stack blocks or tap a rhythm on a drum. Cutting a shape from paper or placing a leaf in a dab of glue requires the eye and hand to work together. Creative movement activities, such as imagining one's body as clay that can be made into different shapes, help the child relate physical movement and concepts. Listening to different types of music has been shown to slow down or speed up a person's heart rate and lower blood pressure (Using music, 2009).

## The Arts Foster Emotional Well-Being

The arts have always been valued for the self-expression they can provide. However, their importance in emotional health goes far beyond this. Purposeful and playful physical movement, such as is found in arts activities, improves emotional well-being by causing the brain to release mood-altering chemicals, such as endorphins, which can heighten attention and provide a sense of well-being.

This is supported by current research on the effect of creative arts expression on healing. Heather Stuckey and Jeremy Noble (2010), in a summary of research done between 1995 and 2007, found a strong connection between each of the art forms and emotional well-being.

- **Music**—Music, which is the most researched of the arts, can control pain and restore emotional balance.

- **Visual Arts**—Visual art allows people to express feelings and thoughts that are difficult to put into words, such as grief, fear, and anxiety. Overall, creating visual art was found to be a positive activity that provided release from anxiety-producing situations, such as severe pain and health issues.

- **Creative Movement**—Creative movement not only improves physical condition but also improves self-awareness and body image.

- **Drama**—Theater training improves both long-term memory and feelings of self-confidence.

In all cases, participating in the arts reduced stress. Therefore, by providing a wide range of **open-ended**, developmentally appropriate arts activities, not only

The arts bring people together in ways that are enjoyable and fun. As these children learn to make music together, they are also learning how to listen to others and to work toward a common goal.

do we set the stage for young children to express their feelings, but we also gift them with a lifelong way to relieve stress and a source of self-healing that will improve the quality of their lives.

## The Arts Build Sensory Perception

The arts help children develop perceptually. Children learn through their senses. They absorb information from the world through touching, seeing, hearing, tasting, and smelling. This is how they acquire concepts about the nature of objects, actions, and events. Children learn better when teachers provide experiences that are sensually rich and varied, and that require children to use their perceptual abilities in many different ways. Children who have sung songs about, drawn pictures of, and acted out the metamorphosis of a butterfly will have a better understanding of the process than children who have only been told about the process.

The arts also enhance perceptive skills by teaching spatial concepts. Creative movement activities, for example, allow children to play with and use spatial concepts such as big/small, long/short, and under/over as they reach high or crawl along the floor. Visual arts activities let children explore the visual and tactile constructs of color, shape, pattern, form, and placement in space as they draw, paint, and play with modeling clay. Singing and playing instruments provide opportunities for children to develop their listening abilities as they investigate pitch, rhythm, and melody.

Most importantly, the arts, especially when integrated with experiences with nature, allow children to use all their senses to develop a sense of wonder and appreciation for the aesthetic qualities of the objects in our world. Chapter 4 presents activities that awaken children to the sensory landscape around them.

## The Arts Create Community

Arts activities can help children develop socially by teaching them to take turns, to share space and materials with others, and to make positive choices in personal behavior. Arts activities often require children to work with others to accomplish a project or to produce a single, unified piece of art or a dramatic story.

Looking at artwork done by people different from oneself, taking a role in dramatic play, and experiencing unfamiliar styles of music are all ways to enhance children's understanding that each person has a different viewpoint and other individuals do not necessarily see things the same way they do. The arts provide the best entry point for developing media literacy (Nakamura et al., 2009). This is an essential skill for thinking critically in a society in which visual images, music, acting, and dance are frequently used in advertisements to entice us to make unnecessary purchases or propagandize one political point of view over another.

## Across Cultures

**Multiculturalism: What It Looks Like in the Arts**

1. **Content Integration:** Information about diverse peoples and cultures are woven into the entire curriculum on a daily basis. *What this looks like:* Crayons and paints in shades of skin tones are available every day in the art center, not just for certain projects. Instruments from Asia and Africa are included in the bin of rhythm instruments, not just brought out on a special occasion.

2. **Knowledge Construction:** Diversity and cultural perspectives are valued and included. Prejudice and discrimination is recognized and addressed. *What this looks like:* A parent from Haiti visits the class and teaches a song she learned as a child. A Thanksgiving poster depicting Eastern Woodland Native Americans in Plains Indian headdresses is replaced with a more accurate image.

3. **Equity Pedagogy:** Teachers change the way they teach so that all students can understand and learn. *What this looks like:* Arts directions are given in a way that non–English speaking children can understand.

4. **Prejudice Reduction:** Teachers address prejudice when they see and hear it and actively celebrate diversity. *What this looks like:* In selecting art posters to share with the class, the teacher makes sure that many different cultures and types of people are represented.

*See Chapters 5 and 7 for more ideas.*

Sharing space and supplies, laughter and tears, and working on group projects with other young artists help children learn the power of cooperation and of empathy (Brouillette, 2010). Jessica Davis (2008) reminds us that the arts "excite and engage students, wakening attitudes to learning, including passion and joy, and the discovery 'I care.'" Chapter 5 presents many ways to foster community through the arts.

Studying the arts of other times, people, and cultures is another way the arts can draw us together as we learn to appreciate and understand the fabulous diversity of creative ideas as represented by unique art forms from around the world. In addition, sharing the arts from the cultures of students and their families is a respectful way to honor the diversity of our children. In Chapter 7 we will explore ways to present the art of others to young children.

**Addressing bias and cultural differences.** Our children come from different social and cultural backgrounds. Derman-Sparks and the A.B.C. Task Force (1989) encourage arts activities that help children accept racial and cultural differences and reject stereotypes. Selecting arts activities that show respect for their family backgrounds, home culture, and language can support children from diverse cultures and make families feel valued. Activities should reflect appreciation for different cultural beliefs, holiday customs, and family traditions, and they should develop a sense of community. Visual art materials should reflect the many colors of humanity; drama, music, and dance activities should reflect the stories, sounds, and rhythms of the world, as well as the local community; and artworks that decorate the walls should represent people from diverse backgrounds. Field trips and guest artists can provide access to culturally diverse musical, dance, and dramatic performances. Through seeing, touching, and talking about a wide variety of art forms selected from both their own culture and different cultures, children learn that the arts reflect the ideas and feelings of all people.

## The Arts Nurture Creativity

The arts occupy the realm of the imagination. The unstructured quality of well-designed arts activities allows children to experiment with their voices, bodies, and familiar materials in new ways. They can use their own ideas and power to initiate and cause change and to produce original actions and combinations. Paint that drips, block towers that fall down, whistles that are hard to blow, and all of the other small difficulties arts activities present challenge children to find their own solutions to emerging problems.

Torrance (1970) defined creativity as being able to see a problem, form ideas about it, and then communicate the results. When children are engaged in the arts, they are creating something new and unique; in doing so, they are being creative. As Chapter 2 will illustrate, creativity is not something that can be taught but, instead, is something that must be nurtured.

---

**Did You Get It?**

**Which of the following is true of the relationship between the arts and child development?**

a. Children first develop their understanding of the world through spoken and written words.

b. The arts have no developmental effect on children before the age of two years, when they can understand arts concepts.

c. Arts activities develop those areas of a child's brain that are not concerned with logic and cognition.

d. The arts allow children to develop socially.

**Take the full quiz on CourseMate**

---

# How Do the Creative Arts Help Children Learn?

Young children do not have a set goal in mind as they begin to create artistically, any more than they start the day with the goal of learning ten new words. They are caught up in the process of responding to and playing with the stimuli around them, such as the way paint drips, the way clay stretches and bends, and the way another child hums a tune.

As teachers, we can see children growing and developing through the arts activities we design. We can watch the changes in behavior that come with increasing experience in the arts—from the first tentative brush strokes of the two-year-old to the tuneful singing of the mature eight-year-old. However, it is also necessary that children grow in ways that will make them more successful in their interactions with the world.

The nature of an early childhood arts curriculum is determined by our philosophy of how children learn. Visits to most preschools, child care centers, and primary school programs will reveal children drawing, painting, singing, and dancing. However, what the children are actually doing as they draw, paint, sing, and dance will vary widely depending on what the adults in charge believe young children are capable of doing, what they think is the correct way to teach them, and how they interpret the role of the arts in education.

To strengthen our philosophy and establish our goals, we need to examine learning theories, contemporary viewpoints, current research, and successful approaches to the arts in the education of children. These ideas will provide direction in the creation of a successful and meaningful arts curriculum for young children.

## Piaget and Constructivism

In the early 1920s Jean Piaget, a Swiss biologist, began studying children's responses to problems he designed. Based on his now-classic research, Piaget (1959) described how children develop their knowledge of the world. His findings have become the basis of the constructivist approach to early childhood education and include the following beliefs about how children learn:

- Children are active learners. They are curious and actively seek out information that helps them make sense of the world around them.

- Children construct knowledge based on their experiences. Because each child has different experiences, the understandings and misunderstandings acquired are unique to each child and are continually changing as the child has new experiences.

- Experience is essential for cognitive development. Children need to physically interact with the people and objects around them.

- Thoughts become more complex as children have more experiences. Although Piaget proposed that cognitive development was age dependent, many researchers today have modified his age categories and believe that complexity of thought follows gradual trends and may vary in different contexts and content areas (Ormrod, 2003).

## TeachSource Video Case 1.1

### 0–2 Years: Piaget's Sensorimotor Stage

Watch the *0–2 Years: Piaget's Sensori-Motor Stage*. Do you think young children think the same way as adults? How does Piaget explain how children think and learn?

**Watch on CourseMate**

**Theory in practice.** Constructivism views children as self-motivated learners who are responsible for their own learning. Open-ended arts activities that offer many creative possibilities and choices are ideal for this purpose. Logical thought is developed by asking children to explain why they chose their particular creative solutions.

## Vygotsky's Sociocultural Perspective and Social Cognitive Theory

Research on children's thinking in the 1920s and 1930s by Lev Vygotsky (1978) emphasized the importance of peers and adults in children's cognitive development. Vygotsky proposed that one way children construct their knowledge is based on past and present social interactions. His major points were the following:

- Complex thought begins through communication with adults and more knowledgeable peers. Watching and interacting with the people around them helps children internalize the thought processes, concepts, and beliefs common to their culture.

- Although children need to experience things personally and make discoveries on their own, they can also learn from the experiences of others.

- Children can perform at a higher cognitive level when guided by an adult or a more competent peer. Vygotsky defined the **actual developmental level** as what the child can do independently, and the **potential developmental level** as what the child can do with assistance.

- According to Vygotsky, most learning occurs when children are challenged to perform closer to their potential developmental level in what has come to be known as the **zone of proximal development**. It is when they are asked to perform tasks that require communication with more skilled individuals that children experience maximum cognitive growth.

- Vygotsky also thought that young children developed symbolic thought through play. Make-believe and dramatic play allow children to represent ideas using substitute objects (for example, pretending that a bowl placed upside down on their head is a hat) and so help children develop the ability to think abstractly.

Social cognitive theory emphasizes the role of modeling and imitation in children's learning. The well-known psychologist Albert Bandura (1973) found, for example, that children who watched a doll being treated aggressively repeated the behavior when alone with the doll.

However, for a child to learn from a role model, four factors need to occur.

1. **Attention:** The child needs to watch the role model perform the behavior.

2. **Motivation:** The child must want to imitate the role model. Bandura found children were more likely to imitate those they liked or respected, or who were considered attractive or powerful (Bandura, 1989).

3. **Remembering:** The child needs to understand and recall what the role model did.

4. **Reproduction:** The child must repeat the behavior enough times to improve in skill.

**Theory in practice.** These theories help us see children as members of a social community in which adults as role models are an important source of information about the nature of the arts. As teachers we

## ▶❙❙ TeachSource Video Case 1.2

### 5-11 Years: Lev Vygotsky, the Zone of Proximal Development, and Scaffolding

Watch the video *5–11 Years: Lev Vygotsky and the Zone of Proximal Development and Scaffolding.* How do Piaget's and Vygotsky's approaches compare? What are some ways you can determine when a child is ready to learn something new?

**Watch on CourseMate**

1. **Linguistic:** The ability to manipulate the oral and written symbols of language

2. **Logical-Mathematical:** The ability to manipulate numerical patterns and concepts in logical ways

3. **Spatial:** The ability to visualize the configuration of objects in both two- and three-dimensional space

4. **Musical:** The ability to manipulate rhythm and sound

5. **Bodily-Kinesthetic:** The ability to use the body to solve problems or to make things

6. **Interpersonal:** The ability to understand and work with others

7. **Intrapersonal:** The ability to understand oneself

can model for children how artists think and behave. This is because the arts lend themselves to what is characterized as the "apprenticeship model" (Gardner, 1993). In an apprenticeship, the child learns not only how to do the task but also how experts think about the task. We can model artistic methods while thinking out loud about the process. We can make well-timed suggestions that guide the child to the next level of understanding, and we can ask children to explain what they are doing so that they make the learning their own. In addition, we can provide models of what the arts can be by introducing children to wonderful artists from all times and cultures. Doing these things will not only help children grow cognitively but will also nurture their ability to think and act as artists.

## Multiple Intelligence Theory

Based on cognitive research, Howard Gardner (1983, 1991) has proposed that there are at least eight intellectual capabilities, or **intelligences.** These intelligences represent biological and psychological potentials within each individual. Everyone has capabilities in each intelligence, with special strengths in one or more of them. Gardner has identified these intelligences as follows:

Open-ended arts activities have no preconceived end result. Instead, they invite exploration of materials and concepts or pose a problem that can be solved in multiple ways. Playing with puppets allows children to express their ideas and feelings in a wide variety of ways as they engage in imaginative dramatic play. Will this dinosaur be angry and bite or will he be friendly? This child can create his own dinosaur story while developing his oral language skills.

8. **Naturalistic-Environmental:** The ability to sense and make use of the characteristics of the natural world

Traditional educational practice has focused mainly on strengths in the linguistic and logical-mathematical domains. Multiple intelligences (MI) theory provides a framework upon which teachers can build a more educationally balanced program—one that better meets the needs of children with talents in other areas. The arts as a learning and symbolic tool is particularly valuable not only because it embraces the talents often overlooked in education, but also because it crosses and links all of the intelligences.

It is important to note that Gardner (1993) does not believe that there is a separate artistic intelligence. Instead, each of the eight intelligences can be used for either artistic or nonartistic purposes. How an intelligence is expressed will depend on a variety of factors, including personal choice and cultural environment. Linguistic intelligence, for example, can be used to scribble an appointment on a calendar or to compose a short story. Spatial intelligence can be used to create a sculpture or to read a map. Conversely, to create a painting, a visual artist must draw not only on visual-spatial intelligence in order to visualize the artistic elements in the work, but also on bodily-kinesthetic intelligence in order to control the brush and logical-mathematical intelligence in order to plan the sequence in which the paint will be applied.

**Theory in practice. MI theory** broadens our view of children's abilities and potentials into a multidimensional view of intelligence. It means that we need to honor the special abilities of every child by creating an early childhood curriculum that includes many opportunities to use all of the intelligences in artistic ways.

Not every activity will engage all of the intelligences, but when activities are chosen that incorporate many of the intelligences, children can learn in whatever way best fits their intellectual strengths or learning style. In this book, Gardner's intelligences have been interrelated with the physical, linguistic, social, emotional, creative, and intellectual growth areas in order to create models of such balanced arts activities.

*For an example of an MI curriculum planning web with correlated objectives, see The MI Planning Web on CourseMate.*

---

**Did You Get It?**

Ms. Fanelli, a preschool teacher, believes in the constructivist approach to learning. Accordingly, she will most likely

a. allow children to physically interact with objects and people around them.

b. evaluate a child's ability to create an original melody by comparing the child's work to that of his peers.

c. develop arts activities that require the children to follow step-by-step directions.

d. view children as requiring constant supervision and direction in arts activities.

Take the full quiz on CourseMate

---

## What Does a Well-Designed Arts Curriculum Look Like?

The Task Force on Children's Learning and the Arts: Birth to Age 8 (1998) has laid out three curriculum strands for arts-based curricula. These incorporate the need for artistic skills and judgments, while at the same time allowing for creative self-expression and cultural understanding. These strands are as follows:

➤ **Children must be active participants in the arts process.** They should create, participate, perform, and respond to carefully selected arts activities that reflect their culture and background experience.

➤ **Arts activities must be domain based, relevant, and integrated.** Arts activities should allow every child to be successful and reflect children's daily life experiences. The arts should be fully integrated into the rest of the curriculum and help children make connections with what they are learning. At the same time, these activities should build artistic skill and competence in the particular art form being used. Verbal and graphic expressive, reflective, and evaluative responses to arts activities can provide the opportunity to build literacy and intellectual skills.

➤ **The learning environment must nurture the arts.** Adequate quality materials, space, and time should be provided with the needs and abilities of the children foremost. Adult engagement should

## Integrating the Arts

### WHAT IS ARTS INTEGRATION?

According to the Kennedy Center Artsedge (http://artsedge.kennedy-center.org) arts integration means that children develop understanding of a concept and demonstrate that new knowledge through an art form. Integrated arts curricula creatively connect language, math, social studies, or science concepts together with one or more art forms so that the learning objectives in both areas are met.

*Integrated arts curriculum design will be examined more deeply in Chapter 8.*

share in and support children in their artistic explorations and reflect input from current research in the field and artists, arts specialists, early childhood teachers, parents, caregivers, and other community resources.

## Developmentally Appropriate Practice and the Arts

The National Association for the Education of Young Children (NAEYC) has  similar recommendations (Copple & Bredekamp, 2009). A developmentally appropriate curriculum provides daily opportunities for creative exploration and aesthetic appreciation in all of the arts forms using a wide range of materials from a variety of cultures. These activities are integrated into the children's total learning experiences and, while introducing arts vocabulary and concepts, and should have an open-ended design that has joy as its central purpose.

## The Reggio Emilia Approach to Arts Education

These principles are well illustrated by the preprimary program of the municipality of Reggio Emilia, Italy. In this program, the arts are highly valued. Each school has an *atelierista*, or art educator, who works directly with the teachers in designing the program. In addition, each school has a beautiful art room where supplies are arranged by color. This attention to aesthetic qualities carries over to the

school itself, which is decorated with children's artwork that has been carefully mounted. Light, mirrors, and color produce wonderful spaces in which children can play and create. In the Reggio Emilia program, the arts are used as an important method of recording the observations, ideas, and memories of experiences in which the children have participated. The *atelierista* offers suggestions as the children work. The children also share their art with other children. Unlike in the United States, where arts experiences are often used as fillers and artwork is usually sent home at the end of each day, in Reggio Emilia, children are asked to return to their artistic works to reconsider, discuss and critique, and then to rework, or repeat their responsive arts activities.

The Reggio Emilia program is an example of **emergent curriculum.** Elizabeth Jones and John Nimmo (1994) describe this approach to teaching young children as one in which teachers are sensitive to the needs and interests of the children and then build on these through the provision of wonderful learning experiences. The teacher and children are coplayers sharing ideas and choices together in a curriculum that is open-ended and constantly adjusting to new ideas and needs. This does not mean that the teacher has no control over the

Creativity is nourished when children are allowed the freedom to express their unique ideas in an accepting environment that values the arts as a form of communication and self-expression. Jason, age four, has painted his own idea of a cat.

curriculum. Rather the guiding adult is more like a stage director, the one who "sets the stage, times the acts, and keeps the basic drama together" (1994, p. 5). In such a curriculum, the arts can play a major role as is seen in the work done by children in the Reggio Emilia schools.

## The Project Approach

Another example of emergent curriculum in action is the Project Approach, as exemplified by the work of Lillian Katz and Sylvia Chard (2000). This approach identifies and investigates a topic based on child interest, and then the arts are incorporated as a rich, vital way to express learning will be examined more deeply in Chapter 8.

## Goals for Learning

What do children need to learn about the arts? This is a key question in designing an effective arts curriculum for young children. According to Lillian Katz and Sylvia Chard (2000), there are four main categories of learning goals.

**Knowledge.** **Knowledge** includes the vocabulary and concepts we want our children to hear and use. In early childhood arts, this means that we must make sure that children will be learning to talk about and identify the elements of each art form, as well as the materials and methods belonging to each. We then want children to be able to apply what they have learned in their artistic performances and creations as well as in their responses to the artwork of others.

Young children construct this kind of knowledge from direct experiences and interactions with more expert peers and adults. It happens when we ask children to tell how they made a particular color in their paintings or when they learn a song from a friend. The knowledge to be imparted can be expressed in the vocabulary words selected, the concepts being applied, and the questions children will be asked as they are involved in arts activities. In the Exploring the Arts section of this book, examples of these are found under the "What to Say" heading.

**Dispositions.** **Dispositions** are the ways we behave as learners and performers. Examples of dispositions include being intellectually curious, using

the creative process, thinking logically, and being generous and helpful. Another way to view dispositions is to think of them as preferred ways of thinking and behaving. We can think and make decisions, as would a creative musician, an inquiring artist, or an observant poet. Dispositions are nurtured instead of being taught directly. They develop best in carefully designed open-ended learning environments that allow creative exploration, provide safe risk taking, and foster creative problem solving.

Many different dispositions can be developed in the creation of art. First and foremost is the disposition to think and to act like a creative artist, musician, dancer, or actor. For example, a young child playing a drum may say, "Look, I am a drummer like in the band. You can march to the beat of my drum." This is nourished through open-ended arts activities using real art skills, materials, and tools presented by a teacher who is passionate about the arts and who verbally and visually models what these artists do. At the same time, thoughtful statements and questions can promote intellectual curiosity, and careful organization of the activity can promote cooperative behavior and nurture the growth of a caring and socially aware individual.

**Feelings.** Feelings describe how children receive, respond to, and value what they are learning and are reflected in the emotional state of the child. Positive feelings about the arts, or any other subject area, develop in an arts program that makes children feel safe; when activities are challenging but possible; when mistakes are seen as positive ways to grow; and where accomplishments are enthusiastically acknowledged.

Children come to value the arts when we prepare a curriculum that provides activities that share with them a sense of wonder and awaken them to the aesthetic qualities of the world in which they live, and encourages them to respond positively to the art of others. In such an arts program, teachers and peers respond to artistic endeavors with heartfelt, thoughtful comments, and provide open-ended arts activities that allow children to express their unique personal feelings and ideas. Most importantly, a well-planned arts program allows all children to feel successful as artists, thereby enabling them to see themselves as competent individuals.

**Skills.** Skills are the observable behaviors used in arts creation, such as cutting out shapes with a scissors or shaping clay into a ball. Although some skills are learned spontaneously, most develop through practice. If we want our children to be able to use paint skillfully, for example, then we need to give them lots of opportunities to explore paint. In addition, skills from the different growth areas can be practiced through the arts. For example, intentionally having two children use the same glue bottle provides them with an opportunity to practice sharing. Talking about how it feels to move like a drop of water allows children to develop their oral language skills. In fact, well-planned arts activities usually address skill development in all of the growth areas.

## National Core Standards for Arts Education

Another way of looking at what children need to learn about the arts is to examine standards for arts education. Standards provide us with a definition of what a good arts education is and provide a structure on which to build a successful arts program. Based on the specific concepts and skills identified in the standards, we can make sure that young children are introduced to a breadth of rich arts experiences through the curriculum units and activity plans we write. In conjunction with forming teaching objectives, the content standards for visual arts, music, dance, and dramatics are provided in Chapters 9 through 12.

The 2013 National Core Arts Standards (National Coalition for Core Arts Standards, 2013) address what competencies children from kindergarten to high school should have in the arts in order to become adults who understand, value, and enjoy the arts.

The 2013 Core Arts Standards are based on the following definition of artistic literacy, which recognizes the importance of the arts in our society:

Artistic literacy is the knowledge and understanding required to participate authentically in the arts. Fluency in the language(s) of the arts is the ability to create, perform/produce/present, respond, and connect through symbolic and metaphoric forms that are unique to the arts. It is embodied in specific philosophical foundations and lifelong goals that enable an artistically literate person to transfer arts knowledge, skills, and capacities to other subjects, settings, and contexts. (p. 13)

To address this goal of artistic literacy for all students the standards delineate expectations in the following areas of competency in the arts:

1. **Creating:** Conceiving and developing new artistic ideas and work.

2. **Performing** (dance, music, theatre), **Producing** (media arts), and **Presenting** (visual arts): Although the various arts disciplines have chosen different words to represent this artistic process, they are clustered here as essentially parallel. This area of competency refers to the physical interaction with the materials, concepts, and techniques of the arts forms as well as the sharing of that process with others.

3. **Responding:** Interacting with and reflecting on artistic work and performances to develop understanding.

4. **Connecting:** Relating artistic ideas and work with personal meaning and contextual knowledge.

The 2013 Core Arts Standards also establish benchmarks starting at the end of second grade that assess the artistic literacy of the children. Early childhood arts education as described in this text will be key in making sure our children reach these high levels of artistic understanding. In addition, because the arts are a vehicle for learning in all areas of knowledge, the arts standards are linked to the National Common Core State Standards in English Language Arts and Mathematics.

Similar arts standards for the education of younger children have been developed by many states.

## Photo Story

## Oceans Integrated Arts Unit

Engaging in dramatic play with sea toys develops creative storytelling skills and at the same time allows a science-related investigation of buoyancy.

Observing and caring for live fish provides inspiration for arts production and performance while developing an understanding of aquatic life. The fish in the children's artworks sprout fins and gills.

Sorting seashells develops sensory and aesthetic perception as well as logical mathematical reasoning skills.

"Rainbow fish" Carved Styrofoam and sponge prints— Emma, Makenzie, Jason, and Jack ages seven and eight

"Shark attack" by Ben age seven

"Fish mobiles" Cut paper—Cynthia, Jake, and David ages seven and eight

For more information on arts standards and to see a sample of state arts standards, visit, *Learning Standards Resources* on CourseMate.

**Did You Get It?**

According to the Task Force on Children's Learning and the Arts: Birth to Age 8, the developmentally appropriate practice for arts education for young children should include

a. daily opportunities for active, creative exploration and aesthetic appreciation.

b. regular offerings of simple arts activities.

c. only materials that are familiar to the children.

d. step-by-step guidance of children as they participate in arts activities.

Take the full quiz on CourseMate

## What Is the Teacher's Role in Creative Arts Education?

In an early childhood program that values the arts, music, dance, dramatics, and visual arts activities are inseparable from the total curriculum. It all seems so effortless. There is a rhythm and flow to a well-planned program that creates the sense that this is what will naturally happen if the children are just told to have fun with a lot of interesting materials. Nothing could be farther from the truth.

Behind that successful program is superb planning by teachers who have knowledge about how children think, learn, and respond to stimuli in their environment. These teachers practice **intentional teaching**. This means that they have a strong knowledge of how children develop in the arts and have practiced ahead of time what they will say and do to encourage young artists so that when that **teachable moment** arises—and it will if open-ended materials and experiences are provided—everything comes together in a moment of wonder and understanding.

We can be those teachers. We can learn what to say about arts production, presentation, and performance, how to say it, and when it is best left unsaid. We can know when to interact and when to wait and watch.

We will seek to be judged not on the children's products but on their growth. We can continually learn and grow along with our young artists from the first contact to the last. We can constantly improve the curriculum we offer, assessing each activity and noting how the children show growth in relation to the goals we have set for them. The result is an arts curriculum of our own creation, both meaningful and thoughtful.

As teachers, we do not need to be professional musicians, dancers, artists, or actors to be effective teachers of the arts. Rather we need to design an art curriculum made up of activities that nurture young artists.

In the end, the teacher is the most important part of the arts curriculum. Teachers are like gardeners, providing the "fertile ground"—the enriched arts curriculum—that gives children a start in thinking and working as artists. As the children grow in skill and confidence, it is our planning, enthusiasm, and encouragement that will allow the child's creativity to flower. It is the purpose of this text to help you become this teacher.

**Did You Get It?**

Intentional teaching means

a. using an idea found on the Internet.

b. using knowledge of children's artistic development to plan arts activities.

c. using materials that have one specific use.

d. ignoring the teachable moment.

Take the full quiz on CourseMate

## Conclusion: The Well-Designed Arts Program

The stage has now been set for developing a rich and meaningful arts program for children. Children are natural artists, in the sense that they play creatively with the elements of the arts that they find in their surroundings. But those surroundings must be provided, determined by a philosophy of what child art is, and what it means. We need to consider why children should do certain arts activities, which ones should be selected, how they should be delivered, and what environment is most conducive to their performance.

This chapter has closely examined why the arts need to be taught. We have learned how the arts help children grow socially, emotionally, physically, intellectually, and linguistically. The following chapters will consider:

1. **How:** We will see how the delivery of arts activities affects what children learn, as well as how the way the child learns affects what activities will be successful.

2. **Where:** We will learn how to design the environment in which child artists will work.

3. **What:** We will investigate the appropriate selection and efficient delivery of arts concepts and skills.

It is the educator's role to nurture the artist within every young child. Although the focus will always be on guiding the artistic development of the child, in doing so the artist within the adult will also be rekindled. Adults and children must become part of the artistic continuum that stretches from our distant human past into the future. To guide young children as they grow through the arts is a deeply rewarding experience.

For additional information about the importance of the arts, arts organizations, and arts standards, see *Online Resources* on CourseMate.

## Teaching In Action

### An Integrated Arts Curriculum

*The arts are integrated into the curriculum through emergent curriculum.*

It is a warm spring day, and sunlight streams through the windows of the large bright room. Photographs of fish and sea creatures decorate one wall. Children's books about the sea are on display on the bookshelf. The teacher has already read several books about the sea to the children and talked to the children about experiences they have had during visits to the beach. Seashells, starfish, fishnets, floats, and other sea-related objects are placed around the room. It is easy to tell that the children have been learning about the ocean. In the center of the room an adult and several children, ages three and four, are hard at work painting a refrigerator box in which round windows and two doors have been cut. They are using yellow poster paint and large paintbrushes. Newspapers cover the floor. One child is painting broad strokes of color across the box, while the other child presses the brush down again and again, making rectangular stamp marks in one small section. In the background, a recording of the Beatles' classic "Yellow Submarine" can be heard.

*Children develop socially by working on a group project.*

*The teacher enthusiastically responds to the artistic elements in the child's work with positive feedback.*

While the painters work away on their submarine, other children are playing at the water table, experimenting with a variety of objects in different sizes, colors, and shapes that either sink or float. At an easel, a four-year-old has filled his paper with waving lines using mixtures of blue, green, and yellow paint. The teacher stops to help the painter at the easel remove his smock. "Look at all the blue-greens and turquoises you have made," she tells him, pointing to examples of those colors.

*(continued)*

## Teaching In Action (continued)

*Arts activities are open-ended. Children choose to use the art supplies in their own creative way.*

At a round table, three children have taken premade paper tubes from the supply shelf and are decorating them with paper, yarn, glue, and crayons. One child asks the teacher to attach a piece of blue cellophane to the end of his "scope." A second child puts her tube up to her nose. "I'm a swordfish. This is my sword. I have a beautiful sword," she tells another girl as she makes a roaring sound through the tube. A three-year-old is exploring what happens when he glues a piece of yarn on the tube and then pulls it off. In another corner, two boys are engaged in noisy, animated play with trucks and blocks. At the computer, a four-year-old is making a multicolored line travel a wiggly path over the screen.

*Visual images from diverse sources enrich the children's experience.*

At the game table, two children are matching pictures. The cards have been made from prints of paintings, sculptures, and crafts from many cultures that illustrate subjects about the sea. These have been cut out of museum catalogs, glued to card stock, and laminated. On the wall behind them is a poster-size print of one of the artworks. One child finds a card that matches the poster and walks over and compares the two pictures. "They're the same, but this one is littler," he notes, holding the picture card up to the print.

*Visitors provide common experiences that lead to integrated learning.*

Suddenly everyone stops working. A special visitor has arrived! A father of one of the children brings in two plastic buckets, and all the children circle round. In the tubs are saltwater creatures borrowed from the pet store where he works. The children closely observe a sea urchin, an anemone, and a sea snake. One child looks at the sea urchin through his cellophane-covered tube. "It changes color," he states with wonder. He shares his tube with the others so they can see the change too.

*Arts and language activities are unified.*

When the visitor leaves, some children head off to a table where crayons, markers, and stapled paper booklets are set out. "I'm writing a story about a sea snake and an 'anoome,'" says one five-year-old girl. She draws a long wiggly line on one page. "Here he is very sad." Then she draws a purple circle. "This is his friend, the 'anoome.' Now he is happy!" When she finishes her book, she "reads" it to her teacher, inventing a long, detailed story to go with her pictures. "You made your anemone the same color as the one Sam's father brought to show us," the teacher says. The girl beams with pride and skips off to read her book to her friend.

*Children explore sensory experiences.*

A three-year-old has settled in with a lump of play dough. He rolls out a long "worm." "Look—I can make it wiggle like a sea snake," he says, as he twists and turns the play dough. Some children take cardboard tubes to decorate. They want to put cellophane on theirs so they can have their own "scopes." Several other children have taken colored paper, markers, and scissors. They talk quietly together as they invent new sea creatures.

"Mine has tentacles like the sea urchin."

"I'm going to give mine a big mouth and teeth," says another. They cut out their creatures and take them to the teacher.

*(continued)*

## Teaching In Action

*Children initiate and choose what they want displayed.*

"Let's put a string on them and hang them up so they can swim in our sea," says one. The teacher hangs their creatures inside a large glass aquarium that has been decorated with sand and shells on the bottom. They join other paper sea creatures, made by other children, which are already afloat on the air currents.

Meanwhile, several other children have moved into the submarine. They are busy arranging blankets and pillows.

"I think it is softer this way," says Peter. Sam lies down and tries it out. He curls up and sucks his thumb.

"I think we should have a yellow blanket in the yellow submarine," says Sue, bringing in a piece of yellow cloth from the dress-up box. Other children look in through the portholes and make faces at their friends.

*Creative movement grows out of the children's dramatic play, and, combined with music, provides a smooth transition to story time.*

"We will be the fish swimming around the submarine!" they tell them. The teacher observes the children's play and puts on Saint-Saens's *The Swan*. The music matches the children's actions as they move around the box inventing fish sounds and motions. The teacher joins the dancers and invites the children in the box to come out and swim in the sea with them. Sue swirls the yellow cloth behind her. "This is my tail," she sings.

*Children have made plans and look forward to the next day.*

"Story time!" says the teacher. "Let's swim to the rug." The dancing children and those working about the room move to the rug and settle around the teacher, who reads the story *The Rainbow Fish* by Marcus Pfister. The children gather round the aquarium and look at their floating sea creatures.

"We need a rainbow fish," says one boy.

"Let's make lots of rainbow fish tomorrow," joins in another.

"I will find some shiny rainbow paper for you," says the teacher. Full of excitement about the next day, the children help put away the materials they have used and then get ready to leave.

# Reflection Page

## Why the Arts?

All of the following have been suggested as important reasons children should be taught the arts. Think carefully about each item and then rank each by its importance. Write a number in front of each, with 1 being the highest rank and 9 being the lowest. Based on your ranking, write a statement that explains why you feel the arts are essential for young children.

_____    The arts are part of being human.

_____    The arts stimulate brain development.

_____    The arts promote early literacy.

_____    The arts improve physical health.

_____    The arts promote emotional well-being.

_____    The arts create community.

_____    The arts foster cognitive growth.

_____    The arts nurture creativity.

_____

_____

_____

_____

_____

_____

_____

_____

_____

_____

_____

# Reflection Page

## How to Have a Successful Observation

Observing children involved in arts activities is an invaluable way to learn how children react to various kinds of arts experiences. As an observer, you are free of the pressure of performing and can devote your attention to the small details that busy, overworked caregivers often miss.

The following checklist will help you and the participants in the program you are visiting have a pleasant and rewarding experience.

### Before the Visit

- Call for an appointment and get permission to visit.

- Write down the names of the people you speak to on the phone and those of the teachers whose children you will be observing.

- If you intend to use a camera or camcorder, make sure you have all the necessary permissions. In many programs, parents must be asked to sign a release form before you can photograph. Some schools may already have these on file.

- Prepare a form on which to record your observations.

### On the Day of the Visit

- Arrive on time and introduce yourself to the teachers. If possible, have them introduce you to the children. If asked, give a simple explanation for your visit, such as, "My name is _____. I can't wait to see what you are doing today."

- Observe and record carefully. Do not bother the teachers. They are there to work with the children, not you.

- When it is time for you to leave, do not disturb the children or the teachers.

### After the Observation

- As soon as possible, review your notes and add any special details that you remember. Some people find it helpful to make an audiotape recording while the experience is still fresh in their minds.

- Write a note of thanks to everyone with whom you had contact. A special handmade card for the children is always welcome.

# Reflection Page

## Observation: The Arts and the Child

The purpose of this observation is to observe young children in a typical learning situation. The observation will focus on the artistic behavior of the children in a group educational situation. This observation may be done in an organized school or a child care setting that services children between the ages of one and eight. The observation should last 40 minutes to 1 hour.

Date of observation: _____          Length of observation: _____

Ages of children: _____          Group size: _____

## Observation

1.  Which arts activities (creative dance, music, dramatic play, and visual arts) are the children involved in?
    _____
    _____
    _____

2.  What are the adults doing?
    _____
    _____
    _____

3.  How are arts activities made available to the children?
    _____
    _____
    _____

4.  How did the children participate in these arts activities? (Examples: tried once, then left; engaged in nonverbal or verbal interaction with children and/or adults; worked alone; length of time at activity)
    _____
    _____
    _____

# Reflection Page

## Analysis: The Arts and the Child

Based on your observation, write a response to these questions:

1.  How do the arts activities relate to the learning theories and arts standards discussed in this chapter?

    _____

    _____

    _____

    _____

2.  Which artistic dispositions for children were being met, and which ones were not? Why?

    _____

    _____

    _____

    _____

3.  What do you think are the guiding principles of the arts curriculum in this program?

    _____

    _____

    _____

    _____

**Digital Download**    **Download from CourseMate**

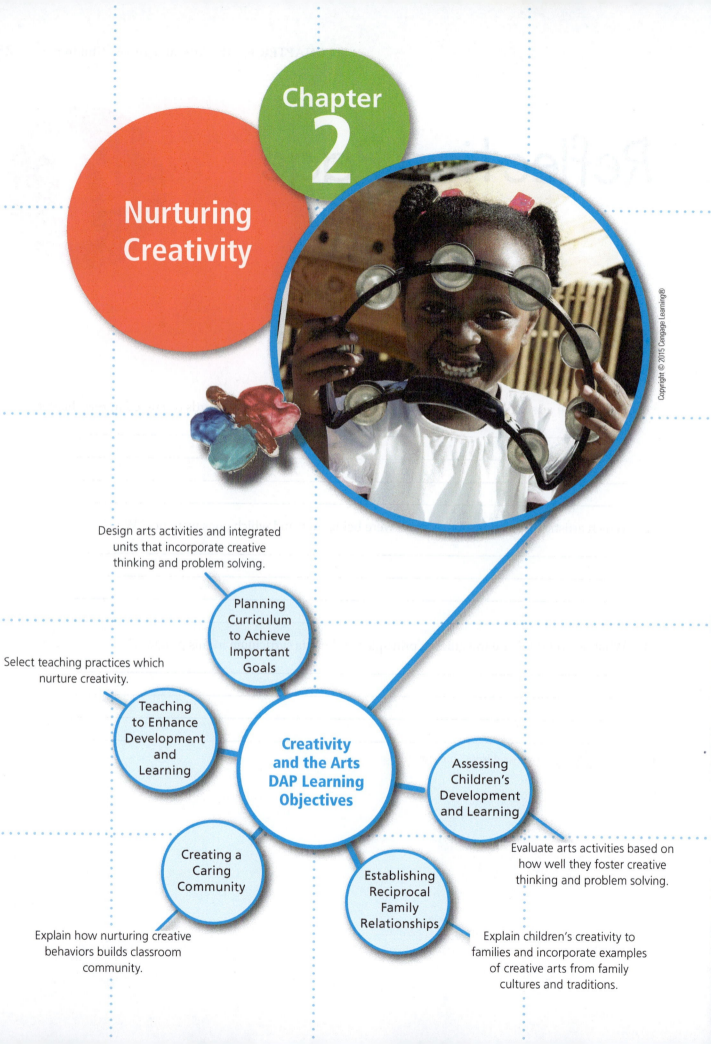

Chapter

2

Nurturing Creativity

Copyright © 2015 Cengage Learning®

Design arts activities and integrated units that incorporate creative thinking and problem solving.

Select teaching practices which nurture creativity.

Planning Curriculum to Achieve Important Goals

Teaching to Enhance Development and Learning

**Creativity and the Arts DAP Learning Objectives**

Assessing Children's Development and Learning

Creating a Caring Community

Establishing Reciprocal Family Relationships

Evaluate arts activities based on how well they foster creative thinking and problem solving.

Explain how nurturing creative behaviors builds classroom community.

Explain children's creativity to families and incorporate examples of creative arts from family cultures and traditions.

## Young Artists Creating

Makalya dabs some white glue with her fingers and then begins to rub it across her paper in a swirling pattern. Although she is usually easily distracted, at this moment she pays no attention to the other children working beside her at the table. Instead of her perpetual chatter, she is silent. Her tongue projects slightly from her mouth as her eyes follow the movement of her hand. If we speak to her at this moment, she may not even hear us, and if she does, she may jump slightly or hesitate before responding to us. In the simple act of spreading the glue in a new way, Makalya has become immersed in the process of discovery and creativity.

# What Is Creativity?

If there is one word most often associated with the arts, it is creativity. We even call them the creative arts. But that doesn't mean that all arts activities are inherently creative or allow children to express themselves creatively. In this chapter we will explore the nature of creativity to learn why it is important to nurture creativity in young children and how to select and design arts experiences that do so.

## Defining Creativity

**Creativity** has been the subject of much research and analysis, yet there is no generally accepted definition. A creative act can be viewed in many ways. What is thought creative behavior in one time and place may not be thought creative in another. Different researchers have offered the following descriptions of creativity.

**Uniqueness.** Creativity is inventing something so unique that it is astonishing to the viewer or user and produces "effective surprise" (Bruner, 1979, p. 12). Thomas Edison's invention of the light bulb or Georges Seurat's use of tiny dots of color to create the style of pointillism are examples of unique products that are considered highly creative.

**Rule breaking.** Creativity is doing something that goes beyond the accepted rules but in a new way that may at first meet resistance, but is eventually understandable and acceptable to a wider audience (Boden, 1990, p. 12). For example, the composer Arnold Shoenberg created a mathematically based twelve-tone method of music composition and introduced atonal music that was initially poorly received.

**Problem solving.** E. P. Torrance (1970) described creativity as the ability to see a problem, form an idea to solve it, and then share the results. The innovative American architect Frank Lloyd Wright thought houses should be inexpensive and fit their environment, so he developed slab construction and designed the "prairie home," which became the prototype for the contemporary ranch-style home.

**An Interactive Process.** Mihaly Csikszentmihalyi (1996, 1997) views creativity as a complex process that reflects an individual's motivation to solve a problem, not alone but in interaction with the requirements of a particular field of study and with other experts in that area of study as well as with the public. For example, a choreographer, in a desire to express a particular idea, invents a new style of dance. The resulting performance reflects the choreographer's experiences and knowledge of how the body can move. This piece will then be judged and accepted or rejected by other choreographers, dancers, and the public.

**Making something new.** Jane Piirto believes creativity is a "basic human need to make new" (2004, p. 37). In this view, creativity is not something unique to a few people who make big changes in the world—what has been called by Mihalyi Csikszentmihalyi (1996) the "Big C"—but is part of each of us (the "little c") that helps us figure out how to arrange furniture in our classroom for optimal learning or design an activity plan that best meets the needs of our particular children.

Most animals have inherited reflexes and responses that enable them to survive from birth. Human beings, on the other hand, must learn almost everything starting in infancy. Creativity is the mechanism by which people use past knowledge and learned skills to meet the needs of a new situation or to solve a problem. If we combine this with Dissanayake's view of the arts as making the everyday special, we can see that the arts are a powerful forum for human creativity.

**Creative Thinking Skills.** Research by Amabile (1983), Feldman and Goldsmith (1986), Gardner (1993), Csikszentmihalyi (1996), and Gruber and Wallace (1999) identifies the following characteristics of creative people:

- They are both passionately interested in and skilled in a particular area of learning, such as science, the arts, or writing, and can identify areas where new ideas are needed or fit and are willing to try something never done before.

- They have the ability to imagine a range of possibilities. They are playful, flexible thinkers who generate many possible ways of doing something or of solving a problem.

- They are energetic and highly persistent and do not give up, even if they fail many times.

- When something goes wrong or fails, they are intrigued instead of discouraged.

- They set high personal standards for themselves and push themselves to learn more and work harder.

They are dissatisfied with what already exists or is known or can be done.

- They are intrinsically motivated, willing to work hard and to struggle with frustration, and yet find great pleasure and satisfaction in the act of creation, or **flow** (Csikszentmihalyi, 2008).

- They have multiple problems and projects that they are working on at the same time.

**Divergent thinking.** J. P. Guilford (1986) proposed a model of intelligence that includes divergent thinking as one of the basic thought processes. Divergent thinking can be defined as the ability to generate many different solutions to a problem and is a key component of creative problem solving. It is characterized by

- **Fluency**—Producing a multitude of diverse ideas or solutions. An example of fluency would be when a child thinks of many different ways to move like a bird.

- **Flexibility**—Seeing things from alternative viewpoints. Flexibility is seen when a child plays several different roles, such as mother, child, and police officer, in pretend play.

- **Originality**—Thinking of ideas or solutions that have never been thought of before. An example of this is when a child takes two magazine clippings of different objects, such as a clock and a bird, and glues them together to create a clock-headed bird.

- **Elaboration**—Improving ideas by adding on or expanding them. Children building with blocks elaborate on each other's ideas when they connect what they have made to someone else's creation, such as when one child makes the garage and the other makes the car to go in it.

## The Importance of Creativity

In the rapidly evolving technological society we live in, creativity and innovation are essential. Our children will grow up in a future that will not only require them to not only build on the past, but also remain ready to solve increasingly complex problems, ones that we cannot even imagine yet. Howard Gardner (2006) has identified creativity as one of the five different "minds" or ways of processing and acting upon information that need to be cultivated if an individual is to be successful in the workplace. He warns that those without creating capabilities can be replaced by computers (p. 23).

Mitchell Resnick (2006) notes that the burgeoning growth in new technologies is increasing the rate of change so rapidly that the future—what he calls the "Creative Society of the 21st Century"—will be based less on what we know, and more on our ability to think creatively. Already young children are more at ease with the technological wonders of today than are their parents. "Childhood," Resnick points out, "is one of the most creative periods of our lives. We must make sure that children's

## ▶❚❚ TeachSource Video Case 2.1

### Kindergarten Curriculum

The video *Play: The Kindergarten Curriculum* discusses the effect of state requirements on kindergarteners' opportunities to be creative. What balance do you think there should be between academics and the arts in early childhood curricula? In this video the teacher has organized a unit for preschoolers around the questions: What are shapes? How has the teacher incorporated the arts? How would you make this unit more exciting and creative for these children?

**Watch on CourseMate**

creativity is nurtured and developed, providing children with opportunities to exercise, refine, and extend their creative abilities" (p. 203). The arts provide a perfect place in which to do so. The College Board (2011) found that of the thirteen identified 21st century skills and habits, creativity was one the top four, alongside communication, critical thinking, and problem-solving, that most aligned with the arts.

### Did You Get It?

**Which of the following is a characteristic of creative people?**

a. After the initial energy for a new idea wears out, they easily give up and move to the next task.

b. When something goes wrong or fails, they are discouraged instead of being intrigued.

c. They work hard and struggle with frustration, yet find satisfaction in the act of creation.

d. They are serious, rigid thinkers who focus on finding one best way of doing something.

**Take the full quiz on CourseMate**

# What Does Creativity Look Like in Children?

Because children are less familiar with the world, they are constantly dealing with fresh circumstances and problems and "creating" a unique response to the situation. The infant finds a dab of spilled milk and creates a design by swirling small fingers through it. The toddler rhythmically taps a spoon on a table. The preschooler finds a stone, adds some crayon marks, and imagines it is a "little creature."

The nature of the creative artistic responses children make will depend upon many factors. An infant does not yet have the ability to create a landscape painting. A toddler cannot produce a symphony. A preschooler cannot carve a marble monument. Nevertheless, even though the children are limited by their skill level and stage of physical growth, their artistic performances are still highly creative. At any moment, each child is at a precise point in development, has a unique set of experiences, and has a personal base of knowledge and skills. These combine to produce creative responses to each stimulus that the child confronts. We should not find it surprising that a one-of-a-kind child produces one-of-a-kind art, music, dance movements, and dramatic play!

In this tempera painting, Elizabeth, age six, shows creative thinking. Using what she knows about animals, she has given her imaginary creature eyes, teeth, and feet. But then she has elaborated by adding color, texture, and pattern to make something totally original.

At the same time, children's creativity looks different than that of adults. Adults bring to the creative process a reservoir of experience and skill. They have technical expertise in their subject matter and knowledge of other creative works. They also have years of living in a particular culture, which may set limits on what is deemed possible or acceptable. Children, on the other hand, are only beginning to obtain experience and expertise and are not yet bound by a rigid concept of what is possible. Therefore, their creative acts are characterized by spontaneity, imagination, and fantasy.

**Spontaneity.** Because children have less expertise than adults and have experienced less pressure to conform, they tend to be freer in their creative ideas and are more willing to share them. This leads to an open and bold approach to arts activities and an increased willingness to explore and take risks.

**Imagination.** When we use our **imagination** or pretend, we are playing with mental images. These images are ideas of things that can be manipulated in the mind and can take visual, auditory, and sensory form. The ability to imagine is particularly strong in young children. Being able to pretend is a key feature of young children's play. A banana becomes a telephone; a bed becomes a boat. Indeed, Jane Piirto sees children's play as the "seed ground of adult imagination" (2004, p. 62).

**Fantasy.** **Fantasy** is the creation of imaginary worlds. It is where the mental images of the imagination are brought to life through story. It is the realm of monsters, fairies, and flying elephants. For young children, the difference between reality and fantasy is not as strongly delineated as it is in adults. This allows children to be less stereotypical in their ideas, an ability that is often envied by adult artists. As Pablo Picasso said, "Every child is an artist. The problem is how to remain an artist once he grows up."

## Creativity and Play

All children are creative. But their creativity is easily stifled. Spontaneity, imagination, and fantasy are foundations of children's natural play and the place where their creativity is born. Children's creative play is essential for healthy development. The link between play and cognitive development is strongly supported by research. Child-initiated play develops memory, self-regulation, oral language, social skills, and leads to more successful adjustment to school (Bodrova & Leong, 2004; Singer, Golinkoff & Hirsh-Pasek, 2006). As they play children gain knowledge and skills. They also discover problems and become motivated to solve them. This is the creative process at work.

However, children today spend much of their time either in adult-organized settings such as school and daycare, or in front of the television or computer screen, and spend less time in child-initiated play. State assessments have increased academic expectations and led to more structured learning at all levels. Time for play and the creative arts is often lost, but it need not be. If we value children's growth and development we can create a playful setting in which academic learning happens, and the creative process is nurtured.

In the following discussion of the creative process, we will see how our behaviors and attitudes, and the decisions we make, can create such a nurturing environment.

---

**Did You Get It?**

**Which of the following is a reason for children's art to be more spontaneous and characterized by fantasy?**

a. They are not bound by a rigid concept of what is possible.

b. They feel more pressure to conform to accepted views of reality.

c. They bring a reservoir of skill and technical expertise.

d. They tend to take less risk with their limited expertise and experience.

**Take the full quiz on CourseMate**

---

## What Is the Creative Process?

Creativity can be seen as the human ability to use one's knowledge and skill to make plans, to try out ideas, and to come up with a response. This creative process or set of behaviors can be witnessed whenever someone solves a problem or produces a unique response to a situation.

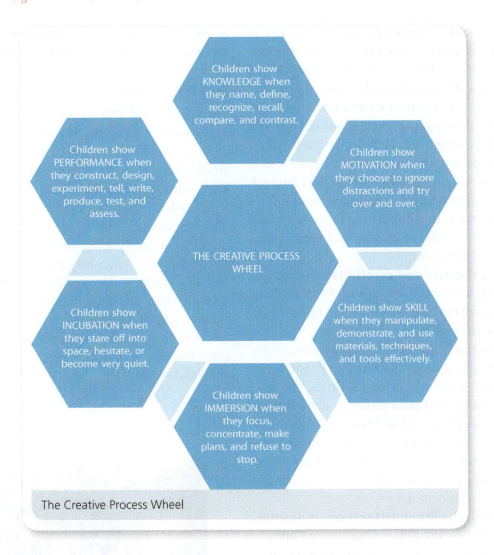

Children show KNOWLEDGE when they name, define, recognize, recall, compare, and contrast.

Children show MOTIVATION when they choose to ignore distractions and try over and over.

Children show PERFORMANCE when they construct, design, experiment, tell, write, produce, test, and assess.

THE CREATIVE PROCESS WHEEL

Children show SKILL when they manipulate, demonstrate, and use materials, techniques, and tools effectively.

Children show INCUBATION when they stare off into space, hesitate, or become very quiet.

Children show IMMERSION when they focus, concentrate, make plans, and refuse to stop.

The Creative Process Wheel

It consists of the following:

* **Knowledge**—What individuals already know about what they are exploring

* **Motivation**—The inner drive to accomplish something

* **Skill**—The development of expertise in using tools and materials or in carrying out an action

* **Immersion**—Being intensely focused on creating something unique with this knowledge and skill

* **Incubation**—A period of time in which individuals think and process what they know and what they wish to do

* **Production**—The active pursuit of a solution or expressive act which may or may not lead to a creative product, presentation, or performance; or

which may be unsuccessful, resulting in the entire process starting over

## Knowledge

Whenever people face a new stimulus or problem, the first thing that comes into play is what they already know and can do. Young children have a much more limited knowledge base than adults, so their responses are often wildly different from those we might expect. The amount of experience children have with an arts material or a technique will influence what their creative response will be. For example, given an assortment of rhythm instruments, a toddler might decide to create a noise by banging the drum with a maraca.

Teachers help children gain knowledge about the arts in several ways.

**Talking about the arts and creativity.** Use a vocabulary rich in artistic language and point out how the children use the different arts elements in their paintings, songs, dances, and make-believe play. For example, children who know what a line is and are aware that there are many different kinds of lines will be able to make a unique line. Activities to use in introducing the art elements are provided in Chapter 4. Use words that describe the creative process. "You thought of many ideas" (fluency). "Your ideas are all so different from each other" (flexibility). "I've never seen that before" (originality). "You made it more interesting by adding more" (elaboration).

**Exploring the arts and creativity.** To enhance fluency, provide a variety of arts experiences that allow children to explore new ways of using their bodies, their voices, and the materials and tools of the arts.

**Experiencing the arts and creativity.** Take children to music, drama, and dance performances and show them the works of visual artists. This encourages flexibility and elaboration as children can take what they experienced and build on it to create something new. For example, after seeing a children's theater production of *Little Red Riding Hood*, a group of children might decide to elaborate and act out the story from the viewpoint of the wolf.

**Accepting individual differences in knowledge.** Each child brings different background knowledge to the arts experience. We must remember that a child's artistic responses may not be what we expect because their knowledge base is limited. Incorporating a used paper towel into a collage can be seen as a creative choice. It demonstrates an ability to categorize it as a piece of textured paper. This represents a highly creative action, equivalent to the famous Spanish painter Pablo Picasso using a piece of real newspaper to represent itself in an early Cubist painting—which art connoisseurs considered unpleasant at the time.

**Set the stage for creativity.** Creativity is not just an individual experience. Groups can work together to come up with creative ideas and solutions. **Brainstorming**—the listing of ideas in an atmosphere of total acceptance and fun develops fluency, originality, and flexible thinking. Creating **topic webs** allows elaboration. **KWL charts**, which display what children already know, and what they wonder about are a way

to elicit child-initiated problems to solve. Ways to use these strategies are discussed in Chapter 8.

## Motivation

The inner drive that causes an individual to want to do something is called **motivation.** Young children are driven by intense curiosity about the world around them. Everything is new and exciting to them. They want to touch everything, see everything, and try everything. How wonderful for the teacher!

Often we have only to present the arts materials or technique and give a few simple instructions, and the children's natural curiosity and desire to explore and play will do the rest. This is called **intrinsic motivation.** When intrinsic motivation is at work, smiling, laughing children gather excitedly around us. They ask curious questions and cannot wait to get started. They spend a great deal of time on their explorations, and want to do more and more.

Motivation cannot be taught. It must be inspired. Open-ended materials that can be used in multiple ways (such as blocks) provide choices, risks, and challenges that spark creativity. These children show intense concentration as they discover if their ideas will work to solve the emergent problem of balancing the blocks.

Giving rewards and prizes is known as **extrinsic motivation.** Prizes or stars for "good" work or competition among students to win a ribbon replace intrinsic motivation with extrinsic motivation and do not belong in an arts program for young children. Such external rewards have been shown to have a limiting effect on creativity. Research by Therese Amabile (1983) found that children produced more artworks when engaged in an open-ended, free play environment than when offered rewards. Another study, in which children were asked to tell stories from a picture book, showed that the group that was rewarded produced stories judged less creative than those by children in the unrewarded group (Amabile, Hennessey, & Grossman, 1986).

In order to create an intrinsically motivating environment, teachers need to be as creative as their students. However, the side benefit to creating a motivating environment is that it also build a classroom community that welcomes and celebrates difference, looks on failure as a way to learn, and provides success for students with special needs. Here are some ways to foster motivation in the arts as well as all areas of learning.

**Provide choice.** Intrinsically motivating activities are always **open-ended.** These are activities that have a multitude of possible results and ways of getting there. When children choose what material they will use or what idea they will express, they take interest in and feel ownership of their work, which will heighten their motivation.

**Be sensitive.** Unfortunately, intrinsic motivation is a delicate force. It may be easily lost through inappropriate organization or presentation of arts activities. Overly restrictive arts activities quickly dampen a child's natural curiosity. Self-motivation in children is diminished by materials that can be used in only one way, projects that must match a teacher-made model, or actions that must conform to a fixed standard.

**Be surprising.** Intrinsic motivation occurs when the mind is active. Get children thinking and asking questions by making sure something new or surprising is always happening in the room. Display new artworks, introduce new materials, play unfamiliar music, wear unusual clothing, tell new stories, and constantly discuss new ideas and experiences.

**Be flexible.** Intrinsic motivation develops from within. Create child ownership of problems and ideas

## Across Cultures

### Creativity Across Cultures

Reading books about creative people from many places and times is a great way to celebrate diversity and introduce children to the ways our creativity can make the world a better place for us all.

Numerous children's books depict people solving problems in creative ways. In Karen Williams' book *Galimoto.* (1991 New York: HarperCollins) an African boy collects a variety of discarded materials to build a toy car. This is an excellent book to use with children to inspire them to be "creators." Follow up reading the story by cleaning up litter around the school grounds. Use what you find to invent something new or that will help people stop littering.

**For more books and activities, see *Books That Celebrate Creativity* on CourseMate.**

by being willing to change direction and follow up on their interests and passions. If a child arrives at school excited because he or she just saw the moon out during the day, take the whole group outside to see it and then together research the moon, read books to learn more, make up stories, songs, and dances to express ideas and feelings about the moon.

**Be encouraging.** Establish an environment in which mistakes are part of the learning process. Eliminate the word *failure* and substitute the word *persevere*. Record children's progress, noting ideas that did not work as learning steps and things learned. Share examples of people who suffered many failures before their ideas worked or were accepted, such as Leonardo DaVinci. Read books that show creativity at work such as Peter Reynold's *The Dot* (2003), in which a young girl who says she cannot draw is encouraged by a teacher to just make a mark and find out where it takes her.

**Be accepting.** Teach children to respect the differing ideas and work of others in an atmosphere where insults and ridicule are banned. Anxiety about making a mistake can prevent children from fully exploring an arts activity.

**Welcome everyone.** In selecting arts activities consider the special needs and skill levels of every child in the group. When activities are truly open-ended and process-oriented, they are inclusive—every child has an equal opportunity to participate successfully in their own unique way. Avoid activities that require lockstep following of directions such as dances with complex footwork, precut shapes that must be put together to look like everyone else's, music that must be played precisely the same every time, and plays that must be performed just as written. All these activities assume a certain level of experience and practice that is usually beyond the abilities of young children, and ignores their personal creativity.

**Value difference. Conformity** occurs when children feel they must be like everyone else or meet some imposed standard. This can make children afraid to express themselves in a new way. For example, fear of getting dirty or ruining something can cause children to be unmotivated to try the messier art materials or venture into a new art form.

**Show confidence.** Teachers who nourish creativity demonstrate a high level of confidence in their students. Their children do not worry about what their final products will look like or how other teachers and parents will judge them. They are more interested in the process the child goes through as they create than in any product that may or may not result.

**Stand back.** If children feel that they are constantly being watched and evaluated, they may be less willing to take risks and try new ideas. If they think we are going to interfere with their investigations, they will hesitate to pursue their own interests. If we solve the problem for them or do the work for them, they will expect that adults always will and become complacent.

**Act playful.** Create opportunities for everyone to laugh, play, and have fun together. Intrinsic motivation happens when both teachers and children are relaxed and happy.

**Look for emergent problems.** Problems that bring forth the most creativity are those that arise in the process of working. A problem that happens when trying to accomplish a task, such as mixing just the right color paint for a painting or attempting to play an original melody on the xylophone, is far more motivating to a child than solving a problem assigned by the teacher. "Messy" or uncertainty problems—such as ones that even the teacher doesn't know the answer to—often elicit the most creative responses (Anderson, 2011). Producing unexpected results from familiar materials is especially intriguing to young children. For example, in the Playful Invention and

## Teacher Tip

### CHOOSING OPEN-ENDED CREATIVE ACTIVITIES

When choosing creative arts activities for young children, ask the following questions:

1. Can children explore on their own?
2. Can children go at their own pace?
3. Can children figure out their own ways to do things?
4. Are there many possible ways to do this activity?
5. Are the rules based on safety and management, not on the end result desired?
6. Is it challenging and complex so that children will want to revisit it again and again?
7. Will children discover problems to solve and solve them in their own unique way?
8. Will it be playful—will they laugh, imagine, and explore?

Exploration (PIE) museums program, children discovered that different foods made different pitches when their electric resistance was tested. This discovery inspired children to create musical instruments and food-eating robots (Resnick, 2006, pp. 201–202).

**Show support.** Cherish, honor, and display the creative ideas, actions, and works of the children. Instead of stereotypical commercial bulletin board patterns and ready-made pictures, make documentation panels that record in words and pictures the children's creative process, both failures and successes, and create visual displays that inform parents. Chapter 8 provides directions for making documentation panels.

**Provide variety.** Boredom arises when the child is constantly offered the same materials with little or no variation. For example, as wonderful as drawing with crayons can be, this cannot be a total visual arts program for young children. In the same way, a housekeeping corner is a great place for dramatic play but should not be the only play center offered all year. Ideas for dramatic play are provided in Chapter 12.

## Skill

The more skilled children are, the more they can concentrate on creatively using the artistic elements, materials, and concepts in their work. Organize activities so that the **techniques** required to accomplish them are appropriate for the ability of the child, providing a significant level of challenge but within the physical and mental capabilities of the child to learn. Arts materials and experiences should stimulate the senses and allow multiple ways to think creatively.

Children move through three levels of skill development as they investigate a new way of working or performing: **exploration, revisitation,** and **responsive.**

**Exploration.** The basis of all arts creation is the exploration of the medium. Exploration, therefore, must be the mainstay of early childhood arts programs. At this level the child is discovering what happens when they use the material or technique. The process of creating becomes secondary. Although this level is most common to infants and toddlers, it is found any time a child or adult tries something new. Even accomplished artists spend time exploring a new material or technique before using it in their work. Children need to know they have the freedom to explore, and that their explorations will not be judged.

Exploration activities are open-ended and allow children enough time, space, and choice in which to develop comfort and control. For example, after a new puppet, art medium, musical instrument, or dance movement is introduced, provide an area or center where children can try them out on their own.

**Revisitation.** At this level the child returns again and again to the same material or action, each time showing more organization and direction. For example, a child after several days or weeks of exploring the xylophone by randomly hitting notes may begin to tap two or three notes repeatedly in a rhythmic pattern.

Children need to be given many opportunities to revisit the same material and technique in order to develop control and skill. Putting out a new art material or musical instrument for a one-time experience, for example, does not help children increase their ability to use it to creatively express their thoughts and feelings.

Instead, furnish art, music, and dramatic play learning centers with open-ended materials that are slowly introduced, explored, and then added to. If an activity or material cannot be revisited and used in different and more complex ways or provide new problems to solve, then it is probably not open-ended in design.

Carefully selected open-ended materials and activities by their very nature invite revisitation. Children rarely lose their fascination with paint, puppets, and musical instruments. However, as children gain skill and confidence, they need more complexity. If you start with two colors of paint or several rhythm instruments, slowly add more. Encourage children to develop more control by challenging them to higher skill levels, such as after children have discovered that red and yellow make orange, ask them to make a darker orange or a lighter one. If they can tap a pattern on a drum, encourage them to play it louder and softer, slower and faster. Revisit movement activities and songs and invite children to add different motions and new words.

**Responsive.** As children gain mastery, their approach changes. They dive into the materials and techniques, no longer worried about how they will control them, but excited instead by the new way they can play and communicate their ideas. This is the responsive level in which the artist is confidently in control and able to plan how to express ideas and feelings.

1. **Planning a responsive activity.** Responsive activities start with thought-provoking experiences,

visual stimulation, and multisensory happenings, followed by opportunities to use the arts in all of their multimedia dimensions. For example, dramatizing how a letter travels from home to the post office and at last to the recipient stretches children's thought processes as they try to creatively represent what they know and feel about getting mail. Another name for responsive activities is **representation.**

2. **Selecting responsive activities.** Activities that require children to communicate ideas and feelings should use materials and techniques with which they are familiar. Making a mural or creating books about a trip to the zoo is not the time to introduce using chalk for the first time. Rather, select a drawing material the children have explored repeatedly and have confidence using.

3. **Encouraging responsive activities.** Children are more likely to express an experience creatively when familiar visual arts, dramatic play, music, and dance activities are readily available following such events as visitors to the classroom, stories that are read or told, science experiments, exciting field trips, and all of the other daily experiences of a young child.

4. **Sharing responsive activities.** Encourage children to share their ideas by providing time to discuss their creations and by recording their oral commentary in class journals, by adding captions to their work or photos of them in action, and make presentation panels that tell what happened.

5. **Valuing children's own expressive forms.** Although the creative work of preschoolers and older children may begin to contain somewhat recognizable images, we must not demand that children produce a recognizable picture or imitate an event precisely. To nurture the creative process, offer only those open-ended activities that do not dictate a uniform end product, but instead allow each child to respond in their own unique way to the event.

**Making it real.**   As the creative arts work done at Reggio Emilia shows, children's creative work in the arts is most expressive when based on real experiences. Reading a book or talking about llamas and then expecting the children to move like llamas and draw pictures of llamas will elicit unique responses. But they will not elicit the passion and depth and creativity that the same activities will do after actually going to the zoo or farm and seeing, smelling, hearing, and touching a real llama.

## Immersion

**Immersion** is the state of being so completely focused on creating something that the passage of time is forgotten, as are personal needs and what is happening around us. In this state the artist feels relaxed and calm. Ideas seem to flow effortlessly from mind to hands. The artist is not concerned with the end product but only with the pleasure of the process itself. Creativity is at work! All of the knowledge, expertise, and motivation of the individual have come together to make this moment possible. Mihaly Csikszentmihalyi (2008) calls this pleasurable feeling of intense concentration and involvement the "flow."

Ann Lewin-Benham (2010) says that flow in young children is the opposite of being bored. A bored infant picks up toys without looking them and discards them. A bored toddler chews his knuckles and looks away as a book is read. A bored kindergartener picks fuzz off the rug while the rest of the group is singing. Flow, on the other hand, is the total concentration of the child on something that stretches the imagination, that puzzles, and that invites creative exploration.

To create the conditions for children to experience flow try the following:

**Provide time to work.**   Plan sufficient time for children to explore and experiment until satisfied. Young children cannot be rushed.

Maria Montessori felt that children needed three hours of unstructured time in which to pursue their investigations. Considering today's busy school schedules, such a length of time is a rarity. So often children are being hustled to circle, to snack, to lunch, to recess, to the bus. For young children the first twenty minutes during unstructured center time is often spent making social connections, exploring the materials, and finding something of interest. If that is all the unstructured time they ever have they will never learn to settle and focus long enough to act out a complex creative story in the dramatic play area, compose an original song in the music center or to paint a series of paintings showing the way the sky changes from morning to night.

Instead of watching the clock, watch the children. Are they deeply engaged? Then push circle time back, set out a snack, and let children eat when they wish. If some children are done before others, engage them in preparing the snack, cleaning up their work, recording their ideas, or gathering materials for the next activity.

Children who feel pressured to finish in a certain amount of time become frustrated, often to the point of crying. When offering an arts activity or center for the first few times, and it is unclear how much time the children will need, present it at the beginning of the session. If children want to start an activity when they will not have sufficient time, it is better to redirect them to something else.

**Avoid interruptions.** It is extremely frustrating for a child to stop when immersed in the creative process. Nevertheless, it will happen, despite the best planning, that children in the act of creating will need to be interrupted. Do so gently. Try to make eye contact before giving a direction. Offer the assurance that the child can continue the activity at another time. It is essential to keep such interruptions to an absolute minimum. If this happens too often, the child will eventually lose the motivation to create.

**Provide intriguing flexible materials.** The arts materials and activities offered to children also make a difference in their ability to concentrate on the creation process and work for an extended time. Make sure to offer well-made, age appropriate materials, and plenty of variety. If the pencil point keeps breaking, if the dress-up clothes are much the same in texture and color, if the musical instruments are all ones to tap, interest will soon fall away.

## Incubation and Performance

The creative process is like a stew in which the ingredients of knowledge and skill are stirred together through motivation and immersion. **Incubation** is the slow simmering of this rich mix, which results in creative ideas and performance. During the incubation stage, young artists are actively engaged in trying out ideas, asking themselves questions, and evaluating their actions. Outwardly, they may study the materials or handle them playfully. They may experiment with an idea or movement and try something new. They may

A child and a spoon set the stage for a playful, imaginative interaction with a teacher who values creativity and wholeheartedly joins in the pretend play.

test the limits of the material, the rules, or the teacher's patience. At other times, they may sit quietly and stare off into space or concentrate intently on what they are creating. Inside they may be thinking such thoughts as, "What will happen if I do this?," "How will these things go together?," "Wow, I didn't expect that to happen!," and "I've never seen anything like this before."

All of this leads to **performance,** in which the ingredients in the stew blend together to form something new, a flavor that has never existed before. At this point, the children have become their creations because each child's knowledge, skills, and motivation are uniquely different from that of any other child who has ever existed. Children's creative performances are an extension of all that they are at that moment. However, at all times we need to remember that it is the process the child went through to get to this moment that is key, not the final product. Process is what we need to celebrate and document and value.

### Did You Get It?

The inner drive that causes an individual to want to accomplish something is called _____.

a. incubation

b. motivation

c. skill

d. process

**Take the full quiz on CourseMate**

# How Do Teachers Foster the Creative Process?

Adults will always be outside of the child's very personal creative process. However, the role we play is crucially important. Psychological studies carried out by Carl Rogers (1976) have shown that an atmosphere of psychological safety is necessary for creative processing to occur. Empathy and acceptance in a nonjudgmental setting lets creativity happen. It is our task to establish an environment and teaching approach in which these conditions can occur.

## Becoming a Teacher of the Creative Arts

Helping children be creative in the arts does not require teachers to be highly skilled professional artists. Research in preschools by Angeloska-Galevska found that teachers who inspired creativity in their children had high levels of rapport, provided open-ended activities, and most importantly valued creativity as essential to learning (Craft, 2002). Such teachers are enthusiastic and passionate about the arts.

For many people, feeling comfortable teaching the arts can be a challenge. How we see ourselves as artists, musicians, dancers, and actors depends on our past experiences in the different art forms and the judgments we or others have made about our artistic abilities. In some cases, we may feel more confident in one art form than another. This personal history sets the stage, but does not have to determine one's effectiveness as a teacher of the arts (Craft, 2002).

**Acknowledge one's personal history.** Becoming more comfortable with the arts begins first with understanding why we feel confident or hesitant about performing in the different art forms. Think back to your earliest experiences in the arts. Did you take dance lessons as a child? Were you told you had a beautiful singing voice? Did another child make fun of a picture you drew? Were you in a play and embarrassed when you forgot your lines? Understanding your own personal struggles and successes in the arts will help you be more aware of and sympathetic to the feelings the children you are working with may be experiencing.

**Learn more about the arts.** If there is an arts area with which you are unfamiliar or feel unsure about, try to learn more by reading about it, attending arts events, and, most importantly, trying your hand at it by attending a class or workshop.

One of the best ways to learn something is to teach it to someone else. Select activities, such as those in this book, that expose children to the arts from a wide variety of times, cultures, and people, and develop an expanded view of the arts together with your students.

**Create together.** Children love when their teachers perform with them. They will not care how our voices sound, what we look like when we are dancing, how well we act out being the big bad wolf, or how well we draw a dog, because they will be busy singing, dancing, acting, and drawing, too.

## Valuing Creativity

It is not enough for teachers to provide wonderful arts experiences for children—they must also value creative behavior.

We value creativity when we:

**Show self-confidence.** No matter how you feel about your own arts skills, always model artistic self-confidence. Would we say to a child, "I'm not a very good reader," or "I can't write the letter 'A' very well," and then expect the child to want to be a good reader or to make a well-formed "A"? However, many adults do not hesitate to tell children that they think themselves poor singers, or that they cannot draw. The child may well think that if this important adult who can read so well and knows so much cannot create in the arts, then it must be very hard to be good at any of the arts.

**Avoid comparisons.** Adults often say to children, "You're a much better artist or singer or dancer than I," even though they would never say to one child that her work or performance was better than her friend's. Putting ourselves down in this way does not build up the confidence of children but instead introduces the element of comparative value. The child thinks, "How can I be better than the teacher? Can some art be better than others?" There should be no "better" or "best" in an early childhood setting, for either children or adults. Instead, differences in skill level should be explained as the result of experience and practice.

**Exhibit enthusiasm.** The children will mirror how we feel about the arts. If we are fearful and tentative about a project, then the children will react with hesitation. If we dislike the feel of a certain material, then the children will sense this and show discomfort. We should avoid using art media or offering activities that we personally dislike. It is important to be able to express enthusiasm. Words full of warmth and joy should be used, such as

*"I can't wait to share this painting with you!"*
*"Look at how this hat makes you look just like a fireman!"*
*"Oooo, this play dough feels so smooth!"*
*"This music makes me feel like dancing"*

**Display the arts.** Personal appearance is a way of showing how people value the arts and of attracting attention to artistic elements and concepts. Dressing in shades of blue when studying the color blue or wearing a wool sweater when talking about fiber art can provide a catalyst for discussion. Appreciation of artwork from other cultures can be shown, for example, by displaying African prints, Guatemalan ikat weavings, Indian embroidery, and Native American jewelry and by playing music from around the world on a regular basis.

**Participate beside them.** It is important for children to see that adults also enjoy the arts, and that they are not hesitant to join in with them. Nevertheless, we must be careful to avoid over participation. There is a difference between showing children that adults enjoy the arts and providing them with an adult model to copy. Look to the children for ideas. For example, if you are leading a creative movement activity about flying like birds, have the children show you their ideas of how birds move and then have everyone try each child's idea, including yourself. If you are writing new words to a song, elicit the words from the children, don't write it by yourself. If you join in a puppet show or dramatic play, ask the children who you might be and let them initiate the interactions. If you join a group of children making collages, do not show them a finished collage you have made or just make a collage alongside them. Instead have them help you decide where to glue down your shapes and talk excitedly about the joy of creating.

## Communicating Empathy and Acceptance

We speak with more than words. Our whole body communicates our meaning. How close we stand, how we move our arms, and the expression on our faces tell children how we feel about them and their creative work. It is important for our nonverbal behavior to match what we are saying to children.

Our faces mirror our feelings. Smiling at a child tells that child that we are pleased with him or her and that we like what he or she is doing. Frowns and cold stares distance us from the child and show disapproval. We need to be aware of the messages we are sending. If a teacher says to a child, "You used the glue in an interesting way" but frowns at the same time because the glue is dripping on the floor, then the positive words do not foster creative development. It is better to react honestly. If the dripping glue is disturbing, deal with the problem first before commenting on the artwork. The teacher might say, "Let's put your collage over here and wipe up all the glue; then we can talk about your collage."

How we move and gesture are also strong expressions of our feelings. It is important to remain at the children's level by sitting or stooping when interacting with them as they participate in the arts process. Using expansive arm motions can signal enthusiasm or inclusion. More subtly, hand signals and **American Sign Language** can be used to introduce the children to other ways of communicating while at the same time providing a quick and nonintrusive way to signal a child without disturbing the other children. For example, signing the word *thank you* can communicate to a child who is wiping up some paint drips that she is doing something that is appreciated.

## Sharing Emotional Responses

No matter how hard we try to cover up our emotions, children seem to sense how we are feeling. It is often better to be open about how we feel. It is hard to shrug off the frustration of a car that would not start that morning or the anger left from sharp words with a friend. The arts can provide a way to express such feelings. Share with the children the source of the feeling and then say, for example, "My car is broken. Here's the sound the engine made this morning. Here's the jerky way it moved," or "I am going to draw a whole bunch of angry lines on my paper and get rid of some of this angry feeling." Showing the children that adults use the arts as an emotional release lets children know that people of all ages use the arts to show their feelings.

## Listening Actively

One of the most important ways a teacher or caregiver can respond to a child is through **active listening.** This should be one of our first responses when children share information about their arts experiences. Especially with new children, it is extremely important to listen before responding verbally, in order to learn more about the child's intent to help us decide what to say to them. We also need to listen to the children we know well to show that we care about what they are saying. Active listening consists of the following components:

- **Waiting**—Do not always respond instantly and verbally to everything a child says. Establish eye contact, and wait for the child to elaborate on what was said. This will also provide time to formulate a thoughtful verbal response if the child does not offer a comment.

- **Looking**—Maintain eye contact with a child while she or he is talking. Remain at the child's eye level if possible.

The exploration level of creative arts activities provides multiple moments for active listening and positive feedback. What would you say to this child about her exploration of the playdough?

- **Responding**—Respond with value-free head nods, appropriate facial expressions, and sounds as the child talks.

## Responding Verbally

Words are powerful. They can transform a humdrum experience into an exhilarating one or destroy a special moment in a second. By choosing words thoughtfully, we not only help children feel good about themselves but expand their thought processes and make the arts experience more meaningful to them. How events are discussed can significantly improve what a child remembers. Research has found that when adults confirm and elaborate on what a child says, and when they ask questions and answer the child's, the child recalls the experience better than when there is no conversation (McGuigan & Salmon, 2004). In another study conversation after the event produced the most accurate recall, talk in the midst of it was the next most effective, and talk before had the least effect, but was better than no conversation at all (Holliday, Reyna, & Hayes, 2002).

Research also indicates that the younger the child, the more important it is to communicate on a one-to-one basis rather than in a large group situation (Lay-Dopyera & Dopyera, 1992). Arts activities provide significant moments for personal dialogue between a child and a caring adult. This relationship is an important one. When there are many warm, positive interactions between adults and young children, there is a beneficial effect on social and emotional development.

What we say to young artists can also have a profound effect on how children view their arts abilities for the rest of their lives. Many adults can trace the origin of their feeling of artistic incompetence to a thoughtless comment they received as a child. We need to take care in offering comments to children, and not speak off the top of our heads or repeat the negative remarks made to us when we were children. What we say and how we respond to children is one of the most significant parts of the educational process, and it takes practice to choose words wisely.

We need to speak with intention. Intentional teaching means that we are prepared ahead of time

## Making Plans

**OPEN-ENDED ACTIVITY:**

**OOPS – A MISTAKE IS GREAT**

**WHO?**    **GROUP COMPOSITION AGE(S):** Suitable for preschool and up

**WHEN?**    **TIME FRAME:** As long as children want to explore and create

**WHY?**    **OBJECTIVES:** Children will develop

- physically, by using the large muscles of the arm and the small muscles of the hand to manipulate the materials. (Bodily-Kinesthetic)
- socially, by interacting with a caring adult and sharing ideas with others. (Interpersonal)
- emotionally, by developing self-confidence from being allowed to handle a variety of materials and tools and by becoming more accepting of mistakes. (Intrapersonal)
- perceptually, by using the senses to observe and to explore changes in their art. (Spatial)
- language skills, by verbalizing their thinking process as they come up with their ideas. (Linguistic)
- cognitively, by observing cause and effect as their manipulation changes the materials and by thinking about their creative thinking process. (Logical-Mathematical)
- arts awareness, by developing knowledge and skill in handling a new and familiar materials. (Content Standard 1 & 2)

**WHERE?**    **SETUP:** On a rug for a large group or a small group at a table.

**WHAT?**    **MATERIALS:** A well-supplied art center, a small stack of damaged paper with paint spills, holes torn it, wrinkles, a paper glued on, etc. A tray or basket big enough for the paper. (It is best if these can be retrieved from papers discarded by the children as a way of recycling.) Also some articles of clothing—hat, vest, socks, and so on for follow-up activities.

**HOW?**    **PROCEDURE:**

**WOW Warm-Up:** Hold up some of the pieces of paper in front of you so the children can see them. "Look at these papers. They aren't perfect. They aren't clean. Each one has a mistake—an *Oops!*"

**What to Do and Say:** *Invite the children's response:* "What can we do? Should we cry because the paper is spoiled?" Shake head no until children agree. "Should we throw the paper away?" Shake heads no. *Frame the activity:* "I know. I will use creative thinking [if you have a hand signal for thinking use it here]." *Intentionally teach the vocabulary of the creative process:* "Creativity is when we think about what we know, what we can do, and how we can put that together to make something new." "Does this spot look like something you know? Does this wrinkled paper have the texture of something you have touched?" Listen to their answers. Say: "Creative people use what they know to get their ideas started." "Which art materials could you use?" Listen to their ideas. Say: "Creative people use their skills to make their ideas happen." Listen to their ideas. Say: "Look at all of our ideas. When we have lots of ideas we are thinking fluently. Look at how they are all different. When we have different ideas we are thinking flexibly."

Say: "I am going to put these *Oops!* papers in the art center in this beautiful tray labeled *Oops!* Now sometimes you will need a perfect piece of paper for your picture. But sometimes—you might want to be a creative thinker and turn an *Oops!* paper into something original." Explain that from now on if they make an *Oops!* they should try and think of something new to make. If they can't, they can put the paper in the *Oops!* tray to await creative use. Say: "Remember sometimes when we make a mistake, that mistake mixed together with our creativity can give us a better idea."

**TRANSITION OUT:** Read the book *Beautiful Oops* by Barney Saltzberg (2010). Ask: "Do you see any ideas in the book that are similar to ones you had?"

**WHAT LEARNED?**    **ASSESSMENT:** Do the children select the *Oops!* papers to use when they go to the center? Do they come up with ideas for the *Oops!* Do they help friends think of what to do when they make a mistake? Are they more willing to complete a picture when they make a mistake? Do they use any of the creative process words when they are working? Do they remember to put damaged papers in the *Oops!* tray? What can be done to improve the experience next time?

**NEXT?**    **EXTENSIONS:** On another day, wear a hat on upside-down, or two non-matching socks, or a piece of clothing backwards. Say: "Oops! I put this on wrong. Is that a mistake? Well, maybe I could imagine that I am a . . ." Ask for their ideas.

so that when a teachable moment occurs we know exactly what to do or say to help the child grow. The arts are full of teachable moments where we can help a child develop better social skills, learn a new vocabulary word, master a technique, or make a cognitive connection. However, without preplanning and a strong knowledge of the individual child's needs, we often fall back on platitudes.

## Using Praise

Probably one of the most common responses to children's artworks and performance is **unconditional praise,** in which a general phrase is said over and over regardless of what the child has done. "Good work!," "Great painting!," and "Nice singing!" are said quickly to the child as the teacher scoops up the drippy painting or hustles the child off to the next activity. The intent is to give encouragement and indicate to children that they have performed successfully.

However, studies indicate that consistent overuse of such praise actually diminishes the behavior being complimented (Kohn, 2006). Said over and over, the words become empty and meaningless. How can every picture be great or wonderful? The children come to believe that the teachers are not really looking at their work. In addition, unconditional praise does not help children think more deeply or make the experience more educational for them.

## Making Judgments

When we say, "I like it!" or "I like the way you . . . ," we are making judgments and expressing our personal values. Besides being overused, such terms open the door to more deleterious results. Many adults prefer realistic artwork that is neat and orderly, music that sounds familiar, and stories that follow familiar plots. They are more likely to respond positively to a painting of a house flanked by two trees and overlooked by a smiling sun than to a dripping paper covered in thick swirls of olive-green paint or be more enthusiastic about a puppet show that retells the story of Cinderella than one that has two outer space aliens talking gibberish.

Expressing adult personal taste in young children's art can lead to some children believing that they are better artists and others feeling like failures. As many arts teachers who work with adults have noted (Cameron, 1992; Edwards, 1979), a large number of people have poor artistic self-images because, as very young children, a piece of their artwork or a song or dance was disliked or compared unfavorably to another's by a significant adult in their life.

In addition, Marshall (1995) and Kohn (2006) warn that by focusing the children's attention on whether or not their behavior is likable, they learn that they must perform to please the teacher rather than to successfully accomplish the learning task. The child's joy in self-expression through the arts is then replaced with the child's conscious effort to produce something likable.

Unfortunately, this sort of judgmental praise naturally flows from our lips. Arguments can be made that in some sense we do want children to behave in pleasing ways; telling them we like something may increase the likelihood that they will repeat the action. However, the creative arts are based on the expansion of new behaviors rather than the repetition of limited actions. Consider what meaningful information a child receives when a teacher says something such as, "I like the way you used green paint today." Does the teacher really want the child to repeat the same use of green paint in every painting, or is there some better way to respond to this child's work?

## Teacher Tip

### WAYS TO PRAISE

Alfie Kohn (1993) suggests the following guidelines when praising children:

- Praise the behavior or product, not the child. Say, "That's a very unique brush stroke," not "You're a very original artist."
- Be specific. Say, "I hear you singing new words to the song," not "That's a nice song."
- Avoid phony sounding expressions. Use a natural, spontaneous voice.
- Avoid praise that creates competition. Praise the whole group, not one individual. Say "I see so many of you dancing to the beat of the music," not "Susie is such a good dancer today."

## Using Positive Feedback

**Positive feedback** tells children precisely what they did well. Instead of saying "Great painting!" the intentional teacher says, "I noticed you wiped your brush on the edge of the paint container so the paint didn't drip." Positive feedback is best used to let children know when they have used a technique well or behaved in a way that will give them further success at the activity.

In order to respond specifically, teachers need to have a clear idea in their minds about what techniques and behaviors are appropriate and possible for the children, and then they must carefully observe the children at work. Positive feedback enhances children's feelings of self-confidence and creativity—it provides information on what they have done well, and communicates to them that adults are personally interested enough in their arts activities to observe specific things they have done.

Even though positive feedback seems more like a wordy description than praise, when it is delivered with the same facial expression and the same warm enthusiastic tone of voice that we would use for "Great job!" the child receives it as praise for being successful in a very specific way.

Positive feedback can take several forms, each appropriate in different situations. With practice, this kind of response can become a natural way of talking to children about their creative work in daily interactions.

**Using descriptive statements.** A **descriptive statement** can be used to make children aware of their behavior and of how they solved a problem creatively, or to increase their understanding of arts concepts. Such descriptive statements show children that teachers value their individuality, because careful observation is necessary to provide a meaningful description. Each child at the same activity can receive a different comment.

These kinds of statements refer to how the child is working either with others or with the materials. They are the easiest statements to formulate and can serve as a good entrance into a conversation with children about their work.

If children are working with a material, comment on how they manipulated it. For example,

*"I noticed that you rolled the clay into a long snake."*

*"You moved the (computer) mouse in a circular way to make those curved lines."*

---

 ## Teacher Tip

### USING POSITIVE FEEDBACK

| **Typical examples of unconditional praise:** | **Ways to use positive feedback instead:** |
| --- | --- |
| Good glue job! | I noticed you put the glue on the back of your shapes and then attached them to your paper! |
| Super effort! | I see you used the maracas to keep rhythm with the music! |
| Nice dancing! | In your dance you made a pattern with your feet. |
| **Typical examples of judgmental statements:** | **Ways to use positive feedback instead:** |
| You are a beautiful bird! | Your arms are moving like a soaring bird's wings. |
| Lovely work! | The lines in your picture swirl in and out like a maze. |
| **Typical examples of imposing statements:** | **Ways to use positive feedback instead:** |
| That's an angry picture! | I see you used lots of black and red and green to show your anger about the accident. |
| What a happy story! | Your story reminds me of a walk I took in my grandmother's garden. |
| It looks like your mother. | I see you used many interesting patterns and shapes in this picture. Is there a story to go with it? |

When children work well with others, describe their behavior.

*"I see that you are singing in tune with your partner."*

Statements can also refer to the amount of effort children have put into an activity.

*"You spent a great deal of time working with Allan on your dinosaur project."*

**Describing artistic decisions.** Verbalizing the steps children have taken to solve a problem or summarizing their solutions are two important ways to make children aware of how they worked through a process.

If the child has struggled to find a solution to a problem, then describe the specific steps taken.

*"I noticed that you tried several ways to attach the tubes together. First you tried gluing them, and then you tried bending them. Now you have pushed one inside the other, and they are holding together well."*

In responding to a finished piece of work, summarize what choices the child has made. Artistic decision statements often contain the following phrases: "you tried," "you found," "you discovered," "you chose." For example,

*"You have chosen to use the drum to accompany your song."*

*"I noticed you found a way to attach that unusually shaped button to your puppet for its nose."*

**Describing arts concepts.** Descriptive statements can increase children's vocabulary, further their understanding of the arts, and make them aware of the sensory qualities of their work. Everyone who works with children and the arts should be familiar with the artistic elements of each of the art forms. Chapter 4 provides a detailed description of these elements, and also of the sensory qualities that should form the basis of this kind of verbal description.

Using arts concepts as the basis of descriptions allows higher-level responses to toddlers' scribbles and arts explorations. For example,

*"Look at all the swirling lines you have made!"*

*"I hear you tapping the rhythm of the tune."*

*"You are dancing with lots of energy!"*

*"Look at the way the wet paint sparkles!"*

**Describing the creative process.** Candace Shively (2011) finds that even young children can be introduced to the idea of flexible, fluent, original, and elaborate thinking, and once familiar with the terms are better able to talk about their own creative decision making process. For example,

*"Look at all the ways you thought of to move like a duck. What a flexible thinker you are."*

*"We came up with so many different ways to make rhythms with our sound makers. What fluent ideas we have."*

*"How original. I have never seen this way of building a block bridge before."*

*"By each of us adding another idea and elaborating on our story we have made it better."*

For more ways to describe the creative thinking process, see *Thinking about Thinking* on CourseMate.

**Paraphrasing and scaffolding.** To **paraphrase,** teachers repeat what children have just said in their own words. This is an excellent way to show children that the teacher has been listening to them. For example,

*Child: "I made lots of green lines."*
*Teacher: "Yes, you made many green lines."*

To **scaffold,** the teacher adds to the child's thought. This helps increase the child's vocabulary and conceptual understanding. For example,

*Child: "I made lots green lines."*
*Teacher: "Yes, you painted many bright green lines with the wide brush."*

**Responding to meaning.** When teachers respond to a child's artistic performance on a positive interpretive level, they model for the child the way the arts communicate to other people. We can refer to a personal sensation or a visual memory by saying, for example, "The story you told about your new puppy makes me remember my first puppy," or "The rectangles in your collage remind me of all the colorful windows in the apartment across the street."

Hall and Duffy (cited in Noyce & Christie, 1989, p. 46) found that when teachers initiated conversations with children by making a statement about their personal feelings or experiences, children gave less stilted, longer, and more spontaneous replies. Used appropriately, such responses can create a wonderful depth of communication between the child and adult.

**Asking questions.** Questioning or making a leading statement is one way to learn directly from the artists what their intent was. Questions can also be used to further children's understanding of the arts process, help them reflect on the consequences of their actions, and assess what they have learned from the arts activity. By encouraging children to verbalize about their artwork, we also help them develop language skills and clarify their thought processes. Questions must be phrased carefully so that they are not intrusive, allow many possible responses from children, and make children feel comfortable talking about the arts.

Before we can expect a child to respond freely to our questions, we must create an atmosphere in which the child feels safe expressing his or her thoughts and feelings. There are four ways to do this.

1. **Provide plenty of opportunities for children to look at artworks, listen to music, and watch dramatic performances and dance.** This will make verbalizing about the arts a natural part of children's experience. If children are used to asking questions about someone else's art, then they will be more comfortable answering questions about their own work.

2. **Express comments about children's artwork in the form of positive feedback.** This provides a model of how the children themselves can describe their own arts performances.

3. **Pay attention to the style of delivery in asking a question.** Questions need to be asked in a tone of voice that contains enthusiastic curiosity. Voices need to be soft, eyes need to make contact, and, once the child begins to respond, we need to practice active listening.

4. **Ask questions at the right moment.** Not every creative performance needs to be explained by a child. Choose carefully the moment to elicit a verbal response. If the child has just finished a painting and is eager to join some friends in the block area, it is not the time to engage the child in a deep conversation about the artwork. At this moment a simple descriptive form of positive feedback will suffice. On the other hand, if a child has been working on a clay sculpture for a long time and has stopped for a moment to get another piece of clay, this may provide an opportunity for a discussion about the work.

**Starting a conversation.** Be careful not to overwhelm children with a long string of questions. Use a question to begin a conversation. Continue the conversation only if the child is interested in doing so, and formulate responses based on the direction the child's answer takes. Learning how to phrase directed questions takes practice. Although when confronted with a dripping puddle of blue and purple paint, or noisy banging on a drum, our initial reaction may be "What is it?" or "What is that supposed to be?" such an intrusive, insulting question should be avoided. Not all child art is intended to be something. Much of a child's initial work with a medium will consist of exploration and experiments with the materials and tools and have no end result. This kind of question is limiting in that it puts all of the focus on the product and places children in the position of having to give an answer they think will please the questioner.

As an alternative to "What is it?" ask children to reflect on their creative performances in much deeper ways. Such questions can take several forms.

1. **Focusing on arts elements.** Questions can focus the children's attention on the arts elements in their work.

   *"What kinds of lines did you make with the crayons?"*

2. **Focusing on process.** The child can be asked to explain the process she or he used.

   *"How do you make those sounds with the tubes?"*

3. **Asking about decisions.** Artistic choices can be explained:

   *"Where on your collage did you decide to put those interesting pebbles you found?"*

**Exploring relationships.** Use questions to focus the children's attention on what they might do next and to see relationships between their behavior and the results. Kamii and DeVries (1993, p. 27) have postulated four types of questions that help children learn about how objects and events are related and foster creative problem solving.

**1. Predicting:**

*"What do you think will happen when you press your fingers into the clay?"*

*"What do you think might happen if you held hands and jumped together?"*

**2. Creating an effect:**

*"Can you make different sounds with the bells?"*

*"What do you think you could do if I gave you these pieces of yarn for your collage?"*

**3. Connecting events:**

*"How did the character in the play turn into this puppet?"*

## Special Needs

### • USING SOLILOQUY TO DEVELOP LANGUAGE SKILLS •

Talking about the arts provides a fertile ground for language development. Non-English speakers and children who need to experience rich language benefit from the process called *soliloquy* which is a way to mediate meaning and language structure that goes beyond baby talk [Feuerstein & Falik (2009)]. Soliloquy is keeping up a stream of rich descriptive words that works particularly well in arts activities.

Lewin-Benham (2010) gives the following examples.

[The teacher is holding hands with her two-and-half-year olds and walking to the painting materials.] "Let's go get the paint. What color do you think it will be?" (Listens to responses.) "Will it be green like the grass or orange like the juicy fruit?" (Listens to responses) "The paint is here on the cart. This is its place." (p. 31)

"'Something crinkly is on this shelf. What do you think it's made of?' She verbalizes for younger ones: 'No, it's not fall leaves! No it's not scrunched up newspaper. Yes! It is silver foil!'" (p. 31).

**4. Finding the cause:**

*"Why don't the pebbles fall off your collage now?"*

## Thinking About Thinking

Short **thinking routines** can be used to help young children construct knowledge, make connections, and develop self-awareness of the creative thinking skills. Angela Salmon (2010) finds that when these routines are used regularly and repeatedly children begin to use the language of thinking in dramatic play, block building, and other areas of learning on their own. Thinking routines help children remember and make connections. However, since thinking is an invisible, abstract process we need to make thinking visible for them. The individual thinking strategy can be written on cards and modeled by the teacher. Thinking routines were originally developed for viewing works of art from a critical perspective. But all of the arts provide a marvelous forum for developing this kind of metaphysical thinking. Here are a few routines from the Project Zero Artful Thinking project to try:

**Think-Pair-Share.** After asking a question, have the children turn to a partner and share their answer. This strategy helps children strengthen their reasoning skills and express their thinking verbally. Because they share with a peer they also model for each other.

**See-Think-Wonder.** After viewing a work of art or an arts performance, ask children to think about what they saw and to wonder why it looks the way it does. This strategy develops observation, focus, and imaginative problem solving.

**Think-Puzzle-Explore.** Use this when a child-initiated problem arises. This routine cues the child to think what the problem is, why it happened, and then prompts them to explore ways to solve it.

Example of a thinking routine in action:

Every time a child puts the crown on his head it falls off.

Teacher: Let's Think-Puzzle-Explore how to fix this. *Think* about why the hat keeps falling?"

Carlos: "It's falling over my eyes, but not in back. It's too big."

Teacher: "Are you *puzzled* by that?"

The intentional teacher is prepared ahead of time with knowledge of what the child knows and is ready to learn so that when that teachable moment presents itself, she knows what to do and what to say.

Carlos: "Yeh. It stayed up yesterday on Mattie's head." He looks over at Mattie. "She has a braid and I don't."

Teacher: "How could you fix it?"

Carlos turns the hat around and looks at the size of the head opening. "It needs something to hold it up."

Teacher: "Let's *explore* what you could use to make it fit." They walk together to the art center.

For more examples of these routines, see *Creative Thinking Routines* on CourseMate.

## How Should Teachers Respond to Problems?

As children participate in arts activities, a variety of difficulties can arise that can limit children's creativity. Some of these are the result of the previous arts experiences children bring with them. If a program is designed around open-ended activities that draw on the children's interests, and if the teachers show children that they value their creative work through thoughtful conversation, then many of these problems will slowly disappear on their own.

**Address fear.** There will always be some children who hold back from participating in arts activities. They may be afraid to take risks because they have had a bad experience with that art form previously or are uncertain what to do. This fear must be respected. It is important to try to find out why they are afraid and then provide the needed assurance. Children may have been scolded for getting dirty or making too much noise, or they may have been made to copy art projects or perform arts skills too difficult for them.

**Be patient.** Never force children to participate in an arts activity. Allow them to watch others performing. If they seem interested, stay nearby and invite them to investigate the activity. Be subtle and positive. Offer materials to use or actions to take, and then slowly withdraw. It is important to keep in mind that children do not develop skills when an adult does the work for them nor do they develop self-confidence in their own abilities if their project is "improved" or "directed" by a teacher. Allow children to explore on their own terms. Remember that, like adults, each child will like some arts activities better than others.

**Take care of personal needs.** Sick, tired, or hungry children will not be able to concentrate and create. If children are worried or nervous, they will be unlikely to take the kinds of risks that creativity requires.

**Provide comfort.** Children cannot be creative artists if they are upset or worried. We need to create a calm, accepting atmosphere that allows children to feel free to experiment and explore. This can be done by modeling an accepting attitude when interacting with children and their art. For example, if one child criticizes another's art performance by saying it is stupid or ugly, then respond immediately with a statement appropriate to the incident, such as in the following example:

- Start by making a positive statement about the artwork in question, such as, "Michelle has used many different textures in her collage." This provides assurance and comfort to the injured child.

**Photo Story**

## An Emergent Child-Initiated Project

# A Playground for Our Mouse

What happens when you combine a mouse, children, and imagination? These second graders imagined that their class pet, Frederick, was bored in his glass tank, so they decided to build him a playhouse. Children used the creative process to design things for Frederick to look at, climb up, and chew on that would also be safe for a little mouse. They used what they knew about mice to select safe materials and built the playhouse using familiar materials from the art center. Then they observed how Frederick liked what they made and thought of new things to try. For months children arrived at school their imaginations soaring, their ideas bubbling over.

Make it clear that the comment made was hurtful and unacceptable, and that uniqueness is valued. For example: "It is hurtful to say that about how someone sings. Everybody sings in his or her own way."

**Provide direction.** If a child is misusing an art tool, musical instrument, or prop, or is struggling with a technique, intervene as subtly as possible. A quiet restatement of the directions, repetition of the safety rules, or quick demonstration is usually sufficient when given directly to the child. If it is not, redirect the child to another activity.

**Build self-confidence.** It is surprising that even very young children often exhibit a lack of confidence in being able to create in the arts. This is because it does not take much to make a child afraid to risk being unique. When a child participates in arts activities, often a product or performance of some kind results, and even if the child is just exploring, in some sense this is an extension of the child. An unkind word, an accident, a well-meaning attempt to make the product or performance fit a preconceived mold, or the attempt to imitate a model that is beyond the ability of the child to copy can all affect artistic confidence.

**Offer open-ended activities.** When children say, "Make it for me," there has been some interference in their natural desire to explore and play with art materials that has diminished their intrinsic motivation. These children need reassurance that their art is acceptable as they choose to make it. Make sure to provide many open-ended arts activities. It is also important to eliminate tracers and models to copy and to maintain a "hands-off" policy. An adult should never work on or "fix" a child's art to make it better.

**Ask questions.** If children insist that they cannot create or perform in the arts, then affirm that difference is valued. For example: "Each artist creates in her own way. Look at all the different ways the other children have used the paint (crayons, paper, boxes . . .)." Then ask an open-ended question:

*"Can you invent a new way to . . . ?"*

*"What would happen if . . . ?"*

*"Have you tried . . . ?"*

## Teacher to Family

### Sample Letter to Families: Responding to Their Child's Visual Art

Families also need to know how to respond to their child's artistic work, particularly in the visual arts. The following letter offers suggestions of ways parents can celebrate the creative process rather than focusing on the product.

Dear Family,

It is a special occasion when your child brings home a piece of art. Each child's artwork is unique, a special part of him or her. Please take a moment to have your child share it with you.

Children have many purposes in creating art. Perhaps today was a chance to explore what happened when blue and yellow mixed together. On the other hand, maybe your child practiced using scissors and glue and discovered a new way to make shapes. To our adult eyes, we may see only some mixed-up colors or odd sticky shapes. But to your child it was an adventure in discovery.

- Ask what did you discover?. You will help your child use words to describe what was learned.
- Ask if there is a story to go with the artwork. You will learn much more about the artist's imagination and assist in language development.
- Describe the lines, colors, shapes, textures, and patterns—and ask your child to do the same. You will help your child build her or his vocabulary.
- Share a memory of a piece of art you created or have seen. You will be teaching your child that many people have created art.

After sharing a piece of art, hang it in a special place for the family to see, such as on a door or a refrigerator. When a new artwork comes home, remove the old one and store it away. Someday your child will enjoy looking at his or her art and remembering that special moment.

Your child's teacher,

**Offer timely help.** When introducing new techniques, they should be within the skill range of the child, and the child must be really interested in learning them. It is helpful to ask, "Do you need help? You look frustrated. Would you like me to show you another way?" Children learn best when the technique that is being taught is delivered at just the right time—the teachable moment—when they need it to solve a problem of their own creation.

**Pair child with a partner.** It takes a high degree of observational skill to be aware of the technical needs of a group of children all actively involved in arts processes. With experience it becomes easier to know which children are ready for a new technique and when they need it. In many cases, a simple pairing of two children of slightly different ages or skill levels may be the best way to increase the skill level of a child without direct adult interference.

---

### Did You Get It?

**Which of the following is true of creative teaching?**

a. Teachers ignore "teachable moments" so as not to interfere with their activity plans.

b. Teachers make models that require children to produce artwork that fits an adult idea of what it should look like.

c. Children are encouraged to go at their own pace and figure things out for themselves.

d. Children's final product or performance is valued more than the process involved in creating it.

**Take the full quiz on CourseMate**

---

## Conclusion: Creativity in Teaching

Creativity is different from the other areas of growth that teachers try to develop in children. It is not something we can teach directly, but we must foster it through our attitude, behavior, and activity choices. Sometimes the children's creative solutions will challenge our tolerance for messiness and disorder. At other times, the inventiveness of a young child will fill us with awe. When selecting and designing arts activities for young children, remember that they will each respond creatively, based on their personally unique previous knowledge, not our preconceived idea of what they will do.

The entire learning environment must be designed around the elements that nurture creative processing. Teachers need to provide opportunities for children to gain knowledge and skill by exploring art media. Children need time to immerse themselves in arts creation, motivated by their boundless curiosity and the search for solutions.

Successful teachers of the arts value curiosity, exploration, and original behavior. They allow children to go at their own pace, figure things out for themselves, and encourage them to try new things. They refrain from making models; from using children's materials in an expert, adult way; and from requiring children to produce artwork that fits an adult idea of how it should appear or sound. They listen to the children and pay attention to what they are thinking. They observe the process that children go through, and pay less attention to the product of this process. Finally, an enthusiastic teacher of the arts provides the children with many opportunities in which they can safely explore and pursue creative activities without interruption.

The line between needed intervention and being directive is a fine one. Teachers do not want to miss the "teachable moment" nor interfere with the children's solving of their own problems. This is the art of creative teaching. Teachers must be in tune with children, understanding their past experiences, sensitivities, and desires. It is not easy. Children are always "dangerously on the brink between presence that they want and repression that they don't want" (Malaguzzi in Edwards, Gandini, & Forman, 2011, p. 58).

It takes a creative person to fashion such an environment. It takes knowledge, skill, and a great deal of motivation to fully bring out creative behavior in children. Like the child, the teacher will say:

*"What will happen if I do this?"*

*"How will these things go together?"*

*"Wow, I didn't expect that to happen!"*

*"I've never seen anything like this before."*

No two individuals approach this task in the same way. This book and experience will provide the knowledge and the skills; teachers must provide their own motivation.

Find additional information on nurturing creativity in young children on CourseMate

## Teaching In Action

### Making a Shape Mural: An Interview

*Q: Have you ever done any printmaking with your child care children?*

*A:* Yes. One of the best experiences I ever had was one of those spur-of-the-moment things. There was only a half-day of school, and I ended up with eight children, ranging in age from one to eight. I didn't want them all just fooling around in front of the TV, so I looked around, and I happened to have some paper plates, some tempera paint, and a roll of brown kraft paper, so I decided to try a printed mural.

*Q: Do you always have art supplies like that?*

*A:* I have found that the arts are something that will get everyone involved. Even the littlest ones can have a part. I try to keep some paint in the cupboard along with other basic supplies.

*Q: How did you get them started?*

*A:* It was a beautiful day, so I took everyone out to the yard, and I began by playing a game of shape tag. I called out a shape and they had to touch something with that shape.

*Q: How did the toddlers participate?*

*A:* I had the older children hold hands with the one-year-old and the two-year-old and find a shape together.

*Q: How did you transition into printmaking?*

*A:* I had brought out my box of printing objects. There were cardboard tubes and potato mashers and wooden blocks and sponges—big things even the little ones could handle. I dumped out the box and asked them to choose an object they thought would make an interesting shape. Then I put a small amount of paint on the paper plates and showed them how to dip an object into the paint and press it to make a shape. I used a piece of newspaper for my demonstration, and then I let them try their shapes on it. I asked the older children to work with the toddlers.

*Q: How did you get the mural going?*

*A:* Well, while they were experimenting on the paper, I rolled out the mural paper on the picnic table and held it down with stones. Then I said, "Who is ready to make a shape trail with their printing tool?" Those who were ready—there were about four—came over, and I told them to start a trail on one edge and make it end on another edge. I challenged them to see how long they could make it. I told them they could cross each other's trails but not cover them up. When they finished, they rinsed their hands in a bucket of water and went to play on the swings and in the sandbox, while the rest came over and finished. The two little ones were in the second group, and I could give them the attention they needed.

*Q: How did you end the activity?*

*A:* After everyone had made their shape trail, we went inside and washed up, and then I gave them some crackers for a snack. We talked about the shape of the crackers. A few children carefully bit of the edges of their crackers to form new shapes. Others made a shape trail with their crackers on their plate. Meanwhile, the mural was drying quickly in the sun. When snack was done, we went out and checked. It was dry, so we brought it inside, and the children had fun counting the shapes in their trails and seeing whose was the longest, whose had the most shapes, whose curved the most, and so on. Then three of the preschoolers played driving their cars along the shape trails. They had a lot of fun with it for many days afterward, and they learned more than if they had spent that time watching TV.

# Reflection Page

## Experiencing the Creative Process: What Is in a Name?

On a piece of paper, write your name in as many different ways as possible. When the paper is full or you run out of ideas, make a list of all the ways they are different in terms of color, size, and thickness.

How many different ways did you invent?

_____
_____
_____
_____

How many look similar to your signature?

_____
_____
_____
_____

How many look different?

_____
_____
_____
_____

List the steps of the creative process you experienced.

_____
_____
_____
_____

# Reflection Page

## Self-Exploration: My First Arts Experience

🖎 What is the earliest arts experience you remember?

_____

_____

🖎 What did you do?

_____

_____

🖎 Where and when was it?

_____

_____

🖎 What materials did you use?

_____

_____

🖎 Who was there with you? What did they say?

_____

_____

🖎 Did anyone comment on your work?

_____

_____

🖎 What emotions did you feel?

_____

_____

# Reflection Page

## Self-Exploration: My Personal Arts Time Line

Fill in all of the arts experiences you remember, at about the age you experienced them. You can include such things as arts courses you have taken, museums and concerts you have been to, a specific artwork you made or performance you have given, a book about any of the art forms you have read, a movie related to the arts that you have seen, a comment made by a teacher or family member about your creative work, and so forth.

| Age _____ | Experience _____ |
|---|---|
| Birth to age 5 | |
| 5 to 10 years | |
| 10 to 15 years | |
| 15 to 20 years | |
| 20 to 30 years | |
| 30 to 40 years | |
| 40 to 50 years | |
| 50+ years | |

**What Does My Timeline Tell Me?**

Study your timeline and ask yourself the following questions:

1.  Do you remember more experiences from your early childhood or more from your later years?

    _____

2.  How many are happy memories?

    _____

3.  Do any memories make you feel uncomfortable?

    _____

4.  Do you remember any of the adults who participated in creating these memories?

    _____

5.  How will these memories affect the way you will approach young children and their creative arts processing?

    _____

# Reflection Page

## Self-Exploration: Defining Creative Behavior

*"Just how broadly creativity is defined is critical to any program planning, for far too often creative ideas are ignored, or worse yet, actively squelched when well-meaning educators are only watching for a creative product that matches their aesthetic standards."*

—*Nancy Lee Cecil and Phyllis Lauritzen (1995, p. 28)*

Analyze each of the following behaviors in terms of whether or not you would consider it creative and what action you would take, if any, to change or control the behavior.

A child eats a piece of play dough because "it looked like a banana."

_____

_____

A child glues his paper to the table because he "didn't want it to slide off the table."

_____

_____

A child runs around the room biting everyone with his imaginary "snake."

_____

_____

A child drums on another child's head.

_____

_____

A child uses a scissors to cut the hair of another child.

_____

_____

# Chapter 3

## Artistic Development

Identify the factors that affect the artistic development of children and use this knowledge to design DAP arts activities.

List the four DAP filters and explain how to use them to select and assess developmentally appropriate arts activities.

**Planning Curriculum to Achieve Important Goals**

**Teaching to Enhance Development and Learning**

**Artistic Development DAP Learning Objectives**

**Assessing Children's Development and Learning**

**Creating a Caring Community**

**Establishing Reciprocal Family Relationships**

Explain how to meet the needs of each child through developmentally appropriate arts activities.

Apply reflective teaching practices and assessment tools to record and assess the process of art creation.

Use documentation, portfolios, and active communication about the arts to establish relationships with families.

Copyright © 2015 Cengage Learning®

## Young Artists Creating

Andy picks up a crayon and grasps it tightly in his fist. He slowly approaches the large white paper before him. Arm held stiffly, he rubs the crayon on the paper. Lifting the crayon, he looks at the smudge he has left behind. With his other hand he touches it, rubs it, and looks at his fingers. The mark is still there. He bends over and sniffs it with his nose. Cautiously, Andy looks up. Is this all right? Can he do this? But no one is stopping him. He returns to the paper. With broad strokes, Andy makes his first true marks on the world. Broad sweeps of color up and down, back and forth. Again and again, on paper after paper, at the beginning of his second year of life, he draws. . . .

## How Do Children Develop in the Arts?

It begins with a line, a sound, a movement—an action that reflects the child's physical control over the body. The infant is at the beginning of a long and complex process, which in the eighth year of life will end with a mastery of arts skills that is remarkably expressive and controlled. Young children do not know that this is where their explorations in the arts will lead; they only know the moment—this pleasurable and exciting moment in which they have acted and produced a result.

All of us were once infants, unable to move on our own. Step by step, we learned to crawl and then to walk. At first, we walked unsteadily, clasping a guiding hand. Soon we could take baby steps on our own, and in no time at all we could run and dance.

In the same way, each child grows artistically. Although no newborn is a musician, dancer, actor, or painter at birth, inside every infant is the potential to grow into one. When the time is right, children start their artistic journey, tentatively making small marks upon the world. Their marks enlarge and change from wavy scribbles to enclosed shapes to symbols that encompass their experience. Their gurgling sounds coalesce, become organized, develop rhythm and pitch, and become song. Their random movements become coordinated, and patterned into a fluid dance. This pattern of increasing competence repeats itself in every young child, everywhere in the world mediated by the unique cultural background and personal life events they experience.

Development in the arts begins in infancy. This infant shows her responsiveness to music and rhythms.

### The Arts and Developmentally Appropriate Practice: DAP

Developmentally appropriate practice (DAP) is based on the idea that teachers need to know how young children typically develop, what variations may occur in this development, and then be able to adjust their teaching to reach each individual child (Copple & Bredekamp, 2009). To do this we must ask ourselves the following three questions, which are the basis of developmentally appropriate practice and which will help us select the best arts activities for our children:

1. What is known about child development and learning? This knowledge helps us identify the child's expected developmental level by directing

us to look at the child's similarity to others of the same age. This is called **normative development.**

2. What is known about each child's individual development? This knowledge will help us discover what makes each child uniquely different from others the same age so we can better meet that child's needs.

3. What is known about the social and cultural context in which children live? This knowledge helps us better understand the communication style, cultural beliefs and attitudes, strengths, and desires of both the child and the child's family.

# What Is Known About Child Development in the Arts?

According to the National Association for the Education of Young Children's Position Statement on Developmentally Appropriate Practice (Copple & Bredekamp, 2009, pp. 1–31), being knowledgeable about **normative development,** or what children are generally like at various ages, allows teachers to make initial decisions about which activities and experiences will be safe, but challenging, for young children.

The normative age divisions used in this text follow those of Copple and Bredekamp (2009). They are intended to provide general guidelines from which appropriate arts activities may be selected.

**Infant.** In this text, **infant** is used to refer to children from birth to 18 months. Infants have the following characteristics:

- Explore first with mouth and later with eyes and limbs
- Use movements, gestures, and vocalizations to communicate
- Have very limited self-regulatory skills and require constant supervision
- Show development of physical control from the head down and from the center of body out to the limbs
- Are strongly attached to caregivers and respond best in one-on-one settings
- Have short memories and attention spans
- Can learn to respond to simple commands

**Toddler.** Throughout this text, **toddler** is used to refer to children between the ages of 18 months and 3 years who may exhibit the following characteristics:

- Need to explore with all their senses and may still put objects in their mouth
- Have limited self-regulatory skills and require close supervision
- Engage in parallel play
- Show developing control over large muscles in the arms and legs
- Have short attention spans, usually less than 10 minutes, and need simple materials to explore
- Need to repeat actions
- Say names of objects and understand more words than they can say
- Are developing a sense of self

**Three- to five-year-olds or preschoolers.** Most children of this age display the following characteristics:

- Show increasing self-control and can work side by side in small groups
- Usually will not put inappropriate items in mouth
- Show developing control over wrists, hands, and fingers
- Have an increasing attention span and can work independently for 10 minutes or more at a time

**Five- to six-year-olds or kindergartners.** Most children in this age range display the following behaviors:

- Show increasing control over wrists and hands and exhibit a more mature grip on drawing tools
- Can concentrate for a period of time, 30 minutes or more, on a self-selected arts activity
- Can work together in small groups of three to six on common projects and are able to share some supplies
- May dictate or be able to write stories with invented spelling
- Can follow a three-step direction

- Can classify objects and make predictions

- Can use words to describe the qualities of objects—color, size, and shape—and begin to sort them by those qualities

**Six- to eight-year-olds or primary age.** Most children in this age range show the following behaviors:

- Hold drawing tools with a mature grip

- Concentrate for an hour or more on a self-selected arts activity and return to an ongoing arts project over a period of several days

- Initiate, participate, and assume roles in cooperative group arts activities

- Begin to read and write stories with the majority using conventional spelling by the end of the eighth year

- Understand that objects can share one or more qualities and can use this knowledge to make predictions and comparisons and to draw conclusions

## Children's Development in the Arts

Much of the artistic performance of young children is determined by their physical development. This is particularly true in the early years. However, as children get older, what they have learned influences their artistic performance as well. As children develop language skills and knowledge about the arts, their artistic performance and works become more complex. In this chapter we will look at how physical growth and experience affect artistic behavior in general. Chapters 9 to 12 look at the specific influences of development in the four art forms.

## The Role of Physical Development in Children's Artistic Performance

Although each of the art forms requires different skills, all of them are influenced by how children develop physically. This is particularly true in the early years. An infant who can sit but not walk will not be able to dance independently.

In young children the development of physical control over the body is usually sequential and predictable. For example, children usually sit up before they walk. This sequence is illustrated in Table 3-1.

Children develop from the head down and from the center of the body out (Cherry, Godwin, & Staples, 1989, p. 53). Infants turn their heads toward sounds and may show preferences for certain types of music. By age one, arm and leg movement shows developing control. They can now grasp musical instruments, crayons, and markers tightly in their fists and make whole arm movements, up and down, back and forth. They can also lift and drop their arms, stabbing and punching the paper with gusto and verbal expression, or beating a drum with wild enthusiasm. This period has been called by some researchers that of the "random or uncontrolled scribble" (Lowenfeld & Brittain, 1987). Watching infants drawing, it does seem at times that their scribbles have a mind of their own, careening off the edges of the paper and onto the table or floor. Listening to them shaking a tambourine, it might seem like they move to the beat of a different drummer. But there is also thoughtful deliberation. Watch the child at play in the arts, pausing in mid-line or mid-tap to express delight. The arm and hand may not yet be under control, but a mind is growing there!

By preschool age, many children can create original dance movements based on the dances they have seen adults doing.

| TABLE 3–1 | Sequence of Physical Development in Young Children | | | |
|---|---|---|---|---|
| **Age** | **Arms** | **Head and Torso** | **Legs** | **Whole Body** |
| At birth | Random movements | Need support | Random movements | |
| Infants *Newborn to 6 months* | Put hands in mouth Reach and grasp objects Bring object to mouth | Turn head Lift head Sit with support | Put feet in mouth Reach and kick objects with feet | Roll over |
| Infants 6 months to 1 year | Pick up objects Drop objects Pass objects from hand to hand | Sit alone Roll | Can bear weight on legs Stand Walk holding on | Cross midline Crawl/creep Imitate actions Move whole body to music |
| Toddlers 1 to 2 years | Throw objects Push and pull | Bend to pick up something | Walk "toddling" Kick object Run | Creep up stairs Climb up but may have trouble getting down Move mainly arms and legs to music |
| 2 to 3 years | Catch large objects Throw underhand | | Walk forward and backward Walk up steps Run with open stride Jump up and down Balance on one foot briefly | Climb up and down using alternating feet and hands |
| Preschoolers 3 to 4 years | Throw overhand Bounce ball | Do somersault | Walk heel toe Balance on one foot Walk on a straight line Climb steps using alternative feet Jump over something Can do a standing broad jump Tip toe | Ride a tricycle Swing May have difficulty judging space and direction Switch quickly from one motion to another |
| Kindergarteners 5 to 6 years | Hand dominance established | | Hop on one foot Walk on balance beam Skip a little Skate | Smooth muscle action Coordinate movements with others |
| Primary Ages 6 to 8 years | Catch/throw small ball Know left from right Can dribble a ball | | Skip on either foot Skip rope Walk forward/backward on balance beam | Remember dance steps Follow complex directions |

*Note: As in all the arts, physical development is strongly influenced by experience. This chart is intended only as a general guideline to what skills might be mastered in terms of age. However, the basic sequence of skill acquisition will pertain to most children.*

**One- to three-year-olds.** Between the ages of one and three, children begin to have more control over their elbows. This increasing physical control is reflected in the child's ability to clap, wiggle, and sway in rhythm to music.

Sweeping arcs are created as children move their arms independently. Lines on paper now have curved edges. They loop and swirl across the paper exuberantly.

With continued physical maturation, toddlers develop control over their wrists and feet. Older toddlers can "dance" by bouncing, bending knees, walking on tiptoe, and swinging arms. They begin to match their movements with the beat. This is also when children start to learn their first tunes, clapping games, and finger plays. When they play, they may hum or sing made-up songs.

Now they can also control the line that issues from their drawing tools. They can start and stop at will and lift the crayon and place it down again close to where they want it. Scribbles begin to be joined into lopsided geometric figures. Control over the fingers is also slowly developing. The tight fist may be replaced by a looser grip, although some children may still have no particular hand preference.

As children persist in repeating motions and creating the resulting lines, figures, sounds, and motions, they develop skill and control, but something else is also happening. One day the child will look at the lines, the mess of scribbles, or stop in the middle of babbling or halt in mid-step and say: "Look at my doggie," or "I made a bear story," or "I sing a happy song," or "I am dancing salsa." And although 10 minutes later the child may give a totally different name to the scribble, the story, the song, or the dance—still unrecognizable to us—those actions have developed meaning for that child. This development is tremendously exciting. We can "see" and "hear" the child

thinking. Table 3-2 shows a normative view of artistic development in children from birth to age 8.

## The Role of Cognitive Development in Artistic Performance

The arts have often been used as ways to investigate cognitive development in preliterate children.

**Gardner Model of Cognitive Development.** Howard Gardner has led the way in investigating the cognitive aspects of early childhood artistic development. In general, Gardner (1991) supports Piaget's idea (1959) that sensory learning dominates the first 18 months of life, and that this is followed by a symbolic period during the preschool years, in which children master the symbolic forms of language, number, and the arts. According to his theory of multiple intelligences, Gardner proposes that cognitive development takes place in waves rather than stages, with burgeoning knowledge developing within a specific intelligence and then overflowing into other intelligences.

| TABLE 3–2 | Development in the Arts | | | |
|---|---|---|---|---|
| **Age Group\*** | **Language/Dramatics** | **Music** | **Visual Art** | **Movement** |
| Infancy to age 1 | Respond to sound<br>Identify different voices<br>Make meaningful sounds<br>Imitate voices<br>Laugh, smile<br>Make faces and show emotions in response to stimuli | Pay attention to music<br>Respond to loud/soft<br>Rock & bounce to music<br>Imitate musical sounds | Random scribbles<br>Use whole body<br>Look at objects and pictures | Grasp and hold objects<br>Move arms & legs<br>Start & stop<br>Match actions to needs<br>Crawl, sit, stand, climb<br>Cross midline<br>Hand-eye, eye-hand coordination<br>Walk with help |
| Ages 1 to 3 | Use words and simple sentences<br>Name objects<br>Make believe conversations<br>Scribble writing<br>Imaginary play | Listen to music<br>Identify types of sounds<br>Make up own songs<br>5 note range<br>Cannot match pitch or keep time<br>Explore instruments' sounds | Basic scribbles<br>Placement patterns<br>Aggregates begin — suns, mandalas, people<br>Action symbols<br>Use whole arm<br>Fist grip<br>Identify items in pictures | Pound & roll play dough<br>Walk, run, jump, hop<br>Go up stairs with help<br>Push & pull<br>Throw |
| Ages 3 to 4 | Recognize letters, some words<br>Invent, retell stories<br>Use invented spelling<br>Take on a role in pretend play<br>Act out invented stories with props | Sing simple songs<br>5 to 8 note range<br>Begin to keep time<br>Begin to match pitch<br>Play simple instruments in group | Recognizable images<br>Spatial relationships<br>Begin to use wrist<br>Finger grip matures<br>Identifies, matches art by style | Catch & throw with both hands<br>Climb stairs one foot at time<br>Walk heel toe<br>Balance on beam<br>Ride tricycle, swing<br>Match movements to rhythms |

*(continued)*

| TABLE 3–2 | Development in the Arts *(continued)* | | | |
|---|---|---|---|---|
| Ages 5 to 6 | Read words and sentences<br>Identify types of books<br>Write story from picture<br>Begin to use conventional spelling and writing process<br>Enjoy jokes, riddles | Sing in tune in a group<br>Identify pitches<br>Add lower notes to range<br>Identify changes in music<br>Keep time<br>Read simple notation<br>Can begin piano, violin, etc. | Cultural symbols<br>Add ground line and sky line Balanced placement<br>Numerical concepts<br>Tell stories through art<br>Recognize styles of art | Make balls from clay<br>Catch & throw large & small balls<br>Climb stairs without support<br>Skip. Jump rope<br>Balance well<br>Ride bicycle<br>Coordinate movements with others |
| Ages 7 to 8 | Read independently<br>Write using most conventions<br>Perform short simple plays | Hear harmony<br>Sing rounds & 2 parts<br>Keep time accurately<br>Read music<br>Play parts on instruments | Repeat established symbols but start to strive for realistic images<br>Control over materials improves | Play group sports<br>Learn dance steps |

*The first wave.* Gardner believes that sometime between the ages of 18 months and two years, children become capable of using symbols to communicate their knowledge that events consist of objects and actions. Although language oriented, this symbolic realization "spills" into other intellectual domains. At this point, if asked to draw a truck, the child scribbles with the marker while making truck sounds.

*The second wave.* At about age three, a second wave called topographical mapping occurs. Now the child can express the spatial relationships of real objects, such as showing two adjoining circles and identifying the top one as a head.

*The third wave.* Around age four, the child begins to use numerical relationships (digital mapping). For example, children may draw four human figures to represent four people in their family, or count the beats as they tap on a drum.

*The fourth wave.* The most educationally important event occurs sometime during the fifth, sixth, or seventh year, when children begin to invent their own notational systems. Children now draw pictures using graphic symbols of their own invention, for such purposes as to remember experiences or to "list" belongings. They may invent ways to record the notes in a song. Gardner, although he points out the influence of seeing adults using notational systems, feels that there is an innate human propensity to create such systems.

Table 3–3 summarizes the relationship between cognitive growth and how it is expressed in children's artistic performance.

### Did You Get It?

Mia teaches a preschool class of three and four-year-olds. Which of the following arts activities will be most suitable for the children in her class?

a. work in groups of ten to create a skit for Parents' Day

b. sing a round

c. fill out activity sheets for an hour

d. sing songs in a 5 to 8 note range

**Take the full quiz on CourseMate**

## What Is Known About Each Child's Individual Development?

As anyone who has ever worked with young children can verify, artistic development in individual children does not follow the nice, neat patterns laid out in textbooks and on normative charts. Although developmental tables such as 3-1, 3-2, and 3-3 can provide useful guides in understanding what might be expected at various ages, they do not present the whole picture. Children are dynamic and ever changing. The second question we must ask as we design a developmentally appropriate arts curriculum is: What are the unique abilities of this individual child at this time and place?

DAP reminds us that children have unique strengths, needs, and interests.

**TABLE 3–3** The Arts and Cognitive Growth, based on Gardner (1991)

| Age | Cognitive Understanding | Arts Production |
|---|---|---|
| Causal Relationships 1 ½ – 2 years | Discovers the relationships between object and event. | Bangs a drum to make a sound.<br>Draws a cat by scribbling and meowing at same time.<br>Makes a funny face and causes someone to laugh. |
| Spatial relationships 2-3 years | Discovers spatial relationships | Can place whole body or a body part in relation to an object or another person.<br>Draws a person by putting a small circle (head) on top of a larger one (body). |
| Numerical relationships 3-5 years | Represents numerical concepts | Counts taps on a drum using fingers.<br>Draws a dog with four legs, two eyes, one nose, two ears, and one mouth.<br>Places dishes on the table in the housekeeping center equal to the number of children playing. |
| Notational Relationships 5-7 years | Invents or learns meaningful symbols of the culture | Makes marks or uses music notes to create an original melody.<br>Draws a picture of his or her family and labels them – "mom," "dad," or by name.<br>Puts on a Spiderman mask and acts like the superhero. |

These may be due to maturational differences, developmental delays, physical challenges, or exceptional gifts. Development does not proceed in lockstep fashion, but rather in growth and spurts.

## Physical Factors

Physical development happens at varying rates in different children. There may be periods of fast growth followed by periods of slower growth.

Sometimes a new ability will suddenly appear. At other times it will take the child months of trial and error before the behavior is exhibited. We see this in the variation that occurs in children learning to walk. Some stand up one day and take off at a run. Others take a step, fall down, crawl some more, and then try again over and over.

Growth patterns are strongly influenced by heredity, nutrition, and exercise. Poorly nourished children will exhibit delayed growth and physical coordination. For example, 40 percent of children in Head Start programs have been found to have delays in motor skill development (Woodward & Yun, 2001). Children who have the space, time, and encouragement to explore large areas physically, such as through creative movement activities, will be better coordinated and have stronger muscles.

Some children have physical challenges such as vision and hearing impairments or trouble controlling their bodies. Others may overreact or underreact to sensory stimuli. Some children may have had negative early experiences that have a delayed impact on language and personality development.

These children need special consideration in planning arts activities so they can enjoy the arts and participate fully in them. In fact, for many children with special needs, the arts can provide an alternate and meaningfully rich way to communicate with others.

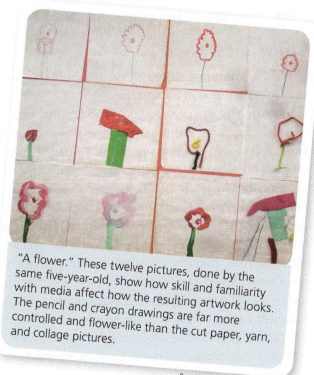

"A flower." These twelve pictures, done by the same five-year-old, show how skill and familiarity with media affect how the resulting artwork looks. The pencil and crayon drawings are far more controlled and flower-like than the cut paper, yarn, and collage pictures.

# What Is Known About the Social, Emotional, and Cultural Context In Which Children Live?

Children also differ in the life experiences to which they have been exposed. Lillian Katz and Sylvia Chard (2000) call this the "dynamic dimension of development." An examination of the emotional, social, and cultural context in which young artists function reveals that there are many important ways in which variations in maturation, educational experiences, and other environmental factors influence young artists.

## Emotional Factors

A child's emotional state will greatly influence how the child performs in the arts.

**Traumatic events.** A child who has just experienced a disturbing event may use the arts as a way to express and release deep emotions. Tornados, earthquakes, accidents, family stressors, and death often elicit scribbling, stabbing at the paper, splashing of paint, and banging on drums from people of all ages. Because the arts can serve as an emotional release, we need to bring sensitivity to our artistic interactions with children. With understanding and encouragement, we can allow children to work through these deep feelings. Joe Frost (2005) found that work, play, and the arts were significant ways to heal children who were affected by Hurricane Katrina. (See Chapter 5 for specific ways to address children's special needs through the arts.)

**Social pressures.** Teachers also need to understand how their own actions and those of a child's family can influence how a child feels about the arts. Children who are pressured to make their arts performance match an adult "ideal," or are frustrated by an arts material or skill that is beyond their physical ability to master, may develop feelings of failure. Such feelings may cause reluctance to participate in future arts activities.

**Rejection.** Similarly, children who feel that their arts performance is rejected or unacceptable also retreat from arts activities. That is why it is equally important that teachers show their acceptance of the child's work and teach families how to encourage their young artists.

## Environmental Factors

Young children may not see the world in the same way adults do, but they are influenced by the pictures they see, the kinds of objects that surround them, and the artistic reactions of their guiding adults to these things.

**The role of culture.** Children's development in the arts is strongly influenced by the culture in which they grow up. McFee and Degge (1981, p. 334) cite studies that indicate that children from cultures with particular stylistic ways of drawing will learn to draw in that style.

Children who have seen examples of a variety of art forms and are taught to value them are more likely to incorporate elements from these examples into their own creative works. Dennis (1966) found that children raised in environments with plentiful visual imagery, surrounded by many drawings of people, had higher scores on the Goodenough-Harris Draw-A-Person Test (Harris & Goodenough, 1963). Exposure to a wide variety of interesting musical styles challenges children to invent new songs or refine existing ones.

**The role of exposure.** Adults determine which artistic behaviors and skills are acceptable for children to learn. They set the limits on what is a creative arts performance and what is not. Smearing finger paint on paper is encouraged; smearing cereal on the wall is not. Are egg cartons an art material? Should we use food products in art? Is banging spoons on fine china making music? The adults' definition of what is and is not an arts activity will be transmitted to the child.

The home culture also influences the type of music, art, dance, and storytelling styles the child has experienced. Being aware of the types of music,

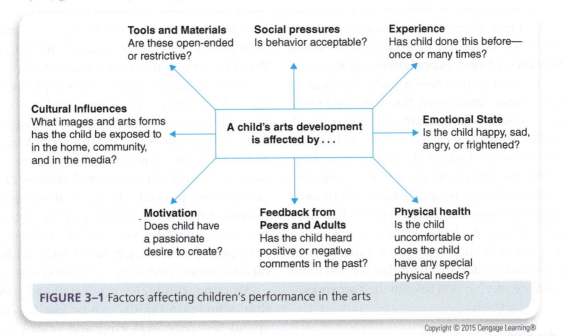

**Tools and Materials**
Are these open-ended or restrictive?

**Social pressures**
Is behavior acceptable?

**Experience**
Has child done this before—once or many times?

**Cultural Influences**
What images and arts forms has the child be exposed to in the home, community, and in the media?

**A child's arts development is affected by . . .**

**Emotional State**
Is the child happy, sad, angry, or frightened?

**Motivation**
Does child have a passionate desire to create?

**Feedback from Peers and Adults**
Has the child heard positive or negative comments in the past?

**Physical health**
Is the child uncomfortable or does the child have any special physical needs?

**FIGURE 3–1** Factors affecting children's performance in the arts

dance, stories, and visual art valued by a child's family and including them in the arts program shows sensitivity and empowers the child.

## The Effect of Experience

Adults also determine how much experience children have with an art form. The more opportunities children have to use arts media, methods, and tools the more comfortable and skilled they will become in the creative arts. All individuals, regardless of their age, need to spend time exploring and revisiting a medium before they can use it expressively.

**Importance of practice.** For example, if young children have many opportunities to draw, they will usually show their highest level of symbol development in their drawings. The same child may produce much less "competent" looking artwork if asked to use an unfamiliar material. Children will quickly revert to scribbles in their first finger painting or watercolor. Repetition and practice are the keys to improving skills at any level. Even adults with excellent fine motor control find themselves scribbling the first time they try to draw freehand using a computer mouse or trackpad.

**Importance of role models.** Children are influenced by the people around them. They are more likely to be interested in creating art if other people around them are as well, and if arts are readily available and highly valued. Young children may make drawings in mud and hum made-up tunes on their own, but they are not going to choose formal

### Across Cultures

**Language Acquistion And The Arts**

Children who speak a language other than English go through sequential stages of language acquisition as they learn English:

1. **Nonverbal:** children listen to and study the patterns they hear.
2. **Rehearsal:** children repeat to themselves silently or by mouthing what they have heard in during activities
3. **Formulaic:** children respond with a single word, such as "yellow" instead of "that is yellow," or imitative phrase such as "sit here."

During these stages it may appear that the child is nonverbal or not learning English, when in fact the child understands much more than he or she can say. Gregory Cheatham and Yeonsum Ro (2010) suggest using intentional teaching in pretend play and storytelling as a way to help the early-stage English Language Learner's language transition. For example, teachers can:

- Suggest the child watch and, when comfortable, participate in pretend play.
- Respond to the child's nonverbal gestures and facial expressions and use of native language with an English response.
- When the child communicates with peers in any way, respond positively.
- As language facility develops, encourage the child to tell simple stories about him or herself.

drawing, singing, or dramatic activities unless parents and teachers have offered such opportunities to them.

**Importance of real experiences.** In the same way, the more opportunities a child has had to participate in real experiences, the richer and more meaningful their arts performance will become. A child who has seen a real chicken will more likely be able to imitate how it behaves in creative movement activities and draw it in more detail than a child who has not. Those who grow up in places where most houses have flat roofs draw house symbols that have flat roofs. Children who have seen that people come in many colors, whether in their community or in pictures, and are comfortable with that fact are more likely to include varying skin color in their artworks.

## Giftedness

Young gifted children are those that exhibit an exceptional level of skill or the potential to learn rapidly in one area of the arts. Such high ability is often due to family values and education, inner motivation, or advanced physical development.

Early exposure to the arts has been shown to accelerate artistic development. In homes where one or more of the arts are highly valued, children are introduced at earlier ages to more complex experiences and skills. For example, all infants are born wired for music, but infants who are sung to and exposed to musical instruments at early ages begin musical expression earlier and are better able to match pitch than children raised in a nonmusical environment, whose only exposure to music is via television and recorded music (Kelly & Smith, 1987). A 2003 research study found that three-year-old children who have more music in their homes had increased auditory sensitivity (Shahin, Roberts, & Trainor, 2003). An enriched music environment for toddlers produced increased voice production (Gruhn, 2002). A study by Christo Pantev found that the younger a child learned the piano, the larger the area of the brain that responds to music (1998).

Another factor that causes some children to excel in one of the arts is motivation. Some children develop a passion for one particular art form. One child may spend hours drawing every day. Another may sing and invent songs. Many children have rich fantasy lives

and make up and act out stories. These children, on their own, put in many more hours practicing their chosen art than their peers and so have advanced artistic skills.

Gifted children, due to variable physical growth, may also exhibit earlier fine motor control. For example, one child might draw realistic-looking faces while most peers are still scribbling. Another child can finger a tune on a violin before others the same age can. Such exceptional abilities are quickly noticed and praised. However, it is important to remember that some children, particularly boys whose fine motor control develops slower than that of girls, cannot express their artistic gifts until later ages when physical development catches up with their creative potential.

Working with highly motivated and skilled children who learn rapidly can be challenging. They spend less time exploring and practicing with a material or technique and are ready to move on to responsive activities before their peers are. Open-ended arts activities that welcome many levels of responses are a good way to meet the needs of these gifted children.

---

### Did You Get It?

**Why is it important to include the styles of art, dance, music, and storytelling that reflect the home cultures of the children?**

a. It shows sensitivity and empowers young children.

b. It makes the arts easier for young children to learn.

c. It increases creativity.

d. It's a good way to help children heal from traumatic events.

**Take the full quiz on CourseMate**

---

## How Do We Make Sense of Children's Artistic Development?

Incorporating these physical, social, and environmental factors, Kindler and Darras (1994; Kindler, 1997) have proposed a model of artistic development that presents artistic production as a two-fold process, as depicted in Table 3-4. One part of the

| TABLE 3–4 | Multimedia Modes of Artistic Production, Based on Kindler and Darras (1994) | | | | |
|---|---|---|---|---|---|
| Child | Mode 1 | Mode 2 | Mode 3 | Mode 4 | Mode 5 |
| **Drama:** Says. . . | Random sounds | Words | Matches sound and action | Naming | Story in cultural style |
| **Visual art:** Draws. . . | Random marks | Shapes | Action symbols | Object symbols | Pictures in cultural style (understandable without verbalization) |
| **Creative dance:** Moves. . . | Random movements | Conscious control | Self-imitation | Repetition | Imitation of cultural style of dance |
| **Music:** Makes. . . | Random sounds | Controlled sounds | Rhythmic sounds | Melody | Song in cultural style |
| ADULT | Media exploration | Simple doodles | Complex doodles | Shorthand symbols (e.g., stick figures) | Detailed, recognizable symbols in style of culture |

process is comprised of biologically propelled physical and cognitive growth. The other is the social and cultural learning, including formal teaching, to which the child is exposed. In this model, individuals do not lose their earlier approaches to arts production but incorporate them or return to them as needed throughout their lives.

Based on the physical, cognitive, and environmental factors affecting an individual child, there is a range of artistic behaviors that child might exhibit. In this model, rather than specific ages or levels, artistic production is organized by modes of behavior. During his or her lifetime, an individual may function in one or more of these modes in varying contexts. For example, upon meeting an unfamiliar medium, most children and adults will operate in the exploratory mode, making random movements as they try to assess the nature of the material. Once they have learned to control a material, they will attempt detailed, graphic, and symbolic expression.

The symbolic communication model shows how a child's arts performance can be viewed a multimedia blend of graphic, verbal, and kinesthetic communication that reveals the child's thought processes, rather than a lockstep process of growth.

## Did You Get It?

**According to the two-fold process in the model of artistic development proposed by Kindler and Darras,**

a. individuals lose their early approaches to arts production and can't return to them at a later stage.

b. rather than specific ages or levels, artistic production is organized by modes of behavior.

c. social factors do not play a role in determining artistic development.

d. biological factors do not play a role in determining artistic development.

**Take the full quiz on CourseMate**

## How Do We Select the Best DAP Arts Activities?

Looking at all the factors affecting a child artist is essential to planning an arts activity or, in fact, any learning activity for that child and assessing the resulting performance. While normative growth charts give us some idea of what to expect from a group of toddlers or primary age children, we should never assume that if a child is a certain age, or is offered the same arts activities as another, we will be able to predict exactly what that child will do with them. But when we understand the range of possible responses, recognize individual difference as normal, and know our children as unique beings with their own histories and passions, we will better choose activities for them.

The growth of young children, from exploring scribblers and babblers to symbol-creating artists, musicians, dancers, and actors, is an amazing journey. This is what makes teaching the arts to children so exciting. Every day is full of fresh, new creative arts performances for their teachers to enjoy.

## Four DAP Filters for Selecting Arts Activities

Based on what we know about how children develop in the arts, we must consider four things in selecting appropriate arts activities for our students.

1. **We must have realistic expectations.** Developmental stage models and an understanding of the factors affecting individual development enhance our understanding of why children's arts performance looks the way it does. But it should not limit our expectations or make us hesitate to try a certain activity. Among young children, we should expect a range of behaviors, from simple exploration based on their level of physical control to complex expressions of their ideas. Within an age cohort, the creative arts produced by children will vary widely, depending on the children's cultural and social experiences and their familiarity with the art form. For example, it is not at all unusual within a group of four-year-olds to witness some children scribbling, some using a limited number of symbolic forms, and some drawing complex graphic symbols. We must accept the scribblers' and babblers' artistic performances as just as valid and important as the more adult-pleasing recognizable pictures, songs, and stories, and select open-ended activities that allow all participants to be creative and personally successful.

2. **We must value children's art production as a developmental process, not as a product.** It is essential to find ways of recording and presenting not just the final product or performance, but the whole process of creation. Anyone who has watched and participated in a child's arts activity knows that the final product may be a letdown. Young dancers may trip and hesitate as they attempt to glide around the stage. Beginning singers may sound out of tune. Arts activities needs to be accompanied by a record of what the children said, the stages the works passed through, and how the children moved as they worked. This is a challenge for a busy, overworked teacher, but it is not impossible.

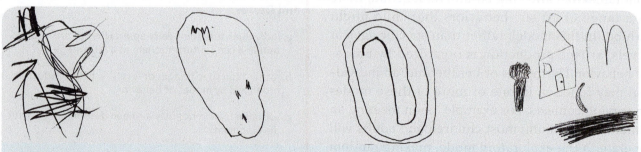

Within an age group, children working in all of the of the artistic modes can be found. (1) Exploration. Marker—Andrew, age three; (2) Initial shapes. Crayon—Kelsey, age three; (3) Action symbol. Marker—Ross, age three; (4) Story symbols. Pencil—Michelle, age three.

3. **We must understand better what the child is thinking.** Knowing the physical, social, cultural, and emotional factors affecting a child helps us better understand and accept the young artist's behavior and resulting creative work. For example, a smiling child banging and stabbing the paper with a crayon is probably not being aggressive, but more likely exploring the possibilities of the crayon. A child doing the same thing, but whose dog has just died, is probably expressing grief.

4. **We must select activities that are suitable for particular children.** Because there will always be a range of abilities in any group, the arts activities that teachers select must be open-ended and allow every child to be challenged. There must always be room for exploration as well as revisitation and responsive work.

---

### Did You Get It?

**Which of the following is good advice for a teacher designing developmentally appropriate practice (DAP) arts activities for children?**

a. A normative growth chart can be used to predict exactly what a child of a certain age will do with the art materials provided.

b. Children within an age cohort will create very similar art displaying a standard set of skills.

c. Children's art must be valued for the final product created, and not the process involved.

d. Developmental stages should not limit our expectations or make us hesitate to try a certain activity.

**Take the full quiz on CourseMate**

---

# How Do We Assess Children's Growth in the Arts?

There are many purposes to assessment. States and governments want to know that schools are doing an effective job at educating children. Standardized tests set the same standard for everyone to meet and pay less attention to factors affecting individual performance. Reflective teachers, on the other hand, want to know that they have chosen the best learning activities for their group of children and that each individual child is benefitting.

The preceding four DAP filters listed help us choose the way we examine children and their artistic performances. In choosing our assessment methods we must be sure we have realistic expectations for each child, record process rather than evaluate the product, elicit what the child is thinking, and evaluate whether the activity we chose was appropriate for the particular child. When we practice reflective teaching, ongoing assessment is incorporated into every activity we teach.

## Setting Realistic Expectations

In order to set realistic expectations we need to know each child well. In the beginning we must rely on information given to us by the child's family and on our own careful observations of the child as the child interacts with arts materials and experiences.

Observing children and watching what they do is an essential component of good teaching. Teachers can learn many things from how children behave and react artistically.

**Observing the individual.** Individual behavior patterns can give us information about the following growth areas:

1. **Physical:** The child's physical control of materials, methods, and skills

2. **Social:** The child's ability to work alone, with adults, and with peers in arts activities

3. **Emotional:** The child's preferences, comfort level with arts materials, and reactions to the art of others as expressed in arts activities

4. **Perceptual:** The child's visual, spatial, and sensory perception skills

5. **Symbolic language:** The child's approach to understanding and creating ways to communicate through the arts

6. **Cognitive understanding:** The child's ability to express arts concepts and vocabulary through movement, sound, visual elements, play, and oral language

**Observing group dynamics.** No child functions alone. We must also place the child in the context of the group. Children learn as much from interacting with their peers as they do from adults. Every group

One of the best ways to observe children's growth and behavior is by carefully watching how they behave and react in different situations.

▶❚❚ **TeachSource Video Case 3.1**

**Progress Monitoring: Using Transitional Time in an Early Childhood Classroom**

Watch the video *Progress Monitoring Using Transition Time*. Can you think of ways to design a similar system to use with arts activities?

**Watch on CourseMate**

has a unique dynamic, and no two groups react in the same way to the arts activities that teachers offer. Observations of the behavior of groups of children can help us see each child more broadly. Group behavior patterns can provide the following information:

- The suitability of the arts experience for the particular group

- The interests of the group

- The role of the child within the group

## Using Observation Tools

To be useful, these observations need to be made regularly and carefully recorded. Two ways to do this are checklists and anecdotal notes.

**Checklists.** A well-designed checklist can be a powerful tool. Watching a child moving to music and recording the way the child moves her arms and legs provides information that can be used to choose a more challenging piece of music for the next movement activity. Over time the checklists can show each child's growth, difficulties, and preferences in the arts.

Checklists strategically placed around the children's environment can provide a convenient way to record

behaviors. Make a list of the children's names and then hang it at the easels, near the blocks, near the listening center, and so on. Use Velcro® to attach a pencil near each list. Develop a simple symbol for the behaviors being observed, such as the initial letters or a shape. Throughout the day, mark the lists with symbols to indicate that a child is in a particular area and what behavior is being observed. Done on a regular basis, these checklists provide a better picture of the child's daily behavior, attitudes, and skill development than memory alone.

**Anecdotal records.** Although more time consuming than checklists, writing down an objective description of a child's interaction with an arts material or a story, and his or her level of expressiveness, can provide rich detail. Anecdotal records provide an ongoing picture of the child's behavior at set times in specific settings. They can be made at the time of the observation or soon after the event. To be useful, the record should document the setting of the event (including the time), the children involved, and any other related information. Anecdotes should be objective, recording only observed behaviors and direct quotes of the children, not the teacher's opinion about the reason for that behavior.

Index cards labeled with each child's name can be carried around in a pocket for a ready way to record quick observations. Labeling the cards with names means no child is missed. Some teachers are more comfortable using clipboards or notebooks with one page divided into sections for each child. Another method is to write on large, self-stick labels, which can then be peeled off and attached to the child's folder.

For examples of arts checklists and anecdotal notes, see *Examples of Checklists and Anecdotal Records for the Arts* on CourseMate.

**Using intentional objectives to focus observations.** One way to focus observations is to think about the objectives you have set for the child, make sure the activity provides opportunity for that objective to occur, and note what that will look or sound like. For example, if your objective is that Michelle, who has difficulty taking turns, will wait for her turn to play the drum, then your assessment part of the objective might be written: "I will know this is happening when I see Michelle standing next to the drum using the strategy I taught her of listening to and moving to the rhythm without touching the drum." Stating objectives this way fosters intentional teaching.

More information on writing intentional objectives will be found in Appendix B.

## Recording the Process

Recording children's creative behavior provides another way to observe their approach to the arts. Today we have a great array of options for dynamic recording of children's creative ventures—running records, photography, video and audio recording, portfolios, and interactive digital devices and media. With the ease of digital media, children can even make their own recordings of their work.

**Running records.** Running records are longer observations that document everything a child does for a set number of minutes (such as a 20-minute period) written down by an objective observer. Although running records are most often used in analyzing reading skills, this type of close observation is very useful for analyzing social behaviors in the arts such as interaction in the dramatic play center or tracking cognitive or language skills during art activities.

**Using photographs.** Anyone working with children should always have a camera close at hand. If the camera is convenient to use and nearby, then it is more likely to be picked up at opportune moments during

the activity rather than used just to record the finished work or a group pose. The camera does not have to be a fancy one, but it should be simple and foolproof to operate. Digital cameras, smartphones, and tablets are ideal for this purpose. Through photos, videos, and digital media, we can capture the excitement and passion of the child along with making a record of the child's performance for future assessment.

1. Photographs and videos of block structures, sculptures, and other three-dimensional projects in construction can be displayed long after the originals are gone.

2. Photo albums of children creating in the arts can be made into class books and kept in the book corner. Audio recordings can be placed in the listening and music centers.

3. Photographs, audio recordings, and videos of children working can be saved in their portfolios, and on class documentation and panels as a visual way to remember how something was done and as a way to emphasize the value of process over product.

4. Photographs of class members, families, friends, and visitors, as well as the children's homes and family events, can be used in portrait lessons and family studies.

5. Photographs of familiar objects shown from unusual viewpoints can challenge children's visual perception.

6. Photographs can be used to record arts activities, setups, and child interactions for teachers to use for reflection on their teaching methods.

7. Digital photos can be saved to a flash drive, CD, or DVD for more compact storage or uploaded into digital photo storybooks, into flipbook software, into PowerPoint presentations, on family pages of school websites, and into teaching materials for interactive whiteboards.

For more information on creating and using digital portfolios, selecting software platforms, and helpful online resources, see *Digital Portfolios* on CourseMate.

For successful photographs, use the following guidelines:

- Try to physically get down to the children's level when taking photographs so that the pictures do not all reflect an adult's perspective.

- If using flash, check the distance from the subject to avoid washed-out pictures.

- Do not shoot against a bright background, such as a window.

**Videotaping.** The availability of camcorders and the video function on digital cameras has made it possible to truly record the multimedia process of arts performances. It can be used to create a time-based record of a child's artistic growth. At regular intervals, record the child dancing, singing, playing an instrument, and creating an artwork. Videos can also be made to record group projects, as part of portfolios, and as a way to assess teaching style.

**Obtaining releases.** Before taking any photographs or making a video, it is essential to obtain a signed release from all families. Many institutions have parents fill out such forms upon enrollment. However, if special use is going to be made of the pictures, such as a public display in an exhibit or at a workshop presentation, then a more specific release should be obtained.

If a family refuses to sign a release, then that request must be respected. When shooting photographs and videos, be careful to avoid taking pictures of children without releases, except when shot from the back.

*For an example of a release, see Sample Model Release on CourseMate.*

## Portfolios

A **portfolio** is a collection of the child's work and related materials made over a period of time. Each child should have either a physical or digital arts folder in which a record of their arts process and development is stored either in the form of the actual artworks and photographs of performances, or, if the equipment is available, in a digitized format. Find a list of what to put in an arts portfolio here.

*For ideas of what to include in a child's arts portfolio, see Suggested Content for an Arts Potfolio on CourseMate.*

**Constructing a folder portfolio.** A short-term portfolio can be made from a very large piece of paper

folded in half, or from two sheets taped together. If it will be used for only a short time, then this will suffice. If the folder will be used over a long period, such as a year or two, then it can be made sturdier by using clear packing tape to protect the edges or it can be made from two corrugated cardboard pieces taped together along one side to form a hinge. The portfolio must be as large as the largest paper used by an individual child. For ease of use, color-code or mark the folders with special symbols as well as names so children and parents can quickly locate their own folders. Find directions for making a portfolio here.

*For directions on making a folder portfolio, see Making a Folder Portfolio on CourseMate.*

CDs, DVDs, and audiotapes that record music, dance, and dramatic activities can be stored separately in shallow gift boxes or trays labeled with each child's name. These boxes can be sent home for the family's enjoyment on a regular basis.

One of the reasons educators hesitate to initiate portfolios is the problem of storing them while still retaining easy access. A pile of large floppy papers is unsightly and heavy. It becomes almost impossible to remove folders on the bottom without handling all of the folders stacked above. One solution is the

 **Classroom Technology**

### *CHILDREN AND CAMERAS*

Including children's participation in recording events using digital photography allows children to create their own documentation record. Bonnie Blagojevic and Karen Thomas (2009) found that young children could learn how to independently take photographs in ways that enhanced their language development while providing insights into how children viewed activities. After children learned how the camera worked, they asked the children what their favorite activities were. After listing their choices, they brainstormed what photos could be taken to show those favorites. The children's photographs were uploaded on to the class computer as a slideshow the children could watch. Then the children picked one photo for a classbook "Our Favorite Things" and dictated an explanation to accompany it. The book was put out for children to read and copies were sent home to families. Families completed a questionnaire and comment sheet as a way to involve the families and to provide feedback.

Photography is a great way to record the artistic process. Allow children to get into the act by letting them film their own work and their peers using inexpensive cameras.

commercially made, vertical, divided storage boxes that are used to store art prints (see Appendix C).

**Digital portfolios.** Saving children's work in digital format solves many of the aforementioned problems. The arts, in particular, lend themselves to this method. Digital photos and video clips of an individual child and of whole group performances can be kept in a folder on the computer and, at the end of a set time period, saved to a flash drive, CD, or DVD to send home to the family.

However, digital portfolios do have some disadvantages.

1. Not all families have access to a computer. In this case, a physical portfolio of actual artworks and photographs is a better choice.

2. Upkeep is more time consuming for the teacher, who must download and save the work to all the different children's folders.

3. It is the adult's task to manipulate the data on the computer, and unless special effort is taken, the children become less involved in the care and organization of their work.

4. In terms of visual art works, having the children look at a photo of their artwork on a computer screen is not the same as being able to touch the real work and experience its true texture, color, and size.

**Combined digital and physical portfolios.** To create the most effective and useful arts portfolio, digital recordings of music, dance, and dramatic activities recorded on a CD or DVD can be combined with a folder containing actual pieces of children's visual artworks.

**Selecting work for the portfolio.** Having a portfolio does not mean that every piece of artwork, every song sung, every creative movement, and every story acted out needs to be recorded and saved. Once children have been introduced to the idea of making a portfolio, they should be asked on a regular basis if they wish to put their artwork or a recording of their performance into the portfolio. If artwork is three dimensional, ask if they would like a photograph taken for the portfolio. The teacher can also select pieces for the folder. Children are more willing to part with their work if they know the reason why. For example, "This painting shows how you have learned to make orange and brown. Shall we put it in your portfolio? Would you like me to write anything about it to go with it?"

**Preparing work for the portfolio.** Artwork and photographs placed in a folder portfolio do not have to be mounted but should not be wrinkled or folded if possible. Each piece should be labeled with name, date, and any comments by the child. Camcorders and digital cameras can be set so the date is automatically included. Files are also dated when they are downloaded to a computer. When taking photographs and videos, be sure to include the child in order to make identification of the work or performance not only easier but more personal. This will help children feel more ownership of their work.

**Timeline for collecting work.** The portfolio should represent a natural timeline, such as one session, 3 months, or a half year. The time period should be long enough to show growth, but not so long that the collection becomes unwieldy. At the end of the time period, the work should be ordered by date to highlight the child's growth or changing interests. If the program is long term, extending over a year or more, then a few pieces from older portfolios can be selected to begin a new one.

Before sending the portfolio home, carry out a self-reflection interview as a culminating activity. This process helps children learn how to assess their own progress.

If using a physical portfolio, always send the entire folder home, and create a new one to use for the next time period. This provides families with a unified presentation of the artwork rather than a hodgepodge of papers, and keeps these simply constructed folders from becoming dog-eared. It is also beneficial for children to reestablish ownership of the portfolio concept through the creation and decoration of a new folder on a regular basis.

## Eliciting Thinking

Whether in digital or folder format, the portfolio system allows arts experiences to be richer and deeper in many ways. Both formats allow the child, the teacher, and the family to look through the portfolio individually and/or together as a way to review past progress.

Sharing a portfolio with a child also provides an opportune moment to start a conversation that helps us know the child better while teaching self-reflective and self-evaluative skills in a non-threatening environment.

**Physical portfolios.** The physical portfolio may contain visual artworks, child-created books, illustrated stories, audiotapes, and photographs of the child. These can be examined and discussed as a way of eliciting self-reflection and deeper thinking on the part of the child. For example:

- After looking at a piece of artwork, the child might decide to add to it, such as using chalk over a painting or painting over a crayon drawing or they may add onto a story or be inspired to revisit or try something new.

- Together the teacher and child can collect, categorize, and make work logs, booklets, or a documentation panel showing growth in skill or knowledge or variations on a theme.

- Together the teacher and child might deliberate and select from a range of work what to put on display. A multimedia one-person show might feature chosen artworks, stories, photographs, and an audio recording playing the child singing.

**Digital portfolios.** Digital media expands these possibilities even more. Once photographs and video clips are stored on the computer, they can be used in a variety of formats.

- Together the teacher and child might decide what they wish to share with the family, the class, or the public. Digitized photos and video clips can be inserted into slide shows and PowerPoint-type presentations as well as newsletters, class web pages, and blogs. Children could have their own blogs or webpages viewable only to their family. Video with child narration can be edited using a simple video editor such as Windows Live Movie Maker, then uploaded to a video-sharing site such as YouTube or Vimeo, and made visible only to family members. Children's work and videos can be made into PDFs or page-turning books that can be viewed on many tablets and e-readers. Digitized photos can be printed out and used in a variety of creative ways such as in collages, class quilts, class books, cards, bookmarks, and identifying labels.

- Digitized photos, audio, and video clips can be saved on CDs, DVDs, and flash drives, and then viewed or listened to on the computer by the child as an activity choice.

- Digitized photos and video clips can be inserted into dictated stories and autobiographies written on the computer.

**Eliciting child-reflection.** Conduct portfolio sessions at intervals to assess changes in attitude to arts activities and to help determine what arts activities will interest the child.

Some questions to ask find out how the child feels about participating in the arts include:

- What is your favorite arts activity?

- What do you like best about creating _____ (stories, paintings, dances, songs, puppet shows, etc.)?

- What is your favorite _____ (artwork, dance, music, song, story, thing to pretend, etc.)?

- Who is your favorite _____ (artist, composer, dancer, actor, story writer, etc.)?

- What is your favorite book about the arts?

- Do you _____ (sing, dance, draw, play and instrument, use playdough, etc.) at home? Tell me about it.

Other questions can elicit information about the child's knowledge of arts concepts and techniques. For example:

🎵 How did you do this?

🎵 What is made from?

🎵 What did you use to _____ (do this, make this sound, act this out, etc.)?

🎵 What were you thinking when you ___ (made, wrote, danced, sang, acted, etc.) this?

🎵 Do you remember how you solved this problem?

🎵 Who did you work with?

🎵 Where did the idea come from?

As we share the portfolio together, we can also encourage self-reflection by asking:

🎵 Which shows something new you learned?

🎵 Which one _____ (took the longest time, was the hardest, was the most fun, etc.)?

🎵 Do you want to add a story or comments?

🎵 Is there anything you want to add or remove from the portfolio? Why?

> ### Did You Get It?
>
> **Lisa has decided to use anecdotal records to record how her students perform in dramatic play activities. Which of the following should she avoid when using this type of record?**
>
> **a.** noting down only observed behaviors of the children
>
> **b.** noting down her opinions of the reasons for their behavior
>
> **c.** noting down only direct quotes from the children
>
> **d.** noting down details such as the setting of the event
>
> **Take the full quiz on CourseMate**

## How Can We Share the Arts with Families?

Families have a very different relationship with their children than do teachers and other caregivers. Children look to their families for exclusive attention and ultimate acceptance as capable people. When children share their creative work with a family member and say, "Look what I made!" they want more than a tepid "That's nice" or an ordinary "Good work." Most importantly, they definitely do not want criticism from this all-important person whom they wish to please. Children really want to know that their families have taken the time to acknowledge their efforts and joy.

Unfortunately, families are far less equipped to give the deep response that children are seeking than are teachers and other trained caregivers. Where the educator sees exploration and creative experimentation, the families may see only what they think is a visible (and perhaps an uncomplimentary) reflection on the quality of their children and their family.

## Ways to Help Families Appreciate their Children's Arts Process

It is the teacher's job to educate families about their children's artistic development. Remember, unless teachers make an effort to record children's creative arts process and educate family members, parents will make judgments based only on what they see—their children's products. To address this try to

🎵 Provide many opportunities for families to review portfolios.

🎵 When talking to families about their children's arts activities, emphasize process and growth rather than the project, and then help family members see this in the artwork. Checklists and anecdotal records will prove invaluable in remembering the specific actions of the children. Instead of saying, "Mary made a painting today," say, "Mary used paint today and learned how to make pink. See the pink spots in her painting." Instead of saying, "Arturo sang a song," say, "Arturo explored the chimes in the music center and invented his own melody and words. He sang his song to the whole group at circle time."

🎵 Schedule "Arts Happenings" and workshops throughout the year at which families and children are invited to create together. This is a good time for group projects, such as murals and rhythm bands, in which everyone can participate. Watching

Reflective teachers work closely with parents, soliciting their opinions and feedback to better understand the child's home culture and provide the best creative experiences for each child.

families interact also gives teachers a better idea of their attitude toward their children's artwork.

🎵 Attach simple, prepared descriptions of arts processes to work being sent home.

🎵 Send home letters or, better yet, institute a regular newsletter that describes the children's arts activities along with other class activities, in terms of process and growth.

🎵 Prepare an attractive booklet, illustrated with children's drawings, that briefly explains the goals of the arts program, what children learn through the arts, and what kinds of arts experiences will be offered.

🎵 Send home suggestions for setting up a simple visual art center in the home. It should not be project based but rather provide a few basic open-ended art supplies that are always available, such as crayons, markers, paper, glue, scissors, and a modeling material such as playdough that children can use in their own ways. Help families by suggesting ways that they can contain messes,

such as by setting up a small area as an art studio, providing an "art table," or, if space is limited, designating a plastic tray as the art spot.

🎵 Describe how to make simple homemade musical instruments, and send home copies of the songs the child has learned so the family can sing them together.

🎵 Make up take-home bags containing a story and simple puppets so the child can dramatize the story for the family.

🎵 Use a home arts survey to find out the artistic background and experience of individual children.

## Ways to Help Families Understand Artistic Development

Families often do not have other children's work with which to compare their children's, and so they cannot tell if what their children bring home is appropriate or not. Teachers need to help families understand the process of artistic development and have them come to understand that exploration in which no final product results is a natural part of every child's artistic performance no matter what the child's age. It is the teacher's job to assure families that their children are performing in ways that are to be expected. There are a variety of ways to do this.

🎵 Display many examples of creative work of all kinds, by children of all ages, either in the public areas where parents congregate, or through exhibits and open houses.

🎵 Hold family workshops in which examples of child art and portfolios from unknown children are shared and concerns about the arts are discussed.

🎵 Send to families, on a regular basis, arts notes detailing what children have accomplished in a specific project.

🎵 Families gain a better appreciation for the creative process if they participate in workshops that allow them to draw, paint, sing, dance, play with puppets, and participate in arts activities similar to those of the children.

## Teacher to Family

### Sample Arts Note (Attach to Portfolios Going Home)

Dear Family Members,

This portfolio presents your child's learning in the arts over the last month. Take time to enjoy the portfolio with your child. Here are some things to talk about:

**Visual Art:** This month we made paintings, drawings and collages in the art studio. Here are the three she chose for the portfolio.

- The painting shows all the new colors your child can mix. Ask her to tell you what colors she used to make them.
- The collage is made from the beautiful things we collected on out nature walk. Ask her to tell you where she found them and why she chose them.
- The drawing was made of a bridge she built in the block center. Ask her how strong it was.

**Music:** At the music center we explored making original melodies using the chimes. Here is your child's melody written in colors. Listen to the tape of her playing it and ask her to show you how to follow along on her written melody.

**Dramatic Play & Creative Movement:** After our nature walk, we studied many different animals that we saw. Then we all imagined living in the woods. Here are photographs of our "Animals in the Woods" creative movement activity. Ask your child what animal she pretended to be.

Your child's teacher,

For more information on digital portfolios, see *Digital Portfolios* on CourseMate

**Digital Download**    Download from CourseMate

### Did You Get It?

**Isabella teaches first grade. When families ask questions about their children's creative work, Isabella should**

a. rave about a particular project which the child did exceptionally well.

b. explain how their child's work compares to normative development in the arts.

c. explain how their child's work compares to that of others in the class.

d. show them their child's portfolio and discuss the process the child went through to create the works.

**Take the full quiz on CourseMate**

## How Can We Practice Reflective Teaching?

Probably the most important assessment we can do is of ourselves. Without self-assessment, teachers cannot grow and improve. Teaching is not a static profession with only one right way to get the job done. The most exciting educators are those who constantly tinker with their programs, try new methods, and are willing to take risks. We need to reflect on our teaching to discover what is working and what is not. This is called **reflective teaching.** When we use reflective teaching practices we do not repeat the same activities day after day and year after year. Instead, we observe, monitor, discover, modify, and experiment in the moment and over time in order to make the best match between our children and our teaching strategies (Carter et al., 2010).

Reflective teaching calls upon us to:

1. Examine our reactions to our children and their behaviors.

2. Observe our children closely in all learning settings.

3. Document what we see and hear.

4. Make time to study our notes and photos.

5. Share thoughts about our observations and ideas with the children, co-workers, and families.

6. Ask for insights from the children, co-workers, and families.

7. Change the environment and materials in order to facilitate new opportunities for play and learning.

# Documenting for Reflection

Because self-reflection is done for ourselves, it is tempting for us to skip this crucial activity when we are exhausted from a busy day with energetic and challenging youngsters. Preplanned, easy-to-use documentation methods make it more likely that we will take the time to assess the arts activities we deliver. The following methods are suggested as ways to accomplish this task. Each provides a different viewpoint; when used in combination, they give an overall view of how we are doing.

**Checklists.** Checklists can be designed to quickly survey almost any area of the program. They provide objective information on the frequency of particular behaviors and areas that may require attention. Checklists do not work if they are buried on a desk or in folders. They need to be strategically placed where they can be seen daily and acted upon.

**Feedback from the children.** It is important to ask children for their response to the activities. This can be done in conversation or through graphing favorites, or through using the arts as communication by having children mime or draw or act out the activity they enjoyed the most.

The checklists and anecdotal records that have been suggested for assessing the children can also be used for program assessment. These checklists reveal which activities attract interest and which are ignored. They document how many children choose to work in certain areas, how long they stay there, how much they interact, and what skills they are exhibiting. They also capture our interaction with the children and provide a picture of what we have said.

For a variety of ways to self-assess, see *Examples of Reflective Assessments* on CourseMate.

**Feedback from others.** The people we work with, especially colleagues working in similar settings are another important source of feedback. For example, Will Parnell (2012) observed co-teachers working at Reggio-inspired preschools benefitted from practicing reflective thinking with each other on a regular basis. Conversation with parents provides another point of view and can point to ways to increase communication with the home.

**Reflective teaching journal.** A reflective journal provides a place for teachers to record their inner feelings about their work. Journaling has been found to be a positive way to develop reflective practice (Mortari, 2012). Teachers need to set aside a time, such as when the children are resting, to write a few reflective sentences on how they personally feel about what has been happening as the children participate in arts activities. One way to approach this task is to respond to these sentence starters:

> *This week I felt competent when . . .*
> *This week I felt frustrated when . . .*
> *This week I felt exhilarated when . . .*
> *This week I had a problem with . . .*
> *This week I discovered . . .*

**"Terrific me" folder.** Place a file folder labeled "TM" in a strategic place. Whenever you receive complimentary notes from parents, children, or others, place them in this folder. Also include copies of materials from workshops attended or given, extra work done, notes about major accomplishments, and any other positive materials and activities. It is human nature to remember the negatives. Reviewing the materials in this folder will provide not only an uplifting experience but also a more rounded view of one's accomplishments.

**Personal arts notebook or portfolio.** Create a binder or portfolio, much like the ones you keep for the children, in which to keep all of the documents you generate while formulating the arts aspect of your program. This serves as a tangible memory of the form and nature of the program. Keep copies of plans, anecdotal records, photos, checklists, and notes on what went well and what actions were taken to deal with difficult or unusual situations. Keep copies of all letters sent home to families. Looking back over this material will be invaluable in making better plans the next time.

## Reflection-in-Action

Donald Shöen (1983) noted that effective teachers observed and acted in the process of teaching. He called this reflection-in-action. In the beginning, practicing reflective teaching while in the process of dealing with active enthusiastic children may seem daunting. However, Deb Curtis and Margie Carter (2010) suggest using a "reflective lens" or set of questions to ask yourself at first after an activity or day is

**Photo Story**

## A Responsive Drawing Activity

## A Visit to the Playground

The children in this kindergarten class made a special visit to their playground. Together with their teacher they looked carefully at the different shapes and forms, and noticed the spaces as well. Then they came back inside and drew pictures to record their experience. Even though they are all the same age, their artwork reflects their different interests and fine motor skills.

"My friends and I like to ride the swings."
Marker—Brittany, age five

Carmela is sharing and playing
safely. Marker—Carmela, age five

"I like to run and jump all over the
playground." Marker—Joe, age five

over, and then, as the questions become integral to your thinking, during the activity itself.

- How do I feel as I observe the children?

- What shows me that the children are learning?

- What are the children thinking and feeling?

- How are materials or environment working?

- What is the influence of family culture and background?

- Are desired learning objectives being met?

- How can I strengthen this to better meet my goals and values?

For ways to use a reflective lens, see *Examples of Reflective Assessments* on CourseMate.

---

### Did You Get It?

**Which of the following is a characteristic of reflective teaching?**

a. repeating the same arts activities day after day for consistency

b. asking for insights from children, parents, and teachers

c. designing arts activities with minimal experimentation

d. assessing the creative work of all children based on a common criteria

**Take the full quiz on CourseMate**

---

## Conclusion: The Child Artist

Artistic development models provide educators with a general overview of children and the arts. But we must remember that actual artistic development of each individual child is a combination of the biological maturation patterns of the body and brain, mediated by social and cultural factors and experiences.

Creative arts for the child is more than the simple manipulation of materials at an art table or putting on a funny hat in the dress-up corner. It is a developmental process. Children's artistic growth is not the step-by-step process so carefully described by the early researchers. It is a multifaceted way for children to develop in the arts through new methods of expression and communication. This process can best be shared through the use of cameras, camcorders, and portfolios. It is our challenge as reflective teachers to continuously recreate the environment, to redesign the activities, and to rearrange the environment so that we nurture this multimedia event in every child.

For additional information on young children's development in the arts, and assessment, see Chapter 3 *Online Resources* on CourseMate.

---

## Teaching In Action

### Open-Ended Arts Activity: Learning About Us

Today was the first day of school. As my first graders entered the classroom, I greeted each one and handed them a piece of paper. "Draw me a picture that tells us something about you." I asked them. At the tables I had set out markers, crayons, and pencils. Soon they were all busy working. Some drew pictures of themselves and their families. Some drew their favorite things. Some drew their houses. I made a picture about me, too.

When they finished, I asked them to join me on the rug with their pictures. We went around the circle and introduced ourselves. We each showed our picture as we talked. Next I read them the book *Everyone is Bob* by T. A. H. Markou (2010). We talked about how boring it would be if we were all the same like the Bobs in the book. How would we know who was who?

Then I wrote "Same" and "Different" on the top of the chart tablet, and we listed things that were the same and things that were different about us. It was amazing. By the end of the first forty minutes of school we all knew so much about each other and appreciated our differences. It was a great way to start the year.

Hillary Clark, First Grade Teacher

# Reflection Page

## Factors Affecting Your Artistic Work

A number of factors affect one's artistic development. Looking back to your own childhood, fill in this graphic organizer with those things you feel most influenced your development in the arts.

| Available Tools and Materials | Social Pressures | Arts Experiences |
|---|---|---|
| Cultural Influences | My Artistic Development | Emotional State |
| Motivation | Feedback from Family, Teachers, and Peers | Physical Health |

**Reflection**

How do you think these factors will affect the way you teach the arts?

_____

_____

_____

_____

# Reflection Page

## Looking at Children's Artistic Development

Using Gardner's and Kindler and Darras's models of artistic growth, reflect on the artistic development of the children described in the following examples and suggest an appropriate follow-up arts activity.

A child holds the paintbrush in his fist and moves it up and down, making large bold lines.

_____

_____

_____

_____

A child taps a spoon on the table in time to a song on the radio.

_____

_____

_____

_____

A child draws a detailed picture of her house that includes a ground line and skyline and writes a description below it.

_____

_____

_____

_____

A child puts on a funny hat, makes a face, and says, "I'm a clown. I can make you laugh."

_____

_____

_____

_____

# Reflection Page

## Documenting Artistic Behavior

Choose one of the following open-ended arts activities and imagine you are teaching it.

- Carpet squares cut into the basic shapes—circles, rectangles, squares, and triangles—are placed on the carpet to make a path. Toddlers are invited to follow the path and say the name of the shape when they step on it. Then they are encouraged to build new paths by moving the shapes around.

- First graders have been asked to collect things that are special to them and arrange them inside a shoebox to make a still-life story about themselves. Each child tells his or her own story orally to a partner.

- After a trip to the zoo, preschoolers decide to turn the dramatic play area into a zoo. Some are building pens with blocks and putting the stuffed animals in them. Some are building a birdhouse, like the aviary they saw, out of a refrigerator box. Some are drawing pictures of birds.

1. Write an intentional objective for each of the developmental areas for your chosen activity.

   Intentional Objective format: The child will be able to . . .

   (socially, emotionally, physically, intellectually, linguistically, perceptually, creatively)

   _____

   I will know this is happening when _____

2. Design a checklist for these objectives.

3. Write three self-reflective questions about the activity using the reflective lens.

# Reflection Page

## Observation: Observing Children and the Arts

1. Plan an arts exploration or practice activity suitable for an infant or toddler.

2. Obtain permission to work with one infant or toddler, either at home or in a child care setting.

3. Set up your activity and observe the infant or toddler at work. Take anecdotal notes. If possible, take photos or videotape the activity (get permission first).

_____

**Age of child:**
**Setup of materials:**
**Length of time of observation:**

_____

1. What did the child do first?

_____

2. What did the child say?

_____

3. How did the child interact physically? (For example, describe position of arms and hands, grip, any other body parts involved.)

_____

4. How long did the child work? (Measure periods of concentration. If child stopped, why? How did the child let you know he or she was finished?)

_____

5. Describe the process the child went through. (What did the child do first? What was repeated? What was surprising? Did you make any changes while working?)

_____

6. Reflect on how you would transform the activity to improve or expand upon it.

Chapter

# 4

## Awakening the Senses

Copyright © 2015 Cengage Learning®

Know why it is important to foster sensory perception in young children.

**Planning Curriculum to Achieve Important Goals**

Practice intentional teaching through sensory-rich interactions with children.

**Teaching to Enhance Development and Learning**

**Sensory Perception and the Arts DAP Learning Objectives**

**Assessing Children's Development and Learning**

Assess children's perceptual develop perceptually and select appropriate activities to meet their needs.

**Creating a Caring Community**

**Establishing Reciprocal Family Relationships**

Plan safe sensory–perceptual arts activities that respect individual children's approaches to learning.

Work with families to select sensory activities that respect their culture and beliefs and personal knowledge of their child.

*Web based on the NAEYC Developmentally Appropriate Practice (Copple & Bredekamp, 2009).*

## Young Artists Creating

"The sand is singing," says Byron as he pours sand into his pail with a soft whir. Mariah looks at her teacher through a tube. "I made you round," she says. Aleko lies down on the grass and says quietly, "I smell the grass growing."

# What Is Sensory Perception?

It is through **sensory perception** that we learn about the world. Tastes, smells, textures, sounds, and sights, most often in combination, stimulate our sensory organs which convert them to neural impulses and send them to our brain for processing. Our eyes, nose, mouth, ears and skin are considered **exteroceptors** because they process external stimuli. The world is a noisy, whirling, colorful place full of sounds that tickle our ears, textures that twitch our fingers, odors that assault our noses, tastes that tempt our tongues and images that dazzle our eyes.

## Our Senses

Each of our senses is uniquely designed to make sense of the multisensory sensory bath we live in and play a major role in arts education.

    **Visual perception.** Discriminating lines, colors, shapes, movement, and dimension is the main function of **visual perception.** Called "visual thinking" by influential psychologist Rudolf Arnheim (1969) this is a cognitive process, as is all sensory perception, that takes images perceived physically by our eyes and gives them meaning. It is the key component that makes visual art possible.

    **Auditory perception.** **Auditory perception** is sensitivity to sounds and noises. It is a key skill in musical development. Learning to discriminate meaningful sounds from the distracting noise that surrounds us is key to developing the ability to focus and attend.

    **Olfactory perception.** **Olfactory perception** is using our sense of smell to identify odors. Although the sense of smell is often less valued than the other senses, it is a very powerful one. Smell stimuli travel directly to the limbic system of the brain, which primarily supports emotions and long-term memories.

Sensory perception is developed by presenting intriguing objects and using rich language to describe how they look, smell, and feel.

Copyright © 2015 Cengage Learning®

A whiff of a familiar odor from the past such as the scent of school glue can make adults feel like they are in kindergarten again. Opening a box of new crayons can bring to mind a drawing made at age five.

    Smell is the first sense to develop, present before birth. Pleasant smells are preferred from early on. Infants smile at the scent of bananas and frown at the stink of rotten eggs. They play more with vanilla scented toys (Biel, 2011). A research study by Schifferstein and Desmet (2007) found that when the olfactory sense is blocked, activities are less pleasant, less predictable, and less emotionally engaging. Experiences relating to smell may be more subtle, often in the background of other activities, but drawing attention to the associated odors or adding pleasant smells will make them more engaging and memorable.

    **Gustatory perception.** Taste is often the forgotten sense in arts education, particularly because teachers must be concerned that children not ingest hazardous art materials and so discourage oral

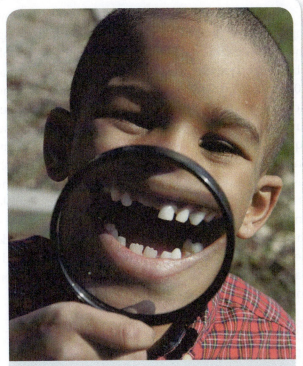

To develop visual perception, invite children to look at familiar things in new ways.

## Special Needs

### • SENSORY INTEGRATION •

**Sensory integration** refers to how we process information from our senses. All the sensations our body is feeling work together to help us understand and control our behavior and responses to stimuli. Children who have **sensory integration dysfunction (SID)** may be overly sensitive or under-reactive to touch, movement, sights, and sounds. Children exhibiting any of these characteristics may react strongly to arts activities by exhibiting fear, yelling, tantrums, or refusal to participate. These children need slow, careful exposure to many sensory activities with calm guidance from a facilitating adult. Many of the sensory and arts elements activities in this chapter provide gentle introductions to arts experiences.

exploration. However, we can emphasize the aesthetic qualities of food as it is served and eaten at snack time and meals. We can create taste centers where tasting is allowed. Dramatic play provides another place where tastes can be imagined and acted out.

**Tactile Perception.** The entire surface of the human body is sensitive to pressure and temperature, as well as to the textural qualities of the matter that makes up the world. This is **tactile perception.** Young children rely heavily on hands-on exploration to acquire knowledge about the characteristics of individual materials and objects and to develop an understanding of how things are spatially arranged and move.

In Montessori sensorial work the tactile sense is broken down into its components: **thermic**—sense of temperature, **baric**—sense of weight or pressure, and **stereognostic**—sensing three-dimensional form by touch alone. In sensorial tasks children order different temperatures of water, differently weighted cylinders, and identify objects hidden in a bag by touch alone.

Touch is not located only in our fingers. Our entire skin is a tactile sense organ. The environment and activities offered to young children should provide continuous opportunities to touch and explore with more than their hands. They can walk on textured surfaces with bare feet, and rub materials against their cheeks and down their bare arms and legs.

## Sensory Perception Development

Every day researchers learn more about the amazing abilities of infants who are born with sensory systems functioning and ready to be refined through interaction with their environment.

**The first months.** Weeks before birth, the unborn child hears sounds and smells the amniotic fluid. Within hours of birth newborns recognize their mother's voice and her unique scent (Winberg & Porter, 1998). While their visual acuity and depth perception are weaker than an adult's, and their eyes still wander, babies in their first days have a sense of size and shape, prefer their mother's face over others, and complex shapes over simple ones (Bornstein, Arterberry, & Mash, 2011). Infants at this stage rely on adults to provide the necessary sensory stimulation that will allow them to grow and refine their reactions.

**The sitting child.** By age four to five months, infants can see a shape inside another, recognize turning three-dimensional forms, and know when one object passes in front of another. They move their heads at first, and then, their bodies toward a sound, can match pitch, and discriminate between rhythmic and non-rhythmic music.

Infants are born ready to learn through their senses in interactions with others. When interacting with an infant it is important to touch and talk and make expressive faces.

By age six to seven months, vision is well developed. Two-dimensional and three-dimensional features, such as shading, relative size, texture gradients, and linear perspective, are used by infants to locate objects around them. Infants at this stage are ready for supervised introductions to many different sensory stimuli.

**Meaning makers.** Not only are babies attracted to sensory stimuli, they also quickly attach meaning to what they perceive. They don't just hear, they listen. They don't just see, but examine. They don't just touch, they reach out or pull away. While newborns prefer faces over shapes, by age five months infants recognize and differentiate between emotional expressions showing anger, fear, happiness, and surprise. By ten months they are attuned to the sounds in their native language, and prefer familiar melodies to unfamiliar ones, and harmonious ones to dissonant ones (Sigelman & Shaffer, 2009, p.155).

Making meaning of what is perceived and knowing how to react develops and becomes refined through the growing child's daily interaction with the people, objects, and experiences in the environment (Cermak, 2009). As the child grows, sensory clues trigger memories based on past physical, social-emotional, and cultural experiences. For example, a toddler sees a brown square. It feels slightly waxy and smells like chocolate, and since the child knows she liked chocolate when she tasted it before, she decides to eat it. The kindergartner at the easel examines turquoise paint, notices its color and fluidity, compares it to a memory of a family trip to the sea, and flicks it on the painting. A second grader hears the teacher sing a folk melody, remembers the pattern and tempo of the notes, and sings along. Sensory perception has set the stage for learning.

> ### Did You Get It?
>
> **Discriminating lines, colors, shapes, movement, and dimension is the main function of _____.**
>
> **a.** visual perception
>
> **b.** auditory perception
>
> **c.** olfactory perception
>
> **d.** gustatory perception
>
> **Take the full quiz on CourseMate**

## Why Is Sensory Perception Important?

Sensory perception experiences are essential for functioning successfully in society. In fact, we rely so heavily on the intake of information through our senses that when deprived of all sensory input for as little as fifteen minutes, adults begin to lose their sense of reality (Mason & Brady, 2009).

## The Effects of Sensory Deprivation

Infancy, in particular, is a critical time for developing sensory perception. When babies are deprived of one type of sensory information, because of a physical issue such as limited vision, hearing loss, or sensitivity to touch, their future growth is affected. Visual

Being held in the lap provides security as an infant explores the sensory stimulus of a crayon.

deprivation in the first seven weeks of life results in impaired recognition of faces (Johnson & Mareschal, 2001). Hearing loss not corrected before six months affects the child's ability to classify and understand distinct sounds, hindering language development. Infants who are under-responsive to tactile stimuli show increased social and communication impairments as they mature (Foss-Ferg, Heacock & Cascio, 2012).

Development can also be affected by a lack of sensory stimulation. Adopted children who experienced sensory deprivation in infancy react adversely to sensory stimuli even twelve years later (Wilbarger et al., 2010). Infants who receive infrequent touching from their mothers eat less and show slower physical growth (Polan & Ward, 1994). Preschoolers with below normal response to sensory stimuli, such as is found in some types of autism, are less able to understand the emotional state of other people (Chasiotis et al., 2006).

## Building Deep Meaning

In addition, young children in this technological age spend less time outside, and are more likely to be sedentary in front of television and computer screens which, while visually compelling, do not provide the physical experience of manipulating real objects in three-dimensional space (Anderson & Hanson, 2010). Television viewing also affects parent–child interactions, vital to effective sensory processing. When adult-oriented television programs play in the background, parents become distracted and interactions with their children playing nearby reduce in quantity and quality (Kirkorian et al., 2009).

As this research shows, sensory perceptual deficits in early childhood often lead to physical, behavioral, and social difficulties, while exposure to television and technology reduces hands-on sensory experiences for many young children.

In addition, when the brain receives too much random, distracting, or general information, the child's brain creates superficial memories rather than deep ones (Caine & Caine, 1994). Surface memory might tell a child that the object in front of him is a round ball. Deep meaning is built up over repeated exposures in an emotionally positive context and tells the child: "This is my ball, the one I play with my brother. It is round and red and has words on it and a scratch on one side and it bounces when I drop it. When I rub it on my face it is bumpy and smells like the bottom of my sneaker. I love playing with my ball." As such, providing rich, meaningful sensory perception activities is a critical component of children's total development.

## The Role of Sensory Perception Arts Activities

Bombarded constantly by sensory stimuli, children cannot pay attention to all of them. Starting at birth, the brain filters the information coming from the senses, discarding some and attending to others. (Merikle, Smilek, & Eastwood, 2001). In order to build deep meaning, the child needs to use **selective attention,** the underlying skill required for effective learning in all developmental areas.

Selective attention requires that the child choose the most important or compelling stimulus, focus on it, discover its meaning, and then react. For example, an infant hears a voice singing a pitch. Ignoring the rub of clothing against its skin, the colors on the wallpaper, the smell of the baby powder under its neck,

Natural objects, such as leaves, allow children to use their tactile perception as they touch the leaf, their visual perception as they examine its shape, their auditory perception as they hear the sound it makes as they crumble it, the their olfactory perception as they smell the damp woodsy odor.

Open-ended arts activities allow children to use their senses as they work with colors, textures, shapes, and patterns. Collage by Jon, age four.

and the trace of milk in its mouth, a baby makes a sound imitating that note.

Ann Lewin-Benham (2010), taking into account the growing body of research on sensory processing and the development of the brain in infants, suggests that experiences with sensory materials be started much earlier with babies than previously thought, and that the arts are an ideal way to develop sustained attention. Sights, sounds, textures, tastes, and smells form the basis of the creative arts and provide an ideal way to entice even the youngest infants to engage and focus in sustained ways.

## Objectives for Sensory Perception Arts Activities

Although all arts activities involve using the senses, specific activities can be selected that enhance and challenge  particular sensory modes, foster the development of selective focus, build discrimination skills, and remedy sensory deficits. At the same time these activities can address growth in all the development areas by creating an enriched learning environment that encourages verbal communication, cognitive processing, and motor development.

Through sensory perception arts activities, children develop:

- **Physically**—*by learning to control bodily movements in the presence of sensory stimuli.* **Kinesthetic awareness** grows as the child reacts to sensory experiences. Neck and torso strengthen and cross-body coordination increases as the child turns towards, searches for, and moves toward sounds and music. Hand movements come to match visual inputs during reaching and grasping arts materials. Finger control develops as the child touches the materials of the visual arts and explores their surfaces. Eyes improve in focusing as they examine visual images and track moving objects during dance and dramatic play.

- **Socially and Emotionally**—*by interacting with peers and adults as they participate in sensory arts activities.* Through interaction with peers and adults, children learn to imitate and model the behavior that is acceptable in their community and culture. They learn to recognize faces and emotional expressions. The smells and tastes of the child's home and culture become familiar and recognized. Through words, touch, and active participation they come to recognize and understand the objects in their environment.

- **Cognitively**—*by attaching meaning to their sensory experiences to understand how the world works.* Arts experiences draw on the senses to improve concentration and memory, provide opportunities for classification and sequencing, and teach cause and effect.

- **Linguistically**—*by providing opportunities to use sound to communicate with and understand others.* Children learn to pick out important sounds from the environment and to ignore distracting sounds as they listen to singing and music. They learn to control sound to communicate needs and emotions when imitating and responding to the sounds of others engaged in arts activities.

- **Creatively**—*by engaging curiosity and risk-taking while developing sustained attention and problem-solving.* When presented with open-ended sensory arts activities, children through control of their own actions can explore, focus on, change, and test the sensory properties of a wide variety of objects, materials, sounds, tastes, smells, and spatial elements.

## Did You Get It?

**A child's ability to tell stories will most likely be affected by sensory deprivation in infancy related to_____.**

a. visual perception

b. tactile perception

c. olfactory perception

d. auditory perception

**Take the full quiz on CourseMate**

# How Should Sensory Perception Activities Be Selected?

Sensory arts activities should be selected based on children's developmental levels and previous arts experiences, while keeping in mind any specific strengths or sensory processing needs of individual children.

Well-designed activities provide multiple opportunities, both novel and repeated, which allow children to perfect their responses to different stimuli, develop memory, create meaning, and build a descriptive vocabulary. While every arts activity addresses all the aforementioned developmental areas, when presenting a sensory perceptual activity the teacher intentionally frames the sensory aspects. This is done by:

- Selecting a sensory-rich experience.

- Alerting the children to the experience.

An unbreakable mirror is an example of an open-ended sensory stimulus suitable for infants. The child can change the visual image by changing facial expression and body position, and by moving closer and further away, or by crawling on it.

Copyright © 2015 Cengage Learning®

## Making Plans

**ONE-ON-ONE ACTIVITY PLAN:**
**INTRODUCING A SQUISHY BAG – A SENSORY ACTIVITY**

WHO?      Group composition age(s): Older infant or toddler

WHEN?     Time frame: 5 to 15 minutes

WHY?      Objectives: Child will develop

- physically, by using the large muscles of the arm and the small muscles of the hand. I will see this happening when the child manipulates the squishy bag. (Bodily-Kinesthetic)

- socially, by interacting with a caring adult. I will see this happening when the child makes eye contact and makes verbal and nonverbal gestures. (Interpersonal)

- emotionally, by developing self-confidence from being allowed to handle the squishy bag. I will see this happening when the child doesn't hesitate to touch the bag. (Intrapersonal)

- perceptually, by visually exploring how colors change as different tactile pressures are applied and by learning that pliant forms change shape. I will see this happening when the child looks at and touches the bag. (Spatial)

- language skills, by verbalizing how the bag feels and looks, and by learning new words for color and shape. I will hear this happening as the child makes verbal responses to my use of these words.(Linguistic)

- cognitively, by observing cause and effect as their manipulation changes the color and nature of the form. I will know this is happening when the child makes the bag change and makes some verbal or non-verbal gesture in response. (Logical-Mathematical)

- arts skill and knowledge, by learning about color, a basic element of visual art, and by developing selective focus and tactile skill in handling a new material. I will see this happening when the child looks when I point my finger and say the name of the colors. (Content Standard 1 & 2)

WHERE?    Setup: Child in a high chair or on an adult's lap at the table. A sealed squishy bag is taped to the high chair tray or table.

WHAT?     Materials: Squishy bag: make one cup of cornstarch finger paint and add two colors that mix well together. (See Appendix D.) Seal bag and cover seal with duck tape. Tape the bag to the table or high chair tray using package sealing tape or masking tape.

HOW?      Procedure:

Wow Warm-Up: Sit with the child and show the child the squishy bag.

What to Do: Model how to poke it and pat it accompanied by enthusiastic words and expressions. Let the child see it, touch it, pat it, and poke it.

What to Say: Use this activity to talk about the tactile qualities of the squishy bag. In an excited voice, use words such as *soft, squishy, pat, poke, push, pull, sticky, press, squash*, and *flatten*. Sensory experiences are a wonderful time to chant or sing with toddlers. Make up some chants to accompany this wonderful activity. For example, chant something like this: *Pat, poke, press that. That's the way we make it flat.*

Transition Out: Let the child spend as much time as he or she wishes exploring the nature of the material. When done, store in a safe place to use again.

WHAT      Assessment: does child respond positively to the squishy bag?
LEARNED?  Does child have sufficient hand strength to change the shape of the material? Does child repeat and use the descriptive terms modeled by the adult?

NEXT?     Repeat the experience with different colors to mix and try different sizes of bags. Follow up with finger painting.

For more examples of sensory activity plans for various ages, see *Sensory Activity Plans* on Coursemate.

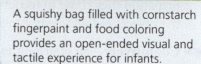

A squishy bag filled with cornstarch fingerpaint and food coloring provides an open-ended visual and tactile experience for infants.

🎵 Allowing a choice of interaction with the stimulus.

🎵 Actively engaging both verbally and nonverbally about the sensory qualities of the experience.

🎵 And as in all good teaching: observing, assessing, adjusting, repeating, and scaffolding as needed based on the children's reaction to the stimulus.

## Selecting Open-Ended Sensory Materials, Objects, and Experiences

Although we tend to think of objects and materials first, sensory stimuli should not be limited to physical objects. Light, shadows, clouds, wind, a visit to a bakery, or a walk in the rain all are full of sensory stimuli. In the same way, while visual and auditory stimuli are more common in children's activities, taste, smell, and touch are powerful senses that can be tapped to motivate and inspire children.

Sensory activities can be designed to help children focus on input from one sense. This type of activity develops important discrimination and classifying skills. However, it is impossible to eliminate the input from all senses. For example, although Montessori sensorial work favors isolating the sensory element to encourage children to order and classify by smaller and smaller increments, children are still receiving input from their sense of touch and their sense of hearing as they observe and then organize, visual materials such as matching pegs with holes, building a graduated block tower, or classifying leaves. Auditory work which asks children to listen closely and match tones or order pitches, also involves feeling the texture and form of the wooden sound cylinders and seeing the colors of the tone bells. Gustatory tasks focus on identifying bitter, sweet, salty, and sour tastes but include the sound and feel of squeezing eye droppers of the solutions into a spoon and sensing the weight and temperature of the spoon in their mouths.

Activities that activate multiple senses also enhance children's cognitive understanding and cement memories. An intentional teacher, for instance, might draw attention to the colors of fruits and their relationship to their tastes by asking questions such as "Do all green fruits taste the same?" Educators in the Reggio Emilia schools purposely mix contrasting sensory experiences to create **synesthetic experiences** that combine visual and tactile, or auditory and shape elements (Lewin-Benham, 2010).

Selecting motivating sensory stimuli requires us to become of aware of our own surroundings, to look at things in new ways, and imagine how our particular children will react to them. While there are many commercial toys that attempt to attract children's attention, found materials and objects made by the teacher will often prove more engaging and are more readily adapted to match children's interests and needs.

A repetitive noise or hard plastic, primary-colored toys decorated with cartoon pictures cannot compete with the intricacies and textures of a veined leaf, a tub filled with soapy water and rainbow-hued bubbles, or the varying quality and expression of the human voice.

**Criteria for selection.** The core of a sensory arts activity is the chosen stimulus or set of stimuli which can be an object, a material, or an event. A carefully chosen stimulus will elicit the sustained attention basic to all learning.

Sand is an open-ended multisensory stimulus that invites active engagement and develops visual, tactile, and auditory sensory perception.

🎵 **The most important criterion in choosing the stimulus is that it allow open-ended exploration.** This means that it should have integral complexity with multiple ways to view it, compare it, change it and use it, such as a mirror which can be viewed from various distances and positions while wearing different expressions, or paper which can be wrinkled, folded, crushed, colored, wet, torn, and cut. Translucent and transparent materials, noise makers, food, and living things make ideal sensory stimuli as they react to children's actions in unexpected ways.

🎵 **It should allow the child to respond and interact with it in a physical and multisensory way.** In our technological world, hands-on experiences are essential. A sturdy basket the child can touch and fill with objects is a better choice for activating the senses than a picture of a basket on a television, on an interactive whiteboard, or on a computer screen.

🎵 **It should introduce novel elements into the child's experience.** This could be something the child has not had contact with before, such as a set of Iroquois ankle bells on a suede strap tied to an infant's ankle or something familiar presented in a new way such, as bubble wrap for toddlers to dance on.

🎵 **The idea for the stimulus should grow from careful observation of children's needs, desires, and input.** For example, after noticing that an infant is beginning to reach out and grasp, provide a sensory stimulus, such as a bell, that the child can hold and shake. If after reading a book about fish, a child wonders if the fish in the book looks like a real fish, it is time to bring a goldfish bowl into the classroom. Pebbles collected by children from the playground can become sensory stimuli as they wash them and watch them change colors as they dry.

🎵 **A well-chosen stimulus will provide opportunities for multiple uses as the child grows and develops sensory perceptual skills.** Repetition develops memory and skill. A bell shaken by an infant's grasping hand can become the bell rung by a toddler to accompany a song, can become part of a set of bells in a preschool comparative sound center, and then, can become part of the musical bells used by primary students to compose an original melody.

For more examples of sensory stimuli, see *Examples of Sensory Stimuli* on CourseMate.

**Safety Considerations.** Select materials with safety in mind, especially with younger children who still put objects in their mouths. Objects shorter than two inches in length and one inch in diameter should not be used by children under the age of three. Materials that are dusty and can be inhaled should be avoided with all children. Seek input from parents about known allergies.

At all times, children should be supervised based on their developmental level and behavioral patterns. A focused teacher in a one-on-one situation can

## Teacher to Family

### *Sample Letter to Families: Child Safety Information*

Dear Family,

All of the arts materials used in our program have been carefully selected to be safe for young children. Some children, however, have special sensitivities. To help us select the safest arts materials for your child, please answer the following questions:

1. Is your child allergic to anything?    yes    no
If yes, please list:
2. Does your child have any respiratory
   problems?    yes    no
If yes, please explain:

3. Is your skin sensitive to anything?    yes    no
If yes, please list:
4. Are there any arts materials that your
   child should not use?    yes    no
Please list and explain.

Thank you for taking the time to complete this form. Together we can make sure that your child will have a safe and fun time creating art.

Your child's teacher,

offer objects that would not be safe left alone with the child, such as a pinecone or sealed plastic bag of colored hair gel or paint. These challenging materials offer the opportunity to teach even infants safe behaviors. When infants go to put inappropriate things in their mouths, make a yucky face and say "No mouth." If they persist, replace with a material that can be safely explored orally and say "This is nicer to chew." More safety tips can be found in Appendix A.

## Introducing Sensory Activities

Once a stimulus is selected, the next task is to alert the children and attract their focus to it, despite all the other sensory distractions vying for their attention. Pointing, modeling, and imitation accompanied by enthusiastic language draw attention and work for all ages, but are especially important for infants and young toddlers.

- **Pointing** helps them train their eyes on the selected stimulus and develop sustained attention. Even young infants will follow a pointing arm with their eyes.

- **Open-ended modeling** demonstrates one or more ways to react and increase skill and interest. Shaking a rattle to show infants that it makes noise increases the likelihood they will try shaking it.

- **Imitation** of the children's reactions tells them they have done something noteworthy.

- **Verbal and nonverbal feedback** that is enthusiastic and encouraging, and is rich in descriptive words builds vocabulary, provides emotional satisfaction, teaches social communication skills, and gives cognitive feedback.

**Wonderful Object of Wonder.** For toddlers and older children, the sensory stimulus should be a **WOW**—a Wonderful Object of Wonder—introduced with questions and wonderings by the teacher. The WOW can be anything that excites the senses and expands the curiosity and experience of the children: a stained-glass window, a bird feather found on the playground, wood blocks in a wooden bowl, or a rhythm tapped on an African drum.

In a sensory arts activity, the children's interaction with the WOW is the focal point. However, a WOW can also be used to elicit wonderment and curiosity when it is the starting point or warm-up in any arts or

Handmade instruments from around the world invite children to touch and explore. They are a good example of the types of sensory stimuli that can be used as Wonderful Objects of Wonder, or WOWs.

other curriculum area activity. See Appendix B for more ideas on the role of WOWs indesigning activity plans.

**Guided discovery.** Preschoolers and older children who have already had many sensory experiences can be alerted through a carefully orchestrated unveiling process. In guided discovery the object or even a center is wrapped or hidden from view to elicit curiosity and create opportunities for children to ask questions and to make predictions based on clues revealed through hints, observations, or a gradual uncovering. See Appendix B for using Guided Discovery in activity planning in general.

### Did You Get It?

Alex is a new teacher of toddlers. He seeks the advice of Linda, a senior teacher at the school, on ideas about selecting a good stimulus for a sensory arts activity. Which of the following should Linda recommend to Alex?

a. The stimulus should clearly indicate to the child what needs to be done with it.

b. The stimulus should allow the child to respond and interact with it in a physical way.

c. The stimulus should be presented on a computer screen or tablet.

d. The stimulus should be specific to one sensory organ, and should not demand multi-sensory uses.

**Take the full quiz on CourseMate**

# How Should Sensory Perception Activities Be Presented?

How sensory activities are presented will depend on the development of the child and the organization of the space.

## Ways to Present to Infants

For infants not yet sitting up or children with physical or sensory issues, cuddling them against the body or holding them on a lap can provide security when introducing something new. As they become accustomed to sensory activities, vary their perspective by placing them on their backs or positioning them to sit facing outward. Be careful about moving objects rapidly toward the face as this can trigger a defensive response. Start slowly with all actions and add energy as the child shows active attention.

Based on careful observation of the way the baby reacts, change and adapt the activity until the baby shows boredom by losing interest, at which time, a new activity maybe started or a rest period given. This type of intimate reciprocal arts activity requires the complete one-on-one attention of the teacher, who provides a constant patter of vocally dramatic description delivered with enthusiasm. For safety, be sure to remove sensory objects and materials from the child's reach when teacher–child interaction is over.

Infants who are sitting up and those who are beginning to turn over, creep, and crawl can be placed on the floor and have the sensory stimulus placed at a distance to encourage them to reach for and move toward it, adding emotional satisfaction to the experience when the child is successful. Placing older infants in pairs encourages increased imitation and can motivate a reticent child. Expand the activities and add challenge by using a larger space and more movements and objects. Include things that roll, bounce, make noise, and change shape when the child moves them, such as long or wide cardboard or plastic tubes, paper bags with noise makers inside, or foam balls and blocks. Strip a crawling infant to her diaper, dip her hands in wet paint, and let her crawl under supervision on a large sheet of paper.

**Visual activities.** If an infant stares at a particular location, observe what is attracting its attention, and then see what happens if a new object or material is placed in that space. Try mirrors, blinking lights, and glittery materials. Move beyond commercial mobiles, and make your own with interchangeable pieces to provide ever-changing novelty. Tracking can be fostered by moving the objects in a constant direction. Spatial depth can be developed by moving the object or material closer or farther away. Building on infants' attraction to faces, move materials that reflect light in different ways, such as paper or velvet in front of your face. To change focus, alternate the baby's position. For example, rest the infant against your body so that the infant faces forward and hold objects out front and to either side so that the child must focus on it against a distracting background.

Make visually interesting items by filling plastic containers and bags with liquids, such as food coloring, water and oil, and small objects, such as pebbles, buttons, or glitter, sealed well with tape or hot glue.

**Auditory activities.** If an infant makes a sound or movement, imitate it. If the baby imitates you, repeat, and elaborate by changing it in some way. Sing songs and recite rhymes accompanied by exaggerated verbal and facial expressions. Look for sound makers that infants can hold comfortably like bells, rattles, and things to tap together. Make your own shakers by filling containers, both opaque and transparent, with different materials and sealing well. As the baby handles these objects describe the sounds and motions the child is making.

**Tactile activities.** Touching materials and objects encourages infants to coordinate eyes and hands and

## Across Cultures

### Using Food in Arts Activities

In selecting food items to use in sensory and other arts activities, be sensitive to family traditions and beliefs concerning foods. In some cultures, certain foods, such as rice, are highly valued and not considered suitable for children to play with. Others may feel that with so many hungry people in our country and all over the world, it is inappropriate to have children play in a sensory bin filled with food items like cereal, macaroni, or beans that will be thrown away when the activity is over.

## Special Needs

### • ADJUSTING FOR SPECIAL NEEDS •

Not all children respond in the same way to sensory stimuli. Some children may need special attention during sensory arts activities.

- **Limited vision.** Stroke from the palm out to the finger tips to increase tactile sensitivity. Use larger objects and sound makers and place within vision range if any. If the child can see some color, use that color. Provide clues that use other senses such applying a particular scent to mark personal toys. Increase tactile, auditory, and movement-based activities. For infants, allow more exploration with the mouth by providing objects that invite sucking. Look for things that vibrate and make noise like drums and rainsticks. Create Treasure Baskets from shallow containers in which everyday objects are grouped. However, minimize ubiquitous plastics in favor of ones that vary in weight and temperature such as fabric, metal, rubber, stone, and wood.

- **Hearing loss.** Emphasize visual and tactile sensory stimuli. Choose objects that reflect and emit light or catch the eye by moving. Make exaggerated visual expressions as you describe the objects. Try mirror, light tables, and sensory bins.

- **Tactile defensiveness.** Some sensory activities that help children become more accustomed to touch sensations include: painting with soap foam and pudding, playing in sand, finding hidden objects in rice or beans, squeezing out white glue, using play dough and clay, and drawing on squishy bags.

- **Distractibility.** Take a box and attach interesting sensory items to the inside. Position the child just inside the opening so that she can see and touch the objects.

- **Oversensitivity.** Lights, tastes, smells, touch, or sounds may cause some children to retreat or panic. These children need a slow, gentle introduction to the experience. Explore using soothing music and massage to calm.

- **Undersensitivity.** Other children may show no reaction to a sensory stimulus or be distracted and unable to focus. These children may need stronger stimuli such as allspice instead of vanilla.

A teacher draws toddlers' attention to the sensory qualities of the materials in a sensory bin filled with water, plastic strips, and pumpkins.

feet. Textures stimulate the skin. Look for materials that make sounds when the baby crunches them or that have unique textures such as aluminum foil and different types of papers and cloth. Laminate colorful paper shapes and natural objects such as leaves and flowers for the infant to handle. Lightly brush objects and materials across the baby's skin, hands, feet, and face.

**Olfactory and gustatory activities.** Accompanied by enthusiastic words, model smelling or tasting a food item and make a surprised or pleased face. Then present the item to the child. Hold pleasant smelling foods, candles, soap, and flowers to the baby's nose or touch the baby's lips with a piece of orange, banana, applesauce, or other pleasant infant-appropriate food.

## Ways to Present to Older Children

For toddlers and older children who have more physical control and increased sensory discrimination skills, complexity can be added through the addition of more objects, materials, and events.

**Sharing.** Children can interact in pairs and small groups as they explore sensory items. Present a unique item to touch, feel, and look at during circle time or during a small group time. Then place it on the observation table, in the drawing center, or another selected location. For example, show a beautiful geode to the group, and have the children pass it around describing what they see and how it feels. Then show them where there are more in a basket for them to explore. Groups are also ideal for listening to auditory stimuli.

**Sensory bins, baskets, and tables.** Containers such as baskets, wooden bowls, dish tubs, and clear plastic storage bins can hold smaller sensory objects or liquids for exploration. Built to contain messy materials, large sand-and-water tables allow a group of children to explore at the same time and can hold many more things besides water or sand, such as hay, shredded paper, and goop made from cornstarch and water.

**For more examples of sensory activities, see** *Sensory Perception Arts Activities* **on CourseMate.**

**Observation table or display.**  Place an unfamiliar object or an arrangement of objects from nature on a small child-height table. If possible, use materials the children have collected and grouped themselves. Add descriptive materials such as photographs of where they come from, identifying labels, and for older children, appropriate observation tools such as magnifiers and tweezers. Make a comment about it to draw attention and encourage the children to look and touch.

*"Look, we have a beautiful conch shell from Florida! How do you think it feels?"*

*"Can you guess what is in the sensory table today? What does it look like?"*

**Learning centers.**  Many sensory experiences lend themselves to learning centers. Small attractively arranged samples of fruits or vegetables or different kinds of bread can be offered at a tasting center. Small boxes or containers containing different materials can be placed at a sound center where children can try to match the sounds or put them in order from softest to loudest.

**Sources of Inspiration.**  Both Reggio Emilia and Montessori programs place a great emphasis on sensory learning. In the Reggio Emilia program, sensory stimuli range from shadows to bird feeders to walking in a crowd (Edwards, Gandini, & Forman, 2011). Many early childhood programs in the United States have documented the ways sensory learning is incorporated into their programs. *In the Spirit of the Studio* (Gandini et al., 2005), *Infants and Toddlers at Work* (Lewin-Benham, 2010), and *Learning Together with Young Children* (Curtis & Carter, 2008) all give examples of effective materials and objects, such as using egg beaters in soapy water, arranging translucent glass beads on mirrors, and making patterns of furry cloth of different types.

An observation table with living things, such as these chicks, provides a wonderful multisensory experience that draws children's attention and wonder.

**Did You Get It?**

Florence, a kindergarten teacher, selects a piece of bubble wrap as a stimulus for a sensory arts activity. Her next task is to

a. initiate interaction between the child and the stimulus.

b. alert the child about the stimulus he is about to experience.

c. explain about the sensory qualities involved in the experience.

d. observe and assess the child as he responds to the stimulus.

**Take the full quiz on CourseMate**

## How Do We Create Sensory Interactions?

The presentation of a sensory stimulus alone is not a complete activity. Planned, intentional interaction between the child and the adult is an essential component. Sensory-rich interactions are made up of a combination of words, actions, and expressiveness that show wonder about and value of sensory qualities and respond to the actions and words of the child.

## Open-Ended Questioning and Wondering

As we have seen in Chapter 2, questioning is one way to elicit children's ideas. When carefully worded so that there is no one right answer, an enthusiastic question can be a useful way to involve a child with a sensory stimulus. To ensure open-endedness, model the wonder of young children and try starting with "why" or "I wonder" instead of "what." Invite comparisons using the word "how" rather than "which."

*Why is this paper sparkling?*

*I wonder how this stone got so round?*

*How is the outside of this peach different from the inside?*

## Building a Sensory-Rich Vocabulary

A sensory element exists in every activity in which children are involved. Instead of seeing blocks, see shapes and forms; instead of glue, notice stickiness. Listen and learn from children. Young children do not hesitate to invite us to "feel this" or "smell that," and we must do the same with them. Find a sensory element, and express it with language rich in adjectives, similes, and metaphors.

*"Look at how the light is shining on your wet paint!"*

*"Oh, the sand is so cool and damp today!"*

*"The yellow paint smells like a field of flowers."*

*"Our tiger teeth fingers are crunching the paper. Crunch. Crunch."*

Use textural adjectives to describe the tactile quality of materials such as silky, soft, smooth, squishy, damp, metallic, bumpy, wet, and rough. Refer to the temperature of the materials: "Oh, this finger paint feels cold!" or "The play dough is warm from your hand." Make them aware of the pressure they are using: "You pressed down with your feet on the floor when you marched," "You banged hard on the drum," or "Your puppet touched me very lightly."

Encourage children to make tactile observations of these items by asking questions such as the following:

*"Is it cold to your touch?"*

*"Are there places you can put your fingers?"*

*"How does it feel on the bottom?"*

## Classroom Technology

### *PLAYING WITH LIGHT*

Young children are fascinated by light. Overhead projectors and interactive white boards are two ways to provide open-ended sensory exploration of light as children move in the cast light. Here are some ideas to get you thinking:

#### On the overhead:

- Explore shining the light on a wall or curtains for shadow play.
- Look for transparent and translucent materials such as cellophane, used theater gels, and plastic wrappings to change the color of the light and the shadows.
- Investigate how a glass tray of water on the overhead can be gently stirred to create the effect of light shining underwater or to create rippled patterns.

#### Interactive whiteboard:

- Project patterns, colors, and shapes using a presentation software such as PowerPoint. Set the show up to change slides at varying intervals and add music if desired.
- Project photographs that set a scene such as a jungle or fire.
- Project children's own drawings and paintings.

Having children trace their shadows on a wall helps them develop their visual perception and increases their understanding of light and shadow.

Compare scents to other natural smells, such as:

*"The paste smells so fresh and clean!"*
*"This play dough smells like pine needles."*

Describe the visual and textural appearance of different foods, such as the rich pink and green of watermelon, the segmented circle shape of a sliced orange, and the bumpy surface of a chocolate-chip cookie.

## What Are the Elements of the Arts?

Another source of sensory language is found in the distinctive sensory-based vocabulary of each of the art forms. Visual art is made up of the visual and tactile elements of lines, colors, shapes, forms, patterns, and textures. Music is composed of the auditory elements of beats, pitch, rhythm, dynamics, harmony, tempo, timbre, and texture. Creative movement incorporates visual tracking and baric perception within the elements of space, distance, direction, flow, effort, and connection. More detail about those elements specific to each of the arts is found in Chapters 9, 10, 11, and 12.

As children pursue arts activities, lavish the young artists with comments based on the arts elements that add sensory qualities to their efforts.

### Line

A **line** can be a mark made by a tool moving across a surface. It may be curved or straight or zigzag or wiggly. Lines can be thick or thin or long or short and are used by artists to make shapes and symbols and by writers to form letters, words, and numbers. Lines can show movement and direction—horizontal, vertical, or diagonal. Most importantly, lines are the mainstay of children's earliest drawings and will continue to remain an important element in all of their art.

Lines are present in visual artwork in all media, but we can also see lines in the positioning of the body in creative dance, in group movements, and in the order of notes in a melody. In nature, lines are the edges, contours, paths, and grooves in natural objects. Line activities are designed to increase children's abilities to look for and focus upon linear elements in their environment.

Searching for lines is one way to develop sustained attention against distracting backgrounds. Find straight lines dividing the tiles on the floor, curved lines hanging from the electric poles, and zigzag lines in the cracks of a frozen puddle. Make up challenges and games that have children step on lines and walk along lines. Line up one behind the other, and make a line of people that moves, wiggles, and sways as they walk in an open space or around furniture.

Music also has a linear element. Play a simple melody and have children follow the melody by drawing a line in the air with their fingers, or give them paint and let them paint lines as they follow along with the music.

Read some of the many children's books that feature lines, and then put out blank booklets for the children to draw their own "line" stories. Study the different lines that make up the letters of the alphabet. Design new ways to write the letters using a variety of lines.

### Color

Teaching the colors has long been a basic of early childhood education. However, color perception is an extremely complex process about which we learn more and more each year.

Infants can see color at birth. In fact, they are born with a fascination for colors, particularly reds (Franklin, Bevis, & Ling, 2010). Infants physically process color with the right sides of their brains. As toddlers acquire language, color perception transfers to the left side (Franklin et al., 2008). In addition, people vary in how they see individual colors. A particular pink may look more orange to one viewer, more bluish to another.

## Integrating the Arts

Using the senses is an important way to activate learning in all subject areas. Wonderful Objects of Wonder attract and hold children's attention and make learning math, science, social studies, or language arts more meaningful.

Instead of counting circles on a paper, provide beautiful beach pebbles or seashells to count. In science, instead of looking at pictures of fish in a book, buy a whole fish at the supermarket to observe, sketch, then make Japanese-inspired gyotaki fish prints.* If the children are studying the rainforest, visit a zoo or pet store to see parrots, frogs, and lizards and a nursery to see tropical plants. When reading a book, look for a real object that relates to the story. It could be a hat, or a food item, something that the character uses, or a sensory object that serves as the starting point for a story.

*To make a gyotaki print, brush water-based printing ink over the surface of the fish. Use thin paper such as rice paper, tissue, or newsprint. Press against the inked fish.

Because not everyone sees colors in exactly the same way, color activities often need to be adjusted. Children who have limited vision or are **color blind,** for example, need to be identified so that they do not feel uncomfortable during color activities and games.

Approximately 6 percent of people have some form of color blindness. Color blindness is more common in boys than girls. Approximately 7 to 10 percent of men in the United States are color blind to reds and greens. Other color combinations, such as blue and yellow, are much more rare. Those color blind for red and green can often differentiate the colors when side by side, but not when the color is viewed alone.

Therefore, children who are color blind often have difficulty with color-related activities. These children quickly learn to try to hide their color discrimination difficulties, especially if they are laughed at by other children when using a color the wrong way, such as drawing a purple tree. Often adults mistakenly think the child does not know the colors yet and will try to force the child to learn them, so it is important to identify color blindness as early as possible. The Ishihara color test, which shows pictures made up of dots of different colors, is an example of a test for identifying color blindness that can be used.

Other children may have limited vision, which makes color identification difficult. Once a color identification problem is identified, try using scented crayons and markers and adding scents, such as vanilla and lemon extract to paints. It also helps to place the colors in the same order at the easel and to line up the markers and crayons in the same color order. When doing color games and activities, have these children work with the colors they can identify.

Color perception is also influenced by the cultural and emotional context in which we learn those colors (Dedrick, 1996; Juricevic, 2010). For example, in some cultures black is associated with mourning, in others, white is. This means that we need to be sensitive to young children's specific cultural backgrounds and experiences.

To develop color discrimination, take time every day to enthusiastically notice the wide range of colors in the children's environment. For example, comment on the colors of the clothing children are wearing; the color of the grass, leaves, and sky when playing outside; and the colors of the fruits and vegetables in their snacks.

Note that there are many varieties of each color and use descriptive or comparative words to identify a variation of a color. For example, "Your sweater is as green as the leaves on our tree," and "Today the sky

## Teacher Tip

### SCENTED MARKERS

Water-based scented markers have pleasant non-toxic odors and can be useful with children who have limited vision in helping them identify colors and for some scent activities. However, caution is advised in using these on a regular basis. Some disadvantages to consider are:

- The scents are similar to candy. For example black smells like licorice, and some children may be tempted to taste them or insert them in their noses.

- The scents are very strong and the smell can be overwhelming in a classroom when several are being used at the same time.

- The scents may become overly identified with a certain color such as lemon with yellow and mint with green, limiting the development of a more discriminating sense of smell.

reminds me of the color of a robin's egg," and "The leaves on that tree are a deeper green than on this one." Point out differences among **hues** in the same color family. Show how colors can vary in **intensity, tone,** and **value.**

Colors get mixed intentionally or unintentionally when painting and printing. Mixing new colors gives the child a sense of power and provides an opportunity for color identification. Finger painting with two or three colors is a very tactile way to combine colors, as is mixing several colors of playdough together.

Providing a preselected palette of colors helps children focus on specific color mixtures. Introduce the **primary colors** of red, yellow, and blue and let children discover how these three colors make the **secondary colors** of orange, purple, and green. Show how adding white makes a **tint**—a lighter version of the color and adding black makes a **shade,** a darker version of the color.

For more ways to mix colors using the color wheel, see *Guide to Mixing Colors* on CourseMate.

## Shape

Everything has a shape. A **shape** is a two-dimensional area or image that has defined edges or borders. A two-dimensional shape has height and width and may be geometric, organic, symbolic, or free form. Many shapes have names based on their properties.

- Geometric shapes follow mathematical principles, such as polygons, squares, rectangles, circles, and triangles.

- Organic shapes come from nature, as in the shape of a leaf or butterfly.

- Symbolic shapes have a special meaning, such as that of letters or numbers or musical notes.

- Free-form shapes are invented shapes that follow no rules.

Each of the four categories of shapes may contain some shapes that are **symmetrical.** If a straight line is drawn through the center of a shape, it will be exactly the same on both sides. Squares, butterflies, the letter "A," and hearts are all symmetrical shapes. All of these shapes will be found in children's artwork, books, and in the classroom environment.

Looking through a tinted view finder adds complexity to how things are perceived, challenging the sensory perception of children as they explore the relationship of color and light.

Copyright © 2015 Cengage Learning®

To help children focus on the qualities of shapes, play games that involve finding specific shapes. Search the room and outside areas for types of shapes. Go on circle, rectangle, and triangle hunts. Hide shapes around the room for children to find.

Develop vocabulary by talking about the qualities of these shapes including and expanding beyond the simple names of heart, square and so on. Present sensory objects that have unusual shapes both symmetrical and non-symmetrical, such as leaves, flowers, and rocks that challenge description. With infants and toddlers, use colorful laminated shapes to make complex shape designs. Differentiate between the edge of the shape and the inside of the shape. Older children can use pattern blocks and tangrams. Take them apart and put them together into new shapes. Make mosaic-like designs by gluing small shapes onto colorful backgrounds.

## Pattern and Rhythm

A **pattern** occurs when anything is repeated several times. Patterns and rhythms occur naturally, as in the designs on a leopard's skin and the chirping of crickets, or can be invented by artists, dancers, and musicians. In the visual arts, a patterned design may be made from repeated shapes, lines, and colors. Musical patterns occur when the same note sequence or rhythm is repeated. **Rhythm** is a time-based pattern. Creative dance is built on the repetition of body movements that create patterns and rhythms. Patterns are important not only in the arts; being able to find and understand patterns is also the basis of language and mathematical understanding.

Encourage children to find examples of pattern and rhythm in the environment. Find the shapes, lines, and colors in patterns on clothing, furnishings, and on nature objects. Physically create patterns to develop memory and meaning. Have children line up in ways that make patterns such as alternating tall and short or those wearing light colors and those wearing dark.

Show surprise and wonder as you comment on patterns in the art they are creating, the music they listen to, and the objects in their environment. Look for natural patterns like the scales on a pine cone and the spots on a Dalmatian. Help children see that a pattern is made up of smaller elements by providing materials that can be arranged in multiple patterns such as color tiles and cloth squares. Provide surprising objects such as books, markers, and shoes and challenge children to arrange them in pattern. Hands-on ordering of objects into patterns is a calming activity. It is also is important for developing connections in the brain. Children who self-generate knowledge through their own actions show better understanding of verbs and objects than those who only observe (James & Swain, 2011).

Explore patterns in dance and music. Read a poem or dance rhythmically, moving different body parts in repetitious ways, and follow the pattern by clapping or playing rhythm instruments. Listen for patterns in the words, melody, and rhythm in musical works. Clap and count the beats in a favorite song. Chart the patterns and rhythms using colors or shapes. For a responsive integrated music and visual arts activity, suggest that children record the song's pattern or create a new one by drawing invented symbols.

The arts elements are found in the clothes children wear and the toys they play with. We can find lines, shapes, colors, textures, forms, patterns, and spaces wherever we look.

## Texture

**Texture** is the way something feels to the touch. Surfaces can be hard or soft, rough or smooth, or bumpy or jagged. Texture is found in all artwork and is an especially important element in collage and modeling activities. Texture plays a role in dramatic play as children dress up in costumes that can feel soft, rough, slippery, and so on against their skin.

We can both feel texture using tactile sensory perception and we can also see texture using visual sensory perception. Help children focus on the tactile qualities of their environment by inviting them to compare the textures of different items in the classroom or in the arts materials. To help develop focus, smooth the tips of an infant's fingers before inviting them to touch. Have older children rub their fingers together before touching a texture. Montessori programs prepare children for tactile discrimination

Providing contrasting textures for collages encourages children to compare and contrast the way the different tactile materials look and behave as they cut them and glue them down.

activities by having them dip their fingertips in warm water and blotting them dry before starting tactile discrimination tasks.

There are many open-ended tactile arts materials that allow children to create their own textures. They can fold and crumple paper, add different amounts of sand to paint, and press natural objects into pliant play dough and clay.

Feet can also explore textures. Check for safety and then allow children to walk on grass, gravel, sand, and cement. Dip into paint and make footprints. Collect carpet squares for children to arrange into textured areas to walk and dance on.

Many children do not have a rich vocabulary to describe the things they touch. Use words that describe textures as the children play and eat their snacks. Compare textures to things they have experienced, such as, "Oh, that's as wet as a rain puddle" or "This feels as soft as Alicia's bunny."

## Form

**Form** is the three-dimensional quality of objects. Forms have height, width, and depth, such as found in spheres, pyramids, cubes, cylinders, and rectangular solids. Childhood physical handling and examination of many forms allow us as adults to recognize the nature of forms just by looking at them.

Forms are complex. They are not always the same on the back or on the bottom as they appear from the front. Point out examples of forms as part of other activities. Ask, "What form is your cup? What form is this block?" Use the correct geometrical term whenever possible, but also include comparisons to familiar objects to enhance understanding, such as, "Look, this rain stick is a cylinder just like our cylinder block, but much longer and fatter. Feel how round it is. See how far around your fingers can go around it. Let's get the block and feel the difference."

Active participation is essential in discovering three-dimensional qualities especially to counteract too much screen time. Block play and clay modeling activities are excellent ways for children to explore

Getting inside three-dimensional forms and crawling through them on the playground is a wonderful opportunity to learn about form and space. Follow up by asking the children questions about the sensory qualities of form and space.

and to create their own original complex forms and to invent their own way to describe them. Construction activities and papier-mâché also involve building in three dimensions. Develop stereognostic sensory perception skills by placing known objects in a touch bag or box for the child to feel and identify.

Creative movement activities allow children to discover the flexible form of their bodies. Encourage them to stretch and bend, to curl up, and lay down to change the forms of their bodies. Older children can create more complex body forms by working together with a partner to make cubes, spheres, and rectangular solids.

## Space

Artists do not just see shapes and forms; they also see the **space** that surrounds them. This may be the empty space of the paper, the open spaces in a sculpture, or the silent rests in a musical composition. Space is an absence of elements that provides a quiet focus in the midst of color, form, texture, line, and pattern. Young children discover space when they look through a tube and see the view contained in a circle, peer through a hole poked in play dough, or clap at the moment when everyone else has stopped.

Because space is the absence of something, it is often invisible. Children need guidance in discovering the role of space in artistic creation. Bend arms and legs to touch the body and point out the openings they encompass. Hold hands with a partner and make bigger spaces. Show how the silent moments in a song (rests) are like holes or spaces. Construct clay sculptures and block structures that are full of holes. Use different objects, such as sticks and geometric-shaped cookie cutters, to form spaces you can see through in the clay. Explore how many and how big holes can be before the structure collapses. Make comments such as, "You have left a rectangular space in the middle of your painting," "You have made round spaces in your play dough. Can you see through them?," "Listen for the silent part in this song," and "Should you leave a big space between the blocks or a small one?"

## Movement

Although **movement** is obvious in creative dance, all the arts are founded on movement. Visual art makes viewers track their eyes across the surface of the work. Dramatic works and stories move from introduction to climax. Music follows a similar sequence. Movement occupies space, takes time, and requires energy.

- *Space*—Movement can follow paths through space that are high, low, horizontal, vertical, and diagonal. They can consume the space or take very little.

- *Time*—Movement has speed and duration. It can range from slow to fast, brief to infinite. It can be rhythmic or arrhythmic.

- *Energy*—Movement can be fluid or sharp. It can flow gently like the melody of a lullaby or be as jerky as a puppet on a string. In the arts, energy most often comes from our bodies whether we are leaping across the room, wiggling a puppet on our finger, acting out a story, or dragging a marker across a piece of paper.

Because movement is so much a part of all the arts, it will be found in every arts activity. When talking about arts activities, try to describe the movement you are seeing. "You put a lot of energy into that high jump," "You are drawing a horizontal line across your page," "You are moving slowly just like the character in the story." Ask questions that help children discover the movements they are making. "Would a mouse make small movements or large ones?," "How is the music moving fast or slow?," and "Are you putting a lot of energy into your brush strokes?"

For more examples of arts elements activities, see *Arts Element Activities* on CourseMate.

---

**Did You Get It?**

**Which of the following is a primary color?**

a. green

b. yellow

c. purple

d. orange

**Take the full quiz on CourseMate**

# How Can We Use Children's Literature?

Children's books are another way to engage children in sensory perception activities and develop focus and sustained attention. Almost any children's book can be used for a line or shape or color hunt. Name a shape that is used in one of the illustrations, and then ask the children to look for it as they listen to the story.

Look for other elements as well. Share stories about sounds, and tastes or that are filled with pictures with patterns, such as the books of Patricia Polacco. Introduce them to books that incorporate texture. Toddlers will enjoy any of the books available that contain actual textures to touch, such as the DK Publishing series *Baby Touch and Feel*. Older children can identify the different textures in the collages that illustrate many children's books such as Eric Carle's *The Grouchy Lady Bug* and then make collages of their own.

*For more books incorporating sensory elements and related activities, see The Annotated List of Children's Books on CourseMate.*

## Making Books

Perhaps one of the best ways to incorporate books and sensory learning is to make your own book or have the children make books of their own. Individual

Children's books show children how sensory and artistic elements can be applied to tell a story.

or class books can be made that encourage children to use multiple senses.

A big book is the perfect size to read to a group of small children. The large pictures can be easily seen by everyone. However, you will not find big books on every topic you may need, nor will the books exactly fit your chosen activities. The ideal solution is to use your creativity and make your own incorporating hands on materials. Here are some examples to get you thinking.

**Book on color.** For example, in a book on color, feature a different color on each page. For each color, have children cut out a variety of shapes from different kinds of paper in that color. Write the color names in crayon and marker in that color. At the back of the book, attach an envelope containing shapes in each color. Invite the children to find the correct page for the "lost" shapes.

**Book on pattern.** For a book on pattern, use handprints, gadget or sponge prints made by the children to illustrate one or more of the following concepts:

- All patterns are made of repeated shapes.
- Some patterns are made from one repeated shape.
- Some patterns are made with two repeated shapes.
- Some patterns are made with three or more repeated shapes.
- Some patterns are made in only one color.
- Some patterns have lots of colors.
- Some patterns are made of different-sized shapes.

Use yarn to attach samples of the gadget objects used to make the prints to the book. Invite children to match them to the patterns, or if using handprints, have them match their hands.

**Book on line.** For a book on lines, have children use marker, crayon, or paint to draw different kinds of lines on each page. Some lines to include are straight, curved, zigzag, jagged, thick, and thin. Try to have each line be a continuation of the one on the previous page. On the last page, put all of the different lines together in a wild line "party." Invite children to follow the lines with their fingers.

**Book on sound.** Create a book of sound clues. Have children draw things that make sounds on each page and label each "How does _____ sound?" Read the book by making the appropriate sounds. Or for a more hands-on experience, attach sound makers to each page using ribbon or yarn. (See Reflection Page 15 for more big book topics.)

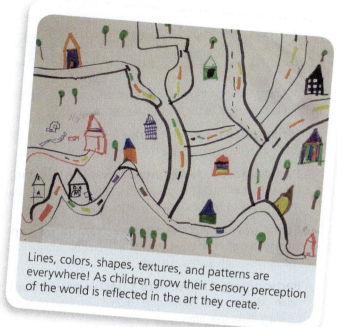

Lines, colors, shapes, textures, and patterns are everywhere! As children grow their sensory perception of the world is reflected in the art they create.

---

### Did You Get It?

If you cannot find a big book on a topic that relates to your curriculum or to the children's interests, you should

  a. skip reading about the topic.

  b. create your own big book.

  c. use a regular size book instead.

  d. write to children's book publishers and demand they publish books on that topic.

Take the full quiz on CourseMate

---

## Conclusion: The Sensitive Teacher

The sensory perception activities presented in this chapter may seem different from more "traditional" arts activities for young children. Some of them may cross into other curriculum areas; others do not use the expected materials. Nevertheless, these explorations, which start with the newborn child, form the basis of how children learn about their world.

It is our job to create an environment that welcomes exploration, is full of wonderful open-ended experiences, allows children to gain pleasure as they use their senses, and rewards children for using their natural learning style.

We must bring excitement and enthusiasm to the classroom daily. We must be open to the sensory wonders that surround us—the pattern of the raindrops on the windowpane, the rainbow in the spilled oil in a puddle, the warm fur of a kitten—and share these with children. If we visualize ourselves as enthusiastic nurturers of young artists' sensory development then the objects, materials, and experiences we provide will make every day special for a young child.

For additional information about sensory learning and the elements of the arts visit, see *Chapter 4 Online Resources* on CourseMate.

---

## Teaching In Action

### SAMPLE PLANS FOR A CELEBRATORY PRESENTATION

**FESTIVAL OF LINES: A SENSORY CELEBRATION FOR TODDLERS AND THEIR FAMILIES**

**Location:** The playground

**Time:** 2:00 to 4:00 P.M.

**Welcome Table:** Program and map; painted or paper streamer lines for visitors to follow to the different activities.

**Art Display (visual perception):** Children's drawings and paintings with associated dictation.

**Photography Display (visual perception):** Photographs of children involved in the activities.

**Interactive Arts Display (visual and tactile perception):** Children's paintings with a set of brushes hung

*(continued)*

## Teaching In Action *(continued)*

on string. Participants are invited to match and trace the lines in the painting with the brush that created them.

**Video (visual perception):** Creative movement and music activities featuring the children are shown.

**Participatory Arts Activity 1 (visual perception):** Large sheet of mural paper, baskets of colorful markers, and an invitation to add some original lines.

**Participatory Arts Activity 2 (tactile perception):** Partner loom is set up with a basket of colorful yarn and an invitation to weave a line.

**Participatory Arts Activity 3 (tactile perception):** Table with paper and white glue colored with food coloring. Children make glue lines.

**Participatory Arts Activity 4 (visual perception and math integration):** Children's paintings are interspersed with bold graphics showing different kinds of lines. Participants are asked to find the total number of each kind of line visible in the paintings. A box and coupons are provided for the guesses. At the end of the celebration, names will be drawn to receive door prizes.

**Puppet Show:** The show put on by parents with help from the children features a simple tale about a magic string, based on the book *Billy and the Magic String* (Karnovsky, 1995).

**Demonstration 1 (visual and tactile perception):** A handspinner demonstrates how wool is turned into yarn. She gives pieces of yarn to participants to use on a partner loom.

**Demonstration 2 (visual and tactile):** Basket weaver creates willow baskets, surrounded by a display of photographs showing examples of lines in nature. Families and children can arrange willow branches in a pattern on a large sheet of paper.

**Demonstration 3 (auditory):** Washtub instrument and cardboard and rubber band "guitars." Families and children can try making different tones by changing length of strings.

**Measurement Table (visual perception and math integration):** Volunteers measure a length of string that is the height of each participant and tape it to a graph.

**Musical Entertainment (auditory perception):** Harp player and/or string players.

**Dance (visual-spatial perception):** A parent volunteer teaches families line dancing.

**Refreshments (gustatory and olfactory perception):** Foods that resemble lines (pretzel sticks, liquorice sticks, breadsticks, carrot sticks and curls, spaghetti).

# Reflection Page

## Reviewing Sensory Perception

Define each of the sensory perception areas and give an example of an open-ended activity that will develop skill in that area.

| | |
|---|---|
| Visual perception | Gustatory perception |
| Auditory perception | Olfactory perception |
| Tactile Perception | Thermic perception |
| Baric perception | Stereognostic perception |

# Reflection Page

## Selecting Sensory Objects, Materials, and Experiences

Choose a place such as your home, backyard, a park, or a store. Make a list of things that have interesting sensory qualities. Next to each item, record what sense or senses it will stimulate. Think of how you would introduce the item to young children and write down one or two things you would say to alert the child to its sensory qualities.

| Sensory Item | Sense Stimulated | Rich Verbal Interaction |
|---|---|---|
|  |  |  |

Review your list. Which ones are suitable for infants, toddlers, preschoolers, or primary children? Choose one item and write a two-part sensory perceptual objective for it. (See Appendix B for directions.)

*Sensory perceptually—the child will . . .*

_____

_____

_____

_____

*I will know this is happening when I observe the child . . .*

_____

_____

_____

_____

_____

_____

_____

# Reflection Page

## Designing A Big Book That Entices the Senses

A big book is the perfect size to read to a group of small children. The large pictures can be easily seen by everyone. However, you will not find big books on every topic you may need, nor will the books exactly fit the needs of your children. The ideal solution is to use your creativity and make your own or with older children have them make them.

**Guidelines for Creating a Big Book that Entices the Senses**

1.   Select one of the senses.

2.   Limit the book to five or six one-sided pages.

3.   Use just a few words.

4.   Illustrations should be made using materials that spark the senses.

5.   Illustrations should be large, bold, and simple. Avoid cute, stereotypical, or cartoon-like drawings. Better yet have the children help make the pictures.

6.   Plan the book so the children can interact with it. For example, include pockets that contain hidden shapes or holes to look through.

7.   Make the pages from heavy oak tag, poster board, or corrugated cardboard. Join the pages with metal, loose-leaf rings.

**Suggested Subjects for Your Big Book**

| Colors | Sounds Around Us | Things We Taste |
|--------|------------------|-----------------|
| Patterns | Textures | Smells We Like |
| Shapes | Things to Look At | Things to Touch |

# Reflection Page

## Observation: A Sensory Experience

Choose one of the senses, and design a sensory experience for children. Present the activity to two or three children, and record what the children do.

**Date of observation:** _____      **Length of observation:** _____

**Ages of children:** _____      **Size of group:** _____

1.  Describe the sensory stimulus and what you said.

    _____

    _____

    _____

2.  What is the first thing the children do? How long do the children investigate the activity?

    _____

    _____

    _____

3.  What do the children say?

    _____

    _____

    _____

4.  Analysis: Using the information in this chapter and what you learned from the observation, defend the inclusion of sensory arts activities in an early childhood setting.

    _____

    _____

    _____

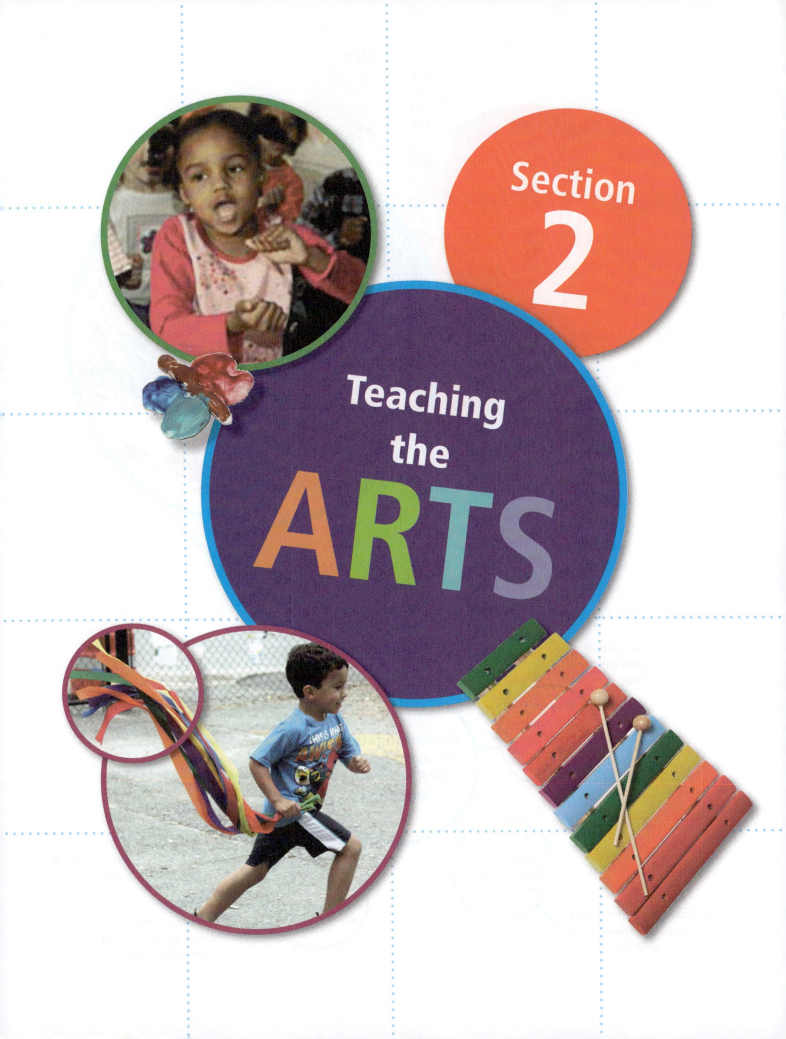

Section
2

Teaching
the
ARTS

Chapter

**5**

Coming Together Through the Arts

Select arts activities that develop children's abilities to work with others in joyful classroom communities.

Plan arts activities that develop social-emotional skills.

Creating a Caring Community

Planning Curriculum to Achieve Important Goals

**Coming Together Through the Arts DAP Learning Objectives**

Establishing Reciprocal Family Relationships

Assessing Children's Development and Learning

Teaching to Enhance Development and Learning

Evaluate the social-emotional developmental needs of all children.

Explain ways to use the arts to form reciprocal relationships.

Identify ways to develop cooperative behavior, nurture cultural respect, and address special needs.

## Young Artists Creating

"Your monkey has really long legs."

"So does yours."

"That's because he's trying to climb up this tree."

"My person is up in the air. He's jumping. You need long legs to do that."

"Yep. My monkey is going to jump when he gets to the top of the tree."

"Oops, the paint is dripping."

"Hurry. Catch it before it runs over Sari's picture."

"Sari will be mad if the paint drips on her dog."

"You are working hard on your paintings for our mural," says the teacher. "I see that you have used two different sizes of brushes."

"Yes, I used Mandie's little brush to paint the buttons, and she used my big brush to paint the long, long legs."

"See," says the teacher, "When we share things, we have more choices of things to use in our art."

## How Can Young Artists Work Together?

Some of the most joyful arts experiences children can have are those in which they work in a group to create something great together—a mural, a box robot, a musical revue, or an original dance. Working together for a common purpose forges children into a group. It becomes "our mural," "our robot," "our songs," or "our dance." It is not surprising that so many of the "class-building activities" of cooperative learning programs are based in the arts. It is easy to incorporate the ideas and skill levels of each individual into an arts activity. Using themes and providing opportunities for arts projects are other ways to foster social-emotional development and promote group bonding.

### Developing Social-Emotional Skills

Social-emotional skills are the basis of rich, rewarding human relationships and an important focus in the early childhood classroom. Research with preschool children indicates that strong social-emotional learning profiles are associated with high social and academic performance ratings (Denham et al., 2012). For example, preschoolers with a high level of social-emotional control have been shown to have higher academic performance in first grade (Neubauer et al., 2012; Walker & Henderson, 2012).

Social-emotional skills include:

- **Confidence.** Being able to recognize our emotions, to understand how emotions affect our thoughts and actions, and to perceive ourselves in positive and realistic ways. Children's beliefs about themselves are influenced by their positive and negative experiences with the adults around them, and the way their culture, social class, religion, and gender are treated (Schiller, 2009).

- **Self-control.** Being able to control our feelings and actions so we can focus full attention on a task, particularly in stressful situations. Self-regulation is strongly associated with adjustment to school, cognitive competence, and positive classroom behavior (Allan & Lonegan, 2011; Garner & Waajid, 2012; Neuenschwander et al., 2012).

- **Empathy.** The ability to recognize and identify with the feelings of others, to trust others, and to

The arts provide time and space for children to learn to work with each other in joyful ways.

Copyright © 2015 Cengage Learning®

## The Arts and Social-Emotional Development

As children mature, their ability to control their behavior and interact effectively with others increases. However, not all children proceed at the same rate. Some children may struggle to focus and wait. Others may have difficulty recognizing the feelings of others and sharing. Children with physical disabilities or who have suffered trauma may lack the ability to communicate their own feelings or to interact effectively with others. Bullying, eating disorders, depression, delinquency, and other problems are associated with poor social-emotional skills often stemming from early childhood (Goleman, 2007, 2009).

Direct teaching of social-emotional skills by integrating them into daily teaching makes a difference

find joy in engaging with them. We are all born with the capacity for empathy. Infants show sensitivity to others at birth, crying in concern when another baby cries (Goleman, 2009), and the part of the brain that feels pain reacts when a child sees another in pain (Willis, 2012). But like creativity, empathy needs to be nourished. Children who have difficulty understanding and responding to the feelings of others are less stable emotionally and less popular (Panfile & Laible, 2012). Lack of empathy and not caring about others is strongly linked to bullying behaviors (Kokkinos & Kipritsi, 2012).

**Cooperation.** Being able to communicate our thoughts and feelings, to work well with others, and to manage social conflict in effective ways. Taking turns, sharing, and helping others are the keystones to better school adjustment and later success in the workplace.

### Teacher Tip

#### STAGES OF SOCIAL PLAY

Regardless of their age, children exhibit different levels of play depending not only on their social and cognitive development, but also on their previous experiences interacting with others. Observing how children play by themselves and with others can give us a better idea of their social skills.

**Observing:** The child watches others playing. This might be found in an infant who is not yet physically capable of joining in or in a child who is new to a group.

**Solitary play:** The child plays by him- or herself. The level of play can range from very simple, such as shaking a toy, to intense, focused imaginary play.

**Parallel play:** The child plays alongside another child, perhaps with very similar toys, but the children do not interact with each other. Parallel play usually begins around the ages of two to three years.

**Cooperative play:** Children play together first in pairs and then in larger groups. In cooperative play children develop language skills as they communicate ideas, needs, and desires. They develop social skills as they learn to share, come to agreement, and take group action. Cooperative play usually appears around the ages of three to four years.

**Organized play:** The ability to participate in games that have rules and winners, such as board games and sports, occurs slowly. It begins to develop around the ages of six to seven, but is most fully developed in eight- and nine-year-olds.

(Willis & Schiller, 2011). The arts provide a fertile ground for doing so because of the natural way they fit into children's play. When activities are creative and open-ended they allow safe risk taking, provide opportunities to express feelings and strengthen self-confidence. Depending on the age of the child and the type of play the child is involved in, there are many ways we can foster social-emotional development through the arts.

**Infants.**  Babies begin life totally self-centered. For example, infants know when they are hungry and demand to be fed regardless of the time of day or night. But as infants mature they slowly become aware that they are separate individuals and show increasing awareness of other people around them. Newborn infants, for example, have been shown to look longer at faces with eyes open than closed, as well as at those with a direct gaze as opposed to those looking toward the side (Bower, 2002). Starting at two to three weeks, infants imitate adult facial expressions and hand movements with increasing sophistication (Bower, 2003). Most of the play of infants is **solitary play** or **observing** the play of others.

Erik Erikson (1963), in his classic analysis of children's social-emotional development, characterizes this period as one in which infants learn to trust other people. With attentive loving care from their caregivers, they will come to see other people as important companions and resources as they explore their world. It is not surprising, therefore, that the arts play

a vital role in developing infants' social skills. Singing and moving together, looking at pictures in a book, and engaging in pretend play with a more knowledgeable peer or adult help infants learn how to explore and create joyfully in an atmosphere of trust.

**Toddlers.**  Children from about eighteen months to three years are, according to Erikson, in the stage of autonomy versus shame and doubt. Toddlers want to be independent and in control, but cling to their caregiver when faced with new stimuli. They may see a toy they want and nothing short of physical restraint will prevent them from grabbing it from another child, or they may hide behind an adult when the booming drums pass by in a parade.

Toddlers work best in situations where they can pursue their arts explorations under the watchful eyes of caregivers. Adults can promote social growth by providing activities in which toddlers can work alongside others but have their own materials and space. Setting up activities in which two toddlers or a toddler and an older child are painting at adjoining easels or are smashing playdough together helps toddlers learn that they can work in close proximity to other children. Toddlers often engage in **parallel play** in which they imitate the actions of a child sitting near them (Einon, 1985). Imitation is one of the ways that children learn skills and behaviors. Adults and other children serve as artistic role models for the young child. One child will begin to pound the clay, and another child will imitate the same action. One child will see another shaking a tambourine and will demand one, too.

**Preschoolers.**  By the age of three, children are beginning to play together in **cooperative play.** They will take on roles in pretend play and will work together to build a tower. At this stage children can work together on all kinds of arts projects, from accompanying a song with handmade instruments to painting a mural. They become enraptured by the excitement of the collective moment and yet are interested in and "see" only the part they personally created. Group arts activities for these children, therefore, do not have the same meaning as those designed for older children and adults in which ideas are arrived at jointly and the project is viewed as a whole. Young preschoolers develop confidence by working on projects that do not have definite end goals but instead allow each child to play an individual part in the process.

Playing side by side and watching each other is one way infants learn social-emotional skills.

**Kindergartners.** When children gain the ability to value and differentiate their own products from those of others, their **cooperative play** becomes more complex. They can start to see that each contribution is a part of something larger—a whole—that is different from each small part but is still partially theirs. Teachers can tell when children reach this stage, because they start to notice the artwork of the other children and will comment, "That is my friend's painting," or "That is Cheri's," when referring to a piece of art they see. They use the terms "we did" instead of "I did" when referring to group projects like "We put on a puppet show" or "we're floating like astronauts." They can identify who created the different parts of a project or played different roles. When children reach this stage, they are ready for more cooperative group activities in which each child works on a designated part of the project, sharing supplies or space.

**Primary age.** By this age children are capable of planning ahead of time what will be needed to accomplish their goal and which part of the project they will work on. At the stage of **organized play** groups begin to set tasks, make schedules, and assign jobs to group members. However, they may still need adult guidance in learning how to incorporate the ideas of each member in a gracious way.

Primary students, who are busy learning about the broader world, enjoy working on long-term projects that involve a common idea, such as turning the classroom into a rainforest complete with a painted mural background, life-size painted animals and paper trees and bushes, accompanied by authentic Brazilian rhythms played on handmade instruments. They can perform parts in a play they have written, enjoy choral reading and group singing, learn folk dances together, and perform in small instrumental groups.

**Did You Get It?**

**If you were to plan arts activities based on Erikson's analysis of social-emotional development, which of the following would you suggest for toddlers?**

a. Ensure that toddlers work on artistic activities alone.

b. Make two toddlers sit together and share materials and space.

c. Expect toddlers to cooperate with other members of a group.

d. Have toddlers work individually in close proximity with others

Take the full quiz on CourseMate

## How Do We Create a Positive Social-Emotional Climate Through the Arts?

As with creativity, social-emotional skills flourish in an environment where children feel self-confident, where they are relaxed, and where they feel secure. A positive social climate develops when children feel that their ideas and feelings are accepted and valued. Qualities such as verbal encouragement, modeling empathy, using emotionally expressive language, and showing emotional warmth to each child have been shown to increase confidence, self-control, empathy, and cooperativeness (Spivak & Farran, 2012).

We model acceptance by giving appropriate time, attention, and assistance to every child. The open-ended nature of the creative arts provides the perfect setting to do this. While engaged in arts activities, we can develop social-emotional skills by:

- Modeling self-control by remaining calm and showing patience in trying situations.

▶❚❚ **TeachSource Video Case 5.1**

**2-5 Years: Play in Early Childhood**

Watch this video showing children at different stages of play. What arts activities would you select for them to foster social-emotional skills?

**Watch on CourseMate**

- Communicating confidence and empathy by using words like we, us, ours, caring, and sharing on a daily basis.

- Providing opportunities to practice self-control and cooperative skills by offering arts activities that inspire children to want to work together.

- Giving positive feedback when children show confidence, act kindly, wait patiently, and share.

- Asking reflective questions such as: Are the children working joyfully? Are they aware of each other's needs?

## Using Positive Guidance to Promote Appropriate Behavior

Working together requires children to exert self-control. Groups of children involved in well-designed arts activities are usually so engrossed that behavioral issues do not play a large role. However, there will always be occasions when children overstep the boundaries of safety and propriety. Responding to inappropriate behavior during arts activities requires a gentle approach that addresses the behavior without restricting creativity nor crushing self-confidence. You can foster safe, creative behavior in three ways: **prevention, redirection,** and **removal.**

### Prevention.

1. Offer only those activities, props, materials, and tools appropriate for the child's skill level.

2. Keep materials and tools not on the child's skill level out of reach and out of sight.

3. Provide each child with adequate space in which to work and move. Dangerous behavior often happens when children accidentally bump or push each other.

4. Provide sufficient supplies to prevent the children from grabbing for that one special item.

5. Closely supervise the children while they work, especially during initial explorations of new materials and tools.

6. Keep group sizes small until the children know how to work safely with a particular technique, material, or tool.

7. Keep arts supplies, musical instruments, and dramatic play materials orderly so that children do not have to dig or grab for what they want. Be sure there is sufficient open space for creative movement.

8. Model safe movement and handling of tools and supplies at all times.

### Redirection.

1. If a child begins to act or to use something unsafely, gently restate the safe way to act or use it, and model the correct behavior, if necessary. For example, if the child puts playdough up to her mouth, say, "Playdough is not food, we use it to make art."

2. Older children can be asked to restate or read the rules or the directions given for the activity.

## Integrating the Arts

### COMMUNITY BUILDING THROUGH THE ARTS

Drama and movement activities can be used to help children get to know one another better and strengthen the class community. Here are some examples.

*Name Game.* Sit in a circle and have the children call out their names. Repeat having the children call out their names in a new way each time—using a different "voice," adding a movement, showing an emotion, or making a funny face.

*Greeting Each Other.* Provide two greeting words, such as *hi* and *bye*. Have the children move around and greet each other. Repeat, adding a movement or singing the greeting.

*What Happened?* Have the children sit in a circle. Ask the first child, "What did you do when _____?" adding an appropriate phrase, such as when you woke up, or when you met a new friend. That child then turns and asks the one sitting next to him or her the same question. Continue around the circle. When children are familiar with the game, try some fantasy phrases, such as "What did you do when your house started dancing?"

*Watch Me.* Stand so that everyone can see everyone else. The leader mimes a brief action, such as meeting someone and shaking hands. The whole group copies the action. The leader then points to another child to be the leader who mimes a new action. Vary the activity by adding a sound to go with the action or mime the next logical step.

**For more group building activities, see *Community Building Arts Activities* on CourseMate.**

With gentle guidance from the teacher, sharing space and materials can help children learn how to work together.

Copyright © 2015 Cengage Learning®

3. If two children want the same supply or tool, provide other similar ones or help them set up a fair way to share it.

**Removal.**

1. When a child's behavior is developmentally appropriate and not unsafe, but annoying to the other children, such as when a toddler draws on other children's papers, gently move the child to a place slightly away from the others but too far away to reach someone else's workspace. Put the move in a positive light by saying, "You will have more space to draw over here."

2. If a child persists in unsafe behavior, redirect her or him to another activity that is more appropriate for that behavior. For example, if a child is snapping the scissors open and closed, explain that the scissors are too sharp to be used that way, but that she can open and close the toy pliers. Remove the scissors, and replace with the pliers.

3. When it is obvious that the activity, tools, or materials are inappropriate for the developmental level of the children, redirect them to another interesting activity, and then remove those supplies. Just because a particular activity may be

recommended for children of a certain age or has been successful for others does not mean that it will be perfect for these particular children. It is better to say that this is not working and end it, than to set up a potentially dangerous situation or one that will cause children to misbehave.

---

**Did You Get It?**

**In which of the following cases is a teacher using a redirection strategy to foster a desired behavior in students?**

a. Sara arranges for the toddlers in her class to work together in groups and share materials.

b. Manuel teaches his class an action song and has them mimic the actions.

c. Tyra sees Michelle grab a drumstick from the child next to her so she moves Michelle to a place on the rug away from the other children.

d. Leanna observes Carla scribbling on the table and records it on her behavior chart.

**Take the full quiz on CourseMate**

---

## How Should Group Arts Activities Be Organized?

Although each child needs to explore the arts in a personally meaningful way, children also need to discover that the arts are not just for individual self-expression. This is best learned by participating in arts experiences as a member of a group. Open-ended creative arts group projects allow children at different ages and skill levels to work together to create something uniquely different from what they would create on their own. When carefully planned, we can participate in many of these activities alongside our children. Great satisfaction is felt when we are part of a successful group arts activity.

Group art activities directly address social-emotional learning. Working with others means children have to control their feelings as they share space, time, and materials with others who have different abilities and needs from their own. Children become more understanding of others' special needs and more appreciative of the creative ideas of those whose background and cultural experiences differ from their own.

Accomplishing this requires the creation of an integrated cohesive unit in which both children and teacher smoothly work together. The challenge of good teaching is to take a group of unique, ever-changing individuals with different levels of social-emotional skills and turn them into a caring community.

We set the stage for group arts activities that are fun, flexible, relaxed, and based on a shared experience when we

**Make it fun.** Include an element of fun when working together. Songs, laughter, and excitement should all be part of the experience.

**Are flexible and open to innovation.** It is the group experience that is important, not the finished product. Value spontaneity and be willing to change course. Avoid the trap of planning an end use for the cooperative project before it is started or having children practice lines of a play over and over for a formal performance.

**Are facilitators.** The teacher's role in a group arts project is to be the guide, not the director. Provide the location, the materials, the excitement, and the beginning of an idea; then let the participants take over. In many activities teachers can participate themselves! The result will be a true expression of each individual's creative moment as a part of that group, at that time, and in that place.

**Reduce stress.** Well-designed group arts activities can provide an excellent way to introduce children to working in a group. However, it is important that children be familiar with the art form and materials to be used in the project and that they have had practice experiences with them. A group activity is not the place to explore something for the first time, but instead provides an opportunity to take pride in using a skill and creating something that requires a level of comfort and control. It is also vital that these projects be designed as open-ended activities, so that every child can participate fully.

**Provide a shared experience.** For preschoolers and up, a collective activity needs to start out with everyone in the group sharing an experience (WOW). This common experience will combine the ideas and actions of each child into a unified whole. The experience should be one in which children participate directly, otherwise they will come to rely on stereotypes and teachers' examples rather than thinking on their own.

The shared experience forms the basis for planning and carrying out murals, creative dances, original songs and music, dramatic play centers, and group sculptures. For example, after a trip to the zoo, children share what they saw, and the teacher makes a class chart of their observations. That chart then becomes the source of ideas for what children will put in their re-creation of a zoo in their classroom.

The shared experience can be the following:

1. a field trip
2. an event that occurs, such as rain, snow, or a parade
3. observation of something real, such as nature objects, animals, machines, or a store
4. reading a story or poem together
5. a class project topic

Some examples of shared experiences and related arts activities include

- Walking in the rain and then making a drip paint mural
- Looking at tire tracks in the mud or snow and then dipping the wheels of toy cars and trucks in paint and rolling them over a big sheet of paper.
- Visiting a flower shop and then making a flower store dramatic play area

**Encourage peer modeling.** Because imitation is one way that children learn new skills, slightly more advanced peers provide better models for young children than adults, whose skills may be far greater than children need or are capable of imitating. Working together on a group arts project provides the perfect opportunity for children to learn from one another.

## Organizing Group Arts Activities

Select activities that each individual, no matter his or her ability level, can participate in fairly equally.

**Group size.** Group size is a critical factor in determining if children will work together successfully. At the Reggio Emilia preprimary schools the teachers have found that different group sizes create different dynamics. For example, pairs of children engage in intense social and cognitive interactions. The addition of a third child can produce solidarity, but also conflict. Groups of four and five have other dynamics (Edwards, Gandini, & Forman, 2011). A general rule should be: the younger the children, the smaller the group.

**Mixed age and ability groups.** Groups that contain a range of ages actually offer one of the best settings in which to develop cooperative arts behaviors. The older children and adults can model respect for each other's work and at the same time supervise the more impulsive little ones.

1. Have members of the group take turns working in pairs or in groups of three. Pair a more expert peer with one who has less experience. The older members should help the younger ones find a place to work and materials to use.

2. In the visual arts allow the youngest group members to go first, because older members will be able to work around one another, whereas the young children may not "see" the work already there and may work on top of it. In the performance arts, the older ones should go first to provide role models for the younger ones.

Arts activities provide a way for groups of children to interact creatively. Using their imaginations, this group of kindergartners turn themselves into a rock band using blocks and rhythm instruments.

## Examples of Group Arts Activities

Types of group arts activities are found in all the arts areas and are limited only by our imaginations. A few ideas are listed as follows. Find more in the Exploring Arts section of this book.

**Drum circle.** Starting with a shared experience such as rain drumming on the roof, the rumble of a train or traffic passing by, or the sound of their feet running on the pavement, give each child a hand drum or show them how they can make different drumming sounds by patting their upper arms, thighs, chests, or the floor. Sit in a circle and start tapping a rhythm. Go around the circle and have each child lead with a new rhythm. With practice this can be accomplished without a break in the drumming.

**Group sculptures.** When many hands contribute to an artwork, incredible energy results. Group sculptures make lively activities for mixed-age groups. Even the youngest child can be helped to place a part on a group sculpture. Group sculptures can be simple and immediate. For example, children on the playground can collect stones or sticks and arrange them into a design on the pavement. Wood scraps collected as part of a visit to a carpenter's shop or trip to a lumberyard can become an amazing structure.

Group sculptures can be built from any easily handled and joined three-dimensional material. Try boxes, paper bags stuffed with newspaper, chenille stems, straws, wooden blocks, corrugated cardboard, telephone wire, or Styrofoam packing material.

Just like all group arts activities, constructions need to grow out of a shared experience. For example, visit a sculpture garden, and then come back and build a class sculpture out of corrugated cardboard. If children are using straws or toothpicks in a counting activity, finish by having the children glue them together into a linear sculpture using a piece of Styrofoam for a base. Walk through the neighborhood and identify different buildings. Then build a model of the community using boxes or pieces of wood.

As children work, encourage them to consider how their part will go with the rest. Describe the work

## Making Plans

**OPEN-ENDED ACTIVITY FEELING FACES GROUP ACTIVITY**

**WHO?**     Group composition age(s): Suitable for toddlers and up

**WHEN?**    Time frame: Depending on age, children will work from 20 minutes to several days.

**WHY?**     Objectives: Children will develop

- physically, by using the large muscles of the arm and the small muscles of the hand to manipulate the various art materials and the muscles of the face to make different expressions. (Bodily-Kinesthetic)
- socially, by interacting with a caring adult, and by sharing materials, space, and ideas with others. (Interpersonal)
- emotionally, by examining their own feelings and those of others in a pleasurable stress-free setting. (Intrapersonal)
- perceptually, by using their senses to observe and select materials for their faces and arranging the faces spatially on a background in concert with others. (Spatial)
- language skills, by using words they know and learning new ones to describe their emotions and those of others. (Linguistic)
- cognitively, by classifying facial features by emotional expression (Logical-Mathematical)
- arts awareness, by manipulating the elements of color and shape to create an expressive face. (Content Standard 1 & 2)

**WHERE?**   Setup:  On a rug for a large group. At table for a small group. One-on-one for special needs.

**WHAT?**    Materials: Markers or crayons, colored papers in different skin colors (white paper plates can be used if children paint them skin tones first), yarn and white glue, large hand mirror(s) (unbreakable), a long sheet of kraft paper long enough for everyone to add at least one face. Chart paper. For extensions: Clippings of faces from magazines, tubes, or cardboard strips.

**HOW?**     Procedure:
WOW Warm-Up: Hold up a mirror and make faces in it. Explore and name different emotions. Let children take turns looking in mirrors and making faces. Ask: "How do our mouth, eyebrows, eyes, and nose look when we feel happy or sad?" and so on.

What to Do and Say: Name feelings that go with different expressions. Encourage children to mirror expressions as you talk about the feelings. For toddlers and up, build emotional literacy by starting a Ways I Feel list including not only pleasant feelings and angry ones, but also neutral feelings like calm, patient, and comfortable (Adams, 2011). For toddlers, provide face-shaped paper in skin tones and let them draw eyes, noses, and mouths. For older children, put out materials at the art center and invite children to create faces showing different feelings using the yarn for hair. When done have children sit together in a group with their faces and take turns gluing them to the long paper to create a mural about feelings. Make cartoon "word bubbles" and have children share what their face is saying.

Transition out: Look at the mural with the children. For younger children, ask them to name the different feelings they see. For older ones discuss places where you see large groups of people, such as at a sporting event, a parade, or a circus. Imagine where your "crowd of faces" might be. Ask: At those events does everybody all feel the same? If there is space, invite children to add more faces when they wish.

**WHAT LEARNED?**   Assessment: Can the children name more feelings after the activity? Do they change the mouths and eyes to show different feelings? When they see another child showing a feeling, can they identify it, and are they more empathetic? Do they use more words about feelings in their play? Do they share materials and space fairly? What feelings are expressed most easily? Which ones are left out? Which feelings were the most difficult to express? *Reflection:* Do I see any expressions of bias? What did the children learn from this activity? What activity should be offered next and why?

**NEXT?**    Extensions: **Stick puppets:** Encourage them to make more faces. They can add a cardboard stick or tube to a face and use their stick puppet to tell stories about feelings. **Literature connection:** Read stories that show children struggling with their feelings such as *When Sophie Gets Angry, Really Really Angry* by Molly Bangs (2004) or Jamie Lee Curtis' *Today I Feel Silly* (1998).

as it changes with each addition: "Look, it's getting taller." Respond positively to each child's contribution: "Your piece helps make it stronger."

**Mosaics.** Because a mosaic is a work of art made from small pieces glued to a cardboard or piece of wood to create a picture or shapes, it is eminently suitable for group arts projects with young children. A wide variety of objects can be used ranging from stones to leaves to cancelled stamps to Styrofoam packing peanuts. Collecting the objects and sorting them by color or shape can be the shared experience from which a mosaic can grow.

**Murals.** The word **mural,** although technically defined as a "wall painting," in literature on children's art, usually refers to a very large, two-dimensional piece of artwork created by a group of children. That is the definition used here. Murals are ideal group projects for children and adults of all ages. They can either be created on the spot in response to an exciting experience, or carefully planned in response to a field trip, study topic, or piece of literature.

Any number of children can contribute to a mural as long as the background is big enough. Do not hesitate to add to the background or to create several murals at the same time, if necessary. Murals enable children of different levels and abilities to work together successfully. One toddler can work with an older child or adult. Preschoolers can work in groups of three and four. Primary students can work in groups of four to six.

**Quilts.** Quilts are ideal for creating a sense of belonging and fit perfectly into teaching units about family and community. Show a finished quilt as the initial shared experience, and if possible, tell the story of how it came to be made. Read a book about quilts such as Anne Jonas' *The Quilt* (1984) or, for older children, Valerie Flournoy's *The Patchwork Quilt* (1985). Children's families can be asked to contribute a square of fabric or help decorate a square of muslin with crayon drawings or with fabric shapes attached with iron on facing. Sewn together the quilt can be used in the story corner or dramatic play areas to soften surroundings and provide comfort. Paper versions of quilts can also be made.

Shared experiences lay the groundwork for successful group activities. After reading the book *Where the Wild Things Are* by Maurice Sendak, a group of children aged four to seven created this mural, working together to paint a night sky background and then adding their own imaginative "wild things" which they drew, cut out, and glued to the background.

**Rhythm Band.** Following a shared experience such as watching a band in a parade or listening to recorded band music, create your own band. Making noise together is a wonderful opportunity for children to practice self-control and cooperation. After children choose their sound maker, teach them a simple hand signal for starting and stopping. Practice following the signals for starting and stopping together. Once they know how, have children take turns conducting the band. When everyone is playing together, try marching around the school.

For more ideas for group arts activities, *see Shared Experiences and Group Arts Activities* on CourseMate.

## Teachers Working Together

Educators also benefit from working alongside their peers. Teaching is often seen as an individual affair. We need to meet often with our peers to share ideas and frustrations. Projects are easier to plan when there are two or three minds brainstorming. We need to involve parents as partners in our programs. Foot painting, creative dancing, and nature collages are easier to manage when there are extra hands. Everyone needs to come together in order to grow together. The program will be richer, and the young artists will show more growth.

## Classroom Technology

### *CAPTURE THE PROCESS*

When engaged in group art projects, remember to record the process. Digital cameras, smartphones, and tablets are exciting supplements to more hands-on methods.

- **Draw it:** Encourage children to make drawings showing the sequence of steps they went through. Clarissa Willis and Pam Schiller, for example, recommend developing self-confidence by asking a child who has succeeded at a challenging task draw a picture of the experience and put it on a wall labeled "I did it" (2011, p. 42).

- **Record it:** Take notes or record what children say during the process. For group-created visual artworks display or play a recording of the children's own words next to the finished piece. For music, drama, and creative dance, display photographs with their words as captions.

- **Capture it:** Take photographs and make video recordings as they work.

- **Reflect on it:** Record the children's description of what they did on an **experience chart,** in a documentation panel, or in e-story form or PowerPoint.

### Did You Get It?

**Which of the following would you use as a guideline for organizing a group activity?**

a. The teacher should plan an end use for the cooperative project before initiating it.

b. The teacher's role should be to guide and not direct.

c. The teacher should not participate in group events.

d. A general rule should be the younger the children, the larger the group.

**Take the full quiz on CourseMate**

## How Are Children with Special Needs Included in the Arts Program?

Because of the open-ended nature of well-designed arts activities, children with special needs can participate fully in most arts programs and group arts activities, often without many modifications. If necessary, changes can be made in the tools and environment to allow active participation. The other children also need to be encouraged to accept and support those with special needs.

## Defining Special Needs

Children with special needs are a tremendously diverse group. Some have obvious disabilities, and others have disabilities that cannot be seen by the casual observer. The **Individuals with Disabilities Act** (Public Law 105–17) has identified ten categories of children who can receive special education services. These include children with learning disabilities, speech and language disabilities, mental retardation, emotional disturbance, multiple disabilities, autism, hearing disabilities, visual disabilities, orthopedic disabilities, and other health disabilities.

In addition, the law mandates that children with disabilities be educated in the least restrictive environment. As a result of this law, many children with disabilities will be found in regular educational settings (Heward, 2000). This has led to many inclusion programs for young children in which special provisions are made so that all children can achieve success.

## Meeting Special Needs

Because children with special needs have unique developmental paths, inclusive early childhood programs need to focus on ways to help them become engaged in learning and in interacting socially with peers. Many of the techniques suggested for working with mixed ages and abilities will also help children with special needs be successful.

**Select open-ended activities.** Exploratory arts activities, which entice children with colors, textures, sounds, movements, and unexpected results, and which can be done alongside peers who are also exploring, can be vital to this process. Arts activities provide an opportunity for children to apply skills needed for further development. Grasping a marker or paintbrush prepares a child for holding a pencil for writing. Pushing and pulling playdough strengthens finger, hand, and arm muscles. Playing a xylophone improves hand-eye coordination.

## Special Needs

### • INCLUSIVE PRACTICE •

Inclusive practice asks us to look at how we can adapt the environment and the activities we offer so that diverse learners can participate to their full extent.

Diverse learners

- are not all the same; they have different needs and abilities
- have the same rights and responsibilities as other children
- are still part of the class even though their ways of performing and learning may be different

Inclusive arts activities

- are available and accessible to **all** students irrespective of class, gender, ethnicity, cultural background, or disability
- are adjusted to meet individual learning requirements
- match the materials and environment to the child's needs

Inclusive teaching

- is proactive, flexible, and reflective
- recognizes that students and teachers process, store, organize, and retrieve information in different ways
- takes into account a diversity of learning styles and learning preferences
- considers the way in which materials will be used
- considers the way in which materials are delivered
- focuses not on the disability, but on the effect the disability has on the student's ability to access, learn, and demonstrate knowledge and skills

Gentle assistance can help a child with special needs participate in arts activities. Here an adult helps a child clap along with a song.

## Using the Arts to Facilitate Growth

Children with disabilities gain social-emotional, language, and cognitive skills more readily when these behaviors are part of play (Davis, Kilgo, & Gamel-McCormick, 1998). Because the arts share so many qualities with children's natural play, they provide a wonderful way to help children with special needs improve in these needed skills.

This is important because children with developmental delays need more time and practice to accomplish educational goals. Therefore, every minute that the child is in an educational setting must focus on the basic skills and behaviors that the child needs to develop and learn. Teachers can facilitate needed development by joining the child in an arts activity and using the time to focus on general instructional goals. For example, if the goal for a particular child is to learn to ask for things rather than pointing, then as part of a collage activity, the teacher may sit beside the child and place some intriguing collage materials to the far side in order to elicit a request from the child.

Research also indicates that when a child talks more, language skills improve (Hart & Risley, 1995). For children with speech delays and disabilities, the teacher may encourage verbalization by asking targeted questions about their creative work and by

**Provide assistance.** When a child needs additional help to be successful, try to provide it in a way that does not draw a lot of attention. Pairing a child with special needs with a knowledgeable child or adult, for example, who can either get the supplies or help the child move in a dance activity without constant teacher direction reduces the chance of the child being singled out.

**Use role models.** Because the child may need to approach the task differently from others, model the method or action in many different ways to the whole group.

## Special Needs

### • BEING THE MOST SUCCESSFUL •

Linda Mitchell (2004) suggests using the MOST (**M**aterials + **O**bjectives + **S**pace + **T**ime) strategies in planning arts activities for all children, including those with special needs.

**M** Choose materials carefully so that all children will be successful using them. Make modifications as needed to meet individual requirements.

**O** Build into the activity objectives taken from individual children's **Individualized Education Plan (IEP)**.

**S** Change the classroom setting to provide the best use of space for every child. This may require designating certain areas for specific activities.

**T** Children with special needs may require more time to engage in and complete an activity.

responding to nonverbal child-initiated interactions by soliciting a verbal response. Talking about the child's creative process and work provides a non-threatening environment in which to do this.

## Adjusting the Activity

The teacher may also need to do a task analysis and break down arts activities into small steps so the child can achieve success. These steps can then be modeled and verbalized for the child, either one by one or in a series based on the child's needs. For example, an exploratory printmaking activity might be broken down into several parts:

1. The child selects a printmaking tool from a tray containing several.

2. The child dips it into the chosen paint color.

3. The child presses the tool onto paper that is taped to the table.

4. The child puts the tool back into the tray.

The steps are then repeated until the print is completed. At each of these steps, the guiding adult should give verbal and visual cues. With each succeeding repetition, the adult can withdraw some of the support until the child can carry out the tasks independently. Another method to help develop social skills with children with autism in the context

of an arts activity is to set up a small dramatic play group of two or three children and provide the child script cards with clues in pictures and words for the child to say during the activity (Ganz & Flores, 2010). Cards might say: "Ask _____ for a turn" or "Ask _____ what he's doing." During the activity the teacher can prompt the child as necessary and slowly withdraw as the child uses the social skills more independently.

## Getting Help

An important part of working with children with special needs is obtaining information and assistance from the child's family. Families play a major role in caring for the child, and they understand much about the child's needs and capabilities. They can share what interactions and modifications of the environment have been successful for them. In addition, an early intervention team or professionals with expertise in the child's area of need can also offer needed assistance.

## The Role of Arts Therapy

All children find emotional release through the expressive nature of music, drama, dance, and arts activities, so it is not surprising that some children may use the arts to work through traumatic experiences. For example, a child who has experienced a natural disaster may draw pictures of houses and trees that are then scribbled over or "destroyed," as happened in the disaster. Gradually, such pictures decrease as the child comes to terms with the occurrence.

For some children, however, the release of otherwise unexpressed feelings and thoughts may require adult help. A child whose pet was killed in an accident may draw increasingly bloody pictures, indicating that the incident is still very disturbing and that there is a need to work through these deep feelings.

Gerald Oster and Patricia Crone (2004) identify several reasons why the arts are a useful way to engage children for therapeutic and psychological assessment purposes.

1. It is less threatening than verbally expressing deep emotions.

2. It provides a product that can be discussed in a variety of ways.

3. The act of creating allows the child to fantasize and try out solutions to problems.

However, it is dangerous for untrained observers to make judgments about a child's emotional state based on just one or a few pieces of artwork. The constant use of one color of paint may simply reflect what color was available or closest to the child. Research indicates that many young children often use paint colors in the order that they are arranged at the easel (Winner, 1982, p. 151). Pictures of family members may reflect attempts by children to control their world. The parents may be shown small and the child huge, a new baby may be left out, or divorce and remarriage may not be reflected at all in the child's "family" portrait. On the other hand, the arrangement of images may just indicate how well the child controls the art medium.

Our role as teachers should be to allow children to use the arts as a personal way to express their thoughts and emotions—a safe place to show their feelings and, incidentally, give adults a peek inside of an often otherwise private world. However, in the case of serious traumatic experiences, arts therapy may be recommended. Arts therapy is a distinct field of study that requires expertise in both art and psychology. The **music, art,** or **drama therapist** functions as an educator who modifies arts activities to

## Special Needs

### • USING MODELING MATERIALS FOR EMOTIONAL RELEASE •

The creation of modeled forms is often accompanied by children's enthusiastic destruction. Pliant modeling materials give children the power to control a small part of their environment. Clay and playdoughs are regularly used by children to release strong feelings in an acceptable way. Clay, unlike other children, bossy adults, or precious belongings, can be hit and smashed, slapped, pinched, and poked, and torn apart and put together again. Children who are having difficulty controlling their social behavior benefit from redirecting this behavior to the forgiving clay.

meet the emotional needs of troubled children. Qualified arts therapists work with a team of professionals to interpret the child's artwork, based on many observations and interactions. They then provide healing arts activities.

## General Modifications for the Arts

All children with special needs are individually unique in terms of how they cope with arts materials and will require individualized adaptations. The following list provides some general ideas. Specific suggestions for each of the art forms will be found in the "Exploring the Arts" section of the book. See also Table 5-1.

| **TABLE 5–1** | **Examples of Ways to Adapt Arts Activities** | | | | |
|---|---|---|---|---|---|
| **Activity** | **Disability** | **Material Modification** | **IEP Objectives** | **Setting Modification** | **Time** |
| Painting | Physical | Use thick-handled brush wrapped in foam | Child will strengthen right arm | Paper will be hung on easel at wheelchair height | Activity will be during open-ended center time |
| Singing a song | Hearing disability | Add signing to song | Child will use sign language to communicate | Child will sit near teacher in circle | Repeat song several times, adding the signs |
| Creative dance | Visual disability | Have children hold hands and move in a circle | Child will hold head erect when walking | Circle will be marked on floor in brightly colored tape | Children will practice walking around the circle |
| Acting out story | Autism | Use familiar objects the child is comfortable with as props | Child will look at others when speaking | Use tape to mark where actors will stand | Before activity have child visit area and see where to stand |

### Meeting needs for muscular control.

1. Put trays across wheelchairs.

2. Provide wheelchair-height tables.

3. Make sure there is sufficient space for wheelchairs to join in creative dance activities.

4. Use pillows to position the child to better manipulate materials and participate in singing and musical activities.

5. Art tools such as crayons, markers, pencils, brushes, and pens, and musical instruments, such as drumsticks, rattles, bells, maracas, and triangles, can be wrapped in foam hair curlers to improve grip. Velcro pieces can be attached to a cotton glove and to the arts object.

6. Attach the drawing tool, paintbrush, or musical instrument to an arm, prosthesis, foot, or headgear. Some children without the use of their arms use their mouths. Drawing tools can be taped into cigarette holders, or a special holder can be made or purchased. Remember, children do not draw or make music with their hands, but with their minds.

7. To facilitate cutting, provide a rotary cutting wheel and a cutting mat instead of scissors.

8. Use no-spill paint containers and thickened paint. Choose brushes in a size that best matches the child's muscle control. Short, stubby brushes may work better than long-handled easel brushes. Foam brushes may make the paint easier to control.

### Meeting visual needs.

1. Place a screen or textured surface under the paper to add texture to drawn lines.

2. Use a fabric tracing or marking wheel to create a raised line. Place pads of newspaper or rubber mats beneath lightweight paper.

3. Use scented crayons and markers; add scents to paint and glue.

4. Provide many tactile materials.

5. Place arts materials and props in the same locations every time, and attach tactile, identifying symbols on supply containers. For example, attach an actual piece of each collage material to collage storage bins. This will allow children to develop independence in obtaining their own supplies.

6. If the child has some vision, find out which colors are easiest to see, and provide many materials in those colors. For example, fluorescent colors and reflective safety tapes may appeal to some children. Mark bold lines on the floor to guide the child during movement and dramatic activities.

### Behavioral and emotional needs.

1. Select activities that have few steps and instant results, such as modeling, painting, making sounds, and puppetry. Expect lots of exploration and physical expression of feelings.

2. For children who are easily distracted, provide work areas that allow plenty of space and that seem separate from the rest of the room.

3. Select and arrange arts supplies carefully to help limit distractions as well.

### Other assistance.

1. Some children who have visual or motor difficulties may need hand-over-hand assistance. Place a hand over the student's to assist with such skills as dipping the paintbrush into the container and then onto the paper, or dipping a finger into paste and then applying it to the object to be glued.

2. Some children may need their base paper taped to the table to keep it from moving or wrinkling when they work.

3. Add picture clues and labels.

4. Use real objects to further understanding (i.e., a real apple as opposed to a picture of one).

5. Incorporate children's communication devices into the activity. For example, a child could play a sound on a communication board to accompany a song.

6. Use multiple delivery modes. Say the directions, show the directions in pictures and words, use sign language, and act out the directions.

## Helping Other Children Accept Those with Special Needs

Although young children can be very accepting of individual differences, they may react in outspoken ways to things that are unfamiliar or strange. We need to be sensitive as we help children learn to live with all kinds of people.

1. Do not criticize children for expressing curiosity. When children notice and ask questions about disabilities and special equipment, answer matter-of-factly with a simple and accurate reply. It is important to be honest when answering. Use correct terminology whenever possible.

   Child:    *"Why does Jared need a special holder for his crayons?"*

   Teacher:  *"Jared uses a holder because he has trouble holding small objects tightly. Jared likes to draw like you do, but he has muscular dystrophy, so we figured out a way that he could do it."*

2. Do not deny differences, but help children see their shared similarities.

   Child:    *"Maya just makes noises with the xylophone."*

   Teacher:  *"Maya likes to make music, just like you do. She has learned how to do many things. Now she is learning how to play the xylophone. Would you like to play along on the drum with her?"*

3. Children need to become familiar with special equipment and devices but also need to learn to respect the equipment of a child with special needs. If possible, rent or borrow a variety of equipment for children to explore, but make it clear that they must respect the personal equipment of the child who must use it.

4. If children are comfortable doing so, have them explain how their special equipment helps them participate in the arts and why it is important to take care of it. If they cannot do this on their own, then have them demonstrate how the equipment is used while an adult explains.

5. Invite artists with disabilities to share their arts. Make sure they are prepared for the sometimes bold questions of children.

6. Reading books about children with special needs is another way to introduce and talk about how similarities and differences. For example, *Moses Goes to a Concert* by Issac Millman (1998) shows how children who are deaf can enjoy a concert.

### Did You Get It?

Aki is a first grade teacher. A child in a wheelchair joins his class. Which of the following would you recommend to Aki?

a. Eliminate all creative movement activities.

b. Have the child leave the room during dance activities.

c. Move the furniture and push the child around the room during creative movement activities.

d. Have the child watch a video of creative movement activities.

Take the full quiz on CourseMate

## How Can the Arts Be Used in Anti-Bias Activities?

Arts activities can be used to help children express their feelings about individual differences. They provide an opportunity for teachers to initiate a dialogue to correct mistaken beliefs and model respect and empathy for others.

In offering the arts to young children, teachers need to be sure that the choice of activities creates an environment in which children from all backgrounds feel comfortable and can be creative in their artwork. Children differ in their racial and ethnic backgrounds. Research shows that children begin to be aware of these individual differences by age two, and that between the ages of three and five they develop a sense of who they are and how they differ from others (Van Ausdale & Feagin, 2001). Before children can feel free to relax and express themselves in creative arts activities, they need to feel valued for who they are, not for how they look, talk, and behave. They need to be treated fairly and have their differences seen as strengths that enrich the learning of all of the children. The visual, physical, and tactile nature of the arts allows children, regardless of their differences, to explore and learn together. Children who speak different languages can learn by observing each other as they create with the arts. Because the arts are common to all cultures, it can be a vehicle through which cultural differences can be explored.

## Creating an Arts Environment that Celebrates Differences

Teachers must take action to encourage the development of an **anti-bias** atmosphere among children. They need to consider the materials they choose to supply and the pictures they display. Activities should be provided that foster discussion and the elimination of the misconceptions that are the basis of many prejudicial beliefs held by young children. The arts can be used in a variety of ways to support an anti-bias curriculum.

**Selecting anti-bias visual images and supplies.**  Children need to see and become familiar with people who look different from them. They also need to develop an authentic self-concept based on liking themselves without feeling superior to others (Derman-Sparks & Ramsey, 2006). Taking the following steps will help children do this:

1. Provide arts materials that reflect the wide range of natural skin tones. Paints, papers, playdough, and crayons in the entire range of skin colors need to be regularly available, along with the other colors.

2. Mirrors and photographs of themselves and their families should be available at all times for children to learn about themselves and each other.

3. Images of people who represent the racial and ethnic groups found in the community and in the larger society need to be displayed. There should be a balance in the images so that there is no token group. It is recommended that about half of the images should represent the background of the predominant group of children in the class. The remainder of the images should represent the rest of the diversity found in society (Derman-Sparks & the ABC Task Force, 1989).

4. When selecting visuals and posters, look for ones that show a range of people of different ages, genders, sizes, colors, and abilities. Display photos of people who are involved in activities that depict current life. Many prints are available that reflect this diversity, including those depicting arts from Haitian, African, African-American, Native American, Mexican, and Asian sources. (See Chapter 7 for suggestions and Appendix B for sources.)

5. Artworks, music, stories, and dances should represent artists of diverse backgrounds and time periods, including the present and counteract stereotypes. This is particularly important for Native Americans.

6. Illustrations in the books read to the children and available for them to use should also reflect society's diversity.

7. Stereotypical and inaccurate images should be removed from display in the room and used only in discussions of unfair representations of groups of people. Avoid so-called "multicultural" materials such as bulletin board kits and patterns that depict people from around the world wearing traditional clothing from the past. These materials leave children with the impression that, for example, all Native Americans wear leather and feathers, all Japanese wear kimonos, and all Africans wear dashikis.

**Selecting anti-bias activities.**  Arts activities can be chosen that help children acquire inner strength, empathy, a strong sense of justice, and the power to take action in the face of bias. Louise Derman-Sparks and Patricia Ramsey note that there are four basic goals of anti-bias education.

1. Help children develop self-confidence and a positive group identity with their home culture and with that of our society.

2. Develop empathy for, and a feeling of, commonality with those who are different.

3. Assist children in developing an understanding of fairness and the knowledge that discrimination and exclusion hurts.

4. Nurture children's ability to stand up for themselves and others in the face of unfairness and prejudice.

## Anti-Bias Arts Activities

Arts activities, because of their open-ended nature and emphasis on working together to accomplish a creative goal, are an ideal way to develop this inner strength. The following activities show how the arts can be used to address racial prejudice based on skin color.

**Mixing my special color.**  Read a book about skin color, such as *All the Colors We Are* (Kissinger, 1994). Help children mix paint that matches the color of their skin. Place the paint in a container that closes tightly. Label the container with the child's name, and have the child give the color a beautiful name. Explain that whenever children want to paint a picture of themselves or their friends, they may use those special paint colors.

**Valuing children's unique colors.** Make sure skin-color paints are available at the easel. Then, when children use the paint color that is closest to their skin color, hair color, or eye color, make a comment about the beauty of that color and express its relationship to the children's coloring, such as: "You are painting with a beautiful almond brown (rich peach, soft beige, deep brown, etc.). It is the same color as your skin (hair, eyes)." Read the book *The Colors of Us* (Katz, 2002) in which different skin colors are given luscious names and then have children create their own names for their color skin.

Read a book that celebrates differences, such as Jenny Kostecki-Shaw's *Same, Same but Different* (2011) in which two pen pals—a boy from a village

Talking about skin color differences and engaging in arts activities that celebrate similarities and differences develop self-confidence and empathy. Here a youngster makes a handprint in her skin color after reading the book *All the Colors That We Are* by Katie Kissinger.

in India and a boy from an American city find they have a lot in common. Collect a variety of paint-chip samples from a paint store. Have children sort them into groups. Then have them find the ones that match their hair, skin, and eye color. Make a graph or chart of the different range of colors in the group.

**Washing up.** This interaction can occur following any messy activity in which the children's hands get covered with an art material—such as finger painting, printing, clay work, or painting. When children are washing up at the sink, say, "What do you think might happen to the color of our skin when we wash the paint off? Look, it stays the same color. Our skin color doesn't come off, only the paint." Also, provide opportunities for children to wash dolls that have different skin colors.

**Color awareness collages.** Children need to learn to cherish all the colors skin can be. Transition into a skin color awareness activity by reading a book that celebrates the colors brown and black, such as *Beautiful Blackbird* (Bryan, 2003). Have the children find or make a list of all of the beautiful black or brown things that they know. Take a neighborhood or nature walk and look for brown or black things. Look at the many different colors skin can be. Put out the collage items, exclaiming over the beautiful color of each material.

## Talking to Children about Differences

When arts materials that reflect skin differences, images of a variety of people, and anti-bias arts activities are introduced to young children, occasions will arise in which biased or unkind remarks will be made, and a response will be required by the teacher. A child may not want to handle black playdough because it is "ugly," or another may say, "My skin color paint is prettier than yours." Whether it is during an arts activity, or at any other time of the day, children's discriminating behavior must be addressed. Such comments, even by very young children, must not be ignored or excused, nor is the teacher's personal discomfort in dealing with difficult subjects a reason not to act. Reacting strongly to biased statements shows children how to act when they see unfairness. The following suggestions may help:

1. Immediately address the child's negative response. A response to the aforementioned statements might be: "All colors are beautiful. Why do you say that?" If the comment is directed to another child, say: "That is a hurtful thing to say. Why do you say that?"

2. Help children figure out why they are uncomfortable. Identify why it was unfair or based on stereotypes.

3. Explain why such remarks are hurtful, and give examples of things the child might say or do instead.

**Did You Get It?**

**Which of the following will help create an anti-bias environment for children?**

a. asking children to mix paint that matches the color of their skin and giving each color a beautiful name

b. avoiding any mention of skin color with children under age 3

c. providing every color of play dough except brown as it makes children act silly

d. using multicultural materials that depict people wearing traditional clothing associated with their ethnicity

**Take the full quiz on CourseMate**

## How Do We Address Cultural Differences Through Arts Activity?

We build children's self-confidence and foster cooperation when we select culturally relevant arts activities that respect children's cultural, linguistic, religious, and ethnic diversity and create a sense of belonging. Faced with a group of young children we see, at first, unique individuals with temperaments, likes and dislikes, and a personal way of doing things in the classroom. But we must also come to see them as embedded in a family, a community, a culture, and a society, all of which will influence how they play, what language they speak, and how they will meld into the classroom community.

**Culture,** like creativity, has many definitions. In the broadest sense it is a group's way of thinking, acting, and responding based on a set of rules or beliefs that make sense of the universe. We value children's cultures when we:

- Use the child's home language in daily interactions, and in bilingual storytelling and reading.

- Select arts activities and materials that reflect the child's home culture.

- Incorporate and welcome family and community members into the classroom as integral parts of the arts curriculum serving as cultural experts, resources of information, and as helpers who can mediate for the child in culturally relevant ways.

## Respecting Family Culture and Beliefs

As teachers we bring our own backgrounds with us into our classrooms. However, the way we were raised may not match that of the children we teach. For example, although play is universal in every child's development, how it looks and what is considered normal and acceptable varies greatly from place to place and culture to culture (Kendall, 1996).

**Environment.** Home environment is one factor. Children who live in crowded apartments where it is not safe to go outside engage in different activities and have a different sense of movement in space then a child growing up on a farm with acres of woodland to explore. This will affect how children respond in creative movement activities such as when they are asked to pretend they are walking outside. Being sensitive to a child's home environment will help us frame our arts activities so that all children feel like they belong.

**Socioeconomic background.** Family economics also has an effect on a child's home culture. Some children grow up with access to many toys and electronic devices, and others have only a few and must create their own playthings from the things they find in their environment. They may be overwhelmed by an overabundance of materials and choices. For example, children who grow up in middle-class homes may be given excess adult clothing and shoes with which to play dress-up, whereas a child from a poor family is happy to have one pair of sneakers. A dress-up corner full of glitzy dresses and glittery shoes may overwhelm such a child. Adding dress-up garments mirroring familiar community occupations and ethnic groups may increase a child's sense of belonging.

**Adult behavior.** Children's art and dramatic play will reflect what they see around them in daily life and on television. Pretend play often mimics adult behavior. While children in hunting societies pretend to hunt, children in the inner city act out gang fights and dodging bullets as they walk to school. Children imitate the action heroes they see in television cartoons. When children act out violent stories in their pretend play, we need to think about why they are doing this and mediate their play with cultural sensitivity rather than punishment or disapproval.

**Gender expectations.** Cultural expectations about gender often determine appropriate play for boys and for girls. Boys are expected to play with trucks and guns while girls are expected to play with dolls and housekeeping. Gender, race, and physical characteristics should not determine what roles children play in a story, or how they are expected to move in a dance. If children object to a child taking a certain role, share a book such as *Amazing Grace* (Hoffman, 1991) in which an African-American girl plays the role of Peter Pan in the school play. Some children may come from homes with only a mother or only a father, or two fathers or two mothers, or homes in which the father stays home and the mother works. Room must be made to welcome all children's families.

In carrying out arts activities, teachers have to consciously stay alert to their own biases. Research has shown, for example, that teachers often react differently to boys than they do to girls (Sadker & Sadker, 1995).

## Teacher Tip

### THE POWER OF CHILDREN'S LITERATURE

Children need to see themselves and others in the books we read to them. Reading books that depict children with similar life experiences develops self-confidence (Brimson, 2009). The book *The Two Mrs. Gibsons* by Toyomi Igus (2001) celebrates love and caring in a family of mixed heritage. Stories about children who are both the same and different from them develops understanding and empathy (Koster, 2005). A story such as *Yo Yes* by Chris Rashka (1993) or *The Other Side* (2001) by Jacqueline Woodson show children ways to make friends with children who are different from them. *Lucy's Picture* by Nicola Moon (1993) in which a little girl creates a touchable collage for her grandfather helps children understand blindness.

**For an annotated list of books that address diversity, see *Books that Make a Difference* on CourseMate.**

## Communicating with Families

In order to better understand our child artists, we need to know about their families and their families need to

## Teacher to Family

Communicating with parents is critical in establishing reciprocal relationships. Because creative arts experiences have the potential to be positives in children's lives, they provide an important resource upon which to build relationships with parents and welcome them into the school community. To do this effectively both one way and two-way forms of communication need to be pursued.

**One-way methods:**

Newsletters highlighting the arts, letters home about arts activities, art notes, school-to-home notebooks about adjustments and successes in the arts, class websites featuring the arts, videos of activities, and portfolios and projects sent home.

**Two-way methods:**

Phone calls and e-mails celebrating creative works, learning "bags" such as an arts bag with a feedback journal, conferences that include the arts as a major component of the child's accomplishments, home visits to talk about the child and interests in the arts, art-home surveys, informal arts shows and performances, invitations to participate in children's projects and fieldtrips, parent visits to share about culture, work, and family arts, parents helping in the classroom with arts projects, parent workshops to explore the arts, and parent-child arts workshops.

understand and contribute to our knowledge. To establish two-way communication with families:

1. Make families feel welcome in the classroom and invite their participation. Arts activities provide a wonderful opportunity to involve parents.

2. Avoid presenting yourself as someone who knows all the answers. Ask questions about parents' goals and hopes for their children. Work together to find solutions to problems.

3. Communicate regularly. Newsletters and arts notes home can share successes in the arts. Set up opportunities for parents to respond in creative ways that take into account the harried lives many of us live.

4. Respect parents' feelings about their child and their culture. Remember if there is a disagreement, the goal is not for you to win and the parent to lose, but rather to find a middle ground in which to find agreement and make the best decision for the child.

## Using a Multicultural Lens

All members of the classroom community should feel welcome in our classrooms. We need to foster children's pride in their own cultural identity but also develop curiosity, enjoyment, and empathy for others' cultural similarities and differences. Derman Sparks and the ABC Task Force (1989) suggest the following as the basis of a multicultural curriculum.

- **Include everyone.** When selecting culturally based activities, build on the cultural backgrounds of the individual children in the class and their families first.

- **Avoid stereotyping a child or a culture.** Not all Mexican-Americans speak Spanish. Not all Indians wear saris. Make references to differences specific to a particular child. Say: "This is what Keena's family does when they visit her grandparents at Thanksgiving." and invite her family to share photographs and stories about their customs rather than saying: "Everyone eats turkey at Thanksgiving." Emphasize similarities as well as differences.

- **Avoid singling out a "minority" child.** Make learning about all children and their similarities and differences the focus. Encourage children to draw pictures of their families and the things they do. Make a class book about the families of children and the staff members. If different languages are spoken, make a class book illustrating some common words in each language.

- **Bring cultural diversity into the classroom every day.** Go beyond a few pictures on the wall. Take walks around the communities the children come from many times. Make class books about the community to be kept in the classroom library. Have families and children share artifacts that reflect their family life such as musical instruments, special bowls and utensils, and the tools they use in their work. Add items to the dramatic play area that reflect their home culture. If a child's parent works in construction, add a hard hat and gloves. If a parent is a nurse, add a lab coat and a stethoscope. If a family prepares rice, add a bamboo steamer and rice bowls.

## Food and Arts

A controversial issue in art for young children is the use of food and food products in art activities. People have strong feelings on both sides of this issue.

**Using food in art activities.** Those who believe it is all right to use food items often give the following reasons:

- Many traditional art materials, such as egg tempera, play dough, and white glue, are made from food products.

- It is easier to determine the ingredients in food products than in commercial art materials so they are safer, especially if the child puts it in her mouth.

- Food items are readily available at the supermarket.

- Children can appreciate the aesthetic qualities of the foods such as when they make a print using an apple half.

- Children are motivated by food and have a lot of fun doing these activities such as when they are told they can lick their hands after finger painting with pudding.

**Avoiding food in arts activities.** On the other hand there are many reasons why food items should not be used in art activities:

🎵 Many children are severely allergic to food items such as milk, wheat, soy, eggs, and nuts.

🎵 Most traditional art materials, such as crayons, chalk, and paper, are not food based.

🎵 Safe art materials for children are widely marketed in department stores, drug stores, and through catalogs.

🎵 Children become confused when told they can eat one art material and not another.

**Using a multicultural lens.** When making a decision on an art activity that calls for food we must consider all of the above plus the cultural message we are sending the children and their families. We need to ask ourselves:

🎵 **Does this use of food respect our families' cultural beliefs?** Some ethnic groups are offended if food they highly value is used for play and not shown respect. For example, some families of Asian heritage may object to the use of rice in sensory play.

🎵 **Does this use of food respect the fact that people are hungry?** Making a necklace out of macaroni or cereal might not bother well-fed middle-class parents and their children, but may distress those who struggle daily to put food on the table. Many children come to school hungry or see hungry people every day on the street.

🎵 **Does this use of food create needless waste?** Food is expensive and should be valued. We tell children not to waste their food. Making prints with apples or bananas or potatoes is a common art activity. But what do children learn when they see all that food thrown into the wastebasket afterward? There are many other things that can be used for printmaking besides foods. Or if there is a specific reason for the activity, consider ways to lessen the waste, such as if the goal is to show the beautiful design inside an apple, use only one apple instead of every child having a half with which to print.

🎵 **Does this use of food teach children healthy eating habits?** Parents may have specific ideas about what they want their children to eat. Giving children candy and sugary cereal to use in art projects highlights these foods in positive ways. Edible playdoughs and finger paints entice children to taste all playdoughs and paints.

For alternatives to use instead of food items, see *Substitutions for Food in Arts Activities* on CourseMate.

## The Role of Holidays

In many early childhood programs, holidays are often a major focus for arts activities. Arts activity books abound with exciting new ways to create holiday art and decorations and perform festive songs and dances. Holidays are fun; they involve rituals, they build a sense of solidarity, and they are part of a society's cultural life. However, it is easy to trivialize a culture when it only makes a once a year appearance in the form of stereotyped art projects, songs, dances, and plays. To develop deeper understanding of different cultures, we need to do the following:

**Celebrate everyone.** Not all holidays are celebrated in the same way by everyone. The holidays of all children in the group must be presented with

Instead of using three perfect circles, snowmen can be made in various ways that allow children to express their own creativity as this snowman by Joseph, age four, demonstrates.

equal emphasis. One holiday should not receive more time and attention than another. Look to parents to provide thoughts, information, and resources on respectful ways of sharing their holidays.

**Celebrate year round.** We need to be sure that a culture is not presented only in the context of a holiday. Presenting artwork and activities that relate to different cultures throughout the year rather than just in the context of a holiday helps prevent children from associating the arts of that culture with only the holiday. For example, Native American arts and culture should be displayed and discussed in many arts contexts—when making masks, working with beads, creating with clay, learning to spin and weave, and examining baskets—not just at Thanksgiving.

**Avoid stereotypes.** One of the hardest things to avoid when dealing with holiday-related arts activities is the stereotypical images related to holidays. These images limit children's creativity and visual imaginations, often do not reflect their home cultures, and undermine their artistic self-confidence as they quickly learn that they cannot replicate the perfection of a commercially made holiday symbol.

The perfect Christmas-tree shape, for example, is impossible for young children to make successfully without resorting to patterns or step-by-step copying, and the image becomes so ingrained that many upper-level arts teachers find that they have to take their students on nature walks just to prove that all pine trees are not symmetrical, and that they can be represented in many other ways in their art. Hearts, egg shapes, bunnies, turkeys, and pumpkins all become bland, perfect symbols instead of reflecting the infinite variety of their actual forms.

It is hard to avoid these symbols because they permeate the markets and media of this society. However, we need to consider carefully which images we want to surround the children in our care. Teachers can take the following actions to expand children's artistic imaginations and fight the prevailing stereotypes.

1. In visual arts provide geometric shapes that children can make into their own creative ideas instead of holiday-related shapes that limit what they can do. Let children draw their own versions of Christmas trees, turkeys, pumpkins, hearts, and other holiday shapes, instead of giving them teacher-prepared paper shapes, holiday cutouts, coloring pages, foam shapes, or stickers.

2. At the playdough and clay center, instead of holiday-shaped cookie cutters, use simple geometric shapes from which children can build their own versions of these symbols if they wish.

3. Provide a range of color choices of materials, not just those of the prevailing holiday.

4. Instead of displaying stereotypical holiday images, provide aesthetic experiences with a collection of pumpkins, piles of pine boughs, a display of turkey feathers, a basket of eggs, or a cage of real rabbits, so the children use their senses to see and touch and discover similarities and differences on their own.

5. Introduce songs and dances from different cultures throughout the year not just at holiday time.

---

**Did You Get It?**

**Which of the following should be avoided when creating an atmosphere of respect for all cultures in class?**

a. displaying images of racial and ethnic groups not represented in the class

b. selecting images that show a range of people of different ages, genders, sizes, colors, and abilities

c. displaying artworks, music, stories, and dances representing artists of diverse backgrounds and time periods

d. using the children's home languages in daily interactions

**Take the full quiz on CourseMate**

---

# Conclusion: Caring For Each Other

Group arts projects can take many forms. From painting a mural to acting out a story, working with others gives children a chance to interact with the arts in a way that is different from individual artistic pursuits. There must be a common vocabulary. "Should we put aqua paint on the fish?" There must be collaboration. "Should this character be a pigeon or an eagle?" And there must be cooperation. "I'll hold the drum for you, and then you can hold it for me."

Photo
Story

# We All Have Feelings

What makes us angry? What makes us happy? What makes us sad? To start off the year, first graders explored their feelings through these questions using pantomime, drawing, painting to music, reading books, and journaling.

"Feeling sick." John Pencil—age seven

"Feeling happy."  By Leah Pastel—age five

"Feeling angry." By Marti, Marker—age six

Documentation Panel for First Grade We All Have Feelings Integrated Arts Unit

The result is more than the sum of its parts. Group arts activities turn "me" into "we" and unite individuals.

Group arts activities can also be used to help children express thoughts and feelings that are hard to put into words. Teachers need to be sensitive to the personal needs and beliefs of their students. Children can and should talk about the differences among them, but actually painting with different skin tones, learning each other's personal likes and cultural backgrounds, and working on the same arts projects with those who are different help children form tangible links. The arts activities that we choose can broaden children's perspectives in ways that will make them more successful participants in a multicultural society.

This chapter has offered ideas that challenge the educator to address sometimes controversial issues.

Overheard comments could be ignored. Black and brown playdough could be avoided, because it makes some children uncomfortable or makes them act silly. Teachers could focus on the more readily available "old masters" instead of looking for the harder-to-locate artwork of African-Americans, Latinos, and those of other cultures. Teachers could give in to the pressure to make commercialized holiday "art," or they can make the other choice, the one that takes a little more effort and haul in ten imperfect pumpkins or take a trip to the turkey farm. They can make a commitment to do what is best for the children, knowing that change happens not all at once but a little bit every day.

For additional information on teaching children to work cooperatively, address bias, and use a multicultural lens, see *Chapter 5 Online Resources* on CourseMate.

## Teaching In Action

### Spaceship Command Center: A Box Project

The following excerpts from a teacher's journal show how the project approach and a flexible approach to room planning was used in a prekindergarten class to correlate children's interests in space with the arts, science, and language studies.

#### Week 1

*Day 1:* The idea: Mike, Bobby, and Jeff arrived all excited. It seems there was a show about space on TV last night. At meeting, all they wanted to do was talk about the spaceship. At blocks, they built a launch pad and used cardboard tubes as rockets.

*Day 2:* Discovering the depth of interest: Today I decided to read Ezra Jack Keats's *Regards to the Man in the Moon* (1981). Then I asked: "What do you think we would need for a trip into space?" What ideas! I couldn't write them down fast enough on the chart. Toby said she has a cousin who went to NASA Space Camp. I wonder if she could come for a visit? I must get in touch. I noticed that many of the paintings and drawings were about space today.

*Day 3:* What do we already know? Today I asked: "What do we know about space?" I made a huge web of children's ideas. I can see they have heard about stars, planets, and the sun, but not much else. There was a discussion about aliens and Star Wars. I must find some factual books about space. Not surprisingly, everyone was building a launch pad today at blocks!

*Day 4:* Building on the interest: I found out about a space exhibit at the discovery center. I called and arranged for a visit the end of next week. That gives me time to plan the bussing and the parent volunteers. We will use this time to read more about space and make a list of questions. I put a sheet up labeled "Our questions about space" in the meeting area. I put up a big poster of the solar system. Then I pretended I was the sun and the children were the planets, and they had a grand time circling around me to the music of "The Planets" by Gustav Holst. I will try to read another two pages and do a movement activity each day at morning meeting.

*Day 5:* Small groups begin: At small group time, I started off by having my group of children look at a picture of the space shuttle and then figure out what the different parts were. I wasn't surprised when Mike, Bobby, and Jeff asked if they could build a spaceship. Everyone started to call out ideas. I said, "Why don't we draw some pictures of our ideas?" Boy, did they work on those pictures! So much detail!

Carol [the aide] had her group looking at photographs of each of the planets and talking about the sizes, colors, and names. Some children in her group wanted to make a mural about space.

#### Week 2

*Day 6:* Group work continues: We found a huge roll of black paper. I hung it on the wall, and the children sat in front

*(continued)*

## Teaching In Action (continued)

of it, and we tried to imagine the blackness of space. I gave them each a tube to look through and turned off the light. It was very effective. At group time we continued to work on sketches for the spaceship. We put out gold and silver tempera paint at the easel, and the children had a grand time painting stars and comets of all kinds to paste on the mural. The spaceship group made tons more sketches. Carol's group made planets.

*Day 7:* Finding direction: I read Gail Gibbons's *Stargazers* (1992, New York: Holiday House). I simplified the text a bit. Then I passed around a telescope for children to look through. They cut out and pasted their stars on the mural. They even made a Milky Way! I can't believe they had such patience to cut out even their little tiny stars. We had so many we even hung some from the ceiling. Then we sat in front of the mural and sang "Twinkle, Twinkle Little Star" and made wishes. Suddenly someone said, I think it was Jeff, "Why don't we make our spaceship in front of the mural so we will be heading into space . . . like we could have a big window. The captain and his mates could sit here and look out."

*Day 8:* Building begins: Toby's cousin couldn't come, but she sent in a videotape of the training. We watched it twice. The second time we looked for ideas for our spaceship. We added seat cushions and seatbelts to the parent wish list by the door. We decided to move a table in front of the mural, and I cut open a large cardboard box. The children drew big windows, and I cut them out. Then they painted it. Now I

have taped it to the table, and it looks great! They have already set up three chairs and sit there counting down.

*Day 9:* Our trip—What did we learn? It was wonderful! The children were so well behaved. I could see that all of our preparations made a big difference. They had a space shuttle model the children could go inside. When we got back, the first thing they wanted to do was make the control panel like the one at the museum. But I got everyone together first, and we wrote down the answers on our question chart. Then I got out some boxes, and everyone helped paint them. It was a good release after being so controlled all morning at the museum.

*Day 10:* The command center: It's done! I can't believe the children had such a great idea. We put some low boxes on the table and the bigger ones on the floor around it. Catie had the idea of using bottle lids for the dials. I attached them with chenille stems so they turn. Then the best idea of all was Louie's. He said, "Why don't we put the computer here?" At the museum, there was a computer in the spaceship. So we did! Some parents even brought in cushions and belts for the chairs. We all took a turn sitting in the command seats. Wow! Next week I will put out paper bags with pre-cut openings so they can make helmets if they wish. But the funny thing was when my colleague, Joanne, poked her head in and said, "What book gave you that neat idea for a computer center?"

"It's not in a book," I said. "It grew in the children's imaginations."

# Reflection Page

## Exploring Ourselves

Knowing our feelings, beliefs, and cultural viewpoint allows us to better understand those of our children and our families. Self-awareness exercises help identify areas we need explore more so that we can be better teachers. Select one or more of the following activities and then reflect on what you learned about yourself and how it might affect your choice or presentation of arts activities.

1.  Choose a popular fairy tale and rewrite it, changing the gender of the characters. Reread the story and think about how the change makes you feel.

2.  Try to accomplish one of the following arts activities while experiencing one of the following handicaps:

    ♪ Wearing a thick snow glove on your dominant hand, or, using your mouth or toes draw a detailed pencil drawing.

    ♪ Wearing a heavy boot on one foot, dance a complete folkdance.

    ♪ Wearing a blindfold or very dark glasses, make a colorful painting or crayon drawing.

    ♪ Place your tongue against the back of your top teeth and sing a song.

3.  Write a story about your childhood about how you learned about your ethnic, racial, and cultural identity. Which aspects were fun and which were unpleasant?

### Reflection: How have your personal experiences affected the way you feel about people different from yourself?

_____

_____

_____

_____

# Reflection Page

## Shared Experiences

Think of one or more open-ended group arts activities that could be done in response to the following shared experiences.

| Shared Experience | Activity Ideas |
|---|---|
| A sudden thunderstorm | |
| A trip to a shoe store | |
| Watching birds | |
| A zookeeper's visit | |
| Studying patterns | |
| Setting up a classroom fish tank | |

# Reflection Page

## Dealing with Difficult Situations

Consider each of the following situations, and decide what you would say and do.

1. A parent picks up her son's painting and says, "Another painting all in black! Why don't you use some pretty colors when you paint?"

   _____

   _____

   _____

2. A little girl refuses to touch the brown playdough. "It's yucky!" she declares.

   _____

   _____

   _____

3. Michael, age five, draws only faces with blood coming out of their mouths.

   _____

   _____

   _____

4. An aide shows the children how to trace their hands to make turkeys.

   _____

   _____

   _____

5. A child with muscular dystrophy is having trouble holding her crayon.

   _____

   _____

   _____

   _____

# Reflection Page

## Observation: Bias in the Environment

Visit a school or childcare center when children are not present, and observe the following:

1.  Are there crayons, paper, modeling clay, playdough, or paints available in a variety of skin colors?

    _____

    _____

2.  Are there child-height mirrors?

    _____

    _____

3.  Are there images or artworks that depict people of different racial and ethnic groups?

    _____

    _____

4.  Are predominant groups represented by the majority of the images or artworks?

    _____

    _____

5.  Is society's diversity represented by the images or artworks displayed?

    _____

    _____

6.  Are books available that reflect society's diversity?

    _____

    _____

7.  Are there any stereotypical or inaccurate images representing certain groups, such as Native Americans?

    _____

    _____

8.  Are there any commercial or stereotypical holiday artworks on display?

    _____

    _____

Based on what you observed, would you judge this a bias-free environment for young children?

______________________________________________________________________
______________________________________________________________________
______________________________________________________________________
______________________________________________________________________

If yes, write a letter to the director telling him or her what you especially liked about what the program offers young children. (Optional: This letter may be mailed to the director, if desired.)

______________________________________________________________________
______________________________________________________________________
______________________________________________________________________
______________________________________________________________________
______________________________________________________________________
______________________________________________________________________
______________________________________________________________________
______________________________________________________________________

If no, make a plan of action that could be used to eliminate bias in the environment. Include cost, time frame, and personnel necessary to accomplish this task. Remember, change occurs bit by bit.

______________________________________________________________________
______________________________________________________________________
______________________________________________________________________
______________________________________________________________________
______________________________________________________________________
______________________________________________________________________
______________________________________________________________________
______________________________________________________________________

Digital Download Download from CourseMate

# Chapter 6

## Creating a Place for the Arts

Explain how to create an arts infused-environment that promotes feelings of comfort, trust, and belonging.

**Creating a Caring Community**

Identify ways to arrange the learning environment to incorporate the arts.

**Planning Curriculum to Achieve Important Goals**

**Creating a Place for Arts DAP Learning Objectives**

**Establishing Reciprocal Family Relationships**

**Assessing Children's Development and Learning**

**Teaching to Enhance Development and Learning**

Apply reflective thinking questions to assess the learning environment.

Use displays of children's creative arts process to welcome and communicate with parents.

List the elements that contribute to an effective arts-infused learning environment.

## Young Artists Creating

Michael takes his paper and crayons and crawls under the table. Lying on his stomach, he draws and draws and draws.

Katina slowly looks through the plastic bins on the shelf. Carefully she selects a piece of ribbon, a gold button, and a piece of shiny silver paper. Then she carries her treasures to the table, eager to make her collage.

Faria listens to a recording of a jazz tune and taps in rhythm on a drum in the music house.

Suddenly it grows dark, and rain starts hitting the windows. The children stop what they are doing and run to the window. One boy puts his finger on the window and traces the path of the raindrops.

## What Kind of Environment Is Needed for the Arts?

**The learning environment** is everything that surrounds us and exerts an influence over us. It consists of space, furnishings, time, and organizing elements. Environment affects our social and emotional sense of well-being. We change to fit different environments. We relax in our living rooms and feel anxious in the doctor's waiting room. Children run and leap in open fields and huddle under beds.

In fashioning the environments in which children will create, there are unlimited possibilities. All of the suggestions in this chapter are starting points, not unbreakable rules. No two early childhood environments need to be alike, nor should they remain static. The environment should change as the children's interests and activities change, or as we explore new ways to create the ideal environment for children. The key element is flexibility. When flexibility is built into the room, we can create the best environment for our children.

How space is organized determines what experiences can be offered to our children and what relationships will be formed. In designing the Reggio Emilia schools Loris Malaguzzi emphasized the importance of the early childhood learning environment, calling it the "third teacher" (Edwards et al., 2011). Charles Schwall (2005) notes "when children live in a space, they own, feel, and find their place within it." That feeling can be one of belonging or one of disconnect. The aesthetics and organization of the surroundings we create will affect the mood, motion, and behavior of the young children in our care.

Developmentally appropriate practice reminds us to consider the needs of the children first when planning  activity areas. Infants and toddlers need different kinds of spaces than do primary children. Infants and toddlers need room to move and freedom to explore in safety. They need challenging sensory materials at their level with places to be private and places for large movement. Older children need personalized spaces that make them feel like they belong, small and large group gathering areas that foster social communication and sharing, and learning centers that recognize their interests and passions while encouraging hands-on learning, independence, and creative thinking. Learning environments for all ages should allow children with special needs to participate fully. Families need to feel

### Did You Get It?

**Steven, an architect, is planning layouts for children's activity areas and classrooms. He should keep in mind that**

a. toddlers need the same kinds of spaces that primary children do.

b. children with special needs must be able to fully participate in the activities.

c. families needn't be considered when designing learning environments.

d. infants need more personalized spaces than older children.

**Take the full quiz on CourseMate**

welcomed into their child's school and classroom. The arts and their ability to make things "special" provide an avenue for doing this.

## How Do We Create an Arts-Infused Learning Environment?

We occupy space with our bodies. For young children who are rapidly developing the ability to control their arms and legs, hands and feet, and fingers and toes, the arts are vitally important. Gross motor skills for coordination, balance, spatial awareness, and strength are exercised during creative movement and dramatic play. The fine motor skills involved in handling arts materials develop hand–eye coordination and finger strength. Daily experiences with dramatic play, creative movement, music, and visual art foster these skills in ways that motivate and excite young children. So push back the tables, the desks and the chairs, and bring the arts in.

### Defining the Instructional Space

The learning environment is the total space children use and how it is arranged. It includes the contiguous outdoor areas as well as any entrances or hallways that the children will pass through or work in. The actual space is less important than its design. It does not matter if the program is in a home, in a large room, such as a church basement, or in classrooms designed especially for young children, when carefully planned almost any space can be effectively arranged to provide an excellent experience for young artists. Jim Greenman (1988) identifies the following characteristics as important elements of environments that surround young children: comfort, softness, safety and health, private and social space, order, time, mobility, and the adult dimension. Making a place for the arts ensures that these elements are addressed.

**Comfort.**   Children feel comfortable when they can use their whole bodies and all of their senses as they explore and learn. Creative movement, large group music activities, and active sensory experiences require open and, preferably, carpeted and padded spaces where infants and children can freely move their bodies in many ways. Small group and independent

Environments for young children should provide both softness and comfort, and moments of privacy and wonderment.

music activities, on the other hand, ask us to provide small, cozy, sound-containing areas where we can rock an infant, or where a kindergartener can sketch while observing an arrangement of flowers. Tables for visual arts activities, low enough for children to kneel, sit, or stand at comfortably beckon small groups to work together. Small, foot-high play tables that straddle the children's legs, picnic benches, and coffee tables all provide toddler-size work surfaces and can be relocated as needed to create privacy or partner work.

**Softness.**   Softness in the environment helps children relax and reduces stress. Soft cushions and bolsters for infants and teachers facilitate communicative interactions. Places where children can curl up while listening to music and ample lengths of colorful fabric to wrap up in and imagine as they play add elements of softness to rooms that are often institutional in design. Fake furs and fuzzy fabric stimulate infant's senses as they crawl and touch. Natural materials and animals add a different kind of softness. Soft, pliable arts materials tantalize fingers. Peaceful background music gentles the sounds of busy children. Clay and glue provide wetness, mushiness, malleability, and stickiness. Dance and dramatic play props add the appealing textures of costumes, dolls, stuffed animals, and puppets. Quiet, relaxed areas with soft furnishings allow children to enjoy beautifully illustrated books and to study art prints and interesting artifacts.

**Safety and health.** Common sense dictates that materials should be safe for the age group using them. There should be no sharp edges or small parts on which children under three might choke. Food and tasting centers need to be differentiated from visual art centers so that toddlers and preschoolers learn not to ingest art materials. See Appendix A for more information on ways to keep children safe.

Although children must be provided with a space that is safe and healthy, small risks give children the opportunity to develop independence and self-confidence. Arts activities provide a way to do this. By handling challenging arts materials, children can learn to deal with such small risks as water cups that spill, paint that drips, and scissors that are sharp. Drumsticks and shakers have to be controlled without injuring others. Actively moving in creative ways requires self-regulating one's body in space and cooperating with others. For preschool and up, using glass or ceramic dishes and metal spoons and forks instead of the ubiquitous plastic in the housekeeping center help children develop focus and fine motor control.

**Privacy and social space.** Foster positive social interaction by careful arrangement of learning zones. Providing places where children can work in large groups, as well as small, private spaces where one or two children can work on a special project helps meet the needs of children with special needs by fostering inclusion. Large puppet stages and dramatic play centers allow needed social interactions for groups of children. On the other hand, a small finger puppet theater or a listening center, furnished with some pillows, a CD or tape player, and earphones, allow children to explore the arts more personally.

Visual arts activities should not be limited to the "art table." There should be times and places for children to take their crayons and paper and work by themselves. The floor is always available as an artwork surface for group projects or solo workers. More private spaces can be found under tables or beside a piece of furniture. "Drawing boards" (small chalkboards

work well) can provide a drawing surface in a carpeted area. Obviously some art media need to be confined to areas that are easy to wipe up or near a sink, but even these spaces can be arranged to provide more privacy for the young artist. Tables for a group of four can be mixed with tables for one or two. Low dividers or storage units can provide a sense of privacy around the easels or modeling areas and at the same time contain these messier materials in a limited space. Some early childhood schools, following the Reggio Emilia model, have set up *ateliers*—separate studio spaces—where children can come to work with clay, paint, fibers, and more (Gandini et al., 2005).

**Order.** More than anything else, order—the intentional structuring of space, time, and materials reflects the educational goals of the teacher. If children are expected to work independently, then the materials and space need to be arranged so children can self-select. If there are materials that children are not to use without adult supervision, such as sharp tools then these need to be placed where children cannot reach them.

Order is especially important in arts pursuits. Open-ended does not mean anything goes, but instead asks us to be intentional and flexible. Open-ended arts activities encourage children to go beyond and make connections. Pinecones in the sensory table might, with permission, be brought over to decorate the table in the dramatic play area. Toy animals might come to live in the zoo built in the block corner. In order for creativity to flourish we need to teach children through modeling, guided discovery, and repeated practice where materials and tools are kept, how they are to handle them, where to use them, and how they are to be returned. They must know when they can move freely across the room and when they must sit quietly and be an audience.

This sense of order cannot be introduced all at once to children. It must be built up over time, slowly adding new expectations, routines, behaviors, materials, and tools as children gain self-control and competence in handling each new addition. For example, one drawing material or creative movement should be introduced, rules established, and then explored for a period of time. Then the next is added, layering on complexity, until the children have access to a wide range of choices, and they can use the techniques and materials in combinations of their choosing. Then they can revisit the materials as needed, and use them in responsive ways.

This leads to richer arts possibilities than, for example, having crayons put out on a table for one week, clay the next, printmaking the next, or offering rhythm band activities on occasion to the whole group instead of having an ever increasing variety of sound makers available in a music center where individuals and small groups can explore sound and rhythm as they revisit on their own.

**Routines.** Regular routines are important for young children. In a dynamic, changeable environment routines add predictability and stability for young children (Copple & Bredekamp, 2009, p. 17). However, routines do not have to be rigid. The arts can play a vital role in facilitating arrivals, snacks, clean up, departures, and transitions from place to place and from small to larger group.

- **Arrivals.** Use the arts to welcome. Singing a welcoming song for infants and toddlers, one that includes a part for the parent, helps ease the child into the room. For older children, setting out interesting natural and sensory objects or drawing materials around the room for the child and parent to explore for a few minutes together helps get the child focused on the exciting day that lies ahead.

- **Snacks.** Snack time provides needed energy and a time to instill healthy eating habits. But breaking off playtime to eat can be disruptive to learning. Consider ways to incorporate snack time into the natural learning cycle through the arts. For example, instead of everyone snacking at the same time, the snack can be offered as a sensory center choice where children are encouraged to explore the shapes and colors, smells and textures of the foods. Math and art can be integrated into the snack center by having children take turns daily drawing a picture menu, and visually showing the number of each type of snack children coming to the center are to take, fostering one-to-one correspondence and counting skills (Curtis & Carter, 2008, p. 189).

- **Clean up and activity transitions.** A short repetitive song, the slow tapping on a drum, a silly set of movements, and the inclusion of everyone's hands can turn chores or a change of activity into a playful event. See Chapters 10 and 11 for music and dance transition ideas.

- **Departures.** Stopping for the day does not have to be a frustration. A creative movement activity can gently cue children to stop, gather belongings, and then gather together for a goodbye song. If parents are picking up children, have them join the song circle.

**Time.** Time is also a part of the environment, although we often forget about it until we glance at the clock and realize it is clean up time. Creative arts explorations—because they mirror natural play so closely—require a flexible view of the time schedule.

At the primary level, so much of the school day is governed by the clock. Lunch, recess, specials, and snacks often limit the amount of time available for arts activities. One solution is to provide learning centers that include the arts during reading and writing workshop times. See Chapter 8 for other ways to integrate the arts into all the areas of learning and to address the National Common Core Standards.

In inclusion settings, a flexible approach to scheduling benefits children with special needs who may require added time at some of the centers, less at others, or perhaps more one-on-one direct teaching and flexible group activities.

Time may seem never-ending when one is in the flow of the creative process, but in childcare and school settings there are times when we must stop. However, creative open-ended arts activities do not always end at clean up time. Provision is needed for the storage or, in the case of dramatic play scenarios or elaborate block buildings, saving of unfinished work to be continued another day. Respecting children's need to engage for longer periods of time shows children that their ideas are valued and develops cognitive memory as children pick up from where they left off. For example, in Reggio Emilia schools there are dedicated areas for long-term project work (Apps & MacDonald, 2012).

**Mobility.** Helen Langer (1989) has written extensively about the importance of mindfulness—the act of being aware of what is going on around us. When everything is fixed in place, it is easy to become set in one's ways or in her words—mindless. When elements in an environment are moved or changed we see them anew. We become alert to new possibilities, and to new combinations. Creativity is awakened.

Mobility is built into an environment when activities can be moved to the most conducive locations or items within a location can be repurposed in another.

For instance, outdoor areas are often underused for arts activities, yet everyone feels bolder outdoors, and there is less concern about damage. Children outdoors can move their arms with aplomb and bounce around while dancing, acting, singing, painting, modeling, or constructing. The outdoors is also a good place for large projects such as murals and refrigerator-box constructions, for noisy active projects such as sound making and singing games, and for wet, messy projects such as painting, murals, papier-mâché, and wet clay.

Mobility also refers to the furnishings. It is important that chairs, tables, rugs, and centers be as flexible as possible to allow us to adjust the room to suit the needs of particular children or activities. Easy-to-move furniture can be pushed back if a large group wants to work together or a bookshelf or table can be called into service to provide a sense of privacy when necessary.

Instead of thinking in terms of the traditional activity areas such as blocks, dramatic play, art center, and so on, we need to view the total environment, consider its inherent qualities, and design mobility into the layout. An open carpeted space allows for creative movement and group music activities, while an uncarpeted area is needed for creative and constructive activities, such as block building and collage making. Wet and messy activities, whether art or science or cooking, might center around the sink or water source. In a home care setting, such work areas might be located in a living room, a playroom, a workshop, or a kitchen.

**Adequate space.** No matter the setting, plan enough space for children to move from one area of the environment to another and to spread out and work comfortably. Younger children need more space than older ones. Allow at least four square feet or more of table surface for each toddler, and at least three square feet for each older child. Children with special physical needs require ample space so they

All children, including those with special needs, should have access to the spaces and materials of the learning environment and feel comfortable, safe, and trusted.

can move easily and safely and have equal access to all areas.

Marlynn Clayton (2001) suggests that the large open space form the heart of the classroom. This multipurpose space allows everyone to sit in a circle, where every child can be seen and feel a sense of belonging. It also provides a special place for dance and dramatic activities. Clayton suggests the following guidelines in planning this meeting space:

- It should be inviting, with well-defined boundaries and clear of obstacles and distractions.

- There should be room for everyone in the class to sit in a circle without touching each other.

- Everyone should be able to see one another.

- It should have several entry and exit points that allow children to move in and out safely and quickly.

- It should be located near an easel or blackboard for displays and by a wall outlet so CD/tape players and other electrical equipment can be used.

**Traffic flow.** When designing the space, reflect on ways the children will move in the room. Will the activity areas attract them? Will there be sufficient room for children to gather around an interesting exploration? How many children can work in an area at a time? Ashley Cadwell (2005) suggests thinking of classroom spaces as streets and paths and organizing them as passages to the main "piazza" in the center. A very low platform in the center of the gathering spot can provide a place for children to better display their work and special objects when sharing, and become a stage for dramatic play (Curtis & Carter, 2008). The learning centers and work areas around the center can be seen as "shops" where different types of learning happens.

The more flexible the room arrangement, the easier it will be for several children to work together. There should be ways to add more chairs, push two tables together, or even move all of the furniture out of the way to accommodate children whose project needs more space.

**Compatibility.** Another concern is to locate learning areas so that they enrich each other rather than distract. A noisy large motor area will distract if in close proximity to a cozy reading nook, but that same active center may create interesting linkages if close to a dramatic play area built by the children to be like the fire station they visited.

## The Adult Dimension

Children are not the only ones occupying the learning environment. Teachers and visiting adults need to feel comfortable in the educational space that they have created.

There should be places where teachers can sit comfortably when they are talking to children about their artworks and portfolios, and when they join children participating in creative movement and dramatic play. There should be room for teachers to move as boldly as the children, and viewpoints from which they can see everything that is going on at once. Parents and grandparents should be able to find places to sit comfortably when visiting. These places should be fully integrated into the environment, not set off from classroom activity in an observation zone or an area that is obviously designed for adults. A few slightly larger chairs that can be moved around, a rocking chair, sofa, or plastic lawn chairs are some ways adults can made to feel welcome.

### ▶❚❚ TeachSource Video Case 6.1

*Video supplied by the BBC Motion Gallery.*

### Reggio Emilia Approach and Preschool Appropriate Learning Environment and Room Arrangement

Watch these two videos and compare the learning environments and how the preschoolers use them. What differences do you see? What similarities? Which of the environmental characteristics are valued the most in each? Which environment do you think is more appealing for young children? Why?

**Watch on CourseMate**

### Teacher Tip

#### REFLECTING ON THE SOCIAL ARTS ENVIRONMENT

| | |
|---|---|
| Space | Is the space adequate or are children squeezed together and bumping into things? |
| | Do children avoid certain spaces or crowd others? |
| | Do children interfere with each other when working? |
| | Does the furniture need to be constantly moved to make room for arts activities? |
| Privacy | Are there places children can work alone but still be visible? |
| | Are children distracted by activities going on nearby? |
| | How can more privacy be added? |
| Comfort | Where are children most quiet and calm when working? |

*(continued)*

## Teacher Tip (continued)

|  | Where are children most noisy and irritable when working? |
|---|---|
|  | Are there some materials children avoid? |
|  | How can more softness be added? |
| Social Interaction | Where do the most positive interactions take place? |
|  | Where do children get upset the most? |
|  | Where do groups of children gather? |
|  | Where do the children seem most joyful? |
|  | Where do they work the longest? |
| Adult Usage | Where do I like to be when talking to a child? |
|  | When visitors come, where do they sit? |
|  | How can adults be better integrated into the classroom activities? |

A well-designed teaching space provides ample room for large motor activities and opportunities for children and adults to work together safely and comfortably.

## How Is an Aesthetic Environment Created?

There is more to designing a space for living or working than arranging the furniture and setting rules for its use. This is particularly true of workspaces for children. In selecting the individual elements that make up the children's learning environment, we must consider the ways in which these elements will enrich the children's sensory-perception and thereby influence their aesthetic and cognitive experience. Although

### Did You Get It?

**Edna is a young facilitator who wants to create an effective learning environment for children. Which of the following things should she keep in mind while making a place for the arts?**

**a.** The actual space is more important than its design.

**b.** All early childhood environments need to be alike.

**c.** Children's sense of well-being is immune to factors in the learning environment.

**d.** Softness in the environment helps children relax and reduces stress.

**Take the full quiz on CourseMate**

people have different aesthetic senses, and room designs will reflect the uniqueness of personal taste, the following guidelines, based on principles of color, design, and children's behavior, are intended as an initial direction from which we can create a beautiful workspace for our children and ourselves.

## Light

Light adds life and focus to a space. When planning a learning area consider the effect of light coming into

The aesthetic arrangement of light, color, texture, and careful arrangement of space transforms everyday work spaces into places where creativity can soar. In this classroom ample light, natural textures, neutral colors, and the uniform use of blue for key accessories creates a beautiful space for learning.

the room through the windows and overhead lights. Ask yourself: How will different zones be lit? Will there be too much light or too little? Which centers need the most light?

**Natural light.** There is nothing better than natural light in the classroom. However, if there is too much sun for part of a day consider temporary ways to shade the windows, such as filmy curtains or shades, or better yet, artwork made by the children. Folded and cut white paper squares can be glued together into a window quilt. Holes can be poked into black paper to create constellations of stars. Tempera paint with a bit of detergent added can be used to create translucent artworks on the window glass. If the windows cannot be blocked, artwork made from tissue paper and other light filtering materials can be displayed in front of the windows.

Or take advantage of that sunlight. Plants love a sunny window and can block out some of the sun. Sunny windowsills also make great places for exploring light and shadows and displaying sensory materials that invite color play such as crystals, prisms, diffusion gratings, glass beads on a mirrored surface, color paddles, cellophanes, and kaleidoscopes.

**Interior lighting.** Florescent light fixtures, common in many schools, can give an industrial feel to a room. Explore ways to soften the lightening such as installing plastic tubes that fit over the bulbs to warm the color and also provide protection if a bulb should break. Or if fire laws allow, suspend fireproofed filmy cloth below the lights. Brighten shadowy areas with small table lamps, clip-on lights, light ropes, or mirrors. In the absence of sun, set up a light table where children can explore the opacity and transparency of materials while the table itself adds light to the area. Netting and see-through fabrics can be strung on lines or frames to delineate boundaries between areas of the room and at the same time change the quality of light and shadow reaching a center.

## Texture

Textures interact with light. Shiny, smooth textures bounce light around a room and reflect colors and movements. Soft, dull textures absorb light and rest the eyes. A classroom needs some of both. Adding smooth and shiny surfaces creates a feeling of space and freedom from clutter. Tiles and linoleum are easy to clean up when wet or sandy and make a good surface for block building, sensory bins, and painting.

The institutional feel of many classrooms can be allayed by adding soft textures. For example, the floor is a large area of texture in any room. Carpeted areas provide softness and absorb sound. They provide cushioning for energetic movement activities, and quiet musical explorations. Area rugs can be used to divide areas visually and texturally. Carpet squares, bolsters, pillows, or small rugs add flexibility as well as texture. They give each child a cozy place to sit at group meetings, but can also be used in other areas, such as in a gross motor obstacle course that provides a safe place for children to climb and pretend. Fabric coverings on bulletin boards not only soften the walls, but hold up longer and fade less than paper.

In planning for infants, we need to include textured surfaces that stimulate their senses. Change ordinary surfaces by covering them temporarily with aluminum foil, bubble wrap, waxed paper, textured fabrics, and similar materials for the infant to explore.

## Color

View the walls and floor as background for the objects that will be displayed in the room. Bright or strongly colored walls or floors are limiting, especially if we consider that many children's toys and the clothing they wear are brightly colored. Linda Apps and Margaret MacDonald (2012), noting the preponderance of saturated primary colors in early childhood settings, suggest that just because these are colors infants notice first does not mean that they prefer them and want to see them all the time. Bright intense colors can also make a room seem smaller, and can be exciting at first, but become tiresome after a while.

Consider the textures and patterns of the various materials on the floors and walls of rooms as well. It is good to have a variety, but keeping the colors of these items closely related prevents the effect from being overwhelming. Here again, neutral earth colors, including beiges, grays, and browns, and soft pastels can provide an unobtrusive background.

Light, neutral-colored backgrounds not only increase the aesthetic quality of a room but can also make the space seem larger. They allow the color scheme of the room to be varied simply by changing the colors in the displays and centers and also provide a neutral background so that children's own artwork stands out. When color schemes expand beyond white and primary colors, children learn to distinguish subtleties in hue and value.

Color families can be used in intentional ways to delineate special zones and work areas. When flexibility is built in by putting up temporary coverings of colored paper or cloth and adding a few accent pieces, colors in an area can be changed to accommodate changing interests and themes or from input given by the children. For example, tints and shades of blue might be used in a "dream-a-story" writing center cushioned with white puffy pillows, and up above, floating from strings, stories written by the children on cloud shapes.

## Storage

Storage containers for items not in use should enrich the environment, not detract from it. Careful selection can actually unify diverse areas and materials. Ann Lewin-Benham (2010) suggests using identical containers to create a storage system that is both easier to arrange on shelves and more aesthetic, with the repetition of the same size, shape, and color creating a restful pattern throughout the room or learning area.

Items can be stored in a variety of containers. Cardboard boxes from the supermarket or household products can be obtained at no cost. If using cardboard boxes, take the time to paint or cover them. Choose a unifying color that goes with the colors of other items in the room. When using purchased plastic bins, dishpans, or containers, try to get them in similar shapes and colors.

## Nature

Adding live plants, aquariums, terrariums, and other displays of natural objects also enrich the aesthetics of the indoor environment and brings the outdoors inside. Set up slowly changing displays of natural objects, such as shells, leaves, or rocks in various places in the room. Arrange the objects by size, texture, or color, and provide magnifying glasses so children can study them more closely. Natural objects, such as acorns, seeds, and pebbles, can be displayed on a shelf or windowsill. Put small items in clear plastic jars and containers that allow light to pass through and are safe for children to turn, shake, and study how the objects move and re-form. Integrate nature into centers. Put a plant on a worktable, put tree slices

and sturdy twigs in the block area, and add real fruit and vegetables to the grocery store center.

If there are windows that give a view of the outside, try to make them a focal point and draw attention to the changes in weather and light. If windows are high hold up infants and toddlers so they can see out on a daily basis. Provide places for older children to record and draw what they see. Consider adding a bird feeder, windsock, flag, snow stick, rain gauge, or similar item for children to observe.

Class pets bring another living dimension to the environment. Small mammals, such as mice, hamsters, and gerbils teach children kindness, caring, and responsibility. Less cuddly creatures such as crickets, worms, caterpillars, ants, tadpoles, Madagascan cockroaches, fish, and tarantulas inspire curiosity and wonder. Keeping paper and pencils nearby encourages children to use art to record what they see.

When considering pets for the classroom, check first for allergies. Have children wash hands before (for the animal's benefit) and after handling the animals. Avoid reptiles, as they are carriers of salmonella.

## Outdoors

Richard Louv (2008) says that never before have children been so disconnected from nature. This lack of contact with nature shows up in children's behavior.

Adding plants, animals, and other natural objects enhances the aesthetic qualities of the classroom as well as encouraging children to help care for their environment.

Children need places where they can explore the wonders of the natural world. Planting flowers and gardens around the school is one way to do this.

For example, children with access to nature show fewer attention deficit disorders (Taylor, Kuo, & Sullivan, 2001). They also have more empathy for animals, a greater sense of oneness, and showed a greater sense of responsibility (Cheng & Monroe, 2012).

Depending on location, access to the outdoors can vary widely. In large cities, playgrounds may be surrounded by high walls or located on a rooftop. Outdoor spaces at schools may consist of a paved yard behind a chain-link fence. In the country, play areas may spread across open fields and wooded areas. No matter the location, when approaching the outside environment, look beyond the typical playground fare and create magical places where children can explore the natural world with their senses and engage their imaginations through the arts and especially dramatic play.

Besides bringing out paint, murals, and rhythm instruments, create aesthetic sensory learning centers in corners of the playground. Collect baskets of leaves in the fall to sort, spill, and crunch as children pretend to be animals searching for food. Shovel piles of snow in the winter to stamp, pat, and shape into labyrinthine houses for snowball people to live in. Suspend bells, wind chines, and shakers from tree branches or attach them to a fence for children to perform music for the birds. In hot weather, gather brushes, bowls, and dishes of water and paint the pavement. In a shady spot under an overhang, below a tree, or under a tent-like canopy set out small branches, stones, gravel, dirt, shovels, and shells to create a fairy kingdom. Make child-sized tables and seats from tree-ringed trunks or large rocks. A garden of flowers or vegetables can be planted anywhere there is some sun. If there is no place to dig, try raised beds or planters.

**For more ideas for designing outdoor areas and equipment, see *Planning an Outdoor Environment* on CourseMate.**

## Technology

Computers, interactive white boards, printers, and tablets have come to occupy most early childhood classrooms. How and where these are located can make a big difference in the role they play in children's learning for preschoolers and up. The American Academy of Pediatrics and the White House Task Force on Childhood Obesity recommend that children under the age of two not engage in screen media at all. For older children, the recommendation is no more than two hours total a day, with limits of half-an-hour in half-day preschools and one hour in full-day programs and elementary schools (National Association for the Education of Young Children, 2012).

Technology works best when it is integrated into learning areas and tied to doing real research so that children begin to see it as resource rather than as a source of entertainment. For example, a computer and printer set up in the writing center can be designated as the class print shop. A computer or tablet with drawing software placed in the block area can be an architect's design hub. A computer or a television with a DVD player showing wildlife videos and animal facts can be placed in a nature area to serve as an animal observation booth. There is another benefit. When computers are dedicated to a specific function, it allows older computers and technology to be kept in service for longer.

Although more and more technology is becoming wireless, much of it is still tied to electrical outlets and includes a maze of wires. Engage children in creating boxes with appropriately placed openings to turn mundane computers into aesthetically seamless parts of the room and to hide the wires. Think of the computer screen as a window that can take you to places far from the classroom. A computer loaded with photos or videos of different places in the community, country, or world can be built into the "windshield" of a cardboard car. Display views of coral reefs and

### Did You Get It?

**Which of the following is a good practice to follow while creating an aesthetic learning environment?**

a. using many florescent light fixtures to brighten the room

b. using strongly colored walls to match children's toys and clothing

c. using bright intense colors to make the room seem larger

d. using light ropes or mirrors to brighten shadowy areas

**Take the full quiz on CourseMate**

undersea life through the porthole in a bathysphere. Deck out the computer as the windows of Mrs. Frizzle's Magic School Bus, and let children imagine touring through deserts, cities, and outer space. With a little imagination the potentials are unlimited.

## How Should Materials Be Presented?

When we take the time to plan how we offer materials, we set the stage for respectful handling by the children. It is the difference between offering a fast food lunch in a bag to be gobbled down and presenting a beautiful arrangement of food served on fine china in a fancy restaurant to be savored slowly.

Arts materials need to be presented in ways that catch the eyes and tickle the senses of our children. Inspiration can be drawn from the Reggio Emilia program where small items in clear jars are arranged by color and carefully selected materials are arranged by shape and size. Lella Gandini calls this "a gesture of offering something precious" (Gandini et al., 2005, p. 123). Children are more likely to choose and treat materials carefully when they are thoughtfully arranged. Children will, for example, carefully consider which piece to take when cut-paper shapes are separated into containers organized by shape and color, but they will root and grab from a box of mixed-up scraps. Costumes thrown haphazardly into a cardboard box will receive less consideration than will those hung neatly from individual pegs.

## Open-Ended Materials and Developmental Growth

If the environment is the third teacher, then open-ended materials must be considered the fourth. Materials is a broad term referring to the physical objects, tools, and supplies that form the basis of all the arts forms. Materials fit different categories depending on children's age, motor skills, and the need for safety. Carefully prepared interactions with materials help children develop.

- **Physically**—*by stimulating the senses and motivating children to investigate and become active investigators, they develop better control over their bodies.* We see this happening when they reach and grasp, hold and release, carry and drop, poke and pull, and squeeze and push. For example, staying within the confines of a hula hoop while dancing improves balance, strength, and muscular control. Pinching threads between finger and thumb in order to pick them up for a collage strengthens fine motor skills and hand–eye coordination.

- **Socially-Emotionally**—*by fostering self-confidence and self-regulation as they successfully handle new challenges and by creating situations that require sharing space and materials with others.* We see this happening when children learn to squeeze a spray bottle to create colors on a mural or when children take turns shaking a rain stick and listening to the sound.

- **Cognitively**—*by comparing, categorizing, and ordering a wide variety of materials and by observing cause and effect.* We see this happening when children compare the handprints they made in playdough or when they drop a bead down a tube and watch it come out the other end.

- **Linguistically**—*by developing a vocabulary of descriptive arts words.* We hear this happening when they use words for colors, shapes, textures, and other sensory qualities.

- **Creatively**—*by engaging curiosity and risk-taking while developing sustained attention and problem solving.* When carefully selected, materials offer

# Making Plans

## OPEN-ENDED ACTIVITY OUR CLASSROOM: A SCALE MODEL

**WHO?**    Group composition age(s): Suitable for toddlers and up

**WHEN?**    Time frame: Depending on age children will work from 20 minutes to many days.

**WHY?**    Objectives:  Children will develop

- physically, by using the small muscles of the hand to cut, fold, bend, and glue manipulate the various materials. (Bodily-Kinesthetic)

- socially, by interacting with a caring adult, and by sharing materials, space, and ideas with others (Interpersonal)

- emotionally, by having their ideas respected and acted upon. (Intrapersonal)

- perceptually, by using their senses to observe and select materials for their designs and arranging objects within a delineated space. (Spatial)

- language skills, by creating and using labels and symbols to mark locations in their designs and room maps. (Linguistic)

- cognitively, by comparing sizes, shapes, and forms with real objects and measurements and exploring the relationships found in working to scale. (Logical-Mathematical)

- arts awareness, by manipulating the elements of color, shape, texture, form, and pattern to create special effects. Content Standard 1 & 2.

**WHERE?**    Setup: Space to move around in the classroom. At table or on floor for a small group. One-on-one for special needs.

**WHAT?**    Materials: A low-sided box close to the shape of the real room. It should be as big as possible so a group can work together. Prepare the box by cutting down the sides so children can reach in easily. Mark the bottom with squares representing 1 square foot in scale with the actual room. Cut out openings where the doors and windows are in the real classroom. Nearby set out age-appropriate materials in attractive low-sided containers to be used for furnishings and objects in the model classroom. For example, for toddlers take photographs of objects in the classroom and glue them to wood blocks and give them varied papers, wallpaper, and cloth or carpet remnants for rugs. Preschoolers and up need more complexity. Add plain blocks of wood or small boxes for furniture, non-hardening modeling clay, chenille stems, wire, varied papers and cardboards, buttons, wallpaper samples, and so on. Have available drawing materials, scissors, and glue, a 1 foot ruler, Unifix cubes and tape measure or trundle wheel.

**HOW?**    Procedure:

WOW Warm-Up: Lead children on a tour of the classroom. Ask: What do we do in this area? What do you like about it? What could we add to make it better?

What to Do and Say: Show them the classroom box model and have them find the doors and windows and compare with the real ones. Measure out one foot square on the floor and compare to the squares in the box. Have children make their own foot measurers using the Unifix cubes [Primary age can make their own individual square foot out of paper] and use these to measure objects in the room. Show them how to use the tape measure or trundle wheel to measure the whole room. Invite children to draw their ideas for how to make the room better and to try their ideas out in the model classroom by arranging the objects and materials in different ways. Assist them in creating written labels for the objects.

Transition out: Listen as the children describe the changes they have made. Take notes and photographs. And then have children clean up by putting away unused items in their proper container.

**WHAT LEARNED?**    Assessment: Do children show a concept of size by comparing the model and the real objects? Do children use the materials to create items that are reasonable in size for the box and do they self-correct when needed? Do they share materials and ideas? Do they label their objects using words or symbols? Does their selection of materials show an awareness of color, shape, textures, form, and pattern?

*(continued)*

## Making Plans (continued)

*Reflection:* Can the children choose the materials they need easily? Are there too many materials or not enough? Which materials are causing problems? What other materials will be needed if they work on the model again? Does the project foster cooperation?

**NEXT?**    *Extensions:* Have children present their ideas to the group and, if possible try some of them out. Expand outside the box and design the outdoor play area. Put out a laminated map of the classroom and washable markers and let children draw different paths to the places they go. Put photographs of the children's faces on small blocks of wood and have them use the model room to tell stories about school.

*Literature connection:* Read stories about houses and buildings such as Gail Gibbons How a House is Built (1996) or Iggy Peck, Architect by Andrea Beaty (2007).

small problems and frustrations that challenge children to think creativity to reach their goal and be successful.

## Offering Materials

Ann Lewin-Benham (2010) reminds us that young children are more capable than we might think and that if arts materials are offered in planned encounters under the supervision of an alert teacher, young children may surprise us with what they can do.

## Offerings for Infants and Toddlers

Infants who are not yet sitting need materials in one-on-one teacher–child interactions such as those described in Chapter 4. When infants become mobile, materials can become grander.

Opportunities to interact with open-ended materials should be planned regularly into the day. Materials like clay, paint, musical instruments, and puppets can be explored as a baby sits in our laps or in a high chair. Larger offerings, such as cardboard tubes, can be placed around the infant on the floor to encourage the child to reach, creep, and crawl. Other materials can be attached to a wall or sturdy framework for the infant to reach for and pull on. For example, sound makers can be tied to thick cord so that they make noise when the child pulls.

Open-ended supplies that invite infant engagement with the arts are often simple materials found readily around us. Most have little or no cost involved. For example, lay out a roll of wallpaper, craft paper, metallic foil, freezer paper, or bubble wrap for infants to explore by crawling and creeping. Spread around a sitting infant cardboard tubes, small boxes, pots and pans, gourd shakers, or natural materials such as large shells, leaves, or stones that meet the choke test and encourage the child to explore by grasping and touching. Objects too small for them to handle safely can be put in sealed clear plastic bottles to shake and watch.

Their increasing gross and fine muscular control means toddlers can handle smaller objects or combine familiar ones in new ways. In supervised planned experiences offer several choices of playdough, paper, or paint brushes by arranging items in low-sided containers that children can see into easily to make their selection. Provide challenges such as painting a cardboard tube that rolls or squeezing color onto paper with eye droppers.

*For more suggestions for intelligent materials, see Materials for Young Children on CourseMate.*

## Offerings for Preschoolers and Kindergarteners

As children's knowledge of their world increases, bring in tools and materials that are real, such as garden tools to use in a real garden, plastic pipes and elbows to design waterways at the water table, or real vegetables for the dramatic play area that will later be made into soup or crudités for snack.

Arts materials should be of good quality and reflect those artists use. Fine-tipped brushes, real drums and recorders, and a full-size puppet theater tell children that the arts are valued and allow them to feel like the artists, dancers, actors, and musicians they really are.

At the same time, provide plenty of materials, such as blocks, sand, clay, sound makers, and lengths of fabric, having multiple possibilities that appeal to the senses, and let the imagination play.

## Offerings for Primary Age

In elementary grade schools, there may be an art or a music specialist who provides group instruction focused on the concepts and skills of the art forms. This may happen on a weekly or intermittent basis. Separate instruction in drama and creative movement in the early grades is much more rare, but may occur. Primary teachers who value the arts appreciate the extra instruction children get from these specialists. They may work closely with them to coordinate and integrate learning as teachers do with the *atelierista* in the Reggio Emilia schools, but they also know that bringing the materials of the arts into the classroom to be used every day will enrich and expand what children learn in all content areas. This can be done by incorporating the arts into math, writing, social studies, and science-based centers, and by setting up arts centers that children can access on their own.

In the primary grades, content becomes important, and activities often reflect themes and unit topics. As part of a study of winter, for instance, the whole class might draw with marker to show how a snowy day makes them feel, sing a song about snow, play rhythm instruments to create the sound of snow falling and crunching underfoot, and move around the classroom imagining shoveling, trudging through snowdrifts, and sledding down slippery hills. All of these bring the arts into the classroom using a few basic materials—markers, paper, and a bin of rhythm instruments.

However, the intentional teacher plans ahead, and provides what Paola Strozzi (2001) calls intelligent materials—in other words, materials that expand thinking. For example, if the children are going to explore snow through all their intelligences and creativity, then we need to provide ample choices of beautifully presented materials that make it possible for them to do so. It is the difference between giving out white paper and snowflake-shaped foam pieces to make snow collages and offering a feast of white and sparkly materials—a range of white papers in varied textures, silvery metallic and plastics, glitter,

white yarns, cotton balls, polyester stuffing, tinsel, beads, gravels, white cloth, and whatever else we, and they, can discover—to be used not only to make a snow day collage, but to be incorporated into snow sound rhythm instruments of their own invention, snowflake props to carry as they move creatively, and in combinations that only they can imagine.

On the other hand, just because these children are older doesn't mean that arts materials must always relate to themes and units. Primary age children still need access to materials that let them set their own goals

## Teacher Tip

### INTELLIGENT MATERIALS

Materials and objects offered to children should be open-ended, inspiring creative decision making and problem solving. Look for items that are

- **Eye-catching** – Does it stand out from the background? Does it have an intriguing shape, color, size, surface reflectivity, or transparency? Does it change appearance when viewed in different ways or when it is cut, folded and manipulated by the child? Examples: foils, fluorescent paper, velvet, colored cellophane and plexiglass, sparkles, watercolor paint, and rolls of one-sided corrugated cardboard.

- **Tactile** – Does it make you want to touch it? Does the texture provide an interesting contrast to the surfaces found in the everyday environment? Does the texture change or make a sound when touched or shaken? Examples: cornstarch gloop (cornstarch and water), clay, transparent colored glass marbles or shapes, colored sand and gravel, metal washers, metal nuts and bolts, feathers, leaves, and pinecones.

- **Unusual** – Is it something from another place, environment, or culture that the children haven't experienced before? Examples: bamboo, peacock feathers, nuts (check for allergies), sea shells and sea life from distance oceans, stones, fabrics, fleece, silk, and musical instruments from other cultures made from native materials.

- **Surprising** – Does it do surprising things when combined with other materials? Examples: Musical instruments make a new sound when combined, mixed colors make new ones.

- **Multipurpose** – Can the material be used in many different ways? Example: Can materials be used to make visual images, props for acting and dancing, and sounds for music?

Intelligent materials are preplanned and beautifully arranged so that children are drawn to them and inspired to use the materials thoughtfully. What would you make with these materials?

The orderly arrangement of supplies allows children to be more independent in their creative work. In addition, early literacy is enhanced by the use of a photograph and words on the label.

and challenges. They still need time and opportunity to pursue child-initiated projects and use their imaginations. They need blocks and paints and sensory experiences, ways to make music, and room to move; all presented in such a way that children make thoughtful choices, manage the materials independently, and clean up after themselves. Chapter 8 will explore ways to address standards and further arts integration in the primary classroom. Chapters 9 to 12 will provide information on specific materials and activities in each of the arts forms appropriate for primary children. Find more on assessing the qualities of the aesthetics and effectiveness of the arts environment here.

*For a checklist for assessing learning environments, see* *Assessing the Arts Environment* *on CourseMate.*

## Presenting Open-Ended Arts Materials

Materials that are freely available for children to choose from should be placed at child height and attractively displayed in uniform containers. Containers should be low-sided and wide enough so that children can easily see what is inside from their vantage point. Clear plastic containers work well for many supplies, as do low baskets, cut-down cardboard boxes, and dishpans.

**Controlling amounts.** Although supplies should be ample, avoid putting out huge amounts of any material. When children see bountiful quantities of a material, whether paper or buttons, they are more likely to use the material wastefully. It is better to display less of something and refill the containers more often.

## Teacher to Family

Set up a materials collection center in the classroom or school where families and community members can donate materials for arts-based exploration. The process of collecting the materials and donating to the program helps tie the school to the community. Asking children to place materials in labeled containers develops sorting and classification skills. Here is a sample letter you might send home:

Dear Family,

The materials center in our classroom encourages you and your child to take a fresh look at the things we discard every day and to see, in place of waste or excess, something full of potential to be repurposed into something new and wonderful. Using these found and recycled materials in our creative work helps our environment and challenges our imaginations.

*(continued)*

## Teacher to Family *(continued)*

Some of the items we can use include:

*Building things*: boxes of all sizes, cardboard, tubes, wood scraps

*Containers*, all sizes and shapes—especially clear plastic and glass, bowls, buckets, Styrofoam trays, squeeze and spray bottles, vases

*Flexible things*: lace, lacing, plastic tubing, ribbons, rickrack, rope, scarves, seam binding, shoelaces, string, ties, twist ties, yarn, wire

*Natural*: coral, driftwood, flowers, fossils, gourds, seashells, seeds, seedpods, starfish, stones

*Papers*: doilies, freezer paper, magazines, newspaper, photographs, posters, wax paper, wrapping

*Shiny & metallic*: cans (with smooth interior edges) cellophanes, colored glass, fabrics, foils, foil papers and wrapping, mirrors, plastic packaging, Plexiglas, ribbon, rods, tinsel

*Small treasures*: beads, bolts & nuts, bottle caps, buttons, corks, gravels, springs, washers

*Textures*: baskets, bubble warp, carpet samples, cotton batting & balls, dried plants, fabrics, foam, netting, packaging, pompoms, sponges, stuffing

*Wood*: bowls, carvings, craft sticks, figurines, logs, scrap pieces, spoons, tree slices and trunks, toothpicks, utensils

As you can see there are so many possibilities. Before you toss something away, together with your child imagine how it might be reused and consider donating it to us. For children's safety please make sure everything is washed and has no sharp edges.

Thank you,
Your child's teacher,

**Digital Download**    Download from CourseMate

---

### Did You Get It?

**Open-minded arts materials foster cognitive growth by**

a. motivating children to develop better control over their bodies.

b. fostering self-confidence and self-regulation as children successfully handle new challenges.

c. developing a vocabulary of descriptive arts words.

d. comparing, categorizing, and ordering a wide variety of materials.

**Take the full quiz on CourseMate**

**Using labels.** Label storage containers, shelves, and hooks so that children can match each item to its place. Labels introduce preliterate children to the printed word and build vocabulary for beginning readers. For infants, toddlers, and preschoolers, include both the word and either a picture or sample of the object attached to the outside of the containers. To develop bilingual skills in all children include labels in home languages. Inviting older children to help make the labels establishes ownership and familiarizes them with the storage system.

Photographs or charts showing how to use the supply and related children's books are another way to add literacy to materials displays.

## How Can We Share Children's Arts Learning?

No matter how much we recognize that process is more important than the finished product, at the end of each day we will be faced with many tangible arts products that will require attention. There will be paintings, child-made books, musical compositions, murals, videos of original playlets, and photographs of creative movements. How do we share these wondrous things? Classroom displays should acknowledge the artistic accomplishment of one or a few children at a time. Public displays can illustrate the learning that is going, or educate the viewer.

### Classroom Displays

The visual arts, in particular, result in both two- and three-dimensional products. Infants and toddlers, who are immersed in explorations, may care little about what happens to their explorations of paint, marker, and play dough and may not even remember making them. Older children will have many different attitudes to their work, depending on their purposes. Some, like toddlers for whom only the process matters, may care little for finished pieces. Others may cherish every piece they have touched. Work that expresses a particular feeling or subject may be highly valued. Art that the child intends as a "gift" will be viewed differently than art that is done just because the materials are there and the mood struck. When children of all ages use the arts as an emotional release or to express feelings, the end result is viewed as an extension of themselves. Its treatment is taken personally.

Because we never know how a child feels, it is always best to treat all children's artwork with respect. This models for the children how deeply we value them and the work they produce. Ways to show respect include

- **Put on names.** For infants and toddlers strive to put names on the back of all pieces of work. Attach pencils or markers to walls and easels with Velcro so that they are always handy and encourage children who can write their own names to do so. Develop a shorthand code, or use initials if pressed for time. If there are different sessions in the program, consider using a different-color marker for each session. For example, all of the green names might belong to the A.M. group, and all of the orange ones to the P.M. group. Label a shelf, cubby, or floor space with each child's name, and teach children to put their projects in their spots. Holding up children's artwork and saying "Whose is this?" tells the children that we did not care enough to notice what arts activities they were participating in that day.

- **Avoid folding artwork.** If artwork is too large to fit in a space, then roll it up. Folded artwork can never be mounted properly. If stored for a period of time, it will tear at the folds. Arts portfolios need to be large enough to hold the largest-size paper that individual children use.

- **Avoid disillusionment.** There will always be a few pieces of artwork that remain unidentified, no matter how hard we strive to label them all. If artwork must be discarded, do so discreetly. When children see artwork in the trash, they worry that the same thing may happen to theirs. Make sure

parents are taught to do the same thing. Many children become disillusioned about creating visual art, because "it will just get thrown away at home."

- **Prepare work attractively.** Make sure that all artwork that goes home or is displayed is properly labeled and presented.

- **Keep hands off.** Children's artwork is their own. Maintain a hands-off policy. Avoid drawing or working on a child's artwork to make it "better." This is insulting to the child artist and reflects a lack of self-confidence on the part of the educator.

## Displaying Children's Work and Performances

Sharing children's work and performances in the classroom are an important part of making them feel like they belong. This type of display is intended to draw recognition from peers, but its main purpose is to develop the child's self-confidence. There are many ways to do this ranging from hanging artwork or photographs at the children's height on a wall or wash line to individual displays.

**Individual arts sleeves.** Mount a clear plastic sleeve protectors or strong two-gallon size plastic bags, if you want something larger, on a bulletin board and label it with the child's name. On a regular basis and in consultation with the child, perhaps as part of a portfolio discussion, decide what to disply in the sleeve.

**Creator of the week.** Another way to share a child's work in the classroom is to establish a creator of the week or month display. Select one child to be the featured artist or musician or dancer or actor, and put up a few pieces of the child's work with photographs of the child in the process of creating or performing. For a musician, record the child singing and playing musical instruments, and then set up a listening center with a CD or tape recorder and headphones. For creative movement display photographs or a looping video or DVD showing the child dancing. For acting show the child participating in dramatic play activities or putting on a puppet show. This same approach can also be used to present a group project.

Focusing on one child or project at a time makes that one child's work special and eliminates the urge to compare the work of one child to another.

Accompany the display with a photograph of the artist, a transcribed interview, and/or dictation about what the child did. Take time to introduce the child and the display to the group. Discuss it with a group in the same way any work or performance would be discussed. Chapter 7 provides lists of questions you can ask.

Hang the display in a place of honor. Because the creator is present, in addition to descriptive questions and statements, questions about technique can be answered. Some teachers finish by asking the other children to write positive comments about the artist.

**Personal space.**  Another place children can display their work is in a personalized location set aside for each child. This could be a cubbie, a space on a shelf, or a stack of similar sized and shaped boxes facing outward on a counter or shelf or attached to a wall. In this enclosed space children can create their own personal changing display of their creations and photographs. This type of system allows children to readily store away their works, provides a place for projects to dry, and reduces the number of unidentified projects. At the beginning of the year or session, create a feeling of ownership by having children paint the insides of their box with their favorite color before creating the display.

**Hooks.**  A row of large coat hooks, one assigned to each child, can be used to display journals, photos in sleeves, and artworks. Taping a string to a corner of most papers will be sufficient to suspend them or, for more long-term or active handling, punch a hole and use looseleaf rings or chenille stems. Hooks can be attached to a wall or under a shelf at child height. This type of system creates a time order as the more recent work will be in front and older work in the back. Hooks will need to be regularly emptied providing a stepping stone toward portfolio creation.

## Creating a Presentation Center

An area may be set up where artworks and photographs are prepared to be displayed, to go home, or to be put into the portfolio. This area can be a small table or shelf containing a stapler, colored paper in various sizes, markers, and preprinted labels.

When children have something they want to save, they can bring it to the table. Ask the child to select a color for the background mount. Staple the artwork or photograph on the mount along with the label and any notes for the family. Digital photographs of the child doing an activity can be printed and glued to cardboard, then cut out and mounted upright onto a box or wood block base. Older children can do this independently. Some children may want to add designs to the frame surrounding the picture. The child then takes the work to a designated storage place or portfolio. If a child does produce a series of artworks on one day or over several days, or a series of photographs are taken, they can be stapled together between two mounting sheets to form a book of art.

Musical compositions, and other arts creations can also be prepared at the presentation table. Children can make a decorative envelope for storing a CD or tape or create a photograph or scrapbook type album.

Sculptures can be mounted on blocks of wood or small boxes the children prepare by painting or attaching materials. Considering how a work will be displayed is part of the arts process and encouraging children to participate fully in the preparation of their work helps develop aesthetic and critical thinking skills.

For directions on mounting work, see *Mounting 2-D and 3-D Artworks* on CourseMate.

## Public Displays of Learning

We need to carefully consider our purpose in displaying the children's creative work to the public. The public arena presents the program to people who have not participated directly in the children's arts process. Public exhibits can also benefit an arts program by educating parents and the community about what the children have been learning.

Public displays should not be for self-satisfaction or competition, but to celebrate the process of creation. When the sole purpose of presentations of children's art is to boost the egos of the children or the educators, then they create pressure situations that are detrimental to the arts process. Fearful of being judged by families or outsiders, we exhort the children to do their best because their families are going to see it, or we select creativity limiting step-by-step projects for the children to do, which we hope will make a good impression. We may display work that we think is most adult pleasing and reject work that looks out of control or unpleasant. We might think, "I can't show this. Their families will be so disappointed in them. They'll think I'm not teaching anything."

Competitions and judged art shows also do not belong in early arts education programs. They emphasize adult-pleasing products and foster the attitude that certain types of art are better than others. Such events may have a positive effect on the winners but can cause the losers to give up on arts creation entirely.

On the other hand, thoughtful public presentation of children's creative work can serve several positive functions that support child artists. Carefully designed exhibits can help families and friends learn more about how and why young children create art. They can also teach about arts concepts and techniques and other curriculum areas, and they can help introduce adults to the arts created by people from other places and cultures. Presentations with such carefully considered purposes will ultimately lead to more genuine ego building than those that have "ego boosting" as their main purpose.

**Thematic displays.** One display method that educates the viewer is to create a display of thematically related works that adds to or creates a unique environment and often elicits the creation of more art. Children can be active participants in creating these displays and deciding how they will look and where they will be placed. For example, for an underwater theme, turn one corner of the room into an undersea environment with child-created sea creatures displayed in a glass aquarium. Hang an undersea mural on the wall. Drape fishnets and shells on the shelving, and place sea-theme sculptures among them. Put the sand or water table in the center. Children's drawings of fish can be displayed by the aquarium, along with fish books and photographs of fish.

Chapter 8 delves deeper into creating and documenting thematic work.

**Artistic growth.** To show artistic growth, create a display showing changes in skill level over time. For example in the visual arts, display a series of works done by one child over a period of months. Accompany the display with photographs of children's hands illustrating different grips on art tools or anecdotal descriptions of how the works were created.

**Arts elements.** To show the arts elements, display a series of works by different children illustrating the use of the elements of that art form such as rhythm, melody, pattern, and pitch in music or line, shape, color, texture, or pattern in the visual arts. Accompany the display with bold graphics representing the arts

Displays of children's work can have many purposes. Including an interactive component, such as the matching question on this printing display, invites the viewer to think about the work and will attract a closer look.

element and children's descriptions of the element in their work. Photographs of children exploring sensory experiences related to the particular element can be included, as can children's books about that element.

**Artistic techniques.** To demonstrate a particular technique, select works using that technique, such as notating a melody using symbols, creative movements on different levels, or making papier-mâché puppets, Accompany the examples with step-by-step photographs of how the children made them and their dictated or written explanations.

**Multidisciplinary.** Learning from other curriculum areas can be displayed by hanging charts and graphs, sample experiments, child-created comments and stories, experience charts, and photographs accompanied by any illustrative artwork or photographs of performances the children created.

**Cultural experiences.** Experiences with artwork from other cultures can be shown by displaying artifacts or prints of the featured pieces, accompanied by descriptions of the culture and how they were made, along with children's artwork and photographs that reflect a related concept. For example, combine printed cloth from India with the children's prints and with photographs of them playing bells and finger cymbals from India.

**Promotional.** A well-put-together public display can introduce a program's best aspects. It can be a multimedia glimpse into the children's daily pursuits.

**Photo Story**

**An Emergent Project**

# An Addition to Our School

When a group of second graders learned that a new addition was planned for their school, they wondered what it would be like. They observed their school, drew floor plans, and then built a model of their idea using a variety of materials.

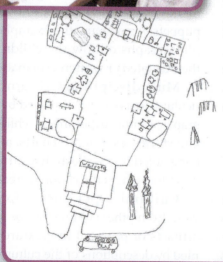

"New Addition" Pencil— Mark, age seven

A promotional display should give a feeling for the experiences in which the children participate. Select one or more works showing a range of techniques and approaches. Accompany the works with photographs of children creating and children's comments or explanations. Label displays with bold signs that attract attention, such as "Our Artists at Work" or "The Wonderful World of Song." Examples of the range of promotional presentations include brochures and calendars, showcases and bulletin boards, and badges and T-shirts, all featuring children's creative work.

## Locating the display

Depending on their purpose, these kinds of public displays can be located in a variety of places. Walls outside of the children's workspace are convenient for educational and promotional displays. Lobbies, hallways, stairwells, doors, offices, bathrooms, and any other space that is visited on a regular basis by the public can be used.

---

### Did You Get It?

**Serena is a second grade teacher. Which of the following should Serena do to show respect for the artwork created by her students?**

a. Gather up all the children's artwork, and at the end of the day hold it up and ask 'Whose is this?'

b. If no one claims a piece of artwork, discard it in the class trash.

c. Roll up large artwork instead of folding it.

d. Draw on their drawings to improve them.

**Take the full quiz on CourseMate**

---

# Conclusion: Creating a Sense of Place

For many years the emphasis on places for children has been on ease of cleaning and efficient functioning. This has been the model for most public schools in the United States. One large space is intended to serve all purposes. It is not surprising that in such an environment, visual arts activities are limited to a multi-purpose table that has to be cleared off at snack time, some boxes of junk, and perhaps a lonely easel. Music and dance rarely occur, and dramatic play is found only in the dress-up corner. In order to create an environment that is conducive to arts creation, some major changes must occur in how we build and equip the basic room.

The key to an enticing, functional place for children is an environment where children can focus on the activities and supplies available, work independently, and clean up when done. We want an environment that is safe and functional and in which children can learn. But the space should also demonstrate that we value the role of the arts, not as a playtime activity, but as an important way that children show us what they are thinking.

Although every space is unique, with careful planning it can meet these requirements. It is well worth the effort.

- Children behave better in environments that consider their needs.

- Space that is arranged so that teachers can move about easily and find needed supplies quickly helps them become more relaxed and attentive to the children as they create art.

- Beautiful workspaces inspire both adults and children to create their best work.

On the whole, our society suffers from a lack of aesthetic vision. Many homes are decorated with an accumulation of well-liked things that do not relate to each other. Our educational settings mirror this.

Sandboxes are filled with so many shovels and containers that there is no room for a child to just play with the sand. Styrofoam trays, wrapping paper, strips of carpet remnants, and some old yarn bits are shoved in a cardboard box, and then children are expected to make something beautiful from them. Dress-up clothes are heaped together in a corner. Adults often feel that children need all of these things to use. But do they? When children are overwhelmed, they do not learn to focus. We need to use intentional teaching and intelligent materials to create the best environment that we can to nourish young artists; need to teach them that there is beauty in each part, and that each part relates to the others to make the whole.

For additional information on creating beautiful environments for learning, *see Chapter 6 Online Resources* on CourseMate.

# Teaching In Action

### *Putting a Group Project Together: Our Neighborhood, Grade 1*

This interview with a first-grade teacher shows how a cooperative arts project can incorporate learning in all the subject areas.

Speaking & Writing

**Q:** How did you begin?

**A:** My first-grade class was very involved in talking about where everyone lived. We began by finding out about where each child lived. The children drew pictures of their houses and shared them with the group. We talked about who lived in the house and the things they did there. Some children brought in photographs of their homes, and we shared them. Then they wrote about their homes in their journals. Everyone had to learn to write their own address and phone number, and we displayed it with each child's house drawing.

Social Studies

We talked about how we are alike and how we are different. I read the children the book *The Big Orange Splot* (Pinkwater, 1977), and we talked about the ways each of their houses is the same and how they are different. We put photographs of each of them with their families by their drawing and talked about how everyone's family was different, too.

Mathematics

We also went for a walk around the school, looking at the houses and stores and counting them. We searched for the house numbers and street names. I told the children to look for different geometric shapes. Then when we got back we made a list of what they

Visual Art

noticed and drew pictures in their journals. By now, houses were a popular subject at the easel and in the block corner. I was pleased to see that the children weren't just making

Creativity

the same old stereotypical house shape either, and they were combining the shapes in new ways and getting very colorful.

Language

**Q:** How did you get them started on the mural?

**A:** Well . . . I drew the streets we had taken on our walk on a large piece of cardboard. I traced our walk on the roads I had drawn and explained that it was like a map. Then I asked children to imagine our walk and to name the different streets, stores, and houses we had passed. I had them use their journals and our chart to help them remember. But it really was amazing how much of the walk they could describe. Next, the children each chose a building to make. They used small blocks of wood that a parent had donated. Doors and windows were drawn on with crayon and marker.

Social Studies

**Q:** Describe how you had the children put the model together.

**A:** We all sat around the cardboard base, with the children holding their buildings. I started at the beginning of our walk, and as I moved my finger along the road, I asked what buildings we would see along the way. The child with that particular building would then come up and place it along the road.

Dramatics & Movement

When we were done, we imagined we were walking around the neighborhood. One child would be the leader and guide us up and down the streets describing things we might see.

Reflection
Intentional planning

**Q:** What do you think the children learned in making this model of their neighborhood?

**A:** They learned which houses and buildings are in the neighborhood of the school, and they were introduced to some beginning mapping. They learned that buildings can be made of many geographic shapes joined in different ways, and that this helped them make more accurate representations of houses and buildings. The children also learned

Family outreach

how to work together in creating the model. I will build on this concept now by introducing how people need to work together to create a community in which all are safe and healthy, and where their rights are respected. I will put out community helper figures in the block area, and costumes and puppets in the dramatic play area. I have also invited parents to come in and share the work they do.

# Reflection Page

## Becoming Sensitive to our Environment

The following activities are designed to provoke thought about the environments in which we exist and the effect they have on our feelings and behavior.

1.  Make a list of places where you feel most relaxed. Categorize them as soft or hard, open or closed, private or social.

    _____

    _____

    _____

2.  Make a list of all of the different environments you spend time in each day, such as the bedroom, kitchen, classroom, bus, and so on. Describe your behavior in each environment in terms of how you move, talk, and dress, and whether you feel comfortable or not.

    _____

    _____

    _____

3.  Based on what you wrote above, describe the perfect environment for you to teach in.

    _____

    _____

    _____

    _____

    _____

    _____

    _____

    _____

    _____

    _____

    _____

# Reflection Page

## Observation: Aesthetics of an Environment

Choose a room in a home or school where children explore the arts or visit a school website that has classroom photographs. Examine this room's aesthetic effect. Use the CourseMate *Assessing the Arts* checklist and the information in this chapter as a guide.

1.  What are the background colors in this room?
    Walls: _____
    Ceiling: _____
    Floor: _____
    Floor coverings: _____

2.  What is displayed on each wall? Be specific. Make a sketch if necessary.
    Wall 1: _____
    Wall 2: _____
    Wall 3: _____
    Wall 4: _____

3.  Are there any sensory displays? If yes, describe them.
    _____
    _____

4.  How are materials displayed?
    _____
    _____

5.  What is the total aesthetic effect of this room? Is there anything you would change to make it more aesthetically pleasing for children?
    _____
    _____

6.  Do you think the room encourages or discourages children's artistic behavior? Is there anything you might change? Draw sketches of your ideas.
    _____
    _____

# Reflection Page

## Designing the Environment

Keeping in mind what the children will be learning about the arts, design an ideal environment.

1.  Outline a 14-by-20-foot room on the graph paper. (Scale: one square equals one foot.)
2.  Trace the scaled pattern pieces shown on Studio Page 24, or design your own.
3.  Cut them out, and try several possible arrangements to create an environment that would be ideal for young artists.
4.  Plan areas for activities that are wet and messy, quiet and comfortable, creative and dramatic, and involve kinesthetic movement.
5.  Consider all of the different arts activities that could take place in each area, and then indicate where supplies would be located.

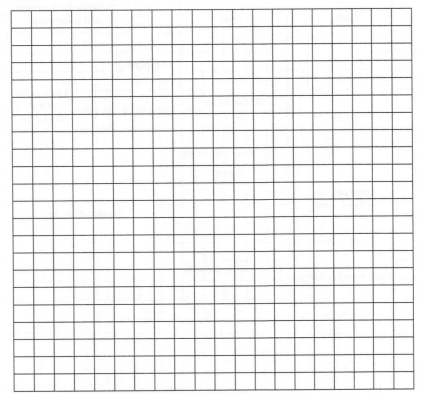

# Reflection Page

## Scaled Furniture Pieces

1 square = 1 foot
Note: Pieces may be used more than once.

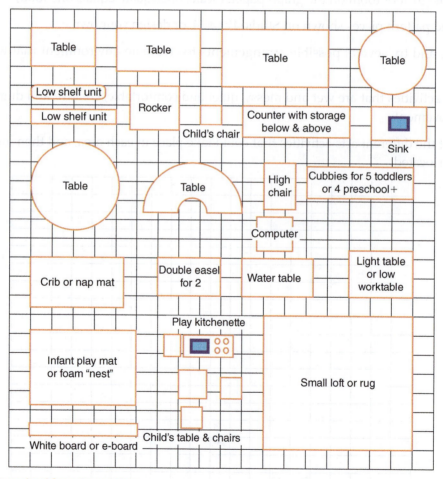

# Introducing the World's Arts

Design responsive arts activities that incorporate the Common Core learning standards in English language arts and the arts.

Planning Curriculum to Achieve Important Goals

Know ways to develop cultural understanding and literacy skills through the arts.

Teaching to Enhance Development and Learning

**Introducing the World's Arts DAP Learning Objectives**

Assessing Children's Development and Learning

List ways to assess children's engagement with artworks and artistic performances.

Creating a Caring Community

Establishing Reciprocal Family Relationships

Understand the importance of sharing the arts of diverse cultures.

Explain how to build reciprocal relationships with families through the arts.

## Young Artists Creating

"What are those things?" Brian whispers.

"I think they're spaceships," his friend Allen replies.

"No, silly, can't you see they're whirlies?" says Shannon.

"What's a whirly?"

"That's when you take a brush and whirl it all around."

"Oh," says Michael thoughtfully, "I do that when I paint, too."

"Well," says the teacher, coming up behind the children, "I see you have discovered our new print, Van Gogh's *Starry Night*. Come over to the rug, and I'll read you a story about the artist. It's called *Camille and the Sunflowers*" (Anholt, 1994).

## How Do Children Learn to Respond to the Arts?

Children absorb many meanings from their environment. The songs teachers select to sing, the pictures they hang on the wall, and the knickknacks on the shelf all show what artistic styles and forms those teachers personally value. In selecting arts experiences, we must look not only to children's own creations but also to the music, dance, drama, and visual arts that express cultural and historical roots. The human-made creative works that surround children when they are young will impact how they will respond to the other artistic works they encounter throughout life.

People tend to like those things with which they feel comfortable and to reject the strange and unfamiliar. It is a basic principle of good advertising to bombard customers' senses until the product is so familiar that they choose it almost automatically. Educators must decide what they would like the objects and experiences in their children's environment to advertise.

### Expanding the Child's Definition of the Arts

Young children naturally create artistic works as part of their way of interacting with and learning about the world, but exposure to the arts of others helps them understand why art is created, who is an artist, and how the arts are a part of their everyday environment. By interacting with carefully selected creative works,

Children's ideas about art are influenced by the artistic works and performances they are exposed to. Laurel, age five, in her drawing of Superman shows her familiarity with the movie.

children learn that the arts are more than just messing around for fun. The arts are not just what they do when they move to music or beat on a drum. When they are engaged with the arts, they are participating in a long chain of human creativity.

In addition, surrounding children with exciting artworks and exposing them to music, dance, and dramatic performances provides them with the impetus to practice the linguistic and cognitive skills of describing and responding to works of art.

## How Do Young Children Perceive the Art of Others?

As teachers, we need to be aware of how we influence children's perception of beauty and the development of their aesthetic philosophy and judgment. Our impact can be felt in two ways. One way we can affect young children's aesthetic perceptions is by creating a pleasing environment with carefully selected, beautiful objects and awe-inspiring performances. The other way is to expand children's definition of beauty by pointing out the aesthetic and sensory qualities in their creative works, performances, and in the environment, and by providing experiences that foster sensory awareness. The goal should be to help children grow into adults who love beautiful things, who value all kinds of art, and who can still find wonder in the beauty of the world.

When experiencing a beautiful artistic performance or a wonderful part of nature, we are overwhelmed by the total effect. But to re-create this experience for someone who has not seen it, we must describe it in terms of the artistic ingredients of which it is composed. These ingredients, or elements, are the building blocks of the artist, dancer, composer, and actor. When we react to something aesthetically, our senses are being affected by the way these elements have been brought together at that moment in time.

Creating with the arts is the process of playing with these elements and arranging them in an aesthetically meaningful way. This is what young children are doing when they explore different art forms. However, they also need to learn how to identify and describe these elements so that they can talk about, understand, and make aesthetic judgments about artistic works.

However, no two people make identical judgments about the arts. People find beauty in different styles of painting, types of music, and ways of dancing because of their personal beliefs, knowledge, or experiences. It is our task to provide an intellectual and critical framework in which children can form their own unique judgments about the arts.

## The Importance of Culture

Children get their first ideas about the arts from their family culture. Many ideas about beauty are held in common by people who share a similar heritage. When a group holds the same ideas about the beauty of some object or experience, this represents a **cultural aesthetic** or **style.** Ideas about style can be based on shared lifestyle, history, or experience. Styles can be handed down from one generation to another, as in the Amish tradition of making quilts from only solid-colored fabrics. Style can also denote works that are based upon a shared set of principles, such as jazz, an American musical style that features strong, flexible rhythms supporting solo and group improvisations.

Although childhood experiences and cultural styles form the core of an individual's aesthetic philosophy, each person's definition of beauty is always changing. Some cultural styles change over time. Eighteenth-century European men felt beautifully dressed when wearing long, curled, and powdered wigs. Sometimes one group of people or an individual will copy or adapt a style from another group, such as when non-Native Americans wear T-shirts decorated with traditional Native American symbols. Children are constantly bombarded with often conflicting ideas about beauty from books, television, and in movies and commercials. These, too, are added to their internal brew of aesthetic experiences and judgments. Taken together, all of these diverse influences form a personal aesthetic philosophy that determines what they think is beautiful and what they like.

## Responding Aesthetically to the Arts: The National Core Arts Standards

Liking a work of art, piece of music, style of dance, or story genre, however, is not the same as understanding and valuing it. The word *beautiful* is not a simple adjective but also a word of judgment. Not all creative works are intended to be beautiful. Some assail the senses with distorted, confused, or unpleasant images or strong emotional messages, and it is hard to separate our emotions about a piece or performance from its value as a creative statement by an artist. We may not like every creative performance done by the children with whom we work or by every professional adult artist, but we can appreciate it, and we can help children appreciate the aesthetic elements in their creations and those of others by developing their ability to respond and make judgments about a wide variety of art forms.

The purpose of the National Coalition for Core Arts Standards is to provide a framework for educating artistically literate citizens. The standards are based on five philosophical principles combined with lifelong goals all of which include on some level responding aesthetically to works of art as shown in Figure 7-1. **Responding** is defined by the NCCAS as "interacting with and reflecting on artistic work and performances to develop understanding." (National Coalition for Core Arts Standards, p. 10).

1. **The arts as communication.** As an important form of communication in our media-driven society, the arts inform our lives. We help our children become artistically literate when we teach them ways to observe, respond to, and to analyze artistic works.

| Philosophical Foundation | Lifelong Goals |
|---|---|
| **The Arts as Communication** | |
| In today's multimedia society, the arts are the media, and therefore provide powerful and essential means of communication. The arts provide unique symbol systems and metaphors that convey and inform life experience (i.e., the arts are ways of knowing). | Artistically literate citizens use a variety of artistic media, symbols, and metaphors to independently create and perform work that expresses and communicates their own ideas, and are able to respond by analyzing and interpreting the artistic communications of others. |
| **The Arts as Creative Personal Realization** | |
| Participation in each of the arts as creators, performers, and audience members enables individuals to discover and develop their own creative capacity, thereby providing a source of lifelong satisfaction. | Artistically literate citizens find at least one arts discipline in which they develop sufficient competence to continue active involvement in creating, performing, and responding to art as an adult. |
| **The Arts as Culture, History, and Connectors** | |
| Throughout history the arts have provided essential means for individuals and communities to express their ideas, experiences, feelings, and deepest beliefs. Each discipline shares common goals, but approaches them through distinct media and techniques. Understanding artwork provides insights into individuals' own and others' cultures and societies, while also providing opportunities to access, express, and integrate meaning across a variety of content areas. | Artistically literate citizens know and understand artwork from varied historical periods and cultures, and actively seek and appreciate diverse forms and genres of artwork of enduring quality/significance. They also seek to understand relationships among the arts, and cultivate habits of searching for and identifying patterns, relationships between the arts, and other knowledge. |
| **Arts as Means to Well-Being** | |
| Participation in the arts as creators, performers, and audience members (responders) enhances mental, physical, and emotional well-being. | Artistically literate citizens find joy, inspiration, peace, intellectual stimulation, meaning, and other life-enhancing qualities through participation in all of the arts. |
| **The Arts as Community Engagement** | |
| The arts provide means for individuals to collaborate and connect with others in an enjoyable inclusive environment as they create, prepare, and share artwork that bring communities together. | Artistically literate citizens seek artistic experience and support the arts in their local, state, national, and global community. |

**FIGURE 7–1** Foundational concepts of the national core arts standards

From the *National Core Arts Standards A Conceptual Framework for Arts Learning* (2013) p. 8 Available from: http://nccas.wikispaces.com

2. **The arts as creative personal realization.** The arts offer ways for every musician, dancer, dramatist, and artist to express her or his personal ideas and feelings. We help our children become artistically literate when we help them refer to their own personal experience of creating artworks when responding to the works of others.

3. **The arts as culture, history, and connectors.** The arts embody symbols, knowledge, and beliefs that may differ from our own or from our children's, but are reflective and informative about the people and cultures that produced them. We help our children become artistically literate when we help them make comparisons and find connections between artworks and the historical and cultural setting that produced them.

4. **The arts as a means of well-being.** Viewing artworks, listening to music, and watching plays and dance are pleasurable activities that enhance our emotional and physical health. We help our children become artistically literate when we teach them how to enjoy viewing artistic works and being receptive members of an audience.

5. **The arts as community engagement.** The arts are a way to form and strengthen groups and communities. We help our children become artistically literate when we engage them in group and community events and settings that value and celebrate the arts.

## Artistic Works as Texts: Arts and the Common Core Curriculum

Responding to artworks and performances also ties in with the Common Core Standards in English Language Arts. The standards for reading, writing, and speaking include discussing, comparing, analyzing, and responding to written materials or "texts." However, artistic works are also communicative materials or "texts" that can be analyzed using the same skills. For preliterate children looking at, listening to, and talking about artistic works and performances provide an introduction to skills they will need to be successful readers and writers. For early literacy learners responding to artistic works is another way for them to apply the reading, writing, and speaking skills they are mastering.

Figure 7-2 shows how literacy skills applied to artistic works or "texts" provide a foundation for the reading, writing, and speaking skills as laid out in the English Language Arts portion of the Common Core.

---

**Did You Get It?**

A teacher would like to encourage children to use the arts for creative personal realization. Which of the following sentences should he use when encouraging his students to paint?

a. Let's see who comes up with the best picture.

b. Your finished paintings will be displayed for evaluation by your peers.

c. Do your best possible work, keeping in mind the techniques learned.

d. Paint a place where you have been, incorporating how the place made you feel.

**Take the full quiz on CourseMate**

---

## How Do We Engage Children with Artistic Works?

Artistic or aesthetic literacy starts with focused awareness and heightened perception. From birth, children are ready to engage physically, sensorially, and cognitively with the objects and events that surround them. Some of those objects and events will be artistic works and performances. At first, those experiences may occur within the home as when a mother sings a lullaby or a father spins the child around in an impromptu dance.

When children enter our programs, it becomes our role to provide experiences with creative art works and performances that supplement and expand on those the child may have experienced with their family. We begin by engaging the child's interest in the texts of the arts.

### Engaging with the Arts

Initially, children respond to the arts performance of others in a sensory way, hearing sounds and rhythms, repeating the words of a story, seeing colors, shapes,

Note: The word "text" as used here refer to artistics works in all art forms.

| Area | Skill | Related to ELA Literacy Common Core Standards |
|---|---|---|
| | | K=Kindergarten<br>1=1st grade<br>2=2nd grade |
| **Reading** | Asks and answers questions about text<br>Compares and contrasts texts<br>Connects pictures and story<br>Describes role of illustrator<br>Describes relationship between illustrations and text<br>Engages with purpose and understanding<br>Identifies meanings of words<br>Identify similarities and differences in texts<br>Interacts with different texts including songs<br>Makes cultural connections to text and self<br>Retells stories based on texts<br>Retells details from texts | L.K.1d<br>RL.K.1–10<br>RI.K.1–7,9, 10<br><br><br>RL.1.1–7,9<br>RI.1–4, 6–9<br><br><br>RL.2.1–9<br>RI.2.1, 3, 6–9 |
| **Writing** | Adds details to strengthen illustrations<br>Creates and presents an artistic work in response to an author or theme studied<br>Gathers information<br>Participates in shared research such as explore a number of books by the same author and express opinion<br>Recalls information<br>Uses combination of drawing, dictating, or writing to express an opinion about a book or topic or to narrate a single event and reaction to it<br>Use digital tools to produce and publish writing | W.K.1–3 & 6–8<br><br>W.1.1–3, 6–8<br><br>W.2.1–3, 6–8 |
| **Speaking & Listening** | Asks and answers questions about texts to show understanding<br>Asks and answers questions to get help or information<br>Comes to a conclusion<br>Communicates with others from different cultural backgrounds<br>Describes familiar things<br>Expresses feelings, thoughts, and ideas<br>Follows rules of discussion<br>Uses drawings or other art forms to add detail to oral presentations<br>Uses new vocabulary correctly | L.K.1d<br>SL.K.1–6<br><br>SL.1.1–6<br><br>SL.2. 1a–c, 2–6 |
| **Foundational** | Engages in language play (alliterative language, rhyming, sound patterns)<br>Recognizes symbols and labels | RF.K.2a |
| **Language** | Sorts & categorizes objects<br>Identify real life connections between words and objects<br>Uses new vocabulary—words and phrases acquired through conversations, reading, being read to, and from responding to texts to describe | L.K.4, 4a, 5a, 5c, 6<br>L.1.4, 5a–d, 6<br><br>L.2.5a, 6 |

**FIGURE 7–2** The arts and literacy skill development
Based on the Common Core Standards for English Language Arts http://www.corestandards.org/ELA-Literacy

and textures, and moving to the music. We can use that sensory attraction and wonderment to draw attention and foster engagement with carefully selected works and performances.

**Making familiar.** In order to "read" the text of an artistic work we must start by familiarizing the child with the work. Starting in infancy we can play music to listen and to move to, hang art posters at their eye level, and act out characters' voices as we read a story to them. We can swirl across the floor with an infant or toddler in our arms amidst a roomful of dancers—all the while engaging their senses and encouraging them to respond by inciting them to look and listen while using enthusiastic description and a vocabulary of the arts.

**Heightening perception.** We add complexity to the engagement by inviting the child to focus on the experience through our excited sharing of our own sensory responses. We can express how the music makes our heart beat faster, how the colors sparkle, how the dancers seem to float, and how the scary story gives us chills.

**Adding emotion.** Experiences with artistic works are tied to our emotions. Facial expressions and nonverbal gestures are ways we share those feelings with our children. We laugh at a comic actor, we sigh upon hearing a beautiful voice, and we pull back when the big bad wolf comes to the edge of the stage and growls at us.

**Creating memories.** We build comfort with artistic works by creating memories through revisiting and retelling. We can replay the music on a recording or hum the tune, point out the similarity in the colors in the painting we saw to the paint at the easel, imitate the dancers' moves, and retell the story of the play.

**Making connections.** When we personalize experiences, we draw on the brain's need to make meaning and increase attention (Caine & Caine, 2008). If you know that the experience relates to one you have shared together, then ask the children if they are thinking of the same one you are. For example, if a familiar song is played on an unusual instrument, you can hum along or sing the words and say: Does this make you think of the same song?

But Eric Jensen (2005a) warns that we must be careful not to assume that what we think is relevant is what the child also thinks is relevant. Connections are stronger when we make them on our own. Provide many opportunities for the children tell you what the artistic work reminds them of. This does not have to be verbally. Even the very young, when prompted, can point to or find things that are similar. For example, after singing a song about a bear, an infant may point to a stuffed bear.

**Adding novelty.** Changing locations or adding something new is another way to attract children's attention to and foster aesthetic engagement with artistic works. Going to performances in a theater and exhibits in museums creates memorable experiences and excites enthusiasm for appreciating artistic works. Setting up a special area of the classroom where children can interact with artistic works is another strategy that fosters engagement. For example, for preschoolers and kindergarteners a dramatic play center can be set up as a jazz café where children can listen to jazz recordings, see photographs of famous jazz musicians, read books about jazz such as *This Jazz Man* by Karen Ehrhardt (2006), and play along on rhythm instruments and kazoos.

**Making it real.** Children need to see and touch "real" pieces of art and actual musical instruments. They need to feel the texture of an oil painting, the flowing form of a stone carving, and the exhilaration of blowing on a mobile. They need to see real actors performing on the stage, and musicians playing in front of them. They will have many of these experiences in the context of creating their own art. They also need to see that it is not just little children, in this room, at this time, who create artworks. In addition, there are many art media and forms that are not safe for or within the skill level of children but that they can experience on an aesthetic level, such as a welded metal sculpture or a symphony played by a full orchestra.

**Making it playful.** The goal of engaging with artistic works and performances is twofold. One goal is learning to appreciate their value as aesthetic creations that communicate, inform, and use arts elements in interesting ways. The second is for sensory stimulation and personal pleasure. Just as we want children to love books, we also want them to love looking at and listening to artistic works and performances. If we set developmentally appropriate goals and choose open-ended activities that match children's interests, if we offer choices, and allow them to be active participants in playful ways, then children will more likely seek out these engagements on their own.

## What Does Aesthetic Engagement Look Like?

When we have selected the right artistic work or performance, have shown enthusiasm, and wonder, and have created the atmosphere that welcomes the arts in, the stage is set for children to become connoisseurs of the arts. Their fascination is visible. We see them

1. Focus on the artistic work.

2. Nod or give verbal clues.

3. Use facial expressions, body language, and signs such as pointing.

4. Listen attentively.

5. Maintain eye contact.

6. Ask and answer questions.

7. Make connections to what she or he already knows.

8. Use vocabulary heard in reference to the work.

Infants' first response to artistic works and performances is sensory. They look, listen, and focus. Remember to match the length of the engagement to the attention span of the child.

## Selecting the Artistic Works and Performances

We, as teachers, are the mediators between our children and the artistic works. In order to select the best creative works and performances to share with children, we must rely on more than our own personal values about what kind of art is pleasing to us. We must expand our knowledge so children will be exposed not only to the styles of the arts with which our heritage and upbringing have made us comfortable, and the arts that reflect their personal backgrounds, but also those works that allow them to experience a wide range of artistic inventiveness across the spectrum of culture, age, gender, time, and technique.

## Criteria for Selection

In selecting works to share, our goal should be to help children value the very essence of artistic creation, regardless of the artist or the origin of the work. By exposing children to a wide range of artistic forms, we prepare them to be accepting of others' creativity wherever they encounter it throughout their lives. As Gardner (1991, p. 101) states, "models initially encountered by children continue to affect their tastes and preferences indefinitely, and these preferences prove very difficult to change."

**Select different styles.** Begin by looking for works that reflect a range of styles. Equivalent to genre in literature **style** refers to the way something is done that is unique to the individual or culture that produced it. Artistic works in the same style have a coherence which helps children find similarities and differences more easily. Consider for example the difference between salsa and the opera, or the conga and the minuet. For more information on different styles, see *Major Styles of Music, Dance, and Visual Art* on CourseMate.

**Select for variety.** As you select works to share with the children, strive for a balanced representation of different subject matters, media, styles, and places of origin.

Selected works should illustrate the following concepts:

1. People of many different ages create works of art.

2. Artistic works have been made by people from many places and times.

## Across Cultures

**Styles of the Arts**
Introduce children to the world's arts by sharing some of these western and non-western styles.

**Some styles of music include:** Aboriginal, Afro-Cuban, Balkan, Caribbean, classical, folk, Hawaiian, Israeli, jazz, Latin, Maori, Native American, rock and roll

**Some styles of dance include:** ballet, conga, flamenco, hora, hula, polka, square dance, twist

**Some styles of art include:** abstraction, African, Chinese, cubism, impressionism, Indian, Japanese, Moorish, Native American, pop art, surrealism

For more examples of style, see *Major Styles of Music, Dance and Visual Arts* on CourseMate.

3. Artistic works tell us about the lives of other people.

4. Artistic works are made using a wide variety of materials, tools, skills, and instruments that reflect the environment and choice of the creator.

5. There are many ways or styles of art.

6. Artistic works are found in many places in our environment.

7. Artistic works have many purposes and meanings.

**Select for family heritage.** Be sure to include artistic works and performances that reflect the cultural background of every child in the group. Include families in the decision making process and draw on their expertise. If possible, have family members share songs, dances, stories, and artworks that are meaningful to them. When children see the arts of their heritage displayed and honored, they feel valued as people.

## Including Multicultural Artistic Works

It is important when selecting artistic works and performances to include examples from diverse cultures. Children can learn about a culture and its people from experiencing its arts and talking about how and why they are made and performed. In the process they come to understand the use and importance of the arts in that culture.

When children see that the arts of their culture and the arts of other cultures contain many similarities, that culture becomes less strange and more appreciated. Lullabies are sung to babies. Folk dances celebrate harvests and weddings. A simple woven basket from Botswana can link a small African village where baskets are used for carrying and storing grains, fruits, and peanuts to a preschool where similar baskets are used to hold their snacks. African masks can be compared to those worn by people on Halloween, by characters on TV, and in plays and movies. All over the world artists have created art, music, dance, and drama for the same purposes—to beautify their homes, to make everyday things special, to make a personal statement, to tell their stories or record their history, and to express their spiritual beliefs. The arts unite all of humankind.

When they see the arts of others treated with respect, they learn to value people who are different. Children model their behavior on adults' behavior. When we share the arts with children, we must consider the message our selection gives about which styles and cultures are important, and how the discussion of these works will affect the children.

In selecting works of art, music, dance, and drama, make sure that they are representative of the culture, and that each piece is accorded respect and understanding.

1. Examples of **multicultural arts** should be displayed and performed in our rooms every day. Avoid trivializing the work of others by showing it only in the context of a particular holiday or art project.

2. Strive for balance. Provide examples from many racial and ethnic groups.

3. Respect the integrity of the works and the particular time, place, and person who created them. Avoid disconnecting the work from its creators by having the children copy the style, symbols, or the design of a work without exploring the original reasons the work was created. Making a paper copy of an African mask in a school setting is not the same as the ritualistic carving of a wooden mask by an African artist.

4. Avoid stereotypes. Present works that show different racial and ethnic groups involved in all kinds of artistic activities. Make sure that the examples are not just from the past, but include creative works made by living musicians, choreographers, artists, and playwrights.

## Selecting Music for Listening

It is important to expose children to many styles and forms of music as early musical listening experiences help establish later musical preferences. Olga Denac (2007) in her study of preschoolers' musical preferences found that the type of music listened to at home influenced what music the preschoolers said they liked. Because popular and country music were listened to most frequently in the home, Denac recommends that teachers make an extra effort to increase children's exposure to other kinds of music, including folk and classical music.

Look for interesting hand-crafted musical instruments and artifacts, such as this African drum and wood carvings, to share with children.

Many musical works pleasing to children have simple harmonies and patterns with a consistent beat. In general, it makes sense to introduce musical works played by a **solo** instrument or small group before listening to a **symphony.** However, simple music should not be the only music they hear. Beatriz Ilari and Megha Sundara (2009), who have done extensive research on infants and their music preferences, note that infant preferences for simpler musical pieces does not mean they are incapable of listening to and enjoying more complex forms of music. Listening to musical works above children's level of performance, such as classical and jazz pieces, just like reading aloud books that are above their reading level, stretches children's minds and improves auditory discrimination skills.

In particular, the baroque period of 1600 to 1750 produced music with rhythms that often match that of the heartbeat. This ties the music to the child's natural body rhythms. The most famous composer of this period was Johann Sebastian Bach, and his work, such as the *Brandenburg Concertos Nos. 1–6,* is considered the most musically complex. His original works, not those watered down for children, should be high on the list of what is played for infants and toddlers (Shore & Strasser, 2006). Chapter 10 provides more information on selecting musical works for young children.

## Selecting Dance Experiences

Dancing experiences for children to observe and investigate should be drawn first of all from places where they can see real people enjoying moving to music ranging from the free-form moves of the rock dancer to a ballerina on her toes. Dancing can be found at parades, weddings, and during halftime at sporting events. Ballet schools and folk dance groups may welcome a visit from young children. Make sure dance performances are geared for young children's short attention spans. Of course, we can also dance for each other. Put on some music and make some moves. Hold infants and toddlers and bounce them to the beat or let older children dance alongside. Chapter 11 provides more information on selecting forms of dance for young children.

## Selecting Dramatic Performances

For infants and toddlers, we are the actors as we retell stories and act out our feelings through gesture and facial expression. Older children can act out skits and stories for each other. Children's theater provides a wonderful introduction to the world of the stage. Short, interactive works performed by adults familiar with young children's attention span and interests will provide role models for children's own dramatic play. Works that act out familiar stories and fairy tales are of particular interest, especially if we read the story to the children before they see it performed. Puppet shows, children's operas, and brief musical productions are appropriate for young children. Although video recorded productions can be shared on a computer or interactive whiteboard, the experience lacks the reality of seeing a play performed on a stage, being little different from watching a television show. It is, therefore, worth the effort to take children to a performance or arrange for performers to visit your program. Investigate what is available locally by contacting local theater groups, high school and college drama classes, local opera companies, and arts-in-education programs. Many nonprofit traveling children's theater groups can be contacted as well.

## Selecting Visual Artworks

The effect of viewing adult art on young children has been particularly well documented in the visual arts. Research shows that young children consistently prefer bright colors and are strongly attracted to colorful artwork (Parsons, 1987; Winner, 1982). Although children as young as two years old can identify pictures as representations of objects they often prefer abstract artwork (Winner, 1989). They like to free-associate imaginary ideas or memories from the picture's image (Parsons, 1987). When viewing artwork, young children tend to prefer simpler and more direct pictures, whereas adult "art experts" would select more complex and intricate ones (Gardner, 1973). Young children tend to have "favorites," works that are personally pleasing. They judge artwork as good based on whether or not they like it (Parsons, 1987). Although they cannot readily identify different art styles, children recognize that art can show imaginary subjects (Gardner, Winter, & Kircher, 1975).

No matter what style is used, children relate best to visual artworks that have subjects that they can identify with on a very basic level, such as faces, children, and people involved in activities, animals, nature scenes,

and places. This does not mean that the pictures can only show familiar subjects, but they should have something on which children can base their understanding. Children who have never seen a red poppy can relate to the flower element of Georgia O'Keeffe's *Red Poppy*. They do not have to have lived in the sixteenth century to identify with the child in Rembrandt's *Girl with Broom*. They will also enjoy **abstract** and **nonobjective** works that resemble their own artwork, and works such as René Magritte's *Raining Cats and Dogs* that involve visual puns or tricks.

## Selecting Arts Artifacts

An **artifact** is a handmade, three-dimensional, cultural art form. Artifacts provide a unique hands-on and inexpensive way of introducing young children to artistic works. Examples of artifacts include baskets, quilts, woodcarvings, musical instruments, and parts of dance costumes or dramatic performances, such as masks. They are often unsigned and made to be used. They may be considered a form of collective **ethnic folk art**. These are not usually museum-quality pieces but are representative of a class of articles from the everyday life of a people and represent the ethnic heritage of a group of people. They are often handed down from one generation to another and carry the family's story with them.

**Look for unique works.** Although they may not be considered fine arts because of the element of repetition of traditional forms and designs, high-quality handmade artifacts retain the creative touch of the artist. They are not made from precut or purchased patterns, but represent a creative variation on a piece that follows a cultural tradition.

When selecting artifacts, choose those that reflect the artist who created it. Each handmade and designed artifact will have a different color, form, and perhaps decorative element from the others. Artifacts will be made from materials that are found in the region in which they were made. A quilt might be made from a family's old clothing or a weaving from the neighbor's sheep wool. A whistle could be carved from a local wood or a mask decorated with native grasses.

If cultural artifacts are being sold, then the sale should benefit the family or community that made them. Beware of items made for the "souvenir" market. Especially on imported items, look for labels that

## Teacher Tip

### INEXPENSIVE SOURCES OF VISUAL ARTWORKS

**Fine Art Posters:** Posters have the advantage of being large enough for a group of children to experience at one time and durable enough to take many years of handling. Fine quality prints can be purchased from most museum gifts shops and online. Look for ones that are on sale. Sources for art prints are listed in Appendix C. Fine art prints can also be borrowed from some libraries.

**Medium-Size Prints:** Smaller art prints can be obtained inexpensively by clipping pictures from some of the many beautiful calendars that feature artworks of all kinds, and from a variety of magazines and catalogs. These prints are too small for large group study or public display but are perfect for use with small groups.

**Mini Art Prints:** Museum postcards and pictures clipped from catalogs and mounted on tag board can be used for a variety of activities by one or two children. These prints are just the right size for small hands, and the freedom they have to handle them makes them very popular with children.

**Digital Images:** The Internet is another source for pictures of artwork and instruments as well as videos of musicians and performers. Images can be viewed on the computer screen, projected, or printed out. DVDs are another possible source of images. However, digital media do not provide the same level of intimacy as does contact with a real work or performer, and, unlike a print, cannot stay on display for a lengthy period of time.

indicate the country of origin. Avoid those that look like they were crudely mass-produced. Before buying an artifact, research its culture to find out if the item is one that is used in the daily life of the people.

**Sources of art artifacts.** The best examples of cultural artifacts are items intended for home, community, or ritual use, not for public display outside of the culture. Teachers may have some artifacts that belonged to their own families, or that they have made themselves and can share with the children. If teachers are willing to share personally valued artifacts, such as grandmother's patchwork quilt, then others are more likely to do so. The families of the children may wish to bring in a special artifact to show the group. If friends have traveled widely or are collectors of a specific type of artifact, then they may be willing

to let the children see one or two pieces or might invite the children to visit the collection. (See the following section on using community resources for specific guidelines.) Sharing cultural artifacts is an excellent way for people of different heritages to bond.

On occasion, a particular artifact may be purchased that will either expand the cultural experience of the children or relate to an activity. For example, share an Indonesian shadow puppet before making shadow puppets with the children.

Artifacts of all kinds are available from many sources, such as department stores, importers, charitable organizations, and craft fairs. Charitable organizations are a good source, because they usually provide information about who made the item and how the money will be used to help the artisans. Craft fairs provide the opportunity to buy directly from the creator and collect the story that goes with the piece.

**Using artifacts.** Many artifacts are relatively low cost and durably made. After all, they are intended to survive the wear and tear of a normal household. Children will especially benefit from being able to touch and perhaps even to use the artifact, such as using an African basket to serve crackers for snack, eating soup from a hand-thrown tureen, wearing a hat

Artistic works from other countries and cultures can show children that artists use the same artistic elements that they do. This mola, an intricate work of applique made by the Guna of Panama, shows color, texture, shape, and pattern.

from Peru in pretend play, or sitting under a handmade quilt made by a grandparent for story time.

For sources for artifacts see Appenix C. For more examples of artifacts, see *Multicultural Artifacts* on CourseMate.

## Children's Literature

The picture books that teachers read to children are also pieces of art. For many children it is the picture that first entices them to the world of books, and books for the very youngest children are often wordless. In selecting books to share with young artists, always consider the importance of the pictures, not just as illustrations of the story but also as aesthetic statements.

Talk about the illustrator as an artist and examine the technique and media used in the illustrations. Understanding the role of the illustrator in adding meaning to the story is one of the ELA Common Core Literacy skills.

**Selecting the books.**   Picture books should be chosen on the same basis as artistic works. Make sure that a variety of artistic media, styles, and cultures are represented in the books that are offered. Specific descriptions of a multitude of children's books are found in the book boxes in each chapter. Make sure to have some examples from the following categories to introduce to the children.

- **Caldecott Winners**—The Caldecott award is given each year to an outstandingly illustrated children's book. Select those that are on the children's level.

For an annotated list of Caldecott winners, see *Exemplary Illustrated Children's Books* on CourseMate.

- **Media**—Look for books that illustrate some of the less common art techniques, such as *Red Leaf Yellow Leaf* (Ehlert, 1991), which uses natural materials in collages to create three-dimensional images.

- **Multicultural**—Include books that feature art forms from other cultures, such as *Abuela's Weave* (Castaneda, 1993), which tells how weaving fits into the life of a girl and her grandmother in Guatemala. Find a listing of books about the arts of other cultures here.

For an annotated list of multicultural books, see *Books about Other Cultures* on CourseMate.

- **Big Books**—For group sharing, have several big books in which the children can easily see the illustrations. More and more books are now available in this format. If you cannot find one on the subject that you need, consider making your own with the children's help.

For directions on making a big book, see *Making a Big Book* on CourseMate.

**Sharing books with children.**   Try some of these techniques to attract and keep their attention when reading to young children:

- If the children are wiggly, simplify the text or skip pages.

- Talk about the pictures. Point out the colors, the media used, and relate them to things the children know or have experienced. Use the illustrations to inspire storytelling and different uses for the book.

- Point to objects in the pictures, and say their names.

- If there are unfamiliar objects in the pictures, introduce them slowly—only a few at a time. Compare them to familiar things that the children know.

- Have one or more real objects that tie in with the story. For example, if the book features a trumpet, as in *Ben's Trumpet* (Isadora, 1991), show a real

Reading books about artists, musicians, dancers, and actors from many times and places is another way to bring the art of the world into the classroom. Big books are especially attractive to young children. Don't hesitate to make your own.

trumpet to the children.

🎵 Invite participation by having children make appropriate sounds or motions as the text is read.

🎵 Use an expressive voice. Change the tone for different characters.

🎵 To develop literacy skills, ask children to predict what will happen next, before the page is turned.

## Teacher as Mediator

However, no matter how carefully we select the artistic works, we need to take the time to learn all that we can about the history and stories that relate to each creative work we present to children. This does

## RESPONDING TO BOOKS THROUGH THE ARTS

### Creative dance

**Retell.** Have children invent movements to go with the story.

**Recreate.** Re-enact the story using no words, only movements of the hands.

### Dramatics

**Change characters.** Ask children to change who the characters are, such as turn a boy to a girl or a snake to a rabbit. Act out the new story that results.

**Create a tableau.** Have children take and hold the poses of the characters, as shown on one page in the story. Have other children try to guess which picture it is.

### Music

**Create an opera.** Inspire children to turn the character's words into songs. Listen to selections from *Peter and the Wolf* by Sergei Prokofiev and see how the composer used different instruments and melodies to represent the characters. Select an instrument and invent a rhythm or melody to represent the characters in another book you are reading them.

### Visual Art

**Revise.** Draw a new ending for the story.

**Retell.** Make scenery and props and use them to retell the story.

**Recreate.** Make a three-dimensional group sculpture that illustrates the theme of the book.

not means we need to be experts. The more we know about a painting, **sonata,** or play, the more confidently we will be able to mediate between the children and the work in order to make it more accessible to them. Being familiar with the work, allows us to

🎵 Plan activities that prepare the children for their first encounter with the work and make that experience more meaningful. For example, if we know what instruments will be played at a concert, we can present each instrument to the children beforehand so they can listen to its timbre and see how it is played.

🎵 Know ahead of time what adjustments we may need to make for children with special needs so they can benefit equally from the experience.

🎵 Decide what we will say about the work to engage the children while developing literacy skills.

🎵 Provide supplementary materials, such as books, web quests, and artifacts that expand on the work or performance.

🎵 Plan follow-up conversations and activities that build on the experience and expand children's thinking.

We can find information about artistic works in the following places.

**Books.**  Many wonderful children's books on artists, musicians, dancers, actors, and playwrights as well as about the many forms of art can be consulted. They can provide interesting facts to share about the selected pieces.

For an annotated listing of resource books about the arts, see *Books about the Arts* on CourseMate.

**Websites.**  In addition, there are websites about almost every type of arts form and about individual musicians, artists, dancers, and dramatic works.

For a list of websites to visit, see *Chapter 7 Online Resources* on CourseMate.

**Museums.**  Many museums and local music and drama groups have guided tours and educational materials available.

# How Can We Talk About Artistic Works?

We can use young children's initial attraction to colorful graphic images, intriguing music, and enticing stories to invite children into a conversation about the works.

## Responding to the Arts Using Literacy Skills

Conversing about artistic works and performances provides an opportunity not only to engage children orally with the works but also to practice the literacy skills of speaking and listening. Rich conversations about artistic works also develop critical thinking skills (Housen, 2002).

## Using a Puppet or Stuffed Animal

The key to engaging the children's interest in a work or artifact is in the way we express our personal enthusiasm and interest in the work. Our voices need to be full of energy and excitement as we discuss the work with the children. Some people find it helpful to use a puppet or stuffed animal. Just like children, adults often feel less inhibited when having "Rembrandt Bear" or "Musical Mozart" talk to the children.

Convert a simple stuffed animal or purchased puppet into an "arts expert" by adding a few small details such as a beret and a smock (with paint splotches, of course) for the "visual arts" or a tux and baton for music. An original puppet can be created using a sock, papier-mâché, or cloth. It helps if the "arms" can be moved so more expression can be added to the presentation. The "arts expert" should be constructed durably, as it will prove a popular friend to the children, who will often model the teacher's art discussions in their play. Make sure to give it a personal history that tells how it came to be so expert in the arts.

Children may also enjoy having their own arts expert. Encourage them to make a puppet with whom they can talk about the arts.

## Asking Questions

Asking and answering questions provides a way to explore an unfamiliar artistic work. Start out with open-ended questions about the work that have a multiplicity of answers and allow all children's responses to be valued.

**Sensory questions.** Upon your first encounter with a group of children, start with simple questions about what they perceive with their senses.

- What do you hear?
- What do you see?
- What do you feel?

**Personal taste.** These questions allow children to express their personal reaction to an artistic work based on their aesthetic response of the moment. Asking children to pick their favorite is a good way to spark interest in an artwork. It is a useful assessment technique to ask children for their personal opinions when first presenting an artistic work, and then again after it has been discussed. Notice if negative initial reactions have changed or become tempered as children become more familiar with the piece.

Be accepting of all responses. Do not tell children that they must like something, but do make them justify their response by asking "Why?" Young children may not be able to express verbally why the piece elicits a certain personal response and may respond with "Because" or "I don't know, I just do." However, asking "why" sets up a pattern in which children learn that a feeling about an artistic work is always based on something. Some of the sophisticated justifications that young children can make are quite surprising, especially after they have looked at and discussed several pieces.

- Do you like this? Why?
- Which of these is your favorite? Why?
- Would you like this artwork to hang in your home? Why?
- Would you like to listen to this music at home? Why?
- Would you like to dance like this? Why?
- Would you like to meet this artist, musician, dancer, or actor? Why?
- Would you like to make an artwork like this? Why?

**How does it make you feel . . . ?** Young children are not always able to express their feelings verbally. Listening to music, for example, can be a very emotional experience, difficult to put into words even for adults. Welcome all responses that the children make to questions about their feelings. When children have different reactions, use this as an opportunity to talk about differences in point of view. To develop point of view and emotional sensitivity, have children try to imagine how the people in artworks, particularly portraits, are feeling, or and how the characters feel in a story or play.

- How did the music make you feel?

- If you were in this story, how would you feel?

- How does the character in this play feel?

- How was the artist feeling when she created this?

- How do you feel when you hear this? Look at this?

- Do you ever feel that way when you paint? Draw? Model? Dance? Sing? Act?

**Thinking strategy questions.** The following set of questions, or thinking routine, asks children to describe their initial or personal response to a work, give an explanation, then examine the work more deeply, and finally, ask their own questions about it. These questions can be used individually or with a group.

- What's going on?

- What do you see or hear that makes you think that?

- What more can we find?

- What do you wonder about?

**Looking at a part.** Create mystery by covering up parts of the work or play only a line of a song or bit of a dance or share a section of a story and ask children questions that foster predicting and imagining.

- What do you imagine this _____ is part of?

- What else do you think might be

- What is special about this one part of the work?

It is not necessary to ask many questions. If the children are very excited about seeing the rest of the work after only one or two questions, then end the questioning by saying: "Let's find out."

**What does it tell you about?** These questions focus on the subject matter or the story of the work. This builds on the natural tendency for children to build narratives around their experiences.

- What is happening?

- Who is this person? Who are these people? What are they doing?

- What do you think the story is about?

- What objects in the work do you know? Use? Are there any you do not know? Use?

**How was it made or done?** These questions help children learn about the different arts techniques while using their arts vocabulary.

- How do you think this was created? How can you tell?

- Have you ever done something like this?

- Does this look like it was made with anything we use?

- What tools do you think the artist used?

- What instruments do you think the composer used to make that sound?

- How did the artist make this texture? Color? Line? Shape? Pattern? Sound? Movement? Sound? Melody? Rhythm?

- How did the puppeteer make the puppet move?

**Can you find?** These questions give the children practice in using arts vocabulary and add a playful game-like quality to the discussion.

- Can you find a line? Shape? Color? Texture? Pattern? Rhythm? Pitch? (Be specific, for example, red rectangle, rough texture, accented beat.)

- Can you trace with your finger a line? Shape? Melody?

- Can you touch or point to a line? Musical note? Shape? Color? Texture? Pattern?

🎵 Did you hear a high pitch? A low one?

🎵 How is the dancer moving? High? Low? Energetically? Slowly?

**What comes next . . . ?** These questions challenge children to make predictions based on the visual clues they see and allow them to practice creative visualization. In designing these questions, make sure there are enough clues to give direction to the child, but that there is no one right answer. Be accepting of all responses.

🎵 What do you think will happen next? Happened before?

🎵 What do you think this person (animal) will do next? Did before?

🎵 What notes will you hear next?

🎵 How will the dancer move now?

**How many . . . ?** Questions can also relate to other curriculum areas, such as math, language arts, social studies, and science.

🎵 How many red circles (blue squares, etc.) can you find? (math)

🎵 Tell me a story about this artwork. (language arts)

🎵 Why are these houses made from reeds? (social studies)

🎵 Do these clouds look like rain clouds? (science)

**Can you do . . . ?** Asking children to respond physically helps them develop their mental imaging skills and allows them to become more involved in the artistic work. There are no right answers to these questions; accept all of the children's responses.

🎵 For a portrait: Can you make your face look like this one?

🎵 After a skit: Can you stand (sit) in the same position as the actor did? How would this person dance?

🎵 After a story: Can you imagine you are doing what this character is doing? (Mime the character's actions.)

🎵 For a photograph of a house: Can you imagine opening and closing this door? Looking in this window? (Mime.)

🎵 After listening to a piece a music: Can you imagine you are playing this instrument in the music we just heard? (Mime.)

**What is the same or different . . . ?** These questions encourage the children to develop the important literacy skill of finding similarities and differences. For very young children, keep the comparisons general and obvious. Older children will enjoy trying to solve trickier ones.

In a single musical work:

🎵 Can you find the high and low notes in the song?

🎵 Which was the fast part? The slow part?

🎵 Which parts sounded the same?

In a single visual artwork:

🎵 In this picture, which person (house, animal) is bigger? Older? Younger? Smaller?

🎵 Can you find the biggest (smallest) square (triangle)?

🎵 Can you find the longest (shortest, thickest, thinnest) line?

🎵 Can you find the brightest (dullest, lightest, darkest) color?

There are many ways to share fine art with young children. Arts games, such as matching art miniprints or pieces of music, are a playful way to engage children with all kinds of art.

In a single dramatic work such as puppet show or skit:

🎵 Which character was the happiest? Funniest?

🎵 Which part was most exciting—the beginning or the end?

🎵 Which character had the loudest voice?

In a single dance performance

🎵 Which dancer moved the most?

🎵 When did the dancers move the fastest? Slowest?

🎵 In which part did they use their arms more—the beginning or the end?

Comparing two works:

🎵 In which play is there a person? A house? An animal?

🎵 Which picture looks more real?

🎵 Which artwork is round (three-dimensional)? Which is flat?

🎵 In which musical piece is the beat is slower? Faster?

🎵 Which dance have we seen before?

**Asking questions about the arts and artifacts of other cultures.** When presenting artistic works and artifacts from another culture, have the children focus on the universal artistic qualities first so that it is clearly identified as an aesthetic work. Ask a selection of questions from any of the aforementioned arts categories before asking about the cultural element. Questions should focus on finding similarities with familiar art forms and investigating possible uses.

🎵 How is this artwork, music, folktale, dance similar to the one we use or do? Listen to? Perform?

🎵 How do you think it is used by the people who created it?

🎵 How is this different from what you have experienced before?

Remember that young children under age eight have a minimal knowledge of the world. They do not know specific geographical information. They respond best when descriptions of how something is made and used in another place are embedded in a story. Children can identify with common human themes such as family, food, and homes; and they love stories that contain animals.

**Revisiting an artistic work.** If they have seen the work or performance before, ask children questions that challenge their memories.

🎵 Do you remember this?

🎵 What familiar _____ are in this work? (sounds, moves, colors, shapes, lines, details, textures, animals, people, plants, or any other element)

---

### Did You Get It?

**Which of the following would you consider good advice for helping children engage with artwork and performances?**

a. Asking children to pick their favorite prevents them from observing the work more closely.

b. Do not make children justify why they like or dislike an artistic work or performance because they are not yet mature enough to do so.

c. It is important to guide children to like an artistic work that is largely accepted or popular.

d. If children have different reactions, use this as an opportunity to discuss differences in opinions.

**Take the full quiz on CourseMate**

---

# How Do We Incorporate Writing Responses to Artistic Works?

In addition to talking about artistic works and performances we can also design activities that involve using responsive arts activities combined with writing activities as a way for children to express their ideas about the works and connect the experience to their own artistic pursuits.

## Aesthetic Responsive Activities for Infants and Toddlers

For infants and toddlers, follow-ups can occur spontaneously after encountering the work. For example, after listening to a song or instrumental melody in a one-on-one setting they can be prompted to echo the song or melody line back. After viewing a painting, they can make a painting. After seeing people dance, they can dance. After watching a puppet show, we can play together with puppets. During these interactions we can

- Develop focus by incorporating the sensory elements of the arts.

- Repeat and reinforce arts vocabulary.

- Wait for the child's response and then teach that a communication involves give and take.

- Recall details to develop memory.

- Refer to things they can do related to the artistic work to build connections.

- Record the children's reactions on an experience chart or documentation panel.

## Aesthetic Responsive Activities for Preschoolers and Kindergarteners

Preschoolers and kindergarteners also benefit from being able to explore hands-on open-ended arts and early literacy activities that relate to the experience but allow children to add their own creative input. We can do this by

**Pointing out similarities.** We can add connection by providing a linkage between the aesthetic experience and their own work. We can note similarities using arts vocabulary: "You are singing the same melody that we heard in the concert," "You are using the same dance move we saw the salsa dancers use," "You mixed the same color paint that the artist used in her painting."

**Recreating the experience.** We can offer materials and activities that invite children to recreate the experience. For example, after viewing a dramatization of the Chinese folktale *Two of Everything* by Lily Toy Tung (1993) in which a magic brass pot doubles everything, we can put out a metal pot filled with doubles of different items in the dramatic play area.

After hearing a high school group play marching tunes, we can put out a CD of John Phillip Sousa marches to listen to at the listening center and we can play the music for creative movement activities.

After visiting a museum we can mount four or five medium-size prints on cardboard and laminate or cover with clear contact paper. Punch two holes in the top of each print, and attach a string or piece of yarn. Hang a child-height hook in the dramatic area, and let the children select and change the displayed art at will.

**Eliciting pre-and post-reactions.** Before an artistic experience children can be asked to draw, dictate, or write about what they expect to see. After the event or viewing of the work they can be asked to look back at their initial idea and add details or make changes based on their new knowledge.

**Recording the experience.** We can have children draw, dictate, and use emergent writing skills to record their reactions, ideas, and feelings in their journals, in a class book, or for a documentation panel. Digital photographs of the experience can be given to the children to paste in their journals as prompts or added to the documentation panel materials.

**Learning more.** With guidance, children can participate in shared research about the artistic works they have experienced. Set out a collection of books about the art form or about similar musicians, artists, and performers or display reproductions, photographs, or videos of different works by the same musician, artist, or performer. Ask children to find similarities and differences and choose their favorites.

**Comparing and contrasting.** Another way to follow up artistic experiences and develop literacy skills is to create simple sorting games. To make your own sorting sets, glue small copies of digital photographs of the artistic works or the performance, or small prints from art magazines, calendars, museum catalogs, or from the Internet to postcard-size tag board pieces. Look for musical instruments, scenes from plays, and ethnic folk art, as well as works by famous artists and portraits of musicians, composers, dancers, and other types of artists. If possible, cover the cards with clear contact paper or laminate them for durability. Children can sort the cards by similarities or differences and play matching games like Concentration and Go Fish.

For more sorting ideas and other arts games, see *Art Games* on CourseMate.

**Sharing the experience.** Children can share their arts appreciation experiences in many ways with their families. One way is to send home arts bags featuring works relating to those that the children are learning about in class.

Use plastic or cloth bags with a handle, or have children decorate sturdy paper bags. In each bag, place a medium-size print of an artwork; an audio or video recording of music, drama, or dance; or a durable, inexpensive artifact along with a book that relates to the artistic work or performance and a toy, game, clothing, or food item that relates to the theme. It is important to select works from a variety of heritages, so parents as well as children become familiar with the world of the arts. Set up a sign-out system. Make sure that the artistic works are labeled, and provide a notebook in which parents can write their comments before they return the bags.

*For more ideas for arts bags see Suggestions for Arts Bags on CourseMate.*

## Aesthetic Responsive Activities for the Primary Grades

All of the activities suggested for preschoolers and kindergarteners can also be used with primary age children. In addition, we can draw on primary students' increasing reading and writing skills by merging looking, talking, and writing responses to artistic works and performances into reading and writing workshops. Use viewing an artistic work or enjoying a performance as texts to get students reading and writing. Here are some examples.

- Fill in a compare and contrast graphic organizer.
- Imagine you were the artist or in the performance. Write about how it would feel.
- Invent a game.
- Make a digital presentation, such as PowerPoint or digital story, about it.
- Make a cartoon about it.
- Research some interesting facts about it.
- Rewrite a dramatic performance changing the setting or characters.
- Write a journal entry.
- Write a review or blog post about it.
- Write a set of questions you would like to ask about what you saw.
- Write a puppet show about it.
- Write a skit about it.
- Write a song about it.

Recording their ideas and feelings about artistic works and performances in their journals helps children develop literacy skills. Crayon and pencil by Laurel, age five.

---

**Did You Get It?**

**Which of the following is an effective way to have children use literacy skills to respond to a performance they have seen?**

a. Have children dictate their reaction to the performance.

b. Have children watch a video of the performance.

c. Tell children it is not necessary to tell their parents about the performance.

d. Review the children's audience behavior and tell them what they did wrong.

**Take the full quiz on CourseMate**

🎵 Write a story about it.

🎵 Write a thank-you letter.

🎵 Write and illustrate a book about it.

# How Can Children Be Introduced to Community Arts Resources?

One way for children to learn about other art forms and the role of art in adult life is for them to meet working artists and to see the arts in the community. Because most young children have short attention spans, these kinds of activities need to be carefully planned. Although a bad experience can do more harm than no experience, it is not difficult to organize a successful artist visit, an arts-related field trip, or a museum experience. The key is to design the experience so that it meets the attention level of the particular children.

## Guest Artists and Performers

The guest artist or performer can be a friend, a colleague, or a family or a community member who creates original art that is relatively portable and not injurious to the children's health. (It would not be a good idea to have someone oil paint or solder stained glass in a room used by children.) The person should genuinely like young children and their infinite curiosity.

When inviting artists and performers to visit, make sure to prepare them for the particular group of children and explain clearly what they should share and say. Have an information sheet prepared ahead of time to give to families and artists who will visit the class. The information sheet should list the times of the various daily activities, the number of children, their ages, and any particular information about items, such as special needs. There should also be a brief outline on how to design a program for children this age.

## Presenting to Infants

Musicians singing and playing an instrument, puppeteers, and storytellers are a great fit for infants. They work best when their presentations are delivered one-to-one so that the performer can adjust the performance based on the infants' reactions.

## Presenting to Toddlers

Toddlers respond best to artists who create fairly large pieces that change appearance quickly. Basket making, painting, drawing, pottery, weaving, and sewing quilt squares together are examples of this kind of art activity. Musicians, dancers, and actors should choose short pieces that children can participate in through movement or singing.

**Setup.**  Squirmy toddlers respond better if the teacher announces the visitor's arrival and directs the artist to a quiet corner, rather than having the visitor offer a group program. The artist then sets up and gives a short performance as children show interest or begins to work on a sample piece of art to attract them. This kind of presentation mirrors Gardner's "skilled master" model (1991, p. 204).

**What the guest should say.**  Toddlers can gather around to watch and ask questions. The visitor should be prepared to answer the children's questions in a simple, understandable way without talking down to them.

**Samples.**  The visitor should bring sample materials and child-safe tools that can be touched by the toddlers. Any dangerous tools should be put away out of sight after each use or, if possible, not used during the demonstration. For example, a quilter could substitute small, blunt scissors for sharp shears when cutting threads.

Visits from guest artists teach children that many different people create art. Ask families if there are any members who play an instrument, sing, paint, work in clay, dance, or act.

## Presenting to Preschoolers and Up

Preschoolers and older children benefit from a slightly longer and more complex visit. Before the guest arrives, tell the children about the visit, and ask questions to find out what they already know about this art form. Relate the visit to any explorations or arts activities that the children have done by asking intriguing questions such as, "Mrs. Kahn will be showing us how she paints landscapes today. I wonder if she will use an easel like you do when you paint?" or "Mr. Chang will be showing us Chinese calligraphy today. Calligraphy means beautiful writing. Do you think he uses a paintbrush or a pencil?" or "Ms. Ganesh will be showing us a dance they do in India. What do you think she will be wearing?"

**Setup.** When visitors arrive and have set up their work, gather the children around and introduce them. Let the guests explain what they do, and give a brief demonstration if the art form is suitable for a large group to see clearly, such as working on a large painting or making a good-size basket. The toddler format described earlier can be used for demonstrations that are best viewed by small groups of children at a time. In the case of visual art, if the process is very long, the guest might bring several samples in various stages of completion and then work on one that is just about complete.

**What the guest should say.** Rather than a lecture, the guest should be prepared with interesting questions to ask the children. For example, a quilt maker might ask, "How many pieces do you think are in one square?" or "How big do you think this quilt will be when I have sewn these six squares together?" A calligrapher might ask, "Do I hold the brush the same way you do?" An instrument maker might say, "What do you use drums for?" Teachers may want to offer possible questions to the guest ahead of time.

The guest or teacher may want to read a children's book that relates to the visit, or visitors may have interesting stories to share about when they were young, or how they became artists.

**Samples.** Just like toddlers, older children need to be able to use their sense of touch as much as possible. Invite the guest artist to bring a sample of materials that the children can touch. For example, a calligrapher could let the children touch the brush and the ink stone instead of the finished calligraphy.

If possible, see if they can give the children a small sample that they can take home with them. A quilter could offer a scrap of cloth that matches the quilt, a basket maker a piece of reed, and a weaver some yarn. Painters can apply paint that matches the painting to a piece of paper; when dry, they can cut it into simple shapes and sign them for the children.

## Concluding the Visit

Prepare a brief letter to send home to families about the child's experience. This helps families understand the child's new knowledge. The child's "souvenir" can be attached to the letter as well so that it will have a context of meaning once it is home.

After the guest has left, have children participate in making a thank-you card. A nice thank-you is a photograph of the visit. Also take photographs to

### Teacher Tip

It is well worth the effort to create an information sheet to send to guests before they visit. A sample follows:

**GUIDELINES FOR GUEST ARTISTS**

1. Visual artists: Bring an unfinished piece to work on and samples of your artwork at various stages. Musicians: Bring an instrument that children can touch and explore. Actors and dancers: Bring costumes or props that children touch or can try on and use.
2. Avoid dangerous items if possible. If you must bring anything sharp or hot, make sure you have a child-proof container for it.
3. Children are more sensitive to toxic materials than adults. Do not bring any solvents, permanent markers, solvent-based glues, oil paints, varnishes, sprays, or dusty materials.
4. Bring only one or two finished pieces that you feel will appeal to young children. Consider how you will display them safely.
5. Bring objects or samples that the children can touch.
6. If possible, bring a "souvenir" of the process or performance that the children can take home.
7. Keep your presentation simple. Prepare questions about your art that you could ask young children. Because children have short attention spans, plan for no longer than 15 minutes.
8. You may also wish to write a letter telling families about your demonstration for the children to take home.

keep in a scrapbook so children can "read" and remember the experience.

## Visiting an Artist's Studio

Taking a group of young children to an artist's studio can be a major undertaking and is most suitable for older children or a small, mixed-age group with ample supervision. The advantages of such a visit are that artists are often more comfortable working in their own surroundings with all of their supplies on hand. The children also get to see the working environment that the artist has created.

The disadvantages are numerous. The workspace may not be large enough or safe enough for young children, and there may be many items that they cannot touch. In cases where visual artists use materials that are hazardous for young children, a visit to the studio is not advised unless those materials can be cleaned up and put away. The workplace of a painter, an **illustrator**, a **calligrapher**, a **weaver**, a **spinner**, a basket maker, a **quilter**, a woodcarver, and a stone sculptor should be relatively safe, with minor adjustments. A printing studio, stained glass studio, pottery studio, or metal workshop may need to be carefully cleaned up, certain processes not demonstrated, and the children closely supervised.

In considering such a field trip, always visit the artist's workspace ahead of time. Check for the following features:

- **Space**—Is there a space large enough for all of the children to gather and observe the artist, or must they take turns? What can the children who are waiting their turn look or do?

- **Safety**—Are there any dangers that cannot be removed? What areas does the artist need to clean up? What parts of the process are dangerous for the children?

- **Preparation**—What do we need to tell the families and children so they will be prepared? Do they need special clothing? What should they look for and point out to the children?

Make sure there is ample supervision for children. Families and other supporting adults should be invited to come and oversee one or two children each. Use the guidelines for guest artists to plan the actual presentation.

## Classroom Technology

### *VIRTUAL FIELD TRIPS*

Although live encounters with musicians, artists, and other performers are essential to making the arts come alive for young children, we can expand upon what is available locally by arranging virtual field trips to museums and performances. Virtual field trips allow children to experience places that may be unsafe or too far way to visit. They can also be used as introductions to traditional field trips the children will take.

Although some prepared virtual field trips are available, Dennis Kirchen (2001) suggests that teachers can better determine the sounds, images, and text that are most developmentally appropriate for their particular children. For ELL children, creating a virtual field trip allows incorporation of the child's home language. For children who have special needs, a virtual field trip may make it possible for them to experience places that are not handicapped accessible or have too many sensory inputs for the a child with sensory integration disorder to deal with. In addition, parents who may not be able to go on a field trip can be invited to watch the virtual field trip either at school or if they have a computer, at home.

Virtual field trips can be created using a word processor, digital photography, a presentation platform such as PowerPoint, and/or free videoconferencing technology such as ooVoo or Skype. With advanced preparation and direction young children can participate in the process and create virtual trips for each other.

Directions for creating a virtual field trip can be found here. http://www.naeyc.org/files/yc/file/201111/Kirchen_Virtual_Field_Trips_Online%201111.pdf

## Visiting Museums

Most museums are not set up to deal with groups of young children. The "look-but-don't-touch" nature of the displays usually means that the children cannot use their natural learning impulses and thus spend the visit constrained and unhappy, leaving them with a dislike for museum-going that may last all of their lives. The exception is the children's museum or children's wing, of which numerous versions have sprung up around the country. These are set up to engage children of all ages in activities that involve the arts and sciences. If such a museum is in the vicinity, do take advantage of the wonderful features it offers. Again, make sure to visit the site ahead of time, and arrange for adequate supervision.

## Teacher Tip

### CREATING A CLASSROOM MUSEUM

A blank wall or divider in one area of the room can be turned into a "museum" by providing a group of varied medium-size prints with yarn attached to hang it by and a row of child-height hooks. Large blocks can be used as bases for any three-dimensional artworks that are durable enough for the children to handle, such as baskets, weaving, and tin ware.

Two books to share with the children as they explore the museum area are *Matthew's Dream* (Lionni, 1991), in which a young mouse decides to become an artist after visiting a museum, and *Visiting the Art Museum* (Brown and Brown, 1986).

This area can also become a gallery or crafts fair. Children can "buy" new art to hang in the home life area, or they can select favorite pieces to take home to share and enjoy for several days. The yarn hanger makes it easy for parents to display the print on a doorknob or other convenient hanging place. Attach a brief history of the artwork, the artist's name, and any special facts about it to the back of any artwork that is sent home.

## Attending Performances

Preparation is key in taking young children to musical, dance, and theatrical performances. Select programs that are especially designed for children and that relate to themes and projects that are ongoing in the classroom. Beforehand, read books about the art form and the artists. See if you can schedule time to meet with the performers after the show or invite them to visit the classroom. After the performance spend time talking about it with the children and then set up a center at which there are props that children can use so they can re-enact what they experienced.

## Other Places to Visit

Many other places allow children to experience the arts. Explore the neighborhood and community for possible experiences for children. Here are some possible ideas:

- **Art store**—Children will enjoy seeing the many different kinds of paints, brushes, papers, and pencils available for visual artists.

- **Music store**—Here is an opportunity to examine instruments up close. If the store gives permission, have children take paper and pencils and draw pictures of what they see.

- **Public sculpture**—Young children may also enjoy a visit to a piece of public sculpture if there is an example within walking distance. Public sculptures are often found in parks or near government and university buildings. Outdoor sculpture gardens attached to museums may also make a good experience. When visiting these locations, go prepared with a list of questions to focus the children on the visual elements of the pieces, and find out something about the artist who made it. Because these sculptural forms are separated from the artist and very different from their own art, children

Field trips provide children with rich, sensory experiences that add meaning to their own artistic work.

## Making Plans

**OPEN-ENDED RESPONSIVE ACTIVITY PLAN: GOING TO THE CONCERT**

WHO?    Group composition age(s): Kindergarten

WHEN?    Time frame: 1 week preparation for the event

WHY?    Objectives: Child will develop

- physically, by improving control over their arms and legs and their body in space. I will see this happening when they mime playing the instruments. (Bodily-Kinesthetic)

- socially, by being respectful audience members. I will see and hear this when they sit quietly in the concert hall, clap at the appropriate times, and follow our "stay safe" rules. (Interpersonal)

- emotionally, by learning that listening to a live concert is very enjoyable. I will know this happening when I see them smiling and sharing how the concert made them feel afterward. (Intrapersonal)

- perceptually, by developing auditory discrimination skills as they listen to the music. I will know this is happening when they identify mystery instruments by their timbre. (Spatial)

- language skills, by answering and asking questions and by recording their ideas using music vocabulary. I will see this happening when we talk about the concert and when they draw, dictate, or write their responses in their journals. (Linguistic)

- cognitively, by comparing and contrasting the three musical selections we hear. I will know this is happening when I hear them identify which one has a fast beat and which one has a slow beat. (Logical-Mathematical)

- music skill and knowledge, by learning the meaning of timbre. I will know this is happening when they match instruments and their sounds and identify the instruments used at the concert. Content Standard 6.

WHERE?    Set-up: Pre-concert: Whole group activities daily, time at the music instrument center and the listening center daily. Attend concert at local high school. Post-concert: Whole group discussion and then writing center time during writing workshop.

WHAT?    Materials: A collection of musical instruments, journals and digital camera. A CD of the musical pieces to be played at the concert, CD player and earphones, a DVD of solos by the five featured instruments (made when the students visit) and another of a concert.

HOW?    Procedure:

WOW Warm-Up: Five high school students will visit and demonstrate their instruments.

What to Do: DAY 1. *Whole group in a circle on the rug:* Following the visit play a timbre guessing game in which they match a picture of the instrument to its sound. Explain about the concert and introduce them to the instruments in the music center and how to handle them. Pass the instruments around the circle so they can feel them and practice safe handling. Explain the writing task at the music center is to choose the instrument's sound they like the best and draw a picture of it and write (or dictate for those with special needs) why they like it. The listening center will have the CD of the music they will hear at the concert to listen to as they wish.

DAY 2–4: Children will cycle through the centers.

DAY: 5 Have the children bring chairs and set up theater seating in front of interactive whiteboard. Go over good audience behavior and when to clap. Then practice as they watch several minutes of the concert.

DAY 6: Attend the concert. Arrive early so they can go on the stage and look at the music and stands and think about how it feels to play in a concert. Take photographs of the children on the stage and beside the students they met with their instruments.

What to Say: After the concert: Ask open-ended critical thinking questions, such as "What did you notice? What did you hear? Which instruments did you see? How did they sound?"

Transition Out: A digital photo will be printed out for each child to be glued in their journal. Children will draw and write about their experience in their journal.

WHAT    Assessment: Did the children enjoy the music centers? Did they choose to go listen to the CD in the listening
LEARNED?    center? Did they use their best audience behavior at the concert? Did they identify the parts in which the different instruments played? Did they use the word timbre? Was the concert developmentally appropriate for all the children? Did they seem excited and happy afterward?

NEXT?    Extensions: Follow up by playing more musical timbre games with different instruments.

## Photo Story

## Integrated Arts Unit: Africa

A guest visitor shares her collection of African masks and carvings as part of a second-grade study of the lands and peoples of Africa. The attention to detail in the children's responsive work reflects the depth of their research.

often have difficulty recognizing them as art and treat them more like unusual playground equipment. Expect such visits to be brief, and perhaps tie them in with a trip to another location.

🎵 **Historic sites**—Reconstructions of older historical homes or farm sites may demonstrate traditional handicrafts from earlier times, such as wool spinning or candle making. These places are usually set up to handle groups, and they may shorten and customize their presentation for young visitors. There is often a real story to make the place come alive for children.

## Audience Etiquette

Prepare children for live performances by teaching them how to behave respectfully. It is a good practice to model and practice audience behavior whenever children present to each other. Children should practice looking at the performer, sitting quietly, keeping their bodies under control, and showing appreciation by clapping at the end.

On the day of the performance, arrive early enough to give children a time to look around the auditorium or venue and ask questions. Explain things that may be unfamiliar such as spotlights, and how the curtains work. Have enough adults on hand to sit among the children and deal with small difficulties as they arise. Although it might seem easier to show a movie in the classroom, nothing is like a live performance. It is worth the extra preparation involved for the memories and inspiration our children will acquire.

## Conclusion: Becoming a Lover of the Arts

The arts are much more than the personal act of creating something. They also involve looking at, talking about, and appreciating the art of others. If we are dedicated to educating the whole child, we must provide children with opportunities not only to explore the process of the arts but also to experience a broad range of artwork and performances. In doing so, we introduce children to the artistic heritage of humankind and the long continuum of creativity that it represents.

It takes effort on our part to do this. Letting children beat on a drum in the classroom is easier than taking a group of wiggly toddlers to experience a drum circle performance in the park. Putting markers out on a table is simpler and more immediate than learning about a piece of artwork and the culture that created it, and then designing a way to explain it to young children. But adults who work with children must never stop making the effort. We must dedicate ourselves to becoming as knowledgeable about the arts as we can be. Our lives will be richer, as will the lives of the children we touch. Together we will approach the crayons on the table, the maracas in the music center, and the dress-up clothes in the housekeeping corner with a new respect and sense of purpose.

*For more resources for teaching about the world's arts to young children, see Chapter 7 Online Resources on CourseMate.*

---

### Did You Get It?

**Which of the following should be considered when planning an artist's presentation for toddlers?**

a. In the case of a long visual demonstration, it is better for the artist to start from the very beginning.

b. Demonstrations for toddlers are most effective when conducted for large groups.

c. Toddlers respond best to artists who create fairly large pieces that change appearance quickly.

d. It is better to provide as little information as possible about the art form prior to the visit.

**Take the full quiz on CourseMate**

# Teaching In Action

*Incorporating the World of Art*

*Why Do We Wear the Clothes We Do? An Integrated Unit of Study for Preschool and Up*

## INTRODUCTION TO STUDY

The type and kind of clothing worn daily is an important facet of a young child's life. Getting into and out of complicated clothing, bundling up in cold weather or dressing lightly in the heat, and feeling comfortable or irritated by the fit or texture of a garment all directly influence how a child feels. Begin the study by building on this interest. We can do this in many ways. One way is to wear an unusual handmade garment, or comment on a new outfit that a child is wearing, and then follow up with any or all of the following:

- Compare this piece of clothing with that worn by other children. Notice the colors and textures in the different garments.
- Make charts and pictographs of the clothing children are wearing.
- Make a web of all of the different items of clothing children can name.
- Ask children how they think clothing is made and how it is colored, and record their ideas on a KWL (what we Know; what we Wonder about; what we want to Learn) chart to return to later in the unit.
- Have children draw pictures of themselves wearing different types of clothing in different settings, such as in school, at night, on a cold day, or at the swimming pool or beach.

## INITIAL EVENT

Follow up the introductory activities with a visit from a fiber artist, such as a weaver, a knitter, an embroiderer, a quilter, or a dressmaker. Try to have this visitor come over a period of several days, and make a complete garment from beginning to end, so children can see the entire process. A small piece of clothing for one of the children's dolls or stuffed animals would be particularly motivating for children. Document the visit by taking photographs or making a videotape of the visitor at work, and have the children record what they see by drawing in theme journals.

## UNIT ACTIVITIES

- Visit a children's clothing store. Have children make drawings of the clothing displays. Older children can put together an outfit and calculate the cost.
- Put out long pieces of wildly printed and richly textured fabric, such as velour and taffetas, and encourage children to make up new outfits for the dramatic play area.
- Investigate special clothing worn for different occupations. Have a firefighter, football player, ballet dancer, or construction worker come and explain why he or she dresses the way he or she does.
- Invite children to wear certain colors or types of clothing on special days, such as sweat suit day or beach day. Plan special activities to go with the clothing. Sweat suit day, for example, could focus on exercising activities.
- Cut out simple vest shapes from brown paper grocery bags, and have children decorate them with printed designs or drawn symbols representing possible future careers.
- Make an attractive display of cloth scraps, laces, ribbons, yarns, and trims, arranged by color and texture, for the collage area.
- Display paintings showing people from different times and places wearing a variety of clothing styles. For example, introduce some of the following (all from the National Gallery): *The Hobby Horse* (Anonymous), *Anne with a Green Parasol* (Bellows), *Little Girl in Lavender* (Bradley), *White Cloud* (Catlin), *Italian Girl* (Corot), and *Marchesa Brigida* (Rubens).
- Explore different ways clothing is fastened—zippers, buttons, laces, and hook-and-loop tape. Add buttons to the collage offerings.
- Extend the study to include footwear, jewelry, hairstyles, and masks.
- Sing the song "Go In and Out the Windows" with children, standing in a circle with their arms raised. Choose one child in turn to weave in and out the "windows" going under the arms of each pair. Compare this play dance to weaving cloth.

# Reflection Page

## Artwork Study

Select an original piece of art, a print, or an artifact that interests you. Record the following information:

Title _____

Artist/Culture _____

Media _____

Description/Story _____

_____

Based on this artwork, write an example of each type of question you could ask children.

1. What does it tell you about?

_____

2. How was it made?

_____

3. Can you find? (arts elements)

_____

4. How does it make you feel?

_____

5. What comes next?

_____

6. How many? (related curriculum question)

_____

7. Can you? (kinesthetic response question)

_____

# Reflection Page

## Comparing Creative Works

Select two pieces of work representing any of the arts and that have some similarity, such as style, subject, media, colors, artist, material, use, theme, or culture. Describe each piece.

**Creative Work 1:** Title _____

Artist/Culture _____

Media _____

Description/Story _____

**Creative Work 2:** Title _____

Artist/Culture _____

Media _____

Description/Story _____

Write three questions that would help children focus on the similarities in the works.

1. _____

2. _____

3. _____

Write three questions that would help children focus on the differences in the works.

1. _____

2. _____

3. _____

# Reflection Page

## Self-Exploration: My Artistic Heritage

What is your cultural background?

_____

_____

What arts did you have in your home when you were growing up?

_____

_____

As a child, did you know anyone who was an artist, musician, actor, or dancer?

_____

_____

As a child, did you visit museums or attend performances?

_____

_____

As a child, did you have any favorite piece or type of art, music, dance, or drama?

_____

_____

As a child, was there any artwork you disliked?

_____

_____

In your home now, do you have pieces of artwork, or musical instruments; do you dance and tell stories?

_____

_____

Do these pieces reflect your artistic heritage, another family member's, and/or choices made based on what you have learned about the arts as an adult?

_____

_____

# Reflection Page

## Self-Exploration: My View of the Arts Now

I think it is important to learn about the arts created by others because:

_____

_____

_____

_____

_____

_____

_____

_____

_____

I would like to learn more about the art, music, dance, or drama of _____
(name a culture). Explain why?:

_____

_____

_____

_____

_____

_____

_____

_____

_____

If I could own any piece of artwork or music ever created, I would choose:

_____

_____

_____

_____

_____

_____

_____

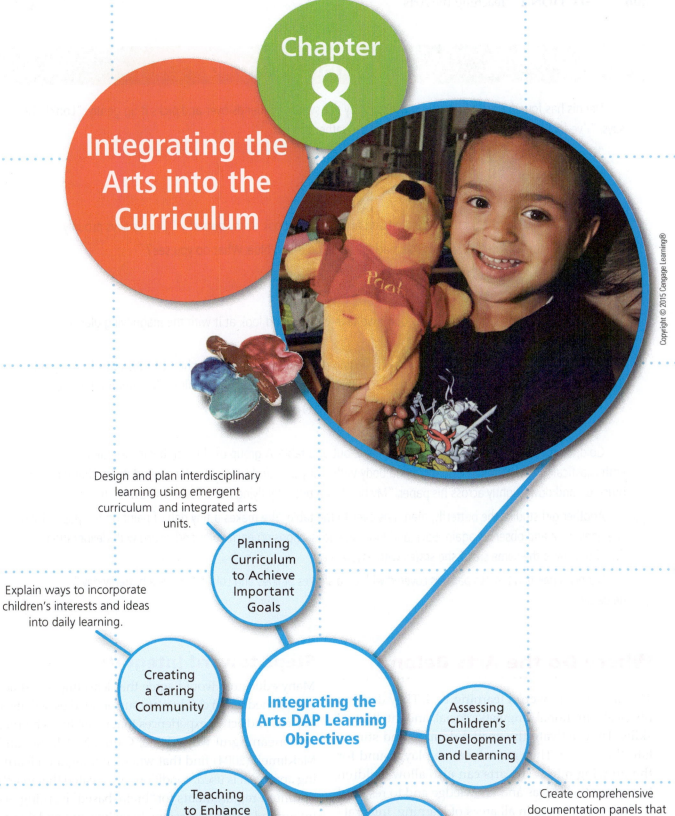

# Chapter 8

## Integrating the Arts into the Curriculum

Design and plan interdisciplinary learning using emergent curriculum and integrated arts units.

**Planning Curriculum to Achieve Important Goals**

Explain ways to incorporate children's interests and ideas into daily learning.

**Creating a Caring Community**

**Integrating the Arts DAP Learning Objectives**

**Assessing Children's Development and Learning**

Create comprehensive documentation panels that demonstrate children's learning.

**Teaching to Enhance Development and Learning**

Design integrated arts activities across the subject areas that foster developmental growth.

**Establishing Reciprocal Family Relationships**

Know ways to welcome families into the classroom using projects and integrated arts units.

## Young Artists Creating

Dennis has found a dead butterfly in the grass by the swing. He bends over and picks it up gently. "Look!" he says, "I've found a butterfly." Several other children gather around.

"I've seen one like that."

"My sister caught a butterfly."

"Can I have it?"

The teacher notices the group of children and approaches. "Look at my butterfly," Dennis says proudly.

"It has so many colors!" responds the teacher. "I see gold and blue. What do you see?"

"Here's some red and yellow," answers Dennis.

"It has lots of feet," Tomas adds.

"Wow, there is so much to see! Why don't we take it inside and look at it with the magnifying glass?" suggests the teacher.

Inside, Dennis places the butterfly on a soft cushion of paper towels, and the children take turns looking at it through the magnifying glass. Some children begin to pretend they are butterflies fluttering around the room. The teacher says invitingly, "Would you like to paint with butterfly colors?"

"Yes," say the children.

Gold, blue, red, yellow, and black paints are put out at a table. A group of children begins to paint enthusiastically. One paints a huge head and body with many legs and swirls of color around it. Another dabs his brush up and down lightly across his paper. "My brush is a butterfly flying from flower to flower," he says.

Another girl studies the butterfly, then runs over to the table. She makes a tiny dab of paint on her paper. Then she goes back and observes again. Back and forth she goes, choosing each color and stroke with deliberation. "My butterfly is the same size," she states with assurance.

Dennis is painting too. His paper is covered with bold strokes of lines and colors. "This is a butterfly day," he declares.

## Where Do the Arts Belong?

The arts are a powerful learning tool. They develop physical, emotional, linguistic, social, and intellectual skills. They activate the spatial domain and stimulate the senses. They are a creative playground for the growing mind. The arts can also allow children to express their ideas and knowledge and to respond to their experiences in all areas of learning. Integrating the arts into the curriculum provides children with the opportunity not only to explore the different art forms in open-ended ways, but also to creatively communicate what they are learning in math, science, social studies, and English language arts.

## Steps toward Integration

Many educators would agree that learning is best accomplished when children are surrounded by activities, objects, and active experiences that relate to each other in a meaningful way. Caine, Caine, McClintic, and McKlimek (2004) find that when an integrated learning approach is used, conditions are created that match optimum requirements for "brain-based" learning. As integrated curricula designs have become widely accepted in early childhood education, teachers have found that unifying the activities presented to young children is both challenging and very rewarding. Integrated activities stimulate both children and teachers to look at the environment around them in new ways.

Integrating the arts into the curriculum requires the teacher to approach the arts in different ways for distinctive purposes. Lessons can be intertwined, so that children acquire arts concepts and skills, while using the arts to connect and increase learning across the disciplines.

**Step 1: Teaching about the arts.** The arts disciplines are discrete subject areas. Dance, drama, music, and visual arts each have unique concepts and skills. A lesson in which we present a new song and then ask children to invent a way to notate it, or one that has children look at a sculpture and then asks them to imagine how the artist made it, is a lesson that addresses the concepts, skills, tools, and work of artists.

Children who have disciplined, specific artistic skills and knowledge can use the arts more effectively and creatively to communicate their ideas. To nourish creative artists, musicians, dancers, and actors teachers must plan thoughtful, well-organized arts activities with clearly stated objectives that focus directly on the arts and artists and that provide many opportunities for arts exploration and practice. The "Exploring the Arts" section of this book suggests ways to meet these objectives. Appendix B explains how to write an activity plan like the ones featured in the Making Plans boxes.

**Step 2: Connecting the arts.** Next, the arts can connect with learning in other subject areas. When children sketch the parts of a flower or sing a song about the seasons they are using the arts to enhance learning in another subject area. These kinds of connected lessons allow children to use skills and techniques of the different art forms to practice and communicate concepts and ideas learned in other subject areas.

Connecting the arts in this way enriches the child's learning experience by providing multiple pathways for children to make what they are learning about more meaningful. The arts can be connected in this way to math, science, social studies, literature, and to each other. The Integrating the Arts boxes found throughout this book provide many examples of ways to connect the arts with other subjects.

Connected arts lessons can develop in several ways. They may be carefully planned as part of the curriculum. Children studying trees might be asked to imagine that they are trees in a creative movement

Drawing can be used to expand and enrich the words of beginning writers as they communicate their ideas. "I like caterpillars." Marker—Ben, age five.

activity. On the other hand, sometimes a wondering question may set the stage for an activity. For example, children measuring water at the water table might wonder aloud what happens when different amounts of water are added to paint. The alert teacher seizes the **teachable moment** and quickly sets up a paint and water mixing activity and invites the young scientists to come explore. Arts activities can also lead to lessons in other curriculum areas. The butterfly painting activity described at the beginning of the chapter could be connected to reading books about butterflies, dramatizing their life cycle, hatching a cocoon, or creating a graph of the different butterflies observed by the children on the playground.

**Step 3: Learning through the arts.** In a fully integrated arts program, the arts are found everywhere in the classroom. Arts pursuits flow into and out of the daily classroom activities as children need them. For example, instead of children passing through a visual art center, each taking a turn at the art medium being offered that day, they are offered a well-stocked art supply center from which they can select familiar tools and media that best meet their expressive needs at that moment.

In such a classroom, children's projects incorporate the arts. Children studying about homes, for example, may make crayon sketches of the houses near the school. In the same class another group might choose to put on a puppet show about building a

the curriculum will be examined in detail—**emergent curriculum** as represented by the **project approach,** and the **integrated learning unit.**

Emergent curriculum starts with an experience or event that inspires children's curiosity and starts them asking questions.

### Did You Get It?

**What is the first step in forming a fully integrated arts program?**

  **a.** teaching about the arts

  **b.** assessing the arts

  **c.** connecting the arts

  **d.** learning through the arts

**Take the full quiz on CourseMate**

house. Individual arts pursuits are also facilitated. One child may spend several days building a complex house of Styrofoam pieces, whereas another paints houses at the easel one day and creates a house from collage materials the next.

In order for this level of integration to occur, the curriculum is organized so as to provide unifying experiences that inspire children to communicate their ideas artistically. In this chapter two ways to integrate

## Special Needs

### • INCLUSION •

Inclusion is the practice of incorporating children with special needs into the classroom and adapting the activities so that they can learn alongside their peers regardless of their disability or academic level. An arts-infused project or integrated unit of study is a powerful way to make all children feel like they belong and can contribute to the group because not every child is expected to produce the same end result. For example, in a project on the firehouse a girl with oral language difficulties who uses a communication device can help her friends compose a song about the firehouse by adding the fire truck siren in a rhythmic way. A nonverbal boy with autism might choose to wear a firefighter coat and hat and pose as the firefighter they are singing about.

## What Is Emergent Curriculum?

Emergent curriculum is created by teachers and children working together to explore ideas that interest them. Topics for study develop from events in the children's lives, daily happenings, and concerns that develop as children work and play.

An emergent unit might begin with listening closely to what children are talking about and observing what they are doing. For example, Dennis's discovery of the butterfly and the children's interest in it could be the start of learning more about insects. The teacher seizes the teachable moment and models enthusiasm and wonder to increase the children's interest. Tantalizing questions can make children look more closely or think more deeply. Instead of dismissing Dennis's discovery of the butterfly with a "That's nice," the teacher draws the children in by pointing out the colors and asking questions about what they see.

If some of the children continue to show interest in butterflies, the teacher might then start to gather resources and think of experiences and activities that relate to this interest. A web about butterflies could be created to help discover ideas to pursue further with the children (see Figure 8-1). Experiences chosen must be rich in sensory and visual stimuli. They

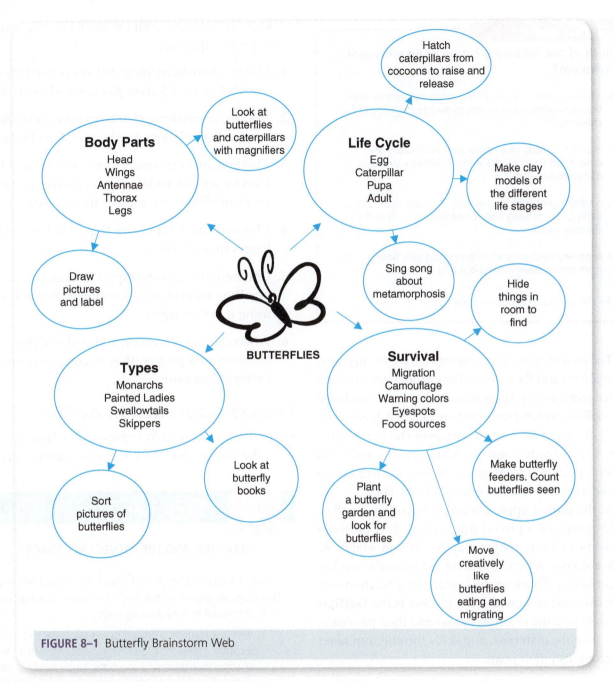

**FIGURE 8–1** Butterfly Brainstorm Web

should be memorable—full of opportunities for asking questions and making observations. Most important, the experiences and activities selected should flow directly from the children's questions and interests.

Throughout an emergent unit we need to be on the lookout for things that spark children's interest. To facilitate the development of an emergent curriculum it is handy to have a reservoir of ideas, books, songs, and arts materials on hand that can be drawn upon at a moment's notice. The Internet can also be a rich source of information.

## What Is the Project Approach?

The project approach is an example of one way to organize and carry out an emergent curriculum. Katz and Chard (2000, p. 2) define a project as "an in-depth study of a particular topic that one or more children undertake." Howard Gardner applauds the project approach, as demonstrated at Reggio Emilia, for the way it guides children in using all of their "intellectual, emotional, social, and moral potentials" (Edwards, Gandini, & Forman, 1993, p. xii).

The project approach starts with a topic of interest to the children and then fosters the children's exploration of that topic as they apply already acquired knowledge and skills in making sense of new material. It is particularly designed to meet the needs of children in preschool, kindergarten, and the primary grades, and it can be very effective in multiage classes, because it draws on the differing skills and knowledge of each child.

In the project approach children work in small or large groups on a project that reflects their personal interests, some of which may be far removed from their everyday experience, and from what the teacher might select. These groups establish a relationship with the teacher in which the teacher is the **facilitator,** soliciting the children's ideas and then providing the concepts, materials, and skills the children need to accomplish their goals.

## The Value of the Project Approach

The project approach engages children's intellects by widening their knowledge and skills at their individual levels of understanding. Unfocused playtime, although beneficial, lacks intellectual challenge and underestimates children's ability to acquire wider meaning from their experiences. An academic approach, on the other hand, forces children to proceed in a lockstep sequence of learning skills and concepts, whether or not these skills are relevant or appropriate for the individual child.

Katz and Chard (2000) list the following benefits of the project approach:

1. Children learn in an integrated manner and the divisions between subjects or play areas is broken down.

2. Teachers are challenged to be creative and to devise constructive solutions to educational problems.

3. Children are intrinsically motivated because it allows for a much wider range of choices and independent efforts on a topic of their choice.

4. Children can select work that matches or challenges their skill level.

5. Children can become expert in their own learning. They are in charge of finding information and using it in new ways.

6. When children reflect on and evaluate their contribution to a project, they become accountable for their own learning.

## Project Approach in Action

In the project approach topics rather than themes form the framework. Topics, unlike themes, can be

**Teacher Tip**

**DRAWING AND THE PROJECT APPROACH**

Sylvia Chard recommends that drawing to record information plays an important role in project work. Drawing can be incorporated in the following ways:

1. The first stage in a project draws upon the children's existing knowledge and experience. To begin, tell a story that relates to the topic to be studied, and then ask children to share their own stories. For example, if the topic is shoes, tell the children about a special pair of shoes and how you felt when you wore them. Follow storytelling by having the children draw memory pictures about their shoes.

2. In the second stage, children do fieldwork to learn more about the topic. In this stage, they can make drawings from direct observation, such as taking off their shoe and drawing it. They can make sketches on field trips, such as at the shoe store, by attaching a few sheets of paper to a clipboard or to a piece of cardboard with a pencil attached.

very specific and are chosen because they relate closely to the children's interests.

**Choosing the topic.** One way to find an emergent topic is to listen to what interests or concerns the children. Did someone just get a letter from a relative who lives far away? That could start a project on the post office. Is a child going to the hospital for surgery? That could begin a project on hospitals. We can also initiate a project by selecting a topic about which everyone has a story or experience to share. For example, we might begin by telling a story about our favorite pair of socks and then ask the children to talk about and draw pictures of their experiences with socks.

Jennifer Kamperman and Mary Bowne (2011) noticed their students blowing into foam noodle tubes to make sounds like elephants and built on this interest by incorporating a large stuffed elephant and a series of mysterious events into a year-long project seeped in literacy activities. They found that by cultivating the interests of the children not only did the children take ownership of their learning and developed in language and social skills, but they as teachers became more creative and sensitive to ways they could incorporate these skills into the project.

**Facilitating learning.** Based on what the children say and draw, learning activities are planned that relate to each individual child's ideas and questions. These activities should allow open-ended exploration of topic-related ideas, and encourage the child to observe, to sense, to explore, and to experiment, both individually and with others. For example, after several children participating in a project on plants comment that all leaves are green, a variety of plants with different color leaves can be put on display alongside containers of different colored dried leaves to use in collages. These activities are then available as a choice for any child to investigate.

**Organizing activities.** Although flexibility is a principle feature of the project approach, projects usually follow a set course. The first phase is devoted to memory work. Children are invited to tell personal stories, to make drawings, and bring in things from home that relate to the topic. The children's knowledge and questions can be made into a KWL chart (see Figure 8-2).

The second phase is devoted to gathering data from observation and experience. During this phase children go on field trips, make drawings from real things, and talk to experts. Children record what they learn through drawings, creative movement, music, dramatic play, and constructions.

The third phase is concluding the project. At this time the teacher helps children select from the work they have done, and what they want to share with other classes and their families. Time is also taken to record conclusions and evaluate what was learned. Figure 8-3 gives an overview of what happens in the different phases.

**Small group work.** One of the key features of the project approach is the importance of working with children in small groups. Teachers meet on a regular basis with groups of children. Together they discuss the initial experiences and pursue questions and ideas that lead into a variety of independent investigations or projects. Small group projects can range from writing a book to making puppets and putting on a puppet show. Children are limited only by their imaginations.

As they work on their projects, the teacher offers guidance, provides requested materials, directs the

| What we Know K | What we Wonder about W | What we have Learned L |
|---|---|---|
| Snakes are long and skinny. | What do snakes eat? | Snakes are reptiles. |
| Snakes live in the grass. | How are baby snakes born? | Snakes shed their skin when they grow. |
| Snakes can bite. | How can you tell if a snake is dangerous? | Snakes eat mice. |
| Some snakes are dangerous. | Why are some people afraid of snakes? | |
| Some of us are scared of snakes. | | |

**FIGURE 8–2** Sample KWL Chart: Snakes

| Phase 1<br>Beginning | Phase 2<br>Data Collecting | Phase 3<br>Conclusion |
| --- | --- | --- |
| Topic ideas are investigated | Resources are collected | Plan culminating event |
| Topic selected | Fieldtrips taken | Complete activities |
| Topic web created by teacher | Guest experts visit | Set up event displays |
| A common experience is shared with the group | Books are read | Discuss and evaluate |
| Stories are shared | Examine artifacts | Create presentation panels |
| Ideas about topic are shared through the arts | Learning is represented through writing and the arts | Invite parents |
| KWL chart created | Revisit KWL chart | Celebrate learning |

**FIGURE 8–3** Life Cycle of a Project

children to sources of information, and teaches specific skills as needed.

**Discussion/representation.** Time is set aside to talk about and share the children's ideas daily. These can be recorded by the teacher in various ways through charts, graphs, dictation, and audio taping. The children's changing ideas can also be documented through their drawings and constructions and through photographs and videotapes made of their activities. This is a very important part of the process; it is the way the different groups' learning is made visible to all of the children.

## Culminating Projects

Completed projects need to be recognized in a special way. One of the main dangers with the project

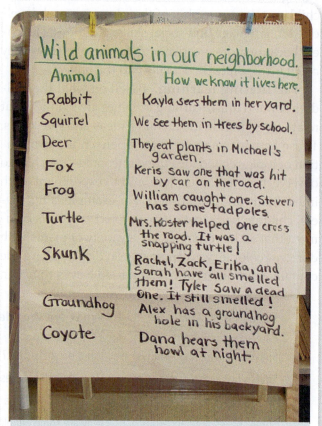

Memory work, the first part of a project, acknowledges what children already know and sets the stage for further research.

A project on how animals survive in the wild emerges when a teacher finds abandoned baby rabbits and brings them to school.

A mural is a great way to culminate a unit of study. "Wild animals in our neighborhood" Tempera—Kerris, William, Zack, Carolyn, Sabrina, Tyler, Alex, Mackenzie, Jenna, Taylor, Erika, and Dana, ages six to eight.

approach is the temptation to focus on the finished products and to ignore the thought and process that went into it. Plan ways to share the children's work through displays of not only the project, but also all of the documentation of the process that went into it. This will be further explained later in this chapter.

---

### Did You Get It?

**Which of the following is a benefit of the project approach?**

a. It helps children become more accountable for their own learning.

b. It requires children to select work that is a few notches higher than their skill level.

c. It helps children learn by separating academics and play.

d. Children rely on teachers to find information for them to use in new ways.

**Take the full quiz on CourseMate**

---

## What Is an Integrated Learning Unit?

An integrated unit is one in which many different subject areas are tied together by relating them to a carefully selected, broad-based concept or theme. This is expressed in the form of an overarching question or a metaphor that ties together the learning areas. For example, if the chosen question is "What is water?" then books about water will be read. Children will experiment with water. They will paint with water, wash the dolls and toys in the play area, and splash in water at the water table. They may take a field trip to a stream or lake and talk about the animals that live in the water.

## Selecting a Unifying Question

Visualizing the possible ways that all the subjects can be integrated around a common question enables us to see beyond the isolated arts activity of the day and allows arts concepts and techniques to be introduced, explored, practiced, and mastered in concert with all the other subject areas. The following guidelines will aid in the selection of appropriate questions for integration.

**Is the question broad-based?** Decide if the question is one that is rich in possibilities for expansion to the different subjects or growth areas and any standards that must be addressed. A subject-based concept web, such as the one illustrated in Figure 8-4, can be used to explore the depth of the unit.

Once the concepts to be learned are laid out on the web, try to brainstorm the activities you might use to teach them. Are there wonderful books to read? Are there related songs and poems? Will there be things to explore through science, visual art, drama, and play? Will children be able to use skills from all of the multiple intelligences to explore this question? Some questions for integrated units have more potential than others. Successful integrated units can be built around questions such as:

- How do animals live?
- How do our bodies work?
- What is a family?
- What is water?

For more examples of open-ended questions, see *Questions for Integrated Units* on CourseMate.

**What resources are available?** Are needed supplies available for certain activities? Are there places to visit or people who could talk to the children about this? Where can books be found that address this question?

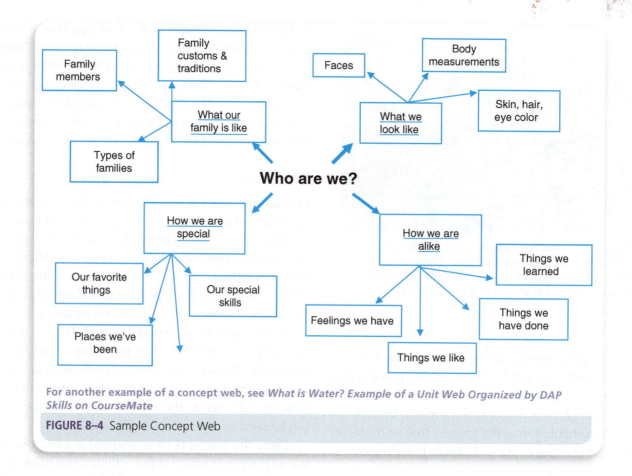

For another example of a concept web, see *What is Water? Example of a Unit Web Organized by DAP Skills on CourseMate*

**FIGURE 8–4** Sample Concept Web

**How much time is there?** The question should be open-ended enough so if the children's interest wanes it will be easy to move on to something else. There should be sufficient time, however, so that if the children become highly interested they do not have to be cut off to "move on." It is not the specific content that teaches. The goal in early childhood education is not to make children experts. Rather the question should be a vehicle that will allow children to explore and learn about their environment within a meaningful context as they master the required subject area skills and concepts as delineated in state standards and the Common Core.

**How can the experiences be made real?** The most important part of unit design is to make sure that it includes plenty of real, **authentic experiences.** It is not enough to read about a subject, watch videos, or search the Internet; if children are studying water they need plenty of activities in which to use water. If they are studying animals, they need to go to the zoo or pet store and see, smell, and touch live animals.

**Can the required skills and concepts be woven meaningfully into this question?** The broader the question the easier it will be to incorporate all of the various subject area objectives. The goal should be to weave in as many as possible. However, in doing so, it is not enough to draw a waterwheel on a subtraction math worksheet and think it is related to a unit on water. In order for learning to be meaningful, the children need to have focused instruction in subtraction, then learn how subtraction relates to the unit question by applying the new math skill in an authentic hands on way. For example, subtraction in a primary unit on the question "What makes the weather?" could be practiced by having each child set out a premeasured cup of water and each day measuring and subtracting to see how much water evaporated.

**What authentic assessments can be used?** An **authentic** or **performance assessment** asks the child to perform a task in which the skill or concept is used to successfully accomplish a real life goal. This type of assessment asks the child to design or create something that shows what they have learned.

Examples of authentic assessments include having children design a creative movement and original song using all the parts of the body after studying about how the body moves or building a boat that floats and holds a certain amount of weight after studying sinking and floating. Authentic assessments often start out with a **rubric** or list of criteria that represents quality work. Rubrics can be individualized to meet each child's abilities and needs or they can be co-designed with input from the children.

## The Arts in Integrated Units

Integrated teaching provides an excellent way to unify the child's arts experiences with the rest of the curriculum. However, it is very important to make sure that the arts activities are open ended. It is a real temptation for the teacher, for example, to want to give the children unit-related pictures to color and patterns to follow, but it must be noted that such directive activities do not foster creative growth, no matter how attractive the results may be.

Do not expect or demand that every child make the same arts projects to take home. The arts allow each child to express a unique view of the unit concepts. Open-ended arts activities can be incorporated into integrated units in many ways (see Figure 8-5).

**Through everyday creative arts activities.** Make sure basic, familiar arts supplies and props are always available. During the unit, children should be free to choose to draw, paint, make a collage, move creatively to music, or create a puppet, whether as a personal exploration or as a reaction to a unit-related experience.

**Through special materials.** Unit-related materials can be offered as a choice. For example, for the unit "What is a tree?" pressed leaves can be added to the collage area, twigs for painting can be placed alongside brushes at the easel, and drums made from hollow tree trunks added to the sound center.

**Through responsive activities.** Encourage children to use the arts as a way to record and respond to special events and experiences by providing opportunities for the children to show what they are learning through activities that incorporate arts skills. For example:

1. Make individual thematic journals by stapling together several sheets of blank or partially lined paper. Then set aside a daily time for children to record in pictures and words their ideas about the topic. Have children share their thematic journals with a partner or a small group.

| Unit Question | Subject | Related Arts Activities |
|---|---|---|
| What do we look like? | Dance | Set up floor mirrors; dance in front of them using different body parts; pair children and have them mirror each other's actions. |
| | Drama | Put mirror in play area. Make funny faces in mirror. |
| | Language Arts | Tell stories about themselves and read books such as *We Are All Alike, We Are All Different* (Cheltenham Kindergarten, 1994), |
| | Math | Measure body parts and graph them. Count numbers of hands, feet, arms, fingers, etc. in class. |
| | Music | Sing "If You're Happy" and add different facial and body expressions. |
| | Science | Study how the different body parts work and help us survive. |
| | Social Studies | Display photographs of class members. Have them learn to identify each other. Hang up photographs of all kinds of people from all over the world. |
| | Visual Arts | Make self-portraits. Make tracings of bodies and add personalizing details. Look at portraits by Rembrandt van Ryn, Amedeo Modigliani, and Pierre Renoir. |

**FIGURE 8–5** Sample Ideas for Integrated Units

2. Set up a storytelling center, such as Vivian Paley (1992) describes. At this center, children can dictate their unit-related stories to the teacher. Later the class can help act out these stories for everyone to enjoy.

3. Set up an author's corner where they can write imaginary stories based on something they have learned during the unit. For example, if they are studying animals, they can write and illustrate a story about one of the animals.

4. Create a music center with thematically related instruments and sound makers where they can compose a musical piece or song. For example, if the group is studying water, the center might feature water drums, water bottles, and rain sticks.

**Through group activities.** Plan one or more group arts activities that relate to the unit concepts. Quilts, murals, and box sculptures can be designed to relate to many theme concepts. Whole group singing and creative movement activities can help make concepts come alive.

## Organizing Integrated Unit Activities

The unit activities selected should span the range of developmental growth areas and tap into all of the domains of the multiple intelligences. Consider questions to be addressed, explorations and experiments to be done, vocabulary to use, and assessments to be made. One way to organize this material is to use an MI planning web or grid (see Figure 8-6).

1. **Put activities in developmental order.** Activities should be planned to logically build on each other. Skills acquired in one activity should recur again at slightly more challenging levels in the next activity. One way to do this is to use index cards or sticky notes on which are written the different activities being considered for the unit. Categorize each activity as introductory, exploratory, revisitation, or responsive, and then lay out the activity cards in sequence from least to most complex on a calendar or grid. As the unit progresses, move the cards to extend or repeat activities as needed. At intervals, take time to revisit the plans and notice what is going well.

Do not be afraid to discard some activities or add others to better match the learning needs of the children. The goal is to produce an integrated unit that flows across the disciplines in concert with the children's developing skills and interest.

2. **Check for comprehensiveness.** The developmental growth areas, in concert with Gardner's Multiple Intelligences (MI), can be used as an organizing framework to make sure that no area of learning is more heavily emphasized than another.

3. **Determine the amount of time needed.** It is important to plan how the activities will unfold over time. Figure 8-7 shows how the arts could be integrated into a one week unit focusing on the question, "How do our bodies work?"

## The Integrated Unit in Action

Integrated units consist of the following components:

**Setting the stage.** Before beginning the unit, allow the children to become familiar with how the workspace or room is organized, what behaviors are expected of them, and how the time is divided during

▶❚❚ **TeachSource Video Case 8.1**

**Exploring Math Concepts through Creative Activities**

Watch the video *Exploring Math Concepts through Creative Activities*. In this video the teacher has organized a unit for preschoolers around the question: What are shapes? How has the teacher incorporated the arts? How would you make this unit more exciting and creative for these children?

**Watch on CourseMate**

| Language Objectives | Cognitive Objectives | Emotional Objectives | Social Objectives |
|---|---|---|---|
| These are behaviors and skills that help children receive and communicate ideas through listening, speaking, reading, and writing. | These are behaviors and skills that help children develop the ability to reason, to think logically, to organize information, to understand mathematical relationships, and to solve problems. | These are behaviors and skills that help children develop independence, understanding, and confidence in their own feelings, preferences, decisions, and abilities. | These are behaviors and skills that help children get along better with others by showing appropriate reactions to others, such as kindness, acceptance, respect, and affection. |
| **Linguistic Activities** | **Logical-Mathematical Activities** | **Intrapersonal Activities** | **Interpersonal Activities** |
| Naming, telling, discussing, describing, defining, retelling, answering, matching lettters to sounds and words, using handwriting, using correct language forms, writing stories, poems, and reports, using the writing process—drafting, editing, and revising own writing and that of others | Identifying properties of objects, predicting, researching, using and manipulating number concepts, measuring, ordering, comparing, contrasting, finding patterns, using graphic organizers, making graphs, planning and carrying out tests | Identifying and expressing personal feelings and preferences, controlling one's feelings and behavior, setting a goal or making a plan and then working to accomplish it, assessing or judging one's own work or efforts | Sharing, helping, taking turns, performing a role in a cooperative activity, using manners, making moral decisions, settling conflicts, making rules, playing games, and learning about other people and cultures |

**Integrative Question:** A broad, overarching question that addresses an important idea

**Concepts:** The specific ideas and information children learn through this thematic unit

| Musical/Rhythmic Activities | Visual/Spatial Activities | Naturalistic Activities | Bodily/Kinesthetic Activities |
|---|---|---|---|
| Identifying and using rhythmic and musical elements, critically listening to music, solving aural problems, singing, playing, and composing music, participating in musical performances | Identifying and using the art elements, looking closely at and evaluating artworks, creating original drawings, paintings, sculptures, and so on, reading and making maps, solving spatial problems and representing ideas using graphic images | Observation, classification and grouping, expressing feelings about nature based on sensory perceptions and outdoor experiences, taking action to protect and care for living things, natural resources, and the environment and grouping, expressing feelings about nature based on sensory perceptions and outdoor experiences, taking action to protect and care for living things, natural resources, and the environment | Sensory activities, exercising, doing physical work, using tools, dancing, moving creatively, dramatizing, cutting, pasting, painting, playing an instrument, doing puzzles, block building and other constructions, driving, and playing sports |
| **Musical Skill Objectives** | **Art Skill Objectives** | **Environmental Skill Objectives** | **Physical Objectives** |
| These are behaviors and skills that help children express their ideas through rhythm and music. | These are behaviors and skills that help children express their ideas through visual imagery, two-dimensional graphic images, and three-dimensional forms. | These are behaviors and skills that help children understand, appreciate, and care for the natural world. | These are behaviors and skills that help children develop their coordination, physical strength, balance, and use of the sense organs for taste, smell, touch, sight, and sound. |

For a completed MI planning web, see *Our Bodies: A Sample MI Web* on CourseMate.

**FIGURE 8–6** Sample MI Planning Web

| MONDAY | TUESDAY | WEDNESDAY | THURSDAY | FRIDAY |
|---|---|---|---|---|
| **Introductory experience** Demonstration by gymnast. | **Introductory experience** Display photos of gymnastic demonstration. | **Introductory experience** Display paintings showing people in action, such as Homer's *Crack the Whip* or a Degas ballet scene. | **Introductory experience** Have children show actions using their puppets. | **Sharing** Have children put on short plays using their puppets. Videotape them. |
| **Language** Discuss how he moved. Imitate motions. Ask: How do our bodies move? Chart their ideas. | **Language** Talk about photos. Name body parts, and tell how they move. Review visit. Write thank-you note together. | **Language** Look at paintings. Ask: What are the ways we can move? Add ideas to word chart. | **Language** Describe ways the puppets moved. Find the ways on the word chart. Look for word patterns such asing. | **Language** Show tape and have children identify movements. |
| **Journal time** Record what they saw. | **Journal time** Draw thank-you pictures. | **Journal time** Show yourself moving in a special way. | **Journal time** Show how the puppets moved. | **Journal time** Show your favorite part of the show. |
| **Read-aloud** *Head to Toe* (Carle, 1997, Scholastic) Do motions. | **Read aloud** *Me and My Body* (Evan & Williams 1992, Dorling Kingsley) | **Read aloud** *The Skeleton Inside You* (Balestrino, 1990, Scholastic) | **Read aloud** *All about My Skeleton* (Black & Ong, 1995, Scholastic) | **Read aloud** *I Can Be the Alphabet* (Bonini, 1986, Viking) Do motions. |
| **Art center** Put out bendable materials such as chenille stems, yarn, and cardboard strips. Encourage children to compare the different ways these bend. Ask: How can you make art that moves? (Exploration) | **Art center** Put out materials for making stick puppets. Set up puppet theater. (Exploration) | **Art center** Introduce paper fasteners. Show how to use to make a bendable "joint." Encourage them to make moving parts on their puppets. (Practice) | **Art center** Encourage puppet making to continue. (Practice) Add other materials for puppets such as yarn, foils, sports insignia clipped from magazines. Invite interested children to create a play using their puppets. (Responsive) | **Art center** Put out paint and play music. Encourage children to move their brushes in different ways as the music changes in pitch, speed, and rhythm. (Exploration) |
| **Music** Teach the "Hokey Pokey." Do motions. | **Music** Review "Hokey Pokey." Do motions. | **Music** Add children's own words and motions to song. | **Music** Use word patterns from word chart to make up a chant. *Example: Running, jumping, hopping, skipping, bending, stopping.* Clap the rhythm, and add body movements. | **Music** Recite chant from yesterday. Have children substitute other words and movements. Sing "Hokey Pokey." |
| **Math center** Put out light and heavy things to explore and move. | **Math center** Add scale to center. Sort items by weight (*small group*). | **Math center** Have children select object, weigh it, and record it on chart (*small group*). | **Math center** Have children select objects of different weights from chart, push them on flat surface, and describe how it feels and the motion they see. Add infor mation to chart (*small group*). | **Math center** Offer a new set of objects. Have children sort them by what they predict they weigh, then weigh them. |
| **Science center** Put out bendable model skeleton, X-rays, and drawing materials. | **Science center** Have children match skeleton's bones to their own bodies (*small group*). | **Science center** Have children find their joints and bend them. Draw pictures of the skeletons inside them. (*small group*). | **Science center** Add boiled chicken bones. Provide mat for sorting bones by size and shape. Ask them to guess what part of a chicken they come from. | **Science center** Put out drawing of chicken skeleton. Invite children to place matching bones on drawing. |
| **Blocks** Put out bendable plastic action figures. | **Blocks** Ask children to describe motions of figures. | **Blocks** Watch how children move and talk about figures. | **Blocks** Encourage children to draw pictures of their figures and their block structures. | **Blocks** Challenge children to think of other ways to move the figures. |

For another sample weekly plan, see *What is Water Integrated Unit Weekly Plan* on CourseMate.

For a blank weekly planner, see *Integrated Unit Weekly Planning Sheet* on Coursemate.

**FIGURE 8–7** Sample Week of an Integrated Unit plan for Kindergarten or Grade 1

the day. Once the unit begins, the children will already know where the basic supplies are and which areas are used for certain activities. Taking time to allow for basic exploration of the environment and getting to know each other beforehand will make it easier for everyone to concentrate more on the theme.

**The initial event.** Once a question is selected, plan an initial event that will be stimulating and provocative, and which gets the children excited about the theme. It should be full of engaging images, ideas, and feelings—a WOW. The event may be one that takes the children beyond the walls of the room, such as a walk or field trip, or it may involve bringing something special to the children, such as a visitor, an animal, or an object. Rearrange the room, and put out new materials, new learning centers, and play items that relate to the unifying theme of the unit. The idea is to raise the interest of as many children as possible.

**Preschool integration.** In a play-based program, unit activities should be integrated into each of the learning centers offered but should not replace them. Children need the continuity of knowing that sand, blocks, home-life/dramatic play, and easel painting will be waiting for them every day. Integrate the unit activities into these areas in small ways such as changing the paint color or texture or the paint tools offered at the easel; providing different containers or toys in the sand; putting out topic-related toys; or providing different dress-up clothes, art to hang, or play food. Although it may not be possible to integrate unit concepts into every area every time, try to find creative ways to touch as many areas as possible.

## Making Plans

**INTEGRATED UNIT CURRIULUM PLAN**

**UNIT OVERARCHING QUESTION: WHAT DO WE SEE?**

WHO?    Group composition age(s): Older infants (with adjustments), toddlers, and preschoolers

WHEN?   Time frame: 1-3-minute introduction, then free choice time at the centers. Each week materials in a featured color will be displayed and discussed.

WHY?    Objectives: Children will develop

- physically, by using the small muscles of their hands and fingers to grip and manipulate the small items. I will see this happening when the children pick up and arrange the items. (Bodily-Kinesthetic)
- socially, by sharing workspace and materials. I will see this happening when children work side by side peacefully, hand itens to each other, and use please and thank you. (Interpersonal)
- emotionally, by feeling pleasure and satisfaction in handling the materials and arranging them in personally pleasing ways. I will see and hear this happening when the children express delight and have happy faces. (Intrapersonal)
- visual and tactile perception skills, by exploring the different colors and textures of the materials. I will see this happening when the children look at and touch materials. (Spatial)
- language skills, by understanding and using arts elements vocabulary. I will see this happening when they point to or pick up an object when given its name or name the color of an object they have noticed. (Linguistic)
- cognitively, by matching objects of the same kind and color together. (Logical-Mathematical)
- arts skills and knowledge, by learning the color names, by matching colors and sounds and movements and by singing simple color songs. (Visual Art Content Standards 1, & 2; Music Content Standards 1 & 2; Dance Content Standard 2)

WHERE?  Setup: Learning centers. (Note before beginning check to see if any child is color blind and adjust activities as needed for that child's success.)

WHAT?   Materials:

Sand Play: Put out containers and shovels, and/or hide blocks or plastic objects of the featured color in the sand for children to find.

*(continued)*

## Making Plans (continued)

Block Play: Put out pieces of cardboard that have been covered on both sides with paper or contact paper in the featured color, and/or add plastic toys of the featured color to the block area.

Dramatic Play: Offer dress-up clothes in the featured color. Put out play food, dishes, or art prints in the featured color.

Easel: Put out the featured color paint, plus white and black.

Drawing/Writing Play: Put out drawing materials, paper, and envelopes in range of hues of the featured color as well as the regular colors.

Sensory Play: Put out play dough or squishy bags in the featured color. Use paint chips to create opportunities for sorting.

Music: Put out a variety of shakers and other simple rhythm instruments plus chimes or a xylophone with different color keys.

**HOW?** Procedure:

WOW Warm-Up: Show the child or children an eye catching object in the featured color and talk enthusiastically about the color. Say: Let's see if we can find this color as we play today.

What to Do: Encourage children to notice the color as they play.

What to Say: As you interact with children at centers, point out the color and use expressive language. Things to say: Wow you found something _____? Isn't that a bright _____? What color do you think this is _____? What does this color look like _____? What does it remind you of? Which sound is like the color? Can we make up a song about the color? For children who can identify the color add complexity by asking them to find things that are all the same color or things that are two different colors. Point out the variation in graduations of a color. Read books about colors such as *White Rabbit's Color Book* (Baker, 1999), *Of Colors and Things* (Hoban, 1993), or *Mouse Paint* (Walsh, 1989).

Transition Out: At end of the day give each child something In the featured color to take home—a sticker, a bookmark, a note to the family.

**WHAT LEARNED?** Assessment: Can child point to the color when named? Does the child use the color name? Can the child find the color? Do the children pick up and manipulate the materials independently? Do the children work well together? Are the children excited about the color, and independently identify and talk about it? Which center is their favorite? Which center has them most engaged with the color?

**NEXT?** Extension: Go on a color scavenger hunt in the classroom and outside. As the children learn more colors, set up more opportunities for sorting and comparisons. Add transparent materials in the colors at the light table or in front of a window. Go on a field trip to a paint store. After colors are done, continue unit to cover shapes, patterns, textures, and forms.

**Primary integration.** In the primary grades integrated activities can be used to unify the different subject areas. For example, if the question is "How do living things survive?," then conduct a science lesson in which children plant seeds and water them. Through this activity they can apply their addition skills as they measure the growth of the new plants, their writing skills as they describe the plants in their journal, and their visual art skills as they draw pictures of the different stages of growth. Integrated arts activities fit especially well into reading and writing workshops where children can read about the theme and then express their ideas in all types of creative ways.

**Ending the unit.** After all the time and effort spent on an integrated unit, it should not be allowed to fizzle away at the end.

**Share**—Provide time for the children to share what they have learned with each other. Children can show the works they have done, and explain how they created it. Consider trying a variety of formats. Although having the child stand up in front of the group is a common method, other possibilities include audio taping or video recording the child's presentation for sharing with the others, having the children write books or design a game, or by creating a digital presentation. These can then be shared with parents as well.

- **Display**—The children can make displays or complete authentic assessment tasks that show what they have learned, and their classmates can circulate among them asking questions and making comments. To keep the group focused on the presentations, provide them with a simple checklist to mark or coupons to collect that show which displays they visited.

- **Evaluate**—The end of an integrated unit is a time for evaluating what has happened. What were the children's favorite activities? What do they remember best? What new things did they learn? What do they want to tell others about their experiences? What have the children learned and accomplished? This is the time for reflective questioning by both the children and the teacher.

## Integrated Units and Projects in Combination

Although the project approach and integrated learning unit have been discussed separately, they are not mutually exclusive. Within the presentation of an integrated unit, topics of interest to one or more children may emerge. For example, during a unit focused on the question "What is water?" three children might become interested in bubbles and want to learn more about them. If the teacher is flexible, these interests can become independent projects.

Whether used separately or in combination, both of these approaches integrate the arts into the total learning of the child. The arts provide the symbolic medium through which children can express what they have observed and thought about. In a dinosaur project, drawings might record how a dinosaur model was built. An original song and creative movement might re-create what was learned about how dinosaurs moved. A puppet show might act out how paleontologists dig up fossils. Nevertheless, these creative works do not stand alone. They are richer and more intense because they are part of a total interconnected experience.

## Teacher to Family

### *Sample Parent Newsletter about an Integrated Unit*

Dear Family,

This week we have been observing water—a perfect activity for such a wet, rainy week. We began by experiencing a variety of water activities. We put ice in the water on the water table, and the children had fun seeing how long it took for the ice to melt. We boiled water and observed the steam rising. Then we used the boiling water to make some delicious mint tea. At the easel, some children experimented with what happens when water is mixed with paint. Tuesday we went outside and splashed in the puddles on the playground. We observed the various ways water looked when it moved.

We talked about different ways to remember what we observed. Some children decided to make charts. Others

made drawings of what they saw. Several decided to make books and used each page to draw pictures of different kinds of water. The children used creativity in inventing symbols to represent ice, steam, and water. They also had to decide which colors to use to represent water. We also imagined we were raindrops and moved creatively as we traveled from the ocean to the clouds and then down to the ground to water the flowers. We learned the song "Sun Soil Water and Air" by the Banana Slug Band and then invented our own movements to go with the song.

Please take time to talk to your child about what he or she learned about water as you enjoy the water projects that are coming home.

Your child's teacher,

Integrated arts activities will be found in all areas of learning. Here children play with plastic farm animals in a sensory bin full of hay as part of an integrated unit on farming.

### Did You Get It?

**Mark is planning an arts-infused integrated unit on how animals behave. Which of the following activities is an example of an authentic experience he could include in the unit?**

a. reading aloud a book on the animal kingdom

b. visiting the pet store to observe animals

c. watching a video on polar bears

d. searching the Internet for the feeding habits of mammals

**Take the full quiz on CourseMate**

## How Can We Share Learning Through the Arts?

There are many ways to share what children have learned.

## Documenting Learning

**Documentation** of what has been learned is an essential part of both integrated and project approaches to curriculum design as well as for individual arts activities. When done well, such documentation provides a rich, thought-provoking, and memorable record of the learning process the children went through.

Julianne Wurm (2005) describes how the documentation kept by teachers in the Reggio Emilia program is used to create **documentation panels** that contain photographs, children's artwork, and written descriptions of what the children said and did. Hung in the classroom, these panels show the children that the process they went through in an arts activity, an integrated unit, or a project is important and provide opportunities for them to revisit their work. Displayed in public spaces for parents and community, the panels show what children can accomplish as they learn.

**Project documentation.** In order to create documentation panels, materials that record how the learning was accomplished must be collected throughout the unit, project, or activity. These records can be anecdotal notes, tape recordings, photographs, and samples of children's work. Materials should be collected at all the stages of the unit or project. Figure 8-8 provides examples of what might be collected.

**Recording group work.** Group work can be recorded on a specially designed sheet that allows input from the children. A large sheet of paper is divided

Handheld tablets and mobile devices provide a convenient way to document children's conversations, songs, and creative movements.

## Classroom Technology

### *USING MOBILE DEVICES TO DOCUMENT LEARNING*

Access to mobile technology is increasing at a phenomenal rate. 93% of 6- to 9-year-olds live in a home with a cell phone. Over 30% have their own cell phone (Shuler, 2009). Tablets are also becoming very popular especially as the larger size makes it easier for preschool children to handle them. Using mobile technology in the classroom allows both the teacher and the children to do the following.

1. Take digital photographs and video of their activities.
2. Send and receive photographs and video images from each other, and from places they may not be able to visit.
3. Send audio and text messages to each other, to the teacher, and to their families.
4. Use the GPS feature to locate themselves and trips they take or imagine taking on a map.
5. Interview people who may be unable to come to the classroom.

Many of these same things can also be done on computers. However, the mobility of cell phones and tablets allows several groups to be recording at the same time. Having several devices to hand means that a spontaneous song going on at the music center and an impromptu puppet show at the dramatic play area are less likely to be missed. Audio of the children talking about their decisions can be recorded at several locations about the room. Devices can be taken on field trips and used to record different impressions.

*For more information on using mobile technology, see Chapter 8 Online Resources on Coursemate.*

into days. Each day the group dictates its accomplishments. Children can also be encouraged to record on the sheet in their own way. Primary children can have one member be the group recorder. Alternatively, each day's work can be recorded on separate sheets that are later bound to create a book about the project.

**Creating a panel.** A meaningful documentation panel should include most or all of the following documents:

1. **A large, easy-to-read title.** A good title draws the viewer to the panel and places the work in context.

2. **Parent information.** There should be brief descriptions of what the children did and learned that make clear the value of doing the project. Unit goals and objectives can be restated in clear, direct language.

3. **Visuals.** The panel should catch the eye. Children's artwork and photographs of the children involved in the processes of learning are an ideal way to do this. Photographs of science experiments, creative movement activities, and other hands-on activities bring what happens in an active classroom to life. The visuals should be carefully mounted on color-coordinated backgrounds.

4. **Captions.** The photographs and children's work should be boldly labeled with quotes made by the children. These can be obtained from anecdotal notes, tape recordings, or by having children offer their own comments (see Figure 8-9).

5. **Actual materials.** Actual samples of tools and materials used, which relate to the theme, and three-dimensional constructions can be attached to the panel or displayed on a table nearby. For example, for a project on the ocean, shells can be glued to the panel.

### DINOSAUR PROJECT RECORDS

Calendar showing days and time project was worked on

Child-dictated anecdotal records

Teacher's anecdotal records

Photos of dinosaur being built

Photos of finished dinosaur and everyone who worked on it

Class graph comparing heights of dinosaur and children in class

Michelle's drawings of finished dinosaur

Frank's story about the dinosaur (dictated and illustrated)

Margo and Toma's story about the dinosaur (recorded on audiotape)

Sheet of comments about the dinosaur written by families and visitors to program

**FIGURE 8–8** Project Documentation: The Dinosaur Project

**Our Dinosaur Project**

Day 1:  We have decided to build a dinosaur. Michelle is making a head out of a box. Frank is making a big tail.

Day 2:  Michelle's mom gave us a big box for the body.

Day 3:  We decided to paint our dinosaur purple. We painted the head today.

Day 4:  Toma and Mark helped us paint the body and tail. Michelle made neat teeth out of a Styrofoam tray.

Day 5:  We tried to put our dinosaur together today. First we tried glue, but it fell off. Then Michelle thought we should use tape. So we taped it, but when Mrs. Denali moved it so we could have reading time, the head fell off. Everyone laughed. Frank was upset. He went and played with the blocks.

Day 6:  Mrs. Denali showed us how to use wire to attach the parts of our dinosaur. She made the holes, and we pushed the wire through. Now our dinosaur is really strong. His head even moves because of the wire.

Day 7:  We named our dinosaur "Purple." Margo wrote the name for us, and we hung it on a string around his neck. We measured him, and he is four feet high. He is taller than we are. We pretended he was wild, and Kate, Toma, and Frank built a pen for him out of the big blocks. We knocked it down and let him out. He is really friendly and guards our room when we aren't here.

**FIGURE 8–9** Sample Project Group Work Anecdotal Note

6 **An interactive.** The best way to involve those looking at the panel is to make sure they are intellectually involved. Ask them to look for particular things or to answer a question, or think about another way to do the same work. For example, for a documentation panel about farming, samples of farm products, such as wool, corn, and hay, can be attached with the question "Can you identify all these farm products?"

## Celebrating with Families

Another way to share the learning of integrated units and projects is to stage a celebration or open house. It takes extra effort, but a celebration or a culminating activity helps solidify all the learning that has taken place. The event may consist of special activities that relate to the topic of study, and/or it may include displays of work and photographs that reflect the activities that have taken place. The entire environment of the room may be changed for the day, and visitors invited with the children as tour guides. It should be a party that celebrates the joy of learning.

Celebrations provide opportunities for parents and children to interact in ways not afforded in the classroom and also provide a way to augment the documentation panels. For example, large play spaces and constructions, such as a store or a hospital, are often created during project work and integrated units, which must be removed to make way for the next learning experience. These can be shared with families during a celebration. A celebration also allows children to develop their oral language skills as they explain the work they have on display or put on performances. Families can also take an active role. Invite parents to help prepare and present the different activities.

**Staging a celebration.** A thematic celebration can have all or most of the following:

- artwork—with descriptions (by children or adults)
- demonstrations—of skills and behaviors they children have learned
- documentation panels
- guest performers—artists, musicians, dancers, storytellers (children or adults)
- interactive exhibits (viewers are asked to respond to a question or survey, or to decide which tool or method was used to make an artwork)
- invitations
- musical and dramatic performances (children, adults, mixed groups, professional)
- participatory activities (such as a mural to which every guest contributes something)
- photographs
- posters
- video of children at work

## Photo Story

## Documenting an Emergent Project

Excited about dinosaurs, a small group of children decided to build their own Tyrannosaurus Rex. These photographs show the children working on it and their drawings recording the process.

Putting on the teeth.

"I drew long arms on Edgar so he could put the teeth on. We are all moving around fast. Working hard." Marker and crayon—David, age seven.

Our finished dinosaur "Purple." Box sculpture—Edgar, age six, David, age seven, Alison, age six, and Erica, age seven.

"Our dinosaur comes to life and leaps off the table." Crayon—Erica, age seven.

Painting the boxes.

Take the full quiz on CourseMate

## Did You Get It?

**How can children's learning in the arts best be shared with families?**

a. through a carefully rehearsed dance performance or staged play

b. through a child-led tour of the classroom and displays of their projects

c. through a quick note home

d. through a report card

# Conclusion: Making the Connection

The arts, as a way of learning and communicating about the world, can enrich every aspect of an early childhood program. Presented with activities that are unified by a deep-seated question, children learn to see and react to the world as an interconnected place. When children's interests provide the starting point for designing arts activities in emergent curriculum, the children see them as meaningful. Self-initiated projects help children develop independent thinking and working skills.

Setting up these kinds of opportunities takes a great deal of work, effort, and creativity on our part. No published unit or project list will work with every group of children every time. Each class is unique in its interests and skills, and the integrated units teachers create must be customized accordingly. It is well worth the effort. When children's interests are aroused, when they are full of enthusiasm, and when they know they have a choice, they respond by thinking more deeply. They care more about what they are doing, and they understand the world better. Integrating the arts into the curriculum also means that all learning becomes more meaningful.

For additional information on integrating the arts into the curriculum, *see Chapter 8 Online Resources* on Coursemate

# Teaching In Action

### A Preschool Teacher's Project Log
### The Store Project: The First Two Weeks

**Monday 10/7.** We took a walk to the store on the corner to buy the ingredients for our fruit salad snack. After we got back, I noticed that the children in the dramatic play area were pretending to go to the store.

**Tuesday 10/8.** I brought in some shopping bags and empty cereal boxes to add to the dramatic play area. Some of the children asked me to help them make a store. We sat in a small group and talked about what we might need in a store. I listed their ideas. They had a pretty good idea about the need for shelves and a cash register. When I asked what we should sell in the store, they had a lot of disagreements.

Later I thought about this and decided we needed to take another trip to the store.

**Wednesday 10/9.** I called the market and made sure we could visit. Then I asked some parents if they could come on Friday for our trip to the market. I announced our trip to the class at circle time and explained that some children wanted to make a store in our classroom. I read them the book *On Market Street* (Lobel, 1989).

**Thursday 10/10.** Today we read *Off We Go to the Grocery Store* (Webster, 2007). I have a child with autism in my class, and this book is designed in a structured format to reduce anxiety about the noises and activities at a supermarket. Afterward we talked briefly about our trip and why we have grocery stores. Later, I met with small groups and made lists of what they thought they would see. I gave them stapled journals to record what they did see, and they wrote their names and decorated the covers with their ideas about the store.

**Friday 10/11.** We visited the market early in the morning when there was hardly anyone else there. The children loved talking to the produce manager, cashiers, and the butcher and drawing in their journals. The store gave us paper bags and hats. When we got back, we shared about the trip. We listed all of the products we saw being sold. Many children

*(continued)*

## Teaching In Action *(continued)*

drew more pictures in their journals. Now everyone wants to help make our own supermarket.

**Monday 10/13.** Wow, such enthusiasm. I shared the photos from our trip, and the children helped me write labels for them. We hung them on the bulletin board as a start to our documentation panel. I read the book *At the Supermarket* (Rockwell, 2010).

We talked about where our store should be and what kind of furniture we needed. Later, some children helped me clear out the area.

**Tuesday 10/14.** Today I read the book *Not So Fast Son-gololo* (Daly, 1989) about shopping in South Africa, and we talked a little about how people shop in different places around the world. We made a list of different types of stores. We talked about what we wanted our store to look like. Tom, Inga, and Monica drew the front of the store on a large paper. Then several other students helped them paint it. Other students made a big sign. Henry and Aaron cut out "cookies" from paper. I sent home a note asking for empty food boxes for the foods on our list.

**Wednesday 10/15.** Anna's mom came in and helped four children make pretend fruit by covering balls of newspaper with papier-mâché. A parent also donated a printing calculator to use as the cash register. I put it out for the children to explore.

**Thursday 10/16.** It is starting to look like a store. Several children arranged the boxes on the bookshelf. The papier-mâché fruit was finally dry, and the group painted their fruit very brilliant colors and patterns. Children are very busy making play dough cakes, pies, hot dogs, and tacos to sell. The best thing was when Susi announced that she was making newspapers to sell in the store. Two other girls and she started a newspaper factory. They spent over an hour folding paper in half and drawing pictures inside. I recorded them talking about what to draw in the newspapers so that they would sell. They drew pictures of our trip to the supermarket and even included advertisements and coupons for our class store—such entrepreneurs!

At the class meeting we talked about how people buy things at the store. The topic of money came up. The children shared their knowledge about and experiences with money, such as how much they get in allowance, and how they felt when they lost a dime. I quickly decided to read the book *Bunny Money* (Wells, 1997) and add some money activities.

**Friday 10/17.** I put out a bin of plastic coins for the children to explore and sort at the math center. I hung up some oversized coins nearby. The coins quickly ended up at the store. Some children spent a lot of time cutting out paper dollar bills and drawing "presidents" on them. Then they had a great time counting them. We put them in a box beside the cash register.

I had brought in a price stamper and some labels. Several children were fascinated with these and made labels for the boxes in the store. I spent some time with them and asked them how they knew the price. They had some interesting ideas about what made something more valuable. Gina thought that the lasagna should cost more than the spaghetti because the noodles were bigger. Michael thought the papier-mâché fruit should be very expensive ($1,000,000) because it was hard to make. Luis said we had the best store because we just could make the money when we wanted to buy something. Michael thought about that and noted that it would take a long time to make a million dollars to buy his fruit. Many children spent time buying things at the store.

Next week I can see we will spend quite a bit of time on money. This will be great for practicing counting skills.

# Reflection Page

## MI Integrated Unit Framework

Select a project topic or integrated unit question of your choice and complete the framework below:

| Language Objectives *Students will* | Cognitive Objectives *Students will* | Emotional Objectives *Students will* | Social Objectives *Students will* |
|---|---|---|---|
| Verbal/Linguistic Activities | Mathematical/ Logical Activities | Intrapersonal Activities | Interpersonal Activities |

**Question:**

**Concepts:**

| Musical/Rhythmic Activities | Visual/Spatial Activities | Naturalistic Activities | Bodily/Kinesthetic Activities |
|---|---|---|---|
| Music Skill Objectives *Students will* | Art Skill Objectives *Students will* | Environmental Skill Objectives *Students will* | Physical Objectives *Students will* |

# Reflection Page

## Arts Activity Plan

Create an arts activity for the integrated unit you planned. (See Appendix B for specific guidelines for activity plans.)

**Activity title**

Who?          Group composition age(s):
              Group size:
When?         Time frame:
Why?          Objectives: In this activity the child will develop . . .

        Socially . . .

        Emotionally . . .

        Physically . . .

        Cognitively . . .

        Linguistically . . .

        Perceptively . . .

        Arts skills and knowledge . . .

Where?        Setup:
With what?    Materials:
How?          Procedure:

        Warm-up (WOW):

        What to do:

        What to say:

        Transition out:

Assessment of learning

Next?

# Reflection Page

## Preparing a Documentation Panel

Select a topic and plan the layout and contents of a sample documentation panel. Include the following:

A large, easy-to-read title          Parent information          Visuals (artwork, photographs)

Captions                             Artifacts                   An interactive activity

# Reflection Page

## Planning a Celebration of the Arts

Select a topic or integrated unit question, and plan a celebratory presentation.
Title:

_____

_____

Welcome:

_____

_____

Educational Arts Displays:

_____

_____

Dramatic Performances:

_____

_____

Musical Performances:

_____

_____

Interactive Exhibits:

_____

_____

Participatory Displays:

_____

_____

Demonstrations:

_____

_____

Graphic Elements (invsitations, brochures, posters, signs, banners):

_____

_____

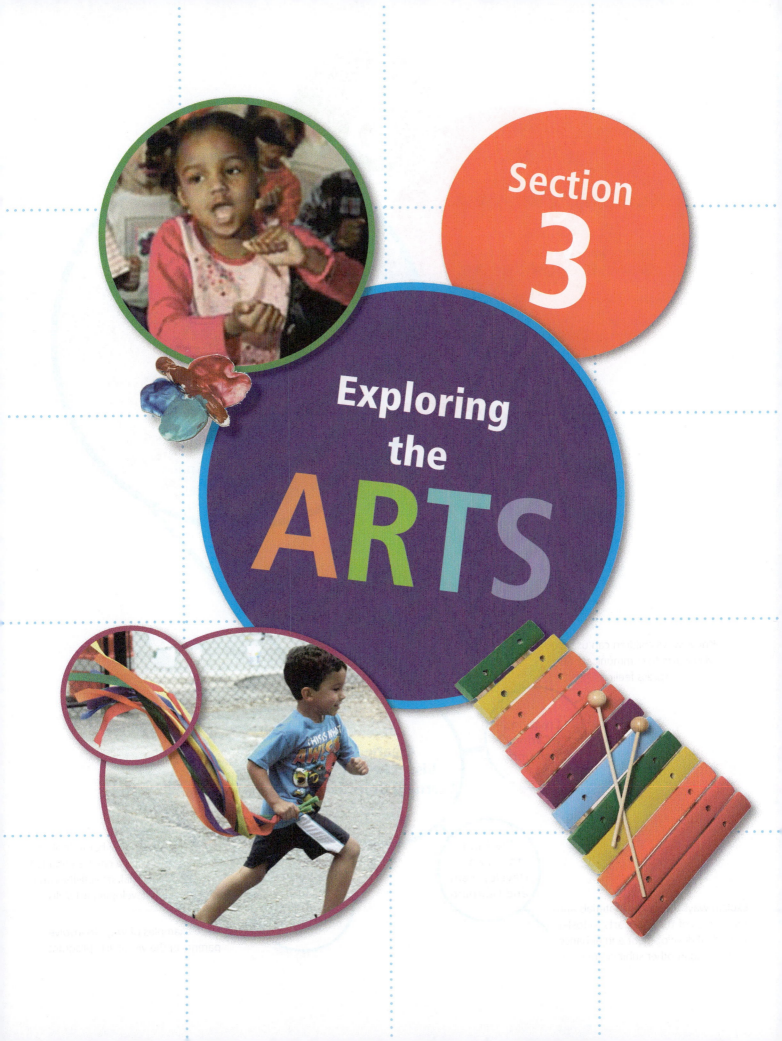

# Section 3

# Exploring the ARTS

# Chapter 9

# Creating Visual Art

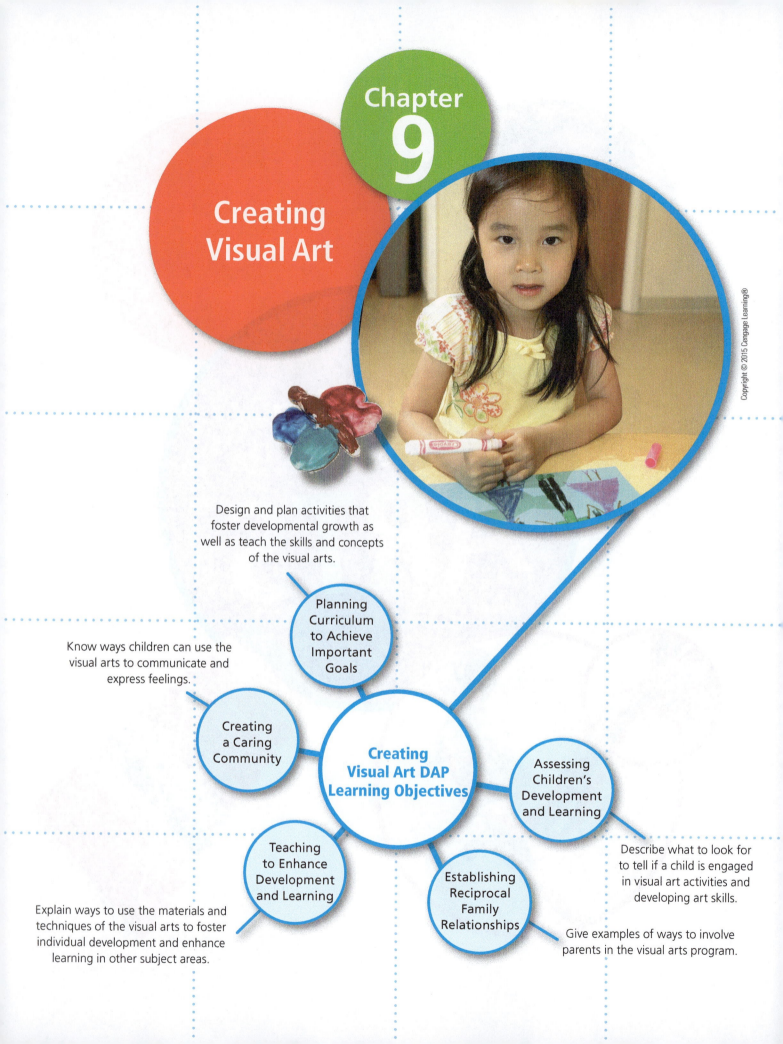

Design and plan activities that foster developmental growth as well as teach the skills and concepts of the visual arts.

Know ways children can use the visual arts to communicate and express feelings.

**Planning Curriculum to Achieve Important Goals**

**Creating a Caring Community**

**Creating Visual Art DAP Learning Objectives**

**Assessing Children's Development and Learning**

**Teaching to Enhance Development and Learning**

**Establishing Reciprocal Family Relationships**

Describe what to look for to tell if a child is engaged in visual art activities and developing art skills.

Explain ways to use the materials and techniques of the visual arts to foster individual development and enhance learning in other subject areas.

Give examples of ways to involve parents in the visual arts program.

## Young Artists Creating

Benjamin, age one, draws a crooked line across his paper.

Alana, age three, dips her brush into yellow paint and then dabs it into the blue paint. "I made green," she says.

"Look I've made a nest," Manuelo, age five, says as he holds up his clay project.

Vanessa and Shakari, both age seven, dip newspaper into papier-mâché paste and wrap it around a cardboard box. "We're making a robot," they say.

## What Are the Visual Arts?

The *visual arts* involve the creation of two- and three-dimensional images that communicate ideas and emotions. The traditional media for doing this includes drawing, painting, collage, printmaking, and sculpture, but in fact, visual art can be made from almost any material imaginable, ranging from natural fibers to industrial waste to computer screens. The key ingredient is the manipulation of the visual and tactile elements of line, shape, color, form, texture, pattern, and space. These elements are arranged by the artist into a composition, which combines the selected materials into a unified whole.

## How Do the Visual Arts Help Children Grow?

Through the visual arts children will develop

- **Physically**—By using the large and small muscles of the arm and hand and eye-hand coordination to handle the different art media. (Bodily-Kinesthetic)

- **Socially**—By working alongside other children and sharing arts materials. (Interpersonal)

- **Emotionally**—By learning to enjoy the act of creating visual art and by developing self-confidence in their ability to control a part of their environment as they handle challenging tools and materials safely. (Intrapersonal)

- **Perceptually**—By exploring new ways to make graphic symbols in two- and three-dimensional space, and by responding to the visual and textual effects they have created. (Spatial)

- **Language skills**—By learning a vocabulary of visual art words, and by learning how to communicate about their artwork and the work of others, orally, with graphic symbols, and, at the primary level, through writing. (Linguistic)

- **Cognitively**—By seeing that their creative actions and decisions can cause the effect of producing a visual image, and by developing the ability to compare and evaluate their own work and the work of others. (Logical-Mathematical)

- **Visual art concepts and skills**—By meeting the Common Core Standards for Visual Art.

**Creating: Students will initiate making works of art and design by experimenting, imagining and identifying content.**

- **PreKindergarten.** Engage in self-directed play with materials

- **Kindergarten.** Engage in imaginative play with materials

- **First Grade.** Engage in collaborative imaginative play with materials.

- **Second Grade.** Collaboratively brainstorm multiple approaches to a problem.

**Presenting: Students will intentionally select and analyze their artwork and the work of others when deciding what artwork to present.**

- **PreKindergarten.** Identify reasons for saving and displaying objects, artifacts and artwork

Drawing is one of the first visual arts experiences young children have. Matthew, age two, has used both broad strokes made with the whole arm and smaller marks made with wrist movements. He is in the scribble stage and learning to control the marks he makes. What drawing materials would you offer him?

Copyright © 2015 Cengage Learning®

---

### Did You Get It?

John, a four-year-old, paints a picture using his imagination. He compares it with his friend's painting and notices they used the same color green. In which of the following ways are the visual arts helping John develop in this scenario?

a. emotionally

b. cognitively

c. physically

d. linguistically

**Take the full quiz on CourseMate**

---

🎵 **Kindergarten.** Select art objects for display and explain why they were chosen.

🎵 **First Grade.** Explain why some objects, artifacts, and artworks are valued over others.

🎵 **Second Grade.** Categorized artwork based on a theme or concept for an exhibit.

**Responding: Students experience, analyze and interpret art and other aspects of the visual world.**

🎵 **PreKindergarten.** Distinguish between images and real objects

🎵 **Kindergarten.** Describe what an image represents.

🎵 **First Grade.** Compare images that represent the same subject.

🎵 **Second Grade.** Categorize images based on expressive properties.

## How Do Children Develop in Two-Dimensional Expression?

In the past 100 years, children's art has attracted the attention of many researchers. Some have collected samples of children's art and looked for patterns (Kellogg, 1969, 1979; Schaefer-Simmern, 1950, Sheridan, 2010). Others have tried to use it to measure intelligence (Cox, 1993; Goodenough, 1926; Harris & Goodenough, 1963). Many have used it to understand how children think (Gardner, 1991; Golomb, 1981; Winner, 1982; Hope, 2008). More recently, children's art has been used to assess emotional needs (Di Leo, 1970; Levick, 1986; Silver, 2002). Over the years, several models of artistic development have been created. These provide one perspective on the teaching of visual art to young children.

However, other research (Kindler, 1997; Wilson, Hurwitz, & Wilson, 1987) indicates that normative sequences do not always reflect the actual development of individual children, but rather visual arts development proceeds in stops and starts and is heavily influenced by a number of factors, including instruction.

### Development in Two-Dimensional Expression

From the 1950s to the 1970s, Rhoda Kellogg (1969, 1979) collected over 1 million drawings done by children from the United States and other countries. These drawings provided the basis for her in-depth analysis of the patterns and forms found in children's art and represent a commitment to the collection of child art unparalleled in early art education research. Kellogg was one of the first to recognize that the scribbles of young children were an important part of the child's development, and that the marks made by young children the world over were more the same than they were different.

1. **Basic Scribbles.** Kellogg isolated twenty kinds of markings (Basic Scribbles) made by children age two and under. The Basic Scribbles consisted of all of the lines the children make, with or without the use of their eyes, whether using a crayon on paper, fingerpaint, or scratching the lines in the dirt. She saw these strokes as representative of the neural and muscular system of the child and forerunners of all of the strokes needed to make art and language symbols. Her descriptions of these Basic Scribbles were offered as a way to describe the art of the very young child.

2. **Placement Patterns.** In addition, Kellogg looked at how children under age two placed these scribbles on their paper. She felt that the Placement Patterns were the earliest evidence that the child was guiding the initial formation of shapes. She hypothesized that children react to the scribbles they make by seeing shapes in the drawing itself rather than trying to represent the shapes seen in the world around them, and that visual and motor pleasure was a motivating factor in causing children to scribble.

3. **Aggregates, Diagrams, and Combines.** Between ages two and three, Kellogg found that children began to draw shapes that they then combined into groups. She termed these groups aggregates, diagrams, and combines. At this stage, children move from unplanned scribbling to being able to remember and repeat shapes they have drawn previously. These shapes become the basis of all the symbols later found in children's drawings.

4. **Mandalas, Suns, and People.** Kellogg was most fascinated by the symbols that often emerged between ages three and four. She noted that the symbols seemed to follow a developmental sequence, and she felt that the mandalas and suns provided the stimuli for the child's first drawings of a person.

At the time Kellogg did her research, most adults considered child art a poor attempt to represent objects and persons in the child's environment and, therefore, worthless or in need of correction. Children were discouraged or even forbidden from scribbling and were encouraged to copy adult models. Kellogg felt that drawing was an expression of the growth of the child's physical and mental processes; it was the process of drawing that was important. She argued that children need plenty of time for free drawing and scribbling in order to develop the symbols that will later become the basis of all drawing and writing.

More recently, Susan Sheridan (2010) has looked at the scribbles and drawings of very young children as brain-building behavior that she characterizes as "one of the predetermined ways a child's brain naturally builds itself" (p. 9). She proposes six stages of scribbling and drawing.

1. **Early Scribbling.** Infants make only a few marks, usually lines and dots. They push and pull and stab at the paper without paying full attention to what they are doing.

2. **Middle Scribbling.** Most toddlers make more and more complex loops and circles.

3. **Mature Scribbling.** They continue to develop more complex patterns using loops and circles and place them in a more controlled manner.

Mandalas, suns, and people. Marker—various children

4. **Early Drawing.** As they reach preschool age, children start naming the scribbles being made; this shows the beginning of representing the natural world and events.

5. **Middle Drawing.** Older preschooler and many kindergarteners show a mix of scribbling and the beginning of recognizable shapes and images, which vary from child to child and drawing to drawing. The child's explanations of the work produced become more verbally complex.

6. **Mature Drawing.** Mastered shapes and movements are combined in new ways to create meaningful and imaginative images during kindergarten and the primary years. They add marks that look like writing, which become words as they learn to write.

However, as we have seen, this development does not necessarily follow in this strict order or time schedule. For children with small motor difficulties this process may take longer. In some cases, children do not obtain sufficient fine motor control to represent their ideas the way they wish until well into the middle years. Outside influences also play a major role in children's graphic skills. The more opportunities children have to draw and use art materials as a way of expressing ideas and capturing visual images, the more skilled they will become.

---

### Did You Get It?

**Which of the following is true of Rhoda Kellogg's in-depth analysis of the patterns and forms found in children's art?**

a. She hypothesized that visual and motor pleasure was a motivating factor in causing children to scribble.

b. She hypothesized that children under the age of two attempt to represent the shapes seen in the world around them through their art.

c. She concluded that children should be asked to avoid scribbling and should be encouraged to copy adult models instead.

d. She discovered that the marks made by young children from different parts of the world have nothing in common.

**Take the full quiz on CourseMate**

---

# How Are Two-Dimensional Activities Designed?

Drawing, painting, collage, and other visual art media can be used by children of all ages, but children vary greatly in maturity level and ability to concentrate on a visual arts activity. The choice of an activity should be based, first of all, on each child's day-to-day behavior rather than on chronological age. In the Making Plans boxes, ages are given only as a guideline.

The presentation of the activity should always be adjusted to the developmental level and needs of the children.

## One-on-One

For infants and young toddlers, who still put things in their mouths, the best way to introduce arts materials and tools is to work with just one child at a time. This allows the child to work under close supervision with a caring adult who can provide immediate positive feedback and share in the child's joyful creation.

## Exploration Centers

Older toddlers and preschoolers will need to spend time discovering how the different art media work. This is the exploration stage. At this level visual art is best presented through art centers where arts materials are arranged in attractive and organized ways that invite independent use. Children should be able to freely choose from a variety of materials and explore on their own as part of their natural play.

## Practice Activities

Once children are familiar with a material, they will need plenty of opportunity to revisit and practice. This is the revisitation stage. Art centers, stocked with beautifully displayed, familiar materials allow choice and continued exploration. Centers allow children to return again and again to familiar materials and tools. In addition, these materials will be at the ready for use in small group or class projects and integrated arts units.

Whether incorporated into the classroom or in a separate space such as the *atelier* in Reggio Emilia type programs, working at beautifully arranged centers should form the backbone of the visual art program from toddler to the primary grades.

## Responsive Activities

Once they have gained sufficient fine motor control and arts skill, children will be able to focus and refine the ideas and feelings they are trying to communicate in their artwork. This is the responsive stage. Responsive activities are often based on common experiences shared by the whole class. In these cases, opportunities for the whole class to make paintings or work with clay at the same time make sense. Working together in this way allows children to see how each of them responds in different ways to the same stimuli. But whole class activities should never replace access to a well-supplied art center.

Vary the drawing experience by providing different sizes of paper, a variety of drawing materials, and demonstrating new ways to draw. Here children draw at an easel.

Copyright © 2015 Cengage Learning®

## The Drawing Experience

Drawing is the most basic of all the visual arts. It is usually the first art experience young children have and is the first step toward literacy.

### Selecting Drawing Materials

Because many ways of drawing are simple and safe, drawing can be offered to even the youngest of children.

**Crayons.** Crayons have been the mainstay of early childhood drawing for many years. Their durability, relative safety, and ease of use will continue to keep them popular. The thick kindergarten size will prove most sturdy for grasping fists. However, other shapes and sizes can be slowly introduced over time. Breakage is to be expected, and removing the paper wrappers expands their creative possibilities. As the children gain better finger control, provide regular-sized crayons. Children can also be offered a much wider variety of colors. Fluorescent crayons, metallic crayons, and multicolored crayons will provide great enjoyment for children at this level. Two or three notches can be cut in the side of a large unwrapped crayon. Rubbed sideways on the paper, it will produce an interesting effect.

**Markers.** Unscented, water-based markers should be the backbone of the drawing program. The smooth, fluid nature of markers allows a level of detail not possible with other drawing materials. Markers are much loved by toddlers. Choose water-based, broad-tipped markers. They create broad sweeps of vibrant color with little pressure. Taking off and putting on the caps provides small muscle practice, although some youngsters may need help doing this for a while.

**Pencils.** Look for pencils with very soft leads, both regular and colored. Using pencils makes young children feel grown up and lets them draw finer lines than they can with the other materials. Children who have some control over drawing materials can also explore using charcoal pencils. The soft lines can be gently blurred with a tissue to create shading.

**Chalk.** Chalk is not suitable for infants because of the danger of inhaling the fine particles. If toddlers are able to keep their hands out of their mouths while working, thick sidewalk chalk used outside on the pavement will provide an interesting color and texture change from using crayons and markers. Avoid the use of chalk on paper or any other surface when working with toddlers. The dust created is hazardous to their health (see Appendix A).

For preschoolers, kindergarteners, and primary age children, regular white and colored blackboard chalk can be offered. To keep dust under control, moisten the paper with liquid starch, milk, water, or thinned white glue. Alternatively, the chalk can be dipped into the liquid and then used for drawing. To prevent inhalation of dust and toxic pigments, use only blackboard chalk, not artists' pastels.

## Selecting Drawing Surfaces

Changing the drawing surface changes the way drawing materials work.

**Paper.** There are many ways to vary the paper offered to children. The size and shape of the paper will affect how the child uses it. Generally, the younger the child, the bigger the paper should be, because smaller paper requires more muscle control to stay within its borders. Newsprint and 50-lb. manila and 50-lb. white drawing paper should be provided for basic drawing activities. Paper can be cut into squares, rectangles, triangles, and circles. Use paper of different colors and textures as well.

**Mural paper.** Long, rolled paper can be hung on a wall, inside or outside, to create a "graffiti" mural. A large sheet can also be laid on the floor, and several children can draw together.

**Other surfaces.** For infants, zip closure plastic bags can be filled with hair gel colored with food coloring and taped closed. Infants can use their fingers to make marks. Older children will enjoy drawing on rocks, on the sides of cardboard boxes, and in sand and rice. With increasing fine motor skills, they can also work on materials with more confining shapes and sizes, such as strips of adding machine tape and sandpaper. Scrap pieces of wood that have been sanded on the edges make an interesting drawing surface. Small, decorated pieces may then be used in wood sculpture constructions.

## Open-Ended Drawing Activities

Provide drawing explorations daily or as often as possible. For infants, provide playful one-on-one experiences.

As infants mature and gain experience, offer more choices of drawing materials and times and places to work. By preschool, children are usually familiar with drawing tools and beginning to develop control over where their lines go. Increased fine motor control allows older children to explore more responsive activities. Figure 9-1 provides a suggested way to introduce drawing as an open-ended activity over a period of five weeks.

Paper and drawing materials are enough to inspire most children. Add variety through small variations that increase choice and creative problem-solving opportunities. Here are some suggested drawing activities to try.

**All one color.** Offer a combination of markers, crayons, and pencils in the same color range, such as all reds or all blues. Then talk about dark and light, and dull and bright. Infant and up.

**Contrasting colors.** Use dark-colored paper with light-colored or metallic crayons. Infant and up.

**Shaped paper.** Paper can be cut into a variety of geometric shapes, but keep these large and simple. Squares; long, thin rectangles; and large triangles are easy to prepare. A paper cutter is invaluable when working with a large number of children. Infants and up.

**Drawing everywhere.** Put paper and crayons or markers in various places around the classroom, such as at the science center and block center. Encourage children to record what they see and do. Preschool and up.

**Bookmaking.** Booklets can be made either from 9-by-12-inch paper or in big book size from 12-by-18-inch sheets. Staple the paper together on either the long or the short side. Start with two pages. As the children develop their story-making skill, increase the number of pages. Tell the children that pages can be added if they need more to complete their story. Show the children how to fold back the pages so the booklet lies flat while they are drawing. Preschool and up.

**Draw what you see.** Set up a still-life arrangement of fruits or flowers or display a live animal. Put drawing materials nearby and invite children to sketch what they see. Preschool and up.

**Drawing boards.** Provide large clipboards with an attached pencil so children can sketch anywhere. Take these on field trips to record what they observe. Preschool and up.

For more open-ended drawing ideas, see *Open-Ended Drawing Activities for Young Children* on CourseMate.

**WEEK 1:** On the first day of class, sit on the rug and open a brand-new box of crayons. Have children name their favorite color. Ask: "How do we use crayons?" Talk about how, when, and where they can be used. Show children where crayons are kept. Have children model getting crayons from the supply area and going to a worktable, and then putting them away. Keep this brief—no more than five minutes. For the rest of the week, have white paper and crayons on the storage shelf. Encourage children to get them and draw. Monitor proper use. Save their drawings for the next lesson.

**WEEK 2:** Start the week by reviewing what the children did with the crayons. Sitting together on the rug, make up a song or movement about lines. Say, "Last week you learned how to get and use the crayons. Here are some drawings you made. What do you see? Do you see lines? What colors do you see?" Let the children respond.

"I will be putting different kinds of papers on the shelf this week. Do you think the crayons will work the same way on them?" Each day put out a different color or texture of paper. Encourage children to compare these to drawings on white paper. Save or photograph their drawings.

**WEEK 3:** Work with a different small group each day. Begin by looking at their drawings. Ask, "What was your favorite paper?" Then say, "Now you know how to get crayons and choose paper. Today I will show you our drawing boards. You can use the drawing board to draw anywhere in the room. You could draw a picture of your block tower. You could draw the fish. You could find a quiet place to draw an imaginary picture. This is how you get a board (demonstrate). Take a crayon container and find your very own drawing place. Draw a picture, and then put away the board and crayons. Gina, can you show us how to put the board and crayons away? Now let's have everyone try it. Find your special place to draw." During the week, encourage children to use the drawing boards.

**WEEK 4:** Start the week by introducing drawing outside. Say, "Today when we go outside, I will take the drawing boards and crayons. Maybe you will find a special place to draw outside." Continue to encourage children to draw inside and outside. By the end of the week, children should be able to get their own drawing supplies and find a place to draw. Now they will be able to do responsive drawings or keep journals as part of thematic units or during projects.

**FIGURE 9–1** From Exploration to Responsive Drawing Activities in Five Weeks

## Reading about Drawing

Read books about drawing or illustrated with drawings such as *The Ish* (Reynolds, 2004) or the classic *Harold and the Purple Crayon* (Johnson, 1998) and its sequels.

For more books featuring drawing, see *Books Celebrating Drawing* on CourseMate.

## Looking at and Talking about Drawings

Expand children's ideas about drawing by sharing drawings by well-known artists. Select art prints that have subjects of interest such as the cave art of the Paleolithic or Picasso's drawings, to share with your group of young children. Encourage them to trace the drawn lines with their fingers.

As children become more familiar with artworks by others introduce art prints that illustrate more complex drawing techniques, such as the work of Albert Durer and M. C. Escher. Challenge children to figure out what drawing material the artists used and provide similar materials for them to try.

Questions to ask about their drawings and those of others:

- What lines do you see?
- Can you trace these lines?

**Did You Get It?**

Cathy works at a daycare center. She wants to organize some visual art activities for the toddlers in her care. Which of the following types of drawing materials should she let them handle?

a. multicolored inks

b. scented oil-based ink markers

c. fluorescent and multicolored crayons

d. regular white and colored chalk

Take the full quiz on CourseMate

🎶 Where do you think the artist start drawing?

🎶 What kinds of lines did the artist make?

🎶 Why do you think the artist choose this materials to draw with?

🎶 What story does this drawing tell?

# The Painting Experience

There is nothing else quite like it. Long tapered brushes dip into liquid color that flows and falls with abandon across a white rectangle of paper. For a moment, the young artist is alone, focused on the interplay of mind and muscle, action and reaction. Painting provides the sensory link between the childish finger that plays in the spilled milk and the masterly hand that painted the Mona Lisa.

Before beginning a painting exploration with children, take a moment to make a tempera painting. Swirl and spread the paint, and concentrate on the way the brush responds to muscular commands and the visual result that is created. Feel the way the brush glides over the surface, and watch how the wet paint catches the light and glistens. Creating a painting is the perfect way to appreciate the importance of process over product to the young child, for whom painting is first and foremost a sensory experience.

For young children, painting is a sensory experience. Watching a young child paint and develop control over a medium that drips and smears is the perfect way to learn to appreciate process over product.

## Selecting Paint

A variety of paints are available that are safe to use with young children. In addition to liquid tempera, other types of paint can be offered. Most of these will work better if used on a table rather than at the easel.

**Fingerpaint.** Commercial **fingerpaint** provides vibrant color in a smooth, easy-to-clean formula and should be the main fingerpaint used. For other fingerpaint explorations, after checking for allergies, try whipped soap flakes or liquid starch colored with a small amount of food coloring or tempera paint. Find recipes for various paints in Appendix D: Recipes.

**Tempera blocks.** This paint comes in dry cakes that fit in special trays. The children must wet the brush to dampen the cube for use. Choose the larger sizes in basic colors and fluorescents. Some adults like the fact that these do not spill. However, the colors and texture of the block paints are not as exciting as liquid tempera paints, so these should never be the only type of paint the children use but, rather, an interesting addition to the program.

**Paint "markers."** These small plastic containers have felt tips. Fill the container with tempera paint, and use like a marker. The stubby shape of the bottles fits well in little hands, and the paint flows out easily. Keep them tightly capped in a resealable plastic bag when not in use (see Appendix C: Supplies for paint marker sources).

**Watercolors.** The small size of the individual watercolors in a set, even in the larger half-pan size, makes them suitable only for preschool and primary age children with well-developed fine-motor control. Watercolors are also more likely to stain clothing than tempera paint. Before giving watercolors to the children to use, wet the color pans and let them sit a short time to soften the paints. Watercolors produce interesting effects when used on wet paper or on top of crayon drawings. Paper can be dampened with a sponge or paintbrush before painting.

## Selecting Brushes

A multitude of commercial paintbrushes are available on the market. Always buy the best quality you can afford. A good brush that is regularly washed out will hold its point and last many years. Poor quality brushes lose their hair rapidly and do not come to a point. Brushes usually come numbered. The higher the number, the larger the brush. Offer children an assortment of brushes to choose from when painting.

**Flats.** These brushes are rectangular shaped and have a straight edge, instead of a point. They are good for painting in broad areas of color, edges, and for making thick even lines.

**Rounds.** These rounded brushes come to a point. These are good for detail work and painting thin lines and dots.

**Easel brushes.** These brushes have a long handle. They are best used when painting at the easel.

**Bristle brush.** A stiff brush made from hog hair.

**Fine hairbrush.** A pointed brush made from ox hair or in the more expensive ones, from sable.

**Polyester or nylon.** A brush made from synthetic material. These are usually very durable.

**Stencil brush.** This is a stubby round brush with very stiff hair.

**Sumi.** A soft-haired brush with a bamboo handle, traditionally used in Japanese painting. It works best in watercolor.

## Selecting Surfaces for Painting

Although plain white paper provides an adequate surface for most types of paint, create exciting sensory experiences by providing a variety of surfaces for children to paint on.

**Brown paper.** Brown kraft paper (or a cut, flattened paper bag) provides an absorbent surface with a color that contrasts well with the lighter colors that are often lost on white paper. Try it with mixtures of pink, sky blue, yellow, and white paint. Try wrinkling the paper and then smoothing it again to create a bumpy texture that is fun to paint on, too.

**Colored paper.** Colored construction paper in dark colors also offers a good contrast for light-colored paints.

**Commercial fingerpaint paper.** This is heavy, with a smooth, shiny surface. Although relatively expensive, children should occasionally have the opportunity to fingerpaint on this paper. Freezer paper, shiny shelf paper, and other sturdy papers can also be used. Paper may be dampened with a wet sponge to make the paint spread more easily.

**Fabric.** Burlap or fabric glued to a cardboard base serves as a challenging texture for painting. This would be a good choice when exploring texture.

**Paper products.** Paper placemats, coffee filters, shelf paper, and thick paper toweling offer different textures for painting.

**Wood and stone.** The varying texture and absorbency of wood scraps and stones provide an interesting contrast to flat paper.

**Other papers.** Some papers are more difficult to paint on for young children. Tissue paper dissolves when it gets wet. Metallic papers and aluminum foil do not take water-based paint well; when dry the paint flakes off.

## Paint Colors

Half of the wonder in the painting experience is using the glorious colors. Tempera paint gives the most painterly effects with luscious colors and a nice thickness. Fight the tendency to use paint right out of the bottle every time. Primary and secondary colors are wonderful, but children need to experience the nuances of color. Using a range of tones allows for more sensory comparisons to be made such as blueberry blue and watermelon pink. Add small amounts of white or black to the primaries to tone them down. Try other mixtures as well. Add yellow to green, purple to red, and green to blue and lighten and darken the resulting colors with white or a dab of black. Having toddlers and older children help mix up containers of new colors is a wonderful activity to engage children in learning new colors.

Store mixed colors in sealed containers such as margarine and yogurt cups. If paint needs to be stored longer, wrap the cups in a sealed plastic bag.

In addition to tempera paint you can make your own. Homemade paint recipes abound. Find a list of paint recipes to try in Appendix D.

## Introducing Painting to Infants and Toddlers

Painting activities for infants need to be safe and carefully supervised but allow plenty of free exploration. The squishy bag activity described in Chapter 4 is one way to "paint" with infants. However, despite the cleanup to follow, don't be afraid to try tempera paint as well. It makes a wonderful sensory activity.

**Exploration.** Work one-on-one with infants and no more than two to three toddlers and be ready with clean up supplies. Strip infants down to their diapers. Have the child sit on your lap or in a high chair or for those who can sit and crawl place them on a large sheet of paper on the floor. Toddlers can sit at a low table.

Pour a small amount of paint in the middle of the paper. Model touching the paint and spreading it around. Allow the child to explore as you make enthusiastic descriptions and encouragements. If a baby tries to eat the paint or mouth a painted hand, gently redirect. If the infant is persistent, it is time to stop and have fun washing up. Repeat as often as possible offering more and different colors of paint each time.

**Using a brush.** Introduce the infant or toddler to using a brush by offering a short-handled brush with stiff bristles that can be grasped in a fist and scrubbed in the paint. Rounds work well for first experiences. Older infants and toddlers with more painting experience can explore other types of brushes. Other objects can also be used to spread the paint such as

## Special Needs

### • DRAWING AND PAINTING MODIFICATIONS •

**Visual:** Children with limited vision should work on a tilted surface or easel so that their eyes are closer to the work surface. Choose the colors of crayons, markers, and paint that they can see best, and add sawdust or sand to the paint so they can feel their finished painting. Different scents can be added to the paint to help with color identification.

**Physical:** Some children with orthopedic handicaps work best if they can lie on the floor when painting. Tape paper to the floor or other work surface so that it does not move while they are working. Wrap foam around the handles of the brushes or drawing tools to make them easier to grip. Use wide, low-sided containers for the paint, such as cut-down margarine or frosting containers. If necessary, use tape to hold paint containers in place.

Accommodate children in wheelchairs by hanging the paper on the wall at a height that allows them to work comfortably. Provide plenty of room for them to extend their arms out full range. If necessary, attach a brush or marker to a dowel to extend the child's reach. Keep the paint thick, and make sure all children have ample working space, so if there are involuntary movements or lack of control, paint does not splatter on the paper or clothing of other children. (See Chapter 5 for more ways to meet special needs.)

plastic net pot scrubbers, sponges, new toothbrushes, bottle brushes, toilet brushes, and vegetable brushes. Look around and see what you can find.

Fill low-sided containers only high enough to color the bristle of the brush. For maximum sensory effect select clear containers so the infant can see the color. Commercial hummus containers or cut down deli containers work well.

## Setting Up a Painting Center

A painting center for toddler, preschool, kindergarten, and primary classrooms can be set up as part of the general art center. It should have both a table and easel. Provide a ratio of one easel for every five children (i.e., if there are 20 children, have four easels set up), or a table on which four children can paint at one time. Side-by-side easels provide the most opportunity for the children to interact. Make sure the easel is low to the floor so the child can reach up to the top of the paper. Cover the table and easel surface with newspaper or other protective material. Kraft paper wrapped around and taped under the table provides a durable and smooth surface. To protect the floor put a piece of heavy plastic under the easels. Use spring-type clothespins to clip the paper to the easel. Provide a place for children to put wet work to dry. To attract children to the center, display clear containers of paint on open shelves and display children's paintings and works by famous artists.

## Open-Ended Painting Activities

Remember that the process of painting is far more important that the final product. Here are some open-ended painting activities to try.

## Teacher Tip

### PAINTING SMOCKS

A good smock that will cover most of the child can be made from a large adult's shirt that buttons up the front.

1. Cut the smock sleeves very short.
2. Put it on the child backwards, and fasten it together in the back with a spring clothespin.
3. Make sure the child's sleeves are pushed up above the elbows.

**Icy paint.** On a hot day add tempera paint to water in ice cube trays and freeze to make colorful ice cubes. If desired, insert a craft stick to serve as a handle or use popsicle molds. The child can move the ice cube around the paper to make colorful marks. Infant and up.

**Water painting.** Give children large brushes and buckets of water. Go outside and paint walls and pavement. Infant and up.

**Table painting.** Put fingerpaint on a smooth, washable tabletop or piece of Plexiglas and let children explore. To save artwork, place a piece of paper on top and press to capture the child's work. Infant and up.

**Lots of colors.** Once the child understands painting procedures, offer new colors. There is no rigid formula for selecting the colors. Let them self-select or mix their own. Infant and up.

**Celebrate a color.** Offer the featured color and related **tints** and **tones** at the paint set-up. On purple day, for example, help children mix up a range of purples, lavenders, and deep indigos. Infant and up.

**Add textures to the paint.** A variety of materials can be mixed into the liquid paint to give it a different feel. Infant and up.

1. The simple addition of a little more water makes a thinner paint and changes the sensory response of the brush as it moves across the paper.

2. Detergent, liquid starch, and corn syrup added to the paint will make it spread differently.

3. To make the paint thicker and textured, add sand, sawdust, cornmeal, flour, oatmeal, dry cereal, or soap flakes.

4. Salt added to the paint will produce a bubbly effect.

5. Salt and Epsom salts sprinkled on the paint produce a glittery effect.

**Varied papers.** In addition to the large newsprint, vary the painting surface by providing colored paper, cardboard, and smooth shelf paper. Cut the paper into a variety of large rectangles and squares, or occasionally into a triangle or circle.

**Draw over paint.** Encourage children to add more details to their dry paintings using marker and crayon. Toddler and up.

**Explore other ways to apply paint.** Paint can be applied with all of the following items: branches, pieces of cardboard, twigs, feathers, feathers, and more. Encourage children to be inventive in figuring out new ways to apply paint. Toddler and up.

*For more ideas for painting activities, see Open-Ended Painting Activities for Young Children on CourseMate.*

## Reading about Painting

Read books about painting and those illustrated with paintings. For example, Tomi de Paola's *The Legend of the Indian Paintbrush* (1988) tells the story the flower "Indian Paint brush" and explains the role of painting in the lives of Plains Indians. This book relates well to painting activities using natural materials such as twigs and plants to apply paint. *The Art Box* (1998) by Gail Gibbons shows tools and materials used by artists for drawing and painting. Karen Beaumont's *I Ain't Gonna Paint No More!* (2005) features a little boy who loves to paint everything. The text is set to the bouncy tune of "It Ain't Gonna Rain No More."

*For more books that celebrate painting, see Books Celebrating Painting on CourseMate.*

## Looking at and Talking about Paintings

Introduce children to colorful paintings with bold shapes such as the work of Wassily Kandinsky, Joan Miró, Georgia O'Keeffe, and Vincent Van Gogh. For preschool and up, use art prints and art cards to introduce different ways of painting. Select works that are noticeably different in style, such as a painting by Vermeer and one by Monet.

Compare art prints, art cards, or digital images of paintings done in different styles or techniques, such as a portrait by Rembrandt and one by Amedeo Modigliani. Then challenge children to make two paintings of the same subject using two different styles or techniques of their own invention.

Questions to ask about their paintings and those of others:

- What colors do you see?

- How do you think the painter mixed that color?

- What do you think the artist painted first?

- What kinds of paint strokes did the artist make?

## Teacher to Family

### Sample Letter to Families about Painting

Dear Family,

Painting is an important part of our art program, and the children will be painting almost every day. In order for your child to have a wonderful time painting, please dress him or her in clothing that is easy to wash. It is important that sleeves are pushed up above the elbows to prevent them from dragging in the paint.

Children will be wearing smocks when painting. However, accidents do happen. The water-based tempera paint we use will come out of most fabrics if it is washed in the following way:

Apply detergent to the spot and rub.

Wash normally.

If the spot still shows, repeat rubbing and washing.

Line dry. Do not put in the dryer until the spot is gone, as the heat will set the color.

It may take several washings to remove the stain completely.

Painting activities help your child grow in many ways, as he or she learns to control the paintbrushes and other painting tools. Please help your son or daughter enjoy painting without the worry of getting paint on clothing.

Your child's teacher,

### Did You Get It?

Daisy works for Redwood Care, a daycare center. She wants to introduce the toddlers at the center to painting. Which of the following should she offer the children?

a. provide each child with an inexpensive brush.

b. provide each child with a set of watercolors

c. provide the children with tempera paint blocks.

d. provide the children with liquid tempera in two or three colors.

**Take the full quiz on CourseMate**

What story does this painting tell?

Is this a **landscape, portrait, seascape,** or **still-life?**

## The Collage Experience

Every art program for young children includes the art activity called "collage." Children are offered various papers, magazine pictures, and small objects to glue onto their pictures. Collage has become one of the most popular art forms for young children. It is also one of the most creative. Young children can arrange their bits and pieces of collage materials in a multitude of ways. Because we do not expect children to produce "realistic-looking" collages, we do not evaluate them in the same way as drawings. Children are extraordinarily free of restraints as they become immersed in the creative process of making a collage.

Every collage experience can be new and different. It is easy to vary the materials that are offered so that the children's motivation to explore and practice will remain high. Children will steadily develop more control over the paste and glue if they are given many opportunities to make collages. The challenge of applying paste to objects of different textures and forms will help develop their hand–eye coordination.

### Selecting Pastes and Glues

#### Glue Sticks

**Advantages**—Large glue sticks are easy for young toddlers to use. Children can grasp them in one or two hands and easily rub the glue on the backing paper. Disappearing-color glue sticks help the child see where the glue has been put. Glue sticks work best for most paper and fabric.

**Disadvantages**—One major difficulty is that caps are difficult for young children to remove and put back on. Often the stick of glue is damaged in the process. This is a skill that needs to be taught and practiced. In addition, children often push up the stick more than needed and apply too much glue. Glue sticks do not work well for three-dimensional objects, so they are limited to only paper collage. Compared to bottled glue, they are also expensive.

### Paste

- **Advantages**—White paste or school paste has many advantages. It is easy to use because it is thick and does not run. Paste holds a variety of materials well. It can be placed on a piece of paper or in a plastic lid and applied with the fingers or a craft stick. It provides a wonderful tactile experience for young children.

- **Disadvantages**—It has a tendency to crack and flake off when dry if applied too thickly.

### White Glue (also called School Glue)

- **Advantages**—This is a strong, durable adhesive that can be used to glue all kinds of objects. Choose only the type that indicates it washes out of clothing. White glue can be thinned with water and spread on a base to provide a pre-glued surface for collage. It will stay wet for 5 to 10 minutes. It easily cleans up with water, and is available in a wide variety of sizes and bottle designs. It dries clear. Squeezing the bottle helps children strengthen and improve control over their hands.

- **Disadvantages**—The runny consistency makes this glue a little more difficult for young children to control. When applied heavily, it wrinkles the paper. Its major disadvantage is that it dries very slowly. Projects must be dried flat for at least 30 minutes before they can be handled. (Tacky or craft versions of this glue can be used in specific situations when instant adhesion is required, but it does not wash out of clothing.)

### Gel Glue

- **Advantages**—This glue is transparent and may be lightly colored. It dries clear, leaving a shiny mark on the paper. It is strong enough to hold a variety of lightweight- and medium-weight objects. It cleans up with water and does not stain

clothing. It is available in bottles similar to that of the white glue, as well as in roller and tube forms.

- **Disadvantages**—This glue is runnier than white glue and is hard for children to control. When gluing fabric, for example, the glue quickly comes right through and wets the fingers. It dries slowly and wrinkles the paper.

**Other adhesives.** Many other pastes and glues are available on the market. Some of them are not safe for young children (see Appendix A). Others are difficult for the children to handle, such as the mucilage, cellulose, and wheat pastes, which are very sticky or runny. Glue pens and rollers are much more expensive (often three times the cost of white glue!) and work best with children who are skilled in handling drawing tools. Find recipes for homemade pastes in Appendix D.

**Tape.** Avoid masking tape and transparent tape. Even though tape is easy to use, it is neither a permanent nor an artistic way to hold arts materials together. Many times, once children become accustomed to using tape, they do not want to use the messier and more challenging paste and glue.

## Selecting Collage Materials

Fascinating materials for collages can be found in nature, from around the house, and from craft activities. Look for interesting papers as well. Send a letter home to parents asking them to contribute found items to the collage center.

## Selecting Cutting Tools

Select scissors that are lightweight and move easily at the pivot. They should be sharp enough to cut paper with very light pressure. They should have a blunt tip. Scissors are traditionally designed for use in the left or right hand, but many children's scissors are now on the market that can be used with either hand. Select ones that work with both left- and right-handed children, if possible. If separate left- and right-handed scissors are used, then color-code them so children know which they should select.

All-plastic, blunt-tipped scissors are a good choice for toddlers and younger preschoolers. These scissors will not cut hair, skin, or fabric. Older children can use pairs with lightweight stainless steel blades and plastic handles. They can also use the children's scissors that make decorative cuts. Other cutting tools include the following.

**Training scissors.** For toddlers or children with impaired finger dexterity, select training scissors that have blunt tips and spring-apart, plastic-coated handles.

**Double-ring training scissors.** These scissors have a pair of outer rings so that as the child holds the scissors, you can guide the actual cutting. They are most useful for children who have dexterity and strength but do not turn the wrist enough to hold the scissors vertically to the paper. This problem is usually manifested when the child tries to cut, but instead the paper folds. Usually the child needs to use them only once or twice. If there continues to be a problem, have the child try the training scissors.

**Rotary hand cutter.** This cutting tool, similar to ones used by quilters, is very sharp and must be used with close supervision. However, this may be the only way some children with special needs can cut. Look for ones designed for use by children that have a protective cover over the blade. Make sure the blade is covered and the handle is easy to grasp. It should have an automatically closing cover. It must be used with a cutting mat underneath at all times. This set-up will allow a child who can grip only with a fist to become quite proficient at cutting.

**Teacher's scissors.** Adults are always cutting many unusual items for collages. Invest in the best quality, all-purpose snips to be found. These usually have stainless steel blades, spring-apart blades, and a lock mechanism, which makes them safer to have around young children. They should be able to cut through heavy cardboard, all fabrics, carpet, leather, branches, pipe cleaners, wire, and more.

## Dealing with Cutting Problems

Children face a variety of challenges when learning to use scissors.

- **Hesitancy**—If children have been forbidden to use scissors in the home, they may be hesitant to begin at first. Give them gentle encouragement to try the scissors.

- **Difficulty holding scissors**—Watch for children who are having difficulty holding the scissors

vertically to the paper. Check that they are using the thumb on top and opposing fingers on bottom to hold the scissors. If they are, gently guide their scissors into the correct position. It may help to hold the paper for them to practice the first few snips. The training scissors can be used to give them a start.

- **Difficulty controlling scissors**—Sometimes the scissors are too heavy or large for the child's hand. In this case, the scissors will tip or wobble unsteadily, and the child will not be able to cut paper. Light, plastic, appropriate-sized scissors should be made available to these children.

- **Hand position**—Some children may need help positioning the hand that is holding the paper. Make sure that they learn to keep their fingers out of the path of the scissors.

- **Paper bends**—One of the most frustrating things for a young child is when the paper bends instead of being cut. This often indicates that they are not exerting enough pressure as they close the scissors. If they keep trying to cut in the same spot, they will never succeed. Suggest that they try cutting in another place or using a different piece. Check that the child is holding the scissors in the correct position, as poor hand position often causes the paper to bend.

- **Wrong paper**—Paper that is either too thin or too thick is difficult for beginner cutters to use. Avoid tissue paper, thin gift wrap, and cardboard when children are still learning. White drawing paper and construction paper have the right amount of stiffness for first-time scissors users.

- **Weak grip**—Children who have difficulty using their fingers, hands, or wrists will find cutting with traditional scissors difficult. Scissors that are squeezed together between the thumb and all of the opposing fingers, and that open automatically with a spring, work well for some children. These are often called "snips." Try to select the lightest-weight pair with the bluntest point. Another option is the use of a rotary cutter.

Making a collage is the perfect way to practice using scissors.

Because there are no preconceived ideas about what a collage should look like, creating a collage is a very open-ended activity that allows unlimited choices. Joey, age three, has glued down precut paper and other materials in his own unique way.

## Setting Up the Collage Center

The collage center can be part of a general art center or can stand alone. Provide a low table where the children can comfortably stand or sit. The tabletop should be bare and easy to wash. If the table must be covered, use an old shower curtain or a plastic tablecloth rather than newspaper, which can stick to the projects. A laminated sheet of construction paper also works well.

Because pasting and gluing with young children is a "messy" activity, and one that can be confused with food, it is important to set up a place where collages can be done away from food areas. This can be a special table that is near a water source. If working in a kitchen area, a large plastic tray or plastic tablecloth can be designated for collage activities, and pasting and gluing can be done only when that surface is set up.

As children gain skill, set up a permanent collage center with attractively displayed paper and objects grouped by texture and color, and set out on low shelving in shallow trays or clear plastic jars and bins.

## Introducing Collage to Infants and Toddlers

Infants can participate in simple introductory collage activities such as these.

**Paper shape play.** Prepare infants and toddlers for future collage activities by cutting out a variety of colorful shapes from heavyweight tag board. If possible, laminate them or use foam. Together, play with the shapes on the high chair tray or table. Describe the shapes and arrange them in different ways. Let the child decide where to put them.

**Tearing.** As a precutting activity, give an older infant or toddler strips of easy-to-tear paper and let the child tear them into small pieces.

**Paper balls.** Show infants and toddlers how to squeeze small pieces of light-weight paper into balls. Drop balls onto sticky-side up contact paper or pre-glued paper.

## Open-Ended Collage Activities

In the beginning, offer only a few types of materials at a time. Slowly, as the children grow in skill, introduce materials that are more difficult to cut, paste, or glue.

**Counting collage.** Have children select paper shapes from the collage offerings and paste to paper. Together, count the shapes used. Infant and up.

**Photo collage.** Print out digital photographs of family and familiar objects. Let children paste pictures onto a stiff paper or tag board background. Infant and up.

**Picture collages.** Preselect pages from magazines and cut them into simple shapes. Initial selections should focus on color, texture, or pattern rather than on objects. Be prepared for the children to paste them down with either side facing up. Toddler and up.

**Cloth and yarns.** Textiles make interesting additions to collages. Most young children cannot cut such materials, so precut them into simple shapes. In addition to fabric, offer ribbon pieces, rickrack, lace, thick yarns, and strings. Cut all of these linear items into short lengths, no longer than 6 inches, to make them easier for young children to handle. Toddler and up.

**Mosaics.** A **mosaic** is a picture made from small objects. Make mosaics from paper cut in 1-inch squares, or any small items, such as seeds, small pebbles, buttons, or tiles. Preschool and up.

**Invent paste.** Set up a center with flour, cornstarch, sugar, water, and milk and small cups for mixing. Provide measuring spoons and explore making a new recipe for paste. Preschool and up.

*Go to CourseMate to find more ideas, see Open-Ended Collage Activities.*

## Teacher Tip

### CHOOSING SAFE COLLAGE MATERIALS

Make sure objects offered for collage are safe for children under age three. Use the choke test to be sure (see Appendix A). Glitter and metallic confetti are also not recommended for young children. These items stick to children's hands and can be rubbed into the eyes. Lick-and-stick papers are not recommended. They give the children the impression that it is all right to put arts materials into their mouths.

*For a list of suggested collage materials, see Collage Materials on CourseMate.*

## Reading about Collages

Numerous books are illustrated with collages. Ezra Jack Keats' classic *Jennie's Hat* (2003) shows a little girl who does not like her hat improving it by adding on all sorts of collaged objects. Lois Ehlert *Mole's Hill* (1998) is illustrated with paper collages inspired by the Woodland Indian tribes' beadwork and ribbon applique. Introduce older children to the collages of Henri Matisse using the book *Drawing with Scissors* by Jane O'Connor (2002). For more books focused on collage, see *Books Celebrating Collage* on CourseMate.

## Looking at and Talking about Collages

The word collage comes from the French word for glue: *coller*. When doing collages share the work of Pablo Picasso. During his cubist period he added real items to his paintings. For example, while sharing Picasso's *Three Musicians*, have children look for the piece of real newspaper. Other artists who made collages include Georges Braque and Kurt Schwitters.

Questions to ask about their collages and those of others.

- What colors, shapes, and textures do you see?
- Which parts looked glued on?
- What materials can you identify?
- What story does this collage tell?

### Did You Get It?

Jeremy has trouble cutting paper. Even though he has the dexterity and the strength, he does not turn his wrist enough to hold the scissors vertically to the paper. Consequently, the paper folds every time he tries to cut it. Which of the following types of cutting tools will allow Jeremy's teacher to guide him as he attempts to cut paper?

a. a rotary hand cutter

b. a pair of double-ring training scissors

c. a pair of training scissors

d. a pair of teacher's scissors

**Take the full quiz on CourseMate**

## Making Plans

**OPEN-ENDED ACTIVITY PLAN: LEAF COLLAGES**

| | |
|---|---|
| WHO? | Group composition age(s): Toddler and up |
| WHEN? | Time frame: 45 to 60 minutes on a fall day |
| WHY? | Objectives: Children will develop |

- physically, children will develop fine motor skills, and gain control and strengthen hands and fingers. I will see this happening when they pick up and glue down leaves squeezing the right amount of glue out of the bottle. (Bodily-Kinesthetic)
- socially, children will develop social skills by participating in a group experience. I will see this happening when they walk in pairs on our trip outdoors and when they share their leaves. (Interpersonal)
- emotionally, children will develop self-confidence. I will see this happening when the leaves stay on their collage. (Intrapersonal)
- visual perception skills, children will develop skill at identifying leaf shapes. (Spatial)
- language, children will develop their vocabulary of descriptive words. I will hear this happening when they use color, texture, and sensory descriptions of the leaves. (Linguistic)
- cognitively, children will develop comparative, sequencing, and computation skills. I will see this happening when they compare, order, and count leaves. (Logical-Mathematical)
- art awareness, children will practice controlling the amount of glue they apply.

| | |
|---|---|
| WHERE? | Setting: With assistants holding their hands, class will go outside under the big maple tree in the yard. Then they will return and use the leaves at the collage center. |
| WHAT? | Materials: Need a basket, leaves, paper, and glue (or contact paper with the backing peeled off). |
| HOW? | Procedure: |

Warm-Up (WOW): Take children outside on a fall day. Try to have one adult or older child paired with one or two children. Together, collect leaves.

What to Do: As children find leaves, help them name the colors and describe how beautiful they are. Put the leaves in an attractive basket. Inside, put the basket of leaves in the collage center and invite them to use them when they make a collage.

What to Say: As the children work at the center talk about the colors and shapes. Count them. Help children remember how it felt to collect them. Ask them why they chose the leaves they did. Describe the colors in exciting language, such as golden reds and brilliant yellows.

| | |
|---|---|
| ASSESSMENT OF LEARNING | Transition Out: When all children have made a collage, read *Red Leaf Yellow Leaf* (Ehlert, 1991) or *Leaf Man* (Ehlert, 2005). Have children point out the leaves in the collage illustrations and see if they match any they found. |

1. Can the children use descriptive terms for color, texture, and shape of leaves?
2. Can the children explain why they chose the leaves they used?
3. Can the children successfully glue the leaves to paper?
4. Are the children enthusiastic? Do they bring in different leaves for the center?

**For more visual art activity plans, see *Sample Visual Arts Plans* on CourseMate.**

## The Printmaking Experience

Printmaking is any art form that involves making a copy of something. Some printing techniques can produce multiple prints, others only one copy **monoprint**. Printmaking can provide another way for young children to explore the sensory characteristics of objects. The children use their sense of touch as they handle the object and apply pressure to make the print. They can compare the stiffness of the object with the slippery wetness of the paint. The print provides a visual image of the texture, pattern, and shape of the object, and the stamping process often creates a rhythmic sound. Printmaking is also a very active art form that requires the children to move their arms with vigor and apply pressure sensitively.

## Selecting Printmaking Materials

Printmaking requires three basic materials—paint, paper, and something with which to make a print.

**Paint.** Choose several colors of very thick tempera paint or fingerpaint. Make sure that the paint colors will not stain hands. White is always a safe choice, as are pastels that are mixed using white and a few drops of a color. If the paint is thin, thicken it with flour. Place a small amount of paint in each tray.

**Trays.** Put the paint in low-sided trays. Use Styrofoam or plastic food trays that have been sanitized

The repetitive quality of printmaking provides the perfect opportunity for children to work together and allows children to explore how shapes can be put together in new ways to create patterns.

(see Appendix A). Ensure that the sides are no higher than half an inch, or try paper plates.

**Printing tools.** For the first explorations, provide the children with large, easily grasped objects that they can dip in the paint, such as a variety of potato mashers or long, cardboard tubes. Place one tool in each tray. As children grow in skill, smaller objects can be added. Look for objects that make different shapes and patterns such as corks, cans, and spools for circles, blocks, erasers, and small boxes for rectangles, berry baskets, pinecones, and small wheeled toys for patterns.

**Paper.** Use paper in the 9-by-12-inch size range. Larger paper makes it difficult for the children to reach the trays and objects without leaning into their prints. Have plenty of extra paper so that children can make more than one print if they wish.

**Drying rack.** A cardboard box drying rack or other wet project storage unit placed near the printmakers will provide a quick place for the prints to dry while still supervising the children. With experience, the children can put their own prints away.

For plans for making a drying box, see *Making a Print-drying Box* on CourseMate.

## Setting Up a Printing Center

For initial printmaking explorations with infants, hold the child on your lap or use a high chair. For older children provide a low table that they can work at while standing. Children usually spend only a few minutes making prints and can do so standing up. This also enables them to reach the trays of paint and objects more easily. Cover the table with newspaper. Have all materials set out before inviting children to begin. Place the trays between the papers or down the middle of the table, depending on the size and shape of the table. Have smocks ready for the children to wear.

Limit the group to one or two toddlers or four older children. Once the children are familiar with the technique and can work more independently, the group size can be increased.

Once children are skilled at printing, consider merging the printmaking center with the painting center by putting the printmaking tools and plates with small amounts of paint near the easels and painting table. This will encourage more innovative work because children can add printed shapes to their paintings.

## Introducing Printmaking to Infants and Toddlers

Handprints and footprints make a good introduction to the concept of making a print.

**Water printing.** Provide a tray of water and let the children make hand or foot prints outside on the pavement.

**Sand prints.** Press a hand or foot into the damp sand. Note: The print can be preserved by pouring plaster over it.

## Open-Ended Printmaking Activities

Printmaking allows you to make multiple copies like a copy-machine. However, unlike a machine copy, each handmade print will be unique in its own way. Once children understand this concept they are ready to try making prints of all kinds.

Some printmaking activities involve stamping the image of some object over and over to make a pattern. This usually produces a one of a kind picture. Others involve making a master "plate" and then making multiple copies of it. The following activities provide ways to make a variety of prints.

**Gadget prints.** Gadget prints are made by dipping an object into paint and stamping it to make a mark. For infants and toddlers, provide large items that the child can easily grasp such as small plastic water bottles, spice jars, and potato mashers and use flat trays or paper plates of tempera paint. Older children can use smaller items like spools, bottle caps, and small blocks of wood or foam. Vary the printing tools, combining new ones with familiar ones. Infant and up.

**Tire tracks.** Dip the wheels of toy cars and trucks in tempera paint and drive around a piece of paper. Infant and up.

**Sponge prints.** Sponges make great printing tools. Cut the sponge into simple geometric shapes. Attach a clothespin to the top of the sponge shape, or, using craft glue, attach a spool "handle" to the sponge. Toddler and up.

**Monoprints.** Make a painting on paper or on a smooth washable tabletop. While still wet, place a piece of paper on top. Lift to see its print. Infant and up.

**"Rubber" stamps.** Commercial rubber stamps are too small for little hands to grasp, but larger ones are easy to make. Cut out simple geometric shapes—square, circle, triangle, rectangle, oval, and so on—from sticky-backed foam. Peel off the backing and affix these shapes to sanded wooden blocks. Toddler and up.

**Splatter prints.** Make a screen box by cutting an opening in a cardboard box and fastening a piece of screening over it. Tape edges well so that there are no rough places. Remove the bottom of the box. Place paper and washable or disposable objects, such as shells, plant stems, lacy doillies, and plastic spoons, under the screen box. Dip a toothbrush in tempera paint and rub across the screen. Remove objects carefully. Toddler and up.

**String monoprint prints.** Dip a piece of yarn or string in tempera paint. Drop the string onto a sheet of paper. Place another piece of paper on top and press. Remove to see the print. Toddler and up.

**Rubbings.** Place flat textured objects, such as pieces cut from plastic berry baskets, under a piece of paper and rub with the side of a peeled crayon to

### Integrating the Arts

**MAKING MATHEMATICAL CONNECTIONS TO THE COMMON CORE**

Visual art activities can be used to reinforce mathematical concepts found in the Common Core Math Standards for K–2.

During drawing activities, children can draw and identify geometric shapes (2.G.A1).

During painting and modeling activities, children can use more, less, and equal as they mix two colors or different size pieces of clay together (K.CC.C6).

When printmaking, children can count orally each time they stamp a shape and add and subtract the numbers of shapes on their paper (K.CC.A.1; K.CC.B4a; 1.OA.A1; 2.OA.B2). They can name the shapes they make and identify their attributes (K.G.A.1-4). They can compare quantities and group and classify (K.CC.C6; 1.G.A1). They can make arrays and identify odd and even groups in patterns (2.OA.C3-4). They can use geometry terms to describe the shapes they make (1.G.A1). They can compose larger shapes using simpler ones (1.G.B6; 2.G.A2).

In fiber art activities children can measure out the length of the materials they will be using and sort by length (1.MD. A1 & 2; 2.MD.A1 &2)

capture the texture. Commercial textured rubbing plates are also available. Toddler and up.

## Reading about Prints

Explore books that feature hand printed illustrations such as Bernard Waber's classic stories *"You Look Ridiculous" Said the Hippopotamus to the Rhinoceros* (1996) and *I Was All Thumbs* (1975), and the beloved *Swimmy* by Leo Lionni (1973).

## Talking about Prints and Patterns

It is easy to find examples of printed materials. Wallpaper, upholstery, rugs, and clothing are often covered with printed designs that form patterns. Expand children's experiences by including examples from home cultures and other places in the world. Look for silkscreen prints by Native American artists of the Northwest coast such as Tim Paul, Bill Reid, Tony Hunt, and others. Also seek hand-printed fabric from India and Africa. Indian wood blocks used for printing cloth can sometimes be found in import stores. Questions to ask about their prints and those of others.

➤ What colors, shapes, and patterns do you see?

➤ Can we match the print to the object that made it? How is it the same or different?

➤ How is this print the same or different from other prints?

➤ What does this print make you think about?

For more ideas for printmaking activities, see *Open-Ended Printmaking Activities* on CourseMate.

## The Fiber Art Experience

**Fiber art** refers to any art form that involves the use of yarn, cloth, or the raw materials that are used to make them. Because fabric plays such an important role in everyday life in terms of clothing and furnishings, it is often seen as a functional object rather than an art form. Yet, even the simplest piece of clothing bears the mark of unnamed artists who determined the shape of its pieces, the drape of the fabric, and its texture and pattern.

Introducing fiber art to children helps them appreciate this often "hidden" and ancient art, which has found unique expression and form throughout time and across cultures. It is an excellent example of an art medium that can serve as a unifying theme for young children. Fiber activities can be used as part of the study of texture, line, and pattern.

In addition, fiber art activities give children experience with counting and the concepts of top and bottom, in and out, over and under, below and above, and in front and behind which are part of the Common Core Mathematics Standards for kindergarteners. Measuring length and using odds and evens are two other math skills that can be applied in the fiber arts and relate to the first- and second-grade math standards.

Weaving on a simple frame loom allows children to explore pattern and texture as they move in a rhythmical pattern.

## Selecting Materials

Yarn and cloth form the basis of most fiber activities and are readily available. People who knit and sew will often donate leftover yarn and cloth to schools.

**Yarn.** Provide children with a wide range of yarns in different colors, thicknesses, and textures. Look for one- and two-ply yarns made from cotton, acrylic, and wool. Use the thicker yarns with very young children.

**Cloth.** Burlap is a sturdy, textured cloth that can be used as a base in stitchery and appliqué activities. Cross-stitch canvas is an open plastic grid that comes in different flexibilities that also provides a sturdy base for beginning stitchers. Unbleached muslin is an inexpensive cotton cloth that can be used to draw on and as a background for appliqué. Felt is easy to cut and handle. More elaborate cloth, such as satins and brocades, provides sensory stimulation. It can often be obtained in discarded sample books from upholstery and carpet stores.

**Basketry materials.** Commercial basket reed is a natural plant material that softens in water and stiffens when dry. It comes in a range of thicknesses. Willow branches collected from neighborhood trees make a good substitute but must be used green as they do not soften in water. Raffia is a strong grassy material that comes dyed in vivid colors.

**Needles.** Choose long 2- to 3-inch plastic needles with large holes for most stitchery activities that use burlap or large-hole cross-stitch as a base.

## Open-Ended Fiber Activities

Remember that, for young children, process is more important than product; do not expect to see perfect baskets or pieces of cloth. Keep activities simple and exploratory and avoid craft kits that limit children's creativity.

Some fiber activities, for example, share many commonalities with collage. Once stitchery and appliqué have been introduced as an activity, yarn and cloth can easily be added to the collage center and cloth cut to size for backgrounds can be offered alongside paper. Other activities such as weaving baskets and fabrics are encouraged by providing a simple framework and allowing children to take turns weaving as they desire.

## Integrating the Arts

### WEAVING A DANCE

The patterned movements found in the weaving process lend themselves to integration with creative movement. Try some of these.

**Threading the needle.** Have children hold hands in a line. The first child is the needle and threads through the line, ducking under the uplifted arms. Still clasping hands, the others follow.

**The Weaver.** Sing the song "In and Out the Window." Have all the children but one stand in a circle holding hands. Children lift their arms as the child weaves in and out under their arms as the song is sung. Continue until all children have had a turn to be the "weaver."

**The Star.** Stand in a circle. Take a ball of yarn and hold on to the end. Toss the yarn to a child on the other side. That child holds on to the yarn near the ball and tosses it to another. Continue until all the children are holding onto the yarn. The resulting design will look like a multi-pointed star. With everyone holding on try different movements while singing a song like "Twinkle, Twinkle, Little Star." Raise and lower the star, come into the middle and move out and so on. This may take some practice to get it going but is very satisfying when successful.

The fiber arts encompass the following techniques suitable for young children to explore the following.

**Cloth pictures. Appliqué** is a design made by attaching pieces of cloth to a fabric background. Reverse applique is when a hole is cut in the top fabric so that the fabric underneath can show. To introduce young children to appliqué, provide precut cloth or felt pieces and a piece of felt or a felt board for the background. Have infants place the cloth pieces as they wish. The pieces will "stick" temporarily. Older children can use white glue to attach the cloth pieces on an individual piece of felt or cloth. Infants and up.

**Stitchery.** Pre-thread large plastic needles with doubled and knotted pieces of various colored yarn about 10–12 inches long. Children can help measure out the yarn to help develop measuring skills. Threaded needles can be poked into a piece of Styrofoam to keep the yarn from tangling. Depending on the age and experience of the children provide cross-stitch canvas, sanitized Styrofoam food trays, or burlap taped to an inexpensive picture frame or stretched in an embroidery hoop. A large piece of stretched burlap can be used for a group stitchery. Children can sit on either side and pass the needle back and forth to each other. When they have mastered the in-and-out pattern, give them buttons or beads with large holes to attach.

Model how to push the needle from the front to the back and from the back to the front. Then let them explore on their own. When they run out of yarn, cut off the needle and tape down the end on the back. Provide one-on-one supportive assistance for infants and toddlers. Preschool and up.

**Handweaving.** To weave children intertwine flexible materials such as yarns, ribbons, strips of fabric in an over-and-under pattern using some kind of frame or **loom** to hold them taut. Anything with regularly spaced openings can be used to weave fibers. Try berry baskets, old dish drainers, and chicken wire.

A simple loom can be made from a piece of cardboard with notches cut at each end. Wrap yarn around and then let the children weave in lengths of yarns and so on that are 2-3 inches longer than the width of the cardboard to create a fringe effect. These weavings can be left on the cardboard for display. A large piece of sturdy cardboard or a wood frame can be used for a group weaving. Preschool and up.

**Basketry.** Baskets are made by intertwining grasses, twigs, and other linear materials to form a container or rigid surface. For young children provide a framework by inserting 6- to 8-inch pieces of thick basket reed into holes punched into the outer edge of a plastic lid to form the basket's ribs. The bigger the lid the better. To help children discover the in-and-out pattern color or mark every other rib with a marker, but don't expect perfection. Children can help collect grasses and willow branches or use yarn, ribbon, and even wire to weave in and out. Preschool and up.

**Quilting.** Making fabric designs from joined pieces of fabric provides an opportunity for a group to work together. Each child can contribute a unique piece of cloth either from a selected fabric or one they have decorated with fabric crayons or even glued-on fabrics if the quilt is intended to be decorative. These pieces can then be sewn together, padded, and backed. Children can help poke threads through to be tied to hold the batting in place. Preschool and up.

**Dyeing cloth and yarn.** The safest way to dye cloth with young children is to use powdered drink mix with a small amount of water added. Food dyes can also be used but will be more expensive. For the cloth, use inexpensive white cotton such as muslin or old sheets. Wool yarn will take the color more vibrantly than cotton.

Natural plant materials are another source for dye stuffs. Try grape leaves, tomato leaves, onion skins, beets, and tea to start. If there are no nut allergies, walnut hulls make a very strong color. Natural materials need to be heated in water and boiled until the water takes on the color. Then dip the cloth in the stained hot water. The longer the material is exposed to the dye, the darker it will be.

None of these colors will be permanent in sunlight but will produce satisfying bright colors during the process. Children can apply the dye using a brush or by dipping in the dye. To **tie-dye** children can fold or pull fabric together and wrap rubber bands around. Wearing rubber gloves while using the dye teaches good safety practices. Kindergarten and up.

## Reading about the Fiber Arts

**Story cloths** are traditional Hmong embroidered appliqués that tell people's life stories. The bilingual English-Hmong *Grandfather's Story Cloth* (Gerdner & Langford, 2008) tells the story of a young boy who helps his aging grandfather remember his past using a story cloth.

Huichol yarn paintings are made by pressing yarn closely together into soft wax to form textured shapes. *When Animals Were People* (Larsen, 2002) is a collection of bilingual English-Spanish Huichol folktales illustrated with yarn paintings. Children can make their own yarn paintings by pressing yarn onto the sticky side of contact paper or into wet glue spread on a sturdy paper.

*M is for Mola* (Striker, 2012) is a multi-lingual alphabet book (Chinese, English, French, Hebrew, Italian, Japanese, Kuna, Portuguese, Russian, Spanish, and Swedish). Each letter is accompanied by a photograph of a mola, an applique method used by the Kuna of Panama as part of their traditional dress.

For more books about the fiber arts, see *Books Celebrating Fiber Art* on CourseMate.

## Looking at and Talking about the Fiber Arts

Talk about and look at the different articles of clothing that can be woven or knitted from yarn, such as sweaters, socks, and hats. Bring in examples of traditional clothing from different places in the world, and look for similarities and differences. Embroidery and handweaving are used in the traditional dress of many cultures such as Ukrainian, Greek, Chinese, and Indian. Have families share special articles of clothing or traditional fiber arts such as knitted items, crocheted and tatted lace, and quilts. Add interesting clothing items to the dress up area and encourage children to ask questions to ask about their fiber art and the art of others.

- What do you see?

- How does it feel?

- How do you think it was made?

- What does it remind you of?

### Did You Get It?

After looking at needlework done by one of her student's parents, Anne wants to engage her kindergarten students in a stitchery activity in which the children will make designs on stretched burlap. While organizing the activity, Anne should choose _____.

a. very thin yarns

b. long 2–3 inch plastic needles

c. artificial permanent colors as dyes

d. metallic needles with small holes

Take the full quiz on CourseMate

## The Digital Art Experience

Very sophisticated conversations about art happen not only at the art table but also between children working at the classroom computer. Computers and digital media have found their way into the hands of

## Classroom Technology

**\*SUMMARY OF THE NAEYC POSITION ON TECHNOLOGY AND INTERACTIVE MEDIA\***

1. Children are spending increasing hours using screen technology (includes television, computers, tablets, mobile phones, etc.).

2. Worries about increasing passivity and obesity suggest that screen time should be limited. Recommendations suggest no more than 2 hours a day total for children between ages 2 and 5 with no more than 1 hour of that during school time. There should be no screen time for infants and toddlers.

3. Total screen time means using any and all digital devices both passive and interactive. It is up to educators to choose the most educative technology activities and to prevent misuse and over use of screen media.

4. It is important for educators to be digitally literate and have sufficient knowledge, skill, and understanding of child development to make wise choices in how screen technology is used with young children.

5. Some children may have little access to the latest technology at home. Integrating technology into early childhood programs is a step towards equity. Technology-handling skills, like book-handling skills, should be in place by age 5.

6. Developmentally appropriate practice should guide decisions about technology integration.

7. Technology activities need to be active and hands-on. They should be playful and involve co-viewing, problem solving, and critical thinking.

8. Technology should be used to enhance home-school relationships, provide those with special needs assistance so they can participate fully, and help dual language learners by providing access to the home language.

Find the complete Position Statement at http://www.naeyc.org/content/technology-and-young-children.

the very young, and they are providing an interactive medium unlike any other art form. Like collage, computer graphics provide an avenue of art exploration that challenges both child and teacher to accept new ways of thinking and working with the elements of art. This section will look at how the use of computers and other digital processes can enhance the visual art program offered to children.

Digital art is here to stay. It is fun and exciting to see one's art appear on the screen. However, care must be taken to limit viewing the screen for long hours. Recent research on the effect on the vision of children by the overuse of computers and hours spent indoors (Seppa, 2013; NAEYC, 2012) strongly suggest that computer exposure be limited.

## The Computer as Art Medium

When the computer is viewed as an art medium rather than as a teaching tool, the logic of its inclusion in any art program involving children becomes apparent. A computer loaded with a simple graphic "paint" program is just another way to create lines and shapes. The monitor screen is the "paper," and the mouse is the tool for applying the lines and shapes and colors. The child manipulates colored light rather than pieces of paper, paintbrushes, or glue, but the artistic decisions are the same.

In this technologically sophisticated society, even very young children are familiar with computers. Being able to create their own "television" picture makes children feel independent and powerful. Properly selected and set up, computer art software provides a wonderful way to introduce children to the computer, beginning a pattern of comfort and success with this technology that will play such a large role in children's futures.

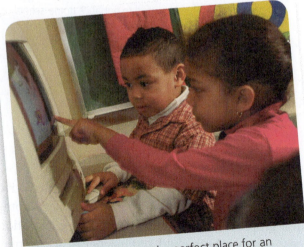

The computer provides the perfect place for an art conversation. An older computer loaded with an open-ended drawing program and with the keyboard placed on top is ideal for young artists.

The computer as art medium can be viewed as another component of the arts program, just like easels and collage centers. It is neither more nor less important than any of the other arts activities offered to children. Like the other arts activities, the computer allows children to play with the art elements in a creative way. Opportunities to work at the computer can be offered as one of the children's daily play choices.

## Selecting Art Software

The computer **software** discussed in this section is of one type only. These are often called "paint," "**graphic**," or "drawing" programs and may come as part of the initial software on the computer; may be the graphic part of "works" programs that combine word processing, spreadsheets, and data processing, may be purchased in special versions designed just for children, or may be downloaded from the Internet. Because the specific software programs available change rapidly, use the following general guidelines for making sure the one selected will work well for young artists.

1. There should be a large workspace of white or black on which to draw.

2. The **cursor** should be large and easy to see.

3. The **menu** of color, shape, and line choices should be visible at all times, either at the side or top of the screen.

4. Menu choice boxes should be large, with logical symbols for line types, shapes, and fill options.

5. The program should have a limited number of menu options. Children do not need such things as multiple pages, graduated colors, and inversions.

6. Programs that load quickly are most convenient. If the only one available requires a complicated loading procedure, be sure to load the program before the children arrive. Turn the monitor off until it is time for the children to work.

7. The ability to save and print the children's pictures allows the children to review what they have done or to put on a computer art show.

8. Most importantly, the program should be open-ended. It should not have pre-drawn coloring-book-style pictures to color, nor should it involve the manipulation of shapes or pictures on an already drawn background. Just because the words *draw, paint, picture,* or *art* are in the title of a program does not mean it is a true art program. Always preview a program before offering it to children.

For suggested software and drawing programs, see *Digital Media Resources* on CourseMate.

## Positioning the Computer

The computer should be located away from heavy traffic and in a "clean-hands" location. There must be an electrical outlet capable of handling the necessary power, preferably with a surge protector. Make sure the computer area will be visible from all parts of the room so that assistance can be offered when needed. Provide space so that two children can work together. It is a perfect way to develop collaborative skills.

## Choosing Equipment

Consider the following equipment when setting up a computer art program.

**Computers.** Any computer that runs the appropriate software can be used. Many child-appropriate art programs can be put on older, lower-powered machines. If the right combination of a program and an older machine can be found, then that may allow one computer to be dedicated to art exploration alone.

**Printers.** A printer is a nice addition, as it provides a way to capture the children's work, but it is not essential. For young computer artists, just as in all of the other art forms, process is more important than product, and the printed versions of children's art are often pale imitations of the glowing images on the screen anyway. For many children, part of the fun seems to be making their pictures disappear when they are done.

**Input devices.** A **mouse** is the best way for young children to draw on the computer. A cordless mouse provides more freedom of movement. Try to put the keyboard out of the way so that the child can focus on the mouse and the screen. On some computers, the **keyboard** can be placed on top of the monitor, or it can be removed and the mouse plugged in directly. If the keyboard is not removable, then it is essential to cover the keys with a protective skin. This will keep sand and other deleterious items out of the keyboard. The keyboard can also be covered with a cardboard box when children are using the mouse to draw. There are also graphic tablets that hook onto a computer like a mouse on which the child can draw freehand with a stylus using Adobe Illustrator. Another alternative is a touch-screen computer or an e-tablet, which lets children work directly on the screen with their fingers. Tablets should be fitted with a protective cover.

## Open-Ended Digital Art Activities

Here are some ways to broaden the digital art experience.

**Adding on.** Have children take turns adding on to a picture. Preschool and up.

**Animate a drawing.** Using the free online drawing program SketchFu, at http://sketchfu.com/, children can draw a picture and then hit a button to see the picture redraw itself. Preschool and up.

**Digital collage.** Use prints of digital designs and photographs to make a collage or add them to a traditional collage. Preschool and up.

**Making multiples.** Children can be taught to insert their digital artworks into prepared layouts or templates created in a software program such as iWorks and Portfolio on an Apple computer, or Publisher, Word, or OpenOffice or Printshop on a PC to create cards, bookmarks, and calendars to share with families. Preschool and up.

**Pattern design.** Create simple and complex patterns using the shape and stamp feature of the software. Preschool and up.

**Slide show.** Children's digital pictures can be saved and incorporated into a show. Some art programs save groups of pictures with a "slide show" feature or in a presentation format such as PowerPoint, Kizoa, or Animato, or made into a flipping pages book using a program like FlipBook or made into a PDF file that can be viewed on some e-readers. Preschool and up.

# How Are Three-Dimensional Activities Designed?

It is important for all children to have many opportunities to work in three dimensions. Infants can explore form by building with blocks and boxes, and through closely supervised one-on-one activities with play dough. By giving children the opportunity to explore a material that has many sides, that can be turned over and around and looked at from different points of view, teachers strengthen children's understanding of the spatial realm in which they exist. Three-dimensional art forms call upon different perceptual modes and different areas of skill development than do drawing, painting, and other two-dimensional activities.

# The Modeling Experience

Modeling, or working with three-dimensional pliable materials, is one of the great joys of early childhood. Soft, smooth clays and playdough are just waiting to be squeezed and poked, to the great delight of the young artist.

When children draw or paint, there is a strong visual response to the marks they make on the paper. In working with modeling materials, although the visual element is still there, the children respond first to the tactile qualities of the forms as they create them. Young children working with play dough or clay will often manipulate the material vigorously while focusing their eyes on something else or staring off into space.

A great deal of talking and noisemaking goes on as children explore clay. Children working on drawings or paintings will perhaps make a comment or two while they work or add a special sound effect, but many at the clay table will pound, slap, and talk incessantly. Modeling materials will provide an opportunity for children to practice their social skills as they respond to each other's actions and exchange pieces of clay or tools.

## Development in Three Dimensions

As in their two-dimensional work, children go through modeling modes that mirror their physical

Ben, age five, has made many pictures using the computer. His picture "House" was made using the online children's art program Tux Paint.

| Mode | Child's Behavior |
|------|------------------|
| 1. Initial Exploration | Manipulates material using all of the senses; uses large motions of arm and hand |
| 2. Controlled Exploration | Begins to make basic forms—pancake, worm, and ball; uses palms and fingers |
| 3. Named Forms | Gives names and labels to modeled forms; begins to use them in symbolic play; uses fingers for shaping |
| 4. Symbolic Forms | Plans the forms that will be used; can attach forms; can pull a form out of a larger piece of modeling material; can use fingers to create small details |

**FIGURE 9–2** The Development of Modeled Form

and cognitive growth. The sorts of forms that children can produce are determined by the amount of control they have over their arms, wrists, hands, and fingers; by their mental ability to imagine a form and then produce it; and by their previous experiences with the material (see Figure 9-2).

**Initial exploration.**  When first confronted with a modeling material, children often approach it with a caution that quickly turns to abandon. They push their fingers into it, pat it, pick it up and put it down, drop it, and squeeze it until it oozes out between their fingers. They may lick it and taste it, rub it on their faces, and stick it up to or into their noses for a good whiff. They will bang it with fists, peel it off their arms when it sticks, and throw it, if not stopped. There is no attempt to make the clay or dough into something but only a pure, multisensory exploration of this exciting material.

This purely exploratory behavior is seen in the youngest children, those between the ages of one and three, and it corresponds in some ways to scribbling in drawing. However, it is often seen in older children as well, especially as they first start to handle a new or an unfamiliar modeling material.

For toddlers, the behavior reflects their lack of small motor control, their reliance on large motor movements of the arm and hands, and their sensory approach to learning about their environment. For older children, this initial exploratory behavior reflects an attempt to understand the material's possibilities and limits. Even adult artists spend time working freely with a medium in order to assess its parameters before beginning to create a sculpture in earnest.

**Controlled exploration.**  After the initial explorations of the modeling medium, children will begin to explore the clay or dough in a more systematic way. At this stage the children may flatten the clay into pancake-like forms using the palm of the hand. With their fingers, they may poke a series of indentations into the surface or pull off small pieces and flatten them. They may stick the pieces back together or create a stack of them. One of the first forms that they can make due to the increasing control over their hands is a long, thin cylinder created by rolling a piece of clay between the palms of their two hands.

In the fourth or fifth year, children discover they can form a sphere or ball by rolling the clay between the palms or between the table and one palm. This is a much more complex skill, as it requires the child to move the hand in a circular motion and is often preceded by much experimentation. Once the ball is perfected, it often becomes the object of manipulative play; it may be rolled across the table, or several may be lined up in a row.

For children who have had many opportunities to use clays, controlled exploration reflects their increasing control over hands and fingers. Older children and adults may also repeat these same manipulations as part of their preliminary explorations of modeling media.

**Named forms.**  The difference between a named form and controlled exploration is not one of form or physical control. It relates instead to the cognitive development of the child. The long, thin cylinder becomes a "snake," the poked pancake becomes a "face," the clay balls become "snowballs." This naming of the modeled forms correlates to the naming of scribbled drawings and reflects the child's developing language skills and the growth of mental imagery.

The manipulative nature of modeling materials allows children at this stage of development to pursue symbolic play in a way that they cannot with two-dimensional art media. Young children "cook" playdough bits in the pots on a toy stove. They offer a "taco" to taste. They make mommy snakes and baby

As children become more skilled with modeling materials, they begin to make recognizable forms. Tina, age three, creates a simple person shape from her playdough.

Elizabeth, age six, has used playdough to create a flower.

snakes that hiss and wiggle around the room and then turn into bracelets wrapped around active wrists. They "bowl" with their clay balls.

Although the child's creations may take on a life of their own, they still are, largely, the result of unplanned manipulation. Once made, they are then "seen" to resemble or represent something. As in drawing, children will repeat these behaviors as they perfect the skills needed to create the basic forms of sphere and cylinder at will.

**Three-dimensional symbols.** In the final mode of modeling development, children are able to plan the forms that they will need to create an object. Instead of using the clay solely as a vehicle for sensory sensation and the release of feelings, the modeling material now becomes a means of self-expression for internal images. These images can be formed in several ways. Some are created by bending, flattening, or distorting one of the basic forms; for example, making a "nest" by poking a hole in a clay ball. Others are produced by joining simple or distorted basic forms, as when a child creates a person from a clay ball and four flattened cylinders. As with the graphic symbols of drawing, the children are not trying to create actual representations of these objects but rather the idea of the object. Once created, they assume a major role in the symbolic dramatic play of the child.

Airplanes fly and drop bombs; animals eat clay bits from the clay bowl; birds sit on eggs in the nest and then fly off to find clay worms.

## Modeling Center Design

Like paste and glue, modeling materials are quite often tasted or eaten. Provide constant close supervision until children have learned not to eat the material. A low, smooth-topped table that is easily washed makes the best working surface. There should be plenty of space for each child. If the tabletop is not appropriate for modeling, or when working at home in a kitchen area, provide each child with a large tray to be used whenever he or she models or does other artwork. Pottery clay requires a different set-up because of the need to keep dust to a minimum (see Appendix A).

## Selecting Modeling Materials

A range of pliable materials is available.

**Playdough.** The safest, most pliable modeling material for young children, especially infants and toddlers, is playdough. Use a commercial brand, or produce a homemade version. Many recipes are available in books on art for children, or consult Appendix D: Recipes.

For the child's initial exploration, the dough should be a nonfood color and have a nonfood scent. A homemade dough has the advantage of being able to be made without scent for the first few explorations. Use only one color of dough for the first experience so the child can concentrate on the tactile qualities of the materials. Provide each child with a baseball-size piece of the modeling dough. If the dough will be reused, offer separate, tightly lidded containers or resealable plastic bags, clearly labeled with each child's name. Preschoolers and primary-age children can be given several colors of playdough at a time, which they will mix with great enthusiasm. Try to pick colors that when combined form attractive new ones, such as red and yellow to make orange, or blue and yellow to make green.

To vary the experience, scents and textures can be added to the dough. Scents should not be food scents that will entice children to taste the dough. Lavander oil and baby powder are two possible scents to try. Sand and coffee grounds can be used to add texture.

**Salt-flour dough.** Children can also mix their own playdough. A salt-flour dough is the easiest for children to use independently. Note: Salt may cause a burning sensation or irritate any small cuts or scrapes that children have on their hands. Check the children's hands first. If children complain about burning, let them wash their hands right away.

1. Work with a small group of three or four children that can be closely supervised.

2. Give each child a bowl, and help each child measure and pour one cup of flour and one-quarter cup of salt. Add one-quarter cup of warm water, and let them knead it together.

3. If the dough is too dry, add some drops of water. If it is too wet, add more flour.

4. Children can add liquid tempera, food coloring, or unsweetened powdered drink mix to the dough to color it.

**Non-hardening clay.** This is an oil-based modeling material, also called *modeling clay*, that does not dry out when exposed to the air. It is more rigid than playdough and suitable for older children who have more developed finger strength. Non-hardening clay, like playdough, is suitable for individual or large group work. Modeling clay should not be ingested. It is not appropriate for children who still try to taste or eat modeling materials. It works best on a smooth, washable surface such as a plastic laminate tabletop, a plastic placemat or tray, or even a laminated piece of construction paper. Do not use it on newspaper, as it picks up the ink.

**Pottery clay.** This is the real clay that comes from the earth and from which pottery is made. It has been used for thousands of years by people around the world. China dishes and stoneware mugs we use every day are made from it.

Purchase only talc-free, moist clay (see Appendix C for sources). Due to dust hazards avoid all powdered or dry clay mixes. Clay contains silica, alumina, and in clay contaminated with talc, asbestos, all of which can cause lung irritation. See Appendix A for specific risks.

Children should wear a smock or covering to keep dust off their clothing. Make sure they keep their hands away from their face to avoid inhaling the fine dust, and they should wash their hands well when done.

Figure one pound of moist clay per child. Store unused clay in double plastic bags that are tightly closed and placed inside a covered plastic can. When used clay is returned to the bag, add a half-cup of water per piece to replace evaporated moisture. Clay will keep a very long time this way. Dry clay can be soaked in water to make it soft again, or it can be baked in a **kiln** to preserve it forever.

For more information on using a kiln and firing pottery clay, see *Firing Pottery Clay* on CourseMate.

Here are some guidelines for working with pottery clay.

1. **Joining.** Two pieces of clay will not join and stay together when dry without special preparation: To join: apply **slip**—a watery clay mixture—to each piece. Press together. Smooth joint so it cannot be seen.

2. **Dampening.** The more the clay is handled, the more it dries out. Overly dry clay cracks and will not stay together. Small amounts of water should be added as needed. It takes a lot of experience

## Special Needs

Children who have limited vision love the tactile nature of modeling materials. Provide a large tray with slightly raised sides for the child to work on—this will make it easier to find small pieces of the modeling material.

to know just how much water to add. Children will quickly learn that too much water reduces the clay to a mud pile. Use this experience to help children see cause and effect.

3. **Location.** Avoid using pottery clay in any multipurpose room or where food is eaten. If possible, use pottery clay outdoors. Indoors, because the fine dust spreads easily, cleanup is very important. The clay-covered newspaper will need to be folded up slowly to not spread the dust. Inside there will be less mess if the children work standing at a table covered with several layers of newspaper.

4. **Clean up.** Wash all tools and wipe down all surfaces. Use buckets for the initial hand and tool rinsing so that the clay-filled water can be dumped outside on the ground where it will not clog the sink drain.

## Modeling Activities for Infants

Because infants readily put things in their mouths, all modeling activities should be one-on-one and last as only as long as the infant is enthusiastically exploring the dough or clay. Begin with brief experiences with unscented homemade play dough or pottery clay.

For an infant, modeling experiences will be primarily sensory. Start when the child can sit securely upright in a high chair. Let the infant touch the dough or clay and move it around as you enthusiastically describe the tactile sensations and the child's actions. When the baby loses interest, remove it and offer it another day.

Over time, demonstrate poking the modeling material with fingers and pulling off bits and sticking them back together. To develop finger strength, avoid providing tools.

## Open-Ended Modeling Activities

Once children are familiar with safe ways to use playdoughs and clays, the modeling activity can be varied in many ways. However, the basic sensory interaction between child and materials should always remain foremost. Too often we surround a child with all kinds of plastic tools, cookie cutters, and rolling pins. Modeling is not a cooking activity, nor is it solely for the creation of flat shapes.

The goal should be on as much direct contact between the hands and the material as possible in the formation of three-dimensional forms. As the children work, encourage this by reminding them to look at their sculptures from all sides and naming the forms they make using geometry terms that are similar, such as cone, cylinder, sphere, cube, and rectangular solid.

**Impressions.** Give the children objects with interesting textures to press into the dough or clay. Try berry baskets, plastic food trays, plastic forks, lids, bottle tops, potato mashers, keys, coins, and any other washable items. Compare the impressions with prints made from the same items. Toddler and up.

**"Stick" sculptures.** Use a lump of dough or clay as a base in which to insert materials such as sticks, toothpicks, pipe cleaners, cardboard strips, craft sticks, beads, buttons, drinking straws, and natural materials, such as pinecones, acorns, shells, dried grasses, and twigs. When the dough has dried, the objects will be securely fastened to the base. Toddler and up.

**Play dough with color.** Let the children color their own playdough by squeezing a drop or two of food coloring or liquid tempera paint onto uncolored, homemade dough and then mixing the color with their hands. Drink mix can also be used to color the dough. Preschool and up.

**Geometric forms.** Older children can use non-hardening modeling clay to make forms such as cubes (made by tapping a sphere on the table to create the sides) and slabs (flat, rectangular "pancakes"), which can be used in building structures. Kindergarten and up.

**Pinch pots.** Making a pinch pot starts by making a roundish ball. To form the pot push a finger or thumb into the center of the ball, and then pinch the dough or clay slowly between thumb and fingers widening the center and thinning the sides until the dough or clay has a bowl shape. Preschool and up.

Pottery clay provides a different sensory experience from playdough. The damp, firm texture helps develop finger strength.

**Animal sculptures.** Children love making animals from play dough, and modeling clay but often have difficulty making the legs and necks strong enough to support the body and head. Talk about how large animals need strong legs. Offer the idea of attaching the animal to a slab base or making it sitting or lying down. Kindergarten and up.

*For more ideas for working with pottery clay, see Pottery Clay Activities on CourseMate.*

## Reading about Modeling and Clay

Reading books about potters around the world who have worked with clay is a great way to help children feel a unity with others. There probably is no more beautiful children's book about clay than Bryd Baylor's class *When Clay Sings* (1972) a poetic ode to the glorious pottery of the American Southwest. *The Pot that Juan Built* (Anderson-Goebel, 2011) is a cumulative book about a clay pot being made by a Mexican potter. *Dave the Potter: Artist, Poet, Slave* (Hill, 2010) is the story of a gifted potter named Dave who lived 200 years ago in North Carolina, but whose pots are widely admired today.

*For more books about modeling and clay, see Books about Modeling and Clay on CourseMate.*

## Looking at and Talking about Modeling and Clay

Introduce children to modeling by sharing a special handmade pottery bowl or dish. Use handmade pottery to serve snacks. Have a potter visit and demonstrate making a pot, or visit a potter's studio.

To encourage children to work in three dimensions, share the sculptures of Henry Moore. His gently rounded human forms are appealing to young children. Compare them to work by other sculptors. If possible, visit a sculpture in the neighborhood, and study and sketch it from different sides.

As contrast, display brightly colored Mexican figurines of roosters and other common animals. Talk about why artists might use color on some sculptures and not on others. *The Sweet and Sour Animal Book* (Hughes, 1997) features Langston Hughes' poetry illustrated with photographs of children's painted clay animals.

Questions to ask children about their modeling and claywork and about that of others include the following.

- How is it shaped?

- How do you think it was modeled?

- How does it look from the other side? From the top? From the bottom?

- What textures do you see or feel?

- Can you imagine modeling the shape with your hands?

- What does it tell you?

### Did You Get It?

**Which of the following is true of controlled exploration with regard to modeling?**

a. It relates to the development of the child's intrapersonal skills.

b. It reflects the child's developing language skills.

c. It relates to the cognitive development of the child and the growth of mental imagery.

d. It reflects the child's increasing physical control over his hands and fingers.

**Take the full quiz on CourseMate**

# The Constructed Sculpture Experience

All children are builders. They create environments. They are the architects of the spaces they inhabit, often creating complex arrangements of toys and furnishings indoors and shelters of sticks and grass outdoors.

Much has been written on the importance of block play for young children (Chalufour & Worth, 2004; Church & Miller, 1990; Gelfer, 1990). In this section, the focus will be on the artistic and creative learning that is developed in building structures with blocks and other materials.

## Selecting Construction Materials

Blocks are often the first construction materials offered to children. Many different kinds are available from which to choose. Other construction materials can later be added to the block center or used on their own.

Blocks allow children to creatively investigate form and structure in open-ended ways. Provide a variety of building materials for children to choose from. Here a child uses sturdy architectural blocks.

**Architectural blocks.** These blocks are based on various architectural styles such as Greek, Roman, and Moorish.

**Boxes.** Empty cardboard boxes are an inexpensive way to provide both units to stack and spaces inside which to build. Jewelry or pudding mix boxes can be used to make miniature houses to be arranged in a model of the neighborhood or town. They can also be made into homes for tiny toys or special treasures, or glued together into unique, three-dimensional structures. Boxes can become homes for beloved stuffed toys. Shoe boxes and cereal, pasta, and oatmeal containers can also be made into houses, homes for treasures, and creatures of all kinds. Giant boxes are instantly appealing to young children, providing an immediate sense of privacy and drawing forth imaginative play. Painting larger boxes provides large motor movement for young children. Appliance boxes can be turned into spaceships or submarines.

**Large blocks.** Made of plastic, wood, cardboard, or foam, large blocks allow children to build structures they can sit on or go inside. They are excellent for dramatic play and for balancing towers. They provide a fun way to discover spatial relationships by building walls to peek over, through, and around.

**Large cardboard pieces.** Pieces of cardboard cut from the sides of boxes can be used to create walls, roofs, and ramps. They can also be fastened together using paper fasteners or chenille stems to make structures that are more elaborate and moveable.

**Light table blocks.** These are transparent plastic blocks that come in a variety of designs to be used on a light table or in combination with other blocks as windows and skylights.

**Pattern blocks.** These small, flat, colored blocks of wood or plastic demonstrate many mathematical relationships. They are excellent for developing ideas of symmetry and pattern, as well as for inventing creative designs.

**Plastic blocks.** Preschool-size interlocking blocks of different designs, such as Duplo® or bristle blocks, allow children to investigate other ways to support what they build.

**Tree cookies.** These are cross-cut slices from branches and logs of different sizes. They may or may not still have the bark on them and maybe sanded or finished with varnish. They can be mixed with regular blocks or used with stumpy cylinders made from thick branches.

**Tubes.** Long cardboard tubes from paper towels and gift wrap make a wonderful building material.

**Unit blocks.** These blocks are usually wooden and come in a variety of geometric and architectural forms. They represent mathematical concepts, such as two right triangles aligning to form a rectangle the same size as the rectangular unit block. This offers the children an excellent opportunity to investigate symmetry and geometric relationships.

**Wood scraps.** Collect small leftover pieces of wood from carpenters or lumberyards, and sand lightly. Children can stack, to glue, or nail together.

## Setting Up a Construction Center Featuring Building Materials

The number of children who can be in a building area will be determined by their ages and the size of the area. Infants work best one-on-one with a caring adult. Two toddlers can work side by side if there are enough blocks and space. If there are only a few blocks in a small, enclosed area, then bumping and grabbing may result.

Preschoolers and primary-school children, who may become involved in cooperative building projects, often can work in larger groups, but attention must always be paid to each child having enough room to move around and get more blocks without knocking over someone else's structure. Use masking tape to mark off a distance from the shelves in which building is not allowed, so that children can get blocks off the shelves without knocking someone's structure down.

Other factors that affect the group size are the size of the blocks and the floor surface. A flat, low-pile carpet makes a good surface because it muffles the blocks when they fall. It is also more comfortable for the children to sit on while working. A smooth wood or tile floor, however, provides a slightly more stable base on which to work and allows smooth motion for wheeled vehicles. A well-designed block area should include both types of surfaces.

## Block Safety

Like other supplies, blocks need to be arranged aesthetically and safely. Low shelves are essential. Blocks stored higher than the child's waist can fall and cause injuries. On the shelves, the blocks should not be stacked more than several high, and each type of block should have its own location. Create a label for each location by tracing the shape of the block on paper and then attaching it to the correct shelf. Put the heaviest blocks on the bottom. Use the top of the shelves for accessories stored in clear plastic bins.

## Adding Drawing to the Building Center

Art materials can be added to the block area to increase the dramatic and architectural possibilities.

1. Paper, markers, and crayons for making maps, and drawing pictures of the buildings.

2. Blue paper and white pencils or crayons to make "blueprints."

3. Cardboard pieces, tubes, and scissors for the construction of roofs, signs, ramps, and more.

4. Fabric pieces to use for rugs and furnishings in houses.

5. Non-hardening clay to make people and animals.

6. Bottle caps and thread spools to add decorative patterns.

7. Aluminum foil to cover blocks for a sparkling effect.

Note: These materials should be slowly added to the block area, so that children have time to investigate the possibilities of each before being overwhelmed by too many choices.

## Working with Papier-Mâché

Papier-mâché is a wonderfully sticky material that dries hard and is paintable. It is a good way to convert flimsy boxes into sturdy constructions, to join boxes together, or to cover rolled newspaper or cardboard tubes to make them solid.

Papier-mâché should be seen as a medium to be used when children have a specific construction problem or project in mind. For example, if children are frustrated because paint will not stick to the box they are painting, suggest papier-mâché. If some children want to build a box robot and the boxes will not stick together, suggest papier-mâché.

Piñatas are also made with papier-mâché. Read *Hooray! A Pinata iñata!* (Kleven, 1996) to introduce papier-mâché to young children. Colorfully illustrated with painted collages, a note at the end explains the Mexican custom of the piñata. To make a hollow form for a piñata cover a balloon with several layers of papier-mâché and pop the balloon when the papier-mâché is dry.

For the paste, use thinned white glue, plain flour and water, or one of the special papier-mâché pastes available. Do not use wallpaper paste, as it contains toxins. If using flour, be on the alert for gluten-sensitive children who may have severe allergic reactions.

Using papier-mâché requires children to follow a set of orderly steps and works best when children work in pairs or small cooperative groups. The papier-mâché process is simple.

1. Demonstrate how to dip a strip of paper into the paste, and then place it on the box or tray. Explain that it is like making your own tape.

2. Encourage children to keep their hands over their paste buckets, which should be set directly in front of them in order to catch drips.

3. Suggest that the children cover the box or item completely, so that nothing shows. One layer is usually sufficient for a first papier-mâché experience. In future experiences, children can be encouraged to put on more layers to make the base sturdier.

4. Place finished projects on a sheet of plastic to dry. They will stick to newspaper. Then place them near a heater or in the sun to speed drying time.

5. When the papier-mâché is dry, it can be painted or collaged.

## Construction Activities for Infants and Toddlers

Safety is the first concern when building with infants. Provide soft blocks with no hard edges such as those made from foam or cardboard or use boxes, cardboard pieces, and cardboard tubes. If the infant is sitting or creeping, place the building materials around the child and encourage exploration.

Boxes are also perfect for toddlers. They are light and can be both stacked and filled. Large ones can be used to build mazes and tunnels. A refrigerator-size box makes a cozy house.

## Open-Ended Construction Activities

Blocks and boxes introduce children to the world of architecture. It is natural for young children to build structures that mirror the buildings they inhabit and see around them. Encourage this connection by pointing out the relationships between the basic geometric forms and their architectural counterparts. Allow plenty of open-ended exploration with building materials for children of all ages. As they develop skill, try some of the following activities.

**Pull-toy.** Attaching a string turns a box into a vehicle in which stuffed toys can ride. Infant and up.

**Special place.** Art can be created inside of the box as well as outside. Color boxes with crayons and markers. Let children glue colored papers to the sides or paint the box using large paintbrushes. Toddler and up.

**Houses.** Boxes make perfect dream houses, houses for toys, and for pets. Spark children's interest by walking around the neighborhood looking at houses and displaying photographs of their homes. Provide wallpaper, fabric, and carpet for decorating the inside of their houses. Blocks of wood, foam, and small boxes can be used for furniture. Preschool and up.

**A personal space.** Plan a day for older children to each be given a small section of the room or playground in which to build her or his own private place using blocks, moveable furnishings, and other delineating materials to form the walls. Share the story *Roxaboxen* (McLerran, 1991) as the perfect complement to this activity. Kindergarten and up.

**Add ons.** Pieces of flat cardboard can be rested against boxes as ramps and roofs or attached onto boxes in various ways, such as with glue or tape. For a sturdy attachment or one that swings like a door, poke holes in the cardboard so that chenille stems can be passed through and twisted closed. Preschool and up.

**Puppets.** Use glue-soaked strips to cover a cereal-type box with papier-mâché. Leave one end open so that it fits over the child's hand. Paint on a face and add yarn hair. Preschool and up.

**Masks.** A cardboard or plastic tray can be used to make a mask-like shape. Cover the tray with two to three layers of papier-mâché strips. Let dry several days. When dry, the tray will fall away. Trim edge into shape for mask and cut out eyeholes. Finish by painting and adding yarn hair. Kindergarten and up.

## Reading about Building

Construction activities provide the perfect opportunity to talk about architecture and three-dimensional design. *Architectural Colors* (Crosbie & Rosenthal, 1993) is one in a series of board books for toddlers and up. On one side there is the name of a color and on the other a building featuring that color. For older children *Architects make Zigzags* (Maddox, 1986) introduces different architectural features.

For an annotated list of books about construction and building, see *Books about Building* on CourseMate.

## Looking at and Talking about Building

Start by looking at actual buildings and how they are made. Explore the school and the neighborhood and find cylindrical columns, triangular roofs, rectangular bricks, arches, and more. Note how doorways are created by placing a crosspiece over two vertical supports (post and lintel), and point out similar constructions in children's block buildings.

Next introduce the children to the artist's role as architect. Display a print of one of Frank Lloyd Wright's buildings. Tell the children about how he loved to build with blocks. Invite an architect or architecture student to come and share his or her sketches, plans, and models of buildings. Such a visit will inspire the children to draw "blueprints" of their own.

Inspire new ways of thinking about building by sharing the box assemblages of Duchamp and Nevelson, such as Nevelson's *Case with Five Balusters* (Take 5: Collage and Assemblage) and then giving children boxes they can use to design their own constructions.

Expand children's ideas about the possibilities of papier-mâché by sharing prints or actual papier-mâché artifacts, such as masks from Mexico.

Improve focus and develop language skills by asking open-ended questions. Questions to ask about their constructions and those of others include the following.

- What do you see?
- How is it different when you look from about viewpoint?
- What forms do you see?
- How are they the same or different from each other?

---

**Did You Get It?**

**Why should young children play with blocks?**

a. They improve their ability to see in two-dimensions.

b. They introduce the children to architectural concepts.

c. They have fun building with them.

d. They are used in all early childhood programs.

**Take the full quiz on CourseMate**

---

## How Do We Share Children's Artwork with Families?

There are many ways to include families in the visual art activities of children. Invite them to visit the classroom any time and paint, draw, and paste alongside their child. Send home artworks and videos of their child at work using the materials of the visual arts and invite them to art workshops where they can learn more about the art of young children and can explore using art media on their own. Parents can also be enlisted to help make playdough and other homemade modeling materials and paint. Welcome home cultures by inviting parents to share artworks that are meaningful for them.

# Conclusion:
# The Power of The Visual Arts

Visual artists have been creating with paper, paint, clay, fiber, and more for thousands of years. Much of what is known about civilizations of the past has been bequeathed to us through the culture's visual artworks. Providing young children the opportunity to work with a wide variety of visual arts media in open-ended ways facilitates the growth of both the mind and hand. It is also a link to our past and our future. As teachers, we need to be sure that all children have the opportunity to explore new media, create graphic symbols, and develop technical skill.

*For additional information on teaching the visual arts, see Chapter 9 Online Resources on CourseMate to young children visit our Web site at http://www.cengagebrain.com.*

## Teaching In Action

### *A Day with Clay: A Teacher's Notebook Entry*

My friend Julian, who is an art student at the local college, came today and showed the children how he makes a clay pot. We set up a table out on the grass by the playground fence. We all gathered around and watched. Outside was perfect. It was very informal and open. The children would watch awhile, go play, and then wander back.

All the while Julian worked he kept describing how it felt. He said things such as, "This is bumpy; I must make it smoother." He also described what he was doing, as in, "I am pushing the clay with my fingers." He was so patient and answered all of the children's questions. He let them touch the clay and the pot he was making, too.

When Julian was done, he invited the children who were standing around him to make pots also. He gave them each a piece of clay and guided them in making it rounded and pushing a hole in the middle with their thumbs. When they were finished, a few others came over and made some pots. Several just wanted to pound the clay flat. Julian showed them how to press sticks and stones into the clay to make impressions. Some children decided to do that to their clay pots. He carved the child's name on each one and took all of the projects to fire in his kiln. He said he thought they would turn out fine. I had a bucket of water for the children to rinse their hands in, and then they went inside to wash up at the sink.

I took lots of photographs. I can't wait to get them back. Then we can make a class book about our Clay Day!

# Reflection Page

## The Elements of Art

In Chapter 4 we learned about the elements of art. For each of the elements listed below, give an example of a visual art activity you could do with children in the age groups indicated.

| Element | Infant or Toddler | Preschool | Primary |
|---------|-------------------|-----------|---------|
| Color   |                   |           |         |
| Shape   |                   |           |         |
| Texture |                   |           |         |
| Form    |                   |           |         |
| Line    |                   |           |         |
| Pattern |                   |           |         |

# Reflection Page

## Planning an Art Center

Select an age group and visual art media. Explain how you will set up the center and introduce the children to it.

**Age Group:** _____          **Media:** _____

Where will the center be located?

_____

_____

What materials will be there?

_____

_____

How will these be aesthetically arranged?

_____

_____

How will you introduce the children to the new center?

_____

_____

What questions will you ask at this center to develop visual arts concepts and skills?

_____

_____

# Reflection Page

## Observation: Children Drawing

1.  Plan a drawing exploration or practice activity suitable for an infant or child up to the age of eight.

2.  Obtain permission to work with the child or children, either at home, at school, or in a childcare setting.

3.  Set up your activity and observe the child or children at work. If possible, take photos or videotape the activity (get permission first). With the child's permission, save one or more of the drawings for your own collection.

_____

**Age of child(ren):**
**Set-up of materials:**
**Length of time of observation:**

1.  What did the child(ren) do first?

_____

2.  What did the child(ren) say?

_____

3.  How did the child(ren) manipulate the drawing tool(s)? (For example, describe the position of the arm and hands, grip, and any other body parts involved.)

_____

_____

4.  How long did the child(ren) work? (Measure periods of concentration. If the child stopped, why? How did the child(ren) let you know the drawing was finished?)

_____

_____

5.  Describe the art produced. (What did the child(ren) draw first? How many drawings were made? What was repeated?)

_____

_____

_____

_____

# Reflection Page

## Observation: Children and Modeling

1. Plan a modeling exploration or practice activity suitable for a child between infancy and eight. Use a modeling material of your choice such as playdough or pottery clay.

2. Obtain permission to work with one child, either at home or in a school setting. If possible, take photos or videotape the activity (get permission first).

_____

_____

**Age of child(ren):**
**Set-up of materials:**
**Length of time of observation:**

1. What did the child do first?

_____

2. What did the child say?

_____

3. How did the child manipulate the modeling material? (For example, describe the position of the arm and hands, grip, and any other body parts involved.)

_____

4. How long did the child work? (Measure periods of concentration. If the child stopped, why? How did the child let you know he or she was finished?)

_____

5. Describe the art produced. (What did the child do first? What actions were repeated?)

_____

6. Reflection: Was the modeling material suitable for this child(ren)? Was the experience enjoyable?

_____

_____

**Chapter 10**

# Making Music

Design and plan music activities that foster children's developmental growth as well as teach the skills and concepts of music.

Know ways to use music to soothe, to express feelings, and give children a sense of belonging.

**Planning Curriculum to Achieve Important Goals**

**Creating a Caring Community**

**Making Music DAP Learning Objectives**

**Assessing Children's Development and Learning**

**Teaching to Enhance Development and Learning**

**Establishing Reciprocal Family Relationships**

Describe what to look for to tell if a child is engaged in music activities and developing music skills.

Explain a variety of approaches to teaching music using listening, music making, and singing to increase children's developmental growth in all areas.

Give examples of ways to involve parents in the music program through sharing music of their musical heritage and their expertise.

## Young Artists Creating

Xavier, age two, picks up a spoon and begins to tap on the high chair tray. "Let's make music," says his caregiver seizing the teachable moment. She claps her hands and nods her head keeping time with his taps. "Now let's count to the beat." she says. "One, two, three, four. One, two, three, four. Hear the rhythm?" Xavier says the numbers and taps harder. His whole body bounces up and down. The caregiver begins to hum the tune to *Row, Row, Row the Boat* as she claps. "Now let's sing Xavier's song," she says. "Tap, tap, tap the spoon. Xavier, tap the spoon. Tap. Tap. Tap. Tap. Xavier taps the spoon."

# What Is Music?

Music is organized sound. One of the tasks of teaching music is to introduce children to the different ways in which music plays with and orders sound. Listening, rhythmic activities, singing, and playing instruments form the basis of creative music experiences, through which the elements of music—rhythm, timbre, dynamics, form, melody, and harmony—are organized into compositions that speak to our mind, our body, and our emotions.

## The Elements of Music

We are all familiar with everyday sounds: the honk of a car horn, the clatter of dishes, children's voices on the playground. On their own these are not considered music. However, any ordinary sound can be turned into something musical. At its most basic music is made up of repeated beats. At its most complex, it is a **composition** of rhythm and **tempo,** dynamics and pitch, timbre and texture, and melody and harmony. These are the elements of music.

**Rhythm.** Rhythm is a time-based pattern that orders sound and makes it musical. A car horn pressed first short and then long repeated over and over creates a rhythm. Each honk on the horn is a **beat.** A rhythm can be varied by changing which beat has the strongest emphasis or **accent.** For example, a long horn blast followed by a short one would consist of a strong or down-beat and a weak or up-beat as in *one* two, *one* two, *one* two and so on. Repeated patterns of strong and weak beats create the **meter** of the rhythm. A waltz or polka meter, for example, is made up of one strong beat followed by two weak beats—*one* two three, *one* two three. **Syncopation,** found in some genres of music such as jazz, is a deliberate change in where the regular stress is expected to come. For example, the stress might come on the weak beat as in one *two* three four or there might be a rest where a strong beat is expected.

**Tempo.** Tempo is the speed at which a rhythm or musical composition is played. It is usually indicated by a term written at the beginning of the piece. Largo, for example means slow. Allegro means lively and fast. Up-tempo or presto means very fast. Within a piece of music the tempo may change many times, or it may remain steady throughout.

**Dynamics.** Dynamics refers to changes in volume from loud to soft and to the accenting of certain tones in a rhythm or piece of music.

**Pitch.** Sound is created through vibration and is measured by the frequency of that oscillation. The lowest sounds most people hear are in the range of 20 Hz. The highest are about 20,000 Hz. The highness or lowness of a particular sound is referred to as its pitch. Many instruments have vibrating parts such as a drumhead on a bass drum, which produces a low pitch, or the strings on a violin, which can produce high pitches. Others such as tubas and clarinets make sound using a vibrating column of air.

**Timbre.** Timbre or **tone color** is the unique quality of a sound. It is how we can tell the sound of a car horn from that of a bird's song or identify the particular voice of a friend on the phone.

**Melody.** A **note** is a single sound or tone. Melodies are created by varying the pitches of notes and playing them in a sequence that may repeat. How the sequence is arranged and repeated creates the form or composition of the musical work. For example, a song might be composed of alternating verses and choruses. The American folksong *The Erie Canal* has this type of form.

**Harmony.** Accompanying the melody may be a sequence of tones that enriches it and makes the sounds blend. Harmony is often created by using a **chord**—several notes played together at the same time. Harmony creates what is called musical texture or a layer of sound that can be pleasant or dissonant to the ear.

## How Do Children Develop Musically?

Musical development starts early. In fact, research suggests that the optimal time for auditory and musical perceptual development is the first year of life although it continues to be refined during the years up to age eight (Trainor & Corrigall, 2010).

### Music Development in Infancy

Unborn babies' ability to hear sounds in the last trimester is believed to set the stage for future musical responsiveness (Parncutt, 2006). Before birth, fetuses can differentiate between a familiar song and a novel one (Abrams, et al., 1998). They also remember what they hear. Right after birth, babies show recognition of tunes heard repeatedly during pregnancy (Hepper, 1991; Wilkin, 1995).

Infants attend to music by turning their heads and making sounds and movements. They show a preference for music over other sounds. For example, infants will concentrate on a musical happening such as

a person clapping or singing despite distracting noises (Bahrick, Lickliter, & Flom, 2004). At two months, infants will turn toward musically pleasant sounds and away from dissonant ones (Weinberger, 2004). Infants in the first year also develop skill in recognizing contrasting pitches and pitch combinations, timbres, textures, and styles (Ilari & Polka, 2006; Krumhansl & Jusczyk, 1990; Trainor, Tsang, & Cheung, 2002). With exposure they can learn to recognize individual works such as folk songs, Mozart piano **sonatas,** and the music of Ravel and remember them weeks later (Ilari & Polka, 2006; Saffran, Loman, & Robertson, 2000; Trainor, Wu, & Tsang, 2004).

With innate attraction to and ample exposure to music, it does not take long for children to become familiar with their cultural musical heritage. Infants begin by matching facial expressions and the voice of the singer (Bahrick, Lickliter, & Flom, 2004). The rhythm and melodic quality of a mother's voice will keep a child's attention, the musicality of speech helping the child acquire language (Mithen, 2006). It is hypothesized that this is one reason adults in all cultures tend to talk to babies in singsong voices called **motherese** and to sing lullabies.

### Music Development in Early Childhood

Music ability and skills continue to develop all through the early years, although as children age, experience, interest and hearing ability make a major

Infants are naturally musical, moving with delight to simple songs and rhythms.

difference in children's performance in the musical area. Toddlers continue to be as fascinated by music as they were as infants. They can repeat sounds, move to rhythms, and start to learn simple songs. During this period their vocal range expands rapidly as does their ability to perceive timbre and identify the sounds of different instruments.

By preschool, children begin to make up their own songs, hold a steady beat, and match body movements to it. Spontaneous music making is a characteristic of the preschool years. Children freely mix tunes and words of their own invention with familiar songs during solitary and group play (Whiteman, 2009).

By kindergarten, children can learn to match and classify sounds, can play singing and movement games, and can reproduce musical patterns. In this period they continue to develop pitch accuracy and an expanded vocal range so that by the start of first grade, 50 percent can sing a full **octave** with 10 percent reaching an octave-and-a-half

(Kreutzer, 2001; Wassum, 1979). They can now indicate changes in pitch by raising and lowering their hands and note a melody with rising and falling lines with dots for beats (Gromko, 2003).

In the primary grades, children improve in their ability to sing in tune and in large groups. Corresponding to their increasing skills in reading and writing, they can learn to read music and to notate melodies and compose original musical pieces. It is during this period that children should begin to learn to play an instrument. Adults who studied an instrument before the age of eight have more brain development in the corpus callosum then those who started formal lessons later (Schlaug, 1995).

Musical development seems to reach a plateau by the age nine (Stellaccio & McCarthy, 1999). This means that the music activities we present to young children are vitally important. The early years are when children learn to sing accurately, acquire their vocal range, and learn basic concepts about rhythm, pitch, and melody (see Table 10-1).

| TABLE 10–1 | Musical Development in Young Children | | | |
|---|---|---|---|---|
| **Age** | **Rhythm** | **Listening** | **Instrument** | **Song** |
| Before birth | Surrounded by rhythm of mother's body | Respond differently to familiar and novel music | Hear music | Hear mother's voice |
| Infants *Newborn to 6 months* | Respond differently to different types of music | Turn toward sounds<br>Notice difference between melodies<br>Respond to loud and soft<br>Recognize and remember different complex musical pieces | Make sounds with objects such as rattles | Babble to musical stimulation<br>Babble on own with pitch and rhythmic pattern<br>Coo in open vowels |
| Infants *6 months to 1 year* | Rock and bounce to music | React to music with sound and motion | Show interest in instruments | Respond to singing by vocalizing |
| Toddlers *1 to 3 years* | Move feet with rhythm of music<br>Cannot keep time<br>Clap to music | Listen to music on radio and recordings<br>Identifies types of sounds<br>Show preferences for certain music<br>Matches sounds and objects | Seek objects to make sounds | Real singing begins<br>Tag on to the end of a song<br>Make up songs and chants<br>Sing on own with recurring pitch center and consistent tempo<br>Have a five-note range<br>Cannot match pitch |

*(continued)*

| Age | Rhythm | Listening | Instrument | Song |
|---|---|---|---|---|
| Preschoolers<br>*3 to 4 years* | Begin to clap on beat<br>Begin to echo clap | Can listen for longer periods while remaining quiet | Tap a beat on an instrument | May sing along with familiar songs with increasing accuracy |
| | Improvise complex rhythm<br>Imitate simple rhythms | Can identify familiar songs<br>Can talk about speed and volume of music<br>Can identify musical phrases<br>Can identify the source of a sound<br>Can identify the sound of familiar instruments<br>Can talk about what they hear using music vocabulary they have learned | Interest in real instruments increases<br>Play simple instruments in small group<br>Play short melodies on tonal instruments<br>Can improvise melodies<br>Can invent original symbols to represent sounds | Can sing in different keys<br>Have a five- to eight-note range<br>Begin to match pitch and echo words in rhythm<br>Spontaneously invents new songs as they play<br>Can sing along with a group |
| Kindergarteners<br>*5 to 6 years* | Can march and clap at same time to music<br>Keep time with music<br>Improvise complex rhythm structure with a climax and conclusion | Identify change in music<br>Recognize a familiar song played on an instrument without words<br>Become active listener and can talk about music heard<br>Can listen respectfully at concerts<br>Can describe the elements and mood of musical pieces | Can tell sounds made by different instruments apart<br>Play sequential and diatonic and chromatic tones on tonal instruments<br>Can learn to read simple notation<br>Focus on one instrument for extended time<br>Can begin lessons on piano, violin, etc.<br>Imitate a rhythm using a different instrument accurately | Make up own songs and write musical symbols<br>Sing in clear tone taking breath at appropriate points<br>Begin to know that a song's melody is fixed<br>Sing in tune<br>Whole steps easier to sing than half steps<br>Descending patterns easier to sing than ascending ones<br>Large intervals more difficult than close ones<br>Most accurate in the A1D1 range (C1 is middle C)<br>Add emotion through facial expression, pitch, dynamics, and tempo to voice |
| Primary ages<br>*6 to 8 years* | Keep time accurately | Can hear harmony<br>Recognize familiar songs played in different contexts<br>Can differentiate between music reflecting different styles and moods | Can learn to read music<br>Play parts on instrument | Can sing familiar songs accurately and has a repertoire of memorized songs<br>Sing more accurately as individual than with group<br>Can reach higher notes<br>Can sing rounds and two-part songs<br>Know that melodies are fixed |

**TABLE 10–1** **Musical Development in Young Children** *(continued)*

*Note: As in all the arts, musical development is strongly influenced by experience. This chart is intended only as a general guideline to what skills might be mastered in terms of age. However, the basic sequence of skill acquisition will pertain to most children.*

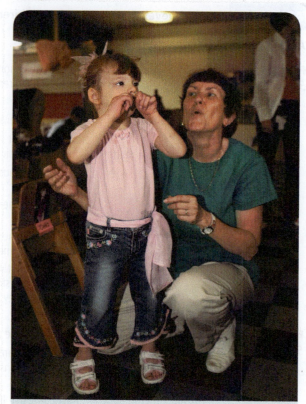

Interacting one-on-one with an adult is essential to music skill development.

# How Does Music Help Children Grow?

Music has been part of human society since the dawn of culture over 30,000 years ago. It has the power to make us cry and to make us feel joy. Beyond pleasure, music positively affects brain development and health affecting development in the physical, social, cognitive, and language areas. When we share music with children, we provide another way to help them grow.

## Music and the Brain

Music has the power to change the brain. Musicians who began their training before age six have hyper-development in some parts of their brains (Rauscher & Hinton, 2003). Even just fifteen months of formal music instruction at age six has been shown to cause growth in multiple areas of the brain (Hyde, et al, 2009; Schlaug et al., 2005). Babies who were exposed to a complex work by Ravel paid more attention to this longer, more difficult piece of music than they did to unfamiliar ones indicating growth in neural networks (Ilari, Polka, & Costa-Giomi, 2002).

Music has also been shown to enhance long-term memory (Wolfe & Horn, 1998). Long-term memory is always forming and reforming interconnections with the information being absorbed (Caine, Caine, McClintic & Klimec, 2008). Adding music to learning activities helps establish memories more quickly and firmly (Stuckey & Nobel, 2010). Many adults, for example, rely on the ABC song, learned during childhood, to assist in alphabetizing.

## Music and Well-Being

Different types of music produce physiological changes in the listener (Krumhansl, 2002). Listening to music has been shown to lower levels of stress, affect the heart rate, and aid healing (Using Music to Tune the Heart, 2009; Nakahara et al., 2009). When premature babies were exposed to music daily, they grew faster and went home from the hospital earlier than those who were not (Sousa, 2001, p. 223).

## Music and Developmental Growth

Music affects a child's total development. Through music activities children develop:

**Physically**—By using the body to participate in and create music. Physical development occurs when children listen, sing, and move to music. Music stimulates and develops a child's auditory perception. Making music with hands and instruments foster the control and coordination of large and small body movements. Research has shown that musicians who play instruments have more ability to use both hands (Weinberger, 2004).

**Socially**—By learning music skills with and from others. For thousands of years music has drawn groups together in song and performance. Young children learn about their culture as they sing traditional songs, and they develop cooperative skills as they work together to create a musical moment. At the same time, music ties together all humanity. All societies have tonal music and sing lullabies to their children (Wade, 2003).

**Cognitively**—By developing the **auditory discrimination** and spatial relationship abilities of the brain. Music allows children to investigate sequencing, and cause and effect. Jensen (1998) notes that playing an instrument helps children discover patterns and develop organizational skills. Although simply listening to music seems to "prime" children's spatial thinking abilities, numerous studies have found a stronger correlation between spatial reasoning and early instruction in music, particularly as related to learning the piano or keyboard (Costa-Giomi, 1999; Graziano, Peterson, & Shaw, 1999; Hetland, 2000; Rauscher et al., 1997).

**Language skills**—By talking about and listening to music. Speech and music draw on the same modalities. The fact that music perception skills have been found to predict reading success indicates that similar auditory processing is needed for both (Anvari et al., 2001). Oral language is developed as children compose their own rhythms and songs to express their ideas. Listening skills increase as children pay attention to the music they hear and play. Causal relationships have been found between music instruction and reading skill (Butzlaff, 2000). Music has also been found to help English language learners. Songs can help children learning a second language to gain skill in pronunciation, grammar, vocabulary, phrasing, and speed of delivery (Scripps, 2002).

**Emotionally**—By using music to express and respond to feelings. Music provides another way for children to express their feelings. Listening to music can also soothe and help children focus better on other tasks (Hetland, 2000). A case study of students who were emotionally disturbed found that they wrote better and had an improved attitude when listening to music (Kariuki & Honeycut, 1998).

**Music concepts and skills**—By meeting the National Common Core Music Standards.

**Creating: Generate and select among multiple musical ideas relevant to a personal experience, interest, or specific purpose.**

**PreKindergarten.** With guidance, explore musical ideas (i.e. move, chant, sing) to use for a specific purpose.

**Kindergarten.** With guidance, explore tonal and rhythmic patterns, and combine selected patterns to create musical ideas relating to a specific purpose or interest.

**First Grade.** With support, improvise tonal and rhythmic patterns, and combine selected patterns to create musical ideas relating to a specific purpose, interest, or personal experience.

**Second Grade.** Generate ideas for an original improvisation and/or composition, using free improvisation and varied sound sources, and select multiple ideas to develop that best relate to personal experience, interest, and specific purpose.

**Performing: Select work(s) to present based on interest, knowledge, ability and context.**

**PreKindergarten.** With guidance, demonstrate (i.e. move, chant, sing) or say which musical selections they would like to perform

**Kindergarten.** With support, demonstrate (i.e., play instruments) or say which musical selection they prefer to perform for a given purpose.

## Special Needs

### • PROVIDING ASSISTANCE TO CHILDREN WITH SPECIAL NEEDS •

#### Auditory Processing

- If the child has partial hearing, the use of earphones and preferential seating near the player may help. The child may also respond to low-pitched drums.
- Children with cochlear implants have poor pitch resolution, which limits recognition of melodies played on a piano or single instrument, although they have normal responses to rhythm. More complex musical pieces that contain multiple clues, such as voice and definitive patterns, are easier for them to recognize and enjoy (Vongpaisal, Trehub, Schellenberg, & Papsin, 2004).
- Percussion instruments are an ideal choice for children with limited hearing. Sprinkling rice or small stones on top of a drum allows the child not only to feel but also see the vibration.
- Children with no hearing respond best to rhythmic pieces, which they can feel through vibrations. If possible, let them touch the speaker as the music plays. Providing a visual element may also help. Media players on the computer often have wave visuals that can accompany the music. The 1995 movie *Mr. Holland's Opus* provides insight into how musical performances can be presented visually to the deaf using lights and visuals.

#### Physical Needs

- Children with motor issues may need help in order to grip an instrument and make a sound. Choose instruments that are easy to hold such as an open tambourine or can be rested on a table or tray such as a drum.
- If the child's muscle control is weak, select instruments that will make a large sound with little effort.
- If the child has limited movement, attach the instrument to the body part the child has the most control over or to a steady surface. Bells and shakers can be attached to arms, legs, or head with hook and loop tape. Triangles can be suspended from a stand or chair.

#### Assistive Technology
**Using Assistive Technology to Make Music**

When children cannot participate verbally or have trouble with motor control, they may need assistive technology in order to participate fully in music activities. One of the assistive tools that can be used very effectively to allow participation in music activities is a touch communication device that can be programmed with a message, words to a song, or music. This device can be a stand-alone specialized communication device, computer software on a computer provided with an extra-large keyboard, or software downloaded on a tablet. Children who use a sound board to communicate may contribute to a rhythm or song activity by pressing a key on the beat or they might use computer software that lets them press the right pitch, say a repeated word in the song, play a recording of the melody, or a recorded line from the chorus at the proper time.

🎵 **First Grade.** Demonstrate or say which musical selection they prefer to perform for a given purpose (e.g., Open House, Grandparents Day).

🎵 **Second Grade.** Demonstrate and explain which musical selection they prefer to perform for a given purpose

**Responding. Support the choice of music for a specific purpose or situation.**

🎵 **PreKindergarten.** With guidance, demonstrate (i.e., move, chant and/or sing) or say/indicate what musical selection(s) they prefer based on personal preference.

🎵 **Kindergarten.** With support, demonstrate or say/indicate what musical selection(s) they prefer to experience or listen to for a given purpose.

🎵 **First Grade.** Demonstrate (i.e., play instruments) or say/indicate what musical selection(s) they prefer to experience or listen to for a given or student-selected purpose.

🎵 **Second Grade.** Demonstrate and explain what musical selection(s) they prefer to experience or listen to for a given or student-selected purpose.

# How Are Music Activities Designed?

Musical activities can be organized in three ways: as individualized instruction, as open-ended, independent exploration, and in organized groups. An effective music program needs to incorporate all these approaches into the curriculum in order for children to develop fully as confident musical creators.

## One-on-One Interactions

For infants and toddlers, in particular, but for all children as well, interacting one-on-one with an adult has been shown to be vitally important in acquiring musical competence. Children, for example, sing more accurately when singing individually than with a group (Goetz & Horii, 1989). Learning to play an instrument proceeds faster when the child receives intensive one-on-one lessons.

One-on-one musical interactions can occur throughout the education of young children. Singing to an infant or toddler while going about daily activities, such as dressing, diaper changing, putting on outerwear, eating lunch, walking places, and so on fit naturally into adult–child interactions. In preschool, kindergarten, and primary classrooms one-on-one echo singing and instrumental solos can be purposely planned into group activities.

## Exploration Centers

Music centers allow children to explore sound, rhythm, and music in playful, creative, and open-ended ways.

A center for exploring sound can be problematic in a busy, noisy preschool and primary classroom. However, it is possible. To muffle the sound, include soft items such as a pile rug, pillows, and draped fabric. A sturdy table covered on three sides with heavy cloth and open in front makes a cozy "music house" in which to listen to music and explore making sounds, but still allows teacher supervision. Several types of music centers address different components of music education.

**Conducting center.** To the listening center add flashlights covered with different-colored cellophane that children can move in concert with the music while shining the light on the wall.

**Composing center.** Alongside instruments of varying kinds, provide a metal tray and magnet-backed notes, plain paper and markers, or paper with staves for older children so they can try their hand at composing.

**Instruments.** Provide handmade and commercial instruments to accompany the recorded music or to use in making up original songs. Make sure there is an assortment of percussive, drums, shakers, and so on, and melodic instruments, such as a xylophone or hand bells.

**Listening center.** Stock the center with a child-friendly CD/music player, or tape recorder, and earphones.

**Sound discovery center.** Set out materials that can be used to make sounds or musical instruments. For example, offer different plastic containers with easy-to-close lids and a variety of small objects, such as pebbles, jingle bells, and buttons that fit inside. Children can use these to make their own shakers to keep time to the recorded music or their own singing.

## Responsive Group Activities

Music is mainly a social activity. Although individuals may play or sing for their own personal enjoyment, music is usually experienced as part of a group. However, the size and purpose of musical groups can vary.

**Small group.** Small groups of children can participate in listening, singing, and composing activities as part of projects and at centers. For example, primary students might compose a song to accompany a skit, or a group of preschoolers may sing a lullaby to the dolls in the housekeeping center.

## Integrating the Arts

### MAKING MATHEMATICAL CONNECTIONS TO THE COMMON CORE

Musical activities can be used to reinforce mathematical concepts found in the Common Core Math Standards for K–2.

#### Preschool
- Children learn one-to-one correspondence as they clap and tap a beat and sing counting songs.

#### Kindergarten
- They can count to 100 orally by ones and tens, recognize cardinality, and learn that the last number is the total beats as they count out the beat in a piece of music.
- They can count forward from a given number when starting in the middle of a line.
- They can write out the number of beats as one way to record the rhythm of a piece of music.
- They can answer questions about how many beats there are, add on beats, and take away beats.
- They classify patterns of beats and count the number of beats in the pattern.

#### First Grade
- Children can continue to count beats to amounts beyond 100.
- Children can solve simple additions and subtraction word problems that ask them to learn or invent a rhythmic sequence and then add or subtract beats or groups of beats from it.
- They can use the clock to time different rhythms, pieces of music, and songs.

#### Second Grade
- Children can count beats by 5s, 10s, and multiples of 100.
- Use addition to find the total number of beats in a song by adding the together the beats in each line.
- Children can count orally each time they tap out a beat.
- Children can use more, less, and equal as they compare groups of beats, two strings of notes, or two different lines in a song or set of songs.
- During rhythmic activities they can compare quantities and group and classify by beats.
- They can identify even groups in rhythmic patterns.

### Did You Get It?

**Which of the following would you recommend for developing the musical abilities of young children?**

a. Have young children practice in groups, rather than individually, to help them sing accurately.

b. Ensure young children are taught how to play music formally, rather than having them experiment on their own.

c. Provide one-on-one rather than whole group activities to teach young children to sing accurately.

d. Ensure young children listen to simplified music, as they will not understand complex music.

**Take the full quiz on CourseMate**

**Whole group.** Many music activities lend themselves to whole group settings. Children can listen to music during a nap or snack. They can sing favorite songs together as part of group meetings as a way to build community. New songs can be taught to the whole group so everyone can sing along. A rhythm band in which everyone participates can show children what can be accomplished when every member works together.

**Transitions.** Music as a form of communication can be used to signal changes in activities, mood, and behavior. Playing calm music while children work and play can create a peaceful, relaxing environment and build a sense of community.

## The Listening Experience

According to Shore and Strasser (2006), an effective music curriculum starts with a developmental series of listening activities. It should include a wide range of music, including complex music. This is based on the research that shows that early listening to complex music by infants leads to richer cognitive and language development.

Listening activities should include music from other times and cultures, as well as listening to natural sounds.

**Selecting pieces for listening.** Music intended solely for children is commonly part of most preschool and primary music programs. However, regardless of the children's ages musical selections should never be limited to only simplified pieces, because all children are capable of more sophisticated listening. Without exposure to complex music, not only in the Western classical tradition, but also that of other cultures, they will not develop the aesthetic awareness and close listening skills needed to truly appreciate and love music.

We cannot begin too early. The early years are critical in the formation of music appreciation. By eight-months an infant can tell the difference between two complex musical works. In doing so they respond more to the **scale** and the meter found in the music they have heard in their home environment (Hannon & Trainor, 2007; Hannon & Trehub, 2005; Lynch & Eilers; 1992; Soley & Hannon, 2010).

Music preferences continue to solidify throughout early childhood. However, research indicates that children up to the age of five are more willing to respond positively to unfamiliar styles than older children and adults (Flohr & Persellin, 2011; Kopiez & Lehmann, 2008). Therefore, the earlier children experience a variety of musical genres and styles the better.

Table 10-2 presents a sampling of music from many cultural traditions that will both appeal to young children while challenging their listening skills.

## Listening Activities for Infants

Sensitivity to sound is one of the most highly developed senses in infants. Listening activities help them learn to focus attention and make sense of the many sounds in their environment.

**Lullabies.** Lullabies are a very special category of song. To soothe infants, play lullabies and rock them gently. The soothing songs help infants learn how to self-regulate and sooth themselves (Parlakian, 2010). Brahms, Handel, and Mozart all wrote wonderful lullabies. Traditional lullabies are available from all cultures. Alice Honig (2005) points out that it does not matter to infants in what language the lullaby is. Nevertheless, families will appreciate a caregiver's initiative in learning lullabies from the child's culture. Singing familiar songs will increase the infant's feeling of comfort and belonging. Try to memorize several

| TABLE 10–2 | Music for Listening and Study |
|---|---|
| **Artist/Producer** | **Title** |
| Puntamayo | *Acoustic Africa* |
| Benedictine Monks of Santo | *Chants* |
| Frederick Chopin | *Sonata No. 3 Op. 58* |
| Hamza El Din | *The Water Wheel* |
| Edward Grieg | *Peer Gynt* |
| Gustav Holst | *The Planets* |
| R. Carlos Nakai | *Dancing into Silence* |
| Inca Sun | *Peru: A Musical Journey* |
| Thelonious Monk | *My Funny Valentine* |
| Wolfgang Amadeus Mozart | *Symphony No. 39 in E Flat* |
| Modest Petrovich Mussorgsky | *Pictures at an Exhibition* |
| Michael Oldfield | *Tubular Bells 1 and 2* |
| Nikolai Andreyevich Rimsky- Korsakov | *Scheherazade* |
| Wayna Picchu | *Folk Music from Peru* |
| Igor Stravinsky | *Petrushka* |
| Vangelis | *Antarctica* |

*Note: These are just a few of a multitude of musical selections that can inspire young children.*

**Digital Download**   **Download from CourseMate**

to sing often to the infant. Vary saying the words and humming the melody.

For a list of multicultural lullaby albums, see *Lullabies from Around thve World* on CourseMate.

**Attention getters.** Sing, hum, or play a lively song to get the baby's attention.

**Clock.** Place a loudly ticking clock near the infant.

**Mobiles.** For non-sitting infants, hang a mobile that makes soft sounds or plays a lullaby. For older infants, securely suspend noise makers that they can reach for and pull. For safety, supervise at all times.

**Movements.** Encourage a young infant to move along to a song you sing or to music you listen to, such as by bouncing and rocking the baby to the music.

**Shakers.** Shake a rattle, set of keys, bells, or play a musical instrument to attract attention. Move the shaker around so the baby follows it with eyes and head. With an older infant, play peek-a-boo with the noisemaker.

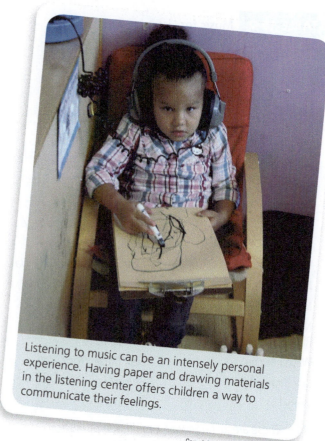

Listening to music can be an intensely personal experience. Having paper and drawing materials in the listening center offers children a way to communicate their feelings.

Copyright © 2015 Cengage Learning®

**Identify sounds.** Make a sound using an object, then hide it, and have the children try to guess what it is. When they are familiar with several, see if they can pick out one from the others only by listening.

**Loud and soft.** Explore ways to make sounds louder or softer. Cover and uncover ears. Whisper and yell. Turn the volume up and down on the player.

**Listen to music.** Play and sing many different kinds of musical pieces from all over the world. Continue to soothe the child with lullabies and gentle classical music. Play dance music for children to move to creatively.

## Listening Activities for Preschoolers and Up

With their longer attention spans, preschool, kindergarten and primary children are much more sophisticated listeners. They can participate in individual and group activities that ask them to compare and contrast sounds and music recognizing the timbre of different instruments and identify instrumental versions of familiar songs. They can start to use the vocabulary of the music to describe what they hear and to share their ideas with others.

Primary students can also begin to write about their listening experiences. This, plus increasing knowledge in the different subject areas, allows activities to become more integrated into other areas of learning.

The following are some suggested activities.

**Body sounds.** Explore all the different sounds you can make with your body—rubbing hands; slapping chest, thighs, or floor; snapping fingers; clapping hands; tapping fingers; stamping feet; clicking teeth; popping cheeks; and so on. Then use these sounds to accompany music as they listen. Preschool and up.

**Collect sounds.** As new sounds are discovered, record them on a class chart. Preschool and up.

**Find the sound.** Have the children close their eyes while one child makes a sound somewhere in the classroom. See if they can identify from where the sound came. Try this game outside as well. Preschool and up.

**Listen to relax.** Provide quiet times when music is listened to solely for enjoyment and relaxation. For preschoolers this can be at naptime. For older children it can serve as a stress-reliever after recess. Preschool and up.

**Singing.** Make singing a daily occurrence. Make up little songs to accompany daily activities from eating to washing up. Vary the loudness of the song and the pitch of the notes sometimes singing higher and sometimes lower.

## Listening Activities for Toddlers

Toddlers are becoming more aware of the sounds around them and can begin to identify the sources of many of them. They are also starting to develop preferences for certain music.

**Sound walk.** Take a walk outside in the neighborhood or in a park and notice the different sounds heard. Look for other places to visit that have interesting sounds, such as a kitchen, a factory, a pool, or beach.

**High low.** Choose a fun word or the child's name and repeat it over and over. Start low and get higher and higher in pitch. As the pitch gets higher, raise your arms over your head. As the sound gets lower, lower arms to your sides.

**Silence.** True listening takes focus. To help children develop auditory focus, make time on a regular basis for silence listening. Stop what you are doing and have everyone stop making noise, close their eyes, and listen. Then share what you heard. Preschool and up.

**Sound scavenger hunt.** Go on a scavenger hunt outdoors. Collect nature objects that can be used to make interesting sounds. Preschool and up.

**Introduce new tunes.** Slowly introduce new music styles so children have time to become accustomed to them, but keep coming back to tunes they already know to maintain recognition. Preschool and up.

**Ordered sound.** Fill small metal cans or film containers with different materials so there is a range from soft to loud. Seal containers shut so the children cannot open them. Let the children explore them at the sound center and think of different ways to group them. Encourage them to put them in order from softest to loudest. Make another set that has matched pairs and see if the children can match them up. Preschool and up.

**Listen closely.** Play a piece of music while the children close their eyes. have them raise their hands when they hear a preselected part, melody, or pattern, or when they hear a change in pitch, tempo, or dynamics. At first play a sample of what to listen for before beginning the activity. Later as the children get more accurate, try it without a sample. Kindergarten and up.

**Classify sounds.** Collect items and instruments that make interesting sounds. Group them by loudness, length of sound, timbre, and pitch. Preschool and up.

**Invent sound machines.** Using boxes, paper, sandpaper, tin foil, Styrofoam, cardboard, straws, and other similar materials, build machines that make an interesting sound. Preschool and up.

**Discover musical forms.** Introduce children to the many styles and forms of music. Listen to children's opera, country dances, symphonies, and jazz sessions. Develop understanding of these forms by comparing and contrasting what makes these types of music different from each other. Could you dance to an aria in an opera? Is it hard to sit still during a country dance or does it make your body want to move?

For a comprehensive list of musical forms, see *Musical Forms* on CourseMate.

**Tell stories.** Most popular music has **lyrics**. Children will be less familiar with instrumental pieces.

Help children listen more closely to instrumental pieces by telling a story about the music that makes it come alive and be memorable. For young children this could be a simple made-up story, such as "Can you hear the birds flying to their nests?" For older children tell stories about the composer, how and why he or she wrote it, and the instruments used to play it. Encourage children to make up their own stories by setting out puppets they can animate to the music or by providing writing materials in the listening center.

## Reading about Music

Numerous children's books introduce composers and their work. Listen to instrumental pieces that tell a story through the music such as *Peter and the Wolf* by Sergei Prokofiev and *The Carnival of Animals* by Camille Saint-Saëns and then read the story. Re-listen to the work to gain deeper understanding of how music can set a **mood** and create character.

Other books introduce famous musicians and music genres such as Celenza's *Gershwin's Rhapsody in Blue* (2006) and Pinkney's *Duke Ellington: The Piano Prince* (2006). Accompany the book with recordings by the musician.

For an annotated list of books about musical genres and composers, see *Books about Music and Musicians* on CourseMate.

## Talking about Music

Research shows that music elicits strong emotional and physical responses in the listener (Standley, 2008). Build on this emotional-physical connection by providing opportunities for intense listening to a musical piece before talking about it. Play the piece numerous times. Invite children to move their hands to the changes in pitch or dynamics, or tap and sway to the rhythms. Allow children to move in the way they best feel matches the music even if it differs from your ideas about the music. When we allow children to move in their own ways, we encourage creativity and foster active listening.

After they have had time to absorb the music through their bodies and make it their own, try asking some of these open-ended questions.

- How did this music make you want to move?
- How did this music make you feel?

🎵 Did you hear any changes in the music that made you move differently or feel differently?

🎵 What did the music remind you of? Or make you think of?

🎵 Did the music tell a story?

*For more ideas for listening activities, see Listening Activities for Young Children on CourseMate.*

---

### Did You Get It?

**When selecting pieces for children under the age of five to listen to, a teacher should \_\_\_\_\_.**

a. have children listen to only simple music from other cultures

b. avoid music that is unfamiliar to the children

c. include complex music from a variety of cultural traditions

d. focus on music intended solely for children

**Take the full quiz on CourseMate**

---

## The Rhythmic Experience

Rhythm is fundamental to life. Each of us carries our own natural rhythm in our heartbeat. Before birth babies respond the sound of their mother's heartbeat (Parncutt, 2006). After birth, infants

Rhythm instruments are ideal for young children. Playing together in a rhythm band teaches children to cooperate and helps them develop mathematical counting skills.

as young as two months notice rhythmic patterns and groupings (Ilari & Polka, 2006; Krumhansl & Jusczyk, 1990; Mithen, 2006). By seven months they can perceive variations in tempo and frequency (Trainor & Corrigall, 2010).

At around two-and-a half toddlers can hear a steady beat and will attempt to match their body movements to it (Provasi & Bobin-Begue, 2003). By preschool children are able to hold a beat and move to it, and by kindergarten most children can identify the rhythmic pattern in a piece of music and match changes in the tempo (Eerola, Luck, & Toiviainen, 2006; Trainor & Corrigall, 2010).

## Designing Rhythmic Activities

Rhythmic activities should develop children's sense of rhythm through open-ended exploration that allows them to create their own rhythm instruments and rhythms. Rhythm activities are naturally engaging to young children and do not have to be complicated. They should involve the child in listening to rhythms and physically responding in some way. Variety can be introduced by using new ways to make sounds and sharing music with different rhythms.

In addition to planned engagements with rhythm we can also incorporate rhythm into daily activities. For example, carry around a small drum or tambourine, or simply clap, to catch and mirror the rhythms of the children at play. As children paint at the easel or jump on the playground, tap out a beat that matches their movement as you bring it to their attention:

🎵 "Listen. Can you hear the tapping beat of the brush?"

🎵 "Listen. Can you hear how fast your feet are stamping as you jump up and down?"

Another way to incorporate rhythm into daily events is to use echo clapping when you want the children's attention. Clap a rhythm and have everyone else clap the same rhythm back. This is an excellent way to get the focus of a group even when they are deeply involved in play.

Rhythmic chants can be used to transition from one activity to another. It is easy to invent your own. For example, when cleaning up chant something like "Clean up. Clean up. Everybody clean up," while

## Teacher Tip

### KEEP A STEADY BEAT

1. Signal the start of the song by tapping a steady beat on your thighs, a table, by clapping or by using a rhythm instrument.
2. Give any instructions as you keep tapping.
3. Give a start signal that matches the beat such as "One Two Ready to Go."
4. Sing the song emphasizing the word syllables that land on the beat.

Example:

**Pol**ly **put** the **ket**tle **on**

**Pol**ly **put** the **ket**tle **on**

**Pol**ly **put** the **ket**tle **on**

We'll **all** **have** **tea**

clapping a regular beat to the words. As children work they can join in and chant along.

To encourage growth, rhythm experiences should occur every day. Rhythm activities can be offered one-on-one, in exploration centers, and as whole group experiences. Here are some activities to try with infant and toddlers.

## Rhythm Activities for Infants and Toddlers

Rhythm activities for this age focus on helping the child discover the rhythm and respond to it. Infants and toddlers benefit most when rhythm is explored one-on-one with a caring adult. Watching our faces and movements as we make rhythmic sounds and movements builds on the natural way infants learn. When we move the child's limbs or as we hold the child and move to a beat the child physically feels the rhythm and our enthusiasm is contagious as we model our own response to the rhythm. We can tell a child is engaged when they rock and bounce along with us.

Infants and toddlers also need opportunities to explore making rhythms on their own.

Introduce infants and toddlers to ways to create sound patterns by providing safe, simple objects for them to shake and tap, such as rattles, spoons, margarine containers, and wooden dowels. Instruments and

sound makers for infants and toddlers should meet the choke and poke test, i.e., be longer than 2 inches in length and 1 inch in diameter and have smooth, rounded ends on sticks and handles and be at least 1 inch in diameter. If needed, wrap handles in foam for added protection and ease of handling.

Use the following activities as inspiration for inventing your own.

**Foot dance.** Attach rattles or bells to an infant's ankles and encourage the child to kick as you sing or listen to music.

**Exercising.** Play a lively tune with a distinct beat. Move an infant's arms and legs in time to music. If the child is able to move on his or her own, model moving to the rhythm.

**Rocking.** Hold the child and rock back and forth in time to music or singing.

**Name rhythm.** Clap out the syllables of the child's name.

**Nursery rhymes.** Select a familiar nursery rhyme or poem and follow the rhythm clapping or using rhythm instruments. Listen for the accented beats.

## Exploring Sound Centers

Set up a sound center where toddlers can explore the sound and rhythms they can make using simple objects they can tap or shake. A list of rhythm instruments follows the next section. Vary the activity by add to or changing the objects.

Preschoolers and older children can make their own sound makers independently if provided with some basic materials, such as containers to fill and tap on. Provide the center with a tape recorder so they can play back their rhythms, paper and markers so they can record their rhythms, or provide a CD player so they can shake, rattle, and tap to the music.

## Whole Group Rhythm Bands

Rhythm sticks make a good introduction to whole group rhythm activities using sound makers starting in preschool. Try to have all the sticks the same color to keep children focused on the sound possibilities rather than who has their favorite color. An inexpensive substitute for commercial sticks is wooden spoons. Child-made shakers or margarine tub drums can also be used.

There are hundreds of different rhythm instruments. Look for instruments all kinds including those from other cultures to share with children. From left to right: maracas, hand drum, castanet, cacho shaker from Peru, sleigh bells, wood tone block.

No matter which sound maker is introduced first, provide plenty of space between each child and show them how to rest the sound maker on the ground in front of them or in their lap until the group is ready to play. Practice picking up the sound maker and putting it down. Teach the children a verbal or visual start and stop signal and practice it. When the children have the idea, put on a march or piece of music with a strong beat and have them tap along. Once they have mastered that, have them think of other ways to make sounds with the sticks or sound makers such as tapping them end to end or gently against their shoe. Play the piece again trying out some of the different ways the children have created.

Incorporate spatial and kinesthetic learning by having them play their instruments to one side or the other, across their bodies, above or below their heads, and using different body parts.

Vary the activity further by playing different kinds of music, tapping along to songs as you sing, and exploring other rhythm instruments like the ones described below. And don't forget to make photographs and videos and audio recordings of your band in action.

## Selecting Rhythm Instruments

Rhythm instruments for young children are usually **percussion**-type instruments, although any instrument can be used to create a rhythm or steady beat. Percussion instruments create sound by being struck or shaken. Although many items found around the house can be used to provide rhythm experiences, a wide range of traditional and nontraditional rhythm instruments can be purchased reasonably. Others are easily made. However, do not rely solely on ones you can make; children need to experience real instruments as well as homemade ones.

**Bells.** All varieties of bells can be used, such as sleigh bells, cowbells, brass bells from India, and gongs. Jingle bells can be attached to elastic wristbands for children who have not yet developed fine motor control or attached to arms or legs to allow infants and toddlers to move their bodies in rhythm.

**Claves.** Made from thick polished sticks, one is held in the palm and the other used to tap it. Explore the sounds made by tapping different sizes and shapes of wood.

**Cymbals.** Children love the large sound they can make with cymbals. Child-size cymbals usually have handles and are designed to fit little hands. Louder cymbals can be made from old pan lids. Finger cymbals come from Asia and because of their small size and high pitch, are ideal for young children.

**Drums.** Drums come in all sizes and shapes ranging from the bass drum to the hand drum. Drums for children should be stable and make a good sound without too much effort. Bongos, tom toms, and the different African drums, such as a *doumbek* or *djembe*, add variety to drumming activities. Drums can also be made from margarine and larger plastic containers with lids, plastic and metal pails, steel pie plates and pots, and five-gallon clean plastic buckets. A quiet drum can be made by stretching a balloon over the top of a coffee can using lacing, elastic bands, or heavy tape to hold it in place. A community drum can be made by using rubber roofing scrap and attaching grommets. Stretch the rubber over a large 3-gallon water tub. Heavy-duty plastic water tubs, intended for farm animals, come in very large sizes and make pleasant-sounding drums when turned upside down.

Electronic drum machines are another way to explore rhythms. Built-in recoded rhythms and songs allow the child to match the beat or play along. Some of them will allow you to record what you play. However, they are expensive, and young children will have just as much fun with homemade drums that allow them to use their whole body.

**Maracas.** Originally made from a dried gourd with the seeds still inside, today they are often plastic. Similar shakers can be made from soda and water bottles filled with different materials, with the lids hot glued on. Preschoolers can fill plastic eggs and margarine-type containers with lids. Put out a selection of items from which to choose, such as sand, gravel, and marbles that make interesting sounds. Paper plates, filled with rice or beans, can be stapled together to make easy-to-use shakers.

**Rainstick.** Purchase a traditional one from an import store or make your own. Insert nails at regular intervals in a cardboard tube, fill with rice, and seal both ends well. Wrap the entire tube in sturdy tape so that nails cannot be removed.

**Rhythm sticks.** These are ubiquitous in children's rhythm bands because they are inexpensive and easy to use. They can be made from well-sanded wooden dowels or wooden spoons. Sometimes they are grooved and a different sound results when the sticks are rubbed up and down against each other.

**Sand blocks.** Two wooden blocks can be wrapped in sandpaper and rubbed together to create a soft scratching sound.

**Strikers.** Depending on the instrument, most percussion requires something with which to tap or hit. Drumsticks are usually too large and loud for children. Hard rubber mallets can be purchased for a softer tone. Soft-sounding mallets can also be made by attaching a tennis ball or rubber ball to the end of a heavy wooden dowel. Cut a hole in the ball, insert the handle, glue, and then wrap in duct tape or cloth so it is firmly attached.

**Tambourines.** A tambourine is a hoop with jingles set into the frame. Some tambourines have a skinhead; others are open. It is an easy instrument for young children to play because it can be either shaken, tapped, or both. Its pleasant sound makes it ideal for creating rhythms to accompany children's activities or for rhythmic transitions.

**Tappers.** A number of instruments make tapping sounds. Castanets are made of clamshell-shaped wood; although plastic ones may be more appropriate for children. They are held in the palm and clicked by opening and closing the hand. Spoons made of wood, plastic, and metal also make good tappers. The spoons, an American folk tradition, are played by holding two metal spoons back to back with one between the thumb and the index finger and the other between the index finger and the middle finger. Hold the palm of the other hand above the spoons and hit the spoons against the knee and the palm to create a clicking rhythm.

**Tongue drum.** The pitched tongue drum is made from hollowed wood and is of Aztec origin. It has wood "keys" that make different pitches when tapped.

**Triangles.** A favorite of young children because of its pleasing high pitch, the triangle is made of a bent piece of metal hung from a string and tapped with a metal stick. Explore the sound made by other metal objects, such as pie tins and old spoons. Suspend the pie tins and spoons from a string so they can vibrate.

**Wood blocks.** These are hollow pieces of wood that create a pleasant sound when tapped.

## Rhythm Activities for Preschoolers and up

By preschool, children have a much better ability to respond on the beat. They can mirror back a rhythm and invent rhythms of their own. Children in kindergarten and older usually can keep time fairly accurately, especially if they have had many rhythmic experiences earlier. They can now play complex rhythms in group activities with small groups or an individual playing a contrasting part. They can start to compare and contrast rhythms, find the accented beat, and combine rhythms in new ways.

The following activities help children practice finding the rhythm, holding it, and matching changes in tempo and dynamics.

**Bubbles.** Blow bubbles. Ask each child to select one bubble to watch. When that bubble pops, they are to say "pop." Repeat, having them make different sounds when the bubble pops. Ask them to listen for any rhythms or patterns that they hear. Do the "pops" come faster as all the bubbles disappear? Follow up by creating a bubble song.

**Body talk.** Select a word of two or more syllables. Say the word and match its syllables by clapping or moving a body part, such as nodding the head, stamping the feet, waving the arms, clapping the thigh, and so forth. Try it using two or more words.

**Clocks.** Find a clock with a loud tick. Have the children say "tick tock" and keep time with claps or rhythm instruments. Follow up by introducing a **metronome,** a device that produces a regular beat that can be changed. Show how the tempo of the beat can be sped up and slowed down. Have child clap or move their rhythm instruments to the beat. Being able to maintain a regular beat correlates with greater achievement in the primary grades (Weikert, Schweinhaer & Larner, 1987).

**Drum circle.** Provide each child with a commercial or homemade drum. Ideally, there should be drums in an assortment of sizes, and hands should be used instead of drumsticks. Sit in a circle and have one child start a rhythm, which is picked up by everyone else. In turn, signal a different child to change the rhythm. The same thing can be done using other rhythm instruments as well.

**Explore rhythm instruments.** Provide plenty of time for the children to explore rhythm instruments on their own before starting any group activities. Introduce new instruments one at a time to the sound center. At the exploration level children will play around with the instruments making sounds, but no recognizable rhythm. As they gain mastery they will start tapping with a regular beat. At the response level they will play a rhythm as they sing a song to themselves. They will vary the rhythm by manipulating instruments or combining two or more in new ways.

**Assess progress.** To assess the ability of an individual child to remember and repeat a rhythm, clap a short rhythm for the child to clap back. Challenge children by making the rhythm longer.

**Heartbeat.** Have the children sit very still and silent, put their hands on their hearts, and feel their heartbeats. Have them tap the floor or their thigh, and shake an instrument with the other hand to match the rhythm. Investigate: Is the rhythm the same for everyone? Does the speed change if you jump up and down? Listen for the heart beat in popular songs. Preschool and up.

**Name rhythms.** Have the children clap out the syllables of their names. See whether children can identify a name just from hearing it clapped. Look for names with the same or similar rhythms. Preschool and up.

**Rhythm pass along.** Have children sit in a circle and hand out a variety of different instruments. Play or sing a familiar song and keep time. At intervals have the children pass their instruments to the person sitting next to them so everyone gets a chance to play

every instrument. Music activities like this encourage turn taking in a rewarding fashion. Preschool and up.

## Reading and Writing Rhythm

Rhythm and poetry are a natural combination. Identification of syllables and understanding how regular beats supply rhythm to a poem or song are skills found in the Common Core Standards. Nursery rhymes are ideal for introducing rhythm and pattern at the preschool level. Have younger children clap or keep the beat using rhythm instruments as they chant "Baa Baa Black Sheep" or "Jack and Jill." Teach older children to write or act out original versions of the rhymes and then add their own rhythmic accompaniment.

Use nursery rhymes to help children learn about meter. Start by saying the rhyme together. Say it again accenting the main beat. This is the start of the **measure.** Next, tap the beat using rhythm instruments. Finally, decide whether the rhythm moves in 2's (strong| weak strong| weak) or 3s (strong weak weak |strong weak weak). Some nursery rhymes with a strong meter are "Humpty Dumpty," "Jack and Jill," and "Jack Be Nimble."

Explore rhyming poems with a strong beat such as the nature poetry of Aileen Fisher in *The Story Goes On* (2005) or Jack Prelustsky's *Read Aloud Poems for the Very Young* (1986) and *It's Raining Pigs and Noodles* (2000). There are also books like Chris Raschka's *Charlie Parker Played Be Bop* (1992) in which the simple text has a jazz rhythm or Matthew Gollub's *The Jazz Fly 2: The Jungle Pachanga* (2010) which introduces Spanish and Latin jazz.

For a list of annotated books with rhythmic text, see *Books with a Rollicking Rhythm* on CourseMate.

Explore writing rhythms by making a large copy of a simple poem and marking the beat with an agreed upon symbol. In the rhythm center have children create their own rhythms to go with a poem or rhyme and invite them to invent a way to write it down on paper using symbols so their friends can play it.

Another way to combine reading, writing, and rhythm is to have the children write stories on a specified topic such as animals or cars, or choose a story from a book. With a partner, add rhythms to parts of the story that reflect what is happening. For example, if a character is walking, then play a slow, even beat. If the character is running, play a quick, heavy rhythm. Invite them to share their stories.

## Talking about Rhythm

Introduce the vocabulary of rhythm by explaining that the beat is like a road or track that keeps everybody together. Use the terms tempo, dynamics, upbeat, and downbeat and together invent hand signals or ways of moving to show changes in these. Play different rhythms using sound makers and have the children describe differences in them using these words. Move on to playing two different musical works and listening to the rhythm. Make a chart listing how the rhythms sound in different styles of music.

As children explore the rhythms they create and those they hear in musical works, use enthusiastic descriptions, lots of movement, and open-ended questioning.

- How does the beat make you feel like moving?

- Does the beat change in any way?

- What else have you heard that has a similar beat?

- What words would you use to describe how this beat sounds?

*For more rhythmic activities to try, see Rhythmic Activities for Young Children on CourseMate.*

---

**Did You Get It?**

Amanda wants to help her preschoolers develop a sense of rhythm. Which of the following activities will best help her achieve this?

a. Amanda should give the children simple percussion instruments to play with.

b. Amanda should play a complex piece of music and ask the children to identify the individual instruments.

c. Amanda should play a piece of music and ask the children to indicate changes in pitch by raising and lowering their hands.

d. Amanda should teach the children songs that they can sing in a group.

Take the full quiz on CourseMate

---

# The Musical Instrument Experience

Rhythmic activities naturally grow into explorations of tonal musical instruments and melody. First experiences with musical instruments should allow children to explore the different sounds they can make.

## One-On-One

Like percussion instruments, tonal instruments should be offered one-on-one at first. Many of them are delicate and need to be explored with supervision. Help children learn to identify the instruments by name. Ask them to describe the shape and sound of each.

## Music Center

Follow up by expanding the sound center into a music center, and provide simple, durable instruments, both homemade and purchased. Make a recording of each instrument's sound, and place it in the music center so the children can explore timbre—the unique quality of the sound—by matching the mystery sound to its instrument.

A computer, MIDI keyboard, and music software can be added as well. As in visual art, an older computer dedicated solely to music exploration is a valuable addition to the arts program. Research has shown that using music software intended for children provides a playful way for them to explore timbre, pitch, and melody (Higgins & Campbell, 2010).

## Whole Group

Expand the rhythm band to include tonal instruments or try creating a melody band of just bells or recorders playing simple tunes and those of the children's own composition. As children gain skill and confidence, stage impromptu parades and concerts. Add child-created tunes to a favorite story or poem. Always remember to keep these activities open-ended and flexible. Performances that require hours of rehearsal and create stress are inappropriate for young children and steal away the child's natural affinity for making music.

## Selecting Musical Instruments

Although rhythm instruments are the most convenient and usually least expensive instruments for

Tonal instruments allow children to explore melody.

children, young children also need opportunities to explore tonality. Providing tonal instruments allows children to discover melody.

**Bells.**  Pitched bells can be a wonderful instrument for young children because they are similar to rhythm instruments and yet they can be used to play a melody. Hand bells are widely available and can be used with all ages. A double set of Montessori bells can also provide excellent training in learning to identify the different pitches.

**Keyboard.**  These instruments usually have keys to press. Those designed for infants and toddlers usually have just a few notes and colored keys. Search the Internet for "baby pianos" to find ones designed just for infants. On the traditional keyboard the white keys are in C major scale and the black keys are sharps and flats. The piano and electronic or MIDI keyboard can be used with very young children, even infants held in a lap, for a variety of music activities. They have the advantage of making it easy to name the notes and play harmony.  If

the keyboard has sufficient range, you can play along with the child either mirroring the same notes or playing chords. Music software that can be played with the MIDI keyboard can teach very young children about the music elements and how to begin to read and compose music. Other keyboard instruments include the accordion, harpsichord, clavichord, and organ.

**Pitched percussion.**  The xylophone and chimes are pitched instruments struck with mallets. Rubber and plastic mallets can be used to soften the sound in the classroom. Simple eight- and twelve-note xylophones allow children to compose and adapt simple melodies as well as explore rhythms. Other pitched percussion instruments include the bell lyre and the vibraphone. These are usually found in full orchestras. The thumb piano or kalimba is an African instrument that is easy for children to play. A simple chime can be made by placing nails on a piece of foam. Select a graduated set of nails in a range of sizes from 10 to 60 penny (2 to 6 inches). To play, tap the nails with a pencil.

**Strings.**  String instruments feature vibrating strings. Guitars and autoharps can be used to accompany children singing and to introduce playing simple melodies. Violin, viola, cello, bass, and harp are usually found in orchestras. Folk string instruments include the ukulele, dulcimers, banjo, zither, and mandolin.

Stringed instruments are found around the world. Each has a unique timbre that gives music from those cultures their characteristic sound. The *oud* is common in Arab countries. The *sitar* and *santoor* are from India. The *bouzouki* is from Greece and the *balalaika* from Russia.

**Wind instruments.**  These instruments are played by blowing air across or into the instrument.

 **Across Cultures**

**Instruments from Around the World**

Display instruments from other cultures, such as Tibetan singing bowls; carved frog and cricket wood rasps from Indonesia; rain sticks and goat hoof chachas rattles from Bolivia; the telavi from Ghana; and woven shakers from Africa, Brazil, and India.

Find information on these and other instruments at https://www.worldmusicalinstruments.com/.

The pitch changes either by varying the amount and direction of the breath or by pressing down keys which change the length of air in the instrument. Woodwinds have keys, which release the air at different lengths down the tube of the instruments. Many woodwinds also have a reed, which vibrates when blown. In order of descending pitch, there is the fife, piccolo, flute, oboe, clarinet, saxophone, and bassoon. There are also many folk wind instruments, such as the bagpipe, harmonica, penny whistle, and recorder. Brass instruments are played by putting lips into a metal mouthpiece, such as the trumpet, trombone, French horn, and tuba. The sound is created by the vibration of the lips.

For health reasons, children need personal wind instruments. Because of this, wind instruments are rare in most preschools and general classrooms. Inexpensive penny whistles and plastic recorders are sometimes used in the primary grades. Children can make kazoos by rubber banding wax paper to the end of a cardboard tube.

## Instrumental Activities for Infants

Because infants up to the age of one explore the world with all their senses instruments are particularly fascinating to them. Safety, of course, is the number-one issue and instruments offered to this age group should be sturdy with no sharp edges. Close supervision is vital and the best experience is one-on-one with the infant in the adult's lap.

**Chime blocks.** Commercial pitched chime blocks make a wonderful introduction to melodic instruments for the infant. If these cannot be found, similar blocks can be made by putting pitched bells inside small sturdy boxes, which are securely taped closed.

These should be used only with adult supervision. Make sure the bells being used pass the choke test.

**Keyboard play.** Play a melody on any keyboard instrument while holding the baby on your lap. Let the child "play" along, demonstrating how to press individual keys with a finger rather than banging with the whole hand.

**Stringing along.** Let the child pluck the strings of any stringed instrument. Be sure the instrument is secure—often you can wedge it between pillows and then hold the child on your lap. As the child plucks a string, finger some notes so different pitches result.

**Chimes.** For very young infants, hang baby-safe chimes where they can kick and bat them. Simple xylophones or chimes set in foam rubber are available for older infants. These should be used with close supervision.

## Instrumental Activities for Toddlers

Toddlers are curious about everything, and instruments are no exception. They are still at the exploratory stage and are more likely to just want to make noise than to create actual melodies. However, the toddler's awareness of and attention to timbre makes tonal instruments very engaging to them.

## Classroom Technology

### *MUSIC SOFTWARE*

Music software for young children can be used to introduce them to timbre, pitch, provide ear training, and reading musical notation. Many programs also allow children to compose original musical pieces and hear them played back. They can add accompanying rhythms and harmonies.

Although many of the programs are recommended for toddlers and up, digital music making should never replace hands-on interactions with actual instruments. Children need to move their bodies to the beat and hear the changes in sound as it moves nearer and closer to them. Use musical software as an addition to all of the other wonderful music activities we can do with children.

Always preview software before offering it to children. Write simple directions using symbols to help little ones know what to do independently.

In selecting music software for children, look for the following:

1. Large, easy-to-click buttons.

2. Limited choices for beats and harmonies.

3. Ability to add a MIDI keyboard. Using a mouse or computer keys is an awkward way for little fingers to play notes.

4. A game-like atmosphere in which children can try again and again to solve puzzles or master a concept rather than drill and practice type activities.

For more information on music software, see *Music Software* on CourseMate

Provide toddlers daily opportunities for playful exploration of sturdy tonal instruments. There are numerous keyboard and chime type instruments made for this age group. Enthusiastic modeling during supportive one-on-one activities is an effective way to guide the child into discovering the melodic possibilities of the instrument. As they play they can learn the names of music instruments and how they look and sound. Older toddlers can also begin to experiment with musical timbres using computer software designed for them.

**Exploring instruments.**  Create a music play area and provide sturdy toy instruments, such as chimes, xylophone, plastic guitar, hand bells, and a child-size piano or keyboard instrument as well as the more common rhythm instruments. Tape the child making music often.

**Music mats.**  Large piano-like mats that children can walk on to make notes, let toddlers explore melody bodily.

## Instrumental Activities for Preschoolers

By the time they enter preschool, children are able to handle instruments more carefully. They still like to explore and need plenty of sturdy instruments, such as those listed for infants and toddlers, but they can also be trusted to handle a guitar or piano with supervision. Preschoolers will freely compose original melodies and songs if given the opportunity to use melodic instruments. A music center for preschoolers should include, if possible, a piano or electric keyboard with a range of several octaves.

**Instrument timbre match.**  Perform a melody on a familiar hidden instrument or play an audio recording and let them try to guess which instrument it is. Once they can do this regularly, try identifying the same instruments being played on recordings of music by famous composers or from other cultures.

**Match the note.**  Place two xylophones or chimes on opposite sides of a screen. Have one child play a note and see whether another child can play the same note back. As children grow in skill, challenge them to match two or more notes up to an entire line of a familiar melody.

**Name the note.**  This is the age when it is important for children to hear the names of the notes in association with playing the note. Provide many opportunities for children to say aloud or sing the note names such as when playing the xylophone, hand bells, or keyboard. For example, instead of saying the words to "Baa Baa Black Sheep" as they tap it out on the chimes sing the note names with the child. Label the notes on other tonal instruments too.

**Melodic music center.**  Preschoolers can explore more varied instruments at a music center. In the beginning they will bang and run the mallet up and down the keyboard. They may snap strings and blow on homemade kazoos without making a tune. With experience and teacher support, they will begin to tap individual keys on the keyboard or hit individual keys on the chimes. Melody begins when the child plays random notes while humming or singing a familiar song and develops as the child begins to raise and lower the pitch to correspond with the song until it matches. Or the child may invent a melody and then sing along with it.

## Instrumental Activities for Kindergarten

By the time they reach kindergarten, children have the hand–eye coordination to handle more complex

## Teacher Tip

### THE SUZUKI METHOD

Dr. Shin'ichi Suzuki believed that any preschool child could learn to play a musical instrument, usually the violin, but others as well, if the right environment was created. This environment consists of the following:

1. Beginning formal lessons between the age of three and five.

2. Teachers who are well trained in the method.

3. Learning by ear before learning to read music and all pieces memorized and reviewed regularly.

4. Playing the same piece together in a group.

5. Frequent public performance so children become accustomed to it.

6. The expectation that parents will attend lessons and supervise daily practice.

The Suzuki method has had much success in getting young children started on instruments, but it has also been criticized for requiring too much formal practice for such young children (Bradley, 2005).

## Teacher Tip

**READING MUSIC**

Introduce older preschoolers, kindergarteners, and primary students to the staff and the names of the notes. The spaces are F, A, C, and E, easily remembered as "face." The lines are E, G, B, D, and F, for which there are several different mnemonic phrases, including "Every Good Boy Deserves Fudge." Once these are known, the whole keyboard makes sense because the white keys go from A to G and then repeat in the same pattern.

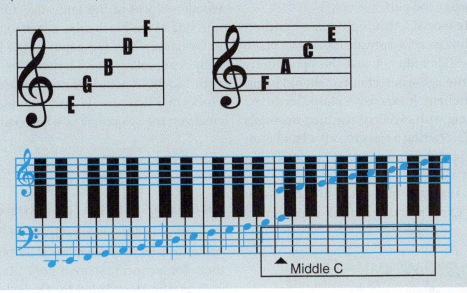

instruments, and can identify many instruments by sound. They can add harmonies to songs they improvise and, if given the opportunity, can start to read music.

**Guess the instrument.** Share a variety of instruments and hang up posters or photos of them. Play notes on the instruments so the children learn how each one sounds. When the children are familiar with them, hide the instrument and play it or play a recording and see whether children can identify it.

**Name that tune.** Make a list of songs children know. Play one of these familiar melodies on a keyboard, piano, xylophone, or guitar. See whether the children can select the song from the list. Vary the game by playing the tune on less familiar instruments, such as a thumb piano.

**Playing with notes.** Make large different-colored notes and a large staff labeled with the letter names of the notes. Put Velcro on the back of the notes and laminate the staff. Hang it in the music center so the children can explore composing a melody and then playing it on a xylophone labeled with the names of the notes. If the xylophone has color

keys and note labels, make sure the notes you make match in color as well.

## Instrumental Activities for Primary Age

Primary-age students can identify familiar instruments by timbre. They can start to understand how instruments work. With instruction they are capable of reading music and playing the piano and violin on their own and in organized groups. Hand bells and recorders can also provide opportunities for group musical experiences. Although formal instruction on the larger string instruments—viola, cello, and bass—and the wind instruments does not usually begin until the end of the primary years, younger children will benefit from many opportunities to explore the basic instruments.

**Make string instruments.** Create a finger harp by wrapping rubber bands around a very sturdy piece of cardboard or wood. Make a guitar by cutting a hole in the top of a sturdy box and wrapping rubber bands around it. Explore how the sound box changes the dynamics of the rubber bands. Explore what happens with different thicknesses and sizes of rubber bands, and different sizes and types of boxes.

**Make wind instruments.** Make simple flutes from marker tops and straws. Blow across the top to create a sound. Select several different types and tape them together in a row from shortest to longest to make panpipes. Plastic water and soda bottles of different sizes can also be used to create different tones. Add water to change the pitch.

**Recorder lessons.** Although some children have families who can afford private lessons on piano or violin, many children do not have this opportunity and yet, this is the age when children should begin to learn an instrument. Inexpensive plastic recorders are available along with excellent teaching materials (see Appendix C). Starting a class recorder band is an excellent way to introduce primary children to playing an instrument in a group.

**Pentatonic scales.** The pentatonic scale only has five notes. On a piano the black keys form a

Ask families if there are any members who play an instrument. An older sister who plays the clarinet makes an ideal role model to inspire young musicians.

pentatonic scale. On a xylophone it is the first, second, third, fifth, and sixth notes. This set of notes always sounds harmonious together and is the basis of many traditional songs, such as *Mary Had a Little Lamb*. Have the children compose melodies using only these notes.

**Improvisation note blocks.** Make a set of music note blocks. You will need eight or more wooden blocks of the same size. On paper that fits one side of the block draw a staff with a note and its letter name. Glue the paper to the block and cover with clear sealing tape. Or draw directly on the block with indelible pen. Have the children arrange the blocks in different ways and then play the tune they create on the xylophone or a keyboard.

For more activities using instruments, see *Activities with Tonal Instruments* on CourseMate.

## Reading about Instruments

To expand children's knowledge of instruments beyond the ones they see in the classroom or to prepare them for a concert share a book about instruments such as Ann Hayes' *Meet the Orchestra* (1995) or *M is for Music* (Krull, 2003).

For an annotated list of books about musical instruments, see *Books about Musical Instruments* on CourseMate.

## Reading and Writing Music

By preschool children are ready to start using written symbols to represent music. They become aware of notes and start to draw lines or dots in one-to-one correspondence to a musical piece (Gromko, 2003). To introduce reading music, give the children paper and crayons and then play a short simple melody. Challenge them to draw the melody on their papers. When they are done, compare the different symbols they invented. Tell them that all of these are great ideas. Then show them sheet music and explain that most composers use the same symbols so that other people can read and play the music.

After this experience, follow up with playful ways to interact with the **notation** of melody such as note card matching games or note reading software on the computer. Be sure to put paper and drawing materials at the listening center so they can write down the music they hear using their own symbols, and in the music exploration center so the children can notate their original melodies.

For kindergarten and primary students, more formal instruction in composition can be started. Introduce them first to the vocabulary. Staff notation in which notes are indicated on a five-line staff is the most common system used today in writing music. The five parallel lines on which music notes are written is called the **staff.** The plural of staff is staves. A scale is a set of notes ordered by pitch.

*For more about teaching children to read and write music, see* Steps to Music Literacy *on CourseMate.*

## Talking about Musical Instruments

Set the stage by providing many different experiences with instruments. For those instruments that the children cannot experience directly, try to provide opportunities for them to hear and see the instruments played. Sometimes older brothers or sisters, parents or local high school students will volunteer to come visit and demonstrate how the instrument is played. Contact the local high school band and orchestra teachers and arrange regular visits. Remind performers to play a very short piece and to share how the instrument is played with the children. If possible, see whether the children can touch the instrument or try it out under supervision. Do not allow the children to blow into a wind instrument, however, for sanitary reasons. Try to find local people who play unusual instruments or create digital music to come share as well.

Open-ended questions to ask about musical instruments.

- How does it sound?

- How does it sound different from _____? (Name another instrument)

- What other instrument(s) is it similar to?

- Does the instrument make a happy (sad, angry, sleepy, tired, etc.) sound?

- How does the sound of the instrument make you feel?

## Making Plans

### CENTER ACTIVITY: COMPOSING A MELODY

| | |
|---|---|
| WHO? | **Group composition age(s):** Preschool, kindergarten, or primary |
| | **Group size:** Four at the center |
| WHEN? | **Time frame:** 10 to 20 minutes |
| WHY? | **Objectives:** Children will develop |

- physically, by using their fine and gross motor control to play the instrument. I will know this is happening when I see the children holding the instruments and using them successfully to create tones. (Bodily-Kinesthetic)

- socially, by sharing ideas with others. I will hear this happening when they work together to make a melody. (Interpersonal)

- emotionally, by developing confidence in their ability to make music. I will see this happening when they smile and share their melodies (Intrapersonal)

- auditory perception skills, by listening for repeated melodic patterns. I will hear this happening when they repeat a pattern back to me and when they tell me they have repeated a pattern in their melody (Musical)

- language skills, by putting words to their melodies. I will hear this happening when they sing their melodies (Linguistic)

- cognitively, by comparing different melodies and making decisions about their own melody. I will see this happening when they listen to each other's melodies and devise a symbol system and record their own music. (Logical-Mathematical)

- music skill and knowledge, by improvising and performing an original melody. I will know this is happening when I see their finished composition and hear them play.

*(continued)*

## Making Plans (continued)

| | | |
|---|---|---|
| WHERE? | **Set-Up:** | At the music center. This area is in a corner of the room. It is carpeted and has instruments displayed on low shelves. On the walls are posters of musical instruments. Children should be familiar with the rhythm instruments at this center. |
| WHAT? | **Materials:** | Child-size xylophone with colored keys labeled with their note names and soft rubber mallets on a low table. A child-friendly tape recorder is nearby. Crayons and paper. |
| HOW? | **Procedure:** | |

**Warm-Up:** Share the xylophone when the children are gathered on the rug. Tap out a short simple melody line of a familiar song like "Row, Row, Row Your Boat." Ask: Could you make up your own melody?

**What to Do:** Let the children explore the xylophone when they visit the music center. Visit the center regularly and demonstrate how to tap out a melody line while pointing out the key colors and names. Encourage the children to use crayons to write their melodies on paper in colored lines or dots labeled with the note names.

**What to Say:** Help the children listen closer. "Does your melody go up or down?" "How many notes do you hear in your friend's melody?" "Are those notes close or far apart? How do they sound different?" Encourage them to write down their melodies. "What color is the first note? What is its letter name?"

**Transition Out:** Collect the melodies the children write and staple them into a class music book. Keep the book in the center for all to use. Play some of the melodies at group time and have the children add words to them. Try joining some of the melodies together into a song.

| | |
|---|---|
| **ASSESSMENT OF LEARNING** | 1. Are the children able to create original melodies? |
| | 2. Are the children able to record the melody using symbols? |
| | 3. Can the children read their symbols and play their melodies? |

**For more sample music activity plans for all ages, see Open-Ended Music on CourseMate**

---

### Did You Get It?

**Which of the following is a tonal instrument that allows children to discover melody?**

a. drums

b. cymbals

c. keyboards

d. shakers

**Take the full quiz on CourseMate**

## The Singing Experience

Children sing spontaneously from as early as age two. They often make up little tunes based on simple, repetitive words while playing. Singing daily helps develop self-confidence, expands vocal range, and helps draw a group of children together into a cohesive group.

Many adults, however, may feel uneasy singing aloud. Nevertheless, all teachers can teach children to enjoy singing. Although we may not like how our voices sound, that does not mean we cannot sing with children. As is true in all arts activities, our level of enthusiasm is far more important than having a trained voice. Children will be more involved in their own participation and learning a new song than in criticizing their teacher's voice.

To develop your confidence, always practice a song first. If possible, learn the song from a fellow teacher or friend. If that is not possible, sing along with a recording. Many children's songs are now available on the Web. The National Institute of Health Sciences has an extensive collection of children's songs, lyrics, and MIDI files. Many of the songs suggested in this chapter can be found on their Web site at http://www.niehs.nih.gov/kids/home.htm. Songs from around the world with both English lyrics and the lyrics in their original languages, plus videos of the songs being sung can be found at http://www.mamalisa.com/.

## Selecting Songs

Choose songs that are short, easy to sing, have a steady beat, and lots of repetition. The pitches of the song should fall within their comfort range, which varies with age. Repetition of the whole song, rather than phrase-by-phrase teaching, seems to foster quicker acquisition of the song (Tarnowski & Leclerc, 1994). Body movements are effective in teaching songs, especially hand gestures indicating pitch and other characteristics of the music.

Children (and adults) usually learn the chorus of a song long before they know all the verses. For example, many people know the chorus to "Jingle Bells," but how many know more than one verse? Use the following guidelines when choosing a song to sing:

- **Infants**—Songs for infants are often very short with lots of repetition. Lullabies are soothing melodies with a slow beat. Teasing songs, such as "This Little Piggy Went to Market," allow adults to interact with the child physically through tickling, finger actions, and sound effects.

- **Toddlers**—Songs for toddlers should have a limited range. The majority of children will sing most comfortably from middle C to G. Middle C is the 24th white key from the left-hand side of the piano (see Teacher Tip: Reading Music). Nursery rhymes and folk songs are often in this range. To appeal to active toddlers, select songs that have interactive elements and movements that draw the child into the song and make it more memorable. Toddlers also love nonsense songs and songs that involve moving their bodies. Songs about feelings help them understand emotions better.

- **Preschool and kindergarten**—For preschoolers, look for songs that tell a story or have words strongly tied to the beat and melody. Many of these are traditional folk songs that have been passed down for generations. Preschoolers particularly like songs that are personal and relate to their everyday lives. Make up songs that feature their names, feelings, body parts, daily activities, and special occasions such as birthdays: Songs can also help them learn to count, spell, and learn other rote material (Wolfe & Hom, 1993; Wolfe & Stambaugh, 1993). Interactive elements and movement are still an important element

in songs for this age and help children remember the words better. Song games encourage children to practice singing and moving to the music.

- **Primary age**—As children get older their vocal range extends to as much as an **octave** above and below middle C. Songs for primary children should use this range because children will lose the high and low notes if they do not use them

## Teacher Tip

### ABSOLUTE PITCH

Absolute or perfect pitch is the ability to identify or sing a named note without reference to other notes. Those with this ability may be able to name all the notes in a chord and even identify the pitch of everyday sounds, such as a car horn. It is a cognitive process of memory that is much like identifying a color. It is believed that there is also a genetic component because children with autism, Well's syndrome, and savants have a much higher incidence of perfect pitch than people in general.

Some research has shown that absolute pitch is a combination of inborn ability and very early exposure to music during a critical period of development in which children between two and four are taught the names of musical tones (Chin, 2003). However, absolute pitch is not required to be a musician or composer. Although Mozart, Beethoven, and Liszt all had perfect pitch, Hayden, Ravel, and Wagner, for example, did not. Most trained musicians have relative pitch in which they can identify notes in comparison to others.

### IMPLICATIONS FOR TEACHERS

Early childhood programs put great emphasis on teaching color names, but almost none on learning the names of the notes. Between the ages of two and four, try to expose children not only to the sound of notes, but also their names. This is done most easily with a piano or keyboard, but any tonal instrument can be used. If you do not know the names of the notes, refer to the piano illustration in this chapter, or use a child's xylophone on which the notes are labeled. Sit the child on one's lap, play a note, and sing its name. Also, play each note in a selected chord, such as C E G, as you sing the letter names. Encourage the child to sing the names, too. Such early exposure may not necessarily result in perfect pitch, but will certainly help in developing relative pitch.

regularly. As children learn more about the world, they enjoy learning the story behind the song. Songs in foreign languages fascinate them. They also enjoy songs from their favorite movies and from radio (see Table 10-2).

**Chants.** **Chants** are words spoken in rhythm with no or limited change in pitch. Often they are half spoken and half sung in a rhythmic, repetitive way. Sometimes a chant is performed on just one note and sometimes on two or more notes. Nursery rhymes, such as "Jack and Jill," and traditional **finger plays** such as "Pat-a-Cake," are good examples of this. Jump-rope rhymes are traditional chants. Some familiar ones are "Miss Mary Mack," "My Name is Alice," "Lady, Lady," and "Touch the Ground." For more fingerplays and jump rope rhymes, see *Finger Plays and Jump Rope Rhymes* on CourseMate. In addition, numerous books and Web sites list jump-rope rhymes.

Chants provide a bridge between early language development and singing and, as such, are very appropriate for infants and toddlers. Because of their simplicity, these are often the first "songs" children sing. Young children will also make up their own chants as they play. Chants are easy to invent on the spot. To help develop a child's singing voice an adult can chant a request to a child and the child can chant it back.

**Invented songs.** Music naturally engages children in learning. In particular, there is a strong link between literacy development and singing. Shelly Ringgenberg (2003) found that children learn vocabulary words better through a song than through conventional storytelling. She suggests that teachers take the melody and rhythm from familiar songs, such as "Mary Had a Little Lamb" or "Twinkle Twinkle Little Star," and add new words based either on a story in a book or that use the concepts or vocabulary being taught.

This type of song is also known as a "story song," "zipper song," or "piggyback song," and many examples can be found in books and on the Web. However, it is just as easy to invent our own to fit the needs of our own children. In addition, allowing children to participate in making up songs based on old favorites is a powerful way to begin a creative music community. Children, if allowed to contribute to the writing of the song will take ownership and pride in the song (Hildebrandt, 1998). Ringgenberg points out some other advantages as well:

Children sing better when you sing with them than when singing along with a recording.

- The melody will be familiar, making it quicker and easier to learn the song.

- Because you choose the content, speed, and length, the song can be tailored to fit the needs of the moment.

- It saves time that would be spent searching for an existing song that might fit.

- No materials are needed except voices and creativity.

## Teaching a New Song

The best way to introduce a new song is spontaneously when it fits what is happening in the children's lives. Singing "Rain, Rain Go Away," for example, will be far more memorable when first heard on a day when rain has spoiled an outdoor playtime or event. Teach a lullaby when children are resting quietly. Introduce a silly song when they need cheering up. Tie songs into integrated units and projects. Sing songs to help chores get done faster.

Children learn a song first by hearing it, then by tagging on to an accented word or phrase, then by joining in on a repeated or patterned part like the chorus, and finally, they can sing it on their own (Wolf, 1994). There are many approaches to introducing a song. Using a combination of them is most effective, but remember, singing with children should always be fun and impromptu. Do not expect young children to learn all the words of a song. It is fine if they chime in on the chorus or on silly words or sounds, and let

## Teacher Tip

### SINGING WITH CHILDREN

Jan Wolf (1994) makes the following suggestions for singing successfully with children:

- Show expression on your face.
- Maintain eye contact with the children.
- Be enthusiastic.
- Signal when to begin, such as with a "Ready, go!"
- Really know the song. Practice it many times beforehand.
- Pictures and props will help the children (and you) remember the song better.
- Choose simple, repetitive songs that are easy to remember.

the teacher sing the verses. Do not expect or demand perfection. If the same song is practiced over and over, it will become boring or a chore to sing. If children become resistant to singing, or lack enthusiasm for a song, it is time to teach a new one.

Songs can be taught to one child, a small group, or a whole class depending on the age of the children and the situation. Children learn songs best from another person's singing rather than from a recording. This is because they are best at matching pitches in their own vocal range and you are free to match their pitch, whereas a recording is preset. Men may find that singing in falsetto may help children sing in better tune. Nevertheless, most young children only begin to sing in tune in the primary grades.

Here are some ways to introduce new songs:

**Whole song method.** Sing the song two or three times. Then sing it again and leave out a key word for the children to fill in or have the children join in the chorus or last line.

**Call and response.** Sing one line of the song and have the children sing it back to you.

**Say it first.** Sometimes it helps to say the words before or after singing the song to help the child understand the words better. We are all familiar with the child who thinks that "Oh say can you see" in the "Star Spangled Banner" is "Jose can you see?"

**Write it out.** For older children, write the words on large chart paper. For beginning readers use a combination of pictures and words. Point to the words as you sing the song.

**Clap the rhythm.** Particularly in songs with a strong beat, clapping or tapping the rhythm helps children feel where the words fit best.

**Act it out.** Many songs lend themselves to movement and dramatic performance. Adding movement helps children remember the words better, as do open-ended songs to which children can add their own words. For example, "Pop! Goes the Weasel" is easily acted out.

**Substitute meaningful words.** Making the song personal also makes it more memorable. The words can be varied by substituting a child's name, a familiar place, or a daily event. For example, instead of singing "Mary had a little lamb" sing "_____ (child's name) has a little _____ (substitute child's pet)."

**Tell the story.** Explain the song as a story, or for primary students, talk about the history of the song. For example, explain that the song "Yankee Doodle" was composed by British soldiers to make fun of the poorly dressed, uneducated Americans, who then adopted the song as their own.

**Make it familiar.** When introducing a new song, play it in the background for a while. This helps children feel more comfortable with it. However, children will not learn a song heard only in the background. There has to be active listening by the child. To learn a song, active involvement in the singing is needed.

**Add signs.** Sing the song accompanied by American Sign Language (ALS). The hand movements make the song easier to remember as well as introduce children to a way they can communicate with those who are deaf. Videos are available for learning how to sign familiar songs (see Appendix C).

## Singing Activities for Infants

Singing activities for infants should build on their developing verbalization skills.

**Sing along.** Accompany the child's movements and activities by humming and singing familiar songs.

**Match it.** Sing along with infant vocalizations. If the child says, "Ba ba" sing "ba ba" back.

**Move to it.** Move the young infant's arms and legs to match the words of the song. Mirror moves for older infants who can sit and crawl.

## Singing Activities for Toddlers

Toddlers are just beginning to sing. At this age children often make up little songs and melodies spontaneously. Nourish this inventiveness by being a responsive partner rather than a leader. Try to match what the child sings. Research shows this leads to a longer engagement in spontaneous song making and more inventiveness over time (Berger & Cooper, 2003; Tarnowski & Leclerc, 1995).

Singing activities for this age group should help them become familiar with the words and melodies of songs in a playful, risk-free atmosphere.

**Move.** Help active toddlers learn new songs by adding motions to accompany simple songs.

**Body awareness.** Foster body awareness by selecting songs that involve body parts such as "The Hokey Pokey" or the French Rhyme "Clic Clac Dans Les Maines (Clic Clap Clap Your Hands)."

**Repeat, repeat.** Choose songs that have repeated words, phrases, and rhymes. This helps toddlers' early literacy development as they hear phrasing and develop phonemic awareness. Try "Blue Bird Blue Bird,"

## Teacher Tip

### INVENTING A STORY SONG

Shelly Ringgenberg (2003) makes the following suggestions for creating an effective story song:

1. Make sure it is developmentally appropriate.
2. Use short, familiar melodies.
3. Choose a key that is comfortable for the children and you. If you are not sure, listen to the children sing and join in with them.
4. Keep it short and rhythmic to hold the children's attention and make it easier to learn.

**Sample story song.** To the tune of "Mary Had a Little Lamb"

*This is how we make an A,*

*Make an A; make an A.*

*This is how we make an A,*

*Up, Down, Across.*

(Note: On the last three words, act out making an A: Move fingers up and down to make the point of A. Then draw a finger across it.) Continue the song using other letters of the alphabet.

"Paw Paw Patch," or the chorus to "Pony Boy." Pause on repeated words and let the children fill in the words.

**Cooperate together.** Toddlers can begin to engage with others through musical interactions. They can each play an instrument and march in a parade. They can hold hands and circle while a short song is sung such as "Ring Around the Rosy."

**Sing it.** Instead of talking, sing to the child while involved in daily activities.

**Keep a steady beat.** The beat of a song is not the same as its rhythm. The rhythm is in the words and the accented syllable marks the beat. We can help toddlers to learn to hear a steady beat by playing songs and marking the beat.

## Singing Activities for Preschoolers

Preschoolers are ready to learn to sing songs on their own and in groups. Design activities that help them remember the words and melodies and that encourage them to create their own songs.

**Picture it.** Use props or a flannel board to dramatize a song. Make a simple flannel board by gluing felt to a thick piece of cardboard. Make your own figures or let the children draw their own ideas on tag board and attach felt to the back.

**Use puppets.** A puppet makes an ideal companion with whom to sing. Use the call-and-response method, with the puppet echoing the song line along with the children. Encourage the children to sing to puppet friends by keeping the puppets at the music center.

**Hands free.** Tape yourself singing a song you want the children to learn as you accompany yourself on an instrument. Play the tape as you teach the song. This will leave you free to add gestures and movements.

## Singing Activities for Kindergarteners

**Singing to learn.** Make letter, word, and number cards to accompany songs with repeated words, ABC, and number songs. Hold up the card at the appropriate time. Once the children are sure of the song let them hold up the cards.

**Singing games.** Play traditional and original singing games with the children. For kindergarten, keep the game simple, active, and noncompetitive. A good example is "The Farmer in the Dell." To play the game, sit or stand in a large circle. The child chosen to be the farmer walks around the circle and chooses the wife. The wife then chooses the animal named next and so on. The game ends when all children have been chosen. It is easy to change the subject of simple songs such as this and keep the game the same. Instead of a farmer, try a zookeeper, or a school bus driver. For example,

> *The keeper of the zoo*
> *The keeper of the zoo*
> *Heigh ho the derry oh*
> *The keeper of the zoo.*
> *Along comes a camel*
> *Along comes a camel*
> *Heigh ho the derry oh*
> *Along comes a camel.*

More singing games are found in Chapter 11.

## Singing Activities for Primary Age

Primary age children can sing much more accurately in a group setting. Singing activities for this age group can begin to introduce part singing as a way of developing the ability to create harmonies.

**Use cue cards.**  Chart the song using words and pictures, such as a rebus as a guide for more accurate group singing and to develop literacy. If singing a song in parts, have separate cards for each part.

**Taking a part.**  Introduce part singing by having some of the children chant a simple phrase while the others sing the melody. For example, for the song "Hickory Dickory Dock" have half the children sing the song and the others chant "tick tock." It helps if the two groups sit with a space separating them.

**Rounds.**  Start with very simple rounds based on the most familiar songs. "Row, Row, Row Your Boat" and "Frere Jacques" are commonly two of the first rounds children learn. Start with two groups and as children gain experience divide them into three and four groups.

For a list of songs to sing with children of all ages, see *Songs for Children* on CourseMate.

### Teacher Tip

#### THE KODÁLY METHOD

Zoltan Kodály (1882–1967) was a Hungarian composer and educator. Kodály believed that every person was a musical being and that singing was the foundation of music education because the voice is the one instrument everyone has. His approach to teaching music has been widely adopted, particularly in public schools. The Kodály approach is founded on the following:

- Music instruction for children should focus first on the folksongs of the child's culture, followed by the works of great composers.
- Music training should be active, using folk dances, singing games, and moving to music.
- The goal of music education is music literacy—the ability to look at written music and hear it in one's head.
- Pitch, intervals, and harmony are taught using hand signals based on the sofège syllables (*do re me fa so la ti do*) that visually show the relationship of the notes. Using hand signals helps make learning to sing a more concrete experience.
- Instruction starts with *sol* and then adds *me* and *la*.
- Visit the Organization of American Kodály Educators Web site for more information: http://www.oake.org/.

Adding movement to songs helps children learn the song faster.

## Reading about Singing

There are numerous books that use the words of familiar songs with attractive illustrations that can be shared with children of all ages. The song can be read in a normal voice and then sung if the children are familiar with the song. Many of these books come with CDs of the song.

Children can also be introduced to singing techniques through books like John Feierabend's *The Book of Pitch Exploration: Can You Sing This?* (2004). Other books tells stories about singing, such as *Opera Cat* (Weaver, 2002), *The Dog That Sang at the Opera* (Izen & West, 2004), or *When Marion Sang* (Ryan, 2002).

For a listing of these types of books, see *Books Based on Popular Songs* on CourseMate.

## Observing and Talking about Singing

Lay the groundwork for talking about singing by giving children plenty of opportunities to sing themselves in different ways and to experience the singing of others. Children may be familiar with popular singers and groups featured on television and radio. Introduce them to different types of performing groups, such as choirs, barbershop quartets, and *a cappella* groups. Videos of singing performances and other children singing can be found on the web. But don't neglect the experience of viewing real performances. Take children to performances by local singing groups and school groups or have groups visit the program. Ask families to come in and share songs.

Center questions on children's own experiences of singing.

♪ Can you clap or move to the beat?

♪ How do the voices sound?

♪ Can you sing along?

♪ What pitches do you hear? Can you sing that high? That low?

♪ How does the song make you feel?

♪ What is another way this song could be sung?

---

### Did You Get It?

Jenna is picking a song for her preschool class to sing as a group. Which of the following characteristics should she consider?

a. It should avoid repetition.

b. It should be long.

c. It should have a steady beat.

d. It should be a classical piece

Take the full quiz on CourseMate

---

## How Do We Share Children's Music with Families?

There are many ways to include families in the musical activities of children. Invite them to visit the classroom any time and join in singing and playing in the band. Send home recordings and videos of their child making music, and invite them to musical instrument workshops where they build instruments for their child to use. For example, parents could work together to make large bucket drums or PVC pipe thunder drums and pipe organs instruments.

For information on building these, see *Making Instruments for Children* on CourseMate.

---

### Did You Get It?

Jazlyn wants to include the families of her pre-schoolers in her music program. What is the best way for her to do this?

a. Invite them to come observe the class singing a special song.

b. Stage a musical production of Jack and the Beanstalk.

c. Invite them to come anytime and join the class rhythm band.

d. Send home a note telling them about the music program.

Take the full quiz on CourseMate

# Conclusion: Becoming Musical

The goal of music experiences for young children is to develop each child into a musical person. A musical person is not a just a consumer of music, nor a professional musician. A musical person is someone who is tuneful, beatful, and artful. A tuneful person carries the melodies of wonderful songs in their head. A beatful person feels the beat of music of all kinds and the natural rhythms of the world around them. An artful person responds to the expressiveness of all music with all their body and soul.

We owe it to the children we teach to give them the gift of music. Music education must start before the child is born and be intensive through the early years. To do this we need to become comfortable ourselves in the world of music. We do not need to be virtuosos. However, we do need to become enthusiastic and confident. Teachers must also be learners. It is never too late to learn to play an instrument or take voice lessons.

For additional information on teaching music to young children, see *Chapter 10 Online Resources* on CourseMate.

---

## Teaching In Action

### A Literacy-Based Integrated Music Activity

"What do you think is in this box?" I ask my class of prekindergarteners.

"A dog!" Billy yells out, forgetting to raise his hand.

"No way. It's too small." Amy says, her large eyes fixed on the box.

"Can I shake it?" Hughie, my little scientist, asks.

I hand him the box.

"Hmmm. Sounds like there's lots of small things inside."

The box passes around the circle of children. Each holds it to his or her ear and gives it a shake.

"They don't bang like metal."

"It's a soft sound."

"I think it's not so many—maybe three or four things."

"I'll give you a hint," I say, after everyone has a chance to listen. "Today we are going to read the story *My Crayons Talk* by Patricia Hubbard."

"It's a box of crayons," everyone says at once. "Open it, Miss Giradi. Open it, please!"

With great majesty I unwrap the box, and show them the nine crayons inside. I hold each one up and the children call out the colors: red, blue, green, yellow, brown, orange, black, pink, and purple.

I read the book to the children, holding up the appropriate crayon when its color is named.

"Now we will read it again in a different way." I open up the plastic container that holds our rhythm instruments. Chloe claps her hands. "Oh, we're going to make music."

"That's right. We're going to make the colors talk. Let's decide which instrument reminds us of each color."

"Yellow goes with the bell, because it's yellow too." Latasha says.

I hand the bell to Latasha.

"I think the drum goes with black, because they are both loud," Billy says.

As each child makes a suggestion, I hand the instrument to them.

"We are going to need some yackity clackers too," I say. I hand out the claves and castanets to the rest of the children.

Now we are going to read the book again. This time when we say a color, if you have the instrument we chose, make a loud sound. When we get to the yackity clakity parts, everyone will play together."

Highly motivated and intently focused each child listens for her or his cue to play as we bring the words in the book to life through the rhythms of the children.

# Reflection Page

## Discovering One's Musical Heritage

What factors have influenced how you feel about music?

1.  What are some family songs you learned as a child? Do they reflect any special ethnic or cultural influences?

    _____

    _____

    _____

2.  Were any members of your family involved in music? What did they do?

    _____

    _____

    _____

3.  Have you ever studied any instrument or had voice training?

    _____

    _____

    _____

4.  What are some of your favorite pieces of music? How often do you listen to them?

    _____

    _____

    _____

5.  What area of music would you like to learn more about?

    _____

    _____

    _____

# Reflection Page

## Selecting Appropriate Music Activities

Based on the information in this chapter, decide what would be the most appropriate age group (s) for each suggested music activity below and explain why.

1. Clap a rhythm and have the children echo it back to you.

   Age group: _____       Why? _____

2. Move a maraca around a child's head while shaking it.

   Age group: _____       Why? _____

3. Hide a familiar instrument behind a box. Challenge a child to guess which instrument it is.

   Age group: _____       Why? _____

4. Have the children write stories and then add rhythms and songs.

   Age group: _____       Why? _____

5. Have the children make up new words for a familiar song.

   Age group: _____       Why? _____

6. Play a musical work by Sebastian Bach while the child is relaxing.

   Age group: _____       Why? _____

7. Have the children invent their own way to write the melody of a song.

   Age group: _____       Why? _____

8. Sing songs in a limited range, such as nursery rhymes.

   Age group: _____       Why? _____

# Reflection Page

## Meeting Special Needs

How would you adjust these music activities to meet the special needs of each child?

| Child | Activity | Adjustments that might be made |
|-------|----------|-------------------------------|
| A child with a cochlear implant | Listening to music | |
| A child with some hearing loss | Playing rhythm instruments | |
| A child with total hearing loss | Having a musician visit the class | |
| A child with poor coordination | Playing a tonal instrument, such as the xylophone | |
| A child in a wheelchair | Playing rhythm instruments while marching around the room | |

# Reflection Page

## Supporting Music Education for Young Children

Why is it important to teach musical skills and concepts in early childhood? Write a letter to the families of an early childhood program, explaining why music activities are part of the curriculum. Justify your reasons using research cited in this chapter.

_____

_____

_____

_____

_____

_____

_____

_____

_____

_____

_____

_____

_____

_____

_____

_____

_____

_____

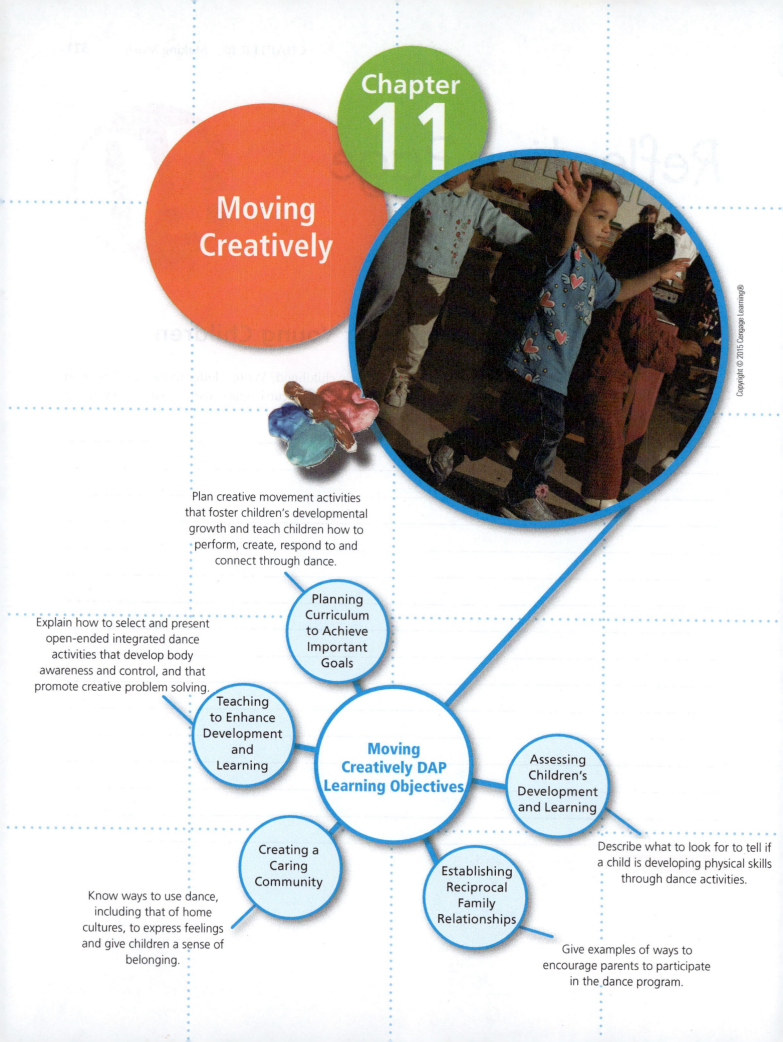

# Chapter 11

## Moving Creatively

Plan creative movement activities that foster children's developmental growth and teach children how to perform, create, respond to and connect through dance.

### Planning Curriculum to Achieve Important Goals

Explain how to select and present open-ended integrated dance activities that develop body awareness and control, and that promote creative problem solving.

### Teaching to Enhance Development and Learning

### Moving Creatively DAP Learning Objectives

### Assessing Children's Development and Learning

Describe what to look for to tell if a child is developing physical skills through dance activities.

### Creating a Caring Community

Know ways to use dance, including that of home cultures, to express feelings and give children a sense of belonging.

### Establishing Reciprocal Family Relationships

Give examples of ways to encourage parents to participate in the dance program.

## Young Artists Creating

"Let's move like the sea turtles we saw at the aquarium," the teacher sings out. Some of the children lie down on the floor. Others get down on hands and knees. A few remain standing.

Kyle pulls in his arms and legs. "I'm inside my shell sleeping," he says.

Franco moves his head forward and back. "I'm looking for a fish to eat," he says.

Maura glides around the room as she swings her arms outward in large circles. "I'm swimming to shore to lay eggs," she explains. "Who's coming with me?"

"I'll swim with you," Taketa replies.

"Look at all the different ways our turtles are moving," the teacher exclaims with a smile.

## What Is Creative Movement and Dance?

The ability to move is a function of three interacting bodily systems. First, our muscular and skeletal system provides support and a framework for action. This framework is guided by kinesthetic awareness—the system of sensors found in our muscles, joints, and tendons, which provides information on posture, equilibrium, and the effort required for a motion to occur. Both these systems are kept balanced by the vestibular sense located in the inner ear, which keeps track of the motion and position of the head relative to the rest of the body. All these parts work together to create the simple and complex actions that we perform unthinkingly each day of our lives.

Our capacity to move allows us to interact with the world and people around us. However, when these movements are organized into a work of bodily art we come to understand how marvelous our bodies are. Through carefully chosen creative movements, we can communicate feelings, tell stories, and become part of the music. We dance.

Creative movement and dance are inherently human and incredibly ancient. Paintings on pottery indicate that dance was as much a part of life in Neolithic times as it is today. Then as it is now, the creative movement of the body was tied to social and spiritual rituals. In the past these rituals were often related to everyday life and needs. The first dances probably imitated the movements of activities such as hunting, harvesting, and planting. Today we dance to feel part of a group, to make friends, and to release bodily tensions.

## Is It Creative Movement or Dance?

The art form based on moving our bodies has been called both *creative movement* and *dance*. Usually in early childhood education, the term *creative movement* is used to emphasize the open-ended nature of movement activities that are developmentally appropriate for young children. Dance, on the other hand, more often refers to formalized styles of movement in which children are taught specific ways to move and particular dance positions and steps, such as ballet or the polka.

In truth, both aspects of movement are essential in the education of young children. All children need the opportunity to use the creative process in discovering their own original ways to move and in using their bodies to communicate their emotions and ideas. However, as they grow they also need to learn how to control their bodies and match their movements to rhythms, music, and the movements of others by participating in simple dances from our own and other cultures. For this reason the term **creative dance** can be used to encompass both these aspects of the movement arts.

Creative movement activities draw children together and create relationships.

## The Core Processes of Creative Dance

The National Dance Educational Organization (NDEO) has identified four core processes integral to dance they call the inner core and which form the basis of the new Common Core Standards in the Arts for Dance (National Coalition for Core Arts Standards, 2013).

**Performing.** Although we usually think of performance as something done in front of an audience, in this definition performance is the actual physical movement that a dancer does. A dance performance can be done alone or with a group, and with or without an audience.

**Creating.** This is the invention of original movements by the dancer either through solving movement problems through improvisation or through choreographing movements to be performed alone or with others.

**Responding.** Responding is when we observe a dance performance and express our ideas about it. Reflections on a dance performance can take many forms ranging from talking and writing about it to creating a movement in response.

**Connecting.** Dance does not exist in a vacuum. It is an expression of ideas, viewpoints, and experiences. It is learned best when the physical, creative, and responsive processes are interconnected and taught together, and when creative dance is integrated into all areas of learning, culture, and life. Because dance develops the strength of and control over the body, it is also connected to healthful living.

## The Elements of Creative Dance

The elements of dance describe a body in motion and so are not separate but simultaneous actions. The National Dance Educational Organization depicts the elements as a concentric circle with the person dancing at the core. See Figure 11-1.

In the center is the dancing self. Each individual is uniquely gifted with personal expression. As we move we express ourselves using the elements of dance. The physical elements are how we move in space. These are time, space, and energy. They are what create individual differences in a dancer's style, form, and expressive meaning. See Table 11-1.

**Time**—We can move our bodies slowly or quickly using varying speeds and duration.

**Space**—Space refers to how we position our bodies in the space that surrounds us. Our bodies can occupy different levels and be open or closed.

**Energy**—This is the effort we use as we move our bodies through distances in that space. Our body can move in a relaxed way or under tension. We can attack and release.

The physical performance of dancing is created in a context of personal and cultural influences which influences the aesthetic quality and meaning of the movements. This context consists of the following:

**Body**—The body is the tool we use to create dances. It is our muscles, bones, tendons, reflexes, and breath. It is the medium through which our ideas and feelings are expressed. Each body is unique in size, shape, and muscular control. This

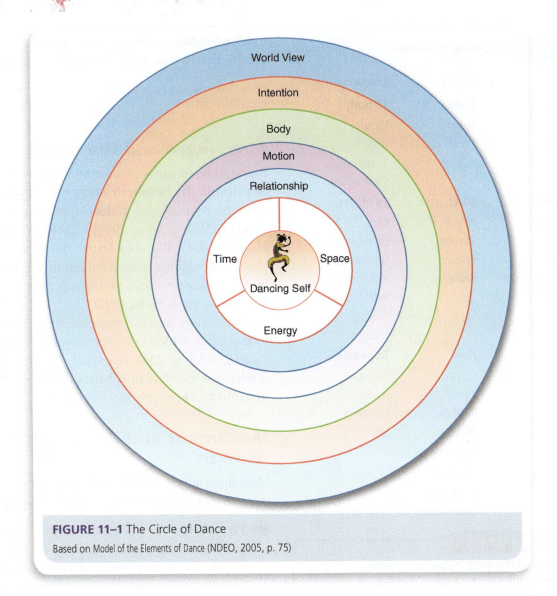

**FIGURE 11–1** The Circle of Dance
Based on Model of the Elements of Dance (NDEO, 2005, p. 75)

makes dance "the most personal of all the arts" (Walter, 1942).

🐾 **Motion**—We use our bodies as an expressive art medium when we move. Creative dance is made up of motions, which consist of streams and pauses in a sequence. Locomotion means the movement moves from one place to another as when we leap, hop, and run. Nonlocomotion refers to those moves we can do standing in one place such as bending, twisting, and swinging. Movements can go in any direction, any distance, and be balanced or unbalanced, large or small.

🐾 **Relationship**—This refers to the way that the dance elements, the body, and motion are combined with each other to communicate the dancer's meaning.

🐾 **Intention**—This is the dancer's or choreographer's purpose for the dance. The performance of the dance fulfills its intention.

🐾 **World view**—Both dancer and the viewer bring unique personal and cultural experiences to the performance which determine what the dance communicates and how that message is received.

| TABLE 11–1 | Describing Movement | |
|---|---|---|
| **Space** | **Effort** | **Connection** |
| **Place** | **Time** | **To body** |
| Size | Speed | Balanced |
| Distance | Duration | Unbalanced |
| | | Stretched |
| | | Compressed |
| **Direction** | **Force** | **To objects** |
| Forward/back | Attack | Close/far |
| Left/right | Tension | On top/underneath |
| Up/down | Release | Side-by-side |
| Clockwise/counter clockwise | Relax | Inside/outside |
| | | In front/behind |
| | | Around |
| | | Through |
| **Level** | **Flow** | **To people** |
| High | Open | Partnered |
| Middle | Closed | Leading |
| Low | Rhythmic | Following |
| | Accented | Solo |
| **Path** | **Distance** | |
| Straight | Near/far | |
| Bent | Short/long | |
| Curved | Wide/Narrow | |

### Did You Get It?

**What is the difference between creative movement and dance in early childhood curriculum?**

a. There is no difference.

b. Dance is only done by trained dancers.

c. Dance is more formal and has set steps and positions.

d. Creative movement is only for children under the age of five.

**Take the full quiz on CourseMate**

# How Does Creative Movement and Dance Help Children Grow?

Movement is basic to life. From birth children spend their waking moments in constant motion. The newborn waves arms and legs, the infant crawls, the toddler toddles, and the preschooler jumps, runs, and climbs. Even in the womb, the fetus swims and kicks.

For an overview of physical developmental milestones, see *Physical Milestones* on CourseMate.

## Movement and the Brain

Being able to move is essential for normal brain development. Research shows that young children use motion cues in developing concepts about objects (Mak & Vera, 1999; Newell, Wallraven, & Huber, 2004). We also know that children with physical disabilities must compensate for their limited motor abilities in order to develop normally (Bebko, Burke, Craven, & Sarlo, 1992).

In addition, physical movement increases oxygen to the brain, which enhances cognitive functioning (Sousa, 2001, p. 230). According to Jensen (2005), academic achievement is better in schools that offer frequent breaks for physical movement.

## Movement and Developmental Growth

Movement affects a child's total development. Through creative movement activities children develop

- **Physically**—By using the body to move with control in the performance of creative movement. Creative movement is a powerful form of exercise in which the body is strengthened and made fit. Introducing young children to creative dance teaches them a pleasurable way to stay fit and healthy. This is especially important because so many of us are prone to be inactive most of the time. A 2004 government survey found that 30 percent of Americans participated in no leisure-time activities and another 30 percent participated only minimally (National Center for Health Statistics, 2006). Moving through dance helps regulate weight, maintain glucose metabolism, and fosters heart health as well. Endorphins are released, which create a state of well-being. Dancing improves posture, balance, physical endurance, and flexibility.

- **Socially**—By learning how to move in concert with others. Creative movement group activities create social unity. Moving with others is an opportunity for children to experience the role of both leader and follower. Children learn how to communicate their ideas to others using only their bodies. Group dances instill collective discipline on the children and make cooperation physically visible as they focus on each other's roles in the performance and note each other's relative position in space to their own. Creative dance also provides the opportunity to learn about and experience culturally different ways of moving as children move creatively to music from other places and perform folk dances from other parts of the world.

🎵 **Cognitively**—By developing thinking and problem-solving skills. Sensorimotor learning has long been recognized as central to early cognitive development in young children (Piaget, 1959). More recently, the powerful relationship between movement and thinking has been supported by the evidence presented by Howard Gardner (1993) for a separate bodily-kinesthetic intelligence. Jay Seitz (2000) outlines two components of bodily thinking that support the deep connection between mind and body. First is the ability of the brain to order movement through motor logic. **Kinesthetic thinking** integrates cognitive, sensory, and emotional experiences, and then responds with the best physical action. Second is **kinesthetic memory,** also known as motor memory, which allows us to remember how to move in specific ways, such as dancing a waltz, by reconstructing the effort, position, and action needed to be successful, even if one has not waltzed in years. In addition, the close relationship between mind and body is shown in the ability to mentally rehearse a physical action through **mental imagery** so that without actual practice one can improve that physical skill.

Open-ended creative movement activities also provide the opportunity for children to use problem-solving skills as they match the movement of their body to the physical challenges being asked of them. For example, if children are asked to move as if they were a cloud, they must first think what a cloud is and how it moves and then decide how they might make their body imitate that movement. Next, they must actually perform

that movement, and follow up immediately with self-assessment to see if they have accomplished their initial goal, and then make any needed correction. Because dance extends over time, this self-correcting feedback between mind and body can continue throughout a dance sequence in a way not always possible in music or fine art.

Spatial and mathematical concepts require children to be aware of their orientation to the environment and how objects behave in space. They need to have a physical understanding of distance, force, and time in order to figure out how objects around them move. This knowledge is obtained by physical investigation and body memory. Dance provides many opportunities for children to move in, around, under, and above the things in their environment cementing these important words in place.

🎵 **Language skills**—By using their bodies to communicate ideas and by a developing vocabulary related to mathematical and spatial concepts. Movement is an essential part of language and communication. Studies show that hand control and speech develop from the same neural systems as evidenced by the fact that gesture precedes speech in infants, and even toddlers will ignore a vocal command if it conflicts with a physical gesture (Seitz, 1989, p. 31). Gesture remains an important form of communication into adulthood. Creative movement activities provide an opportunity for children to explore gesture and body position as a way to express feelings and communicate ideas.

🎵 **Emotionally**—By improving self-confidence and allowing self-expression. Being in control of one's body and feeling fit are essential components of positive mental health. In adults physical fitness has been strongly linked with lower incidences of depression and reduced stress (Fox, 1999). Children who are overweight, clumsy, or uncoordinated are at a disadvantage in most sports activities. Creative dance, which welcomes all bodily responses, provides a safe, pleasurable way for all children, regardless of ability or fitness, to release inner emotions and feel successful.

 **Dance concepts and skills**—By meeting the National Core Dance Standards.

## Connecting: Understand dance in relation to personal identity, values, and beliefs.

 **Prekindergarten.** Recognize a feeling in a dance. Identify an important movement in a dance done at home.

 **Kindergarten.** When watching or performing a dance, describe a feeling. Explain the importance of something observed.

 **First Grade.** Examine feelings and new perspectives evoked by observing, creating, or performing dance.

 **Second Grade.** Express or portray a personal experience and identify expressive movements. Describe or perform personally meaningful movements in a dance from one's own culture and explain how the movement is personally meaningful.

## Creating: Imagine and generate movement using a variety of strategies

 **Prekindergarten.** Respond in movement to a variety of sensory stimuli with teacher guidance. Find a different way to do a basic movement.

 **Kindergarten.** Respond in movement to a variety of stimuli with teacher guidance. Find a different way to do a basic movement by changing at least one of the elements.

 **First Grade.** Explore and improvise movement ideas inspired by stimuli or observed dance in a teacher-guided experience. Explore basic movements by changing the elements.

 **Second Grade.** Explore and improvise movement ideas with awareness of space, time, and energy in a teacher-guided experience. Explore a teacher-directed movement problem and demonstrate a solution.

## Performing: Develop and learn safe movement skills, techniques, and artistry through body-mind connections and practices.

 **Prekindergarten.** Explore and identify whole-body locomotor and non-locomotor movements with teacher guidance. Dance safely using identified isolated body parts.

 **Kindergarten.** Explore and identify a range of same-side and cross-body movement possibilities while safely dancing locomotor and non-locomotor movements with teacher guidance.

 **First Grade.** Explore and identify a range of dance movement possibilities to coordinate body parts and demonstrate safe whole-body locomotor and non-locomotor movements in many directions with cues from the teacher.

 **Second Grade.** Explore and identify a range of dance movement patterns that coordinate body parts and demonstrate whole body organization in locomotor movements while safely moving through space using a variety of pathways and levels, and non-locomotor movement patterns.

## Responding: Perceive and understand artistic intent through sensory, personal, and cultural lenses.

 **Prekindergarten.** Identify a movement in a dance by repeating it. Identify a dance movement done by a family member and repeat it.

### Teacher Tip

#### IS IT CREATIVE MOVEMENT?

Creative movement activities allow children to be creative and make kinesthetic decisions. In selecting activities, ask the following questions:

1. Are the children free to move all parts of their bodies within safe limits?
2. Can the children make their own decisions about how to move?
3. Can the children express their own ideas?
4. Can they do it without tedious practice?
5. Are there a multitude of acceptable movements and few or no incorrect ones?

- **Kindergarten.** Find a movement that repeats in a dance. Describe observed or performed dance movements from one's own culture that repeat.

- **First Grade.** Find a movement that repeats in a dance to make a pattern. Describe observed or performed dance movements from one's own culture that create a style of movement.

- **Second Grade.** Find movements in a dance that develop a pattern. Describe movements in a dance from one's own culture that is different from another style of dancing.

---

**Did You Get It?**

Infants and children with limitations on their motor control are best taught first through _____.

a. exploration exercises

b. group movement sequences

c. many-to-one activities

d. one-on-one activities

**Take the full quiz on CourseMate**

---

## How Are Creative Movement Activities Designed?

Creative dance is concerned with the role of movement in artistic creation. Activities that support this differ from physical exercises and sports, which are also concerned with physical development. In creative movement activities children are asked to imitate and expand on everyday behaviors and actions using their bodies, sometimes with music and props, to create what Jay Seitz (1989) calls a "metaphorical twist" in which the body part is no longer itself but rather a representation of something else. For example, waves can be represented by gently undulating one's arms. Even formal dance has this aesthetic element to it. As the dancers move in choreographed motion, geometric and symbolic patterns are created.

Creative movement activities are best organized by the skill, attention, and experience level of the children.

## One-on-One Activities

Creative movement is by its very nature a social activity and most movement activities for young children are usually done in a group setting. However, infants and children with limitations on their motor control are best taught first in one-on-one and then pair situations where they can practice and develop the skills needed for successful participation in a larger group. For example, while being held in one's lap, an infant's arms might be gently moved to a lullaby. An older child might play a game of hand mirrors with an adult where they sit or stand opposite each other and place hands palm to palm, while they take turns being the leader and moving the hands in different ways.

## Exploration Exercises

Explorations are activities that allow children to explore the possibilities of how to move their bodies and to solve creative movement problems. These can be done one-on-one or with small or large groups of children. In the beginning, these may form the entire movement experience. Later on, they can be used as warm-up exercises for more complex movement experiences.

## Group Movement Sequences

The richest creative movement experiences are those in which a whole group participates. Depending on the age of the children, these can range from having the whole group responding to the same open-ended prompts to elaborate story dances in which individuals and small groups play different roles. Movement sequences, such as those in Table 11-2, can be based on or include traditional and formal dance forms familiar to the group and are best when improvised or choreographed by the children themselves.

## The Reflective Teacher's Role

Although children go through the same patterns of physical development, each child develops according to her or his unique timetable. For example, although most 4-year-olds can leap over an object 6 inches high, a child with physical delays or a child who has never done this before may have difficulty doing so. A child in a wheelchair will experience movement activities

| TABLE 11–2 | Creative Movement Starters |
|---|---|

*Here are some ideas to get the children moving. Ask them how would it feel to be a _____? How would it move?*

| | |
|---|---|
| Cloud blowing | Parachute collapsing |
| Balloon floating | Plane flying |
| Bird peeking | Popcorn popping |
| Cat washing itself | Puppet collapsing |
| Butterfly fluttering | Snake wriggling |
| Detective sneaking | Snowflake floating |
| Egg hatching | Spider creeping |
| Gelatin wiggling | Turtle lumbering |
| Helicopter hovering | Water dripping |
| Ice cube melting | Wind-up toy running down |
| Leaf falling | Worms burrowing |

differently from a child who has limited vision, but both will need to feel included in the activity.

In organizing creative movement activities, the teacher's role is to be a guide or a facilitator providing the framework, positive guidance, and cues that will inspire children to respond using their own creativity and imaginations in their own ways. Developmentally appropriate practice tells us we need to reflect on the needs, expectations, and physical abilities of each child and be prepared for wide variation in response before beginning.

Reflective questions to ask before beginning a creative movement activity include:

- How will each child be able to engage in this activity and will they want to?

- What can I do to prepare the environment so that every child feels less self-conscious and participates freely?

- What guidelines or limitations are needed so the activity is safe but not restrictive?

- What learning domains and skills can this activity address?

- What issues of family background, culture, or exposure to popular media might influence the children's participation and behavior?

- How is my background influencing the music and dance motions I am choosing?

## Creating a Space for Creative Movement

Movement activities require a carefully prepared environment in which children have plenty of space to move boldly and freely. This requires careful structuring of the environment and the creation of safety guidelines.

**Floor.** For very young children who are not yet walking steadily, a carpeted area provides the best surface for movement activities. Once children can walk securely, a bare floor, preferably wood, provides more stability. However, if the surface or undersurface is cement, some kind of cushioned layer or carpet is essential. Movement activities can also be performed outside on the grass in good weather.

Children's shoes should match the surface on which they are dancing. Bare or stocking feet are best for carpeted or carefully prepared grass areas, but be sure nonslip soles are worn on smooth-surfaced floors such as in a gym.

**Space requirements.** Depending on the ages and sizes of the children more or less space will be needed. A general rule is that the children should be able to spread out their arms in any direction and still be an arm's length away from anyone else, a wall, or object.

Adding props helps children accentuate their movements.

**Safety requirements.** Furniture and objects along the edges of the movement area should be closely checked for sharp edges. For example, metal shelving can cut a child who slides into it. The corner of a bookcase can injure a child's eye. It may be helpful to outline the edge of the area with tape or paint so children know where to stop or the edge of the carpet can be the stopping point.

**Creating cues.** As anyone who has worked with young children knows, having a whole group of them in motion at one time can be harrying. Before starting any creative movement activities, it is necessary to have in place easily recognized cues or rituals for starting, stopping, listening, and resting. These signals should be ones you can do easily while dancing yourself, such as a voice command, clapping, or a particular tap on a small drum or tambourine.

No matter the method of cueing, use it consistently and take sufficient time to practice it. One of the goals of initial movement instruction should be to have the children internalize the cues. Ruth Charney (1992) suggests the following steps in teaching children to respond quickly and efficiently to attention signals:

1. First, explain why a cue is needed. "Sometimes we will need to stop dancing and listen so that I can give you new directions."

2. Sound the cue and then model the expected behavior as you explain it.

3. Sound the cue and have individual children model the behavior for the group.

4. Now have several children model the behavior for the group.

5. Last, have the whole group respond to the cue.

6. Repeat as many times as necessary until the whole group performs the task in the expected way.

7. At the start of future activities, always review the cues and have the children practice them as part of a warm-up.

8. If at any time the children do not respond to the cue as expected, take time to practice the behavior again.

## Moving in Concert

Creative movement activities require both sharing space and moving in conjunction with others. Before beginning, set up simple, positively worded behavior rules that foster cooperative behavior and have children role-play what to do in situations such as bumping into another child. Keep the rules simple. It is generally recommended not to have more rules than the age of the child. A good rule for one-year-olds might be "Be safe." Then as children get older add, "Be a friend." "Be a listener." "Be a thinker."

### Teacher Tip

**LEARNING TO RELAX**

To move creatively with young children the teacher needs to feel relaxed and calm. Try these relaxation exercises to get ready to move:

1. Wear loose clothing and sit in a comfortable chair.
2. Inhale through your nose and exhale through your mouth.
3. Inhale slowly, counting to four. Imagine the air flowing to all parts of your body.
4. Exhale, imagining the tension flowing out.
5. Next, as you breathe in, tense one muscle group. As you breathe out, relax.
6. Repeat often.

### Did You Get It?

**Which is the best way to introduce movement activities to infants?**

a. Sit the infant in a high chair and move enthusiastically in front of them.

b. Sit the infant on your lap and move together to music.

c. Put the infant in the crib and play dance music.

d. Put three infants on a rug and play dance music.

**Take the full quiz on CourseMate**

# The Creative Movement Experience

Creative dance may be done with or without music. It is an open-ended approach to moving the body that asks children to solve a problem while making independent choices. It differs from formal dance because it allows many possible responses. At its simplest, it asks children to explore the elements of dance or parts of their body as they develop physical and mental control. Complex creative movement activities let children create a sequence of movements with a beginning, middle, and end that express an idea or feeling.

## Selecting Music for Creative Movement Activities

Movement activities are often accompanied by music. In selecting music, look first of all for pieces that make you feel like moving in different ways. The music should be mostly instrumental because lyrics can be distracting unless they relate directly to the movements being done. Symphonies can also be overpowering in their complexity. Short, carefully selected selections are often more effective. Solos and ensemble performances, for example, have a clear sound quality that makes moving to them easier. In addition, be sure to expose children to a range of musical styles, genres, and instruments from around the world because each evokes different emotions and ideas. For a list of suggestions for music to accompany creative movement, see *Music for Moving* on CourseMate.

## Using Silence and Body Percussion

Movement activities do not need to be accompanied only by music. Sometimes it is best to begin with silence so that children can focus on the cues, your guiding questions, and their own movements. Next, try adding body percussion—clapping and tapping various body parts—or vocalizations—catchy sound effects such as pop, bing, and swoosh. Rhythmic poetry can also be used.

## Adding Props

Props are anything held by the children while moving. Props take the focus off the child's own movements and allow the children to move more

Large group creative dance activities require an open space that allows children to move freely and safely.

Copyright © 2015 Cengage Learning®

freely and with more force. For this reason, they are particularly useful when working with children who are shy, self-conscious, or who have a physical disability. Props enlarge the child's movements and add fluidity. For example, although children can certainly imagine they are moving as if they were planting flowers, holding and manipulating long-stemmed artificial or real flowers will help the child better visualize the needed movements. Scarves and streamers entice children to imagine they are floating and flying as they move. For more suggestions for other props, see *Props for Moving* on CourseMate.

Props can also be used to literally tie a group together. Have young children hold on to a jump rope or scarf as they move. Hula hoops, boxes, carpet squares, and even bubble wrap can be placed on the floor to provide a spot for each child to move within. If using bubble wrap or carpet squares on a slippery floor, be sure to use double-sided tape to hold them in place.

## Planning Creative Movement Activities

Creative movement activities work best when presented in a flexible format that allows the activity to adjust and change in response to the movements of the children. There should be plenty of opportunity for children to provide input and be leaders as well. Depending on the ages, experiences, and physical abilities of the children, creative dance activities can take many forms.

**Assessing Proficiency.**  Creative movement activities should closely match children's physical development. Careful observation of a child's movements can provide important clues to the child's level of physical skill. Graham, Holt-Hale, and Parker (2001) have identified the following four levels:

- **Precontrol**—The same movement cannot be repeated in succession.

- **Control**—The same movement can be repeated somewhat consistently but cannot be combined with another movement or object.

- **Utilization**—The same movement can be repeated consistently and used in new situations and combinations.

- **Proficiency**—The movement is automatic and effortless and can be performed at the same time as other actions as well as modified to fit planned and unplanned situations.

## Open-Ended Creative Movement Activities for Infants

Creative movement is a natural way to interact with infants who are still mainly sensorimotor learners. In general, most infants who do not have a physical or environmental disability develop bodily control from the head down and the center out. In the beginning, the newborn is all head, following objects with the eyes and turning the head toward sounds and objects with arms and legs moving randomly. For infants, initial movement activities focus on moving the head and then the whole body, followed by large arm and leg movements. We can build on this ability by moving together with the child, rocking the child, or moving arms and legs in rhythmic patterns or to music.

By six months infants have gained control over arms and hands and are developing spatial awareness, reaching out for objects and grasping them. In the next six months they develop torso control, learning to sit, crawl, and stand. Older infants who are crawling, creeping, and pulling themselves upright are learning how to move their bodies in space. By holding them

## Special Needs

### • INCLUDING CHILDREN WITH SPECIAL NEEDS •

Susan Koff (2000) points out that the power of creative movement is that it allows all children a way to express themselves nonverbally. Creative movement activities are easily adaptable to meet special needs through **inclusive** practices.

*Physical limitations.*  For children with limited physical control or strength, alter the environment.

- Eliminate hazards, such as low objects that could trip children. Make sure there is room for wheelchairs and walkers to move in the same way as the rest of the children.
- Keep the environment consistent so that children come to know where furniture and objects are located.
- Reduce distances and heights that might be expected in the activity.
- Put low-pile or indoor/outdoor-type carpeting on the floor to cushion falls and prevent slippage.
- Use helpers, either peers or adults, to provide gentle support by holding a hand or shoulder or to push a child in a wheelchair.

*Spatial awareness.*  For children having trouble maintaining their position in an open space, try moving in circles or along the edge of an area rug. Make lines and shapes using tape or paint on the floor for children to follow.

*Visual disabilities.*  Have children hold on to a rope, ribbons, or scarves. If children have difficulty balancing their bodies, provide a bar or study table that they can hold onto as they move or alternatively, pair children up so that everyone, including the child with limited vision, has a buddy.

*Deafness.*  Children who are deaf can participate fully in creative movement activities with minimal changes. Naomi Benari (1995) notes that having in place large, clear visual signals for starting and stopping are essential. She suggests a raised arm or drumstick. Take extra time to be sure children who are deaf understand what each sign means. Play games such as "Follow the Leader" or "Eyes on Me" which require the children to keep their eyes on the teacher as they move. Benari advises using music with a low, loud beat such as Caribbean and African music. Children can also hold on to a piano or kettledrum while moving.

The organization DanceAbility International (http://www.danceability.com/) provides information and examples for integrating everyone into dance activities.

*For more suggestions for creating inclusive creative dance activities, see Inclusive Practices for Creative Dance on CourseMate*

**First counting.** To develop knowledge of body parts and introduce one-on-one correspondence ask the child to move a certain number of body parts in a specified way using voice cues, such as "Wave one hand" or "Shake two feet." With young infants, gently help them respond.

**Creeping and crawling.** Creeping and crawling are essential to cross-lateral development which activates the brain and is important for future learning success (Hannaford, 2005). Put on some music, get down on the floor, and creep and crawl with the infant.

## Open-Ended Creative Movement Activities for Toddlers

Energetic toddlers are always moving, walking forward and backward with the characteristic toddling gait that gives this age group its common identifier. As they develop confidence they discover they can jump and climb, but they may still have trouble balancing and coming to a stop after running or jumping. With their increasing independence of movement, toddlers may invent motions to go with music. They are also primed to imitate dances and moves they see being done by others. While holding hands, they can be led in simple group creative movements.

Tap into that energy with movement activities that let them jump and wiggle as they develop their physical skills.

**Beginning balance.** Develop balancing skills by placing a rope or strip of tape on the floor and have the children imagine it is a "tightrope" to walk across or jump over.

**Beanbags.** To develop balance and body awareness, have children try moving in different ways with a soft beanbag on the head, arm, shoulder, foot, and so on. Stay relaxed; part of the fun is having it fall off again and again.

**Partner up.** Hold the child's hands and have child put their feet on top of yours. Then move together in different ways. Try sliding, hopping, and wiggling to music with a beat.

**Play pretend.** Together, pretend to be some familiar thing that moves in interesting ways and invent movements to express it. For example, pretend to be birds flying, balls bouncing, and flowers growing. Remember that toddlers have very short attention spans so keep the directions to a sentence or

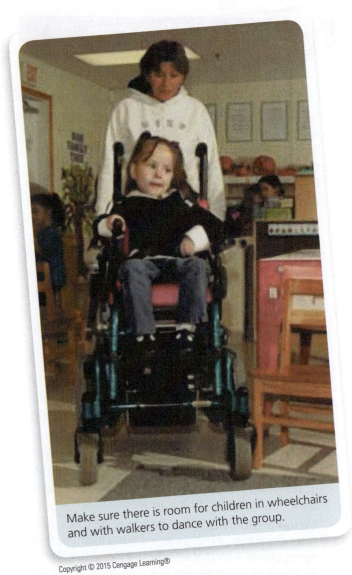

Make sure there is room for children in wheelchairs and with walkers to dance with the group.

with feet barely on the floor and moving to music or hugging them to our bodies and swirling to a song, children can begin their first partner dancing. On their own, they may bounce to musical rhythms while sitting or hanging on the railing of crib or playpen.

Try some of these basic movement activities as a way to engage infants in the wonder of dance.

**Monkey see.** To develop body awareness, make a movement and encourage the child to imitate you. If the child does not respond, imitate the motions the child is making. Say the name of the body part that is moving. This can be done with or without music in the background.

**Rock together.** To develop a sense of time, hold the child and move together in rhythm to music of different kinds.

## Teacher Tip

### PLANNING CREATIVE MOVEMENT ACTIVITIES

| Component | Question to ask yourself |
|---|---|
| Exploration | How will you introduce the movements? |
| Free practice | What will the children do to practice? |
| Rhythmic accompaniment | What instruments, music, or body sounds will you add? |
| Movement control | What signals for start, stop, listen, and rest will you give? |
| Props | What can children use to emphasize or enrich the movement? |
| Extensions | What other themes or topics using these movements can you introduce? |

two delivered with enthusiasm and accompanying motions. For example, say: "Look at those birds flying up there. Let's fly like birds to the tree," as you flap your arms up and down.

*For more movement ideas for infants and toddlers, see Open-Ended Creative Movement for Infants and Toddlers on CourseMate.*

## Open-Ended Creative Movement Activities for Preschool and Kindergarten

With increasing control over their hands and feet and better balance, preschoolers can respond to suggestions that they move their arms, legs, or bodies in a particular way. They will continue to imitate the creative movements of others, but will also initiate original moves in a process of discovery and by recombining movements already mastered. Simple, safe props, such as small scarves and short ribbons, can be held and used to enhance the child's natural movements. With the increasing ability to pretend, children can move as if they were somebody or something else.

Physical growth is very rapid during this period. By kindergarten, children are beginning to have smooth control over their bodies. They can shift their weight from foot to foot, allowing them to skip and slide. They can coordinate their arms and legs and use their sense of balance to move on a balance beam and climb effectively. Following directions, they can move

in a series of patterns and can work together to learn repeated movements and simple folk dances. They can also use their new moves to invent dances of their own.

To introduce preschoolers and older children to creative dance movement activities, use guided explorations.

1. A guided exploration starts with an open-ended question. For example, it could start with pretending to be an animal. Say: How would it feel to be an animal? What animal would you be? How would it walk if it were tired? Hungry? Happy? Allow children to make their own decisions about how the movement should be expressed. Do not say, "Move like an elephant" which makes it sound like there is only one way elephants move. Instead, say, "How do you think an elephant would move?"

2. Then provide plenty of free practice time during which children work individually creating their movement. Take time to allow the children to share their movements by having them pair up and perform them for each other. This is quicker and less frightening than having each child perform before the whole group.

   (If it seems appropriate, consider adding a rhythmic accompaniment such as beating a drum or shaking a tambourine or related prop.)

3. Finally, if the children seem to be deeply involved, add some music that matches the movement.

4. Repeat similar guided movement explorations on a regular basis. For other suggestions for guided group movement explorations, see *Guided Creative Movement Explorations* on CourseMate.

Here are examples of guided creative dance activities to explore with preschoolers and kindergarteners.

**Body shapes.** To develop flexibility and imaginative movements while reinforcing geometric concepts, have the children try to make their bodies into different geometric shapes, such as a circle, a square, and a triangle. Have them start out working alone and then working with a partner. Once they are in position, have them hold still as you count together. Repeat this often and extend the count each time.

**I can be the alphabet.**  To reinforce the letters of the alphabet and to develop critical thinking and problem-solving skills, have the children lay flat on the floor. Call out a letter of the alphabet and have them try to make their bodies into its shape. For some letters, such as M and W, suggest they work in pairs.

**Balancing challenge.**  Continue to help children refine their sense of balance. Lay out a rope or piece of tape on the floor. Challenge the children to try to move in different ways while keeping one or both feet on the line, such as hopping, walking backwards, walking with eyes shut, and so on.

**Worms.**  After looking at worms, snakes, snails, or other wiggly creatures, have the children hold their hands at their sides and wiggle around on the floor. Teach children to control the energy of their bodies by exploring the forces of tension and release as they pull in and stretch out. Have the children think of other wiggly things they could be. Add rhythmic music to develop their sense of time as they explore this way of moving.

**Growing.**  Strengthen children's control over their movements by having them control the amount of energy they expend and the different levels at which they work. Have some children imagine they are seeds or baby animals curled up still, waiting to grow, and have the rest walk around pretending to water them or feed them. Each time they get nourished they should grow a tiny bit. Slowly tap a drum as they grow.

**Floating.**  Have each child stand in a hula hoop or designated spot and imagine how a feather, balloon, winged seed, leaf, or other floating, falling object would move. Focus on moving from level to level smoothly with control. After they have explored their ideas, add clapping, drum beats, music, or props for practicing.

**Tip tap.**  After the children have had time to explore the different levels with their bodies, have them practice moving from level to level by tapping a drum and calling out: up, middle, or down. Vary the speed of the taps, getting faster as they gain more control. Use the same method to practice other contrasting movements, such as turning left and right, forward and back, attacking and releasing, and so on.

**More than one way.**  To foster creative problem solving and critical thinking, challenge children to come up with two or more different movements in response to a creative movement starter, such as "How do you think a small boat might move in a storm on the ocean?" Wait until all the children have completed their movement and then say: "Now show me another way that little boat might move."

**Call and response.**  To refine children's vocabulary of dance, post the words to be practiced such as balance, level, path, and speed (see Table 11-1 for terms) on the wall or write them on cards. Have children take turns leading the group movements by giving verbal cues: "Change your level." "Balance on one foot." "Move in a curved path." "Move your arm fast." Have the performers repeat back the cue.

**Dance makes me feel.**  To develop skill in observing and responding to dancing have children watch a dance performance by their peers, family member(s), guest artists, or a children's performance. If a live performance is impossible, children can watch a video of children or adults dancing. Afterward have the children describe what movements the dancers made and how the performance made them feel. Their responses can be oral, drawn, or shown in a creative movement.

## Open-Ended Creative Movement Activities for Primary Age

Because creative movement is often neglected in the elementary school, children may need to start with simpler activities before trying the more complex ones suggested here. All the activities for preschool and kindergarten can also be used with primary children.

Remember to establish cues and behavioral guidelines at the start. Once in place, using movement to enhance learning is very effective.

The following integrated activities show ways to connect creativity and kinesthetic memory to learning facts and concepts in different subject areas.

**On the Count (math).**  Reinforce counting or adding and subtracting skills by giving the children a number to count to or addition or subtraction problem and challenging them to count off that number or illustrate the problem using movements of their bodies. For example, given the number 10 a child might decide to stamp a foot 10 times or given the addition problem of 3 plus 4, the child might wave a hand 3 times and shake her or his head 4 times while counting up to 7.

**Cycles (science).**  After studying one of the natural cycles, such as the water cycle, the rock cycle, the movement of the sun and moon, or the life cycle, have students work in teams to create a sequence of movements that illustrate it. Children can add props and music to enhance their performance. Remember to ask them to point out how they use the different dance elements in their creative movements.

**Stories (reading).**  After reading a story, challenge the children to retell the story through creative dance movements using props and set to music of their choice.

**Systems (science or social studies).**  Have individual or groups of students read and learn about one part of a system being studied, such as the solar system, a bee hive, a transportation system, a machine, the rainforest, and so on. After learning about the specified part, the students should create a creative movement sequence to represent that part. When everyone is ready, call each part in a logical order. Have each add their unique movements until the whole system is up and running.

For more creative dance activities for preschool, kindergarten, and primary age, see *Creative Dance Activities for Preschool and Up* on CourseMate.

## Making Plans

**OPEN-ENDED RESPONSIVE ACTIVITY PLAN**
**UNDER THE SEA**

**WHO?**  **Group composition age(s):** Primary age: 1st or 2nd grade

**Group size:** Whole class, 20 to 25

**WHEN?**  **Time frame:** Three days, about an hour a day

**WHY?**  **Objectives:** Children will develop

- physically, by moving their bodies with varying force in rhythmic ways. (Bodily-Kinesthetic)
- socially, by combining their ideas to create a unified presentation. (Interpersonal)
- emotionally, by developing self-confidence in their ability to communicate through movement. (Intrapersonal)
- spatial awareness skills, by learning how to locate their bodies in relation to one another. (Spatial)
- auditory awareness skills, by listening and moving in concert with the music. (Musical)
- language skills, by describing their ideas and how they used the element of force. (Linguistic)
- cognitively, by designing a sequence of movements to express an idea. (Logical-Mathematical)
- movement skills and knowledge, by creating an original creative dance sequence using the element of force, which communicates an idea.

**WHERE?**  **Set-Up:** Large, open space in the classroom, outside, or in a gym

**WHAT?**  **Materials:** A small glass fishbowl with a goldfish, an overhead projector, a clear glass pan, chart paper, and markers.

**HOW?**  **Procedure:**

**WOW Warm-Up:** Set up a small fishbowl with a goldfish in it. Place it on the overhead projector. Have students observe the fish and describe how it moves. On chart paper write down their descriptions.

**What to Do:** *Day 1*—Following the fish observation, lead an open-ended guided movement activity: If you were a fish, how would you move? Before starting, review the start/stop/listen/rest signals. Have students stand in a large circle and remain in the circle as they move. After guiding them, play the musical selection *The Swan* from the *Carnival of Animals* by Camille Saint-Saëns as they swim around the room. After a few minutes, have the children sit on the rug and share how it felt to be a fish.

**What to Say:** Guiding questions: "How would you swim?" "How would you turn?" "How would you move if you were resting?" "How would you move if you were being chased by a predator?" "How would you eat your food?"

*(continued)*

## Making Plans (continued)

**What to Do:** *Day 2*—On chart paper, write the heading "Effort" and the words "attack," "tension," "release," and "relax" below it. Have different students act out these different words with their bodies. Put students in groups of three or four and pass out books about sea life. Have students choose a fish or sea creature from the book and then as a group work out how that creature might move. Challenge them to include all four of the effort words in their movement. Allow about 10 minutes for them to explore different ways to move. Then have the group come together on the rug and have each group share the movement they created. Point out examples of tension and release, attack and relaxation.

**What to Say:** "When would a fish be relaxed?" "How does your body feel when you attack or when it is under tension?" "Does it feel similar or different?" "Does it feel good to release the tension from your body?"

**What to Do:** *Day 3*—Set up the overhead projector and place the glass dish on top with a small amount of water in it. Project it on a screen or bare wall. If possible, darken the room. Stir the water to create ripples on the wall. Have the groups from the day before get together and perform their movement in the ripples. Signal stop and listen and then discuss how they could all move together in a beautiful, safe way to create a sea scene. Play *The Swan* again as the class dances in and out of the ripples. Videotape the performance.

**What to Say:** Point out examples of the different forces. Give lots of positive feedback.

**Transition Out:** Give the stop and listen signal and have the students gather together to watch the video of themselves.

**ASSESSMENT OF LEARNING**
1. Can the students incorporate the different forces into their movements?
2. Do they include everybody's ideas in their movements?
3. Do they move in rhythm to the music?

*For more examples of creative movement plans, see* Creative Dance Plans *on CourseMate.*

## Integrating the Arts

### MOVING TRANSITIONS

**Follow the leader.** Form a line behind the designated leader. As the group walks to their destination try to match steps and arm motions with the leader.

**Gathering on the rug.** Move in slow motion or, in contrast, imagine being rockets blasting off and landing on the rug.

**Leaving the rug.** Take tiny steps or giant steps to the next activity.

**Lining up.** Form a train with the teacher or child leader as the engine.

**Quiet moves.** Tiptoe from place to place or imagine being a quiet animal like a bunny or mouse.

**Rest time.** Move slower and slower until you come to a complete stop at the resting place.

### Did You Get It?

**Rylee, a four-year-old, has trouble repeating the same movements in succession during dancing games. Which of the following levels of proficiency is she exhibiting?**

a. Control

b. Precontrol

c. Utilization

d. Proficiency

**Take the full quiz on CourseMate**

## The Creative Dance Experience

Dancing is moving to music in a repeated pattern or using formal positions. Knowing the steps to a dance allows us to easily move in concert with other people. However, for young children, learning to dance should not be for the purpose of public performance or learning perfect steps, but rather to learn how to better control their bodies, and thereby find joy in moving to the music with others.

Formal dancing instruction is not appropriate for young children. However, children can be introduced to styles of dance and then be allowed to incorporate these styles as they move in their own ways to the music. Select dance forms that have a few repetitious movements that closely match the words or accompanying music, such as those found in children's play songs and folk dances. Choose works that allow individual creative movements and do not require rigid conformity to prescribed dance steps or matching one's steps to those of another. For example, a Greek circle dance allows more freedom of movement than does a square dance.

## Selecting Developmentally Appropriate Dances

Young children learn to dance much as they learn to sing a song. They begin by tagging on, repeating one or two of the main movements of the dance over and over. A child attempting to waltz may sway back and forth. Over time and with practice they will slowly add more parts to the dance until they have mastered the entire piece. Dances for the very young should consist of one to three basic movements that match the beat of the music and are open-ended enough that children can invent other ways for doing the dance for themselves. This turns what could be a lockstep performance into a creative arts activity.

A danceable song for young children has a strong beat with lots of repetition. In addition, some children's songs provide directions for how to move. An example of this type of song is "All Around the Kitchen" by Pete Seeger, in which the lyrics provide directions for the movements. There are many wonderful children's albums that feature danceable songs from around the world. For a list of some suggested songs, see *Music for Dancing* on CourseMate.

However, do not be afraid to invent ways of dancing to any favorite song or piece of music. Many songs have obvious places to insert a repeated motion. For example, Woody Guthrie's "Car Song" lends itself to driving motions. There should also be plenty of opportunity for children to make up their own dance moves to teach to others.

## Open-Ended Creative Dance Experiences for Infants

Dance experiences for infants should focus on the joy of moving together with a caring adult.

**Hug me.** Name a body part and hug it in a repeated pattern. Say: "I hug my leg, leg, leg. I hug my head, head, head" and so on. For very young infants, hug their body part for them. Older infants can hug themselves or their caregiver. Change the words to hug other parts of the body or use a different action such as tap, kiss, and so on.

**Bouncing.** Place the infant on one's lap. Put on a catchy tune and bounce the infant gently up and down to the music, providing any needed head and back support. An older child can sit face-to-face holding your hands. Move the child up and down to the music. Say "up" and "down" as you move together. Then explore other ways to move together to the tune.

**Dancing feet.** Play a danceable song and hold the infant upright so that the child can wiggle and kick his or her feet to the music.

## Dance Experiences for Toddlers

Toddlers with their newfound independence need open-ended dance experiences that let them join in as they wish.

**Buddy dance.** Have the toddler put his or her feet on your shoes as you move gently to a dance tune. Then let the toddler dance on his or her own.

**Shake a leg.** Put on a peppy instrumental piece of music and shake different body parts as you dance. Toddlers may have trouble moving each limb separately and keeping their balance. Make sure the floor is cushioned and all forms of movement are accepted.

**March.** Put on a John Phillip Sousa march and parade around the room. Add props and rhythm instruments.

## Open-Ended Creative Dance Experiences for Preschoolers and Kindergarteners

With their better physical control and more fluid movements, three- to five-year-olds are ready to learn simple repetitive dances that they can use as springboards to inventing their own dances.

open-ended dances before trying fancy footwork. Use creative movement activities as warm-ups. Remember that the goal is feeling part of a group, not public performance.

**Open-ended line dancing.** Have the children line up one behind the other. Then have the leader improvise a pattern of changing movements. Play a drum or put on a piece of music and have everybody follow his or her lead. Give everybody a turn at being a leader. Next, try an improvised dance in which everyone holds hands and moves around in a circle.

**Free waltzing.** Play a waltz and have the students invent a dance step that matches the one-two-three beat. Try other types of dances.

**Obstacle course dance.** Create an obstacle course in a large space such as a gym or a grassy lawn. Include large fabric tubes to crawl through, small

A sheet of bubble wrap adds sound effects to a child's movement while at the same time providing a designated spot in which to move.

**Slow motion.** To increase body control, take any dance the children are familiar with, such as "Head, Shoulders, Knees, and Toes," and do it in slow motion. Then do it as fast as you can.

**Chain dance.** Have the children join hands. Put on a tune with a regular beat. The leader starts the chain off by moving the free arm or leg in an interesting way as he or she leads the group around the room. The rest of the children then copy that movement. Have different children take turns being the leader, each of whom improvises a new dance movement.

## Open-Ended Creative Dance Experiences for Primary Age

Children who can perform a sequence of movements are ready to learn and remember more formal dances. Even so, start with dance games and

A rope or tape on the floor helps children control their movements and guides those with special needs.

trampolines, a balance beam, ramp, and so on. Put mats down anywhere children are likely to tumble. Have the children improvise a dance step to a selected piece of music. When they have practiced enough, challenge them to do the obstacle course while dancing to the music. When done, discuss how they had to change the movement to get through the course.

**Foot mat choreography.** After the children have invented a dance step, give them a large sheet of paper and, working with a partner, have them trace their feet in the various positions, and then number the steps taken in order. Give the mat to another student to try. Does the mat dance match the original dance step?

**Invent a dance.** Have children practice choreography by having them work in a group to compose a dance. Have them record the dance by writing down a number of steps and the direction to move in, such as two steps forward, three steps back, four steps to the left. Challenge them to have the dancers end up in the same place they started. Let them try out their dances to different types of music.

## Folk Dancing for Children

Folk dance refers to dances that are at least 100 years old and are not copyrighted. They are usually danced at informal gatherings and have as many versions as the people who dance them. In a folk dance, the dancers can stand in many formations: in a circle, a square, a spiral, a line, or two facing lines. Sometimes participants may dance in small groups of four, as paired partners, or as solo dancers. There may be a caller or leader who gives directions to the dancers such as in American square dancing.

Folk dancing teaches children how to move in a pattern while maintaining a constant rhythm. The predictability and rhythm of the movement and the accompanying song or music helps children learn the sequence of steps and practice counting.

The best way to introduce young children to this kind of dancing is to start with simple singing games in which the song cues the children how to move. Examples of these kinds of games include the well-known "Ring Around the Rosy" and "London Bridge Is Falling Down."

Follow this by introducing the concept of line dancing by having the students march to different dance tunes. When they seem comfortable with

Putting a CD player in the dress-up center encourages children to create their own dance moves.

the rhythm of a tune, have them form two lines and face each other when dancing. This naturally leads into circle dances. Finally, introduce four- and two-partner dances. For some developmentally appropriate dances for young children, see *Dances for Children* on CourseMate.

## The Dance Steps

When selecting folk dances, look for ones that use basic movements. If you wish to try a dance and the moves are too complicated, don't be afraid to simplify them or even invent your own steps to a song or type of music. Here are some basic steps found in many folk dances from which to build original dance combinations:

- *Slide*—In this move one foot moves away from the other and then the other foot moves over to join it. You can slide in any direction and for any number of steps. This is best taught by standing with your back to the children.

*Skip*—This move is very hard to describe in words. Basically, you take a step, hop with a rocking motion on the back foot, then bring that foot forward so you can hop on the other. The hop is shorter than the move and uneven in feel. Skipping is one of the last large motor skills children develop, so be accepting of all children's attempts. Holding a child's hand and slowly skipping with him or her as the motion is rhythmically described is one way to help children improve their skipping.

*Step-Hop*—Although similar to a skip, the step-hop is evenly balanced. The step and hop are equal in timing. Once children can skip, play an even one-two beat on a drum or clap until they can match the beats.

*Cross-Kick*—The foot is kicked out and across the body with the toe pointing outward at a slight angle to the body. Other kicks include back and front. This step requires children to be able to balance on one foot. It helps to have children hold hands or lock elbows in the beginning.

*Jumps*—Some dances involve jumping in place or forward or back on both feet. The "Bunny Hop" is an example of a dance built on jumps.

*Taps*—The dancer taps toe or heel on the floor to make a tapping sound. This is the basis of tap dancing in which shoe soles have metal plates to emphasize the sound.

## Dealing with Gender

Many traditional dances specify different roles and positions based on gender. However, there is no reason to follow these dictates. Instead of separating them into boys and girls, have children line up randomly or have them count off by twos.

## Process Not Performance

For children, moving creatively through dance is the process of learning how to control their bodies in space as well as a delightful way of expressing themselves. As they whirl about the room with their peers, they do not need to worry about how they appear to others. However, expecting them to perform these same movements in front of an audience instantly changes the focus from process to product.

Anyone who has ever attended a dance recital for young children knows that children and teachers become nervous and stressed in such situations. As an

### Across Cultures

**Language Learning and Dance**

Whether a child is an English language learner or a native English speaker, creative dance activities provide an ideal way to practice learning a new language. Many dance story and motion games tie repetition of words together with body movement. Research shows that we learn more when we are moving (Gardner, 1983; Dryden & Vos, 1997, Jensen, 2011).

To get started try the classic "Head, Shoulders, Knees and Toes." Mama Lisa's World (http://www.mamalisa.com/blog/head-shoulders-knees-and-toes-with-an-mp3-recording/) has versions of it in a multitude of languages. Other songs in different language versions can be found doing a search of the Internet.

alternative to staged performances for young children, consider having parents partner with their children, and together perform creative movement activities or learn simple dances in a workshop-type setting.

The best dance activities happen when we watch how children move and build on their ideas.

## Reading about Dancing

One of the best ways to increase the attention span and develop attentive listening when reading aloud to young children is to encourage them to move in concert with the story. Almost any children's book can have movements added to it effectively with a little forethought. If there is a rabbit in the story, you can cue the children to make wiggly bunny ears every time they hear the word "rabbit." If the book is about going on a car trip, cue them to drive the car by turning the steering wheel every time you turn a page. In Bill Martin's *Brown Bear, Brown Bear, What Do You See?* (1995), the children can shade their eyes and turn their heads every time they here the cue words "What do you see?"

There are also many children's books about moving, dancing, and dancers from around the world that can be shared with children. *Spicy Hot Colors: Colores Picantes* (Shaham, 2004) interweaves nine colors and four dance steps with a jazzy bilingual text. *Lion Dancer: Ernie Wan's Chinese New Year* (Waters, 1991) is a photographic essay about a boy preparing for Chinese New Year and his role in the traditional Lion Dance.

For an annotated list of books featuring dance, see *Books that Celebrate Dance* on CourseMate.

## Responding to Dance

All discussions about dancing should start with the body and its movements. Begin with naming the body parts and describing the different ways they can move. Have children describe their motions using their own descriptive language, as well as the vocabulary of the dance elements. Ask questions that make them think critically about their movement choices.

Why did you choose to move in that way ?

What is another way you might have shown that tempo or feeling ?

How could you extend that movement ?

Is there a way to combine these ways of moving ?

Provide opportunities for preschool through primary-age children to record their responses to dance

activities in their journals or at the art center using pictures and words. For example, have children draw pictures of themselves dancing. This is a useful way to assess how children see themselves as dancers. Do they draw themselves alone or with others? Do they show themselves doing active motions or standing still?

Children also need to watch others dancing, not only their peers, but people of all kinds from all cultures. It is easy to bring the world's dance to the classroom using video and the Internet. Dance has long been available through television shows and movies. Early movies featured sweeping dance numbers, such as those of Busby Berkeley, and famous dancers such as Bill Bojangles Robinson, Fred Astaire, Ginger Rogers, Gene

## Classroom Technology

### *DANCE AND THE USE OF MEDIA & TECHNOLOGY*

In recent years, live dance performances have featured a wide range of electronic media ranging from projected images to sensors attached to dancers' bodies that signal changes in lighting and background as they move.

Some ways to incorporate technology into children's creative dance activities include:

- To create a changing background, use a computer and digital whiteboard to project photographs onto the children as they dance. Photographs can be selected to go with an integrated unit or be selected by the children. Set up the photographs to run as an automatic slide show with accompanying music.

- To create the effect of dancing with a digital partner, videotape the children dancing and then project the video on a digital whiteboard while the children dance with themselves either mirroring the moves or moving in response.

- Use Wii technology such as Just Dance Kids, which lets children follow the moves of children dancing on the screen.

- Use an overhead projector to project an image or array of colors on dancing children. Use colored cellophane, overhead transparency shapes, and other translucent materials to create designs or for an underwater effect put a clear glass or plastic tray of water on the overhead and make ripples.

For some examples of digital dance performances, see *Online Resources* on CourseMate.

Kelly, and Shirley Temple. Video excerpts of these old time dancers can be found on the Internet. Today millions of people regularly watch dance-focused reality televisions shows, such as *Dancing with the Stars*, and tune in to watch ice dancing in the Winter Olympics. Classical ballet has been featured in adult movies such as *Mao's Last Dancer, Center Stage*, and *White Nights,* and is also available on the Internet. Feature cartoonslike the Disney classic *Fantasia* also incorporate dancing. For many this is their only exposure to dance being performed, and for children, this is often their first introduction to watching dance. Viewing dance through electronic media is not the same as attending a live performance. However, research has shown that people who are exposed to dance through media are also more likely to attend live performances (Capristo, 2012).

Expand on what children are exposed to on television and in movies by showing videos and DVDs of dances from other places that they are less likely to see at home. Videos of folk dances and classical ballet performed by both professionals and children can be found on the Internet. Show short excerpts that relate to creative movement activities and integrated units.

For a listing of recorded materials available on the Internet, see *Online Resources* on CourseMate.

When watching a dance with children on television, computer monitor, or digital whiteboard, use the opportunity to create a setting much like one at a live performance. Have children sit facing the screen either on the floor or in rows of chairs and review audience etiquette. Encourage the children to clap at appropriate moments as preparation for attendance at actual live performances.

After viewing a performance by their peers, on a video, or at a live performance, have children draw a picture of what they saw in which they imagine they were part of the performance and include themselves in the picture. Alternatively, they can dictate or write a story about what they saw in which they are the main character.

## Making Connections with Dance

Bring the dances of children's home cultures into the classroom by having families teach a favorite dance. Hold dance parties and festivals at which dances from many cultures are shared and enjoyed by families and the school community. Bring in dance groups from local

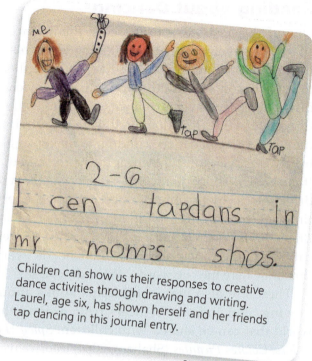

Children can show us their responses to creative dance activities through drawing and writing. Laurel, age six, has shown herself and her friends tap dancing in this journal entry.

Copyright © 2015 Cengage Learning®

dance schools and folk dancing groups to peform classic and folk dances. Provide opportunities for children to compare similarities and differences in the various dances they participate in and observe. Videography of the children dancing provides an excellent way to do this.

Primary children can research dance genres, famous classical ballets, and world culture dancing groups and traditions using the Internet or a teacher-prepared Web quest and then teach their peers about what they learned.

Connect dance to healthy living by emphasizing how dancing makes the body stronger and more flexible. Time how long children can hold a position, jump up and down, or measure how far they can stretch an arm or leg or touch the ground. Do a series of practice activities daily. Then retime and record the new time. Total the scores and make a class graph as a way to visually celebrate the class's improvement without singling out individuals.

## Conclusion: Let's Dance!

The power of creative movement and dance is immense in terms of developing children's ability to think spatially. Yet, it is often the one art form that is missing from young children's educational experience. If children do movement activities, it is usually in the form of simple dance games with little input from the children themselves. Although "Head, Shoulders, Knees, and Toes" and "Ring Around the Rosy" are perfectly fine, simple movement activities for young children, they are not all that creative movement education can be. Creative movement and dance must allow children to think with their bodies. The teacher of creative dance must be willing to improvise along with the children. The best dance activities happen when the teacher watches what the children are doing and builds on their ideas, adding props, music, and enthusiasm as needed.

Remember too that dance happens in a fleeting moment. Unless it is caught on video, there is no record of it happening. There is no artwork to hang on the wall or tune to hum. Today with digital photography and videos, there are more opportunities than ever to capture the imagination of children as they discover the potential of their bodies to communicate ideas and express feelings.

*For additional information on teaching creative dance to young children, see Chapter 11 Online Resources on CourseMate.*

## Teaching In Action

### Open-Ended Creative Movement in Action

**The Bridge:** After visiting a bridge or learning about bridges, have children stand in two lines about 3 feet apart. Play a slow, gentle piece of music and ask children to slowly reach across to the child opposite and join hands to make a bridge. They can make their bridge at any height. As the music plays they should sway with their bodies. Now, have the children go under the bridges one at a time to get to the other end where they form a new bridge with a partner.

**The Machine or Robot:** Have each child think of a machine-like movement and a sound to go with it. Establish a start and stop signal and then have them practice their movement. Now ask everyone to touch someone else to become part of a giant machine or robot.

**Dancing Dolls:** Put out a variety of materials, such as paper, wood, metal, cloth, stuffing. Have children feel these and study how they move. Ask: "Which are rigid?" "Which are flexible?" Have children choose one of the materials and imagine how they would sound and move if their bodies were made out of it. Have them explore their creative moves and then share with others. To extend the activity, have two different materials join together and move in a new way reflecting that combination.

**Dance Cards:** On large paper or poster board, draw different kinds of lines, swirls, spirals, dashes, and dots in different sizes, weights, and directions, as in these examples.

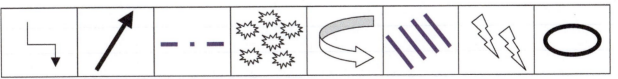

Hold up the cards and ask children to create a movement that relates to the image on the card. Repeat at different speeds and at different levels. Next, add music and move to the beat. For older children have them pair up and combine their two movements.

# Reflection Page

## The Elements of Dance

For each of the elements, give an example of an activity you could do with children that would reinforce the concept.

Movement

_____

_____

_____

Space

_____

_____

_____

Energy

_____

_____

_____

Time

_____

_____

_____

Body

_____

_____

_____

# Reflection Page

## Meeting Special Needs

Creative movement activities can be challenging for children with special needs. Adapt each of these activities to meet the needs of the child described.

| Child | Activity | Adjustments that might be made |
|---|---|---|
| A child who walks with crutches | Pretending to fly like birds | |
| A child who has limited vision | Crawling like worms | |
| A child with total hearing loss | Moving around the room and crossing a "river" made from tape on the floor | |
| A child with Down syndrome | Working with a partner mirroring each other's actions | |

# Reflection Page

## Selecting Appropriate Creative Movement and Dance Activities

Why are the following activities not appropriate for young children? Use what you know about children at different developmental ages to explain why they are not approriate.

1. Teaching toddlers to square dance.

   _____

   _____

   _____

2. Having preschoolers perform an elaborate ballet with many parts in front of their parents.

   _____

   _____

   _____

3. Presenting an activity to toddlers in which everyone has to move in exactly the same way, at the same time, over and over.

   _____

   _____

   _____

4. Putting on loud music and letting a group of preschoolers run all around the classroom.

   _____

   _____

   _____

# Reflection Page

## Observation: Children Moving Creatively

Observe a group of children involved in a creative movement or dance activity.

**Date of observation:** _____      **Length of observation:** _____

**Ages of children:** _____      **Group Size:** _____

1. Do the children have control over their movements as expected for their developmental age?

   _____

   _____

   _____

   _____

   _____

2. Which movements come easily for them? Which types of movements give them difficulty?

   _____

   _____

   _____

   _____

   _____

3. How do individual children express themselves through their movement choices?

   _____

   _____

   _____

   _____

   _____

4. How did the children participate in these dance activities? (Examples: tried once then left; engaged in nonverbal or verbal interaction with children and/or adults; worked alone; length of time at activity)

_____

_____

_____

_____

_____

5. What are the adults doing while the children dance?

_____

_____

_____

_____

6. How are dance activities made available to the children?

_____

_____

_____

_____

7. Suggest some other creative movement and dance activities that would be appropriate for this group of children.

_____

_____

_____

_____

_____

**Digital Download**   **Download from CourseMate**

## Chapter 12

# Nurturing the Imagination

Design and plan dramatic play activities that foster children's overall development as well as teach children the skills of the dramatic arts.

Explain ways to use open-ended dramatic activities to develop focus, self-regulation, creative problem-solving, literacy skills, and a sense of story.

Know ways to use dramatic play to help children express their feelings and develop social bonds with their playmates.

Describe how to use dramatic play to assess children's social-emotional, physical, cognitive, and language skill growth.

Give examples of ways to involve parents in children's dramatic play activities.

**Planning Curriculum to Achieve Important Goals**

**Teaching to Enhance Development and Learning**

**Nurturing the Imagination DAP Learning Objectives**

**Assessing Children's Development and Learning**

**Creating a Caring Community**

**Establishing Reciprocal Family Relationships**

## Young Artists Creating

"The puppet I'm making is going to be a spaceman."

"So's mine!"

"Let's pretend they are going to the moon."

"Okay, but what can we use for a rocket ship?"

"How about the tall drum?"

"That'll work. Hey, we can even drum on it to make it sound like the rocket is taking off!"

## What Are the Dramatic Arts?

Drama and theater are highly integrative art forms. Visual art, music, and creative movement can all be incorporated into dramatic performances whether they are elaborate movie productions or skits put on by children. In addition, problem solving, mental representation, communication skills, language usage, and storytelling play an essential role in the creation of a dramatic work. This means that the dramatic arts are a vital way to foster cognitive and literacy development in young children as well as offering a way to integrate learning across the disciplines.

For children, child-initiated play forms the basis of the dramatic arts curriculum. As they imitate the activities of the adults in their lives, they develop socially, emotionally, creatively, and intellectually.

Copyright © 2015 Cengage Learning®

## The Core Processes of the Dramatic Arts

The Common Core Standards in the Arts for Theater has identified the following core processes integral to dramatic or theater arts (National Coalition for Core Arts Standards, 2013).

- **Performing.** As in dance, performance in theater arts is defined as the actual physical participation in a dramatic experience. A dramatic performance can be done alone or with a group, and with or without an audience.

- **Creating.** This is the invention of an original dramatic performance either through interpretation and problem solving while acting out a role or through creating original dramatizations and stories to be performed alone or with others.

- **Responding.** Responding is observing a dramatic performance and expressing ideas about it. This can take many forms, ranging from talking and writing to creating a dramatic work in response.

- **Connecting.** Participation in dramatic performances provides a safe, playful space in which to connect personal experiences and to express emotions. It affords a way to test out ideas and work out problems, and it can be a healing force in therapy for emotional and mental trauma (Casson, J., 2004).

# What Are the Elements of the Dramatic Arts?

The elements of drama and dramatic play share much in common. First, to be successful as an actor a person must be able to imitate others. This requires proficiency in oral language and in controlling the body. The foundation for imitative behavior is established in early childhood as infants learn how to make themselves understood by parents, caregivers, and older children using gesture, words, and actions.

Second, actors also need to know how to use props, costumes, and settings as a way to enhance the meaning of their performance. Through play, the ten-month-old playing peek-a-boo with his father's hat, the toddler putting shoeboxes on her feet and pretending to skate, and the preschooler "cooking" a meal in the playhouse are all learning how to use parts of their environment for dramatic effect.

Third, theater productions are formed around an aesthetically organized and creative presentation of a message or story. The development of narrative skills is a key feature of children's dramatic play. The toddler pantomiming falling in a puddle, the preschooler playing with an imaginary friend, kindergarteners acting out the story of *Goldilocks and the Three Bears,* and second graders writing and producing their own playlets about life in the rainforest are learning the principles of story creation, structure, and self-expression.

## The Elements of Drama

The ability to use the elements of story and those of drama develop rapidly in the early childhood years. By the age of five most children are capable of creating and performing complex stories, often sustaining them over an extended time period (see Table 12-1).

The elements of drama are the underlying components that add texture and uniqueness thereby bringing stories to life. They include:

- **Focus**—Successful performance in the dramatic arts requires self-regulation and concentration. Actors show focus when they maintain the attributes of a character throughout a performance. Audiences show focus when they mentally and emotionally center their attention on the dramatization they are watching. Children show focus when they assume roles in their pretend play scenarios that may last over several days.

- **Tension and contrast**—Tension is the creation of suspense, conflict, or rising action which carries the play scenario or story towards a conclusion. Contrast is what keeps dramatizations from being boring by creating tension. We watch action movies to see the battle between good versus evil. We respond viscerally when a quiet parting scene is followed by a noisy chase scene through busy

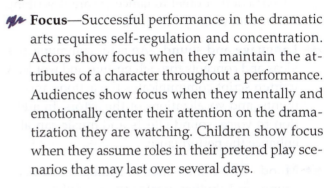

| TABLE 12–1 | Dramatic Elements in Children's Play |
|---|---|
| **Dramatic Element** | **Children's Natural Play** |
| Focus, timing, and rhythm | Watches, imitates, and repeats behaviors of the people around them. Takes on roles. Creates sequences of events with beginning, middle, and end. |
| Language and sound | Imitates vocalizations of people around them. |
| Rhythm and space | Imitates and invents movements in interaction with others. |
| Place and mood | Explores the characteristics of objects and how they are used to create a setting. |
| Symbol | Expresses ideas and feelings by inventing new uses for familiar objects. Creates pretend people, events, objects, and settings. |

**Digital Download**   Download from CourseMate

city streets. The artful combination of tension and contrast is the backbone of effective narrative.

🎵 **Timing**—Timing refers to the manipulation of movements and gestures so that they best match the needs of the dramatic action.

🎵 **Rhythm**—Rhythm is built from tension, contrast, and timing to create the rise and fall of action and emotion in a drama. When we talk about fast-paced action or quiet romance we are describing the rhythm of the production.

🎵 **Language and sound**—An actor communicates ideas and concepts through gesture and words. A written script communicates the actions, movements, and vocalizations of the actors. In addition to voice, sound effects and music can also enhance the performance.

🎵 **Mood**—The combination of setting, movement, sound, and rhythm creates the overall effect or mood. A darkened theater, the sound of drumming rain, and an actor whose head is drooping create one kind of mood. Dorothy dancing down the yellow brick road in the *Wizard of Oz* sets another.

🎵 **Place**—This is the setting in which the story or play takes place. It can be communicated through the arrangement of actual objects and props or created in the imagination through the creative actions and words of the performers.

🎵 **Space**—The area around the performers forms the dramatic space and includes the different levels as in dance.

---

### Did You Get It?

**Which of the following elements of drama is responsible for the creation of suspense, conflict, or rising action which carries the story towards a conclusion?**

a. timing

b. focus

c. tension

d. symbolization

**Take the full quiz on CourseMate**

---

🎵 **Symbol**—Symbolization, the use of one thing to stand for another, is a key element in the dramatic arts and in children's play.

## What Is the Relationship Between the Dramatic Arts and Children's Play?

Historically, theatrical drama has been used most often to entertain an audience. We are all familiar with the plays of Shakespeare and the movie productions of Walt Disney. Both of these are examples of the dramatic arts. However, as we will see, the role of the dramatic arts is very different in the lives of young children.

The presentation of a theatrical production to an audience is the most formal form of the dramatic arts. This level of performance is not developmentally appropriate for children under the age of eight (Edwards, 1993). Requiring children to memorize lines and follow a director are skills beyond the ability of most young children. Instead, dramatic activities need to be built around children's own creative play.

For young children, creative dramatics mirrors their natural form of play. Both play and the dramatic arts are centered on

1. **Using the imagination and solving problems.** Infants play with objects, discovering their properties and uses. Toddlers imitate what they see other people doing. By the age of two most children have entered the world of imaginative and symbolic play in which objects and actions can represent other things (Hyson, Copple, & Jones, 2006). A wooden spoon becomes a magic wand and an old shawl a king's robe. The ability to make-believe and create stories is the main characteristic of play in young children.

2. **Developing a positive identity through self-expression.** Before actors can pretend to be someone else, they must first know who they are and what makes the character they want to be different so they can imagine how that character would move, talk, and react to disaster. In pretend play, children do the same thing as they try on

new roles and see how they fit. In doing so they learn more about themselves and others.

3. **Bonding socially with others.** Through play, children learn about their world and how to interact with the people around them. Like actors on a set, group play requires communication skills and the willingness to both lead and follow others to create a play scenario. They learn to respond to the pretend behaviors, improvisation, and fluid rule-making of their peers as they match their behaviors to the needs of the group.

## The Power of Play

To understand children's ability to imagine and pretend we need to examine the research related to children's play. The basis of current understanding about children's play and the development of young children is the classic work of Jean Piaget (1962) and Lev Vygotsky (1976).

## Piaget's Levels of Play

Piaget believed that play provided children with the opportunity to practice and make sense of new concepts solidifying what they learned through repetition. Piaget identified three levels of play:

1. **Practice play,** in which infants and toddlers at the sensorimotor level of development explore and interact with objects and people using repeated actions, such as when an infant repeatedly knocks an object off the highchair tray.

2. **Symbolic play,** which happens when preschool-age children imitate things they have seen, heard, or experienced. This can be observed when they enact make-believe scenarios such as playing house, taking care of their doll babies, and serving dinner, just like they see their families do.

3. **Game-based play, which occurs during the concrete operational** stage, when children's increasing ability to think logically allows them to enjoy games with preset rules, such as board games and organized sports, and to re-enact the narrative sequence of events in a story or movie they have seen.

## Play and the Emergence of Abstract Thought

Vygotsky studied how children's play contributed to cognitive development. He thought that the object-focused play of infants at the sensorimotor or Piagetian practice level of play represented a stage of cognitive development in which the child was incapable of imaginative thought. The object and its meaning were so fused together in the child's mind that the child could not think of it without actually seeing it. He saw the emergence of the ability of children to make believe as the beginning of abstract thought. Vygotsky also believed that play promoted learning by providing children the opportunity to practice in a safe, accepting setting social behaviors they had not yet mastered. Later researchers have supported this idea. Jerome Bruner (1990, 1996) and Brian Sutton-Smith (1998) see play as the way children learn how to adapt and be flexible in meeting future challenges in their lives. Bruner has also posited that play helps children learn how to think in logical sequence as they create story narratives.

## Play and Flexible Thinking

According to Brian Sutton-Smith, the adaptability fostered through play prepares children to face an unpredictable future as adults. As children pretend, they move in and out of roles assuming different viewpoints. One minute they might be a puppy begging for a bone, and the next, they are the veterinarian coming to heal the puppy's hurt paw. They also have to adjust to other children playing roles different from their normal selves. This ability to fluidly switch roles, point of view, and think metacognitively about their own thinking in relation to others' is important for later school success where to be successful students have to understand and coordinate their own views with those of their teachers and classmates (Bodrova & Leong, 2004).

## Children's Play and the Brain

Current brain research tells us that a child engaged in open-ended play is developing vital brain connections. When children are active participants in play they perform complex movements such as matching their facial expression to a pretend emotion and make novel decisions, such as finding an object to symbolically represent another. This engagement develops the neural connections that form the foundation of future brain development. During play the neocortex or thinking center of the brain is activated as well as the amygdala or emotional center of the brain and the connection between the two centers are strengthened (Jensen, 2005; Johnson, Christie, & Wardle, 2005).

Engaging in play is fun. It reduces stress and facilitates learning. Stress has been shown to impair children's thinking (Jensen, 2005). As children play, the parts of the brain involved in creative thinking and problem solving are more engaged while their stress levels decrease. Children, for example, show fewer nervous habits such as nailbiting while engaged in active play (Johnson et al., 2005).

---

### Did You Get It?

**Jessica and her little brother, Mike, are sitting inside an old cardboard box, pretending to drive a car. Which level of Jean Piaget's levels of play does their behavior demonstrate?**

a. symbolic play

b. practice play

c. game-based play

d. parallel play

**Take the full quiz on CourseMate**

---

## How Do Children Grow Through the Dramatic Play?

Children at play are active, intrinsically motivated, and integrating everything they know into a new creative form. In the act of playing children develop longer attention spans and pursue interests more deeply. They develop creatively, socially, emotionally, and cognitively. Most importantly, they are having fun. Because dramatization calls on so many different abilities dramatic performance is a composite of social-emotional, physical, cognitive, and linguistic skills (see Table 12-2). Because of this the dramatic arts are an ideal way to develop skills in all these areas.

Through dramatic arts activities children develop

- **Physically**—By moving the body to characterize the movements of real and fantasy people,

behaviors, and objects. We see this when children pretend they are driving a car or flying like Superman. The skills and concepts of creative dance are also closely connected to dramatization.

- **Socially**—By learning to make connections to others through facial and bodily behaviors, by trying out new roles, assuming viewpoints other than their own, and cooperating with others to create meaning and narrative. Dramatic play allows children to connect to their own culture and to imagine that of others. We see this when a group of children, after learning about Mexico, pretends they are going to the store to buy tortillas.

- **Cognitively**—By developing the ability to think logically in narrative sequences. Play lets children create and use symbolic thinking as they use one object or action to represent another. It is powerful because it allows children to repeat and analyze their behaviors. For example, a group of children, playing with puppets, may repeat their story several times, each time trying different ways for the puppets to act.

- **Language skills**—By using language to communicate ideas and feelings, and to tell stories. In playing a part, children can explore the control they have over their voices and ways of speaking. Guided participation by the teacher in children's dramatic play has been shown to increase language and literacy skills (Copple & Bredekamp, 2009, p. 14; Bromley, 1998). Organizing play around a theme with ample materials, space, and time helps children develop more elaborate narrative skills. Dramatic arts activities are often the same as early literacy activities. Children build a sense of story from hearing books read aloud, and from telling and acting out their own stories, and those of others. Dramatic play increases children's comprehension and helps them become aware of narrative elements (Vukelich, Christie, & Enz, 2012; Wanerman, 2010).

- **Emotionally**—By giving children a sense of power and control and by reducing stress. In dramatic play, children can take on the roles of the controlling adults in their lives, they can

**TABLE 12–2   Sequence of Development in the Dramatic Arts**

| Age Group | Object | People | Language | Imagination | Narrative |
|---|---|---|---|---|---|
| **Infants** *newborn to 6 months* | Attracted to bright objects, mirrors, pictures, and rattles | Look at familiar faces | React to sounds Match vocalizing Babble Express feelings by crying, yelling, and cooing | | |
| **Infants** 6 to 12 months | Enjoy large toys that move | Play peek-a-boo Mirror facial expressions Solitary play predominates | Communicate with gestures, first words Imitates voices and sounds Respond to name, gestures, and simple commands "Talk" to toys | Pretend familiar actions, such as sleeping, hiding, and talking on phone | Play is disconnected |
| **Toddlers** 1 to 3 years | Like to play with real things, such as pots and pans | Rough and tumble play begins Solitary play leads into parallel play | Use words and simple sentences Name objects Speech grows from 25% to 75% understandable Respond to requests Talk to self Knows 100+ words | Imitate familiar actions and events with realistic toys that resemble the real objects, such as sweeping with a broom Imitate familiar actions of people around them and seen on T V, movies Have make-believe conversations | Story play has no definite structure or end |
| **Preschoolers** 4 to 5 years | Constructive play becomes most predominant, such as blocks and sand | Incorporate other children in play with increasing division of roles | Use voices to match character Speak in full sentences, slowly adding adjectives, prepositions, adverbs. Changes tone to match feelings Listen and make requests in response Talk about things happening elsewhere Use self-talk to control behavior Recite nursery rhymes Know 1000+ words | Play becomes more fictional Can imagine one object is something else Imaginary playmates Role-play imaginary characters | Retell invent, and act out stories Stories have rudimentary plots Invented stories incorporate ideas from stories they have heard |

*(continued)*

| TABLE 12–2 | **Sequence of Development in the Dramatic Arts** *(continued)* | | | | |
|---|---|---|---|---|---|
| **Kindergarteners**<br>*5 to 6 years* | Object and constructive play becomes more orderly | Cooperative play in which there is a shared purpose | Talk about their play<br>Tell stories<br>Tell "jokes"<br>Use past tense consistently<br>Knows 10,000+ words | Fantasy play is more complex and fluid | Use invented spelling and drawing to tell a story |
| **Primary Ages**<br>*6 to 8 years* | Construction becomes more complex<br>Create objects to go with story or play<br>Like games with rules | Enact roles from life, fiction, and media<br>Assign roles in logical, fair ways | Increased control over voice and matching it to role<br>Makes up stories<br>Tells jokes, riddles, and verbal exaggerations<br>Use mostly correct grammar<br>Follow and give instructions<br>Learn 10–15 words a day<br>Knows 20,000+ words<br>Evaluate dramatic performance | Can use very dissimilar objects to represent others<br>Know difference between real and pretend<br>Daydreaming replaces pretend play | Write invented stories from experience or picture<br>Stories can have elaborate plots<br>Create scripts for drama and puppet shows |

*Note: As in all the arts, dramatic arts development is strongly influenced by experience. This chart is intended only as a general guideline to what skills might be mastered in terms of age. However, the basic sequence of skill acquisition will pertain to most children.*

Digital Download    Download from CourseMate

determine what will happen in their play, and they can take risks as they try out new ways of behaving. Through dramatic play children develop independence and self-control. Increased time spent in dramatic play has been shown to correlate with the ability of children to control their behavior in circle time and clean up (Elias & Berk, 2002). Dramatic play allows children to learn how to deal with conflict and diversity and to delay gratification of immediate wants as they share materials, and incorporate the play schemes of others into their own or incorporate themselves into the play narratives of others (Bodrova & Leong, 2004).

**Drama concepts and skills**—By meeting the National Common Core Theater Arts Standards.

## National Standards in Theater

Based on the National Common Core Standards in Theater Arts, children should be able to do the following:

**Connecting: Communicate how and why an awareness of relationships between drama processes, theatre experiences, and the world is used to make meaning of community, cultural, global, and/or historical contexts. Apply ideas, experiences, and elements from different art forms and other disciplines to DAP dramatic activities.**

**Prekindergarten.** With teacher guidance compare themselves and their experiences with those of characters in dramatic play and stories.

**Kindergarten.** With teacher guidance relate characters, stories, and conflict in dramatic play, process drama, and developmentally appropriate theatre experiences to their own lives.

**First Grade.** With teacher guidance connect their personal experiences with characters, stories, and conflict to their dramatic activities.

**Second Grade.** Identify and express in multiple ways how and why relationships are made between themselves and the world during participation in and observation of DAP dramatic activities.

**Creating: Imagine, research, and explore through drama processes, play, and theatre experiences to discover diverse creative ideas.**

**Prekindergarten.** Navigate, with prompting and support, transitions between imagination and reality within dramatic play and process drama occurring in relation to self and others in role and transformation of place and objects.

**Kindergarten.** Transition, with prompting and support, between imagination and reality; share original ideas for problem solving within dramatic activities.

**First Grade.** Work with peers to develop imagined worlds with characters, settings, and stories while problem solving in dramatic activities.

**Second Grade.** Explore and question, collaboratively and independently, ideas about imagined worlds, characters, and stories in process drama while problem solving with peers.

**Performing: Communicate realized artistic ideas in a formal/informal presentation of drama processes or theatre experiences.**

**Prekindergarten.** With teacher guidance, use voice, gestures, body position, and facial expressions to demonstrate basic role-play skills.

**Kindergarten.** With teacher guidance, use voice, body, and facial expressions with detail and variety to demonstrate basic role-play skills.

**First Grade.** Manipulate and sustain, with prompting and support, the voice, body, and face to communicate imagined worlds, characters, and emotions within extended process drama and work shared with peers.

**Second Grade.** Manipulate and sustain, collaboratively and individually, purposeful choices for voice, body, face, and/or design elements to communicate imagined worlds, characters, and emotions.

**Responding: Analyze perspectives, articulate feelings, and critically evaluate on drama processes/theatre experiences using criteria such as aesthetics, preferences, beliefs, and contexts.**

**Prekindergarten.** Recall with prompting and support, plots, preferences, and feelings about stories in DAP dramatic activities, and theatre performances.

**Kindergarten.** Recall and describe, with prompting and support, sequential plot, voluntarily shared preferences/feelings, and details about stories and experiences in DAP dramatic activities and theatre performances.

**First Grade.** Use verbal and non-verbal communication to explain plots, preferences, and feelings about stories and experiences in DAP dramatic activities and theatre performances.

## Did You Get It?

**Why is dramatic play important for developing cultural understanding?**

a. Children get to go to other countries.

b. Children get to celebrate holidays from around the world.

c. Children learn another language.

d. Children get to imagine living in another culture.

**Take the full quiz on CourseMate**

꙳ **Second Grade.** Use verbal and non-verbal communication in groups and individually to discuss plots, preferences, and feelings prompted by stories and participation in DAP dramatic activities and theatre performances.

## How Do We Address Special Needs?

Dramatic activities, because they involve movement and language, require many of the same adaptations as creative movement and dance so that all children can participate fully.

**Children with auditory needs.** For consistency, use the same visual start, stop, listen, and relax signals developed for creative movement and dance activities. Select activities that do not rely exclusively on language. Use picture cue cards for preschoolers and word cue cards for those who can read. Visually mark the area of the performance or play space.

**Children with visual needs.** Start by making sure the children know the location of the props and the boundaries of the area to be used. Survey the area with the child and handle the materials with them before beginning the activity. Give personal asides during dramatic play and performances that let the child know where to find things. Provide a buddy and plan activities for pairs.

**Children with attention-deficit disorders.** Children who have trouble focusing are easily distracted in dramatic play settings where there are many choices and materials. To help these children develop focus, partition off play areas with low dividers that allow visibility for adults but shield one play area from another at the children's eye level. Offer clear directions and simple oft-repeated rules using multiple modalities. Provide plenty of hands-on activities and offer new materials or suggested ideas when the child seems to lose focus. Participate in the play with the child anticipating the child's needs and modeling ways to interact with peers. Have on hand other activities that the child likes and can do independently for use when the child indicates she or he is ready to move on to something else.

**Children with autism.** Because these children have impaired communication and social skills, group play is especially challenging for them, and they often prefer solitary play. With peers they may miss social cues and not be able to follow the improvised narrative script of child-initiated pretend play. Teachers can help foster interpersonal skills by playing one-on-one with these children while modeling ways to interact with others. For example, the one-on-one Floortime Model has been shown to increase social, cognitive, symbolic, and creative behavior in children with autism (Greenspan & Weider, 1998). It utilizes five steps to help children learn how to interact with a playmate. These same steps can also be used to join in the play of all children, especially infants.

1. Observe the child playing and decide how to approach him/her.

2. Join the activity and match the child's emotional tone.

3. Follow the child's lead.

4. Expand on the child's activity by making a gentle suggestion, asking a question, or modeling an action.

5. When a child' responds to your expansion, "the circle of communication" is completed and the process is started over again from step 1.

To help a child with autism participate in group play establish rituals for entering and interacting with peers. Task cards can be used to cue appropriate behaviors. The Integrated Play Group Model is based on Vygotsky's model of learning from expert peers (Wolfberg & Schuler, 1993). Using this strategy, the child with autism is paired with several other children who serve as the play "experts." In the beginning the teacher sets up the play theme and materials and models for the peers how to include the child in their play. The group meets consistently on a regular basis. As the children learn how to interact with each other, the teacher slowly withdraws, becoming an encouraging onlooker, and lets the play evolve naturally.

**Accepting differences.** A large part of the dramatic arts is stretching the imagination. Challenge stereotypes by refusing to accept limiting responses. Gender differences, for example, are established as early as twelve months of age and many children

Through imagination, stories come to life. Dressing up as a firefighter allows a girl to act out being brave, rescuing people, and putting out a fire.

## What Is the Teacher's Role in Children's Play?

Play is the natural activity of childhood. Children the world round, when left on their own, will find ways to make believe, as they have for generations, Yet, despite research showing the value of play, accountability and the need to master academic skills at a young age have come to be seen as more important than playtime for future success by both parents, school administrators, and politicians. Play is viewed as time wasted especially for children with disabilities or economic disadvantages (Snow, 2003; Zieger, Singer, & Bishop-Josef, 2006). More and more time spent in early childhood settings is devoted to direct instruction rather than open-ended play with the assumption that they will get their playtime at home. Unfortunately this is not true, since children are spending increasing time in front of televisions and computers rather than engaging in social bonding with playmates. Opportunity for child-initiated play is also hindered by the fear of many parents to let their children walk around their neighborhoods to play with others.

We can address this increasing lack of playtime by including time for children to play as part of classroom instruction. However, it is important that the play opportunities be designed for maximum developmental growth while not hindering the fluidity and creativity of children's natural ways of playing.

Research has shown that teachers assume a range of roles in interaction with children at play as illustrated in the continuum of teacher participation in

and parents have definite ideas about what toys are appropriate for boys and girls. In dramatic play, there is no reason that a girl cannot play the part of a boy or vice versa. Encourage exploration of many roles by calling the housekeeping center the dramatic play area instead, and including materials that will interest boys as well as girls, such as a tool chest, and by creating more open concept centers such as a bakery or restaurant where roles are less stereotypical.

One way to expand children's story narratives is to read stories that involve character reversals such as Robert Munsch's *Paper Bag Princess* (1992) in which a princess defeats the dragon and saves the knight or San Souci's *Cendrilla: A Caribbean Cinderella* (1998) in which Cinderella is a native of Martinique.

| Uninvolved | Onlooker | Observer | Stage Manager | Co-Player | Mediator | Play Leader | Director |
|---|---|---|---|---|---|---|---|
| Teacher is busy with other things or talks to other adults. | Teacher watches in an encouraging way using positive feedback but does not interfere. | Teacher watches children for a specific purpose and may record the children's behavior or patterns of interaction. Observations are then used to inform future instruction. | Teacher observes the children's natural play and provides assistance with props, and setting but does not enter into play. | Teacher joins in children's play, taking a minor role and following the children's lead, modeling appropriate interaction strategies if needed. | Teacher serves as a conflict manager stepping in as necessary to teach children how to solve problems so that they can play happily and safely. | Teacher takes an active role in initiating the theme of the play and providing props and materials that enhance the children's learning in specific ways or refocus the children to extend the play. | Teacher stands on the sidelines and tells the children what to do or asks questions focused on academic goals that disrupt the play. |

**FIGURE 12-1** Continuum of Teacher Participation in Children's Play

children's play shown in Figure 12-1. At one end of the continuum is non-involvement in the children's play. Uninvolved teachers spend only two to six percent of their time engaging with children at play (Johnson, Christie, & Wardle, 2004). Instead, they spend the time doing work or talking to other adults. In such situations children's play is characterized by simplistic, repetitive narratives, and rough and tumble play, which is often based on characters and superheroes from television, films, and video games.

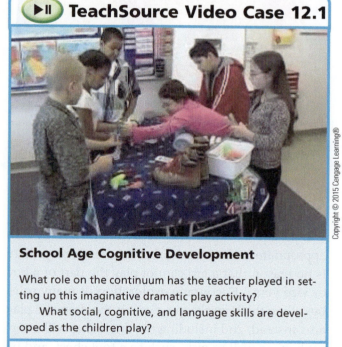

▶❚❚ **TeachSource Video Case 12.1**

**School Age Cognitive Development**

What role on the continuum has the teacher played in setting up this imaginative dramatic play activity?

What social, cognitive, and language skills are developed as the children play?

**Watch on CourseMate**

Joining children's pretend play as a co-player is a wonderful way to enhance language and social skills.

At the other end of the continuum, teachers assume a director's role and tell the children what to do and solve problems for them. This level of direction disrupts children's intrinsic motivation to play and often the activity is abandoned, creating the myth that young children have short attention spans. Elizabeth Jones and Gretchen Reynolds put it this way: "Teacher interruption of play for the purpose of teaching abstract concepts and discrete skills, contradicts everything we know about the learning process of young children" (2011, p. 15).

The roles in the center of the continuum are the ones that are correlated with the greatest growth in cognitive, language, and social-emotional skills. When teachers participated in children's play in effective ways such as these, children's play lasted longer and was more cognitively complex (Sylva, Roy & Painter, 1980; Howes & Smith, 1995). There was also more cooperation and increased amounts of literacy behaviors (Christie et al., 2003).

---

### Did You Get It?

**Andria, a preschool teacher, spends most of her time talking with her colleagues, and little time engaging with her students at play. What effect will her behavior have on her students' dramatic play?**

a. Their play will be characterized by simplistic and repetitive narratives.

b. The children will lose their intrinsic motivation to play and will eventually abandon their activities.

c. The children will work together in a better fashion and show increased amounts of literacy behaviors.

d. Their play will last longer and will become more cognitively complex.

**Take the full quiz on CourseMate**

---

## How Are Dramatic Arts Activities Designed?

In the classroom dramatic play can be used to help children develop their language skills, experience the creative process, consider the visual aesthetics of settings and costumes, and much more. These kinds of dramatics activities should be designed in open-ended ways that allow children to use their imaginations to re-create and express ideas and feelings.

Ideas for play activities can be child-initiated such as in informal play, teacher-initiated, such as using pantomime and improvisation to illustrate new words, or inspired by some special event, such as reading a new story and then acting it out.

## Informal Dramatic Play

Informal dramatic play is characteristically spontaneous, growing out of the natural inclinations of the children. It is child-initiated, but can be supported by teachers when they enter into children's ongoing play and provide facilitation as a co-player, such as by joining a tea party and modeling the use of "please" and "thank you" as part of the play. Elaborating on children's pretend play scaffolds language usage and models positive ways to interact socially.

**Facilitating with words.** Close observation of children at play allows teachers to facilitate language skill development. For example, a caregiver might notice two toddlers playing with toy cars and making car sounds, but not using words. She might walk over to them and join in driving a car too, while asking them questions about where their cars are going to increase their use of oral language.

**Facilitating with props.** Teachers can also enrich play by showing children how to create their own props. An observant teacher functions as a stage manager when he notices that a group of kindergarteners has built thrones and are pretending they are kings and queens. He puts out some paper strips, scissors, glue, and sparkly paper and invites them to make their own crowns.

**Social facilitation.** The flexibility of dramatic play allows everyone to participate. Children, such as those with developmental delays or autism, may not know how to enter into group play situations. We need to be aware of potential social difficulties and be ready to step in. One way to do this is to model how to ask to join a playgroup. Another is to make suggestions that open up the play to more participants. If two children are imagining they are a shopper and a store clerk and another wants to join, the teacher could point out that there are usually many shoppers in a store. Another is to set up rules to make sure that play is fair. Vivian Paley (1992), for example, told her kindergarteners that they could not exclude other children from play, and then enforced the rule through storytelling and ongoing discussions with her students.

## Open-Ended Play Centers

The teacher can also set the stage for informal dramatic play by creating play centers that build on children's natural interests and everyday experiences, such as a playhouse or a store. Other centers can help children learn about how things work or address concerns. For example, many children are fearful of doctor's visits. Creating a doctor's office in which to play can help children work out their fears. Lisa Miles (2009) following up the interests of her preschoolers after reading the *Little House* books by Laura Ingalls Wilder, built an old-fashioned general store stocked with baskets of yarn, ribbon, metal buckets and scoops, a scale, wooden crates, and jars of beans, buttons, and cinnamon sticks. She found that putting a piece of plywood on the floor provided the sound and feel of an old store.

For more center ideas, see *Open-Ended Dramatic Play Centers* on CourseMate.

## Prop Boxes

Prop boxes are similar to play centers in providing children with starting points for child-initiated dramatic play. They have the advantage of being easy to store and ready to use at the opportune moment.

A prop box consists of a collection of objects that will spark children's imaginations. The items can all relate to the same main idea, such as a butterfly net, a wide-brimmed hat, magnifying glass, "cages" made from berry baskets, plastic caterpillars, and butterflies. Other prop boxes can be based on an experience. Prop boxes can include child-safe objects, books, tapes of relevant music, and suggestions for use. Label the box clearly when putting it away for storage so it is immediately ready to use another time.

Prop boxes can be used individually or with small groups of children and are particularly effective when using an emergent curriculum design and for the primary grades, where large play centers are less likely to be found. For example, a teacher might make up prop boxes to go with the children's literature used in the classroom as a way to provide opportunities to revisit the story through role-plays.

Prop boxes can also be used outdoors to spark children to take a new direction in their play and increase their experiences with language and literacy. Celeste Harvey (2010) found that when she provided prop boxes containing chalk, magnifiers, identification guides, and books on insects, children spent time observing lady bugs and drawing them on the sidewalk. Children became so excited they set themselves the task of finding a new bug every day.

For more suggestions for outdoor prop boxes, see *Outdoor Prop Boxes* on CourseMate.

## Addressing Diversity

Diversity and bias can be addressed through dramatic play activities by the careful selection of materials.

**Play centers.**  Play centers can include items that recognize cultural and ethnic differences. In selecting materials, make sure that all the cultural backgrounds of the children in the class are represented. Families are usually quite happy to help out with suggestions and donations of items. Once there is representation of all family backgrounds, expand the offerings to include items from ethnic groups and cultures not found in your classroom. These can become springboards for research and discussion.

**Anti-bias props.**  In choosing culturally diverse props, look for different eating utensils, ethnic foods, unisex materials for different kinds of work, realistic clothing from other cultures, and props for different disabilities, such as wheelchairs, crutches, canes, hearing aids, leg braces, and dark glasses.

**Selecting dolls.**  Dolls for pretend play should be selected to show the different skin tones of the wide range of groups found in the United States. There should also be fair representation of male and female dolls and those with disabilities.

Commercial dolls can be supplemented with "Persona Dolls" (Derman-Sparks & the ABC Task Force, 1989). These are handmade dolls or large puppets that are given specific characters through the telling of their life story by the teacher. Persona Dolls can be customized to represent children with disabilities, diverse ethnicities, or unique family experiences.

Having Persona Dolls in the class provides a way to bring up topics or feelings that would otherwise be difficult. Jan Pierce and Cheryl Johnson (2010) found that when they used Persona Dolls with their preschoolers to solve classroom problems, children identified with dolls with whom they shared similar characteristics. In addition, timid children spoke up more. Derman-Sparks recommends introducing the Persona Dolls that are most like the children in the

## Teacher Tip

### INTRODUCING PERSONA DOLLS

Persona Dolls teach inclusive social-emotional skills and foster self-regulation and problem-solving skills. They provide a safe, engaging way to address difficult issues. To introduce the dolls to children

1. Create a unique personality and background for the doll that shares similarities with one or more of the children in the class. Later introduce dolls that are very different.

2. Introduce the dolls to the children just as you would a new student in the class. Tell the dolls' age, family members, and what their likes and dislikes are.

3. Use your natural voice when speaking for the doll, not a puppetlike one.

4. Have the doll(s) participate in everyday activities such as circle time and during small groups, but do not put them in the housekeeping center. Show the children these dolls are special. Keep them in a place where children can see them and ask for them to play with them when they have a particular dramatic story in which the dolls play a role.

5. When a problem comes up in class, use the doll to rephrase the problem as one the doll is having and ask the children to help solve it.

Open-ended props, such as these foam cushions, increase children's engagement in dramatic play, and help children invent new places to imagine. Perhaps they will cross a mountain or stand on top of a tower.

class first. To allay first-day fears, for example, she suggests having three dolls talk about how they got to know each other, and how they felt when they said goodbye to their parents. If there is a child with a disability in the class, a Persona Doll with that disability can offer opportunities to talk in a more relaxed way about the child's special needs and equipment.

**Adding diversity to prop boxes.** Prop boxes also make ideal ways to integrate multicultural materials into children's play (Boutte, Van Scoy, & Hendley, 1996). For example, seeing an interest among several girls in playing with each other's hair, a teacher could take out the hair dressing prop box. In the box are not only the typical hairbrushes, combs, empty containers of shampoos, and barrettes, but also empty containers of hair products used by other cultural groups. In addition, there could be books about hair, such as *Cornrows* (Yarborough, 1997), *Hairs Pelitos* (Cisneros, 1994), and *I Love My Hair!* (Tarpley, 2001) as well as photographs of men and women from different races and cultures wearing a wide variety of wonderful hairstyles.

## Developing the Imagination

**Mental representation** is at the core of all the arts. It is the ability to produce and act upon **sensory images** in one's mind. These images may involve one or more of the senses, such as visual, auditory, tactile, and olfactory. Although they are not real, these images activate the same parts of the brain as do actual sensory experiences (Kosslyn, Gainis, & Thompson, 2006). The mind is able to combine, remember, and re-create such images to produce new thoughts. This is the realm of fantasy and imagination, and is the basis of literature, which relies on our ability to create mental images as we hear and read stories.

Mental representation is used in the dramatic arts when authors visualize the characters and places in the stories and plays they write, and actors create mental images of the characters they are playing so they can become that person. In the visual arts artists plan their paintings in their minds before they begin.

Dancers mentally rehearse their performance before they step on stage. Musicians and composers hear the music in their mind as they read the notes on a page.

**Benefits of creating mental images.** Creating mental images has been shown to be effective in improving cognitive skills, maintaining energy levels, and strengthening concentration. In one research study, first- and third-grade students who created mental images before reading a story had higher levels of comprehension (Rushall & Lippman, 1997).

Using our imaginations is also an important way to relax. When we are creating mental images, we can escape from everyday life into a world of our own creation. We can daydream ourselves into a favorite place, or do something we can only do in our dreams, such as swim in the deep sea with a mermaid. The relaxation aspect of imagery has been used to help people reduce stress, fear, and pain. Imagery has been shown to help cancer patients feel less stressed during chemotherapy, and to relieve tension during childbirth (Mandle, Jacobs, & Arcari, et al., 1996).

The power of imagery to affect our physical state has been elegantly presented in the well-known work of Ellen Langer (1989). She points out that it is our mental perceptions that influence how we see and understand the world, and not just the external stimuli around us. Langer, in particular, emphases the powerful link between mind and body. She gives the examples of the professor who felt no pain from his severe arthritis when lecturing, and of patients who tolerated surgical pain better when they imagined their surgical wounds came from playing a football game or from an injury from a kitchen knife. There is also the proven ability of placebos to cure patients of disease.

## Planning Guided Imagery Activities

With practice, mental images can become clearer and deeper. **Guided imagery** is one way to develop children's imaginations and get them ready for storytelling and other more active dramatic activities. It is most appropriate for children who have learned to fantasize and can remember what they have imagined, usually by the age of four or five. Start with simple visual imagery games and then proceed to more complex multisensory experiences.

**Mind pictures.** A good introductory activity is to have the children look at an interesting picture. It

could be a photograph or famous artwork. Then have them close their eyes and describe the picture to you.

**Memory pictures.** Have the children close their eyes and imagine a place they have been. Then ask them to describe the place in words or make a drawing of it.

**Imagining the familiar.** After the children have become familiar with the classroom, have them lie on the floor or sit in a circle on a rug and close their eyes. Ask them to imagine they are walking around the room. Describe entering the room and some things you see as you walk around it, such as what is on the walls, on the desks, where the supplies are, and so on. Stop frequently and ask the children if you forgot anything. Accept all their additions to your description. Slowly let the children take over the description as you cue them to where you are standing. When you have made a complete circuit of the room, have the children open their eyes and see if anything was missed.

**Trips of the imagination.** To begin an imaginary trip, have the children sit or lie down and close their eyes. Cue them to relax by saying: "Wiggle your toes. Now let them relax." Repeat for each body part moving up until you reach the head. Next, say: "Today we will be traveling to . . ." or "We will be imagining we are. . . ." Then in a slow, quiet voice describe the trip or characteristics of what is being imagined. Use many descriptive words that describe the sounds, colors, odors, and tastes you encounter. Add more complexity as the children become skilled at creating mental images.

For an example of a script for a guided imagery experience, see *Guided Imagery: A Peaceful Cave* on CourseMate.

**Expressing mental images.** Guided imagery is a good way to introduce arts activities. Follow up imagery experiences with opportunities to create freely such as having an open studio time during which the children can choose to express what they imagined by writing a story, acting it out, drawing a picture, or composing a musical work.

Here are some ideas for guided imagery experiences. Imagine you are:

- A cloud floating over the earth. Describe the different things you can see—birds, planes, forests, rivers, and houses below.

- Water flowing down a stream. Describe how it joins a creek, then a river, and finally reaches the sea.

- Traveling to another planet. Describe the blackness of space, the huge size of the planets as you get near to them, the stars, and the comets swooshing past.

- Traveling to a distant place. Describe all the different ways to travel. Start in a car, get on a train, then take off in an airplane, land, sail on a ship, and finally take local transportation depending on the place, such as a donkey or camel.

# The Pantomime Experience

**Pantomime** is acting out an idea without using words, although it may include sound effects. This type of dramatic play can be child-initiated or teacher-guided and occurs when children are given cues either by the teacher as in guided pantomime, or are influenced by what has been taught, such as dramatizing a book the class read, or reenacting an event from history. One advantage of teacher-guided or **process drama** activities is that they help children explore ideas they might not think of otherwise and provide opportunity to practice dramatic arts skills. Participating in simple pantomimes prepares children for the more complex activities of role-plays and the dramatization of stories.

**Descriptive pantomimes.** In this form of pantomime the teacher or peer leader gives a series of descriptive statements, starting with a statement that cues them that they will be pretending, such as "Imagine you were. . . ." The children respond by inventing facial expressions and motions that reflect what is being described. Topics for descriptive pantomimes include sensory experiences, expression of emotions, characterization, and fantasy.

Begin with simple one-sentence descriptions, such as "Imagine you are smelling a flower" or "Imagine you swimming in the sea." Be careful not to overwhelm the children by trying to do a whole string of them at once. It is better to do one activity a day, perhaps as a warm-up for a morning meeting.

More involved pantomimes can consist of extended descriptions that take the group on a journey or through a process. For example, the leader could think of a place and then guide the group around it. The popular *Going on a Bear Hunt* is an example of this kind of activity. A trip through a castle might start by imagining crossing over the moat on a shaky drawbridge, stomping across a dusty courtyard, banging on the huge wooden doors, climbing the steps to the throne room, and bowing to the giant ogre king. Such pantomimes provide an ideal context, particularly in the primary grades, to review facts and concepts children have learned. If the children have been learning how grain becomes the cereal they eat, a pantomime might have them imagine they are a grain of wheat and go through the process of being harvested, milled, cooked, and shaped into cereal, then boxed, trucked to the supermarket, placed on the grocery shelf, and finally, bought and eaten.

For more ideas for pantomimes, see *Ideas for Simple Descriptive Pantomines* on CourseMate.

**Planning pantomimes.** Brief pantomimes for young children can be spontaneous or even child-initiated; others will require a measure of preplanning. In planning pantomimes, consider the following:

- Is the space adequate? Be sure there is enough room for the children to move actively. If necessary, outline the boundaries for movement or use hula hoops or marks on the floor to keep the children in place.

- Do you know your audience? Be aware of the physical abilities and feelings of the children. Who is shy? Who tends to overreact physically? Adjust the activity to fit the needs of these children so that everyone can be successful and potential

# Making Plans

**GROUP ACTIVITY PLAN:**
**IMAGINING IT**

**WHO?**    Group composition age(s): Preschool and up

Group size: Preferably four to five preschoolers, but can be the whole group if the children are experienced at pantomiming.

**WHEN?**    Time frame: 5 to 10 minutes

**WHY?**    Objectives: Children will develop

- physically, by using their bodies to hold a position. (Bodily-Kinesthetic)
- socially, by working together to create a unified aesthetic event. (Interpersonal)
- emotionally, by gaining confidence to express ideas through pantomime. (Intrapersonal)
- language skills, by describing how the experience felt. (Linguistic)
- cognitively, by seeing that a whole is made up of parts. (Logical-Mathematical)
- dramatic skill and knowledge, by improvising a pantomime and modulating body movements to fit a role. (Content Standards 1 and 2)

**WHERE?**    Setup: Large, open carpeted area

**WHAT?**    Materials: Chart paper and markers

**HOW?**    Procedure:

Warm-Up: Go outside and observe a car or truck. Put the car in park with the emergency brake on and look under the hood when it is running. If possible, take a ride in it. If that is not possible, talk about how it would feel to ride in it. (Option: This could be a fire truck and be done after a visit to the firehouse.)

What to Do: Have the children brainstorm a list of all the parts of the chosen vehicle. Have the children stand up and imagine they are that vehicle, and then have them pretend to drive it around the circle. Next, ask the children to work in a group. Assign each child in the group a role, such as being the engine, the wheels, the driver, the steering wheel, and so on. Have group members take turns being each of the parts. Have them add sound effects like an engine, horn, and so forth, if desired.

What to Say: Use questions to guide problem solving. "How do you think the _____ would move? How will the parts join together? Where should the driver, wheels, and so forth be?" Provide control. "Let's imagine we are driving. Go around in a circle until you are back in your starting spot." Give positive feed-back. "You solved the problem of how to stay together in a workable way by holding hands."

Transition Out: Return to the rug and ask them: How did it feel when just you were the vehicle? Was it hard to get everyone to move together? What are some ways you used? Do you think it is hard to get all the parts of a real vehicle to work together? Follow up this pantomime with others that reinforce the idea that a whole is made up of parts, such as a computer (monitor, keyboard, mouse, plug) or cake (flour, sugar, milk, eggs). For primary students, try pantomiming systems being studied, such as the solar system, an ecosystem, or the human body.

**ASSESSMENT**    1. Do the children work together cooperatively to make a working vehicle?
**OF LEARNING**    2. Can the children describe the differences in the two pantomimes?
3. Do the children understand the concept that the whole is made up of parts?

For more examples of dramatic activity plans, see *Open-Ended Dramatic Arts Activity Plans* on CourseMate.

discipline issues are avoided. Pantomime should be fun for all.

- Are there enough materials or props for everyone and are they safe? If a prop is part of the pantomime, such as a hat or flower, be sure to have one for every child. Make sure all surfaces are smooth and there are no sharp points. Avoid using sticks with active young children because even with care, accidents can happen.

- Can you see everyone? Pantomime has an element of spontaneity and can be adjusted as needed. By watching the children's reactions you can decide whether to expand the activity or stop it. You can also note any children having difficulty and simplify or clarify as needed.

- Can everyone see and hear you? Pantomime leaders, whether teachers or children, should be active participants. Use a loud and clear voice with plenty of enthusiasm.

- Do the pantomimes build on each other? Start simple. Build on the children's skills. When they can follow a one-sentence pantomime, add an extension as in this example: Imagine you are licking a delicious ice cream cone in your favorite

flavor (let them lick for a while)—suddenly a big dog jumps up and knocks it out of your hand. Show how you feel.

- Have you made the rules clear? Practice the start, listen, stop, and relax signals before beginning. Make sure the children know what is acceptable and what is not. Point out the boundaries in which they must stay.

## The Pantomime Experience for Infants and Toddlers

Pantomime is strongly related to gesture, which is the earliest form of communication. We naturally use pantomime as we work with infants and young toddlers. We pantomime feeding ourselves when we want them to eat. We pantomime going to sleep, blowing kisses, being a pretend animal "eating" them up, and more. To make the experience more meaningful it is important to be aware of how we can use this most basic of the dramatic arts to reinforce learning and to develop creative thinking.

**Doing things.** Pantomiming familiar things helps children develop vocabulary and concepts. Together with the children, act out ordinary actions, such as brushing teeth, eating soup, and shoveling snow. Make the activity playful by exaggerating the movements and making silly sounds, such as slurping the soup.

**Being things.** Pantomiming objects in action helps children learn how things work. Together pretend to be inanimate objects. Be a clock, using your arms as the hands. Be a pencil and write with your feet. Be a car, steering the wheel with your hands as you drive around the room.

**Being silly.** Pantomiming with the total body helps develop physical control. Together act in exaggerated ways. Be a floppy rag doll or puppet that cannot stand up. Roll up into a ball and roll around the floor. Be a balloon blowing away in the wind. Be popcorn popping. Add music to enrich the experience.

**Playing with props.** Attach a short string to a piece of paper or a box and have the children interact with the dangling object as if it were a living thing. It can be anything the children imagine or make suggestions, such as a bird, kite, butterfly, or bee.

Pantomime forces children to think of new ways to communicate concepts and ideas. What message do you think these two children are signaling each other?

## The Pantomime Experience for Preschoolers and Kindergarteners

For children between the age of three and six, simple pantomimes that ask them to pretend to be something or do something fit well with their normal fantasy play. These experiences should be short and very open-ended. At the same time, engage in pantomime often and encourage the children to contribute ideas for pantomime time.

**How would?** Ask the children how different things, with which they are familiar, might move or behave. How would a snowflake fall to the ground? How would a bird build a nest? How would a tall person fit under a low bridge?

**Inside the picture.** Have the children study a work of art and then pantomime what they would do if they were inside the picture, or select a piece of music and pantomime how it makes them feel.

**Re-vision it.** Take an ordinary object and pantomime using it in an unusual way. For example, use a shoe for a telephone or a hairbrush for a toothbrush. Pass it around and have each child think of a different thing to do with the prop.

**Be someone.** Have the children act out different jobs and sports activities.

**Statues.** Have the children move about as if they were animals, spaghetti, or made of gelatin. At a pre-established signal have them freeze and hold their positions. Walk around admiring their poses.

## The Pantomime Experience for Primary Age

There is no question that pantomime offers a critical way to reinforce what is being taught across the disciplines. By first and second grade, children can create complex scenarios and can effectively take on the role of leader.

**Messages.** To develop reading skills, put the children in pairs and ask them to imagine they cannot talk. Give each child a written message to communicate solely through gesture, movement, and facial expression. Have primary children write their own messages to act out.

**Invisible objects.** To develop focus and physical control have the children sit in a circle. Describe an object while acting as if you are holding it in your hands.

Then pass the object to the child sitting next to you, who then passes it to the next and so on, each trying to hold it in a way that would be appropriate so that it retains its proper size, shape, and weight. For example, passing an invisible bowling ball will look very different from passing a slippery fish. Vary the activity by having the children change the object each time it is passed or do not say what the object is and have them try to guess it. Have children take turns being the leader.

**Who or what or where am I?** Increase reading comprehension by having the children pantomime an object, character, or setting from a story that is familiar to everyone and then try to guess who, what, or where they are. Extend the activity by having groups pantomime a scene from the story.

**Slow motion.** Develop focus and physical control by acting out familiar activities in slow motion. Challenge the children to line up, write their name, or eat their snack moving as slowly as they can. Vary the activity by asking them to move while shaking violently or bouncing up and down.

**Tableaus.** Another way to develop focus and physical control is to study a work of art or an event in history and re-create the scene holding the pose for a minute without moving. Be sure to record the tableau on camera.

**Verbs.** Learn about action words by writing verbs, such as *swim*, *jump*, and *hop*, on index cards and giving each child a card. Have the children act out the verb.

---

### Did You Get It?

**Which of the following pantomime activities can be used to develop creative thinking among preschoolers?**

a. acting out ordinary actions with the children, such as brushing teeth and eating soup

b. passing a prop around in a group of children and asking them to think of different ways to use the prop

c. asking the children to pantomime familiar activities, such as writing their name or playing basketball in slow motion

d. having a child pantomime a character from a familiar story and asking the rest of the children to guess the identity of the character

**Take the full quiz on CourseMate**

# The Improvisation Experience

Like pantomime, **improvisation** is the representation of an idea through movements, but with the added attraction of using words as well. Like pantomime, improvisation has a spontaneous quality and calls on the creativity of the children to respond to the open-ended problems set by the teacher or peer leader. Role-playing is the most common form of improvisation, but most pantomime activities can also be turned into improvisation with the addition of words.

**Descriptive improvisation.** As in descriptive pantomime, this form of improvisation begins with a leader describing a situation, event, character, or problem and then having the rest act it out. Simple dramatic activities such as these give children a chance to try out different ways of communicating with language and help develop their ability to think on their feet.

For ideas for improvisations, see *Ideas for Open-Ended Improvisations* on CourseMate.

Although for infants and toddlers one-on-one activities work best, in designing descriptive improvisations when working with an older group it is better to have the children perform in small groups or pairs because they will naturally be noisier than when pantomiming, which is done in relative silence. Alternatively, children can take turns performing their improvisation in front of their peers. Another effective method for some activities is to have the children form two concentric circles facing each other.

**Radio or readers' theater.** In this type of improvisation children use only their voices to create the characters. They can make up their own radio program complete with news, weather, ads and talent, retell a story, or in the primary grades act out the part of a character in a book by reading that character's words. A center can be set up to be a radio studio or children can go behind a real or fake radio and pretend to be on air for their peers. For inspiration have children listen to some old radio programs and discuss how different sound effects were made. Old time radio shows can be downloaded for free from the *Internet Archive* http://archive.org/details/oldtimeradio.

**Role-plays.** Role-plays are more involved than simple improvisations. They are most appropriate for kindergarteners and up who are able to work together in a small group.

Role-plays take more preparation than simple improvisation. In a role-play a pair or small group of children assume particular roles to play. For example, one child could be a current student and the other a new student to the school. Once roles are assigned the group is given a **scenario** or situation and each child acts how they think their character would. Role-plays can be used to help children develop dramatic skills, assist children in solving social problems, and help present concepts being studied in a fun and visible way. For example, children can act out a story they have read, or imagine they are traveling to a country they have studied.

For suggested ideas for role plays, see *Ideas for Role Plays* on CourseMate.

In designing role-plays try to make sure that the roles are equal in importance. When a role choice has to be made, a fair method is to write the roles on pieces of paper and have the children draw them out of a hat. This eliminates difficulties that can arise when children feel one part is more attractive than another. As children learn how to be more cooperative, they can be given the choice of roles.

## Using Props for Improvisation and Role-Play

Props play an even more important role in improvisation than in pantomime. Children may feel more self-conscious when speaking a role than they did in pantomime in which they had to think only about what to do with their bodies. As in creative movement, props draw attention away from the performer and make the action clearer. For example, children who are asked to take the roles of different community workers will feel more confident if they can wear a piece of clothing or hat that reflects that occupation. Prop boxes can be an important resource for role-plays. In addition, children can use their imaginations and choose objects they find around the room to be props, such as substituting a yardstick for a cane. Art materials can be used to create masks, hats, paper costumes, and simple scenery as well.

## Masks

Masks, like props, allow children to express themselves in ways that they might not otherwise. Behind

Making their own masks and props allows children to express their creativity. Large eye openings, such as the ones in this paper-bag mask, not only make the mask safer, but also allow children to feel less enclosed.

a mask, children can feel like they are someone else; they may try acting in a new way or attempt things that might be too frightening barefaced.

Commercial masks have sanitary problems when used by more than one child, and often feel suffocating. Instead, encourage the children to make their own masks. Mask-making activities can be done with small groups working at a center, or by individual children who need to create masks to meet some particular requirement of their own self-selected dramatic play activities or for a role-play.

**Materials for masks.** Masks can be made from stiff construction paper, tag board, cardboard, or large paper bags in which eyeholes have already been cut. Chapter 9 explains how to make a papier-mâché mask. Paint, marker, and materials from the collage center, such as yarn for hair, can enhance the character.

**Type of masks.** Children can make three basic masks independently, requiring only a little assistance for the fitting.

1. **Stick mask.** Provide children with face-sized pieces of construction paper or tag board pre-cut into circles, ovals, and other geometric shapes. Eyeholes should be pre-cut. Create the character using crayon, marker, collage materials, or paint. Then glue the mask to a sturdy strip of cardboard or rolled-up tube made from tag board. To use, the child holds the mask in front of his or her face.

2. **Paper bag mask.** Use large paper grocery bags with pre-cut eyeholes. Cut up the side slightly so that the bag rests comfortably over the child's shoulders. Tempera paint works well on the brown paper surface.

3. **Wrap-around mask.** Cut eyeholes in the center of a 12-inch-by-18-inch sheet of construction paper. After it is decorated, wrap it around the child's head, adding an extension strip of paper if needed, and staple it in place so that it rests on the child's shoulders and is loose enough for the child to lift off easily.

**Eyeholes.** Because few young children can manage to locate eyeholes in a safe, usable place, it is helpful if the teacher does this for children up to kindergarten age.. It is important that the eyeholes be large enough to provide safe visibility for children. Make eyeholes circle shaped, not eye shaped, and at least 2 inches in diameter, separated by half an inch. For primary students make a cardboard template they can use to trace eyes for a mask. Show them how to fold the paper and make a snip to start the hole. Note: Mouth and nose openings are unnecessary and can weaken the mask, making it more likely to tear. Draw these on instead.

**Using the masks.** Try to encourage the children not to take their masks home right away after making them. That way they will be able to develop richer dramatic play through interacting with the other children. By using their mask ideas, teachers can find related literature and themes to expand their play. For example, if several children have made animal masks then an interesting zoo or circus could result. A group of robots could lead into dramatic play about outer space.

Ask questions that will help the children develop their characters. What character will you make? How will you show your character's special features? What will its eyes, ears, and so on be like? Think about how your character will talk and move.

## Special Needs

### • DEALING WITH A FEAR OF MASKS •

Adults or strangers wearing masks often frighten young children. Mask-making activities help them deal with this fear. To reassure children who are easily frightened, adults should

- make their own masks using the same materials available to the children.
- avoid masks that show gruesome features.
- always put the mask on and take it off in front of the children.
- play peek-a-boo games with simple masks.

Children may also be frightened or uncomfortable when wearing masks that cover their own faces. Allow them to hold masks up to their faces rather than tying them on. Tie them on only when requested. Always keep eyeholes very large. Some children may not want their full faces covered or may want to make goggles. Have available rectangular pieces of paper or tag board, about 4 by 9 inches, with pre-cut eyeholes. These can be worn by fastening a paper strip around the back of the head.

When several masks are finished, invite different characters to interact with each other. Have them role-play different situations. Which characters do you think have similar characteristics? Which ones are very different from each other? How would this character talk to that one? Do you think they would like each other? How do you think they would shake hands, sing together, go on a trip together, and so forth? How would these characters play together or how would they work together to build something? Talk about how they feel wearing the masks. Ask: "Does wearing a mask change how you act?"

## The Improvisational Experience for Infants and Toddlers

Infants and toddlers will naturally add sounds and words to their dramatic play. The best approach is to enter into their play and model ways to change and control the voice while matching it to one's actions.

**Faces and sounds.** Together, explore making faces showing different emotions with matching sounds and words. For example, laugh for happy or whimper for sad.

**Picture perfect.** Clip interesting pictures of people and animals from magazines. Show a picture to a toddler and ask him or her to act the way that person or animal might act. These pictures can be made part of a dramatic play center.

## The Improvisational Experience for Preschoolers and Kindergarteners

Retain the spontaneous nature of children's play by adding improvisational experiences to play centers where the children have open-ended choices or introduce improvisation while reading a book aloud.

**Clown around.** Make a collection of large, safe, colorful, and fun objects such as a hula hoop, bug net, plastic ladle, child's umbrella, pocketbook, silly sunglasses, and giant elastic tie, and keep them in a box labeled "Inspiration." Children can select an object and improvise a brief performance using words and movement. This box can be kept in a dramatic play center. Add a clown costume to the box for added fun.

**Sound effects.** Add sound effects and motion to the reading of any book. If the book is about a duck, have the children quack and waddle in place every time you say "duck." This is a great way to develop listening skills.

## The Improvisational Experience for Primary Age

As children mature, they become more capable of taking a role in a group improvisation. Role-plays provide a child-pleasing way to integrate subjects.

**Card readers.** Write a familiar word and action on index cards, such as *swim*, or *going in a door*. Pass the cards out at random and have the children say and do what the card says. Start by doing it normally. Then, after the children are familiar with what to do, challenge them to use funny voices, exaggerate motions, or do things backwards. Let them suggest other ways to act out the cards as well. This activity is a great way to practice reading skills, new vocabulary, and spelling words.

**Do as I say.** Have one child describe an action or character while another acts it out.

**Talk back.** Hand out index cards on which is written a character such as a reporter, clown, king,

Descriptive improvisation combines verbalization and action. Imagining an emotion and acting it out helps children develop control over their facial expressions and vocal quality while at the same time providing emotional release.

or troll and have the children pair up and take turns acting out their characters and trying to guess who the partner is. Characters can also be selected from stories being read.

# The Story Play Experience

**Story play** or **narrative drama** is based on children's own stories or on stories children have read or heard. Story play can be very simple. **Finger plays** and nursery rhymes are some of the first stories children learn. It can also be very complex. Primary age students can make up their own **story scripts,** assign roles, and act their story out using their developing reading and writing skills.

No matter what the level, narrative drama contains the following components:

- *Characters*—There may be one or more people, animals, or fantastical characters.

- *Verbal expression*—Stories may be told using words, sounds, or a combination of both as well as through mime.

- *Use of the body*—The characters must act out their roles through carefully planned movements.

- *Plot*—The story is presented in a sequence, the simplest being beginning, middle, and end.

- *Conflict*—Stories are most interesting when there is a problem or conflict that needs to be solved.

- *Setting*—Stories usually occur in a particular time and place.

- *Mood*—Throughout a story the characters may exhibit a variety of moods that relate to what is happening to them and around them.

- *Theme*—This is the main idea or purpose of the story.

## Finger Plays

Finger plays are little stories acted out with the hands and fingers. These are usually accompanied by catchy rhymes. The words either give directions or suggest ways for the children to move their fingers, making the fingers the characters in the story. Because children can learn these when very young and because they involve both language and motion, finger plays are important ways to develop literacy skills. Finger plays can be found in books or learned from others.

## TeachSource Video Case 12.2

**Infant & Toddlers: Emotional Development**

What techniques do the caregivers use to engage infants with finger plays? What other ways could these infants be introduced to story rhymes?

**Watch on CourseMate**

For some examples of finger plays, see *Finger Plays* on CourseMate.

Finger plays help children develop their language and fine motor skills.

Copyright © 2015 Cengage Learning®

## Storytelling

The next level of narrative drama is storytelling. Just like finger plays, storytelling is an ancient art form. Before there were printed books, it was the main way that history and culture were preserved and passed down to the next generation. Today storytelling remains an important practice in some cultures, but has been replaced by books, television, and movies in many others.

Vivian Paley (2004) has developed ways to inspire storytelling by young children. Her method begins with her own invented stories, which she shares daily with the children. In her stories she incorporates real events and problems that occur in the classroom in a fictional format. Next she sets up a storytelling center where her kindergarten children can come and dictate stories to her or another adult. At whole group time she reads the story while other children take the roles of the characters and act the story out in the middle of the circle. Paley finds that children who have participated in this process are likely to write more stories. She has also found that this is an excellent way to include children with

special needs and second-language learners in the group. Aeliki Nicolopoulou, Judith McDowell, and Carolyn Brockmeyer (2006) found that with low-income children, Paley's method transformed the existing journal-writing activity into one that was much more engaging for the children, and in doing so increased their literacy development.

## Storytelling and Literacy

Vivian Paley's model is an important one for teachers of young children to understand and incorporate into their classrooms. Dictation has been shown to be a powerful tool for early literacy development (Cooper, 1993). During the one-on-one time with the child, the teacher can work on many aspects of literacy that best meet the needs of that child. The child gets to watch his or her words turn into letters that can be read back to others. The teacher can suggest words, model how a writer thinks, and ask questions that help the child develop the plot. The teacher can also assess the child's language development and comprehension of narrative elements. However, dictation is a time-consuming process. Elizabeth Kirk (1998) suggests limiting children to one page of dictation by gently saying to the child: "We are getting near the bottom of the page. How do you want to end your story?" That way everyone gets a turn at least once a week to dictate and act out a story.

## Retelling Stories

Narrative drama features the physical retelling of familiar poems, fables, nursery rhymes, and stories. Enacting stories enriches children's language and develops reading comprehension (Bromley, 1998; Furman, 2000). Research by Brian Cambourne and Hazel Brown (1990) shows that retelling stories improved children's vocabulary, comprehension, and writing skills.

Children can retell stories in a variety of ways. Toddlers often make up stories using toys or objects. Preschoolers dress up and become characters in the story, acting it out, and adding their own creative twists. Older children can write their own version of the story, creating scripts, props, costumes, and even scenery.

## Puppetry

Using puppets is another way to retell or create stories. A puppet is really any inanimate object brought

Dress-up clothes allow children to try out new roles, imagining they are community workers or characters in the books they have read.

---

### Across Cultures

**Storytelling for Dual Language Learners**

Storytelling and reading aloud can be used to promote language development in children who are learning English (Gillanders & Castro, 2011). Select a nursery rhyme or a traditional story, or write one of your own, that will allow the addition of hand or body movements and that has many repetitive phrases such as the *Gingerbread Boy* or *Going on a Bear Hunt*.

- To develop vocabulary, select three to five core words and one repetitive phrase essential to the story to emphasize. Before telling the story introduce these words, review their meaning and show pictures or objects illustrating them. Have children repeat the words and suggest gestures to go with them. For example, in the *Gingerbread Boy* every time the phrase "run, run as fast as you can" is said, children could make their fingers run up and down their leg. Alternatively give out the pictures or objects for children to hold up at the appropriate time.
- Tell the story in the child's home language first. If you don't know the language, ask a parent or native speaker to translate for you and tell it with you or make a recording.
- Then repeat the story in English.
- Send home a recording of the story in both English and the home language for the child to share with his or her family.
- Arrange the play centers so that the words and phrase will be repeated and used in new ways throughout the coming days. For example, after telling the story of the *Gingerbread Man*, set up a race course on the playground for children to practice running fast.

---

to life through the active manipulation of a child's hand. Introduce children to the world of puppets by including purchased or adult-made puppets as regular visitors to the program. Most young children do not truly see the actual puppet, but rather the imaginary being it becomes through their play. Puppets can share secrets, read stories, and play with the children. They allow the adult to enter the child's world. Many of the most successful early childhood television programs, such as *Mr. Roger's Neighborhood* and *Sesame Street*, depend heavily on the use of puppets.

In addition to using commercial puppets, children can make their own. Making a puppet should not be a one-time activity, but something the child will return to again and again in order to create a character or persona with which to face the world. After introducing puppet-making supplies at the art center, they should be available on a regular basis for whenever a child wants or needs to create a puppet. It is important, therefore, to keep the design of the puppets quite simple, and within children's ability to create independently, without step-by-step instruction. Try stick puppets, shadow puppets, hand puppets and more.

For more information on making and using puppets, see *Puppetry Resources* on CourseMate.

## Storytelling Experiences for Infants and Toddlers

For children who are just beginning to talk, storytelling experiences should foster a love for story and a development of descriptive language.

**Family stories.** Children's favorite stories are the ones about their own lives, such as when the car broke down on the trip to Florida, getting caught in a thunderstorm while boating on the lake, or grandma's remembrance of her first day of school. Caregivers can share stories about themselves and their families as well as learning some of the child's own stories.

**Read, read, read.** Introduce the world of children's literature to infants from birth. It is never too early to read to a child. Read nursery rhymes, folktales, fairy tales, and traditional stories from the child's ethnic heritage. Based on oral traditions these simple stories provide an introduction to the basis of storytelling—character, setting, and plot. Knowing these also prepares children for reading the great literature of the world, which often is based on or incorporates elements from these traditions.

**Tell me.** Encourage young children who are talking to tell about something they just did. Cue them to use the three part story structure through your questions with a "What happened when you . . . ? What happened next? How did it end?"

## Storytelling Experiences for Preschool and Up

Storytelling is so much a part of the play of young children that the list of possible activities is endless. Here are a few to try:

**Family and school stories.** Continue to tell and retell stories about events in the life of the children and their families. Add stories about happenings in school, such as "Remember the day when the paint spilled all over my pants?"

**Retell.** Model the art of storytelling by retelling familiar tales from memory. Add props, finger movements, and actions. Speak with intensity, using voices to match the characters. These things will help you remember the story and keep the focus of the children as well.

**Puppets.** Put out commercial or handmade theme- and story-related puppets at the puppet theater. For example, animal puppets can be used when studying habitats.

**Masks.** Make masks to represent the different characters in a story and as you read the book hold up the mask at the appropriate time and speak in the character's special voice.

**Take a role.** Give each child a prop, mask, or puppet that goes with the story. As you tell the story have the child do something related to the tale using the prop, mask, or puppet. For example, give out bowls and spoons to go with a telling of Goldilocks. When the bears eat their porridge, the child with the appropriate size bowl stands up and mimics eating.

**Draw it.** As you tell a story illustrate it by drawing simple line drawings. To emphasize story structure

Puppets come to life in children's minds. They provide a safe way for children explore new ways of interacting with others.

divide the paper into three parts for beginning, middle, and end.

**Illustrate it.** Use a felt board to show the setting and characters in the story. Encourage children to make their own felt board pictures to tell stories of their own.

## Storytelling Experiences for Primary Age

By the primary grades, children are developing vocabulary at a rapid rate and learning how to read and write. These new skills can be reinforced and enhanced through dramatic activities.

**Story jar.** Place a number of small objects equal to the number of children in the group in a jar or box, such as toy figurines, jewelry, and pieces of fabric. Have the children sit in a circle and start off a story with an exciting sentence. Pass the jar around the circle and have each child remove one object and add a sentence to the story that includes that item.

**Odd pairs.** Select two words for things that are not usually associated together, like fish and tricycle, and challenge children to invent a story that includes both things.

**Everyone's story.** Sit in a circle and start off a story with an exciting sentence. Each child adds on to the story in turn.

**One word.** Say a word, such as *dog*, and have the children think of other words that mean close to the same thing or go with it, such as puppy, collie, mutt, collar, leash, dog bone, and so forth. Record the words on chart paper and then challenge children to make up a story using all the words.

**"What would happen if. . . ."** Develop imaginative stories by asking "What would happen if . . ." completed with a fantastical occurrence, such as the sky suddenly turned red, the school started to float, or all the fish in the sea started walking around on land. Let the students invent their own "what if" story starters, too. Make up cards with "what if" ideas for times when someone needs a creative spark and keep them at a storytelling center.

**Describe it.** To introduce the use of descriptive language, have the children name different kinds of people, animals, or objects, such as a detective, panda, or pencil. Then on separate paper have them brainstorm a list of descriptive words, such as angry,

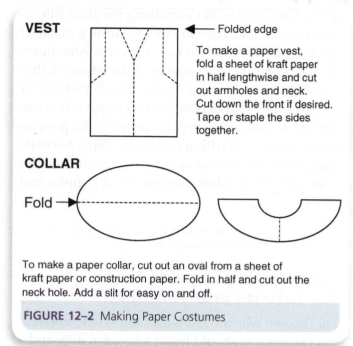

**VEST** — Folded edge

To make a paper vest, fold a sheet of kraft paper in half lengthwise and cut out armholes and neck. Cut down the front if desired. Tape or staple the sides together.

**COLLAR**

Fold →

To make a paper collar, cut out an oval from a sheet of kraft paper or construction paper. Fold in half and cut out the neck hole. Add a slit for easy on and off.

**FIGURE 12–2** Making Paper Costumes

**Did You Get It?**

**Story or narrative play is based on**

a. stories the teacher selects.

b. stories from other cultures.

c. children's improvisations and pantomimes.

d. stories children have invented, read, or heard.

**Take the full quiz on CourseMate**

sneaky, or broken. Put the lists together and have each child select a character and a descriptive word and then tell a story that includes that character. Try two or more of the descriptive words.

**Setting easel.** Make a class collection of settings. On large pieces of tag board, have children draw possible settings, such as a farmyard or an ocean. Then share the settings with the whole group. Ask, "How would you act if you were in one of these places?" Place the settings in turn on an easel and have pairs of children come forward and act out an appropriate event or animate a puppet in front of the scenes.

**Making costumes, hats, and jewelry.** Making costumes, hats, jewelry, and other body decorations is another way that art and dramatic play interact. As with puppets and masks, body-wear items should be simple enough for children to make on their own using simple art supplies.

*For directions for making these items, see Making Costumes, Hats, and Jewelry on CourseMate.*

## How Do We Introduce Children's Theater?

Besides creating their own dramatic play scenarios, young children should have the opportunity to attend drama performances done by older children and adults. Exposure to this level of dramatics will inspire children to expand their own dramatic play and narratives. A backstage tour will introduce children to the role of lighting, stage sets, and costuming in creating the illusion of reality. Being able to see actors in their character roles and as themselves helps them distinguish between fantasy and reality. They will also learn how to behave as an audience.

**Finding performances.**   Children's theater is especially designed to meet the attention span and need for interaction that young children require. Often a local drama group or a high school dramatics club will be willing to perform a program especially for young children.

Local and state arts-in-education programs can often provide information, links to performers, and grants to school groups. More information on these programs can be found at the Arts Education Partnership http://www.aep-arts.org. Many states have Councils for the Arts, which provide grants to groups who perform for schools. Performances geared to children can also be found at street fairs and arts festivals such as the First Night events held in many cities on New Year's Eve.

### Theater Experiences for Toddlers

For children who have only seen recorded performances, a live performance in which they can interact with the actors provides a wonderful model of what the dramatic arts can be. At the same time, we need to remember that young children believe that what they are seeing is real. If possible, have the actors talk to the children first and then put on their costumes. At

Children can respond to dramatic performances in many ways. Paige, age seven, has drawn the characters in a children's play she has seen with herself and her friends in the roles of the actors.

the end actors can remove the costumes and answer children's questions about what they were wearing, why, and how the costumes were made.

For a positive experience we need to make sure the children are comfortable. Because of their high activity levels, initial theater experiences for toddlers should be no more than 20 to 30 minutes long. Holding performances in the classroom or another familiar place is helpful as chairs in an auditorium or theater may be too large and visibility difficult. Having children sit on the floor is one possible alternative. The ideal performance for this age has only one to three actors with minimal staging who carry out their show very close to the children.

### Theater Experiences for Preschoolers

With their longer attentions spans, most preschool age children can attend longer performances about 30 to 60 minutes in length. They particularly enjoy stories and characters they are familiar with and will notice any changes that have been made in the narrative. Like toddlers, preschoolers may still be too small to sit comfortably in adult size seating. Before going to a performance make sure to ask about seating. Some theater groups let the children sit in a circle on the stage or on simple risers. Puppet shows work well because small children can get a good view of the raised up puppet stage.

## Theater Experiences for Kindergarteners and Primary Students

By the age of 5 or 6 children are ready for lengthier performances. They are better able to sit in adult-size theater seats and have a longer attention span. Most children by this age have heard many stories, seen many television shows and movies, and will be aware of the story elements in the play they see. Wanting to know the ending of the story will motivate them to sit through the play to the end.

## Theater Etiquette

Susan Fishman (2010) recommends that adults model how to be good audience members. This begins before the performance during which children are shown how to listen, when to participate, and how to show appreciation by clapping at appropriate times. These skills can first be practiced when viewing performances by peers. Later, when taking a group to a show, invite parents to accompany the group so there is a high adult to student ratio, and be sure to go over audience skills with both children and volunteers. Advise children to watch an adult if they are not sure what to do. If a child cannot sit still and pay attention, or is plainly uncomfortable during a performance, rather than disciplining the child and making the experience unpleasant, just quietly leave early with the child, and then try another performance when the child seems more ready.

With a little bit of effort the wonder of live theater can be shared with children.

## Responding to Dramatic Performances

Books provide an ideal way to introduce the vocabulary of drama and to practice discussing how the elements are used. Books model the narrative structure of beginning, middle, and end essential to all story making and demonstrate how conflict and tension are built to maintain interest. We can look for setting, discuss the characters, and decide on the theme and mood of the story.

Retelling and re-enacting stories from books will enhance children's natural play and develop their comprehension and story writing skills while making them more critical viewers of live and recorded dramatic productions. The story *Hey, Little Ant* (Hoose & Hoose, 1998) is an excellent example of a book that serves multiple purposes. The story tells about a boy who is considering whether or not to step on an ant. The book illustrates a clear beginning with the boy ready to step on the ant, a middle in which the ant defends himself, and an ending where the boy makes his decision. The conflict and tension build as we all wait to find out what the boy will do. Follow up reading similar stories by having preschoolers and older children act it out or retell it in a different way. Ask children to identify the dramatic elements. Ask questions such as

- Did your retelling have a beginning, middle, and end?
- Why did you choose to start there?
- How did you create conflict and tension?
- What mood did you create?
- What was your message?
- What is another way you might have told this story?
- What other ending could you have?

Provide opportunities for them to record their responses in their journals or at the art center using pictures and words. Videography of the dramatic play of the children provides an excellent way for children to see themselves as actors.

Expand on what children are exposed to on television and in movies by showing videos and DVDs of stories from other places that they are less likely to see home. Videos of storytellers and pantomime performed by both professionals and children can be found on the Internet. Show short excerpts that relate to children's dramatic play interests and integrated units.

## Making Connections through Drama

Bring the stories of children's home cultures into the classroom by having families share favorite stories. Create class books featuring these stories and share with families and the school community, such as displaying them in a public library. Bring in storytellers and dramatic performances that reflect different cultures, and provide opportunities for children to compare similarities and differences in the various stories, finger plays, puppet shows, and performances they see. Primary children can research and report on famous actors or folktales using the Internet, a teacher-prepared Web quest, or personal interviews and then teach their peers about what they learned or create their own dramatic act in response.

### Did You Get It?
**Theater experiences for toddlers should**

a. be at about 20 to 30 minutes long initially.

b. be in a large auditorium or theater.

c. include more than five actors to keep the toddlers interested.

d. be viewed on TV or video.

**Take the full quiz on CourseMate**

## How Do We Use the Dramatic Arts to Assess Growth?

Because dramatic play integrates so many of the growth areas, it provides an ideal situation in which to observe and evaluate children's learning.

**Content knowledge.** Teachers can observe the subject matter and concepts being used in children's play. For example, following a trip to the firehouse, a group of kindergartners playing in the dramatic play center might be observed play acting the safety practice of "Stop, Drop, and Roll" when pretending the food they are cooking is burning or children acting out the metamorphosis of a butterfly can be watched to see if they repeat the life stages in the correct order.

**Critical and creative thinking.** Decision making plays a key role in dramatic play. Teachers can observe the choices children make as they act out their ideas. For example, are the events in a logical order? Do the props and costume choices relate to the children's purpose? Are their choices unique and reflective of creative thinking?

**Physical control.** In order to play a role or imitate a behavior, children must exhibit both gross and fine motor control. Pretend play provides a noncompetitive setting in which children can explore the extent of their body motion. A toddler wiggling around pretending to be a worm, or a first grader stretching as high as possible to reach imaginary apples on a tree, are moving their bodies in ways not commonly found in ordinary events. Careful observation of how children handle props and move as they play can provide feedback on general physical development.

**Language development.** Teachers can also assess children's interest in stories and how well they have comprehended them by observing which stories are chosen for retelling and how they are reenacted. They can also note vocabulary usage and sentence structure.

### Did You Get It?
**Which of the following is a way to use dramatic arts to assess children's growth in critical and creative thinking?**

a. by assessing their comprehension of a story

b. by observing if they have improved their fine motor control

c. by asking them to identify a character in a story

d. by noticing the types of decisions they make in their play

**Take the full quiz on CourseMate**

# Conclusion: Imagine It!

The dramatic arts are the world of story and imagination with its roots in children's natural fantasy play. Through dramatic play, pantomime, improvisation, and storytelling, children can learn to control their bodies and words to create personas. They can become anything and anybody. Literacy skills are nurtured and developed as children become enthusiastic storytellers and scriptwriters. Music, dance, and visual art play a role in children's dramatic work.

The processes of pantomime, improvisation, and storytelling can be used to enhance everyday teaching and make facts and concepts more meaningful for students.

Teachers must also be performers. The skills of drama can also enhance how we teach. We can add flair to what we say, intensity to how we move, and story to what we tell.

For additional information on teaching the dramatic arts to young children, *see Chapter 12 Online Resources* on CourseMate. Visit our Web site at http://www.cengagebrain.com.

## Teaching In Action

### Puppets: Transcript of a Student Observation

When I entered the three- and four-year-olds' room, I saw the teacher's aide working with a small group of children. They were sitting on a rug, and the aide was using a puppet made of a cardboard tube and a piece of round paper with a simple face on it. She was using a funny little voice and singing a song that described something about each child. When she said the child's name, she would lightly touch the child's hand with the puppet. The children seemed delighted. They giggled whenever the puppet touched them. Then she asked them if they would like to make a puppet, too. The children seemed very excited by the idea.

She had paper circles in a basket, and she let the children each choose a circle and gave them each some markers in a small tray. The children drew a face for their puppets. I noticed that some of them were already talking in little, high-pitched puppet voices as they drew. When they were done, they went to a table and glued a cardboard strip to the back of the face. The aide had moved to the table and assisted them by asking

if they had put on enough glue and reminding them to hold the paper to the cardboard until it was stuck.

Next, the children began to have their puppets talk to each other. Two of them took them to the housekeeping area and fed them and pushed them in the carriage. Several others joined the aide in singing the song again, this time using their own puppet to touch a friend. When it was time to go home, the teacher asked the children to put their puppets to sleep in the puppet house [a decorated box that looked like a house]. I thought it would be hard to get them to leave the puppets, but the way she said, "Tomorrow you can wake them up to play again" seemed to fit with how the children thought about the puppets—like real playmates—so they all came over and carefully laid their puppets in the box to sleep. When their families picked them up, some children took family members over to see the puppets sleeping. They were so cute. They would say, "Shhh. . . . Don't wake them up."

# Reflection Page

## The Importance of Play

For each of the developmental growth areas, give an example of how dramatic play facilitates skill development.

Social

_____

_____

_____

_____

Physical

_____

_____

_____

_____

Language

_____

_____

_____

_____

Cognitive

_____

_____

_____

_____

Emotional

______________________________________________

______________________________________________

______________________________________________

______________________________________________

**Reflection:** Based on the skills developed by dramatic play, how much time should be devoted to children's play during the school day?

______________________________________________

______________________________________________

Digital Download Download from CourseMate

# Reflection Page

## Using Guided Imagery

Select one of the guided imagery suggestions in this chapter or on CourseMate or make up a scenario of your own. Write a script for this experience that you could use with young children.

Step 1: Relaxation

_____

_____

_____

_____

_____

_____

Step 2: The Journey

_____

_____

_____

_____

_____

_____

Step 3: The Return

_____

_____

_____

_____

**Reflection:** What will children learn from participating in this activity?

_____

_____

_____

# Reflection Page

## Designing a Play Center or Prop Box

Select a developmental age level, an appropriate topic, and learning objectives, and then write a plan of what you would include in a dramatic play center or prop box. Be sure to include a book or two, and multicultural and antibias materials.

**Children's ages:** _____

**Topic:** _____

**Objectives:** Using this center or prop box the children will develop

physically _____

socially _____

emotionally _____

language skills _____

cognitively _____

dramatic skill and knowledge _____

Describe what materials will be in the center or prop box.

_____

_____

_____

_____

_____

**Refelction:** What will be the greatest benefit of having this prop box or center prepared and ready to use at a "teachable moment."

_____

_____

# Reflection Page

## Telling a Story

Prepare yourself for telling a simple story to a group of children.

1. Select a folktale, fairy tale, or create an original story. Write a brief summary of it.

   _____
   _____
   _____
   _____
   _____
   _____

2. List the props you will use to enhance your presentation.

   _____
   _____
   _____
   _____
   _____

3. Describe how the children will actively participate as you tell the story. For example, how will they move or what sounds will they make?

   _____
   _____
   _____
   _____

**Reflection:** Do you feel confident about telling a story to young children? What can you do to prepare yourself beforehand?

   _____
   _____
   _____

# Appendix A

## Safety Guidelines

The following guidelines provide the information needed to create the safest environment possible for young artists.

NOTE: The Art and Craft Materials Institute has a voluntary labeling program. The AP Seal stands for a product certified to contain insufficient quantities of any material that is toxic or injurious to humans or that will cause acute or chronic health problems. The CP Seal means that the product meets manufacturing standards. Always look for these seals on the art supplies you purchase. In addition, for every material being used a Material Safety Data Sheets (MSDS) should be obtained from the manufacturer or seller of materials and kept on file. These sheets contain the raw ingredients and how to treat ingestion of or contamination from the product. Sheets for many products can be found at the National MSDS repository: http://www.msdssearch.com/ or obtained from the manufacturer.

## Material Safety Checklist

Use this checklist to ascertain if a product is safe for young children. Examine the material and circle "yes" or "no" for each question:

1. Is there a high probability that it will be ingested?
   yes          no

2. Is dust produced?
   yes     no

3. Is it difficult to wash off skin and surfaces with water?
   yes     no

4. Will spray, vapor, smoke, or fumes be produced?
   yes     no

5. Are the ingredients unknown?
   yes          no

6. Is it intended for adult use?
   yes          no

7. Will it be difficult for children to handle safely?
   yes          no

Avoid any product that has one or more "yes" answers.

## Guidelines for Safe Teacher Behavior

Use the following suggestions as a guide in choosing and using art materials.

- Any room or space used by children must be totally free of hazardous materials.

- When there is a choice, buy the least hazardous arts materials that will meet personal needs. For example, choose the following:

  Water-based markers instead of permanent markers

  Liquid paint instead of spray paint

  White glue instead of rubber cement

  Tacky craft glue instead of epoxy

- Keep all hazardous materials in a locked metal cabinet.

- Do not use any hazardous arts supplies in front of children. For example, do not use rubber cement while the children use safe white glue.

- When working with dusty materials, wear a dust mask.

- When working with skin irritants, wear rubber gloves.

- When working with solvents or hazardous fumes, wear an approved face mask with the proper filters. This is essential when using fabric dyes or making stained glass.

- Adequate ventilation means the outdoors. Unless there is a sealed glove box that is ventilated to the outside, never use hazardous materials at home or in the classroom, even if children are not present. An open window is not sufficient. Fumes and dust can remain in the air or collect on surfaces and contaminate the children or teacher days later.

- Handle sharp, dangerous tools with care. Pass scissors to children in a safe way. Store the paper cutter where children cannot see or touch it.

## Risk Factors

We need to be extremely protective of young children's health. The following chart shows some of the risks children can be exposed to from art materials.

| Factor | Risks to Children | Action to Take |
| --- | --- | --- |
| Metabolism | Children absorb toxins more rapidly than adults. | Do not use art supplies intended for adults. |
| Body Size | Children's mouths and noses are closer to the work surfaces. | Sit children at child-size tables and chairs. |
| Muscular Control | Children have less developed fine motor control and hand–eye coordination. | Provide child-size tools and ample workspace. Use safety scissors. |
| Behavior | Children have less self-control. | Set clear limits, supervise closely, and remove dangerous items from the setting. Make sure that for children under age three, small items pass the choke test.* |
| Health | Each child has unique health issues. | Check for allergies, asthma, and other health issues that may be irritated by materials. |

*A simple device to check the size of objects can be purchased from most school supply catalogs and stores. A general rule is that objects shorter than 2 inches in length and less than 1 inch in diameter should not be used by children under age three.

## Safe Substitutions

Here are some safe alternatives to use in lieu of toxic materials.

| Category | Art Materials Found In | Safer Alternative |
| --- | --- | --- |
| Solvents: These are poisonous if swallowed, flammable, and cause brain damage if inhaled over time. They are usually labeled "Keep out of reach of children" and "Flammable." | Oil paint, turpentine, and other thinners | Water-based paints |
| | Lacquer and thinners Shellac and alcohol thinners | Coat objects with water-based acrylic gels |
| | Permanent printing ink | Water-based printing ink |
| | Permanent markers | Water-based markers |
| | Rubber cement and thinners Superglue, airplane glue, and epoxy | White or gel glues, craft glue, school paste |
| Aerosol Sprays: Inhaling these can cause bronchial irritation, asthma attacks, and increased susceptibility to respiratory infection. | Spray glue | White or gel school glue |
| | Spray paint | Use a brush |
| | Charcoal/chalk fixatives | Press a paper to finished picture to remove excess dust. Laminate finished work. |

| Category | Art Materials Found In | Safer Alternative |
|---|---|---|
| **Toxic Pigments:**<br>Colors made from cadmium, lead, cobalt, chromium, and so forth are poisonous. | Artist quality paints | Use AP seal paints intended for children. |
| | Artist quality pastels | Use AP seal colored chalks intended for children. |
| | Ceramic glazes | Paint clay with child-safe paints or have adult apply glaze away from areas where there are children. |
| | Copper enameling | Make jewelry in other safe ways. See text. |
| **Dusts:**<br>Inhaling these can cause bronchial irritation, asthma attacks, and increased susceptibility to respiratory infection. Clay dust may be contaminated with asbestos. | Firing clay | Use only wet clay. Make sure clay is labeled "talc free." (asbestos is found in association with talc.) |
| | Ceramic glazes | Paint clay with child-safe paints or have adult glaze the pieces away from children. |
| | Plaster | Do not mix in the presence of children. Avoid carving dried plaster. Due to excessive heat do not make hand casts. |
| | Powdered tempera | Do not mix in the presence of children. Wear a filter mask. Avoid activities that use sprinkled powdered paint. |
| | Chalk | Use on a wet surface. Place newspaper under paper. Have children wash hands immediately after use. |
| **Dyes:**<br>Commercial dyes may contain chemicals that cause bladder cancer and severe allergic reactions. | Fabric dyes | Use natural dyes made from plants or unsweetened packaged drink mix. |
| **Fumes and Toxic Gases:**<br>Strong lung irritants may be released when a material is heated. | Wax | Do not melt in the presence of children. |
| | Plastics | Do not melt or iron in the presence of children. |
| | Crayons | Do not melt or use glues, which contain solvent that melt the plastic. Attach with chenille stems, yarn, or wire. |
| Bacteria Contamination | Styrofoam trays and plastic food containers | Rinse containers and their lids in hot, soapy water. Soak for 1 minute in a disinfectant solution of three-quarters of a cup of chlorine bleach per gallon of water. A final rinse in warm water is necessary to remove the bleach solution. Cover clothing and protect hands from the bleach by wearing rubber gloves. Do not allow children to use this disinfectant solution. |
| | Playdough and other similar shared materials | Older children can be asked to wash their hands or use a tissue before use. For toddlers and young preschoolers, a good solution is to give the children their own pieces of modelling dough and their own storage containers or resalable bags. |
| | Cardboard toilet paper tubes | Substitute rolled paper tubes. A rolled half-sheet of 12-by-18-inch tag board makes a very sturdy tube. Regular construction paper can also be used. |

# Ways to Help Children Distinguish Food from Art Supplies

Some art materials resemble foods, such as play-dough, or smell sweetly enticing, such as paste and paints. Because young children often try to put these in their mouths, it is important to always use non-toxic art materials specifically intended for children. However, even though these are safe, we still need to safety-proof our children by teaching them to never put any art material in their mouths. That way, if they should encounter adult art materials, which may appear to be the same as nontoxic ones but are not, they will know not to ingest them. Here some ways to help children differentiate between food and art materials.

1. Avoid art materials that closely resemble foods or smell like foods. For example scented markers that smell like candy can trick children into to tasting them. Later, those same children may try to taste a toxic permanent marker.

2. If the children will be making something from a food item and eating it, it should be called "cooking" and done in the cooking area. For example, a child told that he may lick his hands after "painting" with pudding will be more likely to lick his hands after painting with tempera paint.

3. Enforce the rule that no art material is ever tasted, eaten, or drunk. If a child persists in trying to put an item in her mouth, remove the materials and try a different activity.

4. Supervise children, and do not let them put their fingers into their mouths when working with art materials. Children and adults often forget and chew or suck on a finger when concentrating on their work. Be alert and gently remind the child to wash his hands first.

5. Mix and store art materials in containers that are visually different from those used for food. If a food container is being reused, cover the outside with a label, or paint it.

6. Insist that children wash their hands after they finish using art materials, but before they work with foods.

## Separate Arts Activities from Food Areas

7. In all arts activities, but particularly gluing, painting, and clay, keep the art activity separate from cooking and eating activities. Children need to learn from the beginning that many art materials are never put in one's mouth nor eaten, and separating these two activities is one way to do this. In a home situation, when the weather does not allow outside artwork, the kitchen may provide the only location for arts activities requiring water. One way to separate art from food activities is to have a special low table, tray, or mat that is used only for arts activities. Never eat on tables that have been used for art projects. If tables must be used for both purposes, give the children trays on which to do their art, or cover the tables with plastic tablecloths when eating on them.

# A Sample Letter to Families: Child Safety Information

Dear Family,

All of the arts materials used in our program have been carefully selected to be safe for young children. Some children, however, have special sensitivities. To help us select the safest arts materials for your child, please answer the following questions:

1. Is your child allergic to anything?                    yes    no
   If yes, please list:
2. Does your child have any respiratory problems?         yes    no
   If yes, please explain:
3. Is your child's skin sensitive to anything?            yes    no
   If yes, please list:
4. Are there any art materials that your child should not use?    yes    no
   Please list and explain.

Thank you for taking the time to complete this form. Together we can make sure that your child will have a safe and fun time creating art.

Your child's teacher,

# Appendix B

## Planning Arts Activities

Whether a curriculum is planned around themes, projects, learning centers, or play areas, the individual components are the activities—the specific things the children and the educator will be doing. It is important to plan these activities carefully, to ensure that nothing is forgotten and to provide a measure against which we can assess our delivery.

Plans for individual arts activities need to take account of the factors that will affect the dynamics of a particular group of children and answer the following questions: who, why, where, when, what, and how? By planning answers to each of these questions ahead of time, teachers are better prepared to guide the arts activities they offer the children.

## Who? Group Composition

Every group of children is unique. The following three characteristics should be considered when making plans.

1. **What are the ages and number of children?** The ages and number of students will affect the amount of time, space, and supervision for which the teacher must plan. Planning an activity with 4 one-year-olds will require very different decisions than designing a program for 20 five-year-olds. If the children are of mixed ages, will all of them be able to work with the same amount of supervision and be successful?

2. **What are the children's previous experiences?** The less familiar children are with an arts medium or technique, the more exploration they need. If the children are competent with a material, then more responsive activities can be planned. If a group contains children of various ages, developmental phases, and experience, then care must be taken that the selected arts activities are open-ended, having many possible ways for children to carry them out. This will allow children to work comfortably at their own developmental levels.

3. **Are there children with special needs?** Check that each activity will be able to be accomplished by every individual. Do the activities need adaptation so that a child with special needs can have success? Select arts activities that can be done by a wide range of children, and modify the materials, tools, and set-up as necessary.

## When? Time Frame

Next, consider the amount of time that will be available for the children to work on their arts activities. Make sure that there will be sufficient time to complete an activity, whether on the same day or over a period of days. Will wet projects be able to dry? Will children be able to reach completion? Be sure to allow time for sharing and discussing as well.

## Why? Goals and Objectives

Good activities have clear educational goals. Goals are the long-term changes in behavior that the activities are meant to foster in children. They are why the activities are selected. These are not changes that will happen after one activity or even two. To reach set goals children need many opportunities in which to learn and to practice. Self-confidence, for example, comes after many successful experiences.

# Writing Objectives

Short-term goals are called **objectives**. An objective is a statement describing a behavior that can be accomplished within the time frame of the activity. Objectives are usually phrased in terms of observable skills and behaviors. One way to write effective objectives is to think of them as having two parts. The first describes the growth area and the skill or behavior to be practiced in the activity. The second describes how we will know that this growth is happening by describing what we should see or hear the children doing. For example, a skill objective for a cutting activity might be written as follows:

**Part 1:** In this activity the children will develop physically as they coordinate eye, hand, and finger movements while using scissors.

**Part 2:** I will know that this is happening when I see the children freely cutting shapes out of the paper.

The first part of this objective focuses our attention on the behaviors we need to facilitate so that the child will be successful. The second part of the objective provides a way for us to immediately assess the child's progress. The following sample objectives show how objectives relate to the growth areas discussed in Chapter 1.

Here are the developmental areas, some suggested *specific* skills, and some examples of well-written objectives.

## Social Objectives

These are behaviors or skills that help children get along better with others.

*Examples of social skills:*

being helpful

patiently waiting a turn

sharing

showing kindness

working cooperatively

taking a role

listening respectfully

following direction

**Complete objective example.** *Children will practice* patiently waiting a turn. I will know this objective is being met when I see the children sitting quietly in the circle and raising hands when they want to speak.

## Physical Objectives

These are behaviors or skills that help *children develop* control over their bodies.

*Examples of gross motor physical objectives:*

throwing and catching

balancing

coordinating movement of arms and legs

being flexible

*Examples of specific fine motor physical skills:*

cutting and pasting

zipping and buttoning

using a writing or drawing tool

picking up small pieces

**Complete objective example.** *Children will practice* balancing. I will know this objective is being met when I see the children walk at least 3 feet on a plank laid flat on the floor.

## Language Objectives

These are behaviors or skills that help children receive and communicate ideas through listening, speaking, reading, and writing.

*Examples of language skills:*

naming

telling or retelling

discussing

describing

defining

answering questions

matching letters and sounds

identifying words

listening to stories and so forth being read aloud

reading words

comprehending

using correct language forms (grammar)

writing stories, poems, and reports

using the writing process—drafting, editing, revising, and publishing

**Complete objective example.** *Children will practice* telling a story. I will know this objective is being met when the children dictate a story to me with a beginning, middle, and end.

**Complete objective example.** *Children will practice* identifying words. I will know this objective is being met when the children, given a card with a verb on it, act out that action.

**Complete objective example.** Children will practice listening to and retelling a story. I will know this objective is being met when I see the children sitting quietly during the story and when they draw pictures of their favorite part in their journals.

## Cognitive Objectives

These are behaviors or skills that help children develop the ability to reason, think logically, organize information, and solve problems.

*Examples of intellectual skills:*

naming

observing

counting

calculating

measuring

comparing and contrasting

predicting

ordering

finding patterns

testing ideas

making a plan

graphing

using a graphic organizer (like a Venn diagram)

**Complete objective example.** *Children will practice* measuring and comparing. I will know this objective is being met when they use a scale to measure some pumpkins and then use what they learn to decide which one is the heaviest.

**Complete objective example.** *Children will practice* combining things they know in a new way. I will know this objective is being met when I see the children taking roles of characters in the story and acting out something different from the story ending.

## Perceptual Objectives

These are behaviors or skills that help children use their senses to perceive and make sense of the characteristics of the objects and environments that surround them.

*Examples of visual perceptual or spatial skills:*

identifying visual elements, such as colors, shape, textures, and forms

matching visual elements

observing placement and relationships between objects

looking from different viewpoints

observing how parts form a whole or vice versa

*Examples of auditory perception skills:*

identifying auditory elements, such as pitches, timbres, tempos, and dynamics

matching auditory elements

matching rhythms with movements

**Complete objective example.** *Children will practice* looking at three-dimensional forms from different viewpoints and describe what they see. I will know this objective is being met when I see the children turning their clay sculptures around and talking with each other about how they look.

## Emotional Objectives

These are behaviors or skills that help children develop independence, self-knowledge, and confidence in their own abilities.

*Examples of emotional skills:*

working independently

evaluating their own work or behavior

using self-control

expressing their feelings or preferences

showing pride in their work

showing trust

**Complete objective example.** *Children will practice* evaluating their own work. I will know this objective is being met when they assess their growth in writing by comparing a journal entry they wrote in September to one they wrote in May and I hear the children saying things like, "Look how I used to make 'A.' Now I make it so much better!"

## Arts Objectives

These are behaviors or skills that help children develop expertise in the particular art form. These objectives may be based on local or national arts standards. See the Exploring the Arts chapters for summaries of the standards for each of the art forms.

## Where? Set-up

This part of the plan describes where the children will be working. How should the furniture be arranged? Where should the supplies be located? What changes will have to be made so that this activity will run smoothly?

In describing the setting is important to remember that the environment includes everything that surrounds children.. It is where the child works and learns. It is the room and any other space used for arts creation—hallways, play areas, and the outdoors. It is how orderly the supplies are and how appropriately sized the furniture is. It is the arrangement of the workspace and the other children in it. How this environment is planned and used will determine how much the child can concentrate on learning about and creating in the arts.

## What? Materials

It is important to list the supplies needed for each activity. This will quickly indicate which items are on hand and what has to be found or bought. It is often possible, with a little creativity, to make substitutions, but the key to success is to keep the materials basic and safe. The more the children can handle the tools and supplies on their own, without constant supervision, the more they will grow artistically.

## How? Procedure

Once an activity is selected, it is necessary to plan how to present it. Every activity has three parts: an introduction or warm-up, what the children will do, and how you will interact with the children.

### The Warm-Up or WOW

First, it is necessary to introduce the materials and procedures to the children. An activity can be started many ways, but the most effective ways are those that entice the children by awakening their natural curiosity. These introductory experiences or "wonderful opportunities to wonder" (WOW) must be rich in sensory and visual stimuli. They should be memorable—full of opportunities for asking questions and making observations. Most important, the experience should flow directly into the arts activities that are offered to the children.

Warm-ups for arts activities can range from something as simple as playing a beat on a drum to something as complex as a field trip to a museum. The type of introduction or warm-up will depend on the age of the children and their previous experiences.

**Real object.** For young children, who are only just beginning to think symbolically, warm-ups should always include a carefully selected real object and related questions that draw them into the activity. But even older children can be inspired by a wonderful object of wonder. Finding a real object takes extra time, but it is worth it. Presenting a real object that draws children's attention makes the difference between an ordinary experience and a wonderful one.

The real object should be something that the children can see, touch, and possibly use. In some cases, a new art material, tool, prop, or musical instrument can be the real object. For example, a teacher might show the children a large paintbrush at circle time and say: "Here is a new brush to try when you go to the easel today. What kind of line do you think it will make?" In other cases, the real object may be a nature object, such as a shell or a colorful leaf. Whatever it is, it should be presented with so much showmanship and enthusiasm that it elicits a "Wow!" from the children.

**A book.** A wonderful children's book is another way to introduce an arts activity. Many examples of books about the arts are given throughout this text. However, no matter how terrific the book is, try to accompany books with a real object as well. Just imagine the difference in the children's creative work between these two examples. In the first, a teacher reads a book about ladybugs and then suggests that the children make ladybug pictures at the drawing center. In the second, a teacher reads a book about ladybugs and then displays a jar of live ladybugs. After the children observe using hand lenses and share what they see, the ladybugs are placed in the drawing center. In the first warm-up, the children have just the memory of the pictures in the book when they go to the drawing center. Only the second warm-up draws children into the activity and sustains it as they go to the center and re-experience the ladybugs.

**Works of art.** Another way to start an arts activity is to display a reproduction of an artwork, listen to a work of music, or watch a recording of a play or dance. These can be done by adults or children. Talking about the work can model how the children can talk about their own work while they participate in the activity. However, these works should never be held up as models for the children to imitate or copy in their own work.

**An experience.** Going outside and touching trees, looking at trees, and laying beneath trees is a wonderful way to introduce a creative movement activity focused on trees. Activity-related experiences that take children out of the classroom can be an inspiring way to begin an activity. Field trips and walks in the neighborhood are rich in such possibilities.

**Guided discovery.** Guided discovery is a form of warm-up that is an ideal way to introduce children ages four and up to a new material, technique, or center. The purpose is to develop interest and excitement in the children while at the same time establishing guidelines for use. Guided discovery consists of three parts.

1. **Unveiling.** Wrap a small item related to the activity in wrapping paper, or put larger ones in an interesting basket, box, or bag. Centers can be covered with a cloth or blocked with a banner or screen. Ask the children to guess what the object is, or what the center might contain. Slowly give clues or unwrap it.

2. **Exploring.** Show the object or parts at the center. Ask questions about how it might be used. Focus on what would be careful, safe ways to handle the materials or to behave in the center.

3. **Rule setting.** Finally, summarize the children's positive suggestions into easy-to-understand words or pictures, and make a sign to post near the center or workspace. When a behavior is inappropriate, refer to the sign as needed.

## What to Do

Although flexibility must be an integral component of teaching, describing step by step what the children and you will be doing can provide guidance in making sure maximum learning takes place.

## What to Say

It is a good idea to plan ahead of time some of the questions and vocabulary words that will be asked during the activity. Often when busy dealing with active young artists it is easy to forget one's good intentions. Consider carefully the kinds of concept-based questions you will ask, and the vocabulary you will use. Make cards or signs listing the vocabulary to display during the activity. Write questions on cards that you display as you ask the questions. List some possible responses you will make to the children's actions and work. It is through teacher–student interaction that knowledge about the art form, skill in performance, the disposition to think as an artist, and feelings of self-confidence in the arts are acquired.

## Transition Out

In the same way, plan how to provide the children with closure at the end of each activity. The transition out should restate the basic concept of the activity while extending the learning in some way.

This could be a statement that summarizes what the children have been doing, or a question that makes them reflect on their learning and then invites them to carry what they learned to a new setting. For example, a creative drama activity focused on panto-miming meeting someone new could end as follows: "Look at all the friendly ways we thought of to make a new friend! Let's try some of these ideas out the next time a new visitor comes to our class."

## Assess the Learning

An activity is not complete unless there is some way to know how the children have gained knowledge and skill. In this section, prepare several reflective questions you could ask or behaviors you could observe that will provide information on what has been learned. In writing these, refer back to the objectives originally set for the activity.

## Writing an Arts Activity Plan

The following is an example of one way to write an activity plan. It is the format used in this book. This or a similar form can be used whenever a new activity is being considered. The outline provides one way to organize the basic information needed to create successful activities.

---

### ACTIVITY PLAN FORMAT

**ACTIVITY:**

**WHO?**      **Group composition age(s):**

          **Group size:**

**WHEN?**    **Time frame:**

**WHY?**      **Growth Objectives:** In this activity children will develop . . .

          Socially

          Physically

          Intellectually

          Linguistically

          Perceptively

          Emotionally

          **Arts Objectives:** In this activity the child will grow as an artist . . .

**WHERE?**   **Set-up:**

**WHAT?**    **Materials:**

**HOW?**      **Procedure:**

          **Warm-up [WOW]:**

          **What to do:**

          **What to say:**

          **Transition out:**

**ASSESSMENT OF LEARNING:**

## SAMPLE ACTIVITY PLAN: A Painting Exploration

**WHO?**   **Group composition age(s):** Three- and four-year-olds

**Group size:** two or three at a time

**WHEN?**   **Time frame:** 3-hour session

**WHY?**   **Growth Objectives:** In this activity children will develop . . .

- Socially, by learning how to get along and talk with other artists. I will know that this is happening when I see them talking about their paintings to each other.
- Physically, by exercising hand–eye coordination. I will know that this is happening when I see them filling scoops, mixing paint with a spoon, and using different paintbrushes.
- Linguistically, by learning new art vocabulary. I will know this is happening when I hear them describe a texture and see them point to one of the textures.
- Cognitively, by observing and describing cause and effect. I will know that this is happening when I hear them making predictions about what will happen to the texture of the paint and then describing the result.
- Perceptively, by making their own choices of what textures and colors to mix together. I will know that this is happening when I see them select a color and texture to combine that is different from the others.
- Emotionally, by strengthening their self-confidence using paint. I will know that this is happening when I see them actively exploring the paint.
- Arts skills and knowledge: In this activity children will grow as visual artists by gaining skill in applying different textures of paint. They will identify the visual art element of texture.

**WHERE?**   **Setup:** Warm-up activity on rug. Painting at the easel, table, or paint center.

**WHAT?**   **Materials:**

Containers of tempera paint in a variety of colors

Labeled containers of different materials to add to paint: sand, salt, soap flakes

Small scoops, brushes, and paper at the easel or on newspaper-covered table

**HOW?**   **Procedure:**

**Warm-Up [WOW]:** Large group: (on rug) Pass around a piece of sandpaper, then a piece of fake fur. Ask the children to describe how it feels. Play the "Texture Search" game: Name a texture; each child then has to find something with that texture and touch it. Have the children take turns naming the textures they find.

**What to Do:**

1. Ask: "What is the texture of paint?"

   "How could we change the texture of paint?"

   "What do you think would happen if you added these things to the paint?"

   "Would you like to add one and see what happens?"

2. Demonstrate how to add one of the materials to the paint. Tell the children that they can add any of the materials to their paint when they come to the painting place.

3. As the children come to paint, supervise them as they add materials to the color of their choice, and then use it in their paintings.

*(Continued)*

**What to Say:**

Descriptive: "You are using the large brush." "You used the textured paint to ___."

Questioning: "Which paint did you like using better?" "Which paint was hard to spread?"

**Transition Out:**

Say: "You had fun painting with the different textured paint. You can add a different texture the next time you paint. Let's put your painting over here to dry. What would you like to do now? I see your friend Ann is having fun with the blocks."

**ASSESSMENT OF LEARNING**

1. Do the children use descriptive words to talk about their textures?
2. Do the children gain more control and confidence in using brushes and paint?
3. Can the children see differences in the paint and identify what was added to change the texture?

# Appendix C

## Teacher Resources

### Arts Supplies

**Boxes,** for storing large prints, big books, and portfolios. Available from:

> **Calloway House** (cardboard storage boxes and units)
> 451 Richardson
> Dr. Lancaster, PA 17603-4098
> http://www.callowayhouse.com

**Paint daubers** (Chapter 9)

**Paint markers, refillable** (Chapter 9)

**Paint scrapers and fingertip painters** (Chapter 9)

**Papier-mâché paste** (Chapter 9)

**Precut mats** (Chapter 4)

**Tempera blocks** (Chapter 9)

**Vertical floor loom** (Chapter 9)

All these items are all available from many arts supply companies, including:

**Dick Blick**

> P.O. Box 1267
> Galesburg, IL 61402-1267
> 1-800-447-8192
> http://www.dickblick.com

**Lakeshore Learning Materials**

> 2695 E. Dominguez
> St. Carson, CA 90749
> 1-800-428-4414
> http://www.lakeshorelearning.com

**NASCO**

> 901 Janesville Ave.
> Fort Atkinson, WI 53538-0901
> 1-800-558-9595
> http://www.enasco.com

**Sax Arts and Crafts**

> P.O. Box 51710
> New Berlin, WI 53151
> 1-800-558-6696
> http://www.saxarts.com

**Triarco**

> 14650 28th Ave. No.
> Plymouth, MN 55447
> 1-800-328-3360
> http://www.triarcoarts.com

## Artifact Sources

**Art Institute of Chicago**

> The Museum Shop
> Michigan Avenue at Adams
> St. Chicago, IL 60603
> 1-800-621-9337
> http://www.artic.edu

**Global Crafts**

> 300 B Flagler Avenue
> New Smyrna Beach, FL 32169
> 1-866-468-3438
> http://www.globalcrafts.org

**Southwest Indian Foundation**

> P.O. Box 86
> Gallup, NM 87302-0001
> 1-505-863-4037
> http://www.southwestindian.com

**Ten Thousand Villages**

> 704 Main Street
> PO Box 500
> Akron, PA 17501-0500
> 1-887-883-8341
> http://www.tenthousandvillages.com/

**Unicef**

> P.O. Box 182233
> Chattanooga, TN 37422
> 1-800-553-1200
> http://www.unicef.org

## Sources of Prints and Posters

**All Posters**

> P.O. Box 60000
> San Francisco, CA 94160
> 888-654-0143
> http://www.allposter.com

> Online source for reasonably priced posters of all kinds

**Art Image Publications**

> P.O. Box 160
> Derby Line, VT 05830
> 1-800-361-2598
> http://www.artimagepublications.com

> Online source for fine art prints and kits

**Art.com**
10700 World Trade Blvd.
Suite 100
Raleigh, NC 27617
800-952-5592
http://www.art.com
Online source of fine art prints

**Art Institute of Chicago**
The Museum Shop
Michigan Avenue at Adams
St. Chicago, IL 60603
1-800-621-9337
http://www.artic.edu
Prints and postcard reproductions from their collection

**Art with Heart**
Syracuse Cultural Workers
P.O. Box 6367
Syracuse, NY 13217
1-315-474-1132
https://www.syracuseculturalworkers.com/

Contemporary posters and postcards, many featuring the work of African American and Native American artists

**Crizmac**
P.O. Box 65928
Tucson, AR 85728-5928
1-800-913-8555
http://www.crizmac.com

Individual and sets of prints, including Take 5, of Native American, Haitian, African, and other art from many times and places

**Crystal Productions**
1812 Johns Drive
Glenview, IL 60025-6159
1-800-255-8629

http://crystalproductions.com
Take 5 poster sets, DVDs, and art games

**Dover Publications**
31 E. 2nd
St. Mineola, NY 11501
http://store.doverpublications.com

Postcards and inexpensive books that can be cut apart to use as prints, featuring Native American, African, Asian, and Central and South American art

**Knowledge Unlimited**
P.O. Box 52
Madison, WI 53707-0052
1-800-356-2303
http://thekustore.com

Posters featuring ancient cultures, Native American, African American, female artists, and others

**Metropolitan Museum of Art**
255 Gracie Station
New York, NY 10028-9998
1-800-468-7386
http://www.metmuseum.org

Print and postcard reproductions of artwork in their collection

**Museum of Fine Arts, Boston**
P.O. Box 244
Avon, MA 02322-0244
http://www.mfa.org

Prints and postcard reproductions from their collection

**Museum of Modern Art**
11 W. 53rd St.
New York, NY 10019-5401
1-800-447-6662
http://www.moma.org

Prints and postcards from their collection

**Nasco Arts and Crafts**
901 Janesville Ave.
Fort Atkinson, WI 53538-0901
1-800-558-9595
http://www.enasco.com

Caraway book series on world art forms, Take 5, and many other print series, and famous artists' postcard sets

**National Gallery of Art**
2000B South Club
Dr. Landover, MD 20785
http://www.nga.gov

Postcards and medium-size prints of works in their collection

**Sax Visual Arts Resources**
P.O. Box 51710
New Berlin, WI 53151
1-800-558-6696
http://www.saxarts.com

Print sets reproducing African American, African, and Native American art and more

# Music Supplies

## Musical instruments are available from:

**House of Musical Traditions**
7040 Carroll Avenue
Takoma Park, MD 20912
301-270-9090
http://www.hmtrad.com/catalog/
Traditional and folk instruments from around the world

**Lakeshore Learning**
2695 E. Dominguez St.
Carson, CA 90895
800-778-4456
http://www.lakeshorelearning.com
Safe rhythm instruments for infants, toddlers, and preschoolers

**Music Kids**
1175 Groveland
Dr. Chuoluota, FL 32766
407-446-6818
http://www.musickidsonline.com/
Instruments for infants and toddlers, including chimes and music mats

**Production Associates**
12 W. Collins Avenue
Orange, CA 92867
714-771-6519
http://www.wesign.com
We Sign music videos in American Sign Language

**Two Little Hands Productions**
P.O. Box 581037
Salt Lake City, UT 84158
801-533-5151
http://www.signingtime.com/
Songs and stories in American Sign Language on video and CD

# Appendix D

## Recipes
### Modeling Doughs

#### COOKED PLAY DOUGH

4 cups flour

1 cup of salt

1 tablespoon cream of tartar

4 cups water

1 tablespoon oil

food coloring (optional)

1. Combine the flour, salt, and cream of tartar.
2. Add the water, oil, and food coloring.
3. Cook over medium heat until thick.
4. Remove from heat and knead when cool.
5. Store in sealed plastic bag or airtight container.

Makes 4 cups

*Note:*

This is a pliant playdough that stays soft for a long time. Add cornmeal, sawdust, coffee grounds, sand, or other grainy items to change the texture.

#### UNCOOKED PLAY DOUGH

4 cups of flour

1 cup salt

4 tablespoons cooking oil

1 and ½ cups water

Food coloring

1. Mix together oil and food coloring and pour into water.
2. Mix together flour and salt.
3. Add water, oil, and coloring mixture to flour.
4. Then stir and knead till smooth and flexible.
5. Store in sealed plastic bag or air tight container.

#### BAKING DOUGH

1 cup flour

½ cup salt

½ cup warm water

Food coloring (optional)

1. Combine all of the ingredients in a bowl.
2. Mix and then knead until smooth.
3. Add more flour if too sticky, more water if too dry.

Makes 1 cup

*Note:*

1. This dough does not keep. Use it in one day.
2. Add 1 teaspoon alum as a preservative if you want to use it longer.
3. This dough can be baked in an oven set at 300°F until hard—approximately 20 to 60 minutes, depending on the thickness of the pieces.

#### ALUM PLAY DOUGH

2 cups of flour

2 tablespoons alum

1 cup salt

1 cup water

2 tablespoons cooking oil

Food coloring as desired

Mix dry ingredients together. Add food coloring, oil, and water. Mix well. Then knead till smooth.

#### SODA CLAY FOR BEADS

Children can make bead shapes from dough made from the following recipe

1 cup baking soda

½ cup cornstarch

⅔ cup warm water

Food coloring or tempera paint (optional)

1. Mix ingredients and heat until as thick as mashed potatoes.
2. Pour on a cool surface, and knead when cool.
3. Add coloring, if desired, during kneading process.
4. Store in plastic bag until ready to use.
5. Shape beads.
6. Use a drinking straw to make holes (holes made with toothpicks are too small for young children to thread).
7. They must air dry a day or two before stringing. To speed drying, bake 10 minutes at lowest oven setting or 30 seconds in a microwave on medium setting.

Makes 1 cup

(Suggestion: Make several batches in different colors.)

## Fingerpaint Recipes

### CORNSTARCH FINGER PAINT OR SLURRY FOR SQUISHY BAGS

3 cups of water

1 cup of cornstarch

Food coloring

1. Mix 1 cup of cornstarch into 1 cup of water.
2. Heat the remaining 2 cups of water to boiling.
3. Mix the cornstarch liquid into the boiling water and stir until thickened.
4. Divide into cups or zipper top bags and add food coloring.

### FLOURY FINGER PAINT

1 cup flour (check for gluten allergies)

2 tablespoons salt

1 ½ cups cold water

1 ¼ cups hot water

Food coloring

Mix together the flour and the salt. Add in the cold water and blend well. Add the hot water while stirring. Boil until thick and remove from heat. Stir until smooth. Color as desired. Refrigerate until use.

### GELATIN FINGER PAINT

1 Tablespoon unflavored gelatin (1 envelope)

Cold water

½ Cup cornstarch

4 Tablespoons liquid dish detergent

Food coloring

Mix gelatin and ⅓ cup cold water, then set aside. Stir cornstarch into 2 ½ cups cold water until cornstarch dissolves. Cook and stir until thick. Remove from heat and mix in the gelatin mixture. Add the liquid dish detergent. Cool and color as desired. Store at room temperature in a sealed container.

### SUPER QUICK RECIPE

Mix ¼ cup liquid starch with 1 tablespoon food coloring or tempera paint. Store in tightly closed container.

### SWEET AND SOAPY

Heat 3 tablespoons of sugar and ½ cup cornstarch in 2 cups of water. Stir until mixture thickens. Add food coloring and a tablespoon of soap flakes or liquid dish detergent. Put in closed container and let cool.

## Homemade Paint

### CONDENSED MILK PAINT

1 cup condensed milk

Food coloring

Add food coloring to the milk until it reaches the desired color. Store in refrigerator until use.

### CORNSTARCH PAINT

½ cup cornstarch

½ cup cold water

4 cups boiling water

Liquid tempera paint or food coloring

Add cornstarch to cold water. Stir well. Add boiling water. Cook over medium heat until it boils. Boil for 1 minute stirring constantly. Cool. Add paint for color. Store in refrigerator until use.

### CORN SYRUP PAINT

4 tablespoons corn syrup

1 ½ teaspoons liquid dish soap

Food coloring or liquid tempera

Mix together the syrup and the detergent and add color as desired.

## CRYSTAL PAINT

1 cup Epsom salts

½ cup water

Food coloring or liquid tempera

Mix salts and water and add coloring. The paint will be sparkly when dry.

## FACE PAINT

1 teaspoon cornstarch

½ teaspoon cold cream

½ teaspoon water

Food coloring

Mix the cornstarch and cold cream together. Add the water and stir well. Add color as desired. Store covered.

## FROTHY PAINT

½ of a quarter-ounce bar of Ivory soap, grated (check for allergies first)

½ cup cold water

Food coloring, optional

Beat soap and water with an egg beater or wire whisk until frothy.

## MILKY PAINT

½ cup powdered milk

Warm water

Food coloring

Add just enough water to make a thick paint. Stir till smooth. Color as desired. Refrigerate until use.

# Homemade Pastes

## FLOUR PASTE

Add water to flour until it reaches a thick but spreadable consistency.

*Advantages:* This is a quick and handy recipe. It is easily made from ingredients found in most kitchens in any amount needed. It works very well on most kinds of paper. It is safe and does not stain clothing. The texture is very different from school paste and provides an interesting change for children. This is one of the few pastes that children can make themselves.

*Disadvantages:* Flour paste cannot be stored and should be used when it is first made. It wrinkles thinner papers and provides a relatively weak bond, so it cannot be used with collage objects. It washes off easily when wet but requires soaking and scrubbing if allowed to dry on surfaces.

## CORNSTARCH PASTE

Mix one part cornstarch to three parts cold water in a saucepan. Add 2 tablespoons sugar and 1 tablespoon vinegar for each part of cornstarch (¼ cup cornstarch and ¾ cups water will make about half a pint). Stirring constantly, slowly heat the mixture until it clears and thickens. Cool before using. Paste can be stored in the refrigerator several weeks if kept in a tightly sealed container.

*Advantages:* Cornstarch paste has a very pleasant texture and is not too sticky. It is a safe, almost colorless paste that dries clear and washes out of clothing. It forms a stronger bond than flour paste and can be used for lightweight items, such as fabric, yarn, ribbon, rice, and thin cardboard.

*Disadvantages:* This is probably one of the better homemade paste recipes in terms of strength, but because it must be cooked, it has to be prepared ahead of time. It is also hard to remove from surfaces when dry, requiring soaking and scrubbing.

# References

Abrams, R. M., Griffiths, S. K., Huang, X., Sain, J., Langford, G., & Gerhardt, K. J. (1998). Fetal music perception: The role of sound transmission. *Music Perception, 15*(3), 307–317.

Adams, E. J. (2011). Teaching children to name their feelings. *Young Children, 66*(3), 66–67.

Allan, N. C., & Lonegan, C. J. (2011). Examining the dimensionality of effort and control in preschool children and its relationship to academic and socioemotional indicators. *Developmental Psychology, 47*(4), 905–915.

Amabile, T. (1983). *The social psychology of creativity.* New York: Springer-Verlag.

Amabile, T., Hennessy, B. A., & Grossman, B. S. (1986). Social influences on creativity: Effects of contracted-for reward. *Journal of Personality and Social Psychology, 34,* 92–98.

Amabile, T., & Hennessy, B. A. (2002). The motivation for creativity in children. In A. K. Boggiaro, & T. S. Pittman (Eds.), *Achievement and Motivation* (pp. 54–74). New York: University of Cambridge.

Anderson, D. R., & Hanson, K. G. (2010). From blooming, buzzing confusion to media literacy: The early development of television viewing. *Developmental Review, 30*(2), 239–255.

Anderson, T. D. (2011) Beyond eureka moments: Supporting the invisible work of creativity and innovation. *Information Research: An international electronic journal, 16*(1). Retrieved May 2013 from http://www.eric.ed.gov/PDFS/EJ925561.pdf.

Anderson-Goebel, N. (2011). *The pot that Juan built.* New York: Lee & Low.

Anvari, S. H., Trainor, L. J., Woodside, J., & Levy, B. A. (2001). Relations among musical skills, phonological processing, and early reading ability in preschool children. *Journal of Experimental Child Psychology, 83,* 111–113.

Apps, L., & MacDonald, M. (2012). Classroom aesthetics in early childhood classrooms. *Journal of Education and Learning, 1*(1), 49–59.

Arnheim, R. (1969). *Visual thinking.* Berkeley, CA: University of California Press.

Bahrick, L. E., Lickliter, R., & Flom, R. (2004). Intersensory redundancy guides infants' selective attention, perceptual and cognitive development. *Current Directions in Psychological Science, 13,* 99–102.

Baker, A. (1999). *White rabbit's color book.* New York: Larouse Kingfisher.

Bandura, A. (1973). *Aggression: A social learning analysis.* Englewood Cliffs, NJ: Prentice-Hall.

Bandura, A. (1989). Social cognitive theory. In R. Vasta (Ed.), *Annals of child development.* Vol. 6. Six theories of child development (pp. 1–60). Greenwich, CT: JAI Press.

Baylor, B. (1987). *When clay sings.* New York: Atheneum.

Beaty, A. (2007). *Iggy Peck, architect.* New York: Henry Abrams.

Beaumont, K. (2005). *I ain't gonna paint no more!* New York: Harcourt.

Bebko, J. M., Burke, L., Craven, J., & Sarlo, N. (1992). The importance of motor activity in sensorimotor development: A perspective from children with physical handicaps. *Human Development, 35,* 226–240.

Beil, L. (May/June 2011). When life stinks. *Autism/Asperger's Digest,* 16–17.

Berger, A. A., & Cooper, S. (2003). Musical play: A case study of preschool children and parents. *Journal of Research in Music Education, 51*(2), 151–165.

Boden, M. A. (1990). *The creative mind.* New York: Basic Books.

Bodrova, E., & Leong, D. (2004). Chopsticks and counting sticks: Do play and foundational skills need to compete for the teacher's attention in the early childhood classroom? *Young children and play.* Washington, DC: NAEYC.

Bornstein, M. H., Arterberry, M. E., & Mash, C. (2011). Perceptual development. In M. H. Bornstein & M. E. Lamb (Eds.), *Developmental psychology: An advanced textbook* (6th ed., pp. 283–325). New York: Psychology Press.

Boutte, G. S., Van Scoy, I., & Hendley, S. (1996). Multicultural and nonsexist prop boxes. *Young Children, 52*(1), 34–38.

Bower, B. (2002, July 6). The eyes have it. *Science News, 162,* 4.

Bower, B. (2003, May 24). Repeat after me. *Science News, 163,* 330–332.

Bradley, J. (2005). When to twinkle: Are children ever too young? *American Suzuki Journal, 33*(3), 53.

Brimson, S. A. (2009). Behold the power of African American female characters. *Young Children, 64*(1), 26–31.

Bromley, K. (1998). *Language arts: Exploring connections* (3rd ed.). Boston, MA: Allyn & Bacon.

Brouillette, L. (2010). How the arts help children to create healthy social scripts: Exploring the perceptions of elementary teachers. *Arts Education Policy Review 111,* 16–24.

Brown, L. K., & Brown, M. (1996). *Visiting the art museum.* New York: Puffin.

Bruner, J. (1979). *On knowing: Essays for the left hand.* Cambridge: Harvard University Press.

Bruner, J. (1990). *Acts of meaning.* Cambridge, MA: Harvard University Press.

Bruner, J. (1996). *The culture of education.* Cambridge, MA: Harvard University Press.

Butzlaff, R. (2000). Can music be used to teach reading? *The Journal of Aesthetic Education, 34*(3), 167–178.

Bryan, B. (2003). *Beautiful blackbird.* New York: Atheneum.

Cadwell, A. (2005). Pedagogical patterns. In L. Gandini, L. Hill, L. Cadwell, & C. Schawall (Eds.), *In the spirit of the studio* (pp. 175–194). New York: Teachers College Press.

Cambourne, B., & Brown, H. (1990). *Read and retell.* Portsmouth, NH: Heinemann.

Caine, R. N., & Caine, G. (1994). *Making connections: Teaching and the human brain.* Alexandria, VA: Association for Supervision and Curriculum Development.

Caine, R. N., Caine, G., McClintic, C. L., & Klimek, K. J. (2008). *12 Brain/Mind learning principles in action for making connections, teaching, and the human brain* (2nd ed.). Thousand Oaks, CA: Corwin.

Capristo, B. A. (2012). *Dance and its use of technology.* Unpublished research thesis. University of Akron, Akron, Ohio. Retrieved May 2013 from http://etd.ohiolink.edu/send-pdf.cgi/Capristo%20Beth%20Ann.pdf?akron1336148430.

Carey, J. (Ed.). (2002). *Brain facts* (4th ed.). Washington, DC: Society for Neuroscience.

Carter, M., Cividanes, W., Curtis, D., & Leo, D. (2010). Becoming a reflective teacher. *Teaching Young Children, 3*(4), 1–4.

Casson, J. (2004). *Drama, psychotherapy, and psychosis.* London: Routledge.

Castaneda, O. S. (1993). *Abuela's Weave.* New York: Lee & Low.

Cecil, N. L., & Lauritzen, P. (1995). *Literacy and the arts for the integrated classroom: Alternative ways of knowing.* White Plains, NY: Longman.

Celenza, A. H. (2006). *Gershwin's Rhapsody in Blue.* Watertown, MA: Charlesbridge.

Cermak, S. (September 2009). Deprivation and sensory processing in institutionalized and postinstitutionalized children. *Sensory Integration Special Interest Section Quarterly.* Bethesda, MD: American Occupational Therapy Association.

Chalufou, I., & Worth, K. (2004). *Building structures with children.* St. Paul, MN: Redleaf Press.

Charney, R. (1992). *Teaching children to care.* Turners Falls, MA: Northeast Foundation for Children.

Chasiotis, A., Kiessling, F., Winter, V., & Haber, J. (2006). Sensory motor inhibition as a prerequisite for theory-of-mind: A comparison of clinical and normal preschoolers differing in sensory motor abilities. *International Journal of Behavior, 30*(2), 178–190.

Cheatham, G. A., & Ro, Y. E. (2010). Young English learners' interlanguage as a context for language and early literacy development. *Young Children, 65*(4), 18–23.

Cheng, J. C., & Monroe, M. C. (2012). Connection to nature: Children's attitude toward nature. *Environment & Behavior, 44*(1), 31–49.

Cherry, C. (1990). *Creative art for the developing child.* Carthage, IL: Fearon Teacher Aids.

Cherry, C., Godwin, D., & Staples, J. (1989). *Is the left brain always right? A guide to whole child development.* Belmont, CA: David S. Lake.

Chin, C. (2003). The development of absolute pitch. *Psychology of Music, 31,* 155–171.

Christie, J. F., Enz, B., & Vukelich, C. (2003). *Teaching language and literacy: Preschool through the elementary grades* (2nd ed.). Boston: Allyn & Bacon.

Church, E. B., & Miller, K. (1990). *Learning through play: Blocks.* New York: Scholastic.

Cisneros, S. (1994). *Hair Pelitos.* New York: Random House.

Clayton, M. (2001). *Classroom spaces that work.* Turners Falls, MA: Northeast Foundation for Chidlren.

College Board (2011). *Arts education standards and 21st century skills: An analysis of the national standards for arts education as compared to the 21st century skills map for the arts.* New York: The College Board.

Cooper, P. (1993). *When stories come to school: Telling, writing, and performing stories in the early childhood classroom.* New York: Teachers and Writers Collaborative.

Copple, C., & Bredekamp, S. (2006). *Basics of developmentally appropriate practice.* Washington, DC: National Association for the Education of Young Children.

Copple, C., & Bredekamp, S. (Eds.). (2009). *Developmentally appropriate practice in early childhood programs serving children from birth through age 8* (3rd ed.). Washington, DC: National Association for the Education of Young Children.

Costa-Giomi, E. (1999). The effects of three years of piano instruction on children's cognitive development. *Journal of Research in Music Education, 47*(3), 198–212.

Cox, M. V. (1993). *Children's drawings of the human figure.* Hove, UK: Erlbaum.

Craft, A. (2002). *Creativity and the early years: A lifelong foundation.* New York: Continuum.

Craft, A. (2010). *Creativity and futures.* London: Trentham.

Crosbie, M. J. (1983). *Architecture Colors.* Washington, DC: Preservation Press.

Csikszentmihalyi, M. (1996). *Creativity: Flow and the psychology of discovery and innovation.* New York: HarperCollins.

Csikszentmihalyi, M. (2008). *Flow: The psychology of optimal experience.* New York: Harper.

Curtis, D., & Carter, M. (2008). *Learning together with young children.* St. Paul, MN: Redleaf.

Curtis, D. & Carter, M. (2010). *The visionary director* (2nd ed.). St. Paul, MN: Redleaf.

d'Amboise, J. (2006). In *Ballet Encyclopedia.* Retrieved April 2013 from http://www.the-ballet.com/ damboise.php.

Daly, N. (1989). *Not so fast Songololo.* New York: Aladdin.

Davis, J. H. (2008). *Why our schools need the arts.* New York: Teachers College.

Davis, M. D., Kilgo, J. L., & Gamel-McCormick, M. (1998). *Young children with special needs.* Needham Heights, MA: Allyn & Bacon.

Dedrick, D. (1996). Color language universality and evolution: On the explanation for basic color terms. *Philosophical Psychology, 9*(4), 497–524.

Denac, O. (2007). A case study of preschool children's musical interests at home and at school. *Early Childhood Education Journal, 35,* 439–439.

Denham, S. A., Bassett, H., Mincic, M., Kalb, S, Way, E., Wyatt, T., & Segal, Y. (2012). Social-emotional learning profiles of preschoolers' early school success: A person-centered approach. *Learning and Individual Differences, 22*(2), 178–189.

Dennis, W. (1966). Goodenough scores, art experience, and modernization. *Journal of Social Psychology, 68,* 213–215.

De Paola, T. (1988). *The legend of the Indian paintbrush.* New York: J. G. Putnam.

Derman-Sparks, L., & the A.B.C. Task Force. (1989). *Anti-bias curriculum: Tools for empowering young children.* Washington, DC: National Association for the Education of Young Children.

Derman-Sparks, L., & Ramsey, P. G. (2006). *What if all the kids are white?: Anti-bias multicultural education with young children and families.* New York: Teachers College Press.

Di Leo, J. H. (1970). *Young children and their drawings.* New York: Brunner/Mazel.

Di Leo, J. H. (1973). *Children's drawings as diagnostic aids.* New York: Brunner/Mazel.

Dissanayake, E. (1995). *Homo aestheticus: Where art comes from and why.* Seattle, WA: University of Washington Press.

Dryden, G., & Vos, J. (1997). *The Learning Revolution.* Auckland, NZ: The Learning Web.

Edwards, B. (1979). *Drawing on the right side of the brain.* Los Angeles: J. P. Tarcher.

Edwards, C., Gandini, L., & Forman, G. (1993). *The hundred languages of children: The Reggio Emilia approach to early childhood education* (2nd ed.). Norwood, NJ: Ablex.

Edwards, C., Gandini, L., & Forman, G. (2011). *The hundred languages of children: The Reggio Emilia approach to early childhood education* (3rd ed.). Norwood, NJ: Ablex.

Edwards, L. C. (1990). *Affective development and the creative arts.* New York: Macmillan.

Edwards, L. C. (1993). The creative arts process: What it is and what it is not. *Young Children, 48*(3), 77–81.

Ehrhardt, K. (2006). *This jazz man.* New York: Harcourt.

Ehlert, L. (1991). *Red leaf yellow leaf.* New York: Harcourt Brace

Ehlert, L. (1998). *Mole's hill.* New York: Harcourt Brace.

Einon, D. (1985). *Play with a purpose.* New York: Pantheon Books.

Elias, C. L., & Berk, L. E. (2002). Self-regulation in young children: Is there a role for sociodramatic play? *Early Childhood Research Quarterly, 17,* 1–17.

Erikson, E. (1963). *Childhood and society.* New York: Norton.

Eerola, T., Luck, G., & Toiviainen, P. (2006). An investigation of preschoolers' corporeal synchronization with music. In M. Baroni, A. R. Addessi, R. Caterina, & M. Costa (Eds.), *Proceedings of the 9th international conference on music perception and cognition* (pp. 472–476). Bologna, Italy: ICMPC-ESCOM.

Feierabend, J. (2004). *The book of pitch exploration: Can you sing this?* Chicago: GIA.

Fein, S. (1993). *First drawings: Genesis of visual thinking.* Pleasant Hill, CA: Exelrod Press.

Feldman, D. H. (1999). The development of creativity. In R. J. Sternberg (Ed.), *Handbook of creativity* (pp. 169–187). New York: Cambridge University Press.

Feldman, D. H., & Goldsmith, L. T. (1986). *Nature's gambit: Child prodigies and the development of human potential.* New York: Basic Books.

Feuerstein, R. & Falik, L. H. (2009). *Mediated soliloquy: Theory, concept, and a guide to practical applications.* Jerusalem, Israel: ICELP Press.

Fisher, A. (2005). *The story goes on.* Brookfield, CT: Roaring Brook Press.

Flohr, J. W., Persellin, D. C., Miller, D. C., & Meeuwsen, H. (2011). Relationships among music listening, temperament, and cognitive abilities of four-year-old children. *Visions of Research in Music Education, 17.* Retrieved March 2013 from http://www. usr.rider.edu/~vrme/v17n1/visions/article1.

Fishman, S. (2010). Theater, live music, and dance: Conversations about young audiences. *Young Children, 65*(2), 30–35.

Flohr, J. W., & Persellin, D. C. (2011). Applying brain research to children's musical experiences. In S. L. Burton & C. C. Taggart (Eds.), *Learning from young children* (pp. 3–22). Lanham, MD: MENC.

Foss-Ferg, J. H., Heacock, J. L., & Cascio, C. J. (2012). Tactile responsiveness patterns and their association with core features in autism spectrum disorders. *Research in Autism Disorders, 6*(1), 337–344.

Fox, K. R. (1999). The influence of physical activity on mental health. *Public Health Nutrition, 2*(3A), 411–418.

Franklin, A., Bevis, L., & Ling, Y. (2010). Biological components of colour preferences in infancy. *Developmental Science, 13*(2), 346–354.

Franklin, A., Drivonikou, G. V., Bevis, L., Davies, I. R. L., Kay, P., & Regier, T. (2008). Categorical perception of color is lateralized to the right hemisphere in infants, but to the left hemisphere in adults. *Proceedings of the National Academy of Sciences, 105*(9), 3221–3225.

Frost, J. (2005). Lessons from disasters: Play, work, and the creative arts. *Childhood Education, 82*(1), 2.

Furman, L. (2000). In support of drama in the early childhood education, again. *Early Childhood Education Journal, 27*(30), 173–178.

Gandini, L., Hill, L., Cadwell, L, & Schwall, C. (Eds.). (2005). *In the spirit of the studio: Learning from the Atelier of Reggio Emilia.* New York: Teachers College.

Ganz, J. B. & Flores, M. M. (2010). Implementing visual clues for young children with autism spectrum disorder. *Young Children, 65*(3), 78–83.

Gardner, H. (1973). *The arts and human development.* New York: John Wiley & Sons.

Gardner, H. (1983). *Frames of mind.* New York: Basic Books.

Gardner, H. (1991). *The unschooled mind.* New York: Basic Books.

Gardner, H. (1993). *Multiple intelligences: The theory in practice.* New York: Basic Books.

Gardner, H. (2009). *Five minds for the future.* Cambridge, MA: Harvard Business School.

Gardner, H., Winner, E., & Kircher, M. (1975). Children's conception of the arts. *Journal of Aesthetic Education, 9*(3), 60–77.

Garner, P. W., & Waajid, B. (2012). Emotion knowledge and self-regulation as predictors of preschoolers' cognitive ability, classroom behavior, and social competence. *Journal of the Pyschoeducational Association, 30*(4), 330–343.

Gelfer, J. (1990). Discovering and learning art through blocks. *Day Care and Early Education, 17*(4), 21–24.

Gerdner, L., & Langford, S. (2008). *Grandfather's story cloth.* Walnut Creek, CA: Shen's Books.

Gibbons, G. (1996). *How a house is built.* New York: Holiday House.

Gibbons, G. (2000). *The art box.* New York: Holiday House.

Gillanders, C. & Castro, D. C. (2011). Storybook reading for young dual-language learners. *Young Children, 66*(1), 91–95.

Goetze, M., & Horii, Y. (1989). A comparison of the pitch accuracy of group and individual singing in young children. *Bulletin for the Council for Research in Music Education,* No. 99, 57–73.

Goleman, D. (2007). *Social intelligence: The new science of social relationships.* New York: Bantam.

Goleman, D. (2008). *Emotional intelligence: Why it can matter more than IQ.* New York: Bantam.

Goleman, D., Kaufman, P., & Ray, M. (1992). *The creative spirit.* New York: Dutton.

Golomb, C. (1981). Representation and reality. *Review of Visual Arts Education, 14,* 36–48.

Gollub, M. (2010). *The jazz fly 2: The jungle patchanga.* Santa Rosa, CA: Tortuga Press.

Goodenough, F. L. (1926). *Children's drawings as measures of intellectual maturity.* New York: Harcourt Brace Jovanovich.

Graham, G. S., Holt-Hale, S., & Parker, M. (2001). *Children moving: A reflective approach to teaching physical education* (5th ed.). Mountain View, CA: Mayfield.

Graziano, A. B., Peterson, M., & Shaw, G. L. (1999). Enhanced learning of proportional math through music training and spatial-temporal training. *Neurological Research, 21,* 139–152.

8 Greenberg, P. (Ed.). (1972). *Art education: Elementary.* Washington, DC: National Art Education Association.

Greenman, J. (1988). *Caring spaces, learning places: Children's environments that work.* Redmond, WA: Exchange Press.

Greenspan, S. I., & Weider, S. (1998). *The child with special needs: Encouraging intellectual and emotional growth.* Reading, MA: Addison-Wesley.

Gromko, J. (2003). Children composing: Inviting the artful narrative. In M. Hickey (Ed.), *Why and how to teach music composition: A new horizon for music education* (pp. 69–90). Reston, VA: MENC.

Gruber, H. E., & Wallace, D. B. (1999). The case study method and evolving systems approach for understanding unique creative people at work. In R. J. Sternberg (Ed.), *Handbook of creativity* (pp. 93–115). New York: Cambridge.

Gruhn, W. (2002). Phases and stages in early music learning. *Music Education Research, 4*(1), 51–71.

Guilford, J. P. (1986). *Creative talents: Their nature, uses, development.* Buffalo, NY: Bearly.

Hannaford, C. (2005). *Smart moves: Why learning is not all in your head.* Salt Lake City, UT: Great River.

Hannon, E. E. & Trainor, L. J. (2007). Music acquisition: Effects of enculturation and formal training on development. *Trends in Cognitive Science, 11,* 466–472.

Hannon, E. E., & Trehub, S. E. (2005). Tuning in to musical rhythms: Infants learn more readily than adults. *Proceedings of the National Academy of Sciences of the United States of America, 102*(35), 12639–12643.

Harris, D., & Goodenough, F. L. (1963). *Children's drawings as measures of intellectual maturity.* New York: Harcourt, Brace & World.

Hart, B., & Risley, T. R. (1995). *Meaningful differences in the everyday life of young American children.* Baltimore, MD: Paul H. Brookes.

Harvey, C. E. (2010). Experiences with an outdoor prop box: Addressing standards during recess. *Young Children, 65*(1), 30–33.

Hayes, A. (1995). *Meet the orchestra.* Orlando, FL: Sea Island.

Hepper, P. G. (1991). An examination of fetal learning before and after birth. *The Irish Journal of Psychology, 12*(2), 95–107.

Hetland, L. (2000). Learning to make music enhances spatial reasoning. *The Journal of Aesthetic Education, 34*(3–4), 179–238.

Heward, W. L. (2000). *Exceptional children* (6th ed.). Upper Saddle River, NJ: Merrill.

Higgins, L. & Campbell, P. S. (2010). *Free to be musical: Group improvisation in music.* Lanham, MD: Rowman & Littlefield.

Hildebrandt, C. (1998). Creativity in music and early childhood. *Young Children, 53*(9), 68–73.

Hill, L. C. (2010). *Dave the potter: Artist, poet, slave.* New York: Little, Brown.

Hoffman, M. (1991). *Amazing Grace.* New York: Dial.

Holliday, R. E., Reyna, V. F., & Hayes, B. K. (2002). Memory processes underlying misinformation effects in child witnesses. *Developmental Review, 22*(1), 37–77.

Honig, A. S. (2005). The language of lullabies. *Young Children, 60*(5), 30–36.

Hoose, P. & Hoose, H. (1998). *Hey, little ant.* Berkeley, CA: Tricycle.

Hope, G. (2008). *Thinking and learning through drawing: In primary classrooms.* Thousand Oaks: Sage.

Housen, A. (2002). Voices of viewers: Iterative research, theory, and practice. *Arts and Learning Research Journal, 17*(1), 2–12.

Howes, C. & Smith, E. (1995). Relations among child care quality, teacher behavior, children's play activities, emotional security, and cognitive activity in child care. *Early Childhood Research Quarterly, 10,* 381–404.

Hughes, L. (1997). *The sweet and sour animal book.* New York: Oxford.

Hyde, K. L., Lerach, J., Norton, A., Forgeard, M., Winner, E., Evans, A. C., & Schlaug, G. (2009). Musical training shapes structural brain development. *Journal of Neuroscience, 29*(10), 3019–3025.

Hyson, M., Copple, C., & Jones, J. (2006). Early childhood development and education. In K. A. Renninger, I. E. Sigel, W. Damon & R. M. Lerner (Eds.), *Handbook of child psychology: Vol. 4. Child psychology in practice* (pp. 3–47). Hoboken, NJ: John Wiley & Son.

Ilari, B., & Polka, L. (2006). Music cognition in early infancy: Infants' preferences and long-term memory for Ravel. *International Journal of Music Education, 24*(1), 7–20.

Ilari, B., Polka, L., & Costa-Giomi, E. (2002). *Babies can un-Ravel complex music.* Paper presented at the 143rd Annual Meeting of the Acoustical Society of America, Pittsburgh, PA.

Ilari, B & Sundara, M. (2009). Music listening preferences in early life. *Journal of Research in Music Education, 56*(4), 357–369.

Isadora, R. (1991), *Ben's Trumpet.* New York: *Greenwillow.*

Izen, M., & West, J. (2004). *The dog that sang at the opera.* New York: Henry N. Abrams.

James, K. I. & Swain, S. N. (2011). Only self-activated actions create sensori-motor systems in the brain. *Developmental Science, 14*(4), 673–678.

Jensen, E. P. (2000). *Music with the brain in mind.* Thousand Oaks, CA: Corwin.

Jensen, E. (2005a). *Arts with the brain in mind* (2nd ed.). Alexandria, VA: Association for Supervision and Curriculum Development.

Jensen, E. (2005b). *Teaching with the brain in mind* (2nd ed.). Alexandria, VA: Association for Supervision and Curriculum Development.

Jensen, E. (2008). *Enriching the brain.* Hoboken, NJ: Jossey-Bass.

Johnson, C. (1998). *Harold and the purple crayon.* New York: HarperCollins.

Johnson, M. H., & Mareschal, D. (2001). Cognitive and perceptual development during infancy. *Neurobiology, 11,* 213–218.

Johnson, J. E., Christies, J. F., & Wardles, F. (2005). *Play, development and early education.* Boston, MA: Pearson.

Jones, E., & Nimmo, J. (1994). *Emergent curriculum.* Washington, DC: National Association for the Education of Young Children.

Jones, E., & Reynolds, G. (2011). *The play's the thing: Teacher's roles in children's play.* New York: Teachers College.

Juricevic, I. (2010). Translating visual art into tactile art to produce equivalent aesthetic experiences. *Psychology of Aesthetics, Creativity, and the Arts, 3*(1), 23–27.

Kamii, C., & DeVries, K. (1993). *Physical knowledge in preschool education: Implications of Piaget's theory.* New York: Teachers College Press.

Kamperman, J. A., & Bowne, M. T. (2011). Teacher, there's an elephant in the room! An inquiry approach to preschoolers' early language learning. *Young Children, 66*(5), 84–89.

Kariuki, P., & Honeycut, C. (1998). *An investigation into the effects of music on two emotionally disturbed students' writing motivations and writing skills.* Paper presented at the Annual Conference of the Mid-Atlantic Research Association, New Orleans, LA.

Katz, K. (2002). *The colors of us.* New York: Square Fish.

Katz, L. G., & Chard, S. C. (2000). *Engaging children's minds: The project approach.* (2nd ed.). Norwood, NJ: Ablex.

Keats, E. J. (2003). *Jennie's hat.* New York: Puffin.

Kellogg, R. (1969). *Analyzing children's art.* Palo Alto, CA: National Press Books.

Kellogg, R. (1979). *Children's drawings/children's minds.* New York: Avon Books.

Kelly, L. & Smith, B. S. (1987). A study of infant musical productivity. In J. C. Peery, I. W. Peery, & T. W. Draper (Eds.), *Music and child development* (pp. 35–53). New York: Springer-Verlag.

Kendall, F. E. (1996). *Diversity in the classroom.* New York

Kent, T., Murphy, H., & Stanton, R. (2010). Television and video viewing time among children aged 2 years. *Morbidity and Mortality Weekly Report, 59*(27), 837–841.

Kindler, A. (Ed.). (1997). *Child development in art.* Reston, VA: National Art Education Association.

Kindler, A., & Darras, B. (1994). Artistic development in context: Emergence and development of pictorial imagery in the early childhood years. *Visual Art Research, 20,* 1–3.

Kirchen, D. J. (2011). Making and taking virtual fieldtrips in prek and the primary grades. *Young Children, 66*(6), 22-26.

Kirk, E. W. (1998). My favorite day is "story" day. *Young Children, 53*(6), 27–30.

Kirkorian, H. L., Pempek, T. A., Murphy, L. A., Schmidt, M. E., & Anderson, D. R. (2009). The impact of background television on parent–child interactions. *Child Development, 80*(5), 1350–1359.

Kissinger, K. (1994). *All the colors we are.* St. Paul, MN: Redleaf.

Kleven, E. (1996). *Hooray! A piñata!* New York: Dutton.

Koff, S. (2000). Toward a definition of dance. *Childhood Education, 77*(1), 27–31.

Kohn, A. (2006). Five reasons to stop saying good job. In B. A. Marlow & A. S. Canestrari (Eds.), *Educational psychology in context* (pp. 200–205). Thousand Oaks, CA: Sage.

Kokkinos, C. M., & Kipritsi, E. (2012). Relationship between bullying, victimization, trait emotional intelligence, self-efficacy, and empathy among preadolescents. *Social Psychology of Education: An International Journal, 15*(1), 41–58.

Kopiez, R., & Lehmann, M. (2008). The "open-earedness" hypothesis and the development of age-related aesthetic reactions to music in elementary school children. *British Journal of Music Education, 25*(2), 121–138.

Kosslyn, S. M., Ganis, G., & Thompson, W. L. (2006). Mental imagery and the brain. In Q. Jing, M. R. Rosenzweig, G. d'Ydewalle, H. Zhang, H. C. Cheng, & K. Zhang (Eds.),

*Progress in psychological science around the world, vol. 1: Neurological, cognitive, and developmental issues* (pp. 195–206). New York: Psychology Press.

Kostecki-Shaw, J. S. (2011). *Same, same but different.* New York: Henry Holt.

Koster, J. B. (1999). Clay for little fingers. *Young Children, 54*(2), 18–22.

Koster, J. B. (2005). *Bookmarking Racism: Challenging White Privilege through Children's Literature and Participatory Action Research in a Suburban School.* Unpublished dissertation, Binghamton University New York: Binghamton University (UMI No. AAT 3203894).

Kreutzer, N. J. (2001). Song acquisition among rural Shona-speaking Zimbabwean children from birth to 7 years. *Journal of Research in Music Education, 49*(3), 198–211.

Krumhansl, C. L. (2002). Music: A link between cognition and emotion. *Current Directions in Psychological Science, 11*(2), 45–50.

Langer, E. J. (1989). *Mindfulness.* Cambridge, MA: Perseus Books.

Larsen, B. (2002). *When animals were people.* Santa Fe, NM: Clear Light Publishing.

Lay-Dopyera, M., & Dopyera, J. E. (1992). Strategies for teaching. In C. Seefeldt (Ed.), *The early childhood curriculum* (pp. 16–41). New York: Teacher's College Press.

Lehman, B. (2006). *Museum trip.* New York: Houghton Mifflin.

Levick, M. (1986). *Mommy, daddy, look what I'm saying: What children are telling you through their art.* New York: Evans.

Lewin-Benham, A. (2010). *Infants & toddlers at work.* New York: Teachers College Press.

Lionni, L (1975). *Swimmy.* New York: Dragonfly.

Lionni, L (1995). *Matthew's Dream.* New York: Alfred Knopf.

Lobel, A. (1989). *On Market Street.* New York: Mulberry Books.

Louv, R. (2008). *Last child in the woods.* Chapel Hill, NC: Algonquin.

Lowenfeld, V., & Brittain, W. L. (1987). *Creative and mental growth.* New York: Macmillan.

Lynch, M. P., & Eilers, R. E. (1992). A study of perceptual development for musical tuning. *Perception and Psychophysics, 52*(6), 599–608.

Maddox, D. (1986). *Architects make zigzags.* New York: Wiley.

Mak, B., & Vera, A. (1999). The role of motion in children's categorization of objects. *Cognition, 71*(10), B11–B21.

Mandle, C. L., Jacobs, S. C., Arcari, P. M., et al. (1996). The efficacy of relaxation response interventions with adult patients: a review of the literature. *Journal of Cardiovascular Nursing, 10*(3), 4–26.

Marshall, H. H. (1995). Beyond "I like the way . . ." *Young Children, 50*(2), 25–28.

Martin, B. (1995). *Brown bear, brown, bear, what do you see?* New York: Henry Holt.

Mason, O. J., & Brady, F. (2009). The psychotomimetic effects of short-term sensory deprivation. *Journal of Nervous and Mental Disease, 197*(10), 783–785.

McFee, J., & Degge, R. M. (1981). *Art, culture, and environment: A catalyst for teaching.* Dubuque, IA: Kendall/Hunt.

McGuigan, F., & Salmon, K. (2004). The time to talk: The influence of timing of adult–child talk on children's memory of events. *Child Development, 75*(3), 669–686.

McLerran, A. (2004). *Roxaboxen.* New York: HarperCollins.

Merikle, P. M., Smilek, D., & Eastwood, J. D. (2001). Reception without awareness: Perspectives from cognitive psychology. *Cognition, 79,* 115–134.

Merryman, R. (1991). *First impressions: Andrew Wyeth.* New York: Harry N. Abrams.

Miles, L. R. (2009). The general store: Reflections on children's play. *Spotlight on Teaching Preschoolers.* Washington, DC: NAEYC.

Millman, I. (1998). *Moses goes to a concert.* New York: Farrar Straus Giroux.

Mitchell, L. C. (2004). Making the MOST of creativity in activities for young children with disabilities. *Young Children, 59*(4), 46–49.

Mithen, S. (2006). *The singing Neanderthals: The origins of music, language, mind, and body.* Cambridge, MA: Harvard University Press.

Mortari, L. (2012). Learning thoughtful reflection in teacher education. *Teachers and Learning: Theory and Practice, 18*(5), 525–545.

Munsch, R. (1992). *The paper bag princess.* Toronto: Annick.

Nakahara, H., Furuya, S., Obata, S., Masuko, T., & Kinoshita, H. (2009). Emotion-related changes in heart rate and its variability during performance and perception of music. In *The Neurosciences and Music III: Disorders and Plasticity: Annuals of the New York Academy of Sciences, 1169,* 359–362.

Nakamura, K. (2009). The significance of Dewey's aesthetics in art education in the age of globalization. *Educational Theory, 59*(4), 427–440.

National Association for the Education of Young Children. (2009). *Position statement on developmentally appropriate practice in early childhood programs serving children from birth through age 8.* Retrieved December 2010 from http://www.naeyc.org/files/naeyc/file/positions/PSDAP.pdf.

National Association for the Education of Young Children. (2012). Position statement on technology and interactive media as tools in early childhood programs serving children from birth to age 8. In A. Shillady & L. S. Muccio (Eds.), *Young children and technology* (pp. 61–72). Washington, DC: NAEYC.

National Center for Health Statistics (2006). *Health, United States, 2006.* (DHHS Publication No. 2006–1232). Washington, DC: U.S. Government Printing Office.

National Coalition for Core Arts Standards (2013). *A Conceptual Framework for Arts Learning.* Retrieved March 2013 from http://nccas.wikispaces.com/file/view/FRAMEWORK%20FINAL1-13-13.pdf/398083540/FRAMEWORK%20FINAL1-13-13.pdf.

National Dance Education Organization (2005). *Standards for dance in early childhood.* Bethesda, MD: NDEO.

Newell, F. N., Wallraven, C., & Huber, S. (2004). The role of characteristic motion in object categorization. *Journal of Vision, 4*(2), 118–129.

Neubauer, A., Gawrilow, C., & Hasselhorn, M. (2012). Watch-and-wait task: On the reliability and validity of a new method of assessing self-control in preschool children. *Learning and Individual Differences, 22*(6), 770–777.

Neuenschwander, R., Rithlesberger, M. Cimeli, P., & Roebers, C. (2012). How do different aspects of self-regulation predict successful adaptation to school? *Journal of Exceptional Child Psychology, 113*(3), 353–371.

Nicolopoulou, A., McDowell, J., & Brockmeyer, C. (2006). Narrative play and emergent literacy. In D. G. Singer, R. M. Golinkoff, & K. Hirsch-Pasek (Eds.), *Play=learning: How play motivates and enhances children's cognitive and social-emotional health* (pp. 124–145). New York: Oxford.

Noyce, R. M., & Christie, J. F. (1989). *Integrating reading and writing instruction*. New York: Allyn & Bacon.

O'Connor, J. (2002). *Drawing with scissors*. New York: Grosset & Dunlap.

Ormrod, J. E. (2003). *Educational psychology: Developing learners* (4th ed.). Upper Saddle River, NJ: Merrill.

Oster, G. D., & Crone, P. G. (2004). *Using drawings in assessment and therapy.* New York: Brunner-Routledge.

Paley, V. G. (1992). *You can't say you can't play*. Cambridge, MA: Harvard University Press.

Paley, V. G. (2000). *White teacher*. Cambridge, MA: Harvard University Press.

Paley, V. G. (2004). *Wally's stories*. Cambridge, MA: Harvard University Press.

Parlakian, R. (2010). Beyond twinkle, twinkle: Using music with infants and toddlers. *Young Children, 65*(2), 14–19.

Parncutt, R. (2006). Prenatal development. In G. McPherson (Ed.), *The child as musician: A handbook of musical development* (pp. 1–32). New York, NY: Oxford University Press.

Panfile, T. M., & Laible, D. J. (2012). Attachment security and children's empathy: The mediating role of emotion. *Merrill-Palmer Quarterly: Journal of Developmental Psychology, 58*(1), 1–21.

Pantev, C., Oostenveld, R., Engelien, Ross, B., Roberts, L. E., & Hoke, M. (1998). Increased auditory cortical representation in musicians. *Nature, 394*(6678), 434.

Parnell, W. (2012). Experiences of teacher reflection: Reggio-inspired practices in the studio. *Journal of Early Childhood Research, 10*(2), 117–133.

Parsons, M. J. (1987). *How we understand art*. New York: Cambridge University Press.

Parsons, M. J. (1994). Can children do aesthetics? A developmental account. *Journal of Aesthetic Education, 28*(1), 33–45.

Piaget, J. (1959). *The child's conception of the world*. (J. Tomlinson & A. Tomlinson, Trans.). Savage, MD: Rowman & Littlefield. (Original work published 1929.)

Piaget, J. (1962). *Play, dreams and imitation in childhood*. New York: Norton. (Original work published 1945.)

Pierce, J., & Johnson, C. L. (2010). Problem solving with young children using Persona Dolls. *Young Children, 65*(6), 106–108.

Piirto, J. (2004). *Understanding creativity*. Scottsdale, AZ: Great Potential Press.

Pinkney, A. (2006). *Duke Ellington: The Piano Prince*. New York: Hyperion.

Polan, H. J., & Ward, M. (1994). Role of mother's touch in failure to thrive. *Journal of American Academy of Child and Adolescent Psychiatry, 33*(8), 1098–1105.

Ponick, F. S. (Ed.) (2007). *National standards for arts education*. New York: Rowman & Littlefield.

Prelustsky, J. (2000). *It's raining pigs and noodles*. New York: HarperCollins.

Prelustsky, J. (1986). *Read Aloud Poems for the Very Young*. New York: Knopf.

Provasi, J., & Bobin-Bègue, A. (2003). Spontaneous motor tempo and rhythmical synchronisation in 2½- and 4-year-old children. *International Journal of Behavioral Development, 27*(3), 220–231.

Rauscher, F. H., & Hinton , S.C. (2003). *Type of music training selectively influences perceptual processing*. Proceedings of the European Society for the Cognitive Sciences of Music. Hannover, Germany: Hannover University Press.

Rauscher, F. H., Shaw, G. L., Levine, L. J., Wright, E. L., Dennis, W., & Newcomb, R. L. (1997). Music training causes long-term enhancement of preschool children's spatial-temporal reasoning. *Neurological Research, 19*(1), 2–7.

Raschka, C. (1992). *Charlie Parker played Bebop*. New York: Scholastic.

Resnick, M. (2006). Computer as paintbrush: Technology, play, and the creative society. In D. G. Singer, R. M. Golinkoff, & K. Hirsch-Pasek(Eds.), *Play=learning: How play motivates and enhances children's cognitive and social-emotional health* (pp. 192–206). New York: Oxford.

Reynolds, P. H. (2003). *The Dot*. Cambridge, MA: Candlewick.

Reynolds, P. H. (2004). *The Ish*. Cambridge, MA: Candlewick.

Ringgenberg, S. (2003). Music as a teaching tool: Creating story songs. *Young Children, 58*(5), 76–79.

Rockwell, A. (2010). *At the supermarket.* New York: Henry Holt.

Rodari, G. (1996). *The grammar of fantasy*. (J. Zipes, Trans.). New York: Teachers & Writers Collaborative. (Original work published 1973.)

Rogers, C. (1976). Toward a theory of creativity. In A. Rothenberg & C. Hausman (Eds.), *The creativity question* (pp. 292–305). Durham, NC: Duke University Press.

Rogers, F. (1982). *Talking with families about creativity*. Pittsburgh, PA: Family Communications.

Rowe, G. (1987). *Guiding young artists*. South Melbourne, Australia: Oxford University Press Australia.

Rushall, B. S., & Lippman, L. G. (1997). The role of imagery in physical performance. *International Journal for Sport Psychology, 29*, 57–72.

Ryan, P. M. (2002). *When Marion sang*. New York: Scholastic.

Sadker, M., & Sadker, D. (1995). *Failing at fairness: How our schools cheat girls*. New York: Touchstone.

Saffran, J. R., Loman, M. M., & Robertson, R. R. W. (2000). Infant memory for musical experiences. *Cognition, 77*(1), B15–B23.

San Souci, R. D. (1998). *Cendillion: A Caribbean Cinderella*. New York: Simon & Schuster.

Schaefer-Simmern, H. (1950). *The unfolding of artistic ability.* Berkeley: University of California Press.

Schifferstein, H. N., & Desmet, P. M. (2007). The effects of sensory impairment on product experience and personal well-being. *Ergonomics, 50,* 2026–2048.

Schiller, M. (1995). An emergent art curriculum that fosters understanding. *Young Children, 50*(3), 33–38.

Schiller, P. B. (2009). *Seven skills for school success: Activities to develop social and emotional intelligence in young children.* Beltsville, MD: Gryphon House.

Schlaug, G. (1995). Increased corpus callosum size in musicians. *Neuropsychologia, 33,*1047–1055.

Schlaug, G., Norton, A., Overy, K., & Winner, E. (2005). Effects of music training on the child's brain and cognitive development. *Annals New York Academy of Science, 1060,* 219–230.

Schwall, C. (2005). The atelier environment and materials. In L. Gandini, L. Hill, L. Cadwell, & C. Schwall (Eds.), *In the spirit of the studio: learning from the Atelier of Reggio Emilia* (pp. 16–31). New York: Teachers College Press.

Scripps, L. (2002). An overview of research on music and learning. In R. J. Deasy (Ed.), *Critical links: Learning in the arts and student academic and social development* (pp. 143–147). Washington, DC: Arts Education Partnership.

Seppa, N. (2012). Urban eyes. *Science News, 183*(3), 22–23.

Seitz, J. A. (1989, August). *The development of bodily-kinesthetic intelligence in children: Implications for dance artistry.* Paper presented at the American Psychological Association Convention, New Orleans, LA.

Seitz, J. A. (2000). The bodily basis of thought. *New Ideas in Psychology, 18,* 23–40.

Shaham, S. (2004). *Spicy, hot colors: Colores picantes.* Little Rock, AR: August House.

Shahin, A., Roberts, L. E., & Trainor, L. J. (2003). *Enhanced auditory envoked potentials in young children enrolled in musical training.* Paper presented at the Brain, Behavior, and Cognitive Society 13th Annual Meeting, McMaster University, Ontario, Canada.

Sheridan, S. R. (2010). *Handmade marks.* West Conshocken, PA: Infinity.

Shore, R., & Strasser, J. (2006). Music for their minds. *Young Children 61*(2), 62–74.

Shuler, C. (2009). *Pockets of potential: Using mobile technologies to promote children's learning.* New York: The Joan Gantz Cooney Center at Sesame Workshop. Retrieved March 2013 from http://pbskids.org/read/files/pockets_of_potential.pdf.

Sigelman, C. K., & Shaffer, D. (2009). *Life span human development.* Belmont, CA: Wadsworth.

Silver, R. (2002). *Three art assessments.* New York: Brunner-Routledge.

Singer, D. G., Golinkoff, R. M., & Hirsch-Pasek, K. (Eds.). (2006). *Play=learning: How play motivates and enhances children's cognitive and social-emotional health* (pp. 192–206). New York: Oxford.

Shively, C. H. (2011). Grow creativity! *Learning and Leading with Technology, 7,* 10–15.

Slavin, R. E. (1995). *Cooperative learning: Theory, research, and practice* (2nd ed.). Boston: Allyn & Bacon.

Schifferstein, H. N. J., and Desmet, P. M. A. (2007). The effects of sensory impairments on product experience and personal well-being. *Ergonomics, 50,* 2026–2048.

Shoen, D. (1984). *The reflective practitioner: How professionals think in action.* New York: Basic Books.

Snow, C. E. (2003). Ensuring reading success for African American children. In B. Bowman, (Ed.), *Love to read: Essays in developing and enhancing early literacy skills of African American children* (pp. 17–30). Washington, DC: National Black Child Institute.

Soley, G., & Hannon, E. E. (2010). Infants prefer the musical meter of their own culture: A cross-cultural comparison. *Developmental Psychology, 46*(1), 286–292.

Sousa, D. A. (2001). *How the brain works* (2nd ed.). Thousand Oaks, CA: Corwin.

Spivak, A. L., & Farran, D. C. (2012). First-grade teachers behaviors and children's prosoccial actions in classrooms. *Early Education and Development, 23*(5), 623–639.

Standley, J. M. (2008). Does music instruction help children learn to read?: Evidence of a meta-analysis. *Applications of Research in Music Education 27*(1), 17–32.

Starko, A. J. (1995). *Creativity in the classroom.* White Plains, NY: Longman.

Sternberg, R. J. (1988). *The nature of creativity.* New York: Cambridge.

Stellaccio, C. K., & McCarthy, M. (1999). Research in early childhood music and movement education. In C. Seefeldt (Ed.), *The early childhood curriculum: Current findings in theory and practice.* New York: Teachers College Press.

Striker, S. (2012). *M is for mola.* Publisher: Susanstriker.com.

Strozzi, P. (2002). Daily life: Seeing the extraordinary in the ordinary. In C. Guidici, C. Rinaldi & M. Krechevsky, (Eds.), *Making learning visible: Children as individual and group learners* (pp. 58–77). Reggio Emilia: Reggio Children

Stuckey, H. L., & Nobel, J. (2010). The connection between art, healing, and public health: A review of current literature. *Journal of Public Health 100*(20), 254–263.

Sutton-Smith, B. (1998). *The ambiguity of play.* Cambridge, MA: Harvard University Press.

Sylva, K., Roy, C., & Painter, M. (1980). *Childwatching a playgroup & nursery school.* Ypsilianti, MI: HighScope Press.

Tarpley, N. A. (2001). *Love my hair!* New York: Little, Brown.

Taylor, A., Kuo, F., & Sullivan, W. (2001). Coping with ADD: The surprising connection to green play settings. *Environment and Behavior, 33*(1), 54–77.

Tarnowski, S. M., & Leclerc, J. (1994). Musical play of preschoolers and teacher–child interaction. *Update: Applications of Research in Music Education, 13*(1), 9–16.

The Task Force on Children's Learning and the Arts: Birth to Age 8. (1998). *Young children and the Arts: Birth to age 8.* Washington, DC: Arts Education Partnership.

Torrance, E. P. (1970). *Encouraging creativity in the classroom.* Dubuque, IA: William C. Brown.

Trainor, L. J., & Corrigall, K. A. (2010). Music acquisition and effects of musical experience. In M. Riess-Jones & R. R. Fay (Eds.), *Springer handbook of auditory research: Music Perception* (pp. 89–128). Heidelberg: Springer.

Trainor, L. J., Wu, L., & Tsang, C. D. (2004). Long-term memory for music: Infants remember tempo and timbre. *Developmental Science, 7*(3), 289–296.

Tung, L. T. (1993). *Two of everything.* Park Ridge, IL: Albert Whitman.

Using music to tune the heart. (2009). *Harvard Heart Letter, 20*(3), 4–5.

Van Ausdale, D., & Feagin, J. (2001). *The first R: How children learn race and racism.* Lanham, MD: Rowman & Littlefield.

Vongpaisal, T., Trehub, S. E., Schellenberg, E. G., & Papsin, B. (2004). Music recognition by children with cochlear implants. *International Congress Series 1273* (pp. 193–196). St. Louis, MO: Elsevier.

Vukelich, C., Christie, J. F., & Enz, B. J. (2012). *Helping young children learn language and literacy: Birth through kindergarten* (3rd ed.). Upper Saddle River, NJ: Pearson.

Vygotsky, L. (1976). Play and its role in the mental development of the child. In J. Bruner, A. Jolly, & K. Sylvia, (Eds.), *Play: Its role in development and evolution* (pp. 537–554). New York: Basic Books.

Vygotsky, L. S. (1978). *Mind in society.* Cambridge: Harvard University Press.

Waber, B. (1996). *"You look ridiculous," said the hippopotamus to the rhinoceros.* New York: Houghton Mifflin.

Waber, B. (1975). *I was all thumbs.* New York: Houghton Mifflin.

Wade, N. (2003, September 12). We got rhythm: The mystery of music and evolution. *New York Times Science,* F1, F4.

Walker, O., & Henderson, A. (2012). Temperament and social problem solving competency in preschoolers: Influence on academic skills in early elementary school. *Social Development, 21*(4), 761–779.

Walsh, E. S. (1989). *Mouse paint.* New York: Harcourt Brace.

Walter, T. (1942). *Invitation to dance.* New York: Barnes.

Wanerman, T. (2010). Using story drama with preschoolers. *Young Children, 65*(2), 20–29.

Wassum, S. (1979). Elementary school children's vocal range. *Journal of Research in Music Education, 27*(4), 214–226.

Waters, K. (1991). *Lion dancer: Ernie Wan's Chinese New Year.* New York: Scholastic.

Weaver, T. (2002). *Opera cat.* New York: Clarion.

Webster, A. (2007). *Off we go to the grocery store.* Bethesda, MD: Woodbine House.

Weinberger, N. M. (2004). Music and the brain. *Scientific American, 292*(2), 89–96.

Weinkart, P. S., Schweinhart, L. J., & Larner, M. (1987). Movement curriculum improves children's rhythmic competence. *HighScope ReSource, 6*(1), 8–10.

Wells, R. (1997). *Bunny money.* New York: Dial.

Wilbarger, J., Gunnar, M., Schneider, M. & Pollak, S. (2010). Sensory processing in international adopted, post-institutionalized children. *Journal of Child Psychology and Psychiatry, 51*(10), 1105–1114.

Willis, C. A., & Schiller, P. (2011). Preschoolers' social skills steer life success. *Young Children, 66*(1), 42–49.

Willis, M. (2012). Insights: Nurturing empathy in the very young and gifted. *Parenting for High Potential, 1*(4), 14–16.

Whiteman, P. (2008). Young children's constructions of the musical knowledgeable other. In L. K. Thompson & M. R. Campbell (Eds.), *Diverse methodologies in the study of music teaching and learning* (pp. 25–44). Charlotte, NC: Information Age Publishing.

Wilkin, P. (1995). A comparison of fetal and newborn responses to music and sound stimuli with and without daily exposure to a specific piece of music. *Bulletin of the Council for Research in Music Education, 127,* 163–169.

Wilson, B., Hurwitz, A., & Wilson, M. (1987). *Teaching drawing from art.* Worcester, MA: Davis.

Winberg, J., & Porter, R. (1998). Olfaction and human neonatal behavior: Clinical implications. *Aeta Prediatr, 87*(1), 6–10.

Winner, E. (1982). *Invented worlds: The psychology of the arts.* Cambridge, MA: Harvard University Press.

Winner, E. (1989). Children's perceptions of aesthetic properties in art. *British Journal of Developmental Psychology, 4,* 149–160.

Wolf, J. (1994). Singing with children is a cinch! *Young Children, 49*(4), 20–25.

Wolfberg, P. J., & Schuler, A. L. (1993). Integrated play groups: A model for promoting the social and cognitive dimensions of play in children with autism. *Journal of Autism and Developmental Disorders, 23,* 467–489.

Wolfe, D. E., & Horn, C. (1993). Use of melodies as structural prompts for learning and retention of sequential verbal information by preschool students. *Journal of Music Therapy, 30*(2), 100–118.

Wolfe, D. E., & Stambaugh, S. (1993). Musical analysis of Sesame Street: Implications for music therapy practice and research. *Journal of Musical Therapy, 30*(4), 224–235.

Woodward, R. J., & Yun, J. (2001). The performance of fundamental gross motor skills by children enrolled in Headstart. *Early Child Development and Care, 169,* 57–67.

Wurm, J. P. (2005). *Working in the Reggio way.* St. Paul, MN: Redleaf.

Yarborough, C. (1997) *Cornrows.* New York: Putnam.

Zieger, E., Singer, D., & Bishop-Josef, S. (Eds.). (2004). *Children's play: The roots of reading.* Washington, DC: Zero to Three.

# Glossary

## A

**abstract**   In art, a work that emphasizes formal elements over subject matter.

**abstraction**   Art that is based on real images but uses them as design elements.

**acrylic paint**   A synthetic, resin-based paint that dries quickly and permanently. Not suitable for use by young children.

**active listening**   A nonverbal way of responding to a child, which includes waiting, maintaining eye contact, and gesturing in response.

**actual developmental level**   Skills or behaviors a child can do independently.

**aesthetic**   Special characteristics that attract one's attention.

**aesthetics**   The study and appreciation of the idea of beauty.

**American Sign Language**   A system of hand, body, and facial gestures used by the deaf community in the United States. Similar systems exist in other countries as well.

**anecdotal records**   Recorded detailed and objective descriptions of a child's behavior. Also known as *anecdotal notes*.

**anti-bias**   An approach that actively addresses discriminatory behavior and actions.

**appliqué**   A design made by attaching pieces of cloth to a fabric background.

**art**   a creative work, most often used to refer to visual art works.

**art form**   One of the arts, such as dance, drama, music, or visual art.

**art therapy**   The use of visual art to help children and adults express their feelings as they work through problems.

**artifact**   A handmade, three-dimensional cultural art form.

**arts**   Expressing ideas and feelings in an expressive way through music, dance, drama, and visual art.

**arts elements**   The basic components of an art form that are found in the particular creative work. In the visual arts these are line, shape, color, pattern, form, texture, and space. In music these are rhythm, pitch, dynamics, melody, harmony, timbre, and form. In creative dance these are space, effort, direction, and connection. In drama these are setting, characterization, language, movement, communication, and narrative.

**auditory discrimination**   The ability to tell the difference between different sounds and notes.

**auditory perception**   Being sensitive to the aesthetic qualities of sounds and music.

**authentic experience**   An hands-on, direct contact engagement with real objects and events.

**authentic assessment**   An assessment that asks the child to perform a hands-on or creative task that applies the skills and concepts being assessed. It often includes a rubric.

## B

**baker's dough**   A modeling compound made from flour, water, and salt, which can be baked in a household oven.

**ballet**   A theatrical art form using dance, music, and scenery to convey a story, theme, or atmosphere.

**baric perception**   To sense weight or pressure.

**basket**   A container woven from twigs, reeds, or another sturdy fiber.

**bodily-kinesthetic intelligence**   In Howard Gardner's theory of multiple intelligences, the ability to use the body to solve problems or to make things.

**brainstorming**   A creative teaching strategy in which spontaneous ideas are rapidly thought of and recorded during which there is no discussion, criticism, or analysis.

## C

**calligrapher** A person who writes beautiful lettering.

**calligraphy** The art of writing beautifully.

**cellophane** A thin, transparent film.

**checklist** An assessment method in which observed behaviors are recorded by checking predetermined categories.

**chenille stems** Fiber-covered wires, also called *pipe cleaners*.

**chord** Three or more notes played together at the same time.

**chorus** A melody line or group of lines that repeats at the end of every verse, emphasizing the theme of the song.

**classroom** The inside area of a location used by the children.

**clay** Any soft modeling compound, but especially that formed from earth.

**clicking** In computer use, pressing the button on the mouse to select an item on the screen.

**cognitive** Pertaining to intellectual reasoning based on the use of judgment, logic, and memory.

**cognitive development** Growth in the ability to think logically.

**coil** A long rope of clay made by rolling it on a flat surface with the palms moving outward.

**collage** A picture containing glued-on objects or paper.

**color** The surface quality of an object or substance as revealed by the light that reflects off of it and is seen as a hue in the spectrum.

**color-blind** Being unable to distinguish some of the visible wavelengths of light.

**compose** Create an original piece of music or adapt a familiar piece.

**composer** A person who writes original pieces of music.

**composition** The arrangement of arts elements into a whole.

**concrete operational** The stage of cognitive development at which, according to Piagetian theory, children begin to think logically about events that they observe. This usually occurs at around the age of seven.

**conformity** Pressure to be the same as everyone else.

**conga** An Afro-Cuban dance performed with people holding on to each other

**connection** In creative movement, the way we use our bodies in relationship to all parts of our body, other objects, and the people around us.

**construction paper** A medium-weight paper that comes in a wide variety of colors.

**contrast** An unlikeness in quality.

**cooperative play** When children interact and communicate in meaningful ways during an activity.

**copper enameling** A process in which copper pieces are covered with melted glass. It is not a safe activity for young children.

**craft** Any art form that produces a usable product, such as a fabric, container, or puppet. Often based on traditional techniques, such as basket weaving, embroidery, glassmaking, quilting, pottery, tinwork, and weaving.

**creative dance** Creative expression based on the movement and positioning of the body in space in which participants can move in their own inventive ways to the music.

**creative movement** Movement activities in which each participant can respond in a multitude of ways.

**creative process** A combination of mental processes that will lead to the final creative product or action.

**creativity** Solving problems or expressing ideas and feelings in unique ways.

**cultural aesthetic** When a group of people shares similar ideas and judgments about beauty.

**culture** A peoples' way of thinking, acting, and responding that grows out of a system of rules or beliefs that help them make sense of the universe.

**cursor** A blinking line or shape that indicates where the first mark will appear on a computer screen.

## D

**dance** To move feet and body in a rhythmic pattern. Creative dance is the process of adding one's own unique interpretation to the movement.

**descriptive statement**   A sentence that gives specific details about what is being discussed.

**dictation**   The act of writing down a child's words or stories.

**disposition**   The attitude or state of mind we have toward a particular behavior.

**documentation**   Materials collected to show the process of creating an artwork or participating in an activity.

**documentation panel**   A display of materials, such as photographs, children's words, and drawings that shows the process of a project or integrated unit of learning. Also called a presentation panel.

**drama**   Creative expression of ideas and feelings through voice, action, and body, such as pantomime, play-acting, and storytelling; a work of art that communicates an idea or story through language and action.

**drama therapy**   The use of the dramatic arts to help people deal with emotional and physical stress.

**dramatic play**   The acting out of roles and behaviors by children.

**dramatics**   The act of participating in a creative work that communicates an idea or story through language and action.

**drawing**   A picture made from any linear art material: pencil, marker, charcoal, ink, chalk, and so on.

**dye**   Any substance that changes the color of a material.

**dynamics**   Changes in volume from loud to soft or soft to loud and the accenting of certain tones.

## E

**effort**   How much time, force, and speed we use as we move our bodies.

**elaboration**   The ability to improve ideas by adding on or expanding them.

**embroidery**   A design made with thread on cloth.

**emergent curriculum**   An open-ended curriculum design in which children's interests provide the springboard for the selection of topics and activities to be taught.

**environment**   Everything that surrounds us—the setting. The physical environment usually refers to the classroom spaces and/or exterior spaces, and the way they are furnished.

**ethnic folk art**   Artistic works reflecting a particular culture or heritage created by anonymous artists.

**experience chart**   A written account of what children say about an event or experience in which they have participated.

**exploration**   Discovering how to use new materials and techniques.

**exteroceptors**   Our external sense organs: nose, eyes, mouth, ears, and skin.

**extrinsic motivation**   Giving rewards and prizes.

## F

**fabric dye**   Any substance that permanently colors cloth. Not all dyes are safe for children to use.

**facilitator**   The role a teacher takes when the ideas and the goals come from the children and the teacher responds by providing the concepts, skills, and materials that allow the children to be successful.

**fantasy**   The creation of imaginary worlds. It is where the mental images of the imagination are brought to life through story.

**fiber**   A fine, threadlike material.

**fiber art**   Art forms, such as weaving, appliqué, and embroidery, that use fibers or materials created from fiber.

**finger paint**   A kind of paint intended to be applied with the fingers.

**finger play**   A little story acted out with fingers.

**firing**   Slowly heating clay in an insulated oven called a *kiln*.

**firing clay**   A modeling compound formed from earth that dries out in the air and becomes hard when fired in a kiln.

**fixative**   Any substance that affixes chalk permanently to paper. Fixatives are not safe to use around children.

**flexibility**   Being able to see things from alternative viewpoints.

**flow**   Being so immersed in and focused on a task or problem that the person notices nothing else going on around them. Also a smooth, gliding motion in dance.

**fluency**   Being able to generate a multitude of diverse ideas or solutions.

**folk art**   Artworks created by people who have not had formal training in art, or who use nontraditional art media in ways that reflect their culture.

**form**   The whole of a work of art; also, the three-dimensional equivalent of shape that has the qualities of mass and volume, or the structure that organizes the elements of music.

**free-form**   An irregular shape.

# G

**genre**   A type of music (e.g., gospel, jazz, lullaby, opera, rock and roll, and sonata) or type of literature (e.g. fable, fairy tale, fiction, non-fiction, poetry).

**geometric**   A shape that conforms to mathematical principles.

**goal**   A statement of the kind of growth in a child's behavior that would be expected over a period of time and after many explorations.

**Goodenough-Harris Draw-a-Person Test**   A test in which children's cognitive developmental levels are assessed by asking them to draw a person.

**graphic**   Something that is pictorial or written.

**greenware**   Clay that has air-dried.

**guided discovery**   A process in which a new activity or center is introduced in the context of establishing guidelines for safe, logical use.

**guided imagery**   Creating sensory pictures in the mind based on prompts or stories provided by a leader.

**guiding adult**   The person who selects and prepares the supplies, maps out the possible routes, and provides encouragement along the way.

# H

**harmony**   A sequence of tones that enrich a melody.

**hue**   Color, such as red or yellow.

# I

**illustrator**   A person who makes pictures to go with a story in a book.

**imagination**   Mental images, which are ideas of things that can be manipulated in the mind. These images can be visual, auditory, and sensory.

**immersion**   Being intensely focused on creating something unique.

**improvisation**   Inventing a dramatic action in immediate response to a cue or scenario; music created spontaneously as it is played.

**inclusive**   Adjusting the environment or activity so that all children regardless of developmental level can participate.

**incubation**   A period of time in which individuals think and process what they know and what they wish to do.

**Individualized Education Plan (IEP)**   A document that details how a child with special needs will be taught and what special adjustments will be made so that child will be successful and make educational progress.

**Individuals with Disabilities Act**   A U.S. federal law, updated in 2004, that guarantees children with special needs a free public education tailored to their needs and delivered in the least restrictive environment.

**infant**   A child from birth to 18 months in age.

**informal dramatic play**   Spontaneous, child-initiated play.

**input device**   A hardware device that transforms and sends information to the computer.

**integrated learning units**   A planned group of activities that are interconnected by a shared meaningful question.

**intelligences (multiple intelligences theory)**   A conception of human cognition, proposed by Howard Gardner, that recognizes eight different realms of intellectual capability within each individual: linguistic, logical-mathematical, spatial, musical, bodily-kinesthetic, interpersonal, naturalistic, and intrapersonal.

**intensity**   The brightness or dullness of a color.

**intentional teaching**   Using knowledge, expertise, and judgment to organize learning for children so that when a teachable moment arises the teacher is ready with the appropriate strategy.

**interpersonal intelligence**   In Howard Gardner's theory of multiple intelligences, the ability to understand and work with others.

**intrapersonal intelligence**   In Howard Gardner's theory of multiple intelligences, the ability to understand oneself.

**intrinsic motivation**    A natural curiosity and desire to explore.

## J

## K

**keyboard**    A set of typewriter-like keys that enable users to enter data into a computer.

**kiln**    An oven made from firebrick in which clay can be fired to temperatures over 1000°F.

**kindergartener**    A child between the ages of five and six.

**kinesthetic awareness**    The system of sensors found in our muscles, joints, and tendons, which provides information on posture, equilibrium, and the effort required for a motion to occur.

**kinesthetic memory**    That part of mental processing that allows us to remember how to move in specific ways.

**kinesthetic thinking**    The ability of the brain to order movement through motor logic.

**knowledge**    The concepts, vocabulary, and understandings that individuals already know about what they are exploring.

**kraft paper**    Medium-weight brown paper similar to what is used for grocery bags, often sold in rolls. Sturdy enough for drawing and other arts activities.

**KWL chart**    A three-column chart listing things that are known, things that are wondered about, and things are learned.

## L

**landscape**    A representation of the outdoors.

**line**    A continuous stroke made with a moving tool. A boundary between or around shapes.

**linguistic intelligence**    In Howard Gardner's theory of multiple intelligences, the ability to manipulate the symbols of language.

**logical-mathematical intelligence**    In Howard Gardner's theory of multiple intelligences, the ability to manipulate numerical patterns and concepts.

**loom**    A frame or machine on which yarn is stretched for weaving cloth.

**lyrics**    The words of a song.

## M

**mandala**    A circular design with radiating straight lines.

**march**    Music with a strong beat designed for marching.

**measure**    A grouping of beats that is repeated.

**medium**    Any art material. Plural: media.

**melody**    A sequence of tones that changes or repeats.

**mental representation or imagery**    The ability to produce and act upon sensory images in one's mind.

**menu**    A list of choices available in a computer program, from which the user can select options using the mouse or keyboard.

**meter**    The repeated pattern of beats per measure.

**metronome**    A device that produces a regular beat that can be changed.

**minuet**    A French dance using small steps to a ¾ time.

**mixed media**    A piece of sculpture made from a combination of materials, such as paint, paper, wire, and fabric.

**mobile**    Three-dimensional art that moves.

**modeling**    Showing how to use a material or tool or perform a technique.

**molas**    Textile art form worn on clothing.

**monoprint**    A printing method that produces only one copy of the original.

**mood**    The way a particular combination of music elements affects the listener.

**mosaic**    A picture made from small pieces, such as stones, seeds, or paper bits.

**motivation**    The inner drive to accomplish something.

**motherese**    Singsong baby talk used with infants, high in pitch with many glides and spaces between vowels.

**mouse**    A handheld device that when rolled in different directions along a surface, controlling the movement of the cursor on a computer screen.

**movement**    The positioning and changing stance of the body in space.

**multicultural art**    Art relating to, reflecting, or adapted to diverse cultures.

**mural**  A large piece of artwork, usually hung or painted on a wall. Also, a very large, two-dimensional piece of artwork created by a group of children.

**music**  Organized sound.

**music therapist**  A trained individual who uses music to help people deal with emotional difficulties.

**musical intelligence**  In Howard Gardner's theory of multiple intelligences, the ability to manipulate rhythm and sound.

### N

**narrative drama**  Play or performances based on children's own stories or stories they have heard or read.

**narrative play**  Dramatic activities based on stories. Also called *story play*.

**naturalistic-environmental intelligence**  In Howard Gardner's theory of multiple intelligences, the ability to sense and make use of the characteristics of the natural world.

**newsprint**  A lightweight, inexpensive, slightly gray paper.

**nonhardening clay**  Modeling compounds that never harden but stay soft and pliable.

**nonobjective**  Art based on geometric and organic shapes and forms.

**normative development**  The level of skills and behaviors a child might be expected to have at a given age.

**notation**  Writing down music using some kind of a symbol system. Staff notation in which notes are indicated on a five-line staff is the most common system used today.

**note**  A single sound or tone.

### O

**objective**  A statement describing a behavior that can be accomplished within the time frame of the activity.

**observation**  Taking particular care in watching something.

**octave**  A musical interval of eight notes, such as C to C or D to D.

**olfactory perception**  Being sensitive to the aesthetic quality of odors.

**open-ended**  Activities that have no right answer and a multitude of possible results and ways of getting there.

**opera**  A play in which the actors sing accompanied by an orchestra.

**orchestra**  A large group of musicians, grouped by instrument, and playing parts together.

**organized play**  Games and sports in which there are set rules for everyone to follow.

**originality**  Being able to think of ideas or solutions that have never been thought of before.

**outdoor area**  A contiguous play area outside the classroom.

### P

**pantomime**  Acting out an idea without using words, although it may include sound effects.

**papier-mâché**  A mixture of paper and paste that can be used to cover objects or formed into shapes and allowed to become dry and hard.

**parallel play**  A form of interaction in very young children in which two children sit side by side and do similar things, but do not communicate or interact directly.

**paraphrase**  To restate what has been said.

**pastel**  A drawing made with chalk composed of ground pigments.

**pattern**  A repeated, recognizable combination of art elements.

**percussion**  The beating or striking of a musical instrument.

**performance assessment**  An alternative term for authentic assessment.

**pitch**  How high or low a sound is.

**portfolio**  A collection of the child's work and related materials made over a period.

**portrait**  A representation of the outer and inner characteristics of a being.

**positive feedback**  A praise statement that includes a description that gives specific reference to what was done.

**potential developmental level**  Skills or behaviors a child can do with assistance.

**potter**  A person who works with natural clay.

**pottery clay**    Fired clay.

**practice play**    A level of play in which infants explore and interact with objects using repeated actions.

**prekindergardener**    A child between the ages of 4 and 5. This classification is often used for children who have birthdays at or around the cut-off point for entrance into kindergarten. Often abbreviated as PreK. They may also be considered preschoolers.

**preoperational**    According to Piagetian theory, the period during which children are focused on learning language and using symbols in imaginative ways, but cannot mentally manipulate information in concrete logical ways. They cannot yet imagine someone else's point of view. It occurs between the ages of 2 and 6.

**preschooler**    A child between the ages of 3 and 5.

**presentation panel**    A display of materials that shows the process of creating works of art.

**prevention**    A form of behavior control in which misbehaviors are anticipated and activities, materials, and settings are adjusted to make the behavior less likely to occur.

**primary age**    Children between the ages of 6 and 8 who are in first and second grade or its equivalent.

**primary colors**    The three basic colors from which all other colors are derived, and which cannot be mixed from the other colors. In painting, these are red, yellow, and blue. In colored light, they are magenta, cyan, and yellow.

**print**    A picture made using any technique that produces multiple copies, including woodcut, serigraph (silk screen), etching, and lithography.

**printer**    A machine that produces a paper copy of what is visible on the computer screen.

**process drama**    An unscripted dramatic activity in which the teacher and children work together to create a scenario.

**production**    The tangible expression or product that is the end result of the creative process.

**project approach**    An emergent curriculum design in which children pursue research on a topic of interest to them.

**prop**    Anything used to assist with or enhance a creative movement, dance, or dramatic performance.

## Q

**quilt**    A fabric design created by piecing together smaller bits of fabric.

**quilter**    A person who makes quilts.

## R

**redirection**    A form of behavior control in which the guidelines or rules are restated.

**reflective teaching**    The ability to evaluate and interpret evidence, modify views, and make objective judgments.

**removal**    A form of behavior control in which a child who is misbehaving is removed from the setting.

**representation**    Communicating ideas and feelings through the arts.

**responding**    Actively engaging with artistic works.

**responsive**    Able to express ideas and feelings using a particular arts material or technique.

**revisitation**    Developing control through repeated use of a material or technique.

**rubric**    A list of criteria that defines what is quality work, often used as part of authentic assessments.

**rhythm**    Time-based pattern that orders sound.

## S

**salsa**    A Latin American dance form of Cuban origin usually performed with a partner to a 4/4 beat.

**scaffold**    To restate what was said while adding more description or vocabulary that is more complex.

**scale**    A set of notes ordered by pitch. In jazz and classical music this is usually eight notes. The pentatonic scale common in folksongs is five notes. Most contemporary music is based on a seven-note scale. Scales are named for the note they start on, i.e. C scale starts on C.

**scenario**    An outline or synopsis of a play.

**sculpture**    A three-dimensional artwork. Sculpture can be made from a limitless variety of materials, including wood, stone, clay, metal, found objects, papier-mâché, fabric, plaster, wax, and resins.

**seascape**    A representation of the sea.

**secondary colors**    The colors created by mixing two of the primary colors.

**selective attention**   The ability to choose from incoming sensory signals which should be ignored and which require reaction.

**senses**   There are five senses: auditory or hearing, visual or seeing, olfactory or sense of smell, taste, and tactile or touch.

**sensorimotor level of development**   Based on Piagetian theory, this is the stage when children depend on their senses and actions in order to understand their world. It usually occurs from infancy to age 2.

**sensory awareness**   To focus on the characteristics of people, objects, and environments using one's senses.

**sensory images**   Images that may involve one or more of the senses, such as visual, auditory, tactile, and olfactory.

**sensory integration dysfunction (SID)**   The inability to make meaning from information acquired by the senses.

**sensory integration**   The ability to combine information from all the senses into a meaningful whole.

**sensory mode**   Processing information using one or more of the senses.

**sensory perception**   Sensory perception is taking in physical sensations through the body's sense organs.

**shade**   A color darkened by the addition of black.

**shape**   A two-dimensional area or image that has defined edges or borders.

**skill**   The development of expertise in using tools and materials or in carrying out an action.

**slab**   A flat piece of clay made by either pressing with the palms or using a rolling pin.

**slip**   Liquid clay made by combining clay with water to form a thick, custard-like substance. It is used to join clay pieces.

**software**   Computer programs, stored on disks, that enable a computer to perform tasks.

**solitary play**   A form of activity in which a child entertains herself or himself independent of others.

**solo**   A performance by one individual or instrument.

**sonata**   A musical form composed for two instruments and having three or four movements played at different tempos.

**space**   An open or empty area in an artwork.

**spatial intelligence**   In Howard Gardner's theory of multiple intelligences, the ability to visualize the configuration of objects in space.

**stereognostic perception**   To be able to make sense of a three-dimensional form by touch alone.

**still life**   A representation of an arrangement of objects.

**stitchery**   A design made with yarn or cloth.

**story cloth**   Appliquéd and embroidered textile, made by the Hmong people of Southeast Asia, that record traditional folktales and personal life stories.

**story play**   Drama activities that are based on children's own stories or on stories children have read. Also called *narrative play*.

**story script**   A written version of a narrative drama.

**storytelling**   Oral presentation of a traditional or original story.

**style**   A particular way of doing something that is characteristic of an individual or group.

**symbolic play**   When a child pretends that one object is really something else, such as a large pot used as a helmet.

**symmetrical**   The same on both sides of a dividing line or a mirror image.

**symmetry**   Equilibrium or balance created by placing art elements equally on both sides of a central axis.

**symphony**   A musical piece written for an orchestra. It usually has four parts, with the first part being a sonata.

**syncopation**   A rhythm found in some genres of music, such as jazz, in which there is a deliberate change in where the regular stress is expected to come.

**synesthetic experience**   An activity that includes stimuli for more than one sense.

# T

**tactile defensiveness**   Having extreme sensitivity to touch.

**tactile perception**   The awareness and appreciation of how things feel to the touch.

**tagboard**   A stiff, smooth, bendable board, also called poster board or oaktag.

**teachable moment.**   An unplanned opportunity to teach a needed skill or strategy.

**tempera**   Also known as *poster paint*, a water-based paint that is available in bright, washable colors and goes on smoothly.

**tempo**   The rate of speed of a musical piece or passage.

**texture**   In visual art the tactile or visual surface quality of an object or artwork. In music the layering of notes to create complex sounds.

**thematic unit**   A form of integrated curriculum in which learning is focused on a teacher-selected theme.

**thermic perception**   To sense of the temperature of an object.

**thinking routine**   A simple set of thinking strategies that help children become more critical thinkers.

**three-dimensional**   Having height, width, and depth.

**tie-dye**   A design made by tying parts of a cloth together and then dying the cloth.

**timbre**   The unique quality of a sound that makes it recognizable.

**tint**   A color lightened by the addition of white.

**toddler**   A child between the ages of 18 months and 3 years.

**tone**   In visual art, the relative lightness or darkness of a color. In music, a sound or note.

**tone color**   Another term for timbre.

**topic web**   A graphic organizer in which a topic is placed at the center and then branches of knowledge are extended outward slowly increasing in specific detail.

**two-dimensional**   Having height and width, but no depth.

## U

**unconditional praise**   A general positive statement that conveys no information related to what is being praised. It typically uses words like good, nice, and great.

## V

**value**   The range of lights and darks of colors.

**valuing**   Seeing the importance of a behavior or personal relationship.

**verse**   In a song, groups of two or more lines that have the same melody, but different words.

**vestibular sense**   Keeps track of the motion and position of the head relative to the rest of the body.

**visual arts**   Expression of ideas and feelings through visual and tactile elements.

**visual perception**   The awareness of and appreciation for how things look.

## W

**weaver**   A person who weaves cloth.

**weaving frame loom**   A simple wooden frame on which yarn is wrapped at even intervals to allow the handweaving of cloth.

**weaving**   The process of creating a fabric by interlocking threads and yarns.

**white drawing paper**   A sturdy paper with a smooth surface.

**WOW**   A "Wonderful Object of Wonder" object, material, or experience that excites the senses and focuses attention. Usually used at the start of an arts activity, but also effective as a stand-alone experience.

## Y

**young artist (child)**   A child from birth to age 8.

## Z

**zone of proximal development**   The point between where a child needs total adult assistance and where a child can work independently. According to Vygotsky, this is when the best learning takes place.

# Index

Note: page numbers followed by an "f" indicate figures; followed by a "t" indicate tables.

## A

A.B.C. Task Force, 9, 131, 135, 354
Absolute pitch, 301
Abstract art, 183
Abstract thought, 345
Abstraction, 181
*Abuela's Weave* (Castaneda), 185
Academic achievement, 316
Accents, music, 276
Acceptance, 39
    communicating, 39
    creativity, 32, 38, 75
    differences, 33, 350–351
    dramatic arts and, 64
    modeling of, 118
    positive social climate and, 118
    rejection vs., 64
    special needs, 33–34, 130
Accommodation. *See* Special needs
Accompanying music, 277, 329, 331
Active listening. *See* Listening
Activities. *See also* Interactive
        activities; Multisensory
        activities; One-on-one activities;
        Open-ended activities
    adjusting, 127
    aesthetic responsive, 190–193
    anti-bias, 9, 130–133
    assessment of, 69–76
    auditory perception, 90, 93, 96
    choice in, 33
    collages, 104, 106, 132, 249–250, 259
    color, 100–102
    community building, 8–9, 119
    construction, 9, 105, 122–123,
        268–269
    cooperative arts project, 168

creative movement, 105, 323–329
dance, 319, 323–328, 329–332
delivery of, 19, 45, 129
digital art activities, 259
directions in, 7, 129
domain-based, 13
drawing, 79, 240–241
emotional objectives in, 7–8
exploration centers, 238, 283
fiber art, 39, 255–256
food, 96, 135–136
food areas and, 249
form, 105–106
general modifications of,
    128–129
goals and objectives for, 15–16
group, 120–125
group composition for, 41, 92, 123
gustatory, 97
holidays and, 136–137
instrumental, 295–298
integrated learning unit, 13
line, 101
listening, 285–288
materials for, 37
modeling, 95, 128, 264–265
movement, 105, 323–329
music, 5, 61t, 67t, 77, 100
musical instrument, 295–298
olfactory perception, 90, 96
objectives for, 13, 16, 71, 80, 90,
    127, 207, 214, 217f
one-on-one, 238
open-ended, 34, 49, 90, 91, 93, 123
painting, 128t, 243–245
papier-mâché, 105
participatory arts, 108
pattern, 103
planning, 41
pottery clay, 263–264
practice, 14, 57
practice, selecting, 14, 93–94, 238
printmaking, 253–254

procedure for, 92, 123, 158, 197,
    220, 251, 300, 327, 358
relevant, 13
responsive, 35–36, 239
rhythm, 103, 289, 291–292, 293
selecting developmentally
    appropriate, 14, 57–58, 68,
    309, 338
sensory, 8, 86, 88, 89, 92, 95, 97, 98,
    107
setup for, 41, 92, 123, 158, 193, 194,
    219, 358
shapes, 102–103, 104, 249
singing, 286, 300–306
space, 105, 148–152, 167, 195, 314,
    320–321, 344
special needs and, 33–34, 97,
    125–126, 127, 128t, 129
tactile perception, 90, 93, 96–97
taste perception, 96
three-dimensional, 5, 88, 260
texture, 103–104
time frame for, 41, 92, 123, 158,
    197, 219, 251, 299, 327, 358
transitioning out of, 41, 92, 123,
    158, 197, 220, 251, 284, 300, 328,
    358
two-dimensional, 5, 88, 238–239
visual perception, 87, 90, 91, 93, 96,
    99, 102
warm-ups for, 41, 92, 123, 158, 197,
    220, 251, 300, 327, 358
writing plans for, 41, 92, 123,
    158–159, 197, 219–220, 251,
    299–300, 327–328, 358
Actual developmental level, 11
Adhesives, 247. *See also* Glues; Paste
Adobe Illustrator, 259
Aesthetics
    activities, 190–193
    art and beauty in, 175
    arts elements and, 175–177
    books on, 191, 192

Aesthetics (*cont.*)
   cultural differences in, 9, 133–137
   description of beauty and, 175
   developing a sense of, 14, 190–193
   dramatic arts, 175–177
   engagement, 180
   environment and, 147, 153–157, 170
   literacy, 177
   personal taste and, 42, 153, 187
   teacher role in, 35, 42, 153, 160
African art. *See* World arts
Aggregates, 237
*All Around the Kitchen* (Seeger), 329
*All the Colors We Are* (Kissinger), 131
Alphabet, creative movement and, 326
Amabile, Theresa, 28, 33
*Amazing Grace* (Hoffman), 143
American Academy of Pediatrics, 156
American Sign Language, 39, 303
Anecdotal records, 70–71
Anholt, L., 174
Animato, 260
Animals
   creative movement and, 326,
      327, 360
   sculptures, 265
   stuffed artifacts, 187
"Animals in the Woods," 77
*Anne with a Green Parasol* (Bellows),
   200
Anti-bias activities, 9, 130–133, 354-355
Anti-bias props, 354
Appliqué, 184, 255, 256
Appreciation
   art, 39
   encouraging in families, 75–76
Apprenticeship model, 12
Arches, 269
*Architects Make Zig Zags: Looking
   at Architecture from A to Z*
   (Maddox), 269
Architectural blocks, 266
Architecture, 268, 269
*Architecture Colors* (Crosbie), 269
Arias, 287
Arnheim, Rudolph, 86
Arrivals, in classrooms, 150
Art
   absence of, 4
   analysis of, 25
   artifacts, 183–185
   bags, 134, 192
   color in, 100–102

   as communication, 176
   as community engagement,
      176t–177
   as creative personal realization,
      176t–177
   as culture, history, and connectors,
      176t–177
   definition, 183
   discarding, 163
   displaying, 39
   elements of, 100–105, 271
   folding, 163
   form in, 104–105
   forms, definition of, 104
   integration in, 14, 101, 206–208
   introducing activities with, 50, 95,
      96–98
   line in, 100
   mounting, 164
   movement in, 105
   multicultural, 181
   name labels on, 163
   pattern in, 103
   prints, 184, 254
   real experiences and, 65
   rhythm in, 103
   scented markers, 101
   shape in, 102
   sources, 19, 80, 107, 139, 167, 184,
      186, 199, 223, 226, 270, 307, 333,
      334, 335, 367, 372
   space in, 105
   storing, 72, 164, 181
   study, 201
   styles, 180, 181
   styles of Western, 285
   texture in, 103–104
   well-being and, 176t–177
*The Art Box* (Gibbons), 245
Art center, planning, 272
Art store visits, 196
Art tables, 76, 80, 149
Artifacts, 183–185. *See also* Objects
   defining, 183
   documenting learning and,
      222–223
   selecting, 183–184
   sources for, 184
   using, 184–185
Artistic development, 8, 56–84
   activity selection for, 68–69, 180–181
   assessing, 69–75
   books on, 33, 36

   children's understanding of, 66–67
   creative movement, 105
   developmentally appropriate
      practice and, 14, 57–58, 68–69
   displays of, 107, 163–164, 165, 221
   dramatic arts, 345–350
   emotional factors in, 64
   environmental factors in, 5, 64–65
   experience in, 7–8, 53, 65–66
   factors affecting, 63, 81
   families and, 75–77
   giftedness and, 66
   growth models, 82
   helping families understand, 49
   individual development, 62–63
   media familiarity and, 63
   musical, 8, 5–6, 10–13
   normative development and, 58–59
   objectives, 217f
   overview, 3–4, 56–57, 80
   physical factors in, 63, 235
   reflective teaching, 77–80
   research on, 58–62
   symbolic communication model
      and, 7, 67t
   teacher self-assessment in, 77–80
   three-dimensional, 260, 262
   two-dimensional, 5, 88
Artistic literacy 16, 177
Artistic works as, 177–178t
Artists
   birth to 8 years, 3–4
   community, 8–9
   famous dancers, 333
   famous musicians, 179, 182, 287
   famous painters, 32
   featured, 163
   guest, 193
   pottery clay, 265
   studio visits, 195
   working together, 115
Arts, 1–25
   children's development in, 59
   community building through,
      8–9, 119
   connecting, 6, 16
   creativity and, 32
   description of, 4–5
   engagement with, 177, 179–180
   expanding definitions of, 16, 174–175
   first language, 6–7
   integrating into the curriculum, 14,
      206–208

learning and, 5–18
learning objectives for activities on, 14, 16
lover of, 199
natural world, 13
of others, perception of, 175
program design, 19–20
reasons to teach, 5–10, 22
teaching about, 18–21, 114–145
using with children, 6–7
world, 5, 6, 9, 10
world without, 4
Arts Education Partnership, 369
"Arts Happenings," 75
Arts sleeves, 163
Arts therapy, 127–128
Arts standards. See Standards
Artwork study, 201
Asian arts, 131, 136
Assessment
    approaches to, 14–15, 152, 209–213
    arts growth, 69–75
    authentic, 214–215
    checklists for, 78
    creative movement, 323
    descriptive approach in, 43–44
    developmental approach in, 69–75
    dramatic arts in, 371
    environment, 131, 133–135, 144, 147–148, 169, 170
    expectations for, 69–70
    families and, 75–77
    feedback, 78
    observation in, 23–24, 69–72, 84
    performance, 215–215
    personal tastes and, 187
    photographs in, 71–72
    portfolios in, 72–74
    process approach in, 71–72
    psychological, 127–128
    recording, 71–72
    reflective, 78, 80
    self-, for teachers, 77–80
    self-, in movement, 317
    state, 30
    tools for, 70–71, 72–74
    video, 72
Assistance, special needs and, 126, 129
Assistive devices, 129, 130, 282
Atelier, 239
Atelierista, 13, 14
Attention
    behaviors and, 11

getters, 285
listening activities for, 285
modeling and, 11
music for getting, 286
Vygotsky on, 11
Attention-deficit disorders, 350
Attention span, 58–59
    dramatic play and, 346
    infants, 58
    listening activities and, 286, 333
    performances and, 182, 183, 193, 369
    preschoolers, 58–59
    primary age children, 59
    theater and, 193, 369
At the Supermarket (Rockwell), 227
Attitude
    assessing, 74
    toward displays, 76, 163
    toward personal artwork, 58, 324
Audience behavior, 197, 199
Auditory discrimination, 182, 197
Auditory perception, 86, 109
    activities, 90, 93, 96, 197, 299
    creative movement and, 97
    description and, 86
    disabilities in, 350
    music and, 108, 277, 281, 327
    objectives on, 86, 281, 287
    pattern and rhythm in, 100, 103, 299
    rhythm instruments and, 103
    special needs modifications, 128t, 282, 350
Autism, 125, 127, 128t, 301, 350, 353
Awareness
    body, 304
    color, 100–102, 132
    kinesthetic, 90
    sensory, 101–105

B
Baby Touch and Feel (DK Publishing), 106
Bach, Johann Sebastian, 182, 309
Bags
    art, 134, 192
    squishy, 92
    touch, 105
Baker, 220
Balance, 324, 326
Ballet, 181, 182, 218f, 334, 338
Bands, rhythm, 124

Bandura, Albert, 11
Bangs, Molly, 123
Banners, 231
Baroque music, 182
Basic Scribbles, 237
Basket makers, 255, 256
Baskets, 97–98
Baylor, B., 265
Beanbags, 324
Beats, 276, 289, 304
Beaty, Andrea, 159
Beautiful Blackbird (Bryan), 132
Beautiful Oop (Saltzberg), 41
Beauty, describing, 175
Behavior. See also Direction
    adult, 134
    audience, 149, 177, 197, 199
    creative, 55
    promoting appropriate, 119–120
    special needs in, 129
Bells, 282, 285t, 290, 294
Bellows, 200
Benari, Naomi, 323
Ben's Trumpet (Isadora), 185
Bias, 9, 144–145
Big books, 185
    making, 106, 111
"Big C" (Csikszentmihalyi), 27
The big orange splot (Pinkwater), 168
Bilingual. See English Language Learners
Bins, sensory, 97–98
Blagojevic, Bonnie, 72
Blocks
    architectural, 266
    building, 175
    construction centers, 267
    interlocking, 266
    large, 266
    music note, 298
    pattern, 266
    plastic, 266
    safety and, 267
    unit, 267
Blueprints, 267, 269
Boards
    drawing, 149, 240–241
    flannel, 304
Boards, drawing, 149, 240–241
Bodily-kinesthetic intelligence, 12
Body
    in the arts, 61
    awareness, 304

Body (*cont.*)
    creative movement of, 324
    development, 57, 59–60t, 61t, 261f
    dance and, 314, 320, 328, 329
    image, 8
    integrated units and, 218f
    language, 180
    motions, books and, 186, 333
    objectives, 217f
    pantomimes and, 357
    percussion, 322
    rhythm, 103
    safety, 94–95
    shapes, 326
    singing and, 304
    size, 316t
    sounds, 286
    talk, in music, 291
Booklets, 20, 74, 100, 240
Bookmaking, 240
*The Book of Pitch Exploration: Can You Sing This?* (Feierabend), 306
Books
    on actors, 185
    anti-bias, 130, 131, 132, 134
    on artists, 185
    arts, 263
    on auditory perception, 106–107
    big, 185
    Caldecott award winners, 185
    celebrating art, 241, 245, 250, 257
    on clay, 265
    on collages, 250
    on color, 106, 220
    on construction, 269
    on creative movement, 33, 36
    on creativity, 33
    on dance, 185, 333, 333
    on differences, 131, 134
    on diversity, 134
    on dramatic arts, 371
    on drawing, 241
    on empathy, 132, 134
    for engagement, 185–186
    on fiber arts, 257
    on instruments, 298
    on integrated curriculum, 186
    on jazz, 179
    on lines, 106
    making, 106–107, 240
    media, 185
    on modeling, 265
    multicultural, 33, 185

    museums and, 196
    on music, 185, 287
    on nature of arts, 207, 209f
    on painting, 245
    on patterns, 106
    on physical and cultural
        differences, 130, 132, 134, 351
    on painting, 245
    picture, 185
    play centers inspired by, 354, 366
    on poetry, 292
    on potters, 265
    on printing, 254
    on problem solving, 33
    on puppets, 123, 218f
    reality and, 36
    on rhythm, 292
    selection of, 185–186
    for self-confidence, 134
    sensory, 106
    shapes in, 43, 256
    sharing with children,
        185–186, 192
    on singing, 306
    skills and, 178f
    on sound, 106–107
    on special needs, 130, 351
    on taste and smell, 106
    teaching about the arts with, 186
    on texture, 106
    texture in, 106
    use of, 106
    on visual perception, 108
    on world art, 175, 179, 182,
        185–186, 191
    on writing rhythm, 292
Boredom, 34, 96
Bouncing, 329
Boxes
    construction with, 266
    improvisation, 361
    props, 322, 354, 355, 376
    role-play, 361
Bradley, 200
Brain research, 5–6, 280, 316
    movement and, 316
    music and, 280
    play and, 345–346
Brainstorming, 32, 209f
*Brandenburg Concertos Nos.* 1–6, 182
Bredekamp, Sue, 14, 58, 150, 346
Bridges, in dance, 335
Bristle brushes, 243

*Brown Bear, Brown Bear, What Do You See?*, 333
Brown, Hazel, 366
Brown, M., 333
Browne, Mary, 211
Bruner, Jerome, 345
Brushes, paint, 242–243
    exploring, 244
    types of, 243, 244
Bubble wrap, 94, 98, 159, 322, 330
Bubbles, 291
Buddy dances, 329
Building activities, 162, 267, 269
*Bunny Money* (Wells), 227
Burlap, 243, 255

## C

Cadwell, Ashley, 152
Caine, Geoffrey, 89, 179, 206, 280
Caine, Renate Nummela, 89, 179,
    206, 280
Caldecott awards, 185
Call and response, 326
Calligraphers, 194, 195
Cambourne, Brian, 366
Cameras, 71, 72, 73, 80, 125
*Camille and the Sunflowers*
    (Anholt), 174
*Can You Hear It?* (Lach), 287
Captions, 223
*Car Song* (Guthrie), 329
Card readers, 363
Cardboard, 266
Cards
    art, 245
    cue, 127, 305, 350
    dance, 335
    handmade, 23
    picture, 20
    print, 259
    task, 350
    thank you, 194
Caribbean music, 181, 323
Carle, E., 106, 218
*Carnival of Animals* (Saint-Saëns),
    287, 327
Carter, M., 78
Castaneda, O.S., 185
Catlin, 200
*Case with Five Balusters* (Duchamp/
    Nevelson), 268
Cause and effect, 6, 41, 92, 157, 281

Celebrations, of color, 131–132
Celebratory presentation, 107, 224, 231
Celenza, 287
Centers. *See* Learning centers
*Center Stage*, 334
Chain dances, 330
Chalk, 239–240
Chanting, 302
Characters, in dramatic arts, 186, 364
Chard, Sylvia, 209–211
*Charlie Parker Played Be Bop*
        (Raschka), 292
Charney, Ruth, 321
Charts
    experience, 165
    musical development, 278t–279t
Cheatham, Gregory, 65
Checklists
    activity assessment, 161, 170
    reflective documentation, 78
    families and, 75
    observations, 70–71
    teacher self-assessment, 78
    visits, 23
Cherry, Clare, 59
Children's theater, 183, 369–371.
        *See also* Dramatic arts
Chime blocks, 295
Chimes, 295
Chin, 301
Choking hazards, 149, 159,
        250, 289, 295
Chorals, 118
Chords, 277, 294, 301
Choruses, 301, 302, 304
*Cendrilla: A Caribbean Cinderella*
        (San Souci), 351
Circle of dance, 315f
Clapping
    audience etiquette, 199, 370
    echo, 288
    listening activity, 286
    in music development, 277
    percussions and, 322
    physical development, 60
    rhythms, 103, 289, 291, 303
Class quilts, 124
Classical music, 181, 182, 286
Classroom cleanup, 150
Claves, 290
Clay
    activities, 265
    books on, 265

firing, 263
    hazards of, 263
    modeling, 8, 128, 265
    non-hardening, 158, 263, 264, 267
    pottery, 262–263
    safety and, 264
    storing, 263
    teaching, 270
    tiles, 103, 154, 250
    well-being and, 7
Clayton, M., 151
Cleanup, 243, 264
Clock music, 286, 291–292
Clocks, 291–292
Cloth. *See* Fiber art
Cloth pictures, 255
Clothing
    creative movement and, 321
    looking at, 257
    painting smocks, 244, 246
Cochlear implants, 282
Cognitive development, 61–62,
    artistic performance, 61–62
    art stimulation, 5
    assessing, 69–71
    creative movement and, 317
    drama and, 61–62
    Gardner model of, 61–62
    language, 61–62
    movement and, 61–62, 317
    music and, 61–62, 281
    objectives, 217f
    observing, 116
    Piaget on, 10–11, 345
    play and, 345
    school age, 352
    sensory arts, 91
    social play and, 116
    teacher's role in, 352
    visual arts and, 61–62, 251, 255
    visual perception and, 86
    Vygotsky on, 11–12
    waves of, 61–62
Collaboration, 137
    anti-bias activities for, 9
    appropriate behavior in, 116–117,
        119–120
    arts activities and, 40, 41, 92, 123,
        137, 139–140
    brainstorming, 235
    caring and, 41, 92
    community engagement and, 119,
        176

cooperative behavior and, 15, 114,
        116, 321
    dramatic arts and, 348t
    enjoying, 116
    group size in, 121–122
    mixed-age and ability, 122
    play and, 116
    positive climate for, 118–120
    skills development, 259, 349
    special needs and, 350
    toddlers and, 304
    visual arts and, 235
Collages, 246–251
    activities for, 249–251
    activities for infants, 249
    books on, 250
    centers for, 249
    color awareness, 100–102, 132
    cutting problems, 248
    cutting tools for, 247–248
    digital, 259
    discussions on, 250
    materials for, 246–247, 250
    paste/glue selection for,
        246–247
    activities for toddlers, 249
    types of, 250
College Board, 29
Color, 154–155
    awareness, 100–102
    celebrating, 245
    drawing with, 240
    environment aesthetics and, 154–155
    infants and, 100, 154, 240
    mixing, 131–132
    modeling and, 263
    painting and, 245
    skin, 131–132
    unique, 132
Color blindness, 101
*The Colors of Us* (Katz), 132
Columns, 269
Combines, 237
Comfort, 47, 49, 148
Common Core Standards in the
        Arts 16
    dance, 314
    music, 281
    theater, 248-249
    visual art, 235-236
Common Core Standards in English
        Language Arts, 177, 178f,
        185–186

Common Core Standards in
 Mathematics, 253, 254, 284
 theater arts, 348
 visual arts, 235
Communication
 assessing, 66–67
 arts as, 176
 development through the arts, 7,
 11, 176f, 317
 dramatic arts, 342, 345, 359
 with families, 134–135
 feedback, 78
 kinesthetic, 67
 skill development in, 11, 95, 317,
 349, 350
 special needs and, 350
 symbolic communication model,
 7, 67t
Community
 artists in, 193, 194
 arts in creating, 8–9, 176t–177
 building through the arts, 119
 guest artists, 193
 resources from, 193–199
Comparison
 avoidance of, in teaching, 38
 colors and, 243
 creative works, 177, 189, 202
 form, 104
 pitch, 301
 questions about, 99
 response to artistic works, 191
 rhythms, 103
 same and different, 189
Compatibility, in environment, 152
Competitions, 165
Compose, 164, 295, 298, 331
Composing center, 283
Comprehensiveness, 216
Computer, 257–259
 activities for, 259–260
 as art medium, 258
 assistive technology, 282
 for auditory processing, 282
 dance and, 333, 334
 equipment for, 259
 location for, 259
 in music center, 293
 overuse of, 258
 portfolios and, 73–74
 software for, 258–259
 video and, 183
 virtual field trips, 195

Computer supplies, 258–259
Concept webs, 213–214
Concertos, 182
Concerts, attending, 198
Concrete operational development
 stage, 345
Conducting centers, 283
Confetti, 250
Confidence
 building, 34, 115
 motivation and, 34
 self-, 38
 singing and, 300
 in teachers, 34
Conflict, in dramatic arts, 343
Conformity, 34
Conga dance, 180, 181
Connected arts lessons, 6
Connecting standard
 common core and, 16
 dance, 314, 318–319
 drama, 348, 349
Connections
 to art, 179, 207, 226
 to the body, 316t
 in dance, 334
 in drama, 370–371
 in dramatic arts, 342
 making, 179
 in storytelling, 370–371
Constructed sculpture, 266–269
 activities for infants, 268–269
 activities for toddlers, 268–269
 block safety and, 267
 books about, 269
 centers for, 267
 discussions on, 269
 materials for, 266–267
 open-ended activities, 268
 papier-mâché, 267–268
Constructions, 122, 151, 224, 269
Constructivism, 10–11
Containers, for materials, 161–162
Content integration, 9
Content knowledge, 371
Contrast, in dramatic arts, 343–344
Control
 creative movement and, 323
 levels of, 62t
 physical, 57, 58, 59, 60–61, 371
Controlled exploration, 261
Conversations, starting, 45
Cookie cutters, 105, 137, 264

Cookies, tree, 266–267
Cooper, E., 304, 365
Cooperation. *See also* Collaboration
 books on, 159
 community and, 9
 creative movement and, 317
 dance and, 5, 317
 defined, 116
 group activities for, 137
 group size and, 121–122
 learning programs, 115
 literacy behaviors and, 353
 mixed-age and ability groups, 122
 through play, 116
 positive climate for, 159
 promoting, 133, 159
 through rhythm bands, 124
 through singing, 304
 social skills and, 116
 teachers and, 124–125, 353
Cooperative play, 116, 117, 118
Copple, Carol, 14, 57, 58, 150,
 344, 346
*Cornrows* (Yarborough), 355
Corot, 200
Costumes
 dance and, 183
 dramatic arts, 168, 194, 343,
 353, 366
 making, 368–369
 presentation of, 157
 role play, 361
 texture and, 103, 149
 toddlers and, 369
Counting
 in art, 250
 collage, 250
 in dance, 323, 326
 in math, 326
 in music, 284
Craft, A., 38
Crafts fairs,184
Crawling, 324
Crayons, 239
Creative arts, description of, 4–5
Creating standard
 common core, 16
 dance, 318
 drama, 342, 349
 music, 281
 visual arts, 235
Creative behavior, self-exploration of,
 55, 141, 203–204

Creative dance, 4–5. *See also* Dance
Creative movement, 312–340
    activities for infants, 323–324,
        325, 329
    activities for kindergarteners,
        329–330
    activities for preschoolers, 329–330
    activities for primary ages,
        326–328, 333
    activities for toddlers, 324–325
    body percussion and, 322
    books on, 333
    brain and, 316
    dance vs., 4–5, 313–314
    definition of, 313
    describing, 105, 313–314
    designing activities for, 319–321
    development and, 8, 316–319
    elements of, 314–315
    finding lines in, 100
    form and, 328, 331, 334–335
    music for, 322
    pattern in, 103
    planning activities, 322–323, 325
    process of, 314
    props for, 319, 320, 322
    response activity plan, 327–328
    sensory perception and, 8, 105
    silence and, 322
    space, 314, 320–321
    special needs modifications, 323
    standards, 16, 314
    transitions and, 328
    unity, in movements, 321
Creative process, 30–37
    fostering, 38–50
    immersion and, 36–37
    incubation and performance, 37
    knowledge and, 31–32
    motivation and, 32–34
    overview, 30–31
    skills and, 34–36
    wheel, 31f
"Creative Society of the 21st
    Century," 28
Creative thinking, 28, 371
Creativity, 26–55
    books celebrating, 241, 245,
        250, 257
    in children, 29–30
    Common Core and, 16
    definition of, 27–28
    emergent problems in, 34

encouragement, 33
    expressive forms, 36
    fostering, 14, 38–50
    importance of, 28–29
    making something new, 27–28
    nurturing, 9–10, 13–14, 26–55
    overview, 50–51
    play and, 30
    process in, 27, 30–37
    sensory perception and, 8, 91
    special needs and, 33–34
    teachers in, 18–21, 38–50
    teaching in, 51
Creator of the week, 163–164
Creeping, 324
Critical thinking, 371
Crone, Patricia, 127
Crosbie, M.J., 269
Cross-kicks, 332
Csikszentmihalyi, Mihaly, 27–28, 36
Cubism, 181
Cue cards, 127, 305, 350
Cultural aesthetic, 175
Cultural differences
    acceptance of, 9, 33, 126, 350–351
    activities for, 133–137
    in aesthetics, 9, 133–137
    anti-bias activities and, 9, 131,
        132–133
    artifacts and, 135, 185, 190
    artistic development and, 9, 131
    books on, 131, 134
    caring and, 137–139
    celebration of, 131
    color and, 66, 123, 131, 132
    discussion of, 132–133
    displays and, 131, 137
    displays featuring, 131, 137
    dramatic arts and, 350–351
    ethnic folk art, 183
    families and, 133–134
    holidays, 136–137
    learning from, 165
    musical instruments, 160
    play and, 354–355
    positive social climate and, 118
    sharing, 179, 181, 184, 185, 192,
        217f, 218f
    Western vs. non-Western art,
        181, 285
Culture 4, 11, 13, 14
    colors and, 101
    creativity and, 33

dance and, 333–334
    dramatic play and, 346
    exposure to, 38–39, 165, 181,
        184–185, 190
    fiber art and, 254
    food and, 96
    music and, 281, 284, 285, 294
    props and, 354
    role in development, 64, 65f,
        67f, 80
    sharing of, 9, 296, 370, 371
    storytelling and, 365
    symbols of, 63t
Curiosity
    motivation and, 32
    natural, 33
    promote, 15, 45, 91, 95, 135, 157
    about special needs, 130
    valuing, 50
    WOW and, 95
Curriculum
    anti-bias, 9, 131, 133, 135
    emergent, 14, 208–209
    for kindergarten, 29
    integrated, 206–208
    integrating arts in, 206–208
    learning goals in, 15–16
    learning philosophies and, 16,
        19, 176f
    personalized, 6
    well-designed, 13–21
Cursors, 258
Curtis, D., 78, 98, 123, 150, 152
Curtis, Jamie Lee, 123
Cutting tools, 247–248
Cycles, 326–327
Cymbals, 290

**D**

Daly, 227
Dance, 328–335. *See also* Creative
    movement
    activities for infants, 329
    activities for kindergarteners,
        329–330
    activities for preschoolers, 329–330
    activities for primary age, 329
    activities for toddlers, 330–331
    assessing, 333
    books about, 333
    celebratory presentation, 108
    circle of dance, 315f
    color and, 333

Dance (*cont.*)
concepts and skills in, 318, 326
connecting to, 314, 334
creative, 4–5, 339–340
definition of, 313
designing activities for, 319–320
development and, 316–319
developmentally appropriate, 329, 338
elements of, 336
famous, 333–334
folk, 331
gender and, 332
guided explorations, 313, 325
overview, 329–330, 334–335
multicultures and, 333
music for, 328–329
process vs. performance in, 332
responding to, 333–334
selecting, 182
special needs adaptations for, 337
standards on, 16, 319
steps, 331–332
styles of, 180, 329
symbolic communication model on, 67t
teaching about, 334, 335
weaving a, 255
Dance cards, 335
"Dance makes me feel," 326
DanceAbility International, 323
Dancing dolls, 335
Dancing feet, 329
*Dancing with the Stars*, 334
Darras, B., 66–67, 82
*Dave the Potter: Artist, Poet, Slave* (Hill), 265
Davis, Jessica, 4, 9
Deafness, 323
Decision making
assessment, 371
describing artistic, 44
families and, 181
materials for, 160
Degge, 64
Demonstrations, 108
de Paola, 245
Departures, in classrooms, 150
Derman-Sparks, L., 9, 131, 135, 354
Description
artistic decisions, 44
arts concepts, 44
colors, 100–102

improvisation, 361, 364
music, 103
pantomimes, 357
of scents, 100, 101
of shapes, 100, 102
of space, 105
in storytelling, 367, 368
of tastes, 92
of textures, 103
of visual experiences, 103–105
Descriptive approach, 44
Descriptive statements, 43–44
Desmet, 86
Detail, attention to, photo story, 198
Development and developmental stages
activity selection and, 68–69, 180–181
artistic, 57, 58–59
arts in, 7, 8, 11
cognitive, 5, 235
concrete operational, 345
developmentally appropriate practice and, 14, 57–58, 147, 257, 320
dynamic dimension of, 64
emotional, 64
integrated learning units and, 20
language, 371
of modeled form, 261f
motor, 90, 282
movement and, 316–319
music and, 277–280, 280–282
normative, 58, 61t–62t
physical, 59–61
play and, 346–350
proximal, 12
sensorimotor level of, 11
sensory, 8, 87–88
social skills and, 116, 127, 211, 251
in three-dimensional expression, 260–262
in two-dimensional expression, 236–238
visual arts, 236–238
Developmental approach, 157–159, 280–283
growth and, 316–319
music and, 280–283
open-ended materials and, 157–159
Developmentally appropriate practice (DAP), 14, 62, 68–69
dancing and, 338

described, 57–58
families and, 134–135
filters for reflection, 68–69
Diagrams, 237
Dialogue, 40, 130
Dictation, 107, 164, 365–366
Differences. *See also* Special needs
acceptance of, 33
anti-bias activities on, 9, 131–132
beliefs, respecting others, 133–134
books on, 131, 134
celebrating, 136–137
cultural, 133–134
displays featuring, 131, 137
dramatic arts and, 350–351
families communication with, 134–135
food and arts showing, 135–136
holidays, 136–137
in knowledge, 32
multicultural viewpoint, 135
positive social climate and, 118–120
questions about, 130
talking to children about, 132–133
valuing, 34
Differentiated instruction. *See* Inclusion
Digital art, 257–260
activities for, 259
computers as, 258
equipment for, 259
overview, 257–258
software for, 258–258
Digital cameras, 125
Digital images, 71, 73, 184, 245
Digital portfolios, 73, 74. *See also* Portfolios
Direction
for activities, 7, 9
intervention vs., 50
motivation and, 32
in movement, 34, 316
pantomimes, 357
physical development and, 60t
providing, 49
for virtual field trips, 194
Discarding works, 89
Discipline, promoting cooperative behavior and, 317
Discovery, guided, 95
Discussions, project approach and, 212
Display tables, 98

Displays, 162–167
  anti-bias, 131
  artistic growth, 165
  artistic techniques, 165
  arts elements, 165
  "Arts Happenings," 75
  arts sleeves, 163
  celebratory presentations, 107, 224, 231
  classroom, 162–163
  creator of the week, 163–164
  cultural experience, 165
  educational, 167
  families and, 76
  guidelines for, 184
  hanging art in, 163
  hooks, 164
  interactive, 107
  locations for, 167
  "look-but-don't-touch", 195
  materials, 33
  mounting works for, 163
  multicultural arts, 131, 137
  multidisciplinary, 165
  nature, 155
  performances, 163–164
  in personal spaces, 164
  photographs, 107, 161, 162
  presentation center, 164
  promotional, 165, 167
  public, 164–165, 167
  selecting works for, 73, 180–181
  shape murals, 51
  teaching, 39
  texture, 154
  thematic, 165
  of visual artworks, 235, 236
  welcome table, 107
  of work, 163–164
Dispositions, 15
Dissanayake, Ellen, 4, 28
Divergent thinking, 28
Diversity. *See* Cultural differences
Doctor's office play centers, 354
Documentation, 56, 222–225. *See also* Records
  artistic behavior, 83
  celebratory events, 107, 224, 231
  emergent project photo story, 225
  group work, 222–223
  mobile devices, 223
  panels, 222, 223–224, 230
  preplanned, 78

  projects, 72, 74, 125, 222
  recording, 71, 125, 223–224
  self, 72
Documentation panels, 222–224
*The Dog that Sang at the Opera* (Izen & West), 306
Dolls, 132, 134, 354–355
*The Dot* (Reynolds), 33
Double-ring training scissors, 248
Dough, play, 104, 135, 260, 264, 265
Drama therapy, 127, 128
Dramatic arts, 342–377
  assessment and, 371
  books about, 371
  celebrations, 224
  children's theater, 369–371
  cognitive development and, 346, 352
  connections to, 371–372
  costumes for, 368–369
  definition of, 5, 342
  designing, 354–357
  development in, 346–350
  diversity and, 354–355
  elements of, 343–344
  emotional well-being and, 8
  guided imagery and, 375
  imagination and, 372
  improvisation, 361–364
  locations for, 344
  narrative, 364, 366
  pantomimes, 357–360
  play and, 344–346, 373–374
  play centers, 354, 376
  process in, 342
  prop box, 376
  selecting, 182–183
  sequence of development in, 347t–348t
  shapes in, 362
  special needs adaptations for, 350–351
  standards in, 16, 342, 348–350
  story plays, 364–369, 377
  symbolic play, 345
  symbolic communication model on, 67t
  tasty pantomimes, 357
  teaching about, 351–354, 372
  texture in, 343
  theater etiquette in, 370
  theater play centers, 354
  uniqueness in, 343
  what they are, 369

Drawing
  books on, 241
  colors and, 240
  discussions on, 241–242
  early, 238
  everywhere, 240
  infants, 238, 240–241
  kindergarten, 240–241
  lines, 100
  locations for, 267
  material selection for, 239–240
  mature, 238
  middle, 238
  modifications for, 129
  observations of, 273
  open-ended activities, 240–241
  planning for, 210, 220, 241
  preschoolers, 238, 240–241
  primary age, 240–241
  project approach and, 210
  special needs modifications for, 244
  storytelling in, 348t, 367–368
  surfaces for, 240
  toddlers, 348t, 367–368
Drawing boards, 240
Dress-up, 167, 366
Drum circle, 122, 292
Drums, 290, 291
Drying racks, 252
Duchamp, 268
Duffy, 45
*Duke Ellington: The Piano Prince* (Pinkney & Pinkney), 287
Durer, Albert, 241
Dust
  chalk, 240
  clay and, 263, 264
  control of, 240, 263
  materials and, 94, 194
  pottery clay and, 262
  safe substitutions and, 263
Dyes, 256
Dynamic dimension of development, 64
Dynamics, 276

**E**

Early drawing, 238
Early scribbling, 237
Easel brushes, 243

Easels, 368
Eating, taste perception and, 87, 88.
    *See also* Food
Echo clapping, 279t, 288
Edison, Thomas, 27
Educational displays, 167
Effects, of sensory deprivation, 88–89
Ehlert, L., 185, 250, 251
Ehrhardt, K., 179
Elaboration, 28
ELL. *See* English Language Learners
Embroidery, 39, 256, 257
Emergent child-initiated project, 48
Emergent curriculum, 14–15, 32, 34,
    208–209
    creativity and, 32, 34
    description of, 14, 208–209
    example of, 19–21
    project approach in, 15, 210–213
Emergent project photo story, 34, 48,
    166, 225
Emotional development
    artistic development, 64, 115–118
    in the arts, 116–118
    creative movement and, 8, 317
    dramatic arts and, 346
    expectations and, 69
    infants, 117, 365
    factors influencing, 64
    foster well-being, 7–8
    in integrated learning units, 119
    for kindergartners, 118
    materials and, 157
    movement and, 317
    music and, 281
    objectives in, 217
    observing, 117
    play and, 116, 346–347
    positive climate for, 118–120
    for preschoolers, 117
    promoting, 39–40
    sensory arts, 91
    social- skills, 115–118
    special needs in, 129
    storytelling, 365
    teachers and, 365
    for toddlers, 117, 365
    visual arts and, 235
Emotions
    adding, in art, 179
    artistic development and, 15
    arts therapy and, 127–128

color and, 101
definition of, 15
emotional well-being, 7–8
expressing in art, 123, 127–128, 129
learning goals and, 15
music 281, 280, 281
pantomimes of, 357, 358
photo story, 138
questions about art and, 45
sharing by teachers, 39–40
teaching journals and, 78
traumatic events and, 64
Empathy
    American Sign Language and, 39
    animals and, 156
    books to develop, 134
    communicating, 39
    definition of, 115–116
    development, 115–116
    fostering creativity and, 118–119
    sharing and, 9
    special differences and, 131
Energy, movement and, 314
English language arts, 177, 178f, 185,
    186, 305
English language learners (ELLs), 7,
    46, 366
Enthusiasm, 39
Envelopes, 220
Environment, 146–172
    for activities, 148–153
    adult dimension, 152–153
    aesthetic, 153–157, 170
    anti-bias, 9, 133
    arrangement of, 152
    art supply organization, 207
    in artistic development, 5–6,
        147–148
    books on, 13
    celebration of differences, 131
    changing, visual perception and,
        96, 154
    creating, 148
    for creative movement, 148
    cultural beliefs and, 64, 133
    definition of,
    designing, 148–152, 171
    development and, 4–6, 13, 64,
        66–67
    displays in, 162–164, 166
    enriched, 5, 18, 66, 90
    exposure, 64–65

families and, 133
food areas in, 149
furniture for, 172
for guest artist presentations, 193
instructional space, 148–152
layout of, 152
least restrictive, 125
material presentation, 157–162
for modeling, 262–264
naturalistic-, 13
nurturing, 10, 13–14, 30, 33, 38,
    50–51
olfactory perception and, 86
order in, 149–150
outdoor, 148, 151, 155–156
positive social, 118–120
for pottery clay, 262, 263, 264
for privacy, 149
Reggio Emilia on, 152
requirements of for arts,
    147–148
routines and, 150
safety and health, 149
sense of place and, 167
sensitivity to, creating, 169
social arts, 152
space in, 148–149, 151, 152
special needs and, 128t–129
traffic patterns in, 151–152
Erikson, Erik, 117, 118
Escher, M.C. 241
Ethnic folk art, 183
Etiquette, theater, 199, 370
Everyone is Bob, 80
Everyone's story, 368
Exercise
    creative movement, 319
    physical development and, 60t
    rhythm activities, 103, 289
Expectations, realistic, 69–70
Experiences
    for art lovers, 199
    in artistic development, 65–66
    of arts, 53
    chart, 125
    cognitive development, 65–66
    dance, 182, 329–331
    emergent curriculum and, 14,
        208–209
    modeled form, 261
    painting, 244
    real, 36, 66

responsive drawing, 241
sensory, 93–95, 110
shared, 121, 124, 142
storytelling, 367–369
synesthetic, 93
theater, 369–370
Exploration
  activity selection and, 325
  arts activities, 35, 218f
  behavior, 261f
  centers for, 98, 238, 283
  controlled, in artistic development, 261
  creative movement, 319
  drawing, 241
  by infants, 58, 244
  initial, in artistic development, 261
  music, 283, 306
  painting, 244
  self-, 53, 54, 55, 141, 203, 204
  three-dimension modeling, 261
Exposure, artistic development and, 64–65. See also Experiences
Exteroceptors, 86
Eye contact, 37, 40, 180, 303

**F**

Fabric. See Fiber art
Faces
  activities, 123, 215
  improvisations and, 363
  and sounds, 363
Facilitation, 121
Fairness, 131
Familiar things, imagining, 347t, 356
Familiarity, in art, 179
Familiarizing songs, 278, 279t
Families
  anecdotal records for, 75
  appreciation of process in, 75–76
  artistic development and, 76–77
  arts therapy and, 128
  assessment and, 134–135
  celebrations, 224, 231
  communication with, 134–135
  digital portfolios and, 73
  documentation for, 223, 230
  heritage, use of, 181
  field trips, 9
  music, sharing with, 306
  newsletters for, 221
  painting information for, 246

in play centers, 354
release forms from, 72
safety information from, 94
social pressure from, 64
special needs and, 127
storytelling and, 367
visual arts, response to, 49, 246, 269
Fanelli, 13
*Fantasia*, 334
Fantasy, 30, 348t
Faria, R., 147
The Farmer in the Dell song, 304
Favorites, musical, 302
Fear
  of masks, 363
  teacher responses to, 47, 363
Featured artists, 163
Feedback
  art concepts, 44
  artistic decisions, 44
  conversations, starting, 45
  creative process and, 44
  descriptive statements, 43–44
  examples of, 43–44
  exploring relationships, 46
  meaning, responding to, 44–45
  nonverbal, 95
  paraphrasing, 44
  positive, 43–46
  questions, 45
  scaffolding, 44
  special needs and, 46
  teacher self-assessment, 78
  verbal, 95
Feelings. See Emotions
Feierabend, John, 306
Feldman, 28
Festival of lines, 107
Fiber art, 253
  activities for, 255–256
  books on, 256
  collages, 255
  definition of, 253
  discussion on, 257
  materials for, 255
  painting in, 243
Field trips, 194
Fine hairbrushes, 243
Fingerpaints, 242
  paper, 243
Finger plays, 302, 364

*Finger Plays and Jump Rope Rhymes*, 302
Finger puppets, 149
Firing, 263
Fisher, Aileen, 292
Fishman, Susan, 370
Flannel boards, 304
Flat brushes, 243
Flexibility
  in the arts, 32
  cooperation and, 28
  divergent thinking and, 28
  environments and, 147
  in groups, 121
  in materials, 37
  motivation and, 33
  physical, 325
  project approach and, 211
  thinking, play and, 345
  traffic patterns and, 151–152
Floating, 326
Floor surfaces, 267
Floors, 4, 154, 320
Flournoy, Valerie, 124
Fluency, 28
Foam painting, 129
Focus
  art elements, 45, 101, 102, 103, 104
  artistic works, 180
  cooperative behaviors and, 163
  development of, 86–93
  dramatic arts, 343
  feedback, 45
  intentional teaching, 35
  on literature, 106
Folders
  portfolios, 72–73
  "terrific me," 78
Folk art, 183
Folk dancing, 331
Folk music, 285t
Food
  avoiding use of, 136
  in art activities, 96, 135–136
  dyes, 256
  materials vs., 135–136
  in multicultural activities, 136
  paste and, 262
  printmaking with, 136
  safety with, 149
Foot dances, 289
Foot mat choreography, 331

Force, dance and, 327
Form, 104–105
Form, musical, 287
Fox, 317
Frames, picture, 256
Free waltzing, 330
Free-form shapes, 102
Frere Jacques song, 305
Frost, Joe, 64
Fun, 121
Furnishings, 149, 151, 266, 267, 268.
    *See also* Environment

**G**

Gadget prints, 253
*Galimoto* (Williams), 33
Galleries, 196
Games
    board, 116
    clapping, 60
    Concentration, 191
    "Eyes on Me," 323
    "Follow the Leader," 323
    Go Fish, 191
    matching, 189, 298
    Name Game, 119
    play based on, 345
    singing, 304
    sorting, 191
    timbre, 197
    Watch Me, 119
    What Happened?, 119
Gandini, L., 50, 98, 122, 149, 157, 209
Gardner, Howard, 12, 13, 28,
    61–62, 210
Gel glue, 247
Gender expectations, 134
Gender roles, dance and, 332
Genetics, 301
Genres, 176, 276, 287, 334
Geometric shapes, modeling, 264
*Gershwin's Rhapsody in Blue*
    (Celenza), 287
Gibbons, G., 140, 159, 245
Giftedness, 66
Gifts, prints, 184
*Gingerbread Boy*, 366
*Girl with Broom* (Rembrandt), 183
Glitter, 96, 160, 250
Glues
    for collages, 246–247
    experiments with, 20

gel, 247
glue pens, 247
glue sticks, 246–247
    selecting, 246–247
    white/school, 247
Goals
    for activities, 180
    in the arts, 15–16
    behavior ordering for, 117
    creative movement, 321
    emotions and, 15
    knowledge and, 15
    lifelong, 16, 176f
    objectives and, 18, 126, 131, 223
    skills and, 16
    special needs and, 131
Godwin, Douglas, 59
Goebel, N., 265
Go Fish, 191
"Go In and Out the Windows" song,
    200, 255
*Going on a Bear Hunt*, 366
*Goldilocks and the Three Bears*, 344
Goldman, E., 28
Goodenough-Harris Draw-A-Person
    Test, 64
Graphic programs, 258
Graphic software, 258–259
Greenman, Jim, 148
*Greeting Each Other*, 119
*The Grouchy Ladybug* (Carle), 106
Grouping
    naturalistic activities, 217f
    rhythm and, 288
Groups, 120–125
    activities, 122–124, 358
    age ranges in, 122
    anti-bias activities for, 9
    appropriate behavior in, 119, 122
    arts activities for, 6
    assembling projects, 269
    auditory stimuli, 97
    caring and, 121
    composition of, 41, 92
    cooperative behavior and, 122
    creative movement in, 319
    creativity and, 32, 92, 123, 158, 197,
        219, 251, 299, 327, 358
    displaying works by, 165
    dramatic, 5
    drum circle, 122
    dynamics in, 122

environment for, 176f, 284
    in integrated learning units, 216
    mixed-age and ability, 122
    mosaics, 124
    murals, 124
    music activities, 5, 283–285,
        289–290
    observing dynamics in, 69–70
    organization of, 35, 120–121
    overview, 120–121, 137, 139
    pantomimes, 358
    positive climate for, 119–120
    project approach and, 211–212
    project example, 168
    quilts, 124
    recording learning in, 70–71, 125,
        222–223
    rhythm band, 124
    sculptures, 122, 124
    selection, 68–69, 91, 93
    sensory perception and, 91
    size of, 121–122, 147, 149, 151, 154
    social skills and, 116, 350
    space for, 167
    special needs and, 125
    teacher, 124–125
    visual arts, 122
Growing, creative movement
    activity, 326
Growth, facilitation for special needs,
    126–127
Gruber, 28
Guess the instrument, 297
Guest artists, 193–195, 198
Guided Creative Movement
    Explorations, 325
Guided discipline. *See* Positive
    guidance
Guided discovery, 95
Guided explorations, 325
Guided imagery, 356–357, 375
Guilford, J.P., 28
Guthrie, Woody, 329
Gyotaki print, 101

**H**

*Hairs Pelitos* (Cisneros), 355
Hall, 45
Hand motions, 301
Handprints, 106, 132, 157, 253
Hand puppets, 367

Hands-off policy, 163
Handwoven, 256
Harmony, 277
*Harold and the Purple Crayon*
(Johnson), 241
Hats, 368–369
Hayes, Ann, 298
Hazardous materials, 86, 195
Head Start programs, 63
"Head, Shoulders, Knees and
Toes," 332
*Head to Toe* (Carle), 218
Healing, 7, 128, 280, 342
Health
dance and, 314, 334
eating habits, 136, 150
effect on development, 65f, 280
emotional, 7
environment and, 149
exercise and, 63, 316
movement and, 314, 316
play and, 30
safety and, 94, 149, 193, 240
well-being and, 6, 7, 177
wind instruments and, 295
visual arts and, 8
Hearing, 89, 93, 97, 128t. *See also*
Auditory perception
Hearing loss, 97
Heartbeat rhythms, 292
Heredity, physical development
and, 63
Hesitancy, 248
*Hey, Little Ant* (Hoose), 370
Hickory Dickory Dock song, 305
High low activity, 286
Historic site visits, 199
History, 176f
Hoban, T., 220
Hoffman, M., 134
Holes
activities with, 93, 154, 297
books of, 164
peep, 105
Holidays, 136–137
*The Hobby Horse* (Anonymous), 200
Hokey Pokey, 304
Hooks, for display spaces, 164
*Hooray! A Piñata!* (Kleven), 268
Hora or horo dance, 181

Housekeeping play centers, 34,
351, 355
*How a House is Built*, 159
Hues, 102
Hug me, 329
Hughes, L., 265
Hula dance, 181
Hula hoops, 157, 322, 326, 357, 363
Hurricane Katrina, 64
Hurwitz, Al, 236

**I**

*I can be the alphabet*, 326
Icy paints, 245
*Iggy Peck, Architect* (Beaty), 159
Igus, Toyomi, 134
Ideas, pantomimes of, 357
If You're Happy and You Know It song
(Warhola), 215
Ilari, Beatrix, 182
*I Love My Hair!* (Tarpley), 355
Illustrators, 178f, 185, 195
Imagination, 341–377
assessment, 371
children's theater and, 369–371
design of, 353–357, 376
dramatic arts development and,
342–344
of the familiar, 356
growth through, 346–350
guided imagery and, 356–357, 375
improvisation and, 361–364
mental imagery and, 355–356
overview, 372
pantomimes and, 357–360
play and, 344–347, 373–374
play centers, 376
prop boxes, 376
puppets and, 372
sensory images and, 355
special needs, 350–351
story play and, 364–369, 377
teacher's role in, 351–353
trips in, 356
Imitation
behavior development, 117
creative movement and, 67t
peer modeling and, 121
sensory activities, 95
skill development, 117
Immersion, 36–37
Imposing statements, 43

Impression making, 264
Impressionism, 181
Improvisation, 361–363
definition of, 361
descriptive, 361
dramatic arts, 361
for infants, 363
for kindergarteners, 361
masks for, 361–363
for infants, 363
for preschoolers, 361
for primary age, 361–362
rhythm, 343t, 344
for toddlers, 363
*In the Spirit of the Studio* (Gandini,
Hill & Cadwell), 98
Intention, in dance, 315
Intentional teaching, 35
Inclusion, 126, 135, 208, 323
Incubation, 37
Individualized Education Plans
(IEPs), 127
Individuals with Disabilities Act, 125.
*See also* Special needs
Infants
activity design for, 35, 95, 96–97,
artistic development, 57–58, 59,
237, 277–278, 278f, 283–284,
343–344
auditory activities, 96, 285–286
brain development, 5–6, 90
collage for, 249
color perception in, 100
construction activities for, 268
creative movement activities for,
323–324
dance for, 329
drama activities, 350, 359, 361,
363, 367
dramatic arts development in, 344,
342, 345, 347t
drawing activities for, 237–238,
240
fiber art for, 255
improvisation for, 363
listening activities, 285
materials for, 159
modeling activities for, 264–265
musical development in, 277, 278t
musical instrument activities
for, 295
musical instruments for, 278t

Infants (*cont.*)
  normative development in, 58, 60t, 317, 319
  olfactory and gustatory activities, 97
  painting activities for, 243–244
  pantomimes for, 359
  physical development in, 59–60t
  presentations to, 193
  printmaking for, 253
  response to artistic works, 190–191
  rhythm activities for, 103, 289
  safety, 95, 239
  screen media and, 257
  scribbling, 237
  sensory development in, 86–89, 100–102
  singing activities for, 303–304
  social-emotional development, 116, 117, 345, 347
  songs for, 301
  storytelling for, 367
  tactile activities, 96–97
  visual activities, 96
  visual development, 87, 88–89, 90–91
*Infants and Toddlers at Work* (Lewin-Benham), 98
Information sources, 98, 184
Initial events, 200
Initial exploration, 261
Input devices, 259
Inspiration, sources of, 98
Instructional space, 148–152
Integrated curriculum, 206–231
  arts in, 206–208
  books on, 220, 226, 227
  components of, 217–219, 220–221
  emergent, 14
  example of, 218f
  integrated learning units in, 221
  making connections in, 226
  MI planning web, 217f
  photo story, 17, 198
  plan, 219–220
  project approach in, 221
  sharing learning in, 217f, 218f
  steps toward, 206–208
  teaching about, 19–21
Integrated learning units, 213–222
  activities, 216, 221, 229
  arts in, 215–216
  examples 17, 19–20
  description of, 213

  framework, 228
  literacy-based music, 307
  organizing, 216
  projects with, 216–219, 220–221
  questions for, 213–215
Integrated Play Group Model, 350
Integrity, 181
Intelligence
  multiple intelligence theory on, 12–13
  visual arts development and, 5–6
Intensity, color, 102
Interactive activities, 5
  art display, 107
  creativity and, 27
  interests, building on individual, 6
  sensory, 98–100
  *See also* Motivation
Interior lighting, 154
Interiors, 4, 154
Interlocking blocks, 266
Internet Archive, 361
Internet, digital images from, 184
Interpersonal intelligence, 12, 217f
  in integrated learning units, 219
  planning web, 217f
Interruptions, 37
Intervention, 50, 127
Interviews, portfolio self-assessment, 74–75
Intrapersonal intelligence, 12
  in integrated learning units, 219, 228
  multiple intelligence theory and, 12
  planning web, 217f
Invent a dance, 331
Invented songs, 302
Invented sound machines, 287
Invitations, 134, 224
Isadora, R., 185
*The Ish* (Reynolds), 241
Ishihara color test, 101
*Italian Girl* (Corot), 200
*It's Raining Pigs and Noodles* (Prelustsky), 292
*I Was All Thumbs* (Waber), 254
iWorks, for PCs, 259
Izen, M., 306

**J**

Jazz, 147, 175, 179, 276
  books on, 292

  famous musicians, 179
  types of, 181, 292
*The Jazz Fly 2* (Gollub), 179
*The Jazz Man* (Ehrhardt), 179
*Jennie's Hat* (Keats), 250
Jensen, Eric, 5, 179, 281, 316, 332, 346
Jewelry, 368–369
Johnson, C., 346, 352, 354
Jonas, A., 124
Jones, Elizabeth, 14, 344, 353
Journals
  class, 36, 191, 226–227, 241, 333, 365, 370, 371
  display, 164
  theme, 200, 215
  use of, 139–140, 168, 197
Joy, engagement of, 9, 75, 116
Judgments
  of beauty, 175
  families and, 75
  overview, 42
  positive feedback and, 42
  by teachers, 42
  untrained observers and, 128
Jumping, 332

**K**

Kamperman, Jennifer, 211
Kandinsky, Wassily, 245
Katz, 132, 209–211
Katz, Lillian, 15, 64
Keats, E.J., 250
Keeping time, 276
Kellogg, Rhoda, 236–237, 238
Kennedy Center Artsedge, 14
Keyboards
  computer, 259, 293
  music, 294, 295
Keys, musical, 220, 294–295, 296, 297
Kilns, 263
Kindergarteners
  auditory activities for, 287
  collage activities, 249
  construction activities for, 268
  cooperative behaviors in, 118
  creative movement, 323–324, 325, 329
  curriculum for, 29
  dance for, 329–330
  dramatic arts development in, 348–349
  dramatic arts for, 353, 360, 363, 370
  drawing activities for, 236, 238

improvisation for, 363
materials for, 159, 264
modeling activities, 264
music activities for, 286–287, 291–292, 296–297, 299–300, 304–305
musical development in, 279, 281, 282
musical instrument activities for, 296–297
musical instruments for, 159
normative development in, 58–59
painting activities for, 243–244
pantomimes for, 360
physical development in, 60t
printmaking for, 253
response to artistic works, 190–191
rhythm activities for, 103
singing activities for, 304–305
social-emotional skills in, 117
social skills of, 227
storytelling for, 367–368
theater experiences for, 370
Kindler, A.M., 66–67, 82
Kinesthetic awareness, 90, 217f
Kinesthetic memory, 317, 326
Kinesthetic thinking, 317
Kirk, Elizabeth, 365
Kissinger, K., 131, 132
Kizoa, 260
Kleven, E., 268
Knowledge
    artistic development and, 9
    constructing, 9
    content, 9, 371
    in creativity, 15
    for curriculum development, 15
    in KWL charts, 211f–211f
    learning goals and, 15
    project approach and, 211
Kodály, Zoltan, 305
Kodály method, 305
Koff, Susan, 7, 323
Kohn, Alfie, 42
Kostecki-Shaw, Jenny, 132
Kraft paper, 51, 123, 243, 244, 368,
Kroll, V., 51, 243, 244, 368
Krull, K., 298
Krumhansl, Carol L., 277, 280, 288
KWL charts, 32, 200, 211f–212f

**L**

Labels
    activities, 226–227

on artworks, 63t
on folders, 71
identifying, 74, 98, 129
language skills and, 158
materials, 162, 183–184
portfolio, 72, 73
using, 162
Landscapes, 194
Langer, Ellen, 356
Langer, Hellen, 150
Language. *See also* English language arts and literacy
    about pattern and rhythm, 103
    art words, 235
    artistic development and, 61t–62t
    arts as first, 6–7
    assessment, 371
    cognitive development, 61–62
    creative movement and, 317
    culture and, 65
    dance and, 332
    developmental norms in, 371
    dramatic arts and, 344, 371
    dramatic arts development and, 347t, 371
    dual learners, 366
    finding lines in, 100
    form and, 104
    integrated learning units, 215
    movement and, 317
    music and, 281
    musical development and, 281
    objectives on, 217f
    observing development in, 69–70
    play and, 343, 346
    sensory arts, 91
    shapes and, 102
    skills development, 178, 235, 281, 317
    space and, 105
    special needs and, 46
    symbolic, 7
    talking about arts and, 32, 46
    talking about differences and, 132–133
    texture and, 103
    touch talk, 97
    visual arts and, 235, 251, 261, 269
    for visual experiences, 235
    word play, 363, 368
*Last Dancer,* 334
Latin music, 181, 292
Layout, environment, 151

Learning and learning theories
    active, 13
    assessing, 69–75
    brain-based, 206
    constructivism, 10–11
    documenting, 222–225
    facilitating, 211
    goals for, 15–16
    multiple intelligence theory, 12–13
    in practice, 11
    project approach and, 211
    singing to learn, 304
    social cognitive theory, 11–12
    for teachers, 307
    through the arts, 5, 10–13
Learning centers. *See also* Play centers
    bias in, 350, 354
    block, 266–267
    collage, 247
    composing, 283
    conducting, 283
    designing, 35
    exploration, 238
    guided discovery and, 95
    in integrated units, 219
    listening, 191, 283, 287
    modeling, 137, 262
    music, 179, 199, 293, 296–297
    painting, 244
    printmaking, 252
    rhythm, 292
    schedule example, 217–218f
    sensory, 87, 94, 97, 98
    science, 240
    sound, 215, 283, 287
    storytelling, 216
    time at, 36–37
    variety in, 34
Learning environment, 147–148
*Learning Together with Young Children* (Curtis/Carter), 98
Least restrictive environment, 125
Left-right activity, 316t
*The Legend of the Indian Paintbrush* (de Paola), 245
Lesson plans, 218
Letters to families
    artistic development, 76
    about painting, 246
    arts notes, 78
    on collage materials, 161
    on integrated units, 221
    newsletters, 134, 135

Letters to families (*cont.*)
   on safety, 94
   on visual arts, 49
Lewin-Benhan, Ann, 35, 46, 98
Lighting, environment and, 153–154
Limits, 30, 64, 318
Line
   on computer, 258
   element of the arts, 100, 254
   festival of, 107
   listening for, 321
Line dancing, 330
Linguistic intelligence, 12, 217f
Lining up, 328
*Lion Dancer: Ernie Wan's Chinese New Year* (Waters), 333
Lionni, L., 254
Listening
   active, 40
   activities for infants, 285–286
   activities for preschoolers and up, 286–287
   activities for toddlers, 286
   art development and, 7
   auditory perception and, 86
   centers, 283
   for lines, 321
   music activities, 182, 285–287
   musical development and, 285–286
   for relaxation, 286
   selecting music for, 285
   skill development in, 178f
   by teachers, 40
Listening centers, 283
Literacy
   artistic standards and, 16, 178f
   arts and, 187
   development of, 6–7, 161–162, 177, 185, 186
   dramatic arts and, 365–366
   labels and, 161
   media, 9
   music and, 299, 307
   responding to the arts, 187–193
Literature. *See* Books
Literature, teaching about the arts with, 134. *See also* Books
*Little Girl in Lavender* (Bradley), 200
Little Red Riding Hood, 32
Logical thinking, 6, 217f
Logical-mathematical intelligence, 12–13, 17, 41, 123, 158, 197, 235, 251, 299, 327, 358

London Bridge Is Falling Down song, 331
Looking, in listening, 40
Looking tables, 98
Looking tubes, 20
Looms, 108, 254, 256
Loud and soft activity, 285
*Lucy's Picture* (Moon), 133
Lullabies, 286
Lyrics, 287, 300, 322, 329

## M

*M Is for Mola* (Krull), 256
*M Is for Music* (Striker), 298
Machine movements, 335
Maddox, D., 269
*Magic String* (Kamovsky), 108
Magritte, René, 183
Malaguzzi, Loris, 147
Marshall, 42
Mary Had a Little Lamb song, 297
**Monet** (Anholt), 245
Making Connections, 179, 334, 370–371
Malaguzzi, Loris, 50, 147
Mama Lisa's World, 332
Mandalas, 237
Manipulative play, 261
*Mao's Last Dancer*, 334
Maps, 158, 217f, 267
Maracas, 291
Marches, 329
*Marchesa Brigida* (Rubens), 200
Marching music, 124, 191
Markers, 239, 242
Markou, T.A.H., 80
Martin B., 333
Masks, 362–363
   constructing, 269, 362
   eyeholes for, 362
   fear of, 363
   in improvisation, 361–362
   materials for, 362
   papier-mâché, 362
   in storytelling, 367
   types of, 362
   using, 362–363
Matching games, 93, 191, 219, 298
Matching sounds, 296
Materials. *See also* Supplies
   for activities, 157–159, 162
   celebrating differences and, 224
   for collages, 6, 246–248

   collection center for, 161–162
   for constructed sculpture, 122
   controlling amounts, 161–162
   for developmental growth, 157, 159
   displaying, 223
   for drawing, 298
   environment aesthetics and, 170
   for fiber arts, 255–256
   flexible, 37
   food vs., 135–136
   intelligent, 160
   labels for, 162
   for masks, 269, 362
   for modeling, 128
   offering, 159–161
   open-ended, 161–162
   organization of, 33
   for painting, 242–243
   for pantomimes, 358, 359
   presentation of, 157–162
   for printmaking, 252
   safety with, 94–95
   sensory, 93–95
   softness in, 148–148
   special needs and, 128
Math. *See also* Counting
   blocks and, 267
   centers, 218f
   Common Core and, 16, 253, 284
   dance and, 317
   exploration of, 216
   fiber art and, 254
   food and, 150
   form in, 104, 168
   in integrated learning units, 41, 101, 108, 150, 160, 168, 189, 253, 284
   lines in, 100
   movement and, 326
   measurement table, 108
   number concepts and, 326
   pattern and rhythm, 103, 266
   questions about, 215
   shapes in, 102
   standards for, 16, 253, 254
   visual arts and, 253
Mats
   foot mat choreography, 331
   music, 296
*Matthew's Dream* (Lionni), 196
Mature drawing, 238
Mature scribbling, 237

McClintic, 206
McCormick, Linda, 126
McFee, 64
McKlimek, 206
McLerran, A., 268
Meaning
  artistic works and, 180–181
  of community, 348
  classroom environments and, 179
  in dance, 314
  development of, 88
  in dramatic arts, 343
  family heritage, 181
  literature and, 185
  reading and, 178f
  responding to, 44–45
  searching for, 89
  sensory stimuli and, 86, 88, 91
Measurement table, 108
Media
  books on, 185
  dance and, 333
Media literacy, 9
Mediator
  teacher as, 186
Meeting space, 151
*Meet the Orchestra* (Hayes), 298
Melodies, 276–277
  composing, 299–300
  notating, 298–299
Memories, creating, 179
Memory pictures, 356
Mental imagery, 355–357
Mental representation, 355
Menus, computer, 258
Messages, pantomime, 360
Metabolism, 316
Metaphorical twist, 319
Meter, in music, 276, 292
Metronomes, 291–292
Mice, computer, 65, 258, 259
Middle drawing, 238
Middle scribbling, 237
Millman, Issac, 130
Mind pictures, 356
**Mindfulness** (Langer), 150–151
Minorities, 135
Minuets, 180
Miró, Joan, 245
*M is for Music* (Hayes), 298
Mitchell, Linda, 127
Mobiles, 286
Mobility, 150–151

Modeling
  activities for infants, 264
  artistic development and, 260–261
  books on, 265
  center design for, 262
  cookie cutters for, 264
  creative movement, 261–262
  discussions on, 265
  for emotional release, 128
  on form, 261
  materials for, 128, 262–264
  open-ended, 95, 264–265
  peer, 121
  pottery clay, 263–264
  social cognitive theory on, 11–12
  social-emotional skills, 118–119
  special needs and, 264
Modeling clay, 263–264
Modigliani, Amedeo, 215, 245
*Mole's Hill* (Ehlert), 250
Mona Lisa, 242
Monkey see game, 324
Monoprints, 251, 253
Montessori bells, 294
Montessori, Maria, 36–37
Montessori programs, 87, 98, 103–104
Mood
  in dramatic arts, 364
  in music, 344
Moon, N., 133
Moore, Henry, 265
Mosaics, 124, 250
*Moses Goes to a Concert* (Millman), 130
MOST strategies, 127
Motion, 315
Motivation
  in creativity, 32–34
  definition of, 31, 32
  extrinsic, 33
  giftedness and, 66
  intrinsic, 32–33
  modeling and, 11
  performance and, 65f
  Piaget on, 10
  Vygotsky on, 11
Motor development
  art environment for, 148, 149
  artistic development photo story, 79
  creative movement and, 8, 105
  dance and, 332
  delays in, 63, 129, 238, 282, 290, 316, 319

developmental norms for, 11
fingerplays and, 365
giftedness and, 66
materials for, 157
musical development and, 277–279t, 282
physical factors in, 63, 66
responsive activities and, 239–240
sensory development and, 90
sequence of development in, 60t
space for, 148, 152
special needs and, 129
visual art and, 240, 242, 266, 290
Motor logic, 365
Mounting artworks, 163–164
  to hang, 164
Mouse, computer, 258, 258
*Mouse paint* (Walsh), 220
Movement
  artistic development, 61t–62t
  in dance, 315, 329, 330, 331, 333
  describing, 315
  in dramatic arts, 342, 344
  in music, 286
Movement, creative. *See* Creative movement
Movement, in art, 3
*Mr. Holland's Opus*, 282
*Mr. Roger's Neighborhood*, 366
Multicultural arts, 9, 135, 181–182. *See also* Cultural differences
Museums, 186
  artifacts, 135, 185
  in the arts, 9
  books on, 185
  in creativity, 33
  curriculum, 135
  inclusion of, 181–182
  materials, 355
  music, 285
  promoting, 135
Multiculturalism, 9, 135
Multidisciplinary education, displays and, 165
Multimedia modes of artistic production, 66–67
**Multiple intelligence** (MI) theory, 12–13
  planning webs, 13
Multisensory activities, 5, 98
  modeling and, 261
  guided imagery and, 356–357

Murals, 124
  in celebrations, 224
  definition for, 124
  group projects, 124
  paper for, 240
  printing, 51
  in the project approach, 213
  shape, 51
Murphy, L., 7
Muscle development. *See* Motor
    development
Muscular control, 129. *See also* Motor
    development
Museum areas, 195
Museum visits, 186
Music, 275–311
  activities for infants, 285–286,
    289, 295
  activities for kindergarteners, 286–
    287, 291–292, 296–297, 299–300,
    304–305
  activities for preschoolers, 286–287,
    291–292, 296, 299–300, 304
  activities for primary age, 297–298,
    299–300, 305
  activities for toddlers, 286, 289,
    295–296, 304
  anti-bias environment and, 9
  bands, 289–290
  books about, 287, 298
  and the brain, 280
  in celebrations, 224
  centers, 293, 296
  color and, 289, 294, 297,
    300, 307
  for creative movement, 215, 322
  for dancing, 182, 328–329
  definition of, 5, 276
  design of activities for, 283–284,
    288–289
  development in, 61t–62t,
    277–279, 307
  development in dramatic arts, 5
  developmental appropriate
    activities, 309
  developmental growth and,
    280–282
  discussion on, 287–288, 293,
    299, 306
  elements of, 276–277
  entertainment, 108
  exploration centers, 283

  exploring instruments, 296
  family involvement, 306
  forms of, 287
  giftedness in, 66
  goal of, 307
  group activities, 283–284, 293
  health effects of, 280
  heritage, 308
  homemade instruments, 95, 290,
    292, 296
  instruments, 291–292, 293–300
  instruments, rhythm, 103
  in integrated learning units, 307
  listening activities, 284–287
  for listening and study, 182
  locations for, 293, 296
  mats, 296
  objectives, 217f
  one-on-one interactions, 283, 293
  in pain control, 8
  pattern and rhythm in, 103
  pitch, 176
  presentation of, 153, 164, 184
  reading, 292–293, 297,
    298–299, 306
  rhythm in, 103, 288–293
  selecting, 291–292, 293–295,
    301–302, 309
  singing, 300–306
  software, 295
  songs for children, 300–301,
    302, 305
  sound centers, 283, 289
  space, 290, 297, 305
  special needs adaptations for,
    282, 310
  standards for, 16, 281–282
  story song, 304
  styles, 180
  styles of Western, 285
  supplies, 119
  support for, 311
  symbolic communication model
    on, 67t
  teaching about, 298, 298,
    302–303, 304, 307
  vocabulary for, 276–277, 299
  well-being and, 8, 280
  world, 181
  writing, 292–293, 298–299
Music centers, 293, 296
Music note blocks, 298

Music store visits, 196
Music therapy, 127, 128
Musical intelligence, 12

**N**

NAEYC. *See* National Association for
    the Education of Young Children
Name activity, 52
Named forms, 261–262
Name Game, 119
Name labels, 163
Name rhythms, 289, 292
Name that tune, 297
Narrative, 364–369
  books on, 351
  in dramatic arts, 346
  dramatic arts development and,
    343, 344, 347t
  elements of, 364
  finger plays and, 364
  -play experience, 364–369
  puppetry and, 366
  repetitive, 352
  storytelling and, 365–368
National Association for the
    Education of Young Children, 14
  position on technology, 257
National Common Core State
    Standards in English Language
    Arts and Mathematics, 16, 177,
    178f
National Core Arts Standards, 16,
    175–177, 348–350
**National Dance Educational
    Organization** (NDEO), 314
National Gallery, 200
National Institute of Health
    Sciences, 300
Native American art, 39, 131, 137,
    181, 254
Native American music, 175, 181
Natural light, 154
Naturalistic-environmental
    intelligence, 13
Nature
  aesthetics and, 155
  collages on, 132, 247
  color in, 132
  displaying, 98, 155
  form in, 92
  integration of, 157–156
  lines in, 100

murals on, 51
objectives, 217f
pattern and rhythm in, 103
scavenger hunts, 220, 287
shapes in, 102
wonder and, 95
Needles, 255
Nevelson, 268
Newsletters, 221
Nimmo, John, 14
Noble, Jeremy, 7
Non-hardening clay, 263, 264, 267
Nonobjective art, 183
Nonverbal behavior, empathy and
    acceptance in, 39
Nonverbal feedback, 95
Non-Western art, 181
Normative development, 58–59
Notation, music, 298–299
Note, in music, 277, 297
Note matching, 296
Note naming, 296
Notebooks
    personal arts, 78
    teacher, 270
    school-to-home, 134
*Not So Fast Songololo* (Daly), 227
Novelty, in art, 179
Number concepts, 217f
Nursery rhyme rhythms, 289
Nutrition, physical development and,
    63. *See also* Food
Nylon brushes, 243

**O**

Obesity, childhood, 7, 8, 257
Objectives, 71
    art skill, 217f
    cognitive, 217f
    emotional, 217f
    environmental skill, 217f
    IEP, 128t
    intentional, 71
    language, 217f
    musical skill, 217f
    perceptual, 90–91
    physical, 217f
    social, 217f
    special needs and, 127
    writing, 235
Objects
    creative movement, 322, 325

dramatic arts development
    and, 361
pantomiming invisible, 360
printmaking, 252
safety considerations, 94–95, 159
sensory material, 93–95
Observation, 69–72
    aesthetics of an environment, 170
    of artistic growth, 69–72, 84, 165
    of bias, 144–145
    checklist for, 70
    of drawing, 273
    of groups, 69–70
    of individuals, 69
    of modeling, 274
    recording, 70–72
    in social play, 352
Observation tables, 98
Obstacle course dances, 330
Ocean integrated unit 17, 19–20
Octaves, 278
Odd pairs, 368
*Of Colors and Things* (Hoban), 220
*Off We Go to the Grocery Store*
    (Webster), 226
O'Keeffe, Georgia, 183, 245
Olfactory perception, 86
One-on-one activities, 319
    creative movement, 319
    for infants, 238, 283, 293
    music, 283, 293
    sensory, 92
    special needs, 123, 158
    squishy bags, 92
    for toddlers, 238, 283
One word activity, 368
Open-ended activities
    art materials, 161–162
    choice in, 33
    classroom, scale model, 158–159
    cognitive development and, 157
    creative movement, 12
    cultural differences and, 80
    definition of, 12
    for developmental growth, 157, 159
    group activities and, 123
    fostering creativity with, 157
    for infants, 238
    line dancing, 108, 330, 331
    modeling, 95
    motivation and, 32
    music, 283

offering, 49
planning, 41, 92
play, 354
questioning, 99
sensory perception, 93–95
special needs and, 123,
    125, 158
OpenOffice, 259
*Opera Cat* (Weaver), 306
Operas, 183
Orchestras, 179, 294
Order, environment and, 149
Organic shapes, 102
Organization, 15, 19, 211
Organized play, 116, 117
Originality, 28
Oster, Gerald, 127
*The Other Side* (Woodson), 134
Outdoors, environmental aesthetics,
    155–156
Oversensitivity, 97
Ownership, creating, 33, 73, 164, 302

**P**

Pain control, 8
Paint
    bags, 92
    fingerpaints, 242
    for painting, 242, 243
    for printmaking, 252–253
Painting, 242–246
    activities for, 244–245
    books on, 245
    brushes for, 242–243
    centers for, 244
    computer software for, 258–259
    discussions on, 245
    families and, 246
    for infants, 243–244
    for kindergarten and primary ages,
        242, 244
    paint selection for, 242, 243
    special needs adaptations for, 128t,
        244
    surface selection for, 242
    tempera, 29, 242
    for toddlers, 243–244
Paint "markers," 242
Paley, Vivian, 216, 365
Panel presentations, 222,
    223–224, 230
Pantev, Christo, 66

Pantomimes, 357–360
  descriptive, 357
  for infants, 359
  for kindergarteners, 360
  planning, 357–358
  for preschoolers, 360
  for primary ages, 360
  tasty, 357
  for toddlers, 359
Paper
  balls, 249
  brown, 243
  for collages, 6
  colored, 243
  commercial fingerpaint, 243
  cutting problems with, 248
  different sizes of, 239
  for drawing, 240
  mural, 240
  for painting, 243
  for printmaking, 252
  shape play with, 249
  shaped, 240
Paper bag masks, 362
Paper Bag Princess (Munsch), 351
Papier-mâché, 362
Parades, 124, 29, 304
Parallel play, 116, 117
Paraphrasing, 44
Parents. See Families
Parnell, Will, 78
Part singing, 305
Participation, active, 13, 39
Participatory arts activities, 108
Partner up movement activity, 324
Partners, 124, 331. See also Groups
Pass patterns, 292
Paste
  homemade, 247
  inventing, 250
  papier-mâché, 235
  selecting for collages, 247
The Patchwork Quilt (Flournoy), 124
Patience, cooperative behaviors and, 47
Pattern blocks, 102, 266
Pattern
  construction, 266, 267
  dance, 325, 330, 331
  dance standards and, 318
  definition of, 103
  design, 259
  in digital art, 259

  in fiber art, 254, 256
  mathematics and, 103, 266
  music and, 103, 278, 278–279t, 281, 282, 287
  pass activity, 256
  in printing, 254
  rythym and, 276, 288, 289, 291, 292
  two-dimensional placement, 237
Pedagogy, equity, 9
Peek-a-boo, 285, 343, 347t, 363
Peers
  in cognitive development, 65
  modeling by, 121
Pencils, 239
Pentatonic scales, 298
People
  developing in drawing, 237
  dramatic arts development and, 347t
Perceptual development
  in the arts, 8, 235
  assessing, 69
  expectations, 69
  objectives in, 260
  visual arts, 235
Percussion instruments, 282, 290–291
  body, 322
  pitched, 294
Perfect pitch, 301
Performance standard
  dance, 318
  music, 281
  theater, 342, 349
Performances
  attending, 179, 196
  children's theater, 199
  concerts, 198
  dance and, 314, 315, 326, 327, 328, 329, 332, 333, 334
  for deaf, 282
  dramatic arts, 342
  finding, 344, 349–350, 369–371
  music and, 293, 306
  responding to, 187–190, 370
  selecting, 180–183
Performers, guest, 193
Persona dolls, 354–355
Personal arts notebooks, 78
Personal arts time line, 54
Personal characteristics of creative people, 28

Personal needs, 47
Personal realization, through art, 176t–177
Personal space, 164, 268
Personal taste, 42, 153, 187
Peter and the Wolf (Prokofiev), 186, 287
Pfister, M., 21
Photographs
  activities using, 36, 99, 131–135, 156, 241, 250, 268
  assessment with, 71–72
  by children, 72–73
  collages of, 250, 259
  displaying, 107, 161, 162–167, 224
  as labels, 98
  portfolios, 71–74
Physical development
  as reflection, 77
  in stories, 74
  in artistic performance, 59–61
  in arts, 60–62, 235
  assessment, 323
  cutting problems and, 248
  developmental factors in, 63–64
  giftedness and, 66
  in integrated learning units, 206
  milestones in, 316
  movement and, 59–61, 316
  music and, 61–62, 281
  objectives, 217f
  observing, 371
  music and, 281
  play and, 346
  sensory perception, 90
  sequence in children, 60t
  special needs modifications and, 129
  visual arts and, 61–62, 235, 244
Physical differences. See also Special needs
  dramatic arts and, 65f
  motor skills and, 282
  rhythm instruments and, 282
  space for, 151
Physical well-being, 7–8
Piaget, Jean, 10–11, 345
Picasso, Pablo, 30, 32, 250
Pictographs, 200
Picture collages, 250
Picture frames, 256

Picture perfect, 363
Pigments, toxic, 194, 240
Piirto, Jane, 27, 30
Pinkney, 287
Pinkwater, D.M., 168
Pitch, 276
    absolute, 301
Place, in dramatic arts, 344
Placement Patterns, 237
Planes, 262, 356
Planning
    activities, 41
    art centers, 272
    creative movement activities,
        323–324
    drawing activities, 210, 220, 241
    integrated learning units, 216–219,
        220–221
    MI planning web, 217f
    MOST strategies in, 127
    pantomimes, 357–359
    special needs and, 127
Play, 344–355
    abstract thought and, 345
    the brain and, 345–345
    cognitive development and, 346
    cooperative, 116, 117, 118
    creativity and, 30
    development through, 346–350
    diversity and, 354–355
    drama and, 343–344, 348
    dramatic, 343, 344–346
    early childhood, 118, 351
    elements in, 343t
    emotional development and,
        346, 348
    flexible thinking and, 345
    game-based, 345
    importance of, 373–374
    infants, 117, 347t
    informal dramatic, 353
    kindergartners, 117, 348t
    language development and, 346
    levels of, 345
    manipulative, 349
    observation and, 116, 117, 352t,
        353, 372
    organized, 116, 117
    parallel, 116, 117
    persona dolls, 355
    physical development and, 346
    play centers, 354

power of, 345
practice, 345
preschoolers, 117, 347t
pretend, 324
primary age, 118, 348t
    with shapes, 249
social skills and, 116, 346
solitary, 116, 117, 347t
special needs modifications for,
    350–351
symbolic, 345
teaching, 351–353
by toddlers, 117, 347t
Play centers, 149, 354, 363, 366, 376
Play dough, 94–95, 262–264
    activities for, 264
    introducing, 262–263
    safety with, 94–95
Playful art, 179–180
Playfulness, in teachers, 34
Plot, 364
Pointillism, 26
Pointing, 95
Polacco, P., 106
Polka, Linda, 277, 280, 288
Polkas, 181, 276, 313
Polyester brushes, 243
Pop art, 181
Portfolio (Apple), 259
Portfolios, 73–74
    combined digital and physical, 73
    construction, 72–73
    definition of, 72
    digital, 73, 74
    folder, 72–73
    labeling, 72, 73
    personal arts, 78
    photographs in, 72, 73
    physical, 74
    preparing artwork for, 73
    questionnaire for, 72
    selecting work for, 73
    self-reflection on, 73, 74–75
    summary statements in,
    timeline for collecting, 73
    using, 72, 73
Portraits
    drawing, 215
    family, 128
Positive feedback, 39, 40, 43–46
Positive guidance, 47, 119–120
Post and lintel, 269

Post office play, 36, 211
Posters, fine art, 184
The Pot that Juan Built (Goebel), 265
Potential developmental level, 11
Pots, pinch, 264
Pottery clay, 263–264
    activities for, 264
    firing, 263
    guidelines for working with,
        263–264
    nonhardening, 263
Powerpoint, 71, 125, 192, 195, 199
Practice, 238
    activities for, 238
    in artistic development, 65
    creative movement, 323
    developmentally appropriate, 14
    play, 345
    singing, 303
Praise
    giftedness and, 66
    positive feedback and, 43–46
    unconditional, 42
    ways to, 42
Precontrol level, 323
Predictions, 59, 95, 189
Prejudice, 9. See also Anti-bias
Prelustsky, Jack, 292
Preschoolers
    aesthetic activities for, 191–192
    auditory activities for, 286–287
    construction activities for, 267
    cooperative behaviors in, 117
    dance for, 329–331
    dramatic arts development in, 347t
    dramatic arts for, 194
    guided discovery, 95
    improvisation for, 363
    materials for, 159–160
    modeling activities for, 263
    murals, 124
    music activities for, 291
    musical development in, 279t
    musical instrument activities
        for, 296
    musical instruments for, 290
    normative development in, 58–59
    pantomimes for, 360
    physical development in, 59–61
    presentations to, 194
    response to artistic works, 191–192
    rhythm activities for, 103, 291–292

Preschoolers (*cont.*)
  scale models, 158
  singing activities for, 304
  social-emotional skills in, 117
  songs for, 301
  sound centers and, 289
  storytelling for, 367–368
  theater experiences, 369
Presenting standard, visual arts, 235
Presentations
  celebratory, 107, 224, 231
  center for, 164
  community resources, 184
  to infants, 193
  panel, 222, 223–224, 230
  to preschoolers, 194
  to toddlers, 193
Pretending, 337. *See also* Imagination
Prevention, of inappropriate
    behavior, 119–120
Primary ages
  artistic art development, 59
  auditory activities for, 286
  collage for, 249–250
  construction activities for, 268–269
  creative movement activities for,
    326–329
  dance for, 327, 333, 334
  documentation, 223
  dramatic arts development in,
    353–354
  drawing activities for, 59, 240, 242
  environment for, 147
  improvisation for, 363–364
  listening activities for, 286
  materials for, 160–161
  modeling activities for, 264–265
  music activities for, 286–287
  musical development in, 279t
  musical instrument activities for,
    297–298
  normative development in, 59
  painting activities for, 244–245
  pantomimes for, 360
  papier-mâché for, 268, 269
  physical development in, 60t, 62–63
  planning projects, 118
  presentations to, 194
  printmaking for, 253–254
  response to artistic works, 192
  rhythm activities for, 103
  singing activities for, 305
  social skills in, 116

  songs for, 301
  storytelling for, 368
Primary colors, 102
Printers, 259
Printing plates, 254
Printmaking, 251–254
  activities, 253–254
  activities for infants, 253
  activities for preschoolers, 253
  activities for toddlers, 253
  center for, 252
  computer art, 259
  discussions on, 254
  fiber art, 254–257
  kindergarteners, 253
  materials for, 252
  primary ages, 253
  special needs and, 127
Prints
  books on, 254
  engaging children with, 253
  featured artists and, 254
  patterns and, 254
  postcard-size, 184
  sources for, 184
Printshop, for PCs, 259
Privacy, 149
Problem solving
  creativity and, 27
  emergent, in creativity, 34
  teacher responses in, 47,
    49–50, 143
Process, 342
  appreciating art as, 75–76
  assessing, 69–75
  auditory, 282
  creative, 30–37
  in dance, 314, 332
  in dramatic arts, 342
  family appreciation of, 75–76
  focus on, 45
  fostering, 38–40
  interactive, 27
  performance and, 332
  project approach and,
    210–213
  recording, 71–72
Process drama, 349
Production, 31
  artistic, 67t
  appreciating process vs., 68
  cognitive growth and, 63t
Proficiency level, 323

Project approach, 14, 209–213
  in action, 210–212
  culmination of, 212–213
  definition of, 209
  discussion/representation in, 212
  documentation in, 125
  drawing and, 210
  emergent curriculum and, 15
  integrated learning units in, 215–221
  KWL chart examples, 211–212
  learning facilitation in, 121, 211
  memory work, 212
  organizing activities in, 211
  small groups in, 211
  topic choice in, 211
  value of, 210
Project logs, 74
Prokofiev, Sergei, 287
Promotional displays, 165, 167
Props
  anti-bias, 354
  boxes of, 354, 355, 376
  creative movement and, 322, 323
  diversity and, 354, 355
  dramatic arts, 361
  improvisation, 361
  pantomimes, 359
  role-play, 361
Publisher, for PCs, 259
Puppets and puppet shows
  artifacts and, 187
  books on, 218, 367
  in dramatic arts, 366, 367
  emotions and, 12
  exploration and, 35
  making, 187, 269, 367
  observations, 372
  papier-mâché, 187
  play centers, 149
  preschoolers and up, 367
  shadow, 184
  shows, 39, 99, 108
  singing and, 304
  stick, 123
  storytelling and, 366–367
  student observation and, 372
  using, 366–367
Puzzles, 217, 295

## Q

Quartets, 306
Questions and questioning
  art appreciation and, 45, 187–190

on artifacts, 187–190
asking, 187
broad-based, 213
on collages, 250
comparisons and, 189
on constructions, 269
creative movement activities
    and, 325
drawing and, 241–242
about feelings, 188
for exploration, 187
integrated, 217f
in integrated learning units,
    213–215
in KWL charts, 200
on modeling, 265
for observation, 188–189
open-ended, 34, 99
on painting, 245–246
personal taste, 187
portfolio self-assessment, 74–75
in positive feedback, 45
on prints, 254
problem solving situations, 49
sensory, 187
thinking strategy, 188
unifying, 213–215
weather, 214
on wondering, 99
Quiet moves, 328
*The Quilt* (Jonas), 124
Quilters, 248
Quilting, 256
Quilts, 124

# R

Raffi, 255
*The Rainbow Fish* (Pfister), 21
*Raining Cats and Dogs*
    (Magritte), 183
Rainsticks, 97, 291
Ramsey, Patricia, 131
Rapport, 38
Raschka, C., 292
*Read Aloud Poems for the Very Young*
    (Prelustsky), 292
Reading, 185. *See also* Books
Reading music, 297
"Real" art, 179
Real objects, 62, 89, 129, 185, 236
Recipes. *See also* Appendix D
    homemade paste, 247
    modeling materials, 262

natural dyes, 256
papier mache, 268
Recitals, 332
Recorders, 298
Records. *See also* Documentation
    anecdotal, 70–71
    experiences, 191
    group projects, 222–223
    lessons, 298
    notes and, 125
    photographs and, 71–72
    process, 71–72
    project approach and, 222, 223f
    progress, 33
    releases, obtaining, 72
    running, 71
    video taped, 72
Red Leaf Yellow Leaf (Ehlert), 185, 251
*Red Poppy* (O'Keeffe), 183
Redirection, of inappropriate
    behavior, 119–120
Reflection, project approach and,
    74–75
Reflective teaching, 77–80
    in-action, 78–80
    documentation for, 78
    multicultural lens, 135–136
    overview, 77
    photo story, 79
Reflective thinking, 78, 79, 371
Refreshment, for celebratory
    presentation, 108
*Regards to the Man in the Moon*
    (Keats), 139
Reggio Emilia, 14–15, 152
Rejection, 64
Relationship, in dance, 315
Relaxation, 286
Releases, 72
Remembering, 11
Removal, of inappropriate
    behavior, 120
Renoir, Pierre, 215
Repetition, 65, 67t, 94, 301
Representation, 183, 212
Reproducing, 11
Resnick, Mitchell, 28–29
Responding and responsiveness
    activities, 35–36, 239
    active listening and, 40
    to artistic content, 318
    to books, 186
    to dance, 314, 333–334

in dramatic arts, 342
infant activities for, 190–191
kindergarteners activities for,
    191–192
learning, 174–177
letters to families and, 78, 134
literacy skills and, 187
in music, 283–284
preschoolers activities for, 191–192
primary grades activities for, 192
standards for, 16, 235, 282, 319, 342
toddlers activities for, 190–191
written, 190–193
Responsive activities, 35
    aesthetic, 190–192
    drawing and, 239
    photo story, 79
Restaurant play centers, 351
Retelling, 366
Re-visioning, 360
Revisitation, skills and, 35
Reynolds, Gretchen 33
Reynolds, Peter 353
Rhapsodies, 287, 217f
Rhythm, 103
    activities for infants, 103, 289
    activities for kindergarteners, 103,
        291–292
    activities for preschoolers, 103,
        291–292
    activities for primary ages, 103,
        291–292
    activities for toddlers, 103, 289
    assessment, 292
    bands, 124, 289–290
    definition of, 103, 276
    designing activities for, 288–289
    discussion on, 293
    in dramatic arts, 343t, 344
    instruments, 103, 291–292
    in integrated learning units, 307
    movement and, 316t, 322, 325
    musical development and, 276,
        278, 279t, 288
    objectives, 217f
    poetry and, 322
    reading and, writing and, 292
    sensory activities, 103
    sound centers and, 289
    writing and, 292–293
Rhythm sticks, 291
Ring Around the Rosy song, 304, 331
Ringgenberg, Shelly, 304

Risk taking
  clay and, 263
  fear and, 47, 49
  feeling of being watched and, 34
  learning goals and, 15
  problem solving and, 157
  safe, 117
  sensory activities and, 91
  space for, 149
  for sustained attention, 157
River crossing, 337
Ro, Yeonsum, 65
Robot movements, 335
Rocking, 289
  together, 324
Rockwell, 227
Rogers, Carl, 38
Rogers, Fred, 366
Rogers, Ginger, 333
Role models
  in artistic development, 65–66
  special needs and, 126
Role-playing, 361
Rosenthal, S., 269
Rotary hand cutters, 248
Round brushes, 243
Rounds, singing, 305
Routines, in environment, 150
*Row, Row, Row the Boat song*, 276, 305
*Roxaboxen* (McLerran), 268
Rubens, 200
Rubber stamps, 253
Rubbings, 253–254
Rugs, transitions and, 151
Rules
  breaking, 27
  setting for activities, 153
Running records, 71
Ryan, P.M., 306

**S**

Safety
  adhesives and, 194
  appropriate behavior and, 119
  with blocks, 267
  clay and, 263
  collages and, 250
  construction activities, 268
  creative movement and, 321
  environments and, 149, 195
  family information form, 94
  field trips and, 195

food vs. materials, 136
health and, 149
letter to families about, 94
materials and, 95–96, 194, 240
musical instruments and, 295
odors and, 101, 162
play and, 94–95
psychological, 38
risk factors and, 15, 117
scissors and, 248
"Stop, Drop, and Roll," 371
substitutions for, 136
teacher behavior guidelines
  for, 119
Saint-Saëns, 21, 287, 327
Salmon, Angela, 46
Salsa dance, 61, 180, 191
Salt-flour dough, 263
*Same, Same but Different* (Kostecki-
  Shaw), 132
Sand blocks, 291
Sand prints, 252
San Souci, 351
Say it first, 303
Scaffolding, 12, 44
Schwall, Charles, 147
Scales, 298
Scavenger hunts, 287
Scents, 100, 101, 263
Scented markers, 101
Schifferstein, 86
Schiller, Marjorie, 115, 117
Schiller, Pam, 124
School glue, 247
Science
  buoyancy and, 17
  centers, 218f, 160
  cycles and, 326–327
  experiments, 36
  investigations, 220
  movement in, 223
  questions about, 215, 189, 213
Scissors, 247–248
Scribbles, development in, 237
Sculptures, 122
  animal, 265
  constructed, 266–269
  group, 122, 124
  public, visiting, 196, 199
  stick, 264
Seascapes, 246
Secondary colors, 102

Seeger, Pete, 329
See-Think-Wonder, 46
Seitz, Jay, 317, 319
Selection
  arts activities, 68–69
  arts artifacts, 183–184
  computer art software, 258–259
  criteria for, 180–181
  dance, 182
  drama, 182–183
  drawing material, 239–240
  for family heritage, 181
  integrated learning units, 213–215
  of multicultural arts, 9
  music, 281, 282
  of music for listening, 283
  musical instrument, 291
  paint, 242–243
  painting surface, 243, 245
  paste/glue, 246–247
  portfolio work, 73
  sensory perception activities,
    91–95
  song, 301–302
  of styles, 180
  for variety, 180–181
  visual art, 183, 239, 242–243, 246–
    248, 252, 255, 258–259, 262–264,
    266–267
  of works and performances, 180
Self-awareness, 8, 46, 141
Self-confidence, 115
  building, 49, 115
  motivation and, 33
  singing in, 300
  in teachers, 38
Self-control, 115
Self-exploration, 53–55, 141, 203–204
Self-expression, 344–245
Self-reflection
  interviews on portfolios, 74–75
  in practice, 77–78
  in teaching journals, 78
Sendak, Maurice, 124
Sensitivity, motivation and, 33, 107
Sensorimotor learning, 11, 317
Sensorimotor level of development,
  11, 345
Sensory awareness, 90
Sensory bins, 97–98
Sensory deprivation, 88–89
Sensory images, 355

Sensory integration, 87
Sensory integration dysfunction (SID), 87
    autism and, 125, 127, 128f, 301, 350, 353
Sensory modes, 90–91
Sensory perception, 85–112. *See also* Sensory deprivation
    aesthetic sense and, 87
    arts activities, role of, 89–90
    auditory, 86, 96
    beauty and, 175
    books on, 106–107, 111
    building meaning through, 89
    color, 100–102
    defining, 86
    development of, 8, 87–88
    elements of art and, 100–105
    form, 104–105
    guided discovery, 95
    gustatory, 86–87, 97
    importance of, 88–91
    infants and, 96–97
    interactions, 98–100
    integration, 87
    modes in, 90–91
    movement, 105
    lines, 100
    objectives of, 90–91
    observation, 112
    olfactory, 86, 97
    one-on-one, 92
    overview, 85–88, 107, 109
    pantomimes of, 357
    patterns and rhythms, 103
    presenting experiences in, 86, 91–93
    selection of activities for, 91–95, 110
    shape, 102
    space, 105
    special needs and, 97
    tactile, 87, 96–97
    taste, 86–87, 91, 93
    texture, 103–104
    visual, 86, 96
    Wonderful Object of Wonder (WOW), 95
Sequencing, skill development in, 6, 91, 281
*Sesame Street*, 366
Setting, in dramatic arts, 364

Setting the stage, 216
Setup, for activities, 193, 194
Seurat, Georges, 27
Shades, color, 9, 29, 155
Shadow puppets, 184, 367
Shadow wall play, 99
Shaham, S., 333
Shake a leg dance, 329
Shakers, 286
Shaped papers, 240, 249
Shapes, 102
Shared
    experiences, 121, 124, 142
    sensory items, 97
    responsive activities, 36, 192
Sharing, 9
    activities, 36, 97
    books, 185
    creative works, 163
    emotional responses, 39–40
    learning through the arts, 192
    music with families, 306
    sensory experiences, 97
    similarities, 130, 355
Shaw, C.G., 132, 281
Sheridan, Susan, 236, 237
Shively, Candace, 44
Shore, Rebecca, 182, 284
Shöen, Donald, 78
Signals, for creative movement, 124, 293, 321, 350
Signs, 167, 180, 231, 267, 303
Silence, 287
Silliness, in pantomimes, 359
Sing alongs, 303
Singing, 300–306. *See also* Music
    absolute pitch and, 301
    activities, 286, 300–306
    activities for infants, 303–304
    activities for kindergarteners, 304–305
    activities for preschoolers, 304
    activities for primary age, 305
    activities for toddlers, 304
    books on, 306
    chanting, 285t, 302
    discussions on, 306
    families, sharing with, 306
    invented songs, 302
    Kodály method, 305
    selecting songs for, 301–302
    special needs and, 128t

    teaching new songs for, 302–303
    vocabulary words, 302
Skilled masters, 139
Skills
    concept web for, 214
    in creativity, 28, 34–36
    definition of, 16, 31
    developing, 115–116
    exploration and, 35, 68, 241f
    learning goals for, 16
    literacy, 187
    mixed-age and ability groups, 122
    music and, 281
    objectives and,
    practicing, 66, 216
    project approach and, 210
    responsive, 35–36, 79, 190–193, 239, 283–284
    selection and delivery of, 19, 281
    social, 42, 116, 117, 127, 251, 350
    visual arts and, 235, 251
Skipping, 332
Slabs, clay, 264
Slide dance steps, 331
Slide shows, 259
Slip, 263
Slow motion dance, 330
Slow motion pantomimes, 360
Smell, sense of, 86
Smith, J.M., 66, 353
Smocks, 244
Snacks, in classrooms, 150
Social arts environment, 152
Social development
    community and, 8–9, 119
    dramatic arts and, 346
    environment for, 157
    movement and, 316–317
    music and, 281
    observing, 69
    play and, 346
    positive climate for, 118–119
    sensory arts, 91
    visual arts and, 235
Social-emotional environment, 118–120
Socioeconomic background, 133–134
Social-emotional skills, 115–118
    appropriate behavior and, 119
    in infants, 117
    in kindergartners, 118
    modeling of, 118–119

Social-emotional skills (*cont.*)
objectives, 217f
overview, 118
positive development of, 118–120
in preschoolers, 117
stages of, 116
in toddlers, 117
visual arts and, 235
Social pressures, 64
Social skills
autism and, 127, 350
modeling and, 260
objectives on, 116
through play, 30,117, 345
role-plays on, 349
teacher's response and, 42
Social space, 149
Sociocultural perspective, 11–12
Softness, 148–149
Software, 258–259, 295
Soliloquy process, 46
Solitary play, 116, 117
Solos, 182
Solvents, 194
Sonatas, 186, 277, 285t
Sorting photo story, 17
Sorting games, 191, 220
Sorting sets, 124, 161, 191
Sound discovery centers, 283
Sound machines, 287
Sound makers, 96, 97, 150, 159, 289
Sound walks, 286
Sounds
classifying, 287
collecting, 286
in dramatic arts, 344
finding, 286
identifying, 285
for improvisations, 363
matching, 296
ordered, 287
scavenger hunts, 287
as signals, 124
Sousa, John Phillip, 191
Space
for creative movement, 105, 320–321
in dance, 314
in dramatic arts, 344
environment and, 151
field trips and, 195
mobility and, 150–151
movement and, 105

for pantomimes, 357
sensory development and, 105
social, 149
for supplies, 14
Spaceship command center project,
139–140
Spatial concepts
creative movement and, 105
movement and, 105
music and, 327
objectives, 217f
sensory development and, 105
Spatial intelligence, 13
Special needs, 127–129
acceptance of, 130
adjusting activities for, 127
artistic development and, 125–130
arts therapy and, 127–128
behavioral and emotional needs,
129
books on, 351
color blindness, 101
creative movement and, 323, 337
dance modifications for, 128t
definition of, 125
dramatic arts and, 350–351
drawing modifications for, 129, 244
general modifications for, 128–129
getting help with, 127, 129
giftedness, 66
growth facilitation with arts and,
126–127
inclusion with others, 126, 208
language skills and, 46
meeting, 125–126
modeling and, 128
muscular control, 129
music and, 129, 282, 310
painting modifications for,
128t, 244
physical factors, 128, 129
rhythm instruments and, 97
sensory development and, 97
sensory integration and,
singing modifications for, 128t
success and, 127
visual needs, 129
*Spicy Hot Colors: Colores Picantes*
(Shaham), 333
Spinner, 195
Spinning, 199
Splatter prints, 253

Sponge prints, 253
Spontaneity, 30
in children's play, 30, 353, 363
for improvisations, 361
for pantomimes, 357, 359
singing and, 278, 279t
Square dance, 181, 329, 331
Staff, in music, 297, 298, 299
Saltzberg, Barney, 41
Standards, 16–18
for arts education, 16–18
Common Core, 16
creative movement, 16
dance, 319
math, 253, 254
music, 16, 281–282
in theater, 16, 349
visual arts and, 16, 235–236
The Star activity, 255
Star Spangled Banner song, 304
Statues activity, 360
Statues pantomimes, 360
Stencil brushes, 243
Step-hops, 332
Stereotypes, 135, 137
Stick masks, 362
Stick puppets, 123
Stick sculptures, 264
Still-lifes, 83, 240
Stitchery, 255–256
Stone, painting on, 243
Storage
art prints, 73
bins, 98, 129
environment aesthetics and,
155, 162
finished work, 150, 164, 252
supplies, 150
Stories. *See also* Narrative
conflict in, 364
creative dance and, 327
creative movement and, 327
learning songs and, 302, 303
power of, 134
for preschoolers, 347t
for primary ages, 347t
retelling, 366
rhythm, 177
setting for, 364
sharing, 212f
sound, 364
Story cloths, 256

*The Story Goes On* (Fisher), 292
Story jars, 368
Story plays, 364. *See also* Dramatic
    arts
Storytelling, 365–366, 367–369
    English language learners, 366
    infants, 367
    literacy and, 365–366
    overview, 365
    preparing for, 377
    preschool and up, 367–368
    primary age, 367–369
    retelling, 366
    toddlers, 367
Strasser, Janie, 182, 284
Stress
    imagery and, 356
    listening and, 286
    music and, 276, 280
    pleasurable, 123
    reducing, 8, 121, 148, 317, 346
    thinking and, 346
Strikers, 291
String instruments, 294, 295
    making, 297–298
    types of, 294
String monoprint prints, 253
Strozzi, Paola, 160
Stuckey, Heather, 7, 280
Studio visits, 195
Styles
    cultural, 175
    dance, 329
    definition of, 175
    music, 180, 181
    painting, exploring, 245
    selection of, 180
    Western art, 181
Styrofoam prints photo story, 17
Subject matter, 30, 180, 188, 371
Submarine play centers, 266
Substitutions, safe, 136
Sumi brushes, 243
Sundara, Megha, 182
Suns, 237
Supplies
    amounts of, 161
    anti-bias, 131
    clean-up, 244
    computer, 258–259
    food vs., 135–136
    locations for, 167

organization of, 119, 161
    posters, 184
    for printmaking, 136, 252
    puppet-making, 367
    safe use of, 119
    sources for, 242
Surprises, 33
Surrealism, 181
Surveys, home arts, 134
Sustained attention, 89–90. *See also*
    Focus
Sutton-Smith, Brian, 345
Suzuki, Shin'ichi, 296
Suzuki method, 296
*The Swan* (Saint-Saens), 21, 327
*The Sweet and Sour Animal Book*
    (Hughes), 265
*Swimmy* (Lionni), 254
Symbols and symbolism, 344
    development and use of, 7
    defined, 344
    dramatic arts, 344
    forms, 261f
    holidays and, 137
    language development and, 7, 69
    play, 344
    shapes in, 102
    symbolic forms, 261f
    symbolic play and, 345
    three-dimensional, 262
    Vygotsky on, 11
Symmetrical shapes, 102
Symphonies, 182
Syncopation, 276
Synesthetic experiences, 93
Systems, 327

**T**
Tableaus, 360
Tables
    art, 80, 148
    coffee, 148
    height of, 129
    light, for special needs, 97
    measurement, 108
    mobility of, 151, 152
    observation, 98
    painting, 245
    play, 148
    privacy, 149
    sand, 98
    social space, 149

visual arts, 148
    water, 98
    welcome, 107
Tactile defensiveness, 97
Tactile perception, 87, 96–97
    activities, 96–97
    baric, 87
    development, 87
    of texture, 103–104
    stereognostic, 87
    thermic, 87
Take a walk, 286
Tambourines, 291
Tap dance, 332
Tape, 247
Tappers, 291
Tapping walks, 289
Task Force on Children's Learning
    and the Arts: Birth to Age 8,
    13, 18
Taste, personal, 42, 153, 187
Taste perception, 86–87
Tasty pantomimes, 357
Taylor, A., 156, 213
Teachable moment, 18, 42, 47, 50,
    207–208
Teachers
    art, 207
    as atelieristas, 14
    becoming creative arts, 38
    books for, 186
    celebratory presentation planning,
        107–108, 231
    clothing for students, 200
    cooperation and, 124–125
    cooperative arts project, 168
    confidence and, 34
    creative movement, 318, 319–320,
        325, 335
    creativity, valuing, 38–39
    in dramatic arts, 353, 372
    emotional development and, 365
    environment and, 152, 153
    equity pedagogy and, 9
    as facilitators, 121
    family communications, 135
    fostering the creative process,
        38–50
    in groups, 121, 168
    help, offering, 50
    intentional teaching, 35
    interactive projects, 226–227

Teachers (*cont.*)
  interruptions by, 37
  journals, 139
  judgments by, 42
  learning, continued, 38
  as mediator, 186
  motivation and, 353
  museums for, 186, 195–196
  music, 289, 296, 297, 301, 303, 304, 305, 307
  noninterference of, 34
  parent newsletter, 221
  participation by, 39
  personal history of, 38
  play and, 351–353
  positive feedback by, 43–46
  portfolios use, 77
  praise by, 42
  puppets and, 372
  relaxation, 321
  resources for, 193–197
  responding to problems, 47, 49–50, 143
  role of in arts programs, 18–21
  safety guidelines for, 94
  scissors, 247–248
  self-assessment for, 77
  sensitive, 33, 107
  sharing emotional responses of, 39–40
  social play, stages of, 116
  social pressure from, 64
  support of creativity, 34
  verbal responses by, 40, 42
  websites for, 186
Teacher's scissors, 248
Tearing, 249
Techniques
  appropriate, 35
  displays featuring, 165
  painting, exploring, 242, 243, 244, 245
  questions about, 213
Technology
  assessment and, 223
  in dance, 333
  in environment, 156–157
  in music, 282
  for play enhancement, 371
Television, 7, 89, 134, 257–258
  in visual art, 156, 334, 370, 371

Tempera paints, 242
  printmaking with, 252, 253
Tempo, 276
Tension, in dramatic arts, 343
"Terrific me" folders, 78
Textiles, 250
Texts, artistic works as, 177–178t
Texture
  activities, 104
  collage, 103
  environment aesthetics and, 154
  modeling and, 103
  in painting, 245
  painting surfaces and, 245
Theater, children's, 369–372 *See also* Dramatic arts
Theater play centers, 371, 366, 363
Thematic displays, 165
Therapy, arts, 127–128
Thinking routines, 46
Think-Pair-Share, 46
Think-Puzzle-Explore, 46–47
*This Jazz Man* (Ehrhardt), 179
Thomas, Karen, 72
Thought processes
  creativity and, 11, 28, 36, 40
  symbolic communication model and, 67
  questions to clarify, 45
Three-dimensional development, 235, 260, 262, 266
Three-dimensional symbols, 262
*Three Musicians* (Picasso), 250
Tie-dye, 256
Tiles, clay, 103, 154, 250
Timbre, 276
  matching, 296
Time and timing
  for activities, 30
  collecting work, 73–74
  for creativity, 36–37
  in dance, 314, 315f
  in dramatic arts, 344
  definition, 105
  for discussions, 212
  environment and, 150
  facilitation of learning and, 211
  movement and, 105, 316t, 334
  offering help and, 50
  personal arts, 54
  portfolio collection, 73
  project approach and, 211, 212

  of questions, 45
  special needs and, 128t
  transition, 70
Tints, 102, 155, 245
Tip tap, 326
Tire tracks prints, 253
Titles, panel, 223
*Today I Feel Silly* (Curtis), 123
Toddlers
  auditory activities for, 286
  collage for, 249, 251
  construction activities for, 268
  cooperative behaviors for, 117
  community resources and, 193
  creative movement activities for, 324–325
  dance for, 329
  dramatic arts development in, 344, 347t, 365
  dramatic arts for, 359, 363, 366, 367, 369
  improvisation for, 363
  materials for, 159–160
  modeling activities for, 264
  musical development in, 278
  musical instrument activities for, 295–296
  musical instruments for, 278t
  normative development in, 58
  painting activities for, 243–244
  pantomimes for, 359
  physical development in, 58, 59–61
  presentations to, 193
  printmaking for, 253–254
  response to artistic works, 190–191
  rhythm activities for, 97, 289
  singing activities for, 304
  social-emotional skills in, 117
  social skills of, 117
  songs for, 301
  storytelling for, 367
Tonality, 294
Tone, color, 102
Tongue drum, 291
Torrance, E. P., 10, 27
Touch bags, 92, 105
Touch talk, 104
Toxic pigments, 240
Traditional practices, defying, 107
Traffic patterns, 151–152
Training scissors, 248
Trains, 122, 328, 357

Transitions
    from activities, 150
    creative movement in, 328
    music in, 284
    rhythmic, 92
Traumatic events, 64
Trays, printmaking, 252
Tree cookies, 266–267
Triangles, 291
Trips, imaginary, 356
Tubes, 267
Tunes, naming, 297
Tung, Lily Toy, 191
Turn taking, 8
Two-dimensional artworks, 217f,
    260–261. *See also* Drawing;
    Painting; Printmaking
*Two of Everything* (Tung), 191
*The Two Mrs. Gibsons* (Igus), 134

## U

Unborn babies, sounds and,
    87, 277
Unconditional praise, 42
Undersensitivity, 97
Under the sea activity, 327
Unique art, 4, 183–184
Uniqueness, creativity and, 4, 14, 27,
    132
Unit blocks, 267
Unveiling, 95
Utilization level, 323

## V

Value, color, 102
Van Gogh, Vincent, 245
van Ryn, Rembrandt, 215
Variety, creativity and, 34, 180–181
Verbal expression, 364
Verbal feedback, 95
Verbs, pantomimes of, 360
Verses, 277, 301, 303
Videography
    in celebrations, 224
    of group projects, 72
    project approach and, 212
    as recording tool, 72
    releases for, 72
    sensory perceptions, 108
View scopes, 20
Vimeo, 74
Virtual field trips, 195

Vision, limited, 97
*Visiting the Art Museum* (Brown &
    Brown), 196
Visits
    artist studio, 195
    guest artists, 194–195
    museum, 186
    to performances, 196
Visual arts, 234–274
    anti-bias activities, 131
    artistic development, 61t–62t
    books about, 241, 245, 250, 254,
        257, 263, 265, 269
    collage center, 249
    collages, 246–251
    colors and, 243
    computers and, 257
    construction center, 267
    cutting problems, 249
    definition of, 5, 235
    designing, 237–239, 260, 262
    development in, 235–236
    digital art, 258–259
    discussions about, 241–242, 245–
        246, 254, 257, 265, 269
    displaying, 235, 236
    documenting learning with, 223
    drawing, 239–242, 273
    elements of, 271
    emotional well-being and, 8
    equipment for, 259
    exploration centers and, 238
    families and, 269
    fiber art, 254–257
    growth from, 235–236
    infants and, 243–244, 249, 253, 264,
        268
    modeling, 260–265, 274
    one-on-one, 238
    open-ended activities, 240, 244–
        245, 249–251, 253–254, 255–256,
        259, 264–265, 268–269
    paint center, 244
    painting, 241–246
    papier-mâché, 267–268
    power of, 270
    practice in, 238
    printing center, 252
    printmaking, 251–254
    responsive activities, 239
    safety issues, 267
    sculpture, 266–269

    selecting, 183, 239, 242–243, 246–
        248, 252, 255, 258–259, 262–264,
        266–267
    skills, 235–236, 251
    software for, 258–259
    sources, 184–240
    standards, 235–236
    styles of, 180
    surfaces for, 240, 243
    symbolic communication model
        on, 67t
    teaching about, 241, 244, 250, 270
    three-dimensional, 260
    toddlers and, 243–244, 249,
        253, 268
    two-dimension, 236–238
Visual disabilities, 101, 125, 323, 350
Visual perception
    activities, visual perception, 87, 90,
        91, 93, 96, 99, 102
    books on, 108
    cognitive development and, 86
    color and, 132
    color blindness, 101
    creative movement and, 8, 100
    description of, 86, 103–105
    development, 87, 235
    looking for lines and, 100
    pattern and rhythm in, 103
    space in, 105
    special needs, 129
    visual arts and, 251, 260
Vocabulary, 7
    architectural, 269
    in art development, 7
    arts elements, 44
    computer, 259
    development of, 32,35,41,44,49
    fiber art, 254
    music, 276–277
    pottery clay, 263
    sensory-rich, 99–100
Vygotsky, Lev, 11–12

## W

Waber, Bernard, 254
Waiting, in listening, 40
Wallace, 28
Walls, 9, 154, 167
Walsh, E.S., 220
Waltzes, 317
Warm-ups, for activities, 95, 330

Washing up, 132
Watch Me game, 119
Water
  bottle tunes, 216
  for collages, 249
  music, 291
  painting, 245
  prints, 253
  table, 19, 159, 165, 207
Watercolors, 242
Waters, 333
*We Are All Alike…We Are All Different*, 215
Weather walks, 156
Weaver, T., 306
*The Weaver*, 255
Weavers, 194, 200
Weaving, 255
Web quest, 186, 334, 371
Webs
  brainstorming, 209f
  concept, 214f
  multiple intelligence planning, 13, 217f
  topic, 32, 221f
Websites, for teaching materials, 186
  children's songs, 300
  core standards, 178
  DanceAbility, 323
  Kodaly, 305
  technology position statement, 257
  virtual field trip, 195
  world instruments, 294
  world songs, 332
Webster, 226
Wedging, instruments, 295
Welcome table, 107
Well-being, through art, 176t–177, 280
Wells, R., 227
West, J., 306
Western art, 181, 285
Wet sensory bins, 98
What Happened? game, 119
"What would happen if…,"368
Wheelchairs, 129, 244, 323, 354
*When Clay Sings* (Baylor), 265
*When Marion Sang* (Ryan), 306

*When Sophie Gets Angry, Really Really Angry* (Bangs) 123
*Where the Wild Things Are* (Sendak), 124
White boards, 99
*White Cloud* (Catlin), 200
White glue, 247
White House Task Force on Childhood Obesity, 156
*White Nights*, 334
*White Rabbit's Color Book* (Baker), 220
Who, what or where am I?, 360
Whole song method, 301, 303
Wiggle jiggle activity, 262, 326
Williams, K.L., 33
Wilson, Bent, 236
Wilson, Marjorie, 236
Wind instruments, 294–295
  making, 298
Winter, J., 183
*Wizard of Oz*, 344
Wolf, Aline D., 302
Wolf, Jan, 303
Wolfe, G., 280, 301
*Wolfgang Amadeus Mozart* (Venzezia), 285t
Wonder
  emergent curriculum and, 15
  See-Think-, 46
Wonderful Object of Wonder (WOW), 95
Wondering, open-ended questions for, 99
Wood blocks
  construction with, 267
  music with, 291
  painting on, 243
Woodcarvers, 195
Woodson, Jacqueline, 134
Word, for PCs, 259
Work spaces, 153
Work surfaces, 148, 149, 244
Workshops, family, 72, 75, 134
World arts, 173–204. *See also* Cultural differences
  African, 39, 131, 139, 181, 182, 198, 290, 323
  artifacts and, 183–184

  books on, 185
  community resources, 193–199
  culture and, 175
  curriculum, 177
  in dance, 182–183, 315
  discussions of, 187
  drawings, 236
  engagement of, 177–180
  expanded definition of arts, 174–175
  incorporating, 200
  instruments, 294
  literacy skills and, 187
  literature and, 185–186
  in music, 182
  presenting, 187–190
  old masters and, 139
  other's artworks, 175
  selecting works for, 180–185
  teachers and, 186
  using with children, 175–177
  value of including,
  in visual art, 183, 184
  written responses and, 190–193
Worms, creative movement and, 326
WOW. *See* Wonderful Object of Wonder (WOW)
Wrap-around masks, 362
Wright, Frank Lloyd, 27, 269
Write it out, 303
Wurm, J.P., 222

**Y**
Yarn
  for collages, 250
  for fiber art, 256
  handweaving and, 256
  painting, 256
*"You Look Ridiculous" Said the Hippopotamus to the Rhinoceros* (Waber), 254
YouTube, 74
*Yo Yes* (Rashka), 134

**Z**
Zone of proximal development, 11, 12